The Official History of the UK Strategic Nuclear Deterrent

Volume I of *The Official History of the UK Strategic Nuclear Deterrent* provides an authoritative and in-depth examination of the British government's strategic nuclear policy from 1945 to 1964.

Written with full access to the UK documentary record, this volume examines how British governments after 1945 tried to build and then maintain an independent, nationally controlled strategic nuclear capability, and the debates this provoked in official circles. Against a background of evolving British ideas about deterrence during the Cold War, it focuses on the strategic, political and diplomatic considerations that compelled governments, in the face of ever-increasing pressures on the defence budget, to persist in their efforts to develop nuclear weapons and to deploy a credible nuclear force, as the age of the manned bomber gave way to the ballistic missile. Particular attention is given to controversies over the portion of the defence budget devoted to the deterrent programme, the effects of the restoration of Anglo-American nuclear collaboration after 1958, increasing reliance on the United States for nuclear delivery systems, the negotiations that led to the Nassau Agreement of 1962 and the supply of Polaris, and discussions within the Western Alliance over the control of nuclear forces. By the time of the October 1964 election, when this volume concludes, previous dismissal of the prospects for successful ballistic missile defence were giving way to growing doubts over the long-term effectiveness of the Polaris system in its role as an independent deterrent, several years before it was due to enter service with the Royal Navy.

This book will be of much interest to students of British politics, Cold War history, nuclear proliferation and international relations.

Matthew Jones is Professor of International History at the London School of Economics and Political Science, UK, and author of, amongst other books, *After Hiroshima: The United States, Race, and Nuclear Weapons in Asia, 1945–1965* (2010).

Whitehall Histories: Government Official History Series
ISSN: 1474-8398

The Government Official History Series began in 1919 with wartime histories, and the peacetime series was inaugurated in 1966 by Harold Wilson. The aim of the series is to produce major histories in their own right, compiled by historians eminent in the field, who are afforded free access to all relevant material in the official archives. The Histories also provide a trusted secondary source for other historians and researchers while the official records are not in the public domain. The main criteria for selection of topics are that the histories should record important episodes or themes of British history while the official records can still be supplemented by the recollections of key players; and that they should be of general interest, and, preferably, involve the records of more than one government department.

The Official History of the Civil Service
Reforming the Civil Service
Vol. I: The Fulton Years, 1966–1981
Rodney Lowe

The Official History of North Sea Oil and Gas
Vol. I: The Growing Dominance of the State
Vol. II: Moderating the State's Role
Alex Kemp

The Official History of Britain and the European Community
Vol. II: From Rejection to Referendum, 1963–1975
Stephen Wall

The Official History of the Joint Intelligence Committee
Vol. I: From the Approach of the Second World War to the Suez Crisis
Michael S. Goodman

The Official History of the Cabinet Secretaries
Ian Beesley

The Official History of the UK Strategic Nuclear Deterrent
Vol. I: From the V-Bomber Era to the Arrival of Polaris, 1945–1964
Vol. II: The Labour Government and the Polaris Programme, 1964–1970
Matthew Jones

The Official History of the UK Strategic Nuclear Deterrent

Volume I: From the V-Bomber Era to the Arrival of Polaris, 1945–1964

Matthew Jones

LONDON AND NEW YORK

First published 2017
by Routledge

2 Park Square, Milton Park, Abingdon, Oxfordshire OX14 4RN
52 Vanderbilt Avenue, New York, NY 10017

Routledge is an imprint of the Taylor & Francis Group, an informa business

First issued in paperback 2018

Copyright © 2017 Crown Copyright

The right of Matthew Jones to be identified as author of this work has been asserted by him in accordance with sections 77 and 78 of the Copyright, Designs and Patents Act 1988.

All rights reserved. No part of this book may be reprinted or reproduced or utilised in any form or by any electronic, mechanical, or other means, now known or hereafter invented, including photocopying and recording, or in any information storage or retrieval system, without permission in writing from the publishers.

Notice:
Product or corporate names may be trademarks or registered trademarks, and are used only for identification and explanation without intent to infringe.

British Library Cataloguing-in-Publication Data
A catalogue record for this book is available from the British Library

Library of Congress Cataloging-in-Publication Data
A catalog record for this book has been requested

ISBN: 978-1-138-67493-6 (hbk)
ISBN: 978-0-367-07610-8 (pbk)

Typeset in Bembo
by Wearset Ltd, Boldon, Tyne and Wear

For Anya, Alec and Sofia

Contents

Preface		ix
Acknowledgements		xvi
List of abbreviations for Volume I		xviii
1	The making of a deterrent force, August 1945–November 1957	1
2	The rise of ballistic missile defence	62
3	In the shadow of Sputnik: the nuclear sufficiency debate and the restoration of Anglo-American nuclear collaboration, March 1957–February 1959	96
4	Breaking the impasse? Polaris and future deterrent policy, February 1959–March 1960	155
5	The future nuclear programme and the cancellation of Blue Streak, December 1959–April 1960	191
6	Skybolt, Polaris and the control of Western nuclear forces, March 1960–May 1961	213
7	An arms race intensifies: ABM defence, nuclear testing and the criteria of deterrence, January 1961–January 1962	260
8	Revising the criteria, January–May 1962	303
9	The prelude to Nassau, June–December 1962	336
10	Securing Polaris: the Nassau negotiations, December 1962–January 1963	364

11 The path to the Polaris sales agreement, January–April 1963 405

12 The origins of a Polaris improvement programme: HR
    169 and the emergence of the Moscow ABM system 458

13 The MLF, the size of the Polaris force and the approach
    of the general election, May 1963–October 1964 495

Index 537

Preface

> The whole and acknowledged point of the [first British atomic] bomb and its successors was that they should not be used except in tests. They were symbols of intent and determination. If they were used, they had failed in their purpose, which was deterrence. If two sides used them in warfare, any victory was bound to be pyrrhic.
> (Margaret Gowing, assisted by Lorna Arnold, *Independence and Deterrence: Britain and Atomic Energy, 1945–1952. Volume 2: Policy Execution* (London, 1974), 497)

The official historian who covers in their work the formation and execution of any aspect of British nuclear policy follows in the footsteps of some very distinguished company. Engaged from 1959 onwards as the archivist and historian of the UK Atomic Energy Authority (AEA), Margaret Gowing provided an incomparable example by producing, along with her successor Lorna Arnold, several authoritative and multi-layered studies, based on an extensive survey of government documents, which covered the early history of Britain's nuclear weapons programme, including the ministerial policymaking that carried it forward.[1] Since the appearance in 1974 of their two-volume work *Independence and Deterrence*, however, which concluded with the accomplishment of the first British atomic test in October 1952 – and despite the original intention to extend the AEA-commissioned series of histories to 1958–59, when Anglo-American nuclear collaboration was fully restored after the rupture experienced in the early post-war years – nothing has appeared under official auspices which adopts a similarly large canvas. Several smaller scale projects did emerge in subsequent years: having assisted Gowing with the compilation and writing of her post-war volumes, Arnold took up her mantle at the AEA with alacrity and generated specialist studies under official sponsorship which looked at UK atomic weapons trials in Australia during the 1950s, the Windscale nuclear accident in 1957, and the road to the first British thermonuclear tests in 1957–58.[2] But in conceiving of a successor volume to *Independence and Deterrence*, Gowing (who had meanwhile moved on to become Professor of the History of Science at Oxford) and Arnold were to find, as the latter admitted, that containing the vast and expanding scope of documents and themes for the period up to 1958–59 was to prove an insurmountable task. Sir Keith Hancock, the great Australian historian who steered the official series of Second World War civil histories through to completion, once advised Arnold that 'there is a limit to the material that can be compressed into a "unified" history'.[3]

A few officially-sponsored projects have also since appeared. With Ministry of Defence (MoD) sanction, a former official, Peter Nailor, produced a slim volume in 1988 which examined the programme that saw Britain successfully design, build and deploy the first of four Polaris submarines by the demanding in-service target date of 1968. Yet Nailor's work was largely absorbed with the administrative process of Polaris programme management – pitched at the level of the Royal Navy's Chief Polaris Executive (CPE) organisation in which he had played a part – and had little to say on high-level policy toward the strategic nuclear deterrent, or the wider context within which the whole programme evolved during the 1960s.[4] A comprehensive history of the Royal Air Force's contribution to the nuclear deterrent role by Humphrey Wynn, working under the umbrella of the RAF's Air Historical Branch, was also published in 1994, and included much illuminating material about nuclear policy in the 1950s and 1960s.[5] There was no sign, however, of a more broadly conceived study. At the end of the century Arnold would speculate that the original AEA series on which she and Gowing had worked was then 'dead beyond hope of resurrection', and that her own most recent book on the hydrogen bomb might represent 'a last hurrah for official nuclear history' in Britain.[6]

The subsequent commissioning in 2008 of a Cabinet Office official history, with sponsorship from the MoD, on the subject of the Chevaline programme – a major, once-secret Cold War project to improve the performance of the UK's Polaris submarine-launched missile force to enable it to penetrate Soviet anti-ballistic missile defences – made Arnold's prediction somewhat premature. The public disclosure of Chevaline in January 1980 by Francis Pym, the-then Secretary of State for Defence, in the House of Commons, and the subsequent controversy that occurred over the project's genesis, rationale and troubled development, marked a significant watershed in post-war British nuclear history.[7] Six months after the existence of the Chevaline was officially acknowledged, on 15 July 1980 another chapter in British nuclear history was opened when the Government finally made its announcement that it had decided to replace Polaris during the 1990s with the US Trident C4 missile system. In March 1982, it was further announced that the much more capable Trident D5 would be procured in lieu of the C4, and in August the first Chevaline patrol was carried out by HMS *Renown*.[8] As with the original arrangements under which the United States had supplied Polaris missiles during the 1960s, warheads for Trident would be designed and manufactured in Britain, while the UK would also produce a new class of nuclear-powered submarines to carry the deterrent.

The decision to acquire Trident, the groundwork for which had actually been laid by the previous Labour Government led by James Callaghan, was a potent symbol of how strong the UK–US relationship remained, with the nuclear component lying near its heart. To its defenders the Chevaline programme would maintain the credibility of the UK independent deterrent during the latter stages of the life of Polaris, bridging the period before the arrival of Trident in the 1990s. Although American assistance had been provided throughout the course of the project, much of the technology employed on Chevaline had nevertheless been derived from UK concepts and engineering designs. During the 1970s, work on the Chevaline warhead and re-entry system at Aldermaston, the home of the Atomic Weapons Research Establishment (AWRE), kept occupied a body of nuclear expertise which could be utilised again when at the end of that decade attention turned to the task of designing a new UK warhead for the Trident programme.

Described by one of those most involved in its history as 'probably in technical terms the most difficult weapon system development ever undertaken by the UK,'[9] Chevaline was representative of a significant post-war tradition, where a whole generation of exceptionally talented and skilled scientists and engineers, tutored in the triumphant successes of British defence science in the war of 1939–45, had turned their collective energies to providing the wherewithal for Britain to maintain its technological edge over the Soviet Union in the Cold War, and demonstrate the UK's continuing technical proficiency to their American allies. At the same time, Chevaline's history was also emblematic of many of the problems that have dogged several of the MoD's large-scale equipment projects. Just at the moment when Chevaline was completing its final trials, it became subject to extensive and controversial criticism, most notably in a House of Commons Public Accounts Committee report produced in March 1982, for its major cost overruns, slips in deployment timescale, and poor programme management, at least during its initial stages. The story of the Polaris improvement programme, from its inception to its introduction into service, was therefore certainly a substantial subject that warranted in-depth historical inquiry, not least for some of the lessons it might hold for subsequent nuclear projects, and where trade-offs sometimes had to be made between secrecy and accountability.

But the history of the development of a weapons system, valuable though this might be on its own terms, would not in itself be enough to fill the notable lacuna, identified above, in British official history covering nuclear policy for much of the Cold War period. That much was quickly apparent to the present author when approached by the Histories section of the Cabinet Office to take on this project. Moreover, it was quite clear that it was impossible to understand the history of the Polaris improvement programme, which had its origins with original acquisition of the missile system from the United States during the 1960s, without placing it within the overall context of the evolution of post-war policy toward the establishment and maintenance of a UK strategic nuclear capability. In this more general sense then, the Chevaline programme of the 1970s was the culmination and result of an entire era of post-war British nuclear thinking and official policymaking. Tracing the story back to the start of this era, and seeing how that official mind-set developed over time, has therefore been a central preoccupation of this multi-volume work.

Across much of the post-1945 period, it is apparent, shifting beliefs and attitudes toward the efficacy of deterrence, alongside differing conceptions of nuclear independence – when Britain was part of a Western Alliance which was dominated by the overwhelming nuclear power of the United States – constituted the well-springs for an often ambiguous policy that eventually mixed alliance commitments with an abiding adherence to national control and operation. It was the continuing attachment to the possibility of independent use of the UK's nuclear force, and the level of capability needed to meet the changing requirements of deterrence when facing the threat represented by the Soviet Union's conventional and nuclear strength in Europe, that was eventually to provide the strategic rationale for a Polaris improvement programme.

But this strategic reasoning also had to be put beside other concerns and interests, sometimes more parochial, which combined to justify a continuing national programme of advanced nuclear weapons development, despite the costs involved. These included, for example, the imperative to sustain a programme of attractive work at AWRE so that the UK's technological capacity for nuclear warhead research and development was maintained, and closely related to this, the concern that in the absence of such significant UK project work, Anglo-American nuclear collaboration, so exhaustively and expensively attained in July 1958 by a crucial agreement which still serves to underpin the relationship, would wither. In addition, the possession of a nuclear force under ultimate national control had important political and diplomatic repercussions, and this in turn would often provide strong arguments for its maintenance as other elements of national power were subject to decline.

The aim of the present history has been to provide a broad study of Whitehall policymaking and attitudes toward the creation and development of a UK strategic deterrent capability, and against this essential background to explore how its effectiveness was viewed, along with the steps that were seen as necessary to assure its continuing credibility. It has been necessary, therefore, for this first volume to return to the origins of British official thinking about deterrence and the requirements of the nuclear weapons programme in the early post-war years, and to chart the growth of debates about the balance between nuclear and conventional forces in defence policy during the 1950s. By the early 1960s, thoughts had turned to successor deterrent systems to the V-bomber force, and the crisis produced by the cancellation of the Skybolt programme led to the Anglo-American agreement over the supply of the Polaris missile system at the Nassau conference of December 1962. Already, however, the issue of ballistic missile defence was becoming a consideration in how the future of the UK force was viewed. Building on this initial base, the second volume of this history reconstructs how the Labour Government elected in October 1964 reacted to the Polaris programme, how proposals for its improvement prompted deep opposition, and the different nuclear futures that ministers and officials were prepared to contemplate. A third volume will examine the evolution of the Polaris improvement programme during the 1970s, showing how it survived a change of government from Conservative to Labour in 1974, encountered numerous problems as costs rose and timescales slipped, until it finally reached fruition with deployment as the Chevaline system in 1982, amid much controversy and recrimination.

The narrative that follows also attempts to put the development of UK nuclear policy in its proper international, political and bureaucratic context. Set against the broad sweep of British foreign and defence policy in the early Cold War period, reference will often be made to technical issues, and the problems posed by the rise of ballistic missile defence in particular. Many of the assumptions, choices and decisions that emerged at this technical and scientific level had connections with and implications for the higher policymaking arena. If the reader is sometimes propelled from the exchanges of senior Whitehall officials in various government departments to the assessments, reports and appraisals of defence scientists, it is to illustrate the crucial links that existed between the two realms. At the same time, no attempt has been made to offer a detailed technical study of the development of the nuclear weapons programme, rather the focus throughout has been on the higher-level considerations that drove warhead requirements.

The prime subject matter of the history has thus been the political, bureaucratic and strategic environment within which the key debates over nuclear policy were conducted, and the interplay between official advice and ministerial decisions. Among my main concerns have been such matters as the nature of deterrence and perceptions of credibility; assessments of the strategic environment and plans for the size, equipment and employment of the nuclear force; relations with the United States and other Western allies in the nuclear weapons field; pressures on the nuclear components of the defence budget from cuts to overall public expenditure; inter-service relations; and the influence of party political considerations during an era when nuclear policy was to become a subject extended and often rancorous political debate. There has also been an attempt to show how nuclear policy was formed at a working level, and to provide illustrations of the heterodox opinions and perspectives that could often be found there. Bureaucratic structures, it is argued, mattered greatly as policy deliberations wound their way through the intricate network of committees and working groups that formed the narrow world of seasoned officials until finally reaching the ministerial office or Cabinet committee meeting. Overall, the history proceeds in general terms through a chronological narrative rather than being organised along thematic lines. The latter has the obvious attraction of allowing one aspect of the story to be followed from origins to fruition, but its fundamental drawback is the loss of the sense in which issues were often intermeshed in both substance and time. Almost invariably policymakers had to deal with their numerous options and problems concurrently, juggling priorities and wider (often political) considerations, while at the same time responding to changes in the international environment.

I have been acutely aware throughout this venture that many serious academic scholars of British nuclear history during the Cold War era have paved the way for others by their often careful and scrupulous examination of the open documentary record.[10] But the constraints of official secrecy have meant that access to some documents in such a nominally sensitive area as nuclear policy has often been restricted, while relatively little attention has been given by scholars to the Polaris phase of deterrent history from the early 1960s onwards. With the benefit of this author's status as an official historian, the current history has been informed by free access to such closed and hitherto inaccessible material across many different departments of government, providing a major opportunity to pursue subjects where the open record has sometimes been incomplete. Hence it has been possible to gather records from the Prime Minister's Office, Cabinet Office, Ministry of Defence, Foreign and Commonwealth Office, Treasury, Atomic Energy Authority, Ministry of Supply, and Ministry of Technology, as well as to use the private paper collections of some of the main participants. As Lorna Arnold once remarked, the relative luxury of official history, where an enormous array of records are available for use, allows us to better 'study the complex relationships between policy, strategy, science, and technology, and to understand more fully the reasons, choices, problems, and constraints involved. The hard realities behind the high-level decisions can be seen more clearly.'[11] Attention has also been given to contemporary discussion about British strategic nuclear policy in the press and parliament where relevant, while developments in US policy, derived from unclassified and open American documentary sources, are also explored for the background this offers on such subjects as attitudes to the UK's independent deterrent, assessments of the Soviet ABM programme and the prospects for ABM limitation.

In accordance with the agenda delineated above, this history starts in its first volume with the origins and early years of the UK strategic nuclear programme, a crucial period which helped to forge the mentalities, beliefs, approaches and organisational structures driving a policy which viewed the establishment and maintenance of a UK strategic nuclear force as essential to security. It was during these years that the rationale for an independent UK deterrent force was developed and debated by ministers; the nuclear relationship with the United States transformed; tensions within the North Atlantic Alliance over the role of national nuclear forces in an era of approaching Superpower nuclear parity rose to the fore; the V-force was supplanted as the prime future platform for the strategic deterrent by negotiation of the Nassau Agreement of December 1962 and the Polaris Sales Agreement of April 1963; early discussions within Whitehall over the size and purpose of the Polaris force were conducted; and, holding very significant portents for the future of that same Polaris force, the emergence of the problem of ABM defence began to be recognised in official thinking.

This current project may be one of the last manifestations of the UK government's ventures into official history, and this melancholy knowledge has imbued in me mixed feelings of responsibility in maintaining a venerable tradition, admiration for the work of my predecessors, and gratitude for the chance to add to the genre. As I hope the reader will appreciate this is a big and wide-ranging story, which I felt could only be conveyed in the detail and scope needed by a long narrative across several volumes. In its writing I have enjoyed free access to both open and currently closed official records, but the statements, opinions, views and interpretations offered, along with any errors, remain mine alone.

Matthew Jones

Notes

1 Margaret Gowing, *Britain and Atomic Energy, 1939–1945* (London, 1964); Margaret Gowing, assisted by Lorna Arnold, *Independence and Deterrence: Britain and Atomic Energy, 1945–1952. Volume 1: Policy Making* and *Volume 2: Policy Execution* (London, 1974).
2 Lorna Arnold, *A Very Special Relationship: British Atomic Weapon Trials in Australia* (London, 1987); *Windscale 1957: Anatomy of a Disaster* (London, 1992); *Britain and the H-bomb* (London, 2001).
3 See Lorna Arnold, 'A Letter from Oxford: The History of Nuclear History in Britain,' *Minerva*, 38, 2000, 201–19.
4 Peter Nailor, *The Nassau Connection: The Organisation and Management of the British Polaris Project* (London, 1988).
5 Humphrey Wynn, *The RAF Nuclear Deterrent Forces: their origins, roles and deployment, 1946–1969* (London, 1994).
6 Arnold, 'A Letter from Oxford,' 212–3.
7 *Hansard*, House of Commons debates (HC), cols 672–82, vol 977, 24 January 1980; see also 'Gasps from Labour at £1,000m Polaris plan,' *The Times*, 25 January 1980.
8 See Cmnd 7979, *The British Strategic Nuclear Force*, July 1980; Defence Open Government Document 80/23, *The Future United Kingdom Strategic Nuclear Deterrent Force*, July 1980.
9 Fred East minute for Sir Robert Armstrong, 'Chevaline,' Td/027, 17 February 1982, PREM 19/694, The National Archives (TNA). All subsequent document references are to TNA material unless otherwise indicated.
10 Notable studies here include John Simpson, *The Independent Nuclear State: The United States, Britain and the Military Atom* (London, 1983); Ian Clark and Nicholas J. Wheeler, *The British Origins of Nuclear Strategy, 1945–1955* (Oxford, 1989); Martin S. Navias, *Nuclear Weapons and British Strategic Planning, 1955–1958* (Oxford, 1991); Ian Clark, *Nuclear Diplomacy and the Special Relationship: Britain's Deterrent and America, 1957–1962* (Oxford, 1994); John Baylis, *Ambiguity and Deterrence: British Nuclear Strategy, 1945–1964* (Oxford, 1995); Richard Moore, *The Royal Navy and Nuclear Weapons* (London, 2001); Peter Hennessy, *The Secret State: Whitehall and the Cold War* (London, 2002); Peter Hennessy, *Cabinets and the Bomb* (Oxford, 2007); Richard Moore, *Nuclear Illusion, Nuclear Reality: Britain, the United States and Nuclear Weapons, 1958–64* (Basingstoke, 2010); Peter Hennessy and James Jinks, *The Silent Deep: The Royal Navy Submarine Service since 1945* (London, 2015).
11 Arnold, 'A Letter from Oxford,' 214.

Acknowledgements

In any work of this scale and nature, support and assistance from many different quarters is a prerequisite and I have incurred numerous debts of gratitude over the past few years. Leading on the official history programme at the Cabinet Office throughout much of this time have been Tessa Stirling and Sally Falk, who have offered sage advice and given encouragement throughout. I have also benefitted from a project board of special distinction, whose members have brought their own extensive experience and knowledge of the nuclear and policymaking world to bear on our discussions of progress, and I would like to register thanks to Richard Alcock, Mike Baker, Sir Lawrence Freedman, Tom McKane, Patrick Salmon, and Simon Webb. As a later addition to the board, Tom, in particular, provided close reading and advice on the contents of my chapters. Mike stepped in at a crucial juncture to provide MoD sponsorship for this official history when it was threatened by the closure of the official history programme at the Cabinet Office, and at MoD itself Tim Digman, Colin Amos and Bob Evans have lent invaluable assistance. My fellow official historians, Ian Beesley, Michael Goodman, and Sir Stephen Wall, have become compatriots and friends, sharing space, frustrations, and camaraderie as we complete our tasks. Gill Bennett, the former head of the Foreign and Commonwealth Office's (FCO's) historical section, has provided valuable advice and counsel. Members of the knowledge and information unit at the Cabinet Office including Sue Church, Wendy Dalton, John Gray, Ron Lawrence, Graeme Ling, Deborah Neal, David Richardson, Sue Wayland, and Nick Weekes, were ever helpful and friendly with my questions and queries about the location and provenance of files.

Availability of Ministry of Defence records was not always straightforward in the early stages of the research work, especially as a result of the asbestos contamination problem in the sensitive file store kept under the Old War Office Building. But from the very beginning of the project Simon Marsh, who was the head of records management at the Ministry of Defence (and now at the Home Office), was an unstinting supporter, and provided all possible assistance in facilitating access to important sources. Quite simply, without Simon's contribution this history – and the kind of wide-ranging account I wanted to write – would not have been possible. Jane Knight offered further invaluable help with retrieving MoD materials for which I am extremely grateful, while Tony Wilson, a Chevaline veteran, was a source of both personal recollections of the project and leads to new MoD and AEA documents that I would otherwise have missed. At the FCO, Russell Pullen was similarly helpful in accessing some highly significant files, and John Walker of the Arms Control and Disarmament Unit has given eager encouragement throughout, as has Seb Cox at the MoD's Air Historical Branch. My work at the AWRE archive was facilitated by Lynn Stringer, while the late Kate Pyne, Aldermaston's resident historian, was a welcoming host on my initial visits.

My feel for the period was enhanced by a series of interviews I conducted with retired officials, defence scientists, and political figures, and it is sad to record that many have passed away since I had the enormous pleasure of meeting them: they included, Lord Armstrong, Tony Benn, David Boucher, Lord Carrington, Roy Dommett, John Freeman, Lord Healey, Peter Jones, Sir Ronald Mason, Steven Metcalf, Sir Richard Mottram, Sir Patrick Nairne, Sir David Omand, Lord Owen, Sir Michael Palliser, Frank Panton, Sir Charles Powell, Sir Michael Quinlan, Sir Peter Ramsbotham, Lord Rodgers, Sir Clive Rose, Sir Kevin Tebbit, and David Young.

Amongst academic friends and colleagues, I express my thanks to Richard Aldrich, Josh Botts of the US State Department's Office of the Historian, Bill Burr, David Edgerton, James Ellison, Frank Gavin, Lord Hennessy (a participant, when in his early incarnation as a journalist, in the events surrounding the unveiling of Chevaline), James Jinks, Fred Logevall, Paul McGarr, David Milne, Richard Moore, Andrew Preston, Kevin Ruane, Bevan Sewell, Marc Trachtenberg, and John Young. The LSE's International History Department has provided a wonderfully conducive and supportive environment for my study and research. During the past few years I have also been fortunate to enjoy many stimulating conversations about Soviet nuclear history with David Holloway of Stanford University, an *exemplar* amongst the fraternity of nuclear historians. My doctoral supervisor from Oxford days, Sir Michael Howard, who once set the highest possible standards of scholarship and erudition when engaged as an official historian of grand strategy during the Second World War, has kept a distant, watchful eye on my progress. Throughout the long process of compiling this work my wife and children have provided all the support that a busy academic historian could wish for, and the dedications for the volumes reflect the huge and unsung contribution they have made.

Abbreviations for Volume I

ABM	Anti-Ballistic Missile
ACSA(N)	Assistant Chief Scientific Adviser (Nuclear)
AEA	Atomic Energy Authority
AEC	Atomic Energy Commission
ARPA	Advanced Research Projects Agency
AWRE	Atomic Weapons Research Establishment
BNDSG	British Nuclear Deterrent Study Group
CAS	Chief of the Air Staff
CDS	Chief of the Defence Staff
CEA	*Commissariat a l'energie atomique*
CENTO	Central Treaty Organization
CGWL	Controller of Guided Weapons and Electronics (Ministry of Supply)
CIA	Central Intelligence Agency
CIGS	Chief of the Imperial General Staff
CNS	Chief of the Naval Staff
COS	Chiefs of Staff
CPE	Chief Polaris Executive
CSA	Chief Scientific Adviser
DAWD	Director of Atomic Warhead Development (Ministry of Supply)
DDRE	Director of Defense Research and Engineering (US Department of Defense)
DOPC	Defence and Overseas Policy Committee
DRPC	Defence Research Policy Committee
EASAMS	Elliot Automation Space and Advanced Military Systems
EEC	European Economic Community
EFTA	European Free Trade Area
FO	Foreign Office
HMG	Her Majesty's Government
ICBM	Intercontinental Ballistic Missile
IRBM	Intermediate Range Ballistic Missile
JCAE	Joint Congressional Committee on Atomic Energy

JCS	Joint Chiefs of Staff
JIB	Joint Intelligence Bureau
JIC	Joint Intelligence Committee
JIGSAW	Joint Inter-services Group for the Study of All-Out War
JOWOG	Joint Working Group
JPS	Joint Planning Staff
JRSWG	Joint Re-entry System Working Group
JSTG	Joint Steering Task Group
LMSC	Lockheed Missiles and Space Company
MDA	Mutual Defence Agreement
MLF	Multilateral Force
MoA	Ministry of Aviation
MoD	Ministry of Defence
MoS	Ministry of Supply
MRBM	Medium Range Ballistic Missile
NATO	North Atlantic Treaty Organization
NIE	National Intelligence Estimate
NRDC	Nuclear Requirements for Defence Committee
ORC	Operational Requirements Committee
PIPSC	Polaris Interdepartmental Steering Committee
PSA	Polaris Sales Agreement
PUS	Permanent Under Secretary
PUSD	Permanent Under-Secretary's Department (Foreign Office)
R & D	Research and Development
RAE	Royal Aircraft Establishment
RAF	Royal Air Force
REB	Re-entry Body
RES	Re-entry System
RRE	Royal Radar Establishment
RV	Re-entry Vehicle
SAC	Strategic Air Command
SACEUR	Supreme Allied Commander Europe
SAM	Surface-to-Air Missile
SEATO	South East Asia Treaty Organization
SLBM	Submarine Launched Ballistic Missile
SPO	Special Projects Office
USN	United States Navy
WDC(NS)	Weapons Development Committee (Nuclear Sub-Committee)
WSCC	Warhead Safety Coordinating Committee

1 The making of a deterrent force, August 1945–November 1957

Shaping a national programme

In retrospect it is clear that the decision to proceed with a British nuclear weapons programme after the end of the Second World War, taken by the Labour Government which assumed office in July 1945, was not a matter of serious doubt once the prospects for a benign post-war security environment had vanished. During this period, ministers and officials were subject to a mix of influences and basic reactions that would figure prominently in many subsequent discussions of the direction of British strategic nuclear policy. There was an evident belief, partly derived from concerns over the physical vulnerability of the homeland to aerial attack, in the efficacy of a policy of deterrence; the conviction that Britain's role as a major power in post-war international affairs demanded and was reinforced by nuclear status; the imperatives of the Anglo-American relationship, where it was felt that influence over Washington could be strengthened through an indigenous nuclear programme; and the confidence that the British scientific and technical establishment – building on the many triumphs of the war years and its innate talents and skills – could rise to the task. Indeed, it is important to recall that it had been British scientists, along with their gifted émigré colleagues, who had played a leading role in establishing during the early stages of the Second World War that production of an atomic bomb from the fission of atoms in enriched uranium was feasible. The MAUD Committee's seminal report of July 1941, as well as detailing the practicality and necessity of a wartime atomic programme, had recommended that even should the war end before a bomb had been produced, 'the effort would not be wasted, except in the unlikely event of complete disarmament, since no nation would care to risk being caught without a weapon of such decisive possibilities.'[1]

Until early 1942 research and development work on a UK atomic bomb project, with some important exceptions, had remained a step ahead of that which was also taking place in the United States. The establishment of a joint wartime programme with the Americans, formally reached with the conclusion of the Quebec Agreement in August 1943, had not overridden expectations that UK efforts in the nuclear field would continue once the war was over. Steadily increasing in importance after 1945, furthermore, was the hope that national progress with nuclear development would help persuade Washington to open the doors to full post-war nuclear collaboration with Britain, a collaboration which had been closed in peremptory fashion by Congressional passage of the McMahon Act in August 1946. As officials and ministers came to appreciate, some of the post-war economic burdens imposed by pursuit of a purely national nuclear programme could be eased if access to the most advanced technical developments in US weapons design were made available to the UK. As the later chapters of this history will show, the paradox of much nuclear policy during the 1950s was that the pursuit of independence also had as a goal the re-establishment of a nuclear relationship with the United States that some – at both home and abroad – would see as compromising the exercise of national sovereignty. At the same time, for others, it was only the construction of a healthy degree of Anglo-American nuclear cooperation that would allow Britain to avoid the debilitating costs of a purely national programme, and so retain the capacity to deploy a UK-controlled strategic nuclear capability.

After 1945, the idea that possession of a national means of retaliation was the most effective way to prevent another major and destructive war in Europe from occurring was certainly one of the most important drivers of the UK nuclear programme. While Britain's immediate post-war strategic nuclear policy clearly developed in a Cold War environment defined by the prevalence of growing tension and distrust with the Soviet Union, it was also informed from its very earliest stages by long-held views on the physical vulnerability of the homeland to bombing from the air and a consequent strong and historically-derived attachment to the concept of deterrence – through accumulation of the means of reprisal – as the only realistic response to the inescapable facts of geography and demography.

Towards the end of August 1945, only a few weeks after the dropping of atomic bombs on Hiroshima and Nagasaki, Clement Attlee, the matter-of-fact Prime Minister of the new Labour Government, composed a personal and characteristically incisive memorandum which considered the implications of recent events for the future pattern of warfare and for international relations more generally. Previous ideas about post-war military planning, for example the need to disperse essential industries to make them less susceptible to aerial bombardment, had, Attlee conjectured, been rendered 'quite futile' as nothing could 'alter the fact that the geographical situation of Britain offers to a Continental Power such targets as London and the other great cities.' Measures of civil defence were also likely to prove a 'futile waste'. Discussion of imperial defence or of the need for strategic bases in the Mediterranean seemed plainly anachronistic when 'the vulnerability of the heart of the Empire is the one fact that matters.' At the recent Potsdam Conference, where the victorious Allied powers had gathered to discuss the political settlement in Europe after Germany's defeat, the Prime Minister had noticed that the participants still talked of river lines and frontiers as if they held any military significance, whereas it had to be realised that

> ...the modern conception of war to which in my lifetime we have become accustomed is now completely out of date. We recognised or some of us did before this war that bombing could only be answered by counter bombing. We were right. Berlin and Magdeburg were the only answer to London and Coventry. Both derive from Guernica. The answer to an atomic bomb on London is an atomic bomb on another great city.

Convinced that the secret of the atomic bomb was bound to be disseminated to other states and that this could have destabilising consequences, Attlee proceeded to ruminate on the idea that the wartime alliance of the United States, Great Britain and the Soviet Union should now work toward a new world order where war was banished as a feature of international politics and where 'the rule of law' was established. In the past, he noted, this sort of thinking had been regarded as a 'Utopian dream' but he now thought it 'the essential condition of the survival of civilisation and possibly of life in [sic] this planet.'[2]

Attlee's hope, shared by many contemporaries, had been that the general realisation of the destructive power of the bomb would create the conditions whereby an effective world organisation to preserve the peace would come into being. As he told the Cabinet in November 1945:

> power politics, though they might for a time produce an uneasy equilibrium, were bound to lead in the end to a violent clash of interests and to war; and that the only hope for world peace was that all should lay aside nationalistic ideas and strive without reservation to bring about an international relationship in which war was entirely ruled out. The realisation of the destructive power of the atomic bomb might, he hoped, have brought the peoples of the world into a condition of mind in which they were more ready than ever before to recognise the validity of this general thesis.[3]

But visions of post-war cooperation through the United Nations to transform the nature of international relations, or to construct mechanisms for the international control of atomic energy, were already beginning to founder, as the tensions of the Cold War started to take hold in Europe. Instead, the major states of the international system would have to learn to adjust to the new realities presented by the development of nuclear weapons, and the unnerving possibility they might be used again in a military clash. Nonetheless, Attlee had managed to touch, in his typically direct manner, on much prevailing thinking about the significance of a weapon which had underlined the way in which whole civilian populations, and the densely-packed urban areas of advanced industrial societies, had become the regular – even accepted – targets for all combatants in the total war that had just ended. Moreover, through his mention of retaliation as the only response against the use of such weapons, he had also tapped into a recurrent seam of British thinking about the notion of deterrence and its place in defence policy that had long antecedents.[4]

One of the dominant beliefs and anxieties of a large and influential group of British politicians and military commentators in the years leading up to the outbreak of the Second World War was that wholesale bombing would be a principal and inevitable feature of any future conflict, and was summed up by the famous phrase 'the bomber will always get through,' first coined by Stanley Baldwin in a speech to the House of Commons in November 1932.[5] Strategic bombing, directed against the industrial heartlands of an enemy and its urban-centred populations, offered the prospect of bringing future wars to a swift and successful conclusion by attacking at source the enemy's means and will to continue fighting without having to engage in a costly struggle of attrition involving massed armies on land. Inflicting large-scale civilian casualties over a short time period, it was often supposed, would induce social breakdown, economic collapse and political paralysis. Mounting an effective defence against such sustained aerial bombardment was widely regarded as an impossibility making the outlook grim for those states and their peoples caught up in the next war.

During the 1930s, air power advocates, many of them to be found in the upper reaches of the Royal Air Force, were also ready to articulate the idea that the possession of a strategic bombing force, as well as offering the key to victory if a conflict should breakout, could serve to deter hostile powers from embarking upon aggression in the first place for fear of the terrible consequences that would result. The same fears, however, could also serve to push governments supportive of the status quo toward policies that avoided the likelihood of a military confrontation. In the latter part of the decade, and contrary to initial British presumptions, it was the rapid build-up of German air power that helped to induce caution over adopting a more forceful response to the gathering Nazi threat; it was also anxiety over German bombing potential (even though the German Air Force was not geared for use in a strategic sense) that led the RAF's leaders and civilian politicians to put a greater onus on improved measures of air defence from 1937 onwards.[6]

The assumptions encapsulated in Baldwin's famous prediction were, indeed, to prove only partially correct, and the subsequent effects of conventional strategic bombing were soon seen as less than clear cut. During the Second World War, increasingly sophisticated defensive measures in the form of radar detection, faster and more powerful fighter aircraft, and anti-aircraft artillery, made it possible to inflict heavy losses on attacking bomber formations, which along with the inherent inaccuracies of conventional bombing and the vagaries of the weather, often mitigated the effects on civilian morale and productive output that might otherwise have been expected. Civilian populations themselves proved more resilient to the effects of sustained bombing than had been commonly supposed.[7]

Perhaps more than any other area of the conflict, the air war between 1939 and 1945 provided the opportunity for major strides in science and technology to affect the balance of particular phases of the struggle, offering a compelling example of the need for states engaged in modern war to mobilise, organise and direct such resources. One particularly telling illustration of the destructive potential of technological breakthroughs was provided on 8 September 1944 when the first German V-2 rocket struck London, giving Britain the unhappy distinction of being the first state to suffer the effects of ballistic missile attack. A new dimension had now been opened to the aerial struggle. Unlike the bombing fleets employed up to then (and even with the case of the powered V-1 'glider-bomb' which had been unleashed against Britain two months earlier), interception of such missiles seemed virtually impossible, and the development of completely effective countermeasures infeasible. Hundreds of V-2 attacks followed, before eventually German launching sites were overrun by Allied ground forces in North West Europe, reinforcing the British sense of vulnerability that was to presage later Cold War anxieties. Indeed, the V-2 offensive proved a powerful initial spur into early British studies of ballistic missile defence, an effort that was to continue throughout the following decade.[8]

After the atomic attacks against Japan it did not take long for defence analysts and commentators to speculate that rockets would soon be married with nuclear weapons in order to inaugurate a new kind of 'push button' war, with intercontinental missiles crossing the oceans and obliterating major cities such as London, Paris or New York. Although most informed opinion recognised that this frightening prospect was still many years away – the United States, holding a monopoly of atomic bombs, had only a limited stockpile, and missile technology was still in its infancy with major problems of guidance, accuracy and reliability to be overcome – there seemed few means of active defence that could counter-act this threat.[9]

To some cold-blooded strategists this suggested that pre-emption should be the goal of nuclear planning: if an all-out war involving two powers armed with strategic nuclear weapons should occur, then whoever struck the first blow would hold an immense advantage, perhaps even able to destroy an opponent's nuclear forces before they could be launched (especially if they still relied on aircraft at easily-targeted airbases for delivery), leaving the rest of their society open to further strikes and with little option remaining but capitulation for the unfortunate survivors. But this kind of attack, as well as involving the problematic notion that war might have to be initiated – in a manner that to all appearances was an act of blatant aggression – before its inevitability had become completely clear and manifest, presumed an ability to neutralise the entire nuclear inventory of an enemy. Even the smallest miscalculation of the effects of a pre-emptive strike could still leave an attacker open to a highly-destructive retaliatory blow. Irrespective of these kinds of analyses, moreover, was the 'commonsense' appreciation, increasingly shared across a wide spectrum of political and military opinion, that any use of nuclear weapons would have incalculable, widespread and possibly catastrophic consequences for those states and societies which were involved.

In such circumstances, and given the absence of suitable international controls over nuclear materials or general and comprehensive measures of disarmament, it was felt by many that a policy of nuclear deterrence seemed the rational response for a vulnerable state looking to preserve security while avoiding war. The individual who gave most notable expression to some of the changes that would be brought to strategic thinking at the outset of the nuclear age was the American military theorist Bernard Brodie, who in *The Absolute Weapon: Atomic Power and World Order*, the edited work of 1946 that helped to establish his reputation, coined his much-quoted axiom that, 'Thus far the chief purpose of our military establishment has been to win wars. From now on its chief purpose must be to avert them. It can have almost no other useful purpose.'[10] It was the sheer destructiveness of nuclear weapons that changed the character and purposes of war between major powers, and that reinforced the importance of deterrence (rather than war-fighting per se) as the prime goal of strategic policy and force posture. As Brodie also saw, ballistic missiles would eventually render the potential of nuclear weapons even more threatening by virtually ensuring their swift delivery into the heartlands of an adversary.[11]

Amassing the means of retaliation should therefore, in Brodie's view, become the first and essential step of a defence programme.[12] It was to take several years before the fundamental precepts of deterrence theory were to find ready acceptance in US military circles: the American nuclear monopoly in the initial stages of the Cold War seemed to render such thinking moot, while some assumed that atomic weapons – still relatively small in size and limited in number during the late 1940s – would not necessarily be decisive in delivering a knockout punch in war against the Soviet Union. Brodie's insights, it was appreciated, were primarily directed toward an environment where two potential adversaries might both be endowed with the mutual capacity for large-scale destruction, and at least for the time being the Russians were still devoid of any nuclear capability, let alone a large stockpile of bombs and the means to deliver them.

The position for British officials and observers, with their far more acute sense of physical vulnerability, however, was very different. Even before Brodie was giving expression to his ideas, a clear set of beliefs around the importance of the notion of deterrence was already being formulated in British official circles.[13] In a report issued in mid-June 1945, for example, an ad hoc scientific committee charged by the Chiefs of Staff (COS) with looking at future technical developments in warfare, and chaired by Sir Henry Tizard – who in October 1946 would become the newly-created Ministry of Defence's first scientific adviser – had arrived at conclusions Brodie would have recognised. Although the first successful nuclear test in the New Mexico desert was still a month away, and the members of Tizard's Committee had not been privy to the innermost secrets of the atomic bomb programme in the United States, enough was known about the potential explosive power of atomic energy to speculate about its significance. In advocating a post-war British programme of research into atomic energy, the Committee's report concluded that the 'only answer that we can see to the atomic bomb is to be prepared to use it ourselves in retaliation. A knowledge that we were prepared, in the last resort, to do this might well deter an aggressive nation. Duelling was a recognised method of settling quarrels between men of high social standing so long as the duellists stood twenty paces apart and fired at each other with pistols of a primitive type. If the rule had been that they should stand a yard apart with pistols at each other's hearts, we doubt whether it would long have remained a recognised method of settling affairs of honour.'[14]

We have already seen how the new Prime Minister shared this kind of appreciation. Writing to President Harry S. Truman in late September 1945, Attlee observed that, 'Never before has there been a weapon which can suddenly and without warning be employed to destroy utterly the nerve centre of a great nation,' and the 'emergence of this new weapon has meant, taking account of all its potentialities, not a quantitative but a qualitative change in the nature of warfare.' There now existed

> a weapon of small bulk capable of being conveyed on to a distant target with inevitable catastrophic results. We can set no bounds to the possibilities of airplanes flying through the stratosphere dropping atomic bombs on great cities. There are possible developments of the rocket for a similar purpose. I understand that the power of the bombs [sic] delivered on Nagasaki may be multiplied many times as the invention develops. I have so far heard no suggestion of any possible means of defence. The only deterrent is the possibility of the victim of such an attack being able to retort on the victor. In many discussions on bombing in the days before the war it was demonstrated that the only answer to the bomber was the bomber. The war proved this to be correct.

At the same time, the Prime Minister expressed his concern that despite the fear of reprisal, cities had still been subject to heavy bombing attack; this underlined to him the vital importance of achieving post-war cooperation among the great powers if 'mutual annihilation' was to be avoided.[15]

In October 1945, the Chiefs of Staff had enunciated their own opinion that in the absence of international controls over atomic weapons – and with the implicit assumption that the Soviet Union was working on its own nuclear programme – possession of the bomb would be vital to post-war security. As Attlee was informed by the Secretary of the COS Committee (in a paraphrase of the views of the COS), 'the best method of defence against the new weapon is likely to be the deterrent effect that the possession of the means of retaliation would have on a potential aggressor.' Atomic research leading, as soon as possible, to the development and production of the weapons themselves was considered essential, and any delay 'pending the outcome of negotiations regarding international control might well prove fatal to the security of the British Commonwealth.'[16]

As well as such military considerations, British governments believed they had the scientific prowess and ingenuity to sustain a major nuclear effort. Due to its leading pre-war scientific work in the area of nuclear physics, and its involvement in the wartime project to produce an atomic bomb, Britain had a strong self-image as a nuclear pioneer in the years immediately after the end of the war. There was a firm and proud conviction, to those with privileged access to knowledge of the programme, that the Manhattan Project was a joint Anglo-American undertaking, where British experience and know-how had been important to its eventual success (how far this was the case was, in the opinion of Margaret Gowing, impossible to gauge, though she cites one opinion that the British contribution at Los Alamos may have hastened the production of the bomb by a few months).[17] Indeed, the wartime agreements on atomic collaboration concluded between Winston Churchill, the then Prime Minister, and President Franklin D. Roosevelt, at Quebec in August 1943, and at Hyde Park in upstate New York in September 1944, were explicit in acknowledging the shared nature of the venture. The experiences of the war years, moreover, had instilled in British science a self-confidence that came with the introduction of new technologies, from radar to jet propulsion to sonar detection systems. Post-war research into atomic energy and its military applications was regarded by many as nothing more than a natural progression from what had been achieved during wartime, building on the momentum generated by the mobilisation of scientific manpower by government.

The practical groundwork for a post-war national programme began to be built when the first government atomic energy research establishment was inaugurated at Harwell, south of Oxford, in October 1945. At the end of that same month, even as it was being asked by ministers to investigate the possibilities for international control, the Advisory Committee on Atomic Energy, an influential interdepartmental group of officials under the experienced chairmanship of Sir John Anderson, was recommending that 'we should undertake production of bombs on a large scale for our own defence as soon as possible.'[18] Although no immediate decisions were forthcoming, the subsequent tone of ministerial discussion was pessimistic about the likelihood that effective international safeguards over nuclear use could be constructed – perhaps via a coercive 'non-use' regime – with Ernest Bevin, the Foreign Secretary, setting the mood of sombre realism with his comment that, 'lasting peace could only be ensured if the Great Powers would agree to abandon power politics. But there was no sign of this at present.'[19]

How large a nuclear force would be needed – an evaluation which was required as a yardstick for future planning – was a question which, for the moment, defied any ready and obvious answer. Asked for their opinion on the optimum size of a UK nuclear stockpile so that production needs for fissile material could be calculated, all the COS could offer, in a paper issued at the beginning of January 1946, was the view it was 'not possible now to assess the precise number which we might require but we are convinced we should aim to have as soon as possible a stock in the order of hundreds rather than scores.'[20] They had based this assessment – which one study notes 'suggested the breadth of their ignorance and the height of their ambition' – on the likelihood that an unnamed potential aggressor would have dispersed industries and population, but it took little imagination to see that it was the Soviet Union that was in mind.[21]

In that same month, the Joint Technical Warfare Committee, a subcommittee of the COS set-up to continue the work of Tizard's initial group, and with help from the COS's Joint Planning Staff, had produced a list of Soviet cities with over 100,000 inhabitants (based on figures from 1939), and their distances from Norwich, Nicosia in Cyprus, and Peshawar in India, all locations selected as they were 'in British territory from which the best minimum range coverage is obtainable.'[22] By April 1946 operational research groups at the Air Ministry had compiled crude estimates of the numbers of bomber sorties and atomic bombs that, taking into account likely losses, would be required to destroy all such large cities in the Soviet Union, as well as in the UK, for a conflict that might occur a decade in the future.[23] The Joint Technical Warfare Committee's updating of Tizard's earlier report, produced in July 1946, anticipated that the most likely objects for attack with atomic weapons would be 'concentrations of population [and] centres of distribution and communication,' concluding that it might take 'the rapid delivery of several hundred bombs on target' to bring about the collapse of the Soviet Union.[24]

Production facilities for fissile material for the nuclear programme were also set up during this period, while an Air Staff Operational Requirement for an atomic bomb – reflecting the climate of official opinion as to the necessity of its development – was first issued in August 1946. A few months later the Air Ministry produced a specification for a new high-performance bomber which could carry the weapon when it was finally manufactured.[25] The resulting competition led to contracts for not one, but three different varieties of aircraft, a programme which was to reach fruition in the latter half of the 1950s with the entry into service of the famous V-bomber force of Valiants, Victors and Vulcans.

It was also apparent by mid-1946 that if the United Kingdom was eventually to develop and produce its own stockpile of nuclear weapons it would have to do so alone. Hopes for continuation into the post-war era of the close scientific cooperation with the United States that had been witnessed during the final stages of the Manhattan Project were to be disappointed. Despite President Truman agreeing with Attlee during November 1945 that there was a need for 'full and effective collaboration' in the nuclear field between the two states, by April 1946 it was clear the Combined Policy Committee, set up in 1943 to provide joint direction to Anglo-American atomic development, had ceased to function in any effective manner.[26] An appeal from Attlee to Truman for the continuation of wartime patterns of collaboration, made in a letter delivered in June 1946, went unanswered (the US administration being concerned, so it was avowed, that the propagation of nuclear knowledge stood in conflict with its continuing interest in the Baruch Plan for the international control of atomic energy under the auspices of the United Nations). Estrangement was made complete by the passing of the McMahon Act in August 1946, a piece of legislation which prohibited – by stern punishment – the transfer of classified atomic energy information to foreign countries.[27]

A mixture of motives informed this development, including concerns over the security of sensitive information (news of a Communist spy ring in Canada had broken in early 1946) and nationalist urges to retain a monopoly of control, while legislators had been in ignorance of the substance of the wartime agreements covering collaboration reached between Churchill and Roosevelt.[28] The McMahon Act also brought into being the Congressional Joint Committee on Atomic Energy (JCAE) which served as a powerful watchdog in subsequent years to ensure that the provisions of the legislation were being adhered to by whatever US administration was in office. Subsequent espionage scandals, most importantly the case of the naturalised-British atomic spy Klaus Fuchs in early 1950, were to put paid to any lingering hopes that a fresh basis for nuclear collaboration could be found, with many Americans having grown distrustful of British security standards (it is sobering to recall, for example, that one Donald Maclean was the British Secretary to the Combined Policy Committee in Washington between late 1946 and September 1948).[29] The umbilical cord which had tied together the military nuclear efforts of the United States and Britain was now comprehensively severed, leaving British scientists, engineers and technicians to plough their lonely nuclear furrow for the next 12 years.

The termination of nuclear collaboration with the United States, it should be stressed, served as no check on the determination of ministers and officials to press ahead with a national programme of nuclear weapons development. Indeed, it was soon to be appreciated that only by demonstrating its nuclear expertise would Britain, in time, be readmitted to a close nuclear relationship with Washington. A final decision to develop and manufacture an atomic bomb – in some senses, as we have seen, more a ratification of a course of policy toward acquiring a nuclear capability that had already been firmly established by the government – was taken by a small Cabinet Committee, GEN 163, chaired by the Prime Minister, in January 1947. Although some were to express reservations about the costs involved (including the Chancellor of the Exchequer, who was, one should note, missing from the crucial GEN 163 meeting), the consensus of senior ministers was that Britain had to have the new weapon, as other states would surely proceed along a similar path of weapons development. Towards the end of the previous year the Foreign Secretary had been adamant that Britain had to have the bomb if it was to speak with sufficient weight in its relations with the United States, and now Bevin told his colleagues that it was

> important that we should press on with the study of all aspects of atomic energy. We could not afford to acquiesce in an American monopoly of this new development. Other countries also might well develop atomic weapons. Unless, therefore an effective international system could be developed under which the production and use of the weapon would be prohibited, we must develop it ourselves.[30]

In Gowing's estimation, the January 1947 decision was 'not the result of careful strategic calculation but rather the reflex action of a still great power with great military commitments.'[31]

It is, therefore, worth recalling the strategic picture that held sway when the key decisions for a national programme were made. Dominant here was the uncomfortable reality that Britain faced a perilous and uncertain post-war world, where the atomic bomb might be crucial for national defence, made all the more dangerous with the swift breakdown of the wartime Grand Alliance. Since even before the defeat of Germany the COS had begun to forecast that Britain's most likely post-war military adversary would be the Soviet Union, and there was a widespread assumption that during the war years the Russians had also been engaged in nuclear research.[32]

To many observers, the Truman administration's policy toward the Soviet Union and European commitments generally seemed very unsettled during 1946, with several signs that a retreat to pre-war patterns of isolation might be in the offing. For a Britain that had had to stand alone in 1940, and at the end of the war held no guarantee that the United States would agree to participate in future measures of collective Western defence, initiating a nuclear programme seemed the only wise and prudent course to adopt. Moreover, possession of a nuclear capability accorded with the status of being, alongside the United States, the leading Western power responsible for ensuring that international peace and security were upheld. Indeed, far from enjoying any peace dividend with victory in the recent war, defence planners had to readjust to the menacing presence of Soviet military power in the heart of Europe, behind which lay a totalitarian system of government equipped with an ideology that predicted the demise of capitalism in the West, and which was busy consolidating – with the assistance of local communist parties and using brutal, police state methods – its firm hold over the peoples of Eastern Europe.

Britain had emerged from the war as one of the 'big three' victorious powers, with a permanent seat on the United Nations Security Council and substantial military forces deployed around the globe, but her economic condition had been seriously weakened by the exertions of the war years.

Numerous challenges would have to be faced if she was to live up to her Great Power billing, manage the processes of change sweeping across the colonial empire, and engage in the necessary task of post-war reconstruction and welfare provision at home. Thus, as well as coping with Soviet pressure in Central Europe, British defence policy had to respond to the problems of policing an empire which, when not already on the road to self-government and independence, was increasingly beset with nationalist unrest in the Middle East, Asia and Africa, unrest which, it was anticipated with some foreboding, the forces of international Communism would soon be in a position to exploit.

Policymaking frameworks

The bureaucratic machinery within Whitehall that was to oversee defence policy in this challenging environment went through significant change in the immediate post-war years. The basic building blocks for the central organisation of Britain's post-war defence had been established by a White Paper and subsequent legislation passed in October 1946 which had given the Prime Minister 'supreme responsibility' in this field, and called into existence a new Defence Committee of the Cabinet, which replaced the former Committee of Imperial Defence.[33] As the professional military advisers to the Government, the Chiefs of Staff had responsibility for making recommendations on the most appropriate strategy to adopt in response to international circumstances and available resources, preparing strategic plans for the Cabinet's Defence Committee, and, finally, carrying them out. To perform their tasks the COS could call upon the assistance of two subsidiary bodies, the Joint Planning Staff (JPS) and the Joint Intelligence Committee (JIC). The COS had begun meeting in Committee as early as 1924, but their collective identity was now considered to be a part of a separate Ministry of Defence (MoD), which was officially constituted on 1 January 1947.

The new Ministry was supposed to provide a degree of coordination to the formulation of defence policy that had hitherto been so sorely lacking, but the formal powers of the 'Minister of Defence' – a post created by Churchill in 1940 precisely so that he could combine the premiership with his predilection for intervening in military affairs – however, remained amorphous and decidedly limited in the immediate post-war years. Despite being designated deputy chairman of the Defence Committee, and in theory being able to chair the COS Committee when desired (as Churchill had done on numerous occasions during the war), the Minister of Defence's role was largely confined to formulating common administrative policies and, with the help of a tiny staff, allocating resources to the different services in accordance with the requirements of the Defence Committee. Moreover, the service ministries – Admiralty, Air Ministry and War Office – with their well-established, numerous, and intensely-territorial staffs, were powerful fiefdoms, whose ministers sat on the Defence Committee and vied for their share of the defence budget. It was the service ministers who proposed and decided the weapons programmes which would be introduced to meet the Cold War requirements of defence policy, with the Defence Research Policy Committee (DRPC) set up in January 1947, and chaired by Tizard, the MoD's Chief Scientist, largely a rubber stamp at the end of the process.[34] The connections between the military policies enunciated by the COS and the atomic programme of the government were, moreover, also ill-coordinated for much of the early post-war period.

When the Attlee Government took its initial decisions to proceed with atomic energy research and development in October 1945 consideration had been given as to whether a single minister should be appointed to give their whole attention to the field of atomic energy. The Prime Minister decided, however, that this 'would not be practicable' as the subject raised so many questions that cut across different policy realms, not least in relation to defence and foreign affairs. It was left to the Foreign Secretary, Ernest Bevin, to suggest that 'just as in the United States final authority on these questions lay with the President, so in this country the general responsibility ought to rest with the Prime Minister.' Attlee agreed, adding that he would 'continue to consult his colleagues on major questions of policy as they arose.'[35]

As it transpired, atomic energy subjects featured only ten times on the Cabinet's full agenda during the Labour Governments that held office between 1945 and 1951, with the majority of these devoted to the Prime Minister's visits to Washington in November 1945 and December 1950. The principal vehicle for discussion of nuclear policy issues during the first two years of Attlee's premiership was a small ad hoc Cabinet committee, GEN 75, which he chaired and to which only a few selected ministers were invited. As was noted above, the Government's eventual decision to proceed with a British atomic weapons programme was taken in January 1947 by an even smaller ministerial gathering – GEN 163 – and so helped to consolidate the pattern for subsequent high-level political discussion of strategic nuclear policy. The senior ministers involved in the case of the GEN 163 Committee included just the Prime Minister, Foreign Secretary, Lord President of the Council, Secretary of State for the Dominions, Minister of Defence, and Minister of Supply. It was this style of confined conclave which was to be replicated throughout most of the post-war period, with few decisions about weapons development being reported to Cabinet (the exception being Churchill's handling of the decision in 1954 to develop and manufacture a hydrogen bomb).[36]

A problem that became apparent during this period and was to become a recurring feature of the management of nuclear policy was lack of coordination between different government departments. Responsibility and oversight for the nuclear programme lay with the Ministry of Supply, but its links to the Ministry of Defence and the services were often tenuous and a cause of tension, while its own control of the atomic project has been described as weak.[37] The COS themselves gave little direct advice on the size or composition of the nuclear programme, despite their ostensible role in aligning such requirements with the specific needs of the services, while they displayed, in general, ambivalence over how nuclear weapons would be used in any confrontation with the Soviet Union, at least up to the period when Moscow acquired a nuclear capability of its own.[38]

All this can hardly be deemed surprising. As the nation demobilised and defence budgets shrank, British forces were stretched around the globe and engaged in a bewildering array of tasks, ranging from occupation duties in central Europe, to maintaining the British position in the Middle East in the face of nationalist pressures and violent unrest – being forced to leave Palestine in 1948 – to coping with the outbreak of a major insurgency in Malaya. Senior officers were exhausted after long years of war, and now faced adapting to an unruly world where the dangers and threats were of an entirely new order. Formulating nuclear strategy and finding the appropriate place for nuclear weapons in more general strategic plans was one more original and demanding challenge faced by a defence establishment already under immense strain.

Another notable feature of the early phase of British nuclear policy, and one which was to become the established norm, for accepted and obvious reasons, was that it was shrouded in high levels of secrecy. The revelation of Soviet espionage efforts during and just after the war, apparent after the Gouzenko defection in September 1945, Alan Nunn May's arrest in March 1946, and, most traumatic of all, the Fuchs case in 1950, put an even greater premium on security.[39] As the official historian of these first years of nuclear development put it, 'Mr Attlee and his closest colleagues wanted the public to know as little as possible lest an enemy learn even more.' Costs of the programme were buried in the defence research and development estimates for the Ministry of Supply. Official acknowledgement that atomic weapons were being developed was provided to the House of Commons by the Minister of Defence in May 1948, but the barest of information was given, and an advance D-notice was issued by the MoD to prevent extensive press speculation and further inquiry.[40]

Lack of parliamentary scrutiny also meant, however, that a programme could avoid attracting any controversy, or critical public comment, an increasingly important consideration as the demands of post-war defence cut into the resources available for domestic reconstruction and social provision. Atomic energy was never made the subject of debate in the House of Commons during Labour's term in office. The 'principles and procedures of peacetime Cabinet, ministerial, departmental and Parliamentary government' were circumvented when it came to the military nuclear field, and would remain so, in general, whichever complexion of government was in power over subsequent years.[41] When Churchill came back to the premiership in October 1951 he was surprised by the large scale of the nuclear programme and how it had been possible to conceal its scope from parliamentary scrutiny. Nevertheless, he saw no good reason to alter the practice during his own administration.[42]

The organisation with the responsibility for developing Britain's initial nuclear weapons capability grew out of the Ministry of Supply's wartime Armament Research Department, which had its main establishment at Fort Halstead in Kent. In charge of all kinds of weapons research and development as Chief Superintendent of the Department from January 1946 onwards was the key figure of William Penney, then only 36 years old. With a pre-war high-flying academic background as a mathematical physicist of prodigious natural gifts, Penney had been made an assistant professor at Imperial College London at the age of 27, but in 1940 war work at the Admiralty, where he began by specialising on blast wave properties, took him away from the academic world into a long career in government service. At Los Alamos, where he was sent as part of a 30 strong British team in early 1944, Penney had made several important contributions to the atomic bomb project and provided ideas about its utilisation. He had earned lasting American scientific respect as a result, and forged many personal and professional friendships. Along with Group Captain Leonard Cheshire, he witnessed the dropping of the second atomic bomb over Nagasaki, was an early inspector of the blast damage at Hiroshima, and became an expert assessor of atomic effects and yields as a result of his work in Japan. Even after the curtailment of Anglo-American nuclear collaboration in the early post-war years, the Americans remained keen to use his expertise. With his unique experience, formidable problem-solving intellect and easy-going charm, Penney was an obvious choice to lead the British nuclear weapons programme (while virtually all the other members of the British contingent at Los Alamos had moved back into academic work, were no longer interested in weapons development, or were engaged in more basic atomic research at Harwell). In June 1947, having been entrusted with the critical and Herculean task of developing and producing Britain's first atomic bomb, Penney set about energising a small group of scientists and engineers at Fort Halstead to engage in what was described with cryptic ambiguity as 'high explosives research'.[43]

Within a short time it was apparent that Penney's group, now expanding in number, would need a separate establishment, set apart from their non-nuclear counterparts in Armaments Research, where the programme's special requirements, not least in terms of safety and security, could be accommodated. Starting to formulate his ambitious conception of such an establishment in November 1948, Penney was clear it would have to be in the nature of a 'factory', eventually capable of producing upwards of 50 atomic bombs a year, so that by 1957 the COS's requirement to have amassed a UK stockpile of 200 weapons would have been met.[44] In fact, Penney soon came to resist the relocation of facilities, fearing the inevitable disruption that would result, but at the start of April 1950 the former wartime RAF station at Aldermaston in Berkshire began to be occupied as the site for a new Atomic Weapons Research Establishment (AWRE), where purpose-built workshops, laboratories and offices could be established.[45]

With personnel divided between their old and new locations, Penney's weapons group embarked upon a remarkably swift programme of research, design and fabrication. Wartime knowledge from British involvement with the Manhattan Project was certainly important – Gowing's comment was that as a result of the presence of a British team at Los Alamos, 'In so far as "know-how" went the British were well equipped for the construction of atomic bombs' – but there were still huge challenges to be overcome in numerous fields of new scientific and technical work, such as the processing of fissile material and the engineering of components to extremely fine tolerances.[46] A crucial limiting factor in the whole process was the supply of plutonium, sufficient quantities of which for a test device did not begin to become available until about March 1952.[47] Severe staff shortages at times also hindered Penney's progress, and in its final stages, with the date for an initial test fixed for the autumn of 1952, the project became a 'frantic race against time with serious problems solved only at the eleventh hour'.[48]

The Cold War strategic context

When Penney's hard-pressed staff began their work on the British bomb project in mid-1947 the international climate seemed filled with fresh dangers and uncertainties. While most commentators did not credit the Soviet leadership with the intention of launching an all-out general war during this period, tensions with the West could be anticipated over such issues as the treatment of an occupied and divided Germany, or the maintenance of the Western enclave in Berlin. At its first meeting of January 1947, the COS heard and largely endorsed a presentation on the future pattern of war from the Commandant of the Imperial Defence College, General Sir William Slim, which held that 'Russia by reason of her policy, Government and mentality can be taken as the only potential aggressor. While it is not considered that Russia intends to embark on a major war, she may, by reason of her forward policy unintentionally over-reach the point at which other Powers would be forced to take up arms against her.' Russia would henceforth have to be 'taken as the yardstick for our defence preparations.' If she did decide to attack the UK in the future this was most likely to take the form of an air offensive with atomic or biological weapons directed against major British industrial centres and ports; a land advance across Western Europe to the Channel ports, putting Britain within range of short-range rockets; and submarine attacks on the UK's vital sea communications. The vulnerability of the UK to modern forms of air and missile attack, and the impracticality of finding effective measures of dispersion or civil defence led to the conclusion that,

> Real defence in the atomic age must lie in making an aggressor realise that while he may wreck the nation he attacks, he will at once be subjected to such a counter blow that, whatever success he gains in his initial attack, will be purchased too dearly. Our main defence should be a

counter offensive force, in readiness to deliver such a counter blow the moment we are attacked, and the knowledge that it exists.

The counter-offensive strike would have to be delivered by air with the latest atomic weapons, with long-range rockets probably replacing aircraft over the much longer term.[49]

This kind of thinking was also reflected and amplified in the major report on future defence policy produced by the Chiefs of Staff in May 1947, which was equally gloomy in tone. In a stark portrayal of the looming threat from Russian territorial and ideological expansion, it was admitted that Soviet land forces could easily overrun Western Europe if they chose, putting the United Kingdom within range, once they had been developed, of shorter-range Soviet rockets. When she acquired nuclear weapons, the COS argued, the 'only means' whereby their use by Russia in war might be prevented

> is by facing her with the threat of large-scale damage from similar weapons if she should employ them. This threat can only be achieved by evidence of our ability to use weapons of mass destruction on a considerable scale from the outset. In addition we believe that the knowledge that we possessed weapons of mass destruction and were prepared to use them would be a most effective deterrent to war itself.[50]

Nevertheless, on the part of both Attlee and Bevin during 1946 and early 1947 there was still a strong reluctance to automatically accept the bleak analyses offered by the COS and the military establishment, and an unwillingness to give up on any idea that some accommodation with the Soviet Union might be possible. The Foreign Secretary retained aspirations that Britain could play the role of a 'third force', standing with its West European and Commonwealth partners between the United States and Soviet Union, while the Prime Minister, for his part, was concerned that if faced by too much overt Western pressure Moscow could become even more belligerent during a period when Washington's support was not assured.[51]

The sharp deterioration in East-West relations which was witnessed during 1948, including events such as the Czech coup and Berlin blockade, marked the end of hopes that agreement over a European settlement might be possible and put paid to any idea that tensions with the Soviet Union could be averted. Now with Bevin to the fore, assiduous efforts were made by British diplomacy from the spring of 1948 onwards to encourage the United States to adopt a binding commitment to the security of Western Europe, culminating in the formation of the North Atlantic Alliance in April 1949.

Four months after the North Atlantic Treaty Organization (NATO's) creation the Soviet Union carried out its first test of an atomic bomb, an achievement that came far sooner than most Western intelligence assessments had anticipated. Anxieties regarding the potential for Soviet conventional military power to overrun the shallow defences of Western Europe were now coupled with the growth of Moscow's own nuclear capabilities, putting an even greater onus on Western nuclear forces to offer an effective deterrent to outright Soviet aggression. In this context, membership of the Western alliance afforded Britain some degree of assurance. Indeed, ever since the deployment of US B-29 bombers to the UK at the time of the Berlin blockade crisis in July 1948 (and despite the fact that the aircraft were not actually equipped for atomic operations) there had been an implicit assumption that a US nuclear guarantee – with Washington still enjoying a monopoly on such weapons – operated when it came to the defence of Western Europe.[52]

The shape of the nuclear offensive which might be directed at the Soviet Union began to receive some official attention during this period. In the autumn of 1948 the Joint Intelligence Committee, working alongside the Joint Planning Staff, was asked by the COS to examine how atomic weapons might best be used offensively in a war against Russia in order to achieve 'a rapid and decisive victory.' The outbreak of such a war was assumed to occur in 1957, and Allied belligerents would include the UK, USA and other members of the soon to be signed North Atlantic Pact.[53] The resulting report was eventually produced in early August 1949. It presented the argument that

> effective atomic attack on all the towns which are centres of control – political, economic and administrative – is the best method of creating conditions in which the functions of Government and of the Soviet Police would break down. This would necessitate attacking about 100 large towns in the Soviet Union; moreover, it would be essential to attack all these centres within as short a period as possible. An additional advantage of such a plan would be that about 15 per cent of the total population of the Soviet Union would either become casualties or be displaced. This might weaken the will of the people to resist. Unless, however, the administration is broken, fear of the Secret Police, the fundamental patriotism of the Soviet people, and their capacity to endure hardships, together with their Communist upbringing, would be sufficient to make the Russian people follow their leaders and support Soviet war policy.

To achieve such a large scale attack on Soviet urban areas, it was calculated, would take somewhere between 400 and 575 atomic bombs. 'The destruction of these [100] cities,' the report concluded, 'would be a national disaster of such magnitude that it might also be expected to shatter the faith of the Russian people in their leaders and would seriously weaken both their will and ability to continue the war.'[54]

Within only a few weeks of the production of this report, the Soviet Union would also have the capacity to retaliate against a nuclear attack, or even to initiate the use of nuclear weapons itself, underlining even further Britain's ultimate dependence on the United States for security. However, this uncomfortable fact also carried its own dilemmas. In any confrontation with Moscow, and especially before Soviet nuclear forces had any kind of intercontinental delivery capability, it would be the UK mainland, and the advance airbases it was willing to provide the bombers of the US Strategic Air Command, that would become a prime target for any initial Russian nuclear attack, with all the devastating consequences that would follow.

During the early 1950s, when a British nuclear capability was still incipient, ideas about target priorities in military circles were to be influenced by this powerful sense of the physical vulnerability of the UK to Soviet air attack and move away from the JIC's earlier assumptions. The best way to limit the massive damage that might be caused in such an eventuality, it was believed, was to neutralise it at source by directing the allied atomic air offensive against the airfields of the Soviet long-range air force and known sites of nuclear storage and production, as well as other significant military targets. Only the United States, however, had the resources to mount such an offensive, but American atomic planning, except in barest outline, remained very much an unknown quantity to British officials.[55]

Britain's exposed geographical position also made its leaders concerned that precipitate or belligerent American actions, particularly in Asia after the outbreak of the Korean War in June 1950 and the onset of sustained Sino-American confrontation following later Chinese intervention in that conflict, might trigger a course of events that could lead to a general war with the Soviet Union over issues which were not considered vital, and under circumstances which were not of the government's own choosing. These general political considerations were also important in providing impetus to the drive for a national nuclear force, as it was felt one of the keys to giving London a voice in the central decisions of war and peace that might arise over the coming years.

The heightened international tensions following the first Soviet nuclear test in August 1949, combined with the outbreak of the Korean War, also emphasised the need to reinforce by a substantial margin the then meagre military resources available to the NATO Alliance. Within the UK's defence establishment a lively inter-service debate had, in fact, been underway since early 1948 over the degree of commitment to a conventional defence of Western Europe that should be entertained and the land forces that would have to be allocated to this task. The Foreign Office was keen that Britain's new Western European allies should be given some tangible sign that they would be defended as far to the east as possible, not least as it might help to persuade them to bolster their own contributions, a view which naturally found favour in Army circles. Nevertheless, the Navy saw it as vital to maintain the security of Britain's sea communications in the event of war, while the Air Force stressed defence of the UK homeland and the build-up of a strategic deterrent force. A tussle over the proper allocation of resources ensued, and the ill-coordinated machinery of defence decision-making then in existence, crowned by the weak powers of the Minister of Defence, did not aid the production of a coherent policy.[56]

To some defence planners who considered the changes wrought to the situation by the Soviet test, British nuclear capabilities would now arrive too late to make much difference to a strategic balance that seemed to be shifting very rapidly in the direction of the Sino-Soviet bloc. Previous estimates that the Soviet Union would not be in a position to contemplate a military clash with the West until 1957 (the date when the COS had stipulated that a UK stockpile of 200 atomic weapons should be available) now looked decidedly optimistic. This new appraisal suggested that resources might have to be switched away from the nuclear programme and a greater emphasis placed on forces for conventional defence which could be made available more quickly. Indeed, in the spring of 1950 the COS moved to recommend, and the Defence Committee to accept, that British ground forces should be committed to the defence of Western Europe in the event of a Soviet attack.[57] On the other hand, no slackening in an indigenous nuclear programme seemed prudent when the arrival of the Soviet atomic bomb contained the potential over the longer term to negate the effect of the US nuclear guarantee.[58] Anglo-American disputes over the conduct of the Korean War during the winter of 1950–51 underlined the political disadvantages that could follow excessive dependence on Washington and the need to assert an independent voice in the affairs of the Alliance.[59]

The advocates for a greater emphasis on the conventional defence of Western Europe appeared to have achieved their goal of a more balanced policy by the autumn of 1950 as the need to bolster NATO's ability to withstand a Soviet ground offensive became more widely recognised. The Americans proved ready to offer a substantial troop presence on the Continent, and to supply a General (in the form of Dwight D. Eisenhower) to give NATO overall military leadership, but the bargain that had to be accepted by the West Europeans was that the controversial process of German rearmament should form part of the whole package.[60] By the end of the year, under the spur of the Korean War, the Labour Government – at no little cost to party unity – had endorsed a new and ambitious programme of rearmament that broke decisively with the previous downward trends in defence spending. At its Lisbon meeting in February 1952 the NATO Council, much to the pleasure of the Truman administration, agreed a number of ambitious targets for the build-up of the Alliance's conventional forces. However, the Lisbon force goals soon proved to be far beyond the political will and economic preferences of its members to meet. Instead, the development of tactical nuclear weapons offered a ready substitute for deficiencies in conventional strength, while their prospective use in the event of a Soviet invasion seemed to be a viable proposition when Soviet deployment of similar weapons still lagged some years behind. Indeed, the US Army, a large proportion of whose forces were stationed after early 1951 in support of NATO's Central Front, increasingly considered that a nuclear posture in Western Europe – where tactical nuclear weapons would be used in support of ground operations – was the only way to achieve a forward defence of the theatre.[61]

The election of a Conservative Government in Britain in October 1951 brought with it the widespread realisation that the rearmament measures so recently introduced were placing an intolerable burden on the economy and could prejudice the social provision that the electorate expected from their political leaders. In January 1952, having acceded to the Treasury's increasingly strident warnings, Churchill decided to stretch out the rearmament programme and look for cuts in defence spending. Taking their cue from the top, and with the balance of payments in a dire position, at the end of April 1952 the COS met over several days at Greenwich in order to get to grips with some of the major issues of strategic policy raised by the repercussions of the arrival of a Soviet nuclear capability for the military balance in central Europe that was set to become such a defining feature of the Cold War. The dominant voice amongst the COS at this time on strategic matters was Air Chief Marshal Sir John Slessor, the Chief of Air Staff (CAS) between 1950 and 1952, who was to use his tenure in office to give the cause of the RAF's nascent nuclear role a large boost.

As a group the COS were animated by the growing belief that the immediate threat of a Soviet attack had passed, and that the Cold War was likely to be a protracted and drawn out struggle, where domestic economic health and vitality would be an essential feature of defensive preparedness. They were also impressed by the exponential growth in US atomic capabilities that had been witnessed over the previous 18 months, a development which made them think that any Soviet conventional aggression was unlikely until Moscow had also amassed a significant nuclear armoury. The result of their deliberations at Greenwich was the production in June of a paper on 'Defence Policy and Global Strategy' which concluded that since 'in the foreseeable future' there could be no defence against nuclear attack, primary stress should be placed on deterrence and the threat of retaliation as the best way to forestall Communist aggression. 'The first aim of allied policy,' the paper had reminded its readers, 'must be to prevent war.'[62]

Although by no means novel, the analysis presented by the COS paper was designed to dispel any notion that a purely conventional defence was a viable option for the NATO Alliance if it should face a direct invasion from Soviet bloc forces deployed in Europe. Despite the Royal Navy's insistence that there be inclusion of the concept of 'broken-backed' warfare, where some fighting might still continue after a series of devastating nuclear exchanges (and in what was a reflection of the inter-service differences that still blighted the formation of a coherent defence policy), the ability of the Allied strategic air forces to wage an intense atomic offensive against the Soviet Union in the short initial phases of a world war was nevertheless seen as the decisive factor in deterring war, or even winning it should it nevertheless breakout. The June 1952 COS paper was to prove influential in underlining the importance of deterrence in British strategic planning, and through its attempts to diminish the role of conventional forces in a 'hot' war with the Soviet Union (in the expectation of some that this would permit reductions to defence spending to be made). At the same time, the compromises it contained, including its admission that some forces might still be needed after an initial nuclear exchange, and its warnings against any precipitate cuts in the forces then deployed in central Europe or the Middle and Far East, set the stage for the struggles over the defence budget that were to feature for the rest of the decade.[63]

In the developing Cold War, the COS were particularly insistent about the need for better cooperation between Britain and her allies, and of the importance of close Anglo-American relations. It was the United States, after all, that would have to provide the West's principal share of nuclear capability. Reliance on the United States, while retaining as much influence as possible, had by now become a key feature of British foreign and defence policy. As the United States projected its post-war power into regions of the world which had formerly been dominated by British interests, such as in the Middle East and South East Asia, it became incumbent on governments to persuade and guide Washington to follow policies which allowed Britain to either maintain her position, or provide time and opportunity for careful withdrawal rather than hasty retreat. 'It is becoming clear,' Anthony Eden, the Foreign Secretary, had explained for the Cabinet's benefit in June 1952, 'that rigorous maintenance of the presently-accepted policies of Her Majesty's Government at home and abroad is placing a burden on the country's economy which it is beyond the resources of the country to meet. A position has already been reached where there is no reserve and therefore no margin for unforeseen additional obligations.' But since Britain's position as a world power depended on maintaining its external responsibilities, and any vacuum created might offer the Soviet Union opportunities to exploit, the Foreign Office looked toward transferring some of the obligations they entailed rather than looking toward a drastic policy of wholesale withdrawal. Hence, according to Eden's paper, 'Our aim should be to persuade the United States to assume the real burdens ... while retaining for ourselves as much political control – and hence prestige and world influence – as we can. As regards the defence of Western Europe, we should seek to induce the United States to assume a larger share of the common burden.' Nevertheless, 'a policy of this kind will only be successful with the United States in so far as we are able to demonstrate that we are making the maximum possible effort ourselves, and the more gradually and inconspicuously we can transfer the real burdens from our own to American shoulders, the less damage we shall do to our position and influence in the world.'[64]

In their own Global Strategy paper, the COS had been quite categorical that a British nuclear capability, operating alongside the Americans, was an essential component of defence policy and could offer several military and political advantages. For one, it could not be certain that the US nuclear effort would be directed at all the targets that were of most significance to the UK, including Soviet air and submarine bases which could pose a direct threat to Britain and her vital communications. But providing a contribution to the overall Western deterrent might also give Britain an entrance card into the currently closed world of US nuclear planning and even allow a restraining influence on hasty or over-zealous American action to be exercised. As the COS expressed it, 'to have no share in what is recognised as the main deterrent in the Cold War, and the only allied offensive in world war, would seriously weaken British influence on American policy and planning in the Cold War, and in war would mean that the United Kingdom would have no claim to any share in the policy or planning of the offensive.'[65]

It became doubly important to defence planners therefore, that the scale and speed of the UK nuclear programme should be stepped up over the next few years and imperative that Britain's own V-bomber force should be brought into operation as soon as practicable. Without a nuclear capability, the UK's bomber resources would necessarily have to be used to complement the air strength available to NATO, as stipulated by the US Supreme Allied Commander Europe (SACEUR). Directives issued by the Air Ministry to the C-in-C Bomber Command during the early 1950s, when the only aircraft then available to the force were obsolescent Lincolns and the new Canberra light bombers (all carrying conventional weapons), had in fact stressed the support that should be given to NATO's frontline in central Europe. As one senior officer put it in late 1952, '…until the C-in-C Bomber Command receives more modern equipment, the first priority for his force will be to attack those targets which will do most to reduce the scale of attack by land and air on Western Europe, including the UK. In this connection he will work in close conjunction with SACEUR and receive a target list of priorities from time to time.'[66]

The case for accelerating Britain's nuclear efforts was put forward most forcefully during this period by Lord Cherwell, who after October 1951 as Paymaster General (with a seat in the Cabinet) and someone with long experience of the UK atomic programme, acted as Churchill's chief adviser on nuclear matters. Cherwell was convinced that Britain had to have her own stock of bombs, a position which did not find automatic favour with the Prime Minister. Churchill had been intensely critical of the loosening of nuclear collaboration with the United States that had been seen during the Attlee Governments, and he had anticipated in notably sentimental fashion that his return to Downing Street in October 1951 would bring about an improvement to the situation, and a resurrection of the 'combined' spirit of the 1943 Quebec Agreement. At one early point Churchill had even contemplated giving up on the idea of manufacturing nuclear weapons in the UK once the first British test had been completed in the expectation that the United States would be willing to meet British requirements from its own stockpile.[67] But in the face of the restrictions posed by US atomic energy legislation, and the guarded position of US officials in the Truman administration, this was always highly unlikely.

Nevertheless, there were still major uncertainties over the number of weapons that Aldermaston would eventually be expected to produce. It will be recalled that Penney had originally envisaged the establishment as being able to generate a stockpile of 200 bombs by 1957, but this was very much an arbitrary figure offered by the COS in 1948 (based on the UK delivering one third of an air atomic offensive mounted in concert with the United States) and there had thus far been little attempt to match such estimates to rudimentary war planning.[68] The problem was given candid expression by Lieutenant General Sir Frederick Morgan, the Controller of Atomic Energy at the Ministry of Supply, who wrote to Penney in early 1952:

> As we go today, the whole of our atomic energy project in England derives from a requirement for weapons expressed in terms of delivery of a stated number of these over a defined period. Were it not for this, all we should own would be a comparatively small research and development organisation devoted to the pursuit of somewhat vague objectives both nuclear and nebulous.
>
> As I understand it, the output figures for weapons agreed upon was arrived at originally by some sort of process akin to that known as a Dutch Auction. It seems to be that the requirement has never been keyed in any definite way to any plan or strategy or tactics. This is in a way understandable since we know that the atomic bomb, ever since the original handling of the publicity concerning Hiroshima and Nagasaki, has been regarded as a political far more than a military weapon…[69]

In order to satisfy Morgan's wish for more concrete nuclear planning, however, a degree of effective coordination with the United States was a prerequisite, and of this there seemed little immediate prospect.

During the Prime Minister's visit to Washington in January 1952, amid outward signs of amity, it was apparent that the Americans remained very reluctant to divulge anything about their nuclear war planning against the Soviet Union beyond the barest outline.[70] Evelyn Shuckburgh, a Foreign Office official with the British delegation, recalling in his diary the mood of the meetings, wrote that Truman was inclined to be 'quite abrupt', and after Churchill's delivery of another soliloquy on Anglo-American solidarity would 'cut it off with a "Thank you, Mr Prime Minister. We might pass that to be worked out by our advisers." A little wounding. It was impossible not to be conscious that we are playing second fiddle.'[71] The advice from Slessor, who had a good feeling for the currents of US opinion, was that without an atomic capability of its own, the British voice in matters of overall strategic planning would be muted.[72]

Furthermore, no advance toward technical cooperation with the Americans would be entertained in Washington, it was clear, until Britain's own nuclear development had reached a much more advanced stage, and while memories of lax British security procedures were still so fresh. An announcement was made in February 1952 that Britain's first atomic test would soon be forthcoming, but Cherwell was far from convinced that the existing administrative structures were adequate to provide the rapid advance in the weapons programme that was now felt needed, particularly as service requirements for new variants began to be formulated.

Dissatisfaction with the constraints and inflexibility that placing the programme within ordinary civil service administrative structures seemed to entail had in fact become fairly widespread by the early 1950s. The chief innovation propounded by Cherwell was to liberate the UK nuclear programme from civil service control by creating a public corporation, at arms-length from government, which would take charge of all matters relating to atomic energy. After much inter-departmental wrangling, and only after the first atomic test had been completed was the Cabinet finally persuaded in April 1953 to accept the case for the creation of a semi-independent public corporation, able to recruit staff and operate with greater freedom than if the nuclear project had remained under the direct control of the Ministry of Supply. The following year legislation was passed by Parliament leading to the creation of the UK Atomic Energy Authority (AEA), which brought within its areas of responsibility the developing civil reactor programme, and what was now termed Penney's 'Weapons Group' at AWRE.[73] It was under this new organisational dispensation – with the AEA expected to produce the nuclear weapons needed by the services, and with their requirements still being filtered through the Ministry of Supply – that Aldermaston's scientific staff were to face their next great challenge: the design, development and eventual testing of a British hydrogen bomb.

The thermonuclear revolution

The success of the first British atomic test – Operation Hurricane – conducted at the Monte Bello islands off the north-west coast of Australia on 3 October 1952, certainly demonstrated the ability of Britain's scientists and engineers to master the new technology, and brought a great sense of relief that the huge industrial and scientific effort involved had paid some dividend. But this landmark event, although undoubtedly important for reasons of status and prestige, did not yet offer the UK a capability that made any appreciable strategic difference. Initial Blue Danube nuclear weapons were not delivered to RAF Wittering until November 1953, when service training in their handling and maintenance could begin in earnest.[74] The V-bombers still remained under development, however, and no aircraft would be capable of carrying the new bombs until the first Valiants began to arrive at RAF stations in 1955. It was not until January 1956, in fact, that a Valiant squadron equipped with Blue Danube was finally declared operational, and only in October of that same year was the first actual test of a weapon dropped from a Valiant carried out at the Maralinga range in Australia.[75]

Entry into the nuclear club had been achieved after a major effort (and with an estimated expenditure of £150 million), but it was soon apparent that the costs of maintaining a subscription would become even more onerous. Only a month after the Monte Bello test the United States detonated the world's first thermonuclear device – not yet a deliverable bomb – at Eniwetok atoll, a huge blast which destroyed the island test site and registered an unprecedented yield in excess of 10 megatons. The Americans, it was reported, had not been particularly impressed with the first British atomic test; a UK breakthrough in the thermonuclear field would, however, represent a wholly different proposition.[76]

Details of what had occurred during the 'Mike' test of November 1952 were not officially released by the US authorities until February 1954, but awareness of the enormous destructive potential that had been unleashed was widely rumoured and reported.[77] With weapons soon to be available many hundreds of times more powerful than the bombs dropped on Hiroshima and Nagasaki – one aircraft equipped with a single hydrogen bomb could carry the destructive force of all the conventional explosives dropped on the Axis powers in the Second World War – it was clear that another step change in thinking about the consequences of nuclear war was in the offing.

To the incoming Eisenhower administration in Washington, which took office in January 1953, US nuclear superiority over the Soviet bloc was regarded as fundamental to how Communist threats and pressures were to be met. Determined to make economies in the ballooning defence budgets that had been occasioned by the Korean War, by the end of that year US defence policy had begun to embrace the 'New Look', where nuclear weapons were to be integrated into the inventories and operational doctrine of the US services and the special distinctions that had typically been drawn with conventional weapons broken down.[78] Public expression of this new stance was given by the US Secretary of State, John Foster Dulles, in a January 1954 speech to the Council on Foreign Relations in New York where he avowed there was 'no local defense which alone will contain the mighty land power of the Communist world,' which would henceforth have to be 'reinforced by the further deterrent of massive retaliatory power.' In future, Dulles announced, US policy would 'depend primarily upon a great capacity to retaliate instantly by means and at places of our own choosing.'[79]

The term 'massive retaliation' was soon employed as a short-hand for the reliance that was to be placed on an immediate nuclear response to instances of Communist aggression, although what specific actions would trigger such a response, the scale and scope of the retaliation that would follow, and the consequences that would flow from it, were subjects of major contention. Tactical nuclear support for US military units in Europe began to arrive during the year, and in December 1954 the new approach was made formal in NATO terms when the North Atlantic Council adopted MC-48 as the basis for Alliance military strategy and planning. This important document made plain that any large-scale Soviet aggression in Europe was to be met by the Alliance with an immediate and all-out nuclear offensive; there would be little hope of mounting any kind of protracted conventional defence, it was reasoned, while the best hope of finishing a war rapidly (and even successfully

– if such a term could be used in the awful circumstances which would ensue) was to strike at the sources of Soviet military power with the most destructive weapons in the Western arsenal.[80]

Almost as soon as the new strategy was being promulgated, however, it was subjected to sustained criticism from strategic thinkers and military commentators, including on the British side such notable figures as Patrick Blackett, Anthony Buzzard and Basil Liddell Hart, for the stark choices it presented and the unlikelihood that the Communist powers would believe that the West would use its full retaliatory power when faced with local aggression or limited war scenarios, especially when the Soviet Union itself had the means to retaliate with nuclear weapons. Some critics began to advocate a policy of 'graduated deterrence' (or what would several years later be labelled 'flexible response'), where an escalating series of steps would be taken to meet each level of Communist aggression, so improving the credibility of deterrence, and if war should occur, giving time for fighting to stop – perhaps through negotiation – before an all-out nuclear exchange was triggered.[81]

A policy based on massive retaliation, in the eyes of many strategic commentators, was predicated above all on the overwhelming nuclear superiority that was still enjoyed by the United States over its Soviet rival. But already, in August 1953, the Soviet Union had mounted its own test of a boosted fission weapon of around 400 kilotons, where thermonuclear reactions had been demonstrated, underlining the point that the lead of the West in the nuclear arms race was narrowing very rapidly.[82] Senior military and Foreign Office officials were also certainly concerned about the implications of the new US policy as expressed by Dulles, especially as there was continuing ambiguity over responses to minor or local aggression. In February 1954, during one meeting called to discuss the overall strategic picture, the Chief of the Imperial General Staff, Field Marshal Sir John Harding can be found telling his fellow Chiefs, as well as senior Foreign Office officials, that,

> The major deterrent to Global war had, up to now, been the Western World's lead over Russia in their ability to launch an atomic air offensive. As Russia became possessed of the same ability, our lead was shortened and the only deterrent facing both sides would eventually be the fear of committing mutual suicide. When both sides held more or less equal ability to wage advanced forms of war, the value of the Western Powers' existing deterrent no longer held good even against local and minor wars. The United Kingdom would not consider using atomic weapons in cases of minor local aggression. The question was whether or not the United States really intended so to retaliate against Russia in such minor cases.

Officials remained convinced, however, that in the event of a major conflict with the Soviet Union, nuclear weapons would have to be used immediately. 'It would be important that Ministers should appreciate,' the meeting agreed, 'the fact that if we went to war with Russia, we must regard the atomic weapon as any other and use it from the outset.'[83]

An even more significant event for public and private perceptions of the terrible properties and the huge destructive potential of nuclear weapons was the American test of its first deliverable hydrogen bomb at Bikini atoll in the Western Pacific on 1 March 1954. The 'Bravo' shot registered an unprecedented yield of 15 megatons, far higher than American expectations, and after a sudden shift of prevailing winds spread fallout across several inhabited Pacific atolls and into the path of the *Lucky Dragon*, a Japanese fishing trawler whose crew were sailing 80 miles from the blast and outside the exclusion zone that had been announced around the testing site.[84] The furore that followed helped to galvanise a world-wide anti-nuclear movement whose initial goal was to ban the testing of nuclear weapons in the atmosphere.[85]

In Britain, the repercussions of Bravo were felt at several different levels: popular anxieties over the prospect of nuclear war were demonstrated through the voices of peace activists, trade unionists and religious leaders, with many adherents to the growing anti-nuclear mood found in the grass-roots ranks of the Labour Party. In the face of mounting unease, Churchill had defended American thermonuclear testing at the end of March in Cabinet, and went on to do the same on the floor of the House of Commons – where his performance was very uncertain – amid widespread Opposition calls for an East-West summit and increased efforts toward global disarmament.[86] Around 100 Labour MPs subsequently signed a demand that all tests of hydrogen bombs be stopped and urged that a ban on all nuclear weapons should be negotiated.[87] In private, moreover, the Prime Minister also had his doubts and concerns, writing to Eisenhower on 9 March to express his horror at the power of the new weapons, while taking the chance to underline how concerned he was over the vulnerability of the densely-packed British Isles, where London in particular presented such an inviting target.[88] That same day a worried Cabinet Secretary, Sir Norman Brook, had sent a minute to Churchill recommending the need for a fundamental reassessment of general strategy and policy.[89]

The advent of the hydrogen bomb altered previous perceptions of the consequences of all-out war with the Soviet Union. It was readily apparent that the detonation of only a few such weapons over the UK would bring about death and destruction on an almost unimaginable scale, and in all probability cause the total breakdown of society and government. NATO's formal acceptance of the primacy of nuclear weapons in its military posture underlined the disastrous implications of any outbreak of war in Europe for the security of the United Kingdom. But in the face of economic realities and the overwhelming preponderance of Soviet conventional military strength there seemed little viable alternative to that of reliance on a very rapid resort to nuclear retaliation in the event of Communist aggression. With an eye on domestic opinion, the matter was put with commendable succinctness in his diary by Harold Macmillan in November 1954, when serving as Minister of Defence:

I fear that the public will be rather alarmed to discover that we really cannot fight any war *except* a nuclear war. It is quite impossible to arm our forces with two sorts of weapons – conventional and unconventional. The Air Force and in course of time the Army will be largely equipped with nuclear weapons of one sort or another. This means that if the Russians attacked (which is *very* unlikely) with conventional weapons only, in the first instance, we should be forced into the position of *starting* the nuclear war, with all that is implied – including the counter-attack on the UK. From a purely military point of view, there is no way out. We should be utterly crushed in a conventional war. But, politically, it is full of danger, at home or abroad, and may lead to a fresh outburst of defeatism or neutralism.[90]

An even higher premium than ever was placed on the need to prevent any war breaking out in the first place through a much stronger emphasis on deterrence in the government's policy, but to make this credible it was increasingly felt necessary to have under national control the most advanced weapons that were capable of being produced.

It was certainly the case that thermonuclear technology offered 'second tier' states such as Britain the potential to build a stockpile of weapons which, though relatively small in absolute numbers, held very considerable destructive power. UK nuclear scientists had known about thermonuclear principles since their participation in the wartime Manhattan project, but AWRE's efforts in the early 1950s had been overwhelmingly directed at developing the first Blue Danube bombs and then working on the designs of lighter kiloton-yield warheads that could be carried by smaller aircraft than the V-bombers, or might even be adapted for naval or army use.[91] There was also the fundamental problem that Penney and his Weapons Group had no clear idea how a thermonuclear weapon could be designed, but by early 1954 the former, helped by snippets of American information, was nevertheless coming round to the view that it would be within the capacities of AWRE to produce a hydrogen bomb within about five or six years.[92]

For the Prime Minister, entering his final year in office, the advent of the huge destructive power of the new class of weapons induced a mixture of reactions and emotions that was common to many. Alongside his belief that deterrence was the best means preventing the outbreak of a cataclysmic major war, Churchill experienced dark forebodings of what might befall mankind if deterrence should fail. It was for this reason that he put such great store on negotiating a relaxation of Cold War tensions with the post-Stalin Soviet leadership.[93] There was also the conviction, held very strongly by Churchill and other senior ministers, that possession of hydrogen weapons would give Britain a greater influence over US policy and the crucial issues of war and peace. This seemed all the more necessary considering that many saw the Eisenhower administration's public rhetoric, and even the President's own private correspondence with Churchill, as appearing so belligerent and confrontational.[94]

American plans to use nuclear weapons at an early stage in the event that the Korean armistice agreed in July 1953 was broken by the Communist side had prompted concerns in London, and some open dissent from Eden, in particular, at the Bermuda Conference of December 1953. During the Indochina crisis in the spring of 1954, which coincided with the fevered atmosphere that had greeted the Bravo test, it had been the British Government's restraining voice that had helped to persuade the Eisenhower administration that its plans for intervention would attract little international support. British diplomacy had subsequently helped to quell the fighting through the settlement reached at the Geneva Conference in July 1954, but for many officials the whole episode had served to reinforce fears that some Americans contemplated the prospect of a 'showdown' with the Communist bloc with comparative equanimity, and were keen to use their nuclear preponderance before it disappeared. As Cherwell put it in one of his missives to Churchill in May 1954:

> If I were an American I am sure I would resent – as many of them do – being asked to fight Communism in peripheral wars at enormous expense with conventional weapons and not being allowed to finish them (as the Americans think they could) by using the extraordinary weapons they have developed at such great cost and which they have available. And this resentment would not be diminished by the knowledge that all the while the Russians were feverishly working to increase their stocks of hydrogen bombs and improve their means of delivering them.[95]

Less than a year later, warning against spreading 'panic' about the effects of thermonuclear weapons, Churchill reminded the House of Commons that there were 'many countries where a certain wave of opinion may arise and swing so furiously into action that decisive steps may be taken from which there is no recall'.[96] Once Britain had its own nuclear capabilities – including the new hydrogen weapons – it was hoped that greater influence could be secured over the decision-making process in Washington, particularly if it came to the critical issue of at what stage to take nuclear action in the face of Communist aggression.

From AWRE, Penney himself was very much in favour of taking the thermonuclear step. Towards the end of April 1954 he wrote to Brook and offered the view that it was 'very likely' hydrogen weapons could be made at 'very little extra cost or factory effort' than had been needed for fission bombs. Ideas that there should be a moratorium on nuclear testing were best opposed: 'I think we would be rash to agree to anything that stops us from having hydrogen weapons if US and USSR have them. The day is coming, if it is not already here, when one country can destroy another. Are we prepared to stand aside when a little further effort will give us at least the bargaining power that comes from being able, if necessary, to strike back?'[97]

In the wake of the Bravo test military opinion also swung strongly behind thermonuclear development. The COS found in unequivocal terms in June 1954 that should a global war occur the United Kingdom would be the major target in Western Europe for initial Soviet nuclear attack. They warned that

> Though we can count on the allied strategic air forces being able to strike an immediate and crippling blow at the sources of attack and centres of control, we cannot be certain that the counter-offensive would be in time. Thus, if war did break out, we should have to expect that the United Kingdom would be devastated in the opening days to such an extent that it could no longer function as a main support area. Indeed, the real problem might well be one of mere physical survival.

The COS were accordingly led to the conclusions that

a   Short of sacrificing our vital interests or principles, we must do everything possible to prevent global war which would inevitably entail the exposure of the United Kingdom to a devastating nuclear bombardment.
b   The ability to wage war with the most up-to-date nuclear weapons will be the measure of military power in the future.
c   Our scientific skill and technological capacity to produce the hydrogen weapon puts within our grasp the ability to be on terms with the United States and Russia.

It was, moreover, argued that 'an immediate and overwhelming counter-offensive with the most powerful nuclear weapons offers the only hope of preventing the enemy from completely devastating this country.' It was reasoned from this that Britain had to contribute to the Western deterrent by producing a stockpile of nuclear weapons, including hydrogen bombs, and the means of delivering them.[98]

That there would be no relaxation in the pattern of British nuclear development was finally confirmed during July 1954, when over the course of three meetings of the full Cabinet – for once brought into the decision-making process over nuclear weapons policy – it was agreed that the development and production of a hydrogen bomb was to go ahead.[99] Churchill had, in fact, made this momentous decision with a smaller conclave of senior ministers on 16 June, but when on 7 July he informed the Cabinet as a whole of the conclusion that had been reached, the protests from some of his colleagues over his handling of the issue led him to allow a wider debate.[100]

Churchill's contribution to the Cabinet's deliberations was to remind his colleagues (some of whom expressed unease at the prospect) that 'we could not expect to maintain our influence as a World Power' unless the most modern weapons were acquired. 'The primary aim of our policy,' he had continued, 'was to prevent major war; and the possession of these weapons was now the main deterrent to a potential aggressor. He had no doubt that the best hope of preserving world peace was to make it clear to potential aggressors that they had no hope of shielding themselves from a crushing retaliatory use of atomic power.'[101] He was also clear that the most effective way to ensure that the United States was not tempted into a so-called forestalling attack during the period it still held nuclear supremacy over the Soviet Union, was to earn influence in Washington by playing a major role in deterring aggression through the build-up of thermonuclear strength, rather than leaving the Americans to face Communist power without company.[102]

The daunting task of developing and manufacturing a new class of thermonuclear weapons would now be assumed by AWRE, working under the new AEA which had been brought into existence in the summer of 1954. Over the next few years, Aldermaston – the location of the site in Berkshire soon becoming synonymous with the establishment itself – was to experience a major expansion in staff numbers and scope of work, as it attracted new scientific talent (in critical areas such as theoretical physics) to the challenging assignment that, it was optimistically hoped, would assure Britain retained a place in the front rank of powers. In September 1954, Penney, now knighted after the successful atomic bomb test, was given a new deputy director at AWRE in the shape of William Cook from the Royal Naval Scientific Service. Although without prior nuclear knowledge, Cook was to assume crucial responsibilities for the hydrogen bomb project and later in his long career would play a leading role in the history of the Polaris improvement programme. Having joined the scientific civil service in 1928, when he was only 23, Cook carried out early work on ballistics and rockets, and after the war became the first head of the Ministry of Supply's new rocket development establishment at Westcott. In 1947, he went to the Admiralty to become Director of Physical Research, and three years later succeeded Sir Frederick Brundrett as head of the Royal Naval Scientific Service. By mid-1954 Penney had singled out Cook as the person he wanted to bring into AWRE to help with the new project, and Brundrett (who by then had taken over as Chief Scientist at the MoD) confirmed the high opinion in which Cook was held. In combination with Penney (a team sometimes called 'the two Bills'), it was Cook who provided much of the organisational drive and dynamism of what many later looked back on as Aldermaston's golden years of the late 1950s, when resources were relatively abundant and a steady stream of achievements seemed to validate the efforts that had been made to push forward Britain's nuclear programme. As chair of AWRE's Weapons Development Committee after 1956, and much admired for his skills as a project manager, Cook was credited with having made a major contribution to the eventual success of the thermonuclear programme, not least through his supervision of the Grapple series of tests in the Pacific during 1957–58.[103]

'A contribution of our own'

Announcement of the Government's decision to proceed with the development and manufacture of the hydrogen bomb was made in the annual Defence White Paper published on 17 February 1955. It began with the statement that the emergence of thermonuclear weapons had overshadowed all else during 1954 and that 'new and revolutionary problems' were now posed to the framers of defence policy. Accuracy of aim was now of less importance when delivering such massive explosive power, meaning attacks could be delivered by aircraft at great height and speed, making defence against such an aerial threat even more difficult than previously. The document stands as a landmark in post-war British nuclear history for its presentation of the gruesome and fearful results if such weapons were used, with special prominence given to the effects of radioactive fallout. War would be a disaster, and the paper questioned whether any recognisable civil society could survive such a cataclysmic event. But the risk of such a major war had also, in the Government's view, been reduced by the deterrent effect of the same nuclear weapons that presented such dangers. The central theme of the paper was the need to strengthen deterrence even further as the only way to prevent such an awful eventuality:

> ...in a situation in which the Communist world maintains large and increasingly powerful armed forces, the strength of our forces and those of our Allies must also be developed and sustained against the possibility of a major war. To this end, increasing emphasis must be placed on the deterrent. This deterrent must rest primarily on the strategic air power of the West, armed with its nuclear weapons. The knowledge that aggression will be met by overwhelming nuclear retaliation is the surest guarantee that it will not take place. [...] We must therefore contribute to the deterrent and to our own defence by building up our own stock of nuclear weapons of all types and by developing the most up-to-date means of delivery. We must, moreover, in making our plans for dealing with aggression against our alliance, not flinch from the necessity to use these weapons. For in the knowledge of our resolve lies the best hope, and it is a real hope, that it may never be put to the test.[104]

The subsequent debate over the White Paper in the House of Commons witnessed Churchill's final parliamentary performance before retirement, where he offered a robust and sombre defence of the deterrent. The revelations of the previous year about the power of the hydrogen bomb had, he noted, caused 'the entire foundation of human affairs' to be 'revolutionised, and mankind placed in a situation both measureless and laden with doom.' Negotiations to secure some easing of the arms race seemed to some the best course to follow, but in the absence of effective means of securing general disarmament, the government had resolved to follow a policy of 'defence through deterrents.' Moreover, if general war should break out there were a large number of targets that we and the Americans must be able to strike at once. There are scores of airfields from which the Soviets could launch attacks with hydrogen bombs as soon as they have the bombers to carry them. It is essential to our deterrent policy and to our survival to have, with our American allies, the strength and numbers to be able to paralyse these potential Communist assaults in the first few hours of the war, should it come … There are also big administrative and industrial targets behind the Iron Curtain, and any effective deterrent policy must have the power to paralyse them all at the outset, or shortly after. There are also the Soviet submarine bases and other naval targets which will need early attention. Unless we can make a contribution of our own … we cannot be sure that in any emergency the resources of other Powers would be planned exactly as we would wish, or that the targets which would threaten us most would be given what we consider the necessary priority in the first few hours. These targets might be of such cardinal importance that it could really be a matter of life and death for us.[105]

It was essential, furthermore, that a UK hydrogen bomb should be developed, along with the nuclear strike force to carry it, in order that some overall and less tangible influence over US policy should be exerted: 'I cannot feel,' the Prime Minister told the House, 'that we should have much influence over their policy or their actions, wise or unwise, while we are largely dependent, as we are today, upon their protection. We, too, must possess substantial deterrent power of our own.'[106]

Such official pronouncements on declaratory policy still raised many questions over the role and mission of the strategic nuclear force that was being built. The overwhelming assumption in the early and mid-1950s was that the V-bomber force would eventually operate in tandem with the US Strategic Air Command, with targets in the Soviet Union allocated between the two forces as most appropriate. But little detail was known of US nuclear planning, and it was increasingly apparent from contacts between the respective air forces that until the UK's bombers were actually operational, there was no prospect of achieving the necessary degree of coordination. The embryonic planning for the nascent V-force reflected a 'counterforce' emphasis where the prime targets would be the Soviet air bases from which nuclear attacks against the UK mainland would have to be staged. In anticipation of the arrival in service of the first V-bombers, the Air Ministry directive for the C-in-C Bomber Command began to be re-written in August 1954. The role of the new medium bomber force in peacetime, as defined by one draft version of the revised directive, was 'to act as a deterrent against aggression,' and in war 'to reduce the enemy offensive and defensive power as quickly as possible with the ultimate aim of destroying his will to continue the war.' In order to accomplish the latter task, the C-in-C Bomber Command was ordered to prepare strikes against targets which if war should occur would reduce the scale of attack by land or air against the UK and Western Europe and to counter the threat to the UK's sea communications. The medium bomber force, in particular, was directed against the airbases from which Soviet long-range aircraft could mount offensive operations.[107]

At the higher political level, the Cabinet was informed in November 1954 that the V-force was of 'cardinal importance' to the 'prime aim' of defence policy of discouraging aggression through deterrence. Although no final political decisions had yet been made over its eventual size, current Air Ministry plans called for a front-line force of 240 aircraft by 1962, the main purpose of which was to

> put us in a position to knock out the Soviet air bases from which attacks would be delivered against this country. In addition, it could be used to assist on holding back the Russian land offensive in Europe and could also undertake missions against strategic targets, though we regard these roles as secondary in importance to that of counter-attacking the Russian bomber bases.[108]

Justifying the numbers of aircraft included in his forward programme, Lord De L'Isle, the Secretary of State for Air, had written to Macmillan in March 1955 arguing that while the strategic air offensive had to be an Anglo-American undertaking where the V-bomber force would join with the US Strategic Air Command, among other things, in striking 'immediately and in overwhelming strength the arteries of Russian life – her centres of Government, production and communications' and in attacks designed at 'limiting the Russian nuclear offensive by destroying her airfields and nuclear potential,' within this set of goals 'the primary objective of the British bomber force' was the 150 or so Soviet airfields from which a nuclear attack against the UK could be launched: 'In the face of the thermonuclear threat the destruction of these airfields must be immediate.'[109]

This whole approach was, however, gradually subject to revision as the tremendous shift in destructive power that came with the advent of thermonuclear weapons began to be absorbed. Counterforce targeting, which focused attention on the military forces and assets of an adversary, was to be superseded by a countervalue approach when the V-force was operating in a national or independent capacity, where the onus was placed on large-scale destruction of urban targets. This was, after all, the purest way to achieve a deterrent effect: to inflict such a level of destruction on a society and state that it might cease to function in any recognisable manner, making the potential gain of any initial aggression seem insignificant and even ridiculous against the disastrous consequences that would follow as a result.

An independent capacity for retaliation against the Soviet Union had generally been conceived of as insurance against the need to hit counterforce targets which were not a priority for the Americans, and this had been the main line of argument Churchill had pursued in the House of Commons in March 1955. But on that occasion Churchill had also alluded to the important point that the advent of the hydrogen bomb made it an especially effective weapon 'against nations whose population hitherto has been so widely dispersed over large land areas as to make them feel that they were not in any danger at all,' for it was now the 'enormous spaces and scattered population' of the Soviet Union which was put in a position of 'equality or near-equality of vulnerability with our small densely-populated island and with Western Europe.'[110]

In a strategic environment where the UK's delivery capabilities were decidedly limited but the power of the weapons carried much increased, the attractions of countervalue targeting became steadily more apparent. The need to settle on an agreed target policy was underlined by the arrival of the first Valiant in squadron service in February 1955. Asked to comment on the terms of his draft directive in April, the C-in-C Bomber Command, Air Chief Marshal Sir George Mills, expressed his dissatisfaction and his own wish that the V-force should be assigned to what were called 'morale targets'; there was a need, as he put it, to be 'more specific about the deterrent role.'[111] In fact, Mills had been unhappy with the initial presumption from the Air Ministry that his main focus should be on attacking the Soviet long-range bomber force. Much better for the purposes of deterrence was to be able to threaten the population and administrative centres of an aggressor. As Mills put:

> ...I am sure for the enemy's edification as well as our own we must be specific in saying that our aim in retaliation is to hurt him where it really hurts; if we don't keep this firmly in mind we are going to be ridden off on all sorts of defensive ideas which would ruin or seriously diminish our deterrent value. Whoever would be afraid of launching a sudden attack if he thought the greater part of our retaliation would come back on his airfields? I do pray that we keep our minds absolutely crystal clear on this issue.[112]

In his own re-write of the directive, Mills asserted that the V-force had to be 'trained to attack centres of administration, industry, and population with a view to destroying the enemy's will to start a war.'[113]

The final directive issued to Mills by the Air Ministry in May 1955 did not incorporate all his suggestions but now reflected the stronger emphasis on deterrence. The main task of the V-force was seen, in peacetime, as acting 'as the principal British deterrent to global war by providing the means of meeting aggression with immediate nuclear retaliation against those targets which will hurt the aggressor most.' In war, the force was to 'destroy the enemy's will and ability to fight in the shortest possible time.' Mills was expected to direct the main efforts of his force to the twin tasks of:

a   Reducing the scale of attack by air on the United Kingdom and by air and land attack on Western Europe.

b   Destroying the enemy's will to continue the war by attacks on centres of administration and population and upon his communication system.
c   Countering and containing the threat by air and sea to the United Kingdom's sea communications.

Precise targets were to be allocated by the Air Ministry, except when parts of the V-force had been assigned to support a specific theatre commander, as might occur for NATO.[114]

A further indication of Britain's adherence to an 'independent' strategic nuclear role over the longer-term was the project, announced in the February 1955 White Paper, to design, develop and deploy Blue Streak, a land-based Intermediate Range Ballistic Missile (IRBM). The origins of Blue Streak date back to 1953 when the Air Ministry began to exhibit active interest in an indigenous ballistic missile programme. Influenced by the belief that by the late 1960s the manned bomber would be highly vulnerable to interception, in March 1954 the Ministry of Supply had been asked for detailed proposals for a large-scale missile project. In August 1954 Duncan Sandys, the Minister of Supply, had made an important but largely unsung agreement with Charles Wilson, the US Secretary Defense, which provided for close collaboration and exchange of information over ballistic missile technology, including between private contractors. A service requirement finally emerged from the Air Staff in August 1955 for a ballistic missile capable of carrying a one megaton warhead across a range of up to 2,000 nautical miles (although with the capability for further development to extend maximum range to 2,500 nautical miles), and authorisation was given for the first tranche of expenditure of a £50 million programme of preliminary research and development extending across a ten year period.[115] In early 1956, a more detailed development programme was produced, involving expenditure of £105 million across the next seven years, with introduction into service anticipated for 1963.[116]

Intended to supersede the V-bomber force in the primary deterrent role from the mid-1960s onwards, Blue Streak was soon seen by many critics as flawed in conception, its liquid-fuelled engines meaning it needed lengthy pre-launch preparation, raising concerns it would be open to pre-emptive attack once the Soviet Union was able to deploy a substantial missile force of its own (one remedy introduced was the proposal for underground silo basing for Blue Streak, but this carried additional financial implications).[117] Blue Streak's great virtue, at least in the eyes of the Air Ministry, was that it was, as one historian of the subject has noted, 'an important symbol of genuine British independence.' In practical terms the project could be run according to UK specifications, or as the Air Ministry put it when Blue Streak came under sustained criticism from the Treasury and Admiralty: '…we should insist on keeping it in our programme not only because we want it but also because, politically, we cannot afford to be dependent upon America for this vital weapon. Operationally and technically we must be free … to develop and modify the weapon to meet our appreciation of the operational situation.'[118]

The need to provide an invulnerable nuclear force capable of retaliation even after the launching of a Soviet nuclear attack – one of the main grounds on which Blue Streak was seen as deficient – had already begun to turn a few Navy minds to the alternative of a submarine-launched ballistic missile system. Most important here were the contacts being forged by Admiral the Earl Mountbatten of Burma, the First Sea Lord and Chief of Naval Staff between 1955 and 1959, with his US counterpart Admiral Arleigh Burke. From November 1955, Burke was to keep Mountbatten closely informed of the progress that the US Navy was making in this area, and which was to lead to the development of a revolutionary submarine-launched solid-fuel IRBM (the whole project acquiring the name Polaris in December 1956).[119]

The US programme was eventually to culminate on 20 July 1960 with two successful launches of a Polaris A1 missile off Cape Canaveral from a submerged nuclear-powered submarine, the USS *George Washington*. By this time a Royal Navy liaison officer was attached to the staff of the US Navy's Special Projects Office (SPO) in Washington, an organisation dedicated to marrying and pushing forward the complex threads that made up the whole Polaris programme and which reported directly to the US Secretary of the Navy.[120] Although after 1955 many elements in the Royal Navy remained sceptical about the merits and wisdom of pressing for intensive study of a UK Polaris option as a competitor to Blue Streak – both because it could mean diversion of resources away from the surface fleet and there was as yet no sign the Americans were prepared to offer such an advanced system to the UK – a strong inter-service rivalry between the Royal Air Force and Royal Navy over the future of the deterrent was incipient with the emergence of an effective under-water missile system such Polaris, which held some obvious advantages over aircraft or land-based missiles which were tied to vulnerable and easily identified fixed sites.

For the moment, however, such inter-service tensions were made manifest during the mid-1950s in the battles fought over the eventual size of the V-force. While the RAF had a strong vested interest in arguing that priority should be given to the strategic nuclear deterrent, both the Army and Navy stressed the need for adequate provision for coping with the insurgencies and brushfire wars that accompanied Britain's world role and end of empire defence commitments, as well as limited wars that could occur in the Middle East and Asia where nuclear weapons might not be used from the outset. What these debates made clear was that there was as yet no national 'criterion of deterrence', or level of destruction, which it was considered would be sufficient to deter the Soviet Union from an attack on vital British interests, or the UK mainland itself, and which could be used as a yardstick against which the size of the V-force could be measured.

By the end of 1955, in fact, the key consideration was the balance to be struck between what it was felt could be afforded in the defence budget, and whether Britain's allies would see the eventual size of the V-force as a respectable contribution to the strength of the regional alliances of which Britain was a leading member. Apart from Britain's role in NATO, these included significant extra-European commitments to the South East Asia Treaty Organization (SEATO) after September 1954, and, in the Middle East, to the Baghdad Pact which had been formed in February 1955, and which three years later, following the Iraqi revolution of July 1958, was to become the Central Treaty Organization (CENTO). All three alliance systems were to involve some degree of declared nuclear commitment by the late 1950s, a fact which the Air Ministry was happy to use when arguing that the numbers of V-bombers be kept as high as possible.

The issue of the reliability of the American nuclear guarantee to Western Europe had also begun to figure in the thinking of British officials by the mid-1950s. A situation could now be foreseen, perhaps in only a few years' time, when the Soviet Union would have acquired enough thermonuclear strength to directly threaten the continental United States, making it seem less sure that Washington would, in all circumstances (especially if the Soviet Union refrained from using nuclear weapons at the outset of a war), intervene with its strategic nuclear forces in the event of a conflict in central Europe. It would now be the United States which would be deterred from acting in a decisive fashion for fear of the retaliation that would result.

This uncomfortable prospect might be assumed to have influenced in important ways the motivation for developing an independent nuclear force in the mid-1950s. For example, the COS had argued in June 1955 that it would be 'strategically unacceptable to rely entirely on the United States to provide the deterrent. Moreover with the rapidly increasing yield of nuclear weapons it would become progressively more difficult for the United States to come to our aid if we alone were threatened in view of the consequences to her of such action.'[121] Yet in the prolonged discussions over the size of the V-force there was little assessment of what would be a viable number of aircraft and weapons to constitute a fully 'independent' deterrent against the Soviet Union, where nuclear action, retaliatory in nature, would be unilateral (the United States, by implication, having eschewed using its own strategic forces). With the V-force just forming, and the only weapons available the first generation Blue Danube atomic bomb, this was entirely understandable. The production of thermonuclear weapons in the UK could, it was true, give a small nuclear force the capacity to inflict major damage on an adversary, but the initial priority for staff planners was to discuss coordination of plans and to share knowledge with their American counterparts as part of a concerted allied effort.

Within this context, economic considerations tended to be paramount in ministerial deliberations and the progressive reductions in the planned numbers of V-bombers that took place between 1955 and 1957. In this tight budgetary environment, the initial tendency for the Air Ministry was to retain an emphasis on counterforce targeting as it was an approach which could be used to defend the need for a higher number of aircraft to tackle the many dispersed military targets in the Soviet Union that presented themselves, even when the nuclear offensive was conducted in concert with the Americans. Indeed, by early 1955 the Air Ministry was arguing that its current favoured figure of 240 V-bombers ought to be higher on military grounds, but was the maximum size of force that could operate effectively given the requirements for trained aircrew and maintenance personnel.

In an Anglo-American nuclear offensive, the V-bomber force would be expected to attack several different target systems in the Soviet Union. 'The attack on Russian centres of government and administration, production and communications would be a formidable undertaking,' one draft letter from the Secretary of State for Air observed.

> It would be simple if we could believe that a few well-placed thermonuclear bombs on Moscow, Leningrad, Stalingrad and other centres would bring the war to an immediate end by its effect on the morale of the Russian people. But this would not necessarily occur. The Russian armies would be advancing and their air forces flying; industry would continue to operate; if adequate measures had been taken to decentralise control effective orders could continue to be given. As long as their organisation continued the Russians could continue the war. Accordingly the strategic offensive against the Russian war-making power behind their armed forces involves more than the destruction of a few major centres; it involves the destruction of a large number of targets over a very wide area within a very short time, so as to disrupt the ability of the Russians to conduct organised war.[122]

The result of this whole process was often confusion over exactly how the deterrent force might be employed if war should come, and how a declaratory stress on an independent contribution to the Western deterrent was translated into war plans and the projected size of the force. In July 1955, for example, the COS endorsed a JPS paper which argued that the UK contribution to the allied bomber force

> should not absorb an undue share of the Defence Vote but it must be big enough for the United Kingdom to have a say in Allied strategic policy. The important thing is that Allied research should always keep our means of delivery ahead of the enemy and of his means of defence, and that our selection of the means of delivery should be governed by its being the most effective and economical available.[123]

The view of the then CAS, Marshal of the Royal Air Force Sir William Dickson, was that there were two justifications for the size of the V-force then planned. In political terms it was considered 'essential that our contribution should be of such size and quality as to enable us to play our part in the formulation of allied strategic (and particularly strategic bombing) policy.' Militarily, since the number of targets that would need to be attacked in the short initial phase of a war was then considered beyond current US capabilities, a V-force of 240 aircraft was felt to be a valuable and visible reinforcement of the American effort.[124] During the subsequent long round of debates that took place over lowering the size of the force the argument that the UK had to be seen by the Americans as making a worthwhile contribution to the overall Western deterrent was pushed forward on a consistent basis by the Air Ministry.

A contrasting view on the overall approach to defence spending was put forward, in a typical example of the differing perspectives that were held at this time, by Reginald Maudling, the Minister of Supply (and a future Chancellor of the Exchequer). According to Maudling, in a letter he sent to the Minister of Defence, Selwyn Lloyd, in August 1955, there were simply not sufficient resources to defend against every possible threat. Allied or friendly support would not be available to tackle internal unrest in colonial territories, or to meet aggression from minor powers. Therefore, he reasoned, weapons to fight these kinds of conflicts should have a first call on national resources. In larger limited wars, or in a major war involving the Soviet Union, though, reliance would have to be placed on the United States. It was evident that Britain could do no more than make a 'marginal contribution' in a global nuclear war and so expenditure on the deterrent should be seen as less of a priority:

> We must recognise that any provision we make to add to the United States striking power is in practice more a political than a military provision. It is sometimes described as the entrance fee to the club. I doubt myself whether there is much wisdom in paying an entrance fee so high that you cannot afford to patronise the bar when you get there.[125]

A firm refutation to this line of argument was immediately delivered by the Secretary of State for Air, in a counter-submission for Lloyd:

> We must I agree rely on the United States in some spheres which are not the most vital to us in the hydrogen age. But I am most strongly opposed to the suggestion that we must consider ourselves subordinate to the United States in all military spheres other than those in which we are alone concerned. Such complete subordination is I consider neither true in fact nor a desirable object of policy. Indeed to maintain our position in world affairs and at the same time command the continuing support of the United States we must at the very least show our determination to defend ourselves in these islands against nuclear attack as effectively as possible. It is generally conceded that nowadays air defence mainly lies in the power of counter-offence with nuclear weapons. Certainly our policy must be to avoid global war, but from the knowledge that we have both

the will and the power to counter attack with nuclear weapons and that we shall not yield our vital interests to blackmail derives the deterrent, and hence the political value, of a strategic bomber force. And this knowledge affects the minds not only of foes but of friends as well.[126]

Ministers of defence, on the other hand, under consistent pressure from the Treasury, and with concerns over how the budget was stretched to meet all the commitments and demands of the Cold War – whether in Central Europe, the Middle East, or South East Asia – looked to make progressive reductions in orders for the expensive V-force, especially when Blue Streak development was also underway.

In July 1956, as the whittling down process in the numbers of V-bombers entered a new phase, Air Chief Marshal Sir Dermot Boyle, who had replaced Dickson as the CAS, told his fellow members of the COS Committee, that it was 'extremely difficult to calculate a firm figure for the size of the "V" Bomber Force on purely military grounds.' His latest recommendation for a force of 200 aircraft was, he averred, because it was 'highly desirable to build up our deterrent force quickly if we were to gain the essential influence we needed with the United States to participate in the counter-offensive, and to obtain bombs from them until such time as we had an adequate supply of our own.' The other point Boyle mentioned was simply that 'NATO strategy was based on the effectiveness of the deterrent and we had agreed to contribute to it. NATO nations were expecting and awaiting this contribution.' When it came to answering questions from his sceptical colleagues over the size of stockpile of thermonuclear weapons that would eventually be required for the V-force – amid concerns over the impact on conventional forces of the nuclear programme – all he could say was that 'until we had a sufficient force to persuade the United States to co-ordinate their planning with us, we could not say with certainty what targets and, consequently what weapons, we would need.'[127]

Overriding importance was still given, therefore, to securing agreement with the Americans for combined planning for operations in the event of general war, where Bomber Command, in the initial wave of allied nuclear forces, would attack a variety of jointly assigned targets, both military sites such as airfields and ports, and urban areas. Yet as Boyle's comments indicated, virtually nothing was known about Strategic Air Command's detailed target planning, while UK reconnaissance resources could not possibly cover all the targets of potential interest in the Soviet Union. There was a pressing need to prevent overlap in target allocation, coordinate mission sorties, timings and tactics, share target intelligence, and to ensure that economy of effort was achieved by the combined resources of the two strategic bomber forces. Low level approaches at a staff level aimed at making a start with such coordination had proved fruitless during 1954, and by the following year the Air Staff were anxious that a high-level political overture to the US authorities, perhaps through the Prime Minister should be made.[128]

It was apparent that until the UK's nuclear contribution was given substance through deployment of the first V-bombers, the Americans would not be prepared to talk on an official level. Dickson finally held discussions in Washington with his opposite number, the Chief of Staff of the US Air Force, in September 1955 over the need for cooperation, but it was not until August 1956 that the first serious contact between British and US air staffs over coordination of nuclear strike planning took place in London – Valiants, it will be recalled, having by then entered squadron service – and by the end of the year a 'concept of allied nuclear operations', and an 'outline plan of action' had been drawn up, and approved by the US authorities. Throughout these early conversations the US stress had been on a rapid retaliatory atomic air offensive directed against military targets, and Soviet nuclear capabilities in particular.[129]

There is every indication that these first contacts were highly tentative and that little operational detail was explored between staffs. When the COS approved the documents presented by the Air Staff as a result of these preliminary conversations with the Americans, there were some misgivings as it was feared that commitment to a particular concept of operations could imply commitment to a specific size of V-force, when the latter subject was still very much a matter of debate. Admitting there were some differences in how the two air forces were approaching the task of coordination, the CAS nevertheless stressed that the 'important thing was to get joint planning with the Americans started.' When supporting documentation on the next series of approaches to the Americans over joint planning was sent to the new Minister of Defence, Duncan Sandys, in January 1957 there was included the caveat that 'coordination of operational plans would not in any way imply any relinquishment of our national control of the Royal Air Force bomber force.'[130] Working in concert with the Americans, therefore, was not to involve any diminution of the notion of an independent contribution to the strategic deterrent forces of the Alliance.

The Sandys White Paper and the creation of a national strategic target policy

The combative figure of Sandys had been brought to the MoD by Harold Macmillan when the latter had assumed the premiership from Eden at the start of 1957 after the debacle of the Suez crisis. That the crisis propelled Macmillan into Downing Street was significant for the immediate future of defence policy as he had first-hand experience of the need for reform at the Ministry of Defence and was convinced that change would be required if essential reductions in defence spending were to be made (not least as the crisis had helped to underline the frailty of Britain's international economic position).[131] During the early 1950s, in the wake of the rearmament set in train by the Korean War, the central staff of the Ministry of Defence underwent expansion, as it ran a growing plethora of inter-service committees, and oversaw military research, development and production. For successive ministers of defence, service domination of the defence policy field became increasingly frustrating as he and his staff – sometimes without access to the necessary information – had to resolve the conflicting demands that the differing programmes of the armed forces presented, particularly once pressures for greater controls on defence spending began to come from Downing Street and the Treasury. Writing in his diary on taking up his new duties as Minister of Defence in October 1954, Macmillan complained: 'This new Ministry of mine is a queer kind of affair. I have no power; yet I am responsible for everything – esp[ecially] if its goes wrong … When I ask for a small meeting with the Service ministers, about 40 to 50 people turn up!'[132]

The individual service ministries clearly remained in the ascendant, and the minister of defence, despite in theory being responsible for the overall formulation of defence policy, struggled to do much more than monitor existing programmes and attempt to steer service prerogatives in a coherent direction. With criticism of the existing state of affairs becoming increasingly widespread and some grip on defence spending seen as essential, in October 1955, Eden, the then Prime Minister, had attempted to bolster the position of the Minister of Defence by making him responsible for the 'composition and balance' of the armed forces, involving him more with the content of the defence programme, and giving him a direct channel of communication to the COS Committee by creating a new and additional position of Chairman, a post which would be filled by one of the existing Chiefs (and who was to represent the Committee's corporate views to the Minister of Defence and the Cabinet's Defence Committee). But with only a small briefing staff and no power to resolve differences within the Committee itself, the Chairman's role – its first incumbent was Dickson – was soon shown to be less influential than those keen on reform had initially hoped.[133]

As we have seen, the debates over the size and role of the V-bomber force had been conducted against the background of intense rivalries between the services over the balance of resources each should command in the defence budget. Patently unhappy with the overall state of affairs, Eden had instigated a major review of defence spending in 1956. The Suez crisis delayed action on the results of the review, but when arriving in Downing Street Macmillan was determined that Sandys should be given the additional authority to push through the changes that he considered necessary. Sandys himself had considerable experience of the nuclear programme and the problems of controlling spending on defence research and development when serving as Minister of Supply between 1951 and 1954, where he had also been exposed to the debilitating effects of inter-service competition over major projects.[134]

The so-called 'Sandys era' in British defence policy was to be accompanied by reforms in the higher organisation of the Ministry of Defence that heralded the eventual arrival of fully-centralised decision-making machinery – in theory at least – rather than the service-based structures of the past. With the full backing of the new Prime Minister, in January 1957 Sandys was given 'authority to give decisions on all matters of policy affecting the size, shape or organisation and disposition of the Armed Forces, their equipment and supply (including defence research and development) and their pay and conditions of service.'[135] His subsequent Defence White Paper of April 1957, although in many respects representing the culmination of a number of lines of strategic thought that had been drawing together since the early 1950s, made crystal clear his intention that it would henceforth be the Minister of Defence who would determine the main contours of defence policy and the character of the forces which were to carry it out. Yet Sandys' forceful personality often had to substitute for a set of clearly defined means or an organisational structure to fulfil his new responsibilities.[136]

A White Paper on the *Central Organisation for Defence* was published in July 1958, creating a new Defence Board, composed of the Minister of Defence, the service ministers, the Chief Scientist, the Permanent Under Secretary (PUS), and the COS, but it never became an effective tool for high-level policy discussions. The White Paper also announced that the Chairman of the COS Committee was to be turned into a fully-fledged Chief of the Defence Staff (CDS), who, with the assistance of an increased staff, was intended to be the principal military adviser to the Minister of Defence.[137] Rotated between the three services, whoever held the CDS post was supposed to both chair the COS Committee in an impartial manner, and present its unified opinions and recommendations. The CDS was, however, only to offer his own independent advice when the Committee as a whole could find no agreement, while the individual service Chiefs of Staff retained their rights of direct access to the Minister of Defence and even Prime Minister.[138] As with so much defence policymaking machinery during this era, the effectiveness of the CDS role tended to depend more on the personality of the individual that filled it than on its formal constitutional position in the MoD hierarchy. The fact that its occupant from July 1959 onwards was the imperious figure of Admiral Mountbatten ensured that the position would become a powerful voice in the new moves to centralise defence organisation that were to be made during the early 1960s.

Nevertheless, the strong single-service directed mentalities of most military planners and staffs remained entrenched. The Joint Planning Staff which served and carried out the instructions and studies mandated by the COS Committee, for example, was composed of separate service directors of plans, and they had no conception of adopting the unified approach personified by the CDS role, which made Mountbatten all the more determined to build-up his own staff element and give it more control over the planning machinery. To compound such problems, the Minister of Defence, who had been assigned the responsibility, under the 1958 White Paper reforms, for 'the formulation and general application of a unified policy', still did not have an adequate centralised staff organisation to carry out his allotted role of controlling, rather than merely coordinating, the activities of the service ministries. The service ministers themselves, although no longer able to sit in the full

Cabinet, retained their membership of the Cabinet's more significant Defence Committee, and were able to muster parliamentary lobbies when defending their parochial interests. That they would have much to argue over was apparent from the substantive changes in policy introduced during the turbulent months that followed the arrival of Sandys at the MoD.

In much the same spirit as the 1955 Statement on Defence, the Sandys White Paper of April 1957 had reiterated that '…the overriding consideration of all military planning must be to prevent war rather than to prepare for it … [and] the only safeguard against aggression is the power to threaten retaliation with nuclear weapons.' At the same time defence spending had to be kept in line with the UK's economic means, the White Paper had warned, and it was considered to be necessary 'to revise not merely the size, but the whole character of the defence plan.' In the nuclear field Britain could only make what was called 'a modest contribution' to the defence of the West which relied overwhelmingly on the US strategic nuclear forces, but Britain also had to possess 'an appreciable element of nuclear deterrent power' of its own, not least to allow for reductions to be made in conventional forces – most notably through the abolition of national service. The overall aim of the White Paper was to cut defence spending from its current total of ten per cent of Gross National Product to seven per cent by 1962, with armed forces manpower dropping from 690,000 to 375,000.[139]

Whereas the COS's 1952 Global Strategy paper, with its rhetorical stress on the nuclear deterrent, had not been followed by any appreciable reductions in the strength of Britain's conventional forces in favour of nuclear, over the next few years the Sandys period of defence policy would witness major battles over resources as budgets were squeezed. The problem was compounded by the fact that there was to be no concurrent reduction in Britain's worldwide military commitments, which remained just as onerous as they had been since the end of the war, not least as the struggle against Communism or revolutionary nationalism was pursued in far-flung corners of Asia, the Middle East, and Africa. Sandys himself became a figure 'universally reviled in military circles' (as one historian has put it), his relationship with the COS deteriorating rapidly in early 1957 as he refused to relent over his demands for major cuts in manpower and ran roughshod over their views.[140]

Before the publication of the White Paper, in February 1957 the new Prime Minister had explained his own line of thinking to the Defence Committee over how the reductions in the overall numbers of the regular forces which were planned over the next five years would be offset by equipping them with nuclear weapons. Macmillan had argued that

> Our objective should be to remain a nuclear power [and] for this purpose we would need the capacity to make both atomic and hydrogen weapons and the means of delivering them. It was a matter of judgment how much production was necessary in order to maintain our influence in this field. Nuclear weapons could be used for tactical, strategic or defensive

purposes. ... In the strategic field, nuclear strength could not be used in circumstances short of global war. We could, therefore, assume that we should not use strategic nuclear weapons except in alliance with the United States.

Yet at the same time, it was necessary to

have within our control sufficient weapons to provide a deterrent influence independent of the United States. The number of kiloton and megaton bombs which we should produce for this purpose would depend on further assessments of the costs involved. The objective, however, should be to provide the minimum required to give us an independent deterrent influence.[141]

It was this imprecise notion of an 'independent deterrent influence' that was to form a central feature of the Macmillan Government's approach to strategic nuclear policy over the next few years.

To the Prime Minister, the trauma of Suez had served not only as a painful reminder of Britain's financial dependence on the goodwill of Washington, and the dangers of operating out of step with the US administration, but also of the potential unreliability of US policy in a crisis situation. Macmillan's whole approach in the field of foreign affairs after assuming the premiership was predicated on rebuilding a close relationship with the Eisenhower administration and he saw Britain's growing nuclear capabilities as a key component of how this goal could be achieved, not least in their role in helping persuade the Americans to restore the nuclear collaboration that had been cut-off by the McMahon Act of 1946. In this he followed a train of thought that had been implicit in the hydrogen bomb decision of 1954. When suggestions were floated in January 1956 that plans for the development and production of thermonuclear weapons should be reversed on economic grounds, they had been adamantly opposed by the COS and Brundrett, the Chief Scientist at the MoD.

Considering the reductions in Britain's force commitments to NATO which were likely over the next few years, Brundrett thought that the UK's position in the Alliance would become impossible if the megaton weapon programme were also brought to an end. The COS Committee as a whole agreed that any such action 'would remove the foundation stone of United Kingdom strategic policy which was based on our remaining an independent power possessing and being able to deliver the primary deterrent.' Failure to develop megaton weapons would 'sacrifice immediately and in perpetuity our position as a first class power. We would have to rely on the whim of the United States for the effectiveness of the whole basis of our strategy. Furthermore, our views would no longer have any weight with Russia and our status would be lowered in the eyes of the United States.' The technical knowledge which came with a thermonuclear programme, it was maintained, also meant that the United States was more likely to share their own information in this field, as only by having something useful to offer in return would the Americans be ready to engage in such an exchange.[142]

The Sandys White Paper consolidated previous trends by elevating nuclear deterrence, at least in rhetorical terms, to become the foundation stone of British defence policy. Only the counter-threat of nuclear retaliation, the COS had argued in their own contribution to the defence review, could deter the 'probability of nuclear bombardment [from the Soviet Union], against which no adequate defence is foreseeable. The safety of the United Kingdom, they had continued, depended on the 'Allied Strategic Bomber Force and on the continued cohesion of NATO, including the continued involvement of the United States in Western Europe.' But at the same time, the COS believed that it would be 'wrong to leave the United States as the only providers of the deterrent, as this would leave the ultimate defence of the United Kingdom and of United Kingdom interests solely in American hands.'[143] During the presentation of the Defence White Paper, moreover, Sandys had given clear expression to the view that a nuclear capability under national control played some role as an insurance against the future reluctance of a US administration to commit itself to the defence of Western Europe.

> 'So long as large American forces remain in Europe, and American bombers are based in Britain,' he had told the House of Commons in April 1957, 'it might conceivably be thought safe – I am not saying that it would – to leave the United States sole responsibility for providing the nuclear deterrent. But, when they have developed the 5,000 mile intercontinental ballistic rocket, can we really be sure that every American Administration will go on looking at things in quite the same way? We think that it is just as well that an appreciable element of nuclear power shall in all circumstances remain on this side of the Atlantic, so that no one shall be tempted to think that a major attack could be made against Western Europe without the risk of nuclear retaliation.[144]

What constituted an 'appreciable element of nuclear power' was, however, very much a matter of debate, and the Air Ministry, above all, were to grow frustrated that Sandys was uncommitted – and even uninterested – in the long fight with the Treasury over the numbers of V-bombers that were to operate in the front-line force. Indeed, the most visible manifestation of Britain's nuclear ambitions under the new government, and the means by which mastery of the most advanced elements of weapons technology was to be demonstrated to the Americans, was the Grapple test series, which began in the Pacific on 15 May 1957 with the air drop by a Valiant bomber of a new design of warhead, Short Granite, intended to demonstrate some of the principles of staging and radiation implosion that AWRE had been trying to establish over the previous year.[145]

The ultimate success of the Grapple series of experiments over the next year was to pave the way for the design of more efficient and powerful types of thermonuclear warhead at Aldermaston. For Sandys, nevertheless, the 'independent' aspects of nuclear deterrent policy took their clearest form in his backing for the Blue Streak IRBM programme. Blue Streak was intended to provide the backbone of the deterrent from the mid-1960s onwards, when it was assumed that the effectiveness of the V-bombers – even when carrying a new British-designed short-range stand-off rocket – would be negated by improvements to Soviet air defences; it was also a project with which Sandys had been closely associated since his days at the Ministry of Supply, not least as it was his approach to the US Secretary of Defense in 1954 which had helped secure invaluable exchanges of information with the Americans on ballistic missile technology. Concerned with maintaining operational independence, major bureaucratic support for Blue Streak also came from the Air Ministry, along with Brundrett and his MoD central scientific staff (although Brundrett tended to see guided missiles as a ready substitute for manned aircraft in the future defence programme).

By 1957 Blue Streak was, nonetheless, coming under renewed and critical scrutiny from the Treasury, who were concerned over its rising estimated costs. The original Ministry of Supply submission on Blue Streak costs, made in May 1955, had mentioned a figure of £50 million to cover development, including new test facilities and hardware. But this was acknowledged to be very much a speculative estimate and took no account of the requirement for a full production programme. As estimates rose during 1956, projecting total expenditure of £105 million with a view to achieving some initial operational capability by 1963, one MoD official recalled having to defend 'the very existence of Blue Streak against savage attacks by the Treasury.'[146] The MoD and Ministry of Supply were forced to cut the full programme figure to £75 million in the spring of 1957, with first deployment not now expected until 1965/66, in order to fend off calls for cancellation from the Treasury. But Sandys was warned by Aubrey Jones, the Minister of Supply, in October 1957 that this 'austere' level of spending – with no contingency or allowance for alternative lines of development – was unlikely to result in a successful programme delivered according to timetable. Jones now advocated use of an estimate of at least £150 million, and the Treasury was told by the MoD that same month that final expenditure could be in fact range from £160–200 million.[147]

As well as Treasury opposition to its mounting costs, Blue Streak also faced scepticism from within the Admiralty, where some Naval officers recognised that deployment of a land-based ballistic missile would put paid to their own growing interest in a submarine-based system such as Polaris. The Prime Minister's lukewarm support for the programme also became apparent in early 1957, when he indicated he was open to the idea of acquiring the US Thor IRBM instead of proceeding with Blue Streak, should Thor be available on acceptable terms.[148] As with so much strategic nuclear policy of this period, the costs of maintaining independence were frequently set against the palpable financial and technical advantages of pursuing 'interdependence' with the United States, especially as the Anglo-American relationship recovered from the rupture of the Suez crisis.

Despite the increasingly discernable strength of British nuclear capabilities and a rhetorical adherence to independence, the emphasis of military planners remained on securing joint arrangements with the Americans over targeting. High level transatlantic political approval for respective air staffs to take forward arrangements over coordination was finally achieved through an exchange of letters between the Minister of Defence and the US Secretary of Defense which took place in late January 1957, and this understanding was reaffirmed when Macmillan met President Eisenhower on Bermuda in March. Much still had to be done, nevertheless, to bring practical expression to the principles being gradually established.[149]

In January 1957, as part of its review of the conduct of Allied strategic nuclear attack in conditions of global war, the Joint Planning Staff had recommended that detailed target selection for the British strategic nuclear force should be undertaken by the Air Ministry, but that this work should be carried out under a broad target policy that was decided by the government of the day, as advised by the COS.[150] In particular, the Air Ministry now needed to consider the different Soviet target systems which the V-bomber force should be directed to attack, the probability it would achieve the objectives which had been set, and the results which might be expected from the delivery of such a nuclear offensive. Only with such information – crucially – could detailed target planning with the Americans begin. The Air Staff was hence instructed in May 1957 to develop a target policy under two distinct eventualities (and the order held significance):

a   Retaliatory action where the Royal Air Force attack is co-ordinated with that of the United States Air Force.
b   Action on an emergency basis in a situation in which the United Kingdom is forced into unilateral retaliation.

Planning guidance also made clear it should be assumed the Soviet Union had initiated aggressive action against the West, involving both conventional *and* nuclear weapons at the very outset. This reflected a strong belief that Soviet military planners, if they did decide to take the gamble of an invasion of Western Europe, would be unlikely to forgo the obvious advantages brought by the first use of nuclear weapons. Bomber Command target policy at this stage was therefore explicitly retaliatory in nature.[151]

The impetus for a unilateral, national plan, it is therefore important to note, derived in the first instance from the Air Staff's need to give instructions to the target planners at Bomber Command to carry forward the work they had begun with their American opposite numbers to develop a coordinated nuclear strike plan. Moreover, the Air Ministry's enthusiasm for moving forward with target planning in late 1956 and early 1957 had been somewhat curbed by the reservations of the other Chiefs of Staff that agreement to a particular target plan (especially with the Americans) would involve commitment to a particular size of V-force, when this might absorb resources from other areas of the defence budget. Further talks between senior officers on the Air Staff and their US counterparts on the procedures for coordination of UK-US target planning eventually took place in May 1957 (leading to the negotiation of a formal memorandum of understanding in July), and it was at this juncture that COS approval was sought for the Air Staff to begin to prepare their paper on Bomber Command's overall target policy.[152]

The Air Staff's subsequent task was rendered easier by the Defence Committee's ruling in August 1957, against the recommendation of the Minister of Defence, that the eventual size of the V-force when fully deployed should be limited to 144 aircraft, of which 104 were to be the more advanced and longer-range Mark 2 Vulcans and Victors.[153] By setting a precise figure for the numbers of the V-force, the Defence Committee allowed the Air Staff to be more explicit about the eventual force they could contribute to a combined strike with the Americans, and the damage potential that it would possess. While in theory an assessment of a sufficient degree of damage which could deter the Soviet Union from embarking upon aggression should have been compiled as a guide to the optimum size of the strategic deterrent as it began to materialise during the late 1950s, in practice it was the finite capability of the force itself that helped to generate evaluations of the level of destruction that had to be achieved for independent deterrence to be effective.

A basic conclusion made by the Air Staff paper that finally emerged from this process in October 1957 was that attacks against Soviet nuclear and military target systems, such as airfields or weapon production facilities, in a scenario where the UK was acting alone, would do little to reduce the scale of the nuclear offensive that the Soviet Union would be capable of delivering against Britain. There were, however, 131 Soviet cities with a population of 100,000 or more, 54 of which were classed as of 'major importance' as they were centres of government, administration or military and economic control. Destruction of these centres, it was concluded, would do irreparable damage to the Soviet organisation for security, paramilitary and military control, as well as disrupt the entire economy, communications and transportation system of the country. This would have a 'definite and immediate effect on the ability and will of the USSR to continue a war.' Bomber Command's growing inventory of V-bombers would soon allow many of these city targets to be reached, though the number of targets which could be hit was likely to vary over time as the strength and capability of the V-force altered and Soviet air defences developed and improved. Nevertheless, the paper asserted that

> under any foreseeable hypothesis Bomber Command has an increasing capability to strike powerfully and with telling effect against Russian

cities and administrative centres. It is felt that this would be the most damaging retaliatory blow we could deliver if the Russians were to launch an attack against us and, therefore, the most effective deterrent against such an attack ever being launched.

Nowhere in the Air Staff paper was there, it should be noted, any specific number of cities mentioned as the target set for a unilateral V-bomber retaliatory strike. Instead, it was observed that of the major Soviet cities, 44 were then within range of the Mark 1 V-bombers which were then entering Bomber Command service; when the longer-range Mark 2 variants of the Vulcan and Victor aircraft arrived, however, 98 cities could be reached (indeed the latter number was being quoted in Air Ministry papers from May 1957 which looked at the numbers of larger cities which could be reached by the Mark 2 V-bombers operating at their maximum 2,100 nautical mile range from airbases in East Anglia).[154]

The COS Committee was given their first collective look at the Air Staff paper in September 1957. Boyle explained that its aim was to show what could be done by the UK force in a situation where the Soviet Union had attacked the UK alone; in conjunction with the United States in the event of a joint attack; and 'in the unlikely event of Soviet aggression against the West with conventional weapons [but] without simultaneous nuclear attacks, what we could do if we decided to retaliate with nuclear weapons.' Mountbatten thought that the plans for coordinated action with the United States should have the greatest priority, and wanted it stressed that the UK-only plans were explicitly retaliatory in nature. 'It must be made clear beyond possible doubt,' the First Sea Lord intoned, 'that if we were to take unilateral action against the USSR, though we could do grave damage to them, they could strike a mortal blow against the United Kingdom; it was not possible therefore to contemplate unilateral action except only in case of retaliation.'[155]

A revised version of the paper was endorsed by the COS the following month. Their discussion gave Mountbatten a chance to raise his doubts that even the scale of destruction that was anticipated would 'quickly break the Russian will to continue the war,' but he now withdrew his original suggestion that the policy directive should be prefaced with a paragraph explaining why it covered 'the highly improbable course of unilateral retaliation by the United Kingdom.' The Chief of the Air Staff was prepared to concur with Mountbatten's reservations over effects of carrying out the 'national' plan, saying that though the power of the V-bomber force should not be underestimated, he 'agreed it would not be wise to give Ministers the impression that we could deliver a blow that would necessarily be decisive.' Nevertheless, he wanted high-level endorsement of the target policy so that Bomber Command's tentative start to planning with the US Air Force could continue.[156] The final COS paper which emerged from the discussion – COS(57)224 – as well as confirming the principles of a combined offensive with the US Air Force, agreed that 'if the UK should be forced to take unilateral retaliation against the USSR, the target policy of Bomber Command should be to attack the Soviet centres of administration and population. This is the most effective system for our limited resources.' In the 'unlikely event' that the nuclear offensive was initiated by the Western air forces, rather than taken in retaliation to Soviet aggression which also employed nuclear weapons from the outset, it was considered that 'Allied strategic target policy should be to concentrate initially on destroying the enemy's ability to launch a nuclear attack against the West.'[157]

The COS had anticipated that such a major item of business should be dealt with by the Cabinet's Defence Committee; high level political endorsement for strategic target policy had, after all, had been one of the JPS recommendations made in January 1957 when the subject began to be mooted.[158] However, Sandys decided in November 1957 that COS(57)224 should not be referred to his colleagues, at least for the moment. His stated reason was that he felt 'it was better to wait until we know more of the American plans from the joint Air Force talks which are taking place.' Approving COS(57)224 'as a basis of planning', he asked that the COS update him after a few months 'in the light of the further knowledge we hope to gain about American intentions and about the targets which are allotted to the British Bomber Force in the joint Strategic Plan.'[159]

With the assistance of the Joint Intelligence Bureau (the body within the MoD responsible, amongst other things, for scientific and technical intelligence), the Air Ministry proceeded to grade according to priority those 98 cities which featured in the national target policy as being within reach of the Mark 2 V-bombers, with population, administrative and economic importance, as well as transportation links, playing a part in how each was ranked.[160] The new city target list then featured in the annex that was provided with the basic command directive issued in November 1957 to the C-in-C Bomber Command, and it was his headquarters that thereafter carried out detailed target planning. Meanwhile, talks between Bomber Command and US Air Force planning staffs took place in early 1958, and led to agreement on a combined plan which covered all available Soviet targets; neither side, however, revealed the yields of nuclear weapons they would be using, or numbers in their national stockpiles.[161] The first 'national' nuclear retaliatory strike plan, based on COS(57)224, seems to have come into effect in April 1958, by which date 76 nuclear weapon-carrying V-bombers were available as a front-line strike force. By July, the coordinated plan involving the US Strategic Air Command, where Bomber Command was assigned a much wider range of targets than if operating alone, had also entered into effect.[162]

The unilateral 'national' target policy enunciated in COS(57)224 was, in fact, never explicitly referred to senior ministers for consideration and approval, even though it would become the first 'criterion of deterrence' which would be employed by the UK's strategic nuclear force when operating in an independent role. Although over the years to come specific aspects of targeting would be re-examined by different bodies, and be subject to revision, it is instructive to observe that even into the 1970s the staffs responsible for national nuclear strike planning staffs – many drawn from RAF backgrounds – would still make reference to COS(57)224 as offering the basic guidance which informed their more detailed work.

This basic policy enshrined a full-blown commitment to a countervalue targeting philosophy, where deterrence would be predicated on holding the enemy's major population centres subject to devastating and large-scale retaliatory action if major aggression were to occur. It was an approach that was considered the best means for a modest-sized nuclear force to assure the purest form of deterrence in a political context where the credibility of the US nuclear guarantee to the Western alliance could not always be assumed. But it is important to underline that the primary aim of the UK strategic nuclear force during this period was to make a contribution, through combined planning and operations with the Americans, to the overall Western deterrent; as Mountbatten had been at pains to highlight, the contingency of an independent retaliatory strike by a Britain standing in isolation from her other Western allies was thought highly improbable by many.

By the time of COS(57)224's approval by the Chiefs of Staff in the autumn of 1957 the shape of the UK strategic nuclear force had become clear. A ten-year programme to design, develop and manufacture a force of the most up-to-date medium-range jet bombers was bearing fruit, with the V-bombers entering service in steadily increasing numbers equipped with the first generation Blue Danube atomic bomb. Designs for new thermonuclear weapons were also well advanced, supported by an energetic atmosphere nuclear tests series and led by an experienced and versatile team of scientists and engineers at Aldermaston. As a result of the productive meeting between Macmillan and Eisenhower on Bermuda in March 1957, there had been outline agreement to site 60 US Thor IRBMs at British bases, where they would eventually operate under 'dual-key' arrangements, with firing of the weapons to be a matter of joint decision between governments. Finally, Blue Streak development promised to give the UK its own indigenous ballistic missile capability by the mid-1960s, when it was assumed that steady improvements in Soviet air defences would make it unlikely that the V-force would be able to penetrate to targets deep within the Soviet Union.

The presumed vulnerability of the manned bomber to interception from ground-launched guided missiles had been one of the principal reasons why Blue Streak's advocates had seen it as so important to maintaining the credibility of the deterrent (although the Air Ministry was careful to argue that the missile should be seen as complementing, rather than supplanting, the inherent flexibility of a bomber force). 'If we are to maintain a medium range bombardment threat,' the Operational Requirement for Blue Streak issued in 1955 had intoned, 'the ballistic missile offers the best chance of delivery of nuclear weapons since no effective defence against such a missile is now known.'[163] As the following chapter will show, however, concurrent developments in ballistic missile defence technology were soon to challenge the categorical nature of such assessments and to open up a new dimension to the nuclear arms race.

Notes

1 See Margaret Gowing, *Britain and Atomic Energy, 1939–1945* (London, 1964), 76–8, 395.
2 GEN 75/1, 'The Atomic Bomb,' memorandum by the Prime Minister, 28 August 1945, CAB 130/3, The National Archives (TNA). All subsequent document references in this volume are drawn from the TNA unless otherwise indicated.
3 See Attlee's comments in Confidential Annex, CM(45)51st Conclusions, item 4, 8 November 1945, CAB 128/4/2.
4 See the discussion in Clark and Wheeler, *British Origins of Nuclear Strategy*, 66–77.
5 See Lawrence Freedman, *The Evolution of Nuclear Strategy*, 2nd ed (London, 1988), 5.
6 For background see Richard Overy, *The Bombing War: Europe, 1939–1945* (London, 2013), 19–55; Charles Webster and Noble Frankland, *The Strategic Air Offensive Against Germany, 1939–1945, Volume I: Preparation* (London, 1961), 6–11, 54–68, 86–91; Donald Cameron Watt, 'Restraints on War in the Air Before 1945,' in Michael Howard (ed.), *Restraints on War: Studies in the Limitation of Armed Conflict* (Oxford, 1979), 57–78; Uri Bialer, *The Shadow of the Bomber: The Fear of Air Attack and British Politics, 1932–1939* (London, 1980); Clark and Wheeler, *British Origins of Nuclear Strategy*, 20–24.
7 Overy, *Bombing War*, 614–24.
8 See Jeremy Stocker, *Britain and Ballistic Missile Defence, 1942–2002* (London, 2004), 20–33.
9 Freedman, *Evolution of Nuclear Strategy*, 22–33.
10 Bernard Brodie (ed.), *The Absolute Weapon: Atomic Power and World Order* (New York, 1946), 76. On Brodie see Fred Kaplan, *The Wizards of Armageddon* (New York, 1983), 9–32; Ken Booth, 'Bernard Brodie,' in John Baylis and John Garnett (eds), *Makers of Nuclear Strategy* (London, 1991), 19–56.
11 Brodie, *Absolute Weapon*, 31–3.
12 See, for example, Freedman, *Evolution of Nuclear Strategy*, 41–4.
13 A point made by Clark and Wheeler, *British Origins of Nuclear Strategy*, 66–71.
14 COS(45)402(O), 'Future Developments in Weapons and Methods of War,' report by Sir Henry Tizard's "Ad hoc" Committee, 16 June 1945, DEFE 2/1251; and see Gowing, *Independence and Deterrence*, I, 32–3, 163.
15 Attlee letter to Truman, 25 September 1945, Annex I to GEN 75/3, 'Note by the Prime Minister,' CAB 130/3, and in PREM 8/116; also reproduced in *Documents on British Policy Overseas, Series I, Volume II, Conferences and Conversations 1945: London, Washington and Moscow* (London, 1985), 544–7.
16 Major General Leslie C. Hollis minute for Attlee, 10 October 1945, PREM 8/116, and as COS 1449/5 annexed to COS(45)246th mtg, 10 October 1945, CAB 79/40.
17 See Gowing, *Britain and Atomic Energy*, 238–68.
18 GEN 75/10, 'International Control of Atomic Energy,' report by officials, 29 October 1945, CAB 130/3.
19 GEN 75/7th Meeting, 1 November 1945, CAB 130/2.
20 GEN 75/22, 'Large Scale Production of Materials for Use as a Source of Atomic Energy,' Note by the Secretary of the Cabinet, 2 January 1946, covering Chiefs of Staff minute for the Prime Minister, 1 January 1946, CAB 130/3; and see also Gowing, *Independence and Deterrence* I, 169, and Wynn, *RAF Nuclear Deterrent Forces*, 13.
21 See Clark and Wheeler, *British Origins of Nuclear Strategy*, 47.
22 TWC(45)44(Revise), 'Target Ranges,' note by the Joint Secretaries, 5 January 1946, DEFE 2/1252.

23 TWC(46)14, 'A Preliminary Note on Air Effort and Loss in Atomic Warfare,' memorandum by the Scientific Adviser to the Air Ministry, 13 April 1946, DEFE 2/1252.
24 TWC(46)15(Revise), 'Future Developments in Weapons and Methods of War,' report by the Joint Technical Warfare Committee, 1 July 1946, DEFE 2/1252; reproduced in Wynn, *RAF Nuclear Deterrent Forces*, 556–9.
25 See Gowing, *Independence and Deterrence*, I, 174, 234; Wynn, *RAF Nuclear Deterrent Forces*, 17–8, 26–7, 44–7.
26 For the Truman-Attlee agreement, see *Documents on British Policy Overseas, Series I, Volume II*, 627–30, and Richard G. Hewlett and Oscar E. Anderson, Jr, *The New World, 1939/1946: A History of the United States Atomic Energy Commission, Volume I* (Pennsylvania, 1962), 466–8.
27 Ibid, 477–81, 501.
28 Gowing, *Independence and Deterrence*, I, 92–108.
29 Arnold, *Britain and the H-Bomb*, 195–8; on Maclean see Gowing, *Independence and Deterrence*, I, 48.
30 GEN 163/1st Meeting, Confidential Annex, 8 January 1947, CAB 130/16, and for Bevin's views see Alan Bullock, *Ernest Bevin: Foreign Secretary 1945–1951* (Oxford, 1983), 352.
31 Gowing, *Independence and Deterrence*, I, 209.
32 See, for example, Julian Lewis, *Changing Direction: British Military Planning for Post-war Strategic Defence, 1942–1947*, 2nd ed (Abingdon, 2003), 122–35, 349–53.
33 Cmd 6923, *Central Organisation for Defence*, 1946.
34 For the essential background see Franklyn A. Johnson, *Defence by Ministry: The British Ministry of Defence, 1944–1974* (New York, 1980), 15–34; Michael Howard, *The Central Organisation of Defence* (London, 1970), 1–7; Lewis, *Changing Direction*, 284–5.
35 GEN 75/3rd Meeting, 3 October 1945, CAB 130/2; see also Gowing, *Independence and Deterrence*, I, 27.
36 See Gowing, *Independence and Deterrence*, I, 19–22, 182–3; and see also Peter Hennessy, *Cabinet* (London, 1986), 135ff.
37 Gowing, *Independence and Deterrence*, I, 39–45.
38 See Baylis, *Ambiguity and Deterrence*, 64–7.
39 See Christopher Andrew, *The Defence of the Realm: The Authorized History of MI5* (London, 2009), 341–7, 386–90.
40 Gowing, *Independence and Deterrence*, I, 211–2; and see Nicholas Wilkinson, *Secrecy and the Media: The Official History of the United Kingdom's D-Notice System* (London, 2009), 222–4.
41 See Gowing, *Independence and Deterrence*, I, 26–7, 51–6.
42 Ibid, 406.
43 See Gowing, *Independence and Deterrence*, II, 4–7, 15–18, 442; and Lord Sherfield, 'William George Penney,' *Biographical Memoirs of Fellows of the Royal Society*, 1994, volume 39, 283–302.
44 Penney letter to Portal, TS 20/2, 10 November 1948, and attached memorandum, 'The Atomic Bomb Production Establishment,' AB 49/26.
45 Gowing, *Independence and Deterrence*, II, 446–54.
46 Gowing, *Britain and Atomic Energy*, 267. See also Gowing, *Independence and Deterrence*, II, 456.
47 Wynn, *RAF Nuclear Deterrent Forces*, 33.
48 See Gowing, *Independence and Deterrence*, II, 72–6, 472.
49 Confidential Annex to COS(47)1st meeting, 1 January 1947, DEFE 4/1.
50 DO(47)44, 'Future Defence Policy,' report by the Chiefs of Staff, 22 May 1947, CAB 131/4.
51 See Baylis, *Ambiguity and Deterrence*, 60–64.

52 See, for example, Freedman, *Evolution of Nuclear Strategy*, 52–3; the initial deployment was of three groups of aircraft, see DO(48)18th Meeting, 13 September 1948, CAB 131/5.
53 JIC(48)116(Terms of Reference), 'Defence Aspects of Atomic Energy,' note by the Secretary, 2 November 1948, CAB 158/5.
54 JIC(48)116(Final), 'The Use of Atomic Bombs in a War Against the Soviet Union,' report by the Joint Intelligence Committee and the Joint Planning Staff, 4 August 1949, CAB 158/5.
55 See Baylis, *Ambiguity and Deterrence*, 72–4.
56 See Baylis, *Ambiguity and Deterrence*, 76–84; Moore, *Royal Navy and Nuclear Weapons*, 55–9.
57 See David French, *Army, Empire and Cold War: The British Army and Military Policy, 1945–1971* (Oxford, 2012), 92–3.
58 See Baylis, *Ambiguity and Deterrence*, 102–3.
59 See Gowing, *Independence and Deterrence*, I, 315.
60 See Marc Trachtenberg, *A Constructed Peace: The Making of the European Settlement, 1945–1963* (Princeton, 1999), 96–108.
61 See Marc Trachtenberg, 'The Nuclearization of NATO and US-West European Relations,' in his *History and Strategy* (Princeton, 1991), 156–9.
62 D(52)26, 'Defence Policy and Global Strategy,' paragraph 71(b), report by the Chiefs of Staff, 17 June 1952, CAB 131/12.
63 See Gowing, *Independence and Deterrence*, I, 440–3; Freedman, *Evolution of Nuclear Strategy*, 78–81; Baylis, *Ambiguity and Deterrence*, 126–51; Wynn, *RAF Nuclear Deterrent Forces*, 43–4.
64 C(52)202, 'British Overseas Obligations,' paragraphs 4, 29–30, memorandum by the Secretary of State for Foreign Affairs, 18 June 1952, CAB 129/53.
65 D(52)26, 'Defence Policy and Global Strategy,' paragraph 92, report by the Chiefs of Staff, 17 June 1952, CAB 131/12.
66 Air Vice-Marshal T. G. Pike letter to Air Vice-Marshal Sir Harry Broadhurst, 20 November 1952, AIR 2/15917.
67 See Gowing, *Independence and Deterrence*, I, 407.
68 See ibid, 215–6.
69 Morgan letter to Penney, 29 February 1952, AB 49/26.
70 See Elliot to COS, ELL 252, 23 January 1952, DEFE 20/1; Gowing, *Independence and Deterrence*, I, 315–8, 411–6; and see in general Matthew Jones, 'Great Britain, the United States, and consultation over use of the atomic bomb, 1950–1954,' *Historical Journal*, 54, 3, 2011, 797–828, especially 808–17.
71 Evelyn Shuckburgh, *Descent to Suez: Diaries, 1951–1956* (London, 1986), 32.
72 John Young, *Winston Churchill's Last Campaign: Britain and the Cold War, 1951–1955* (Oxford, 1996), 79–80.
73 See Gowing, *Independence and Deterrence*, I, 408–9, 425–34; Simpson, *Independent Nuclear State*, 96–7; Arnold, *Britain and the H-Bomb*, 71.
74 See Wynn, *RAF Nuclear Deterrent Forces*, 92.
75 Ibid, 115–8.
76 See Gowing, *Independence and Deterrence*, I, 450.
77 See 'Hydrogen Blast in '52 Dug Mile-Wide Crater in Sea and Wiped Out Island,' *New York Times*, 18 February 1954.
78 See Richard M. Leighton, *History of the Office of the Secretary of Defense, Vol III: Strategy, Money, and the New Look, 1953–1956* (Washington DC, 2001), especially 151–3; Robert R. Bowie and Richard H. Immerman, *Waging Peace: How Eisenhower Shaped an Enduring Cold War Strategy* (New York, 1998), 44–8, 97–8, 184–6; John L. Gaddis, *Strategies of Containment: A Critical Appraisal of American National Security Policy during the Cold War* (New York, 2005), 132–4;

Matthew Jones, *After Hiroshima; The United States, Race, and Nuclear Weapons in Asia, 1945–1965* (Cambridge, 2010), 162–78.
79 'Text of Dulles Statement on Foreign Policy of Eisenhower Administration,' *New York Times*, 13 January 1954.
80 See Freedman, *Evolution of Nuclear Strategy*, 83–4, and Paul Buteux, *The Politics of Nuclear Consultation in NATO, 1965–1980* (Cambridge, 1983), 1–4; and for MC-48 in particular, Baylis, *Ambiguity and Deterrence*, 193–4; Trachtenberg, *A Constructed Peace*, 158–60.
81 See Freedman, *Evolution of Nuclear Strategy*, 93–119.
82 See David Holloway, *Stalin and the Bomb: The Soviet Union and Atomic Energy, 1939–1956* (London, 1994), 303–9.
83 'United States Strategic Policy: record of an informal meeting between the Chiefs of Staff and representatives of the Foreign Office held in the Ministry of Defence at 3.15pm on Monday, 22nd February 1954,' CAB 301/173.
84 See Jones, *After Hiroshima*, 182–93.
85 See Lawrence Wittner, *Resisting the Bomb: A History of the World Nuclear Disarmament Movement, 1954–1970* (Stanford, 1997), 1–26; Robert Divine, *Blowing on the Wind: The Nuclear Test Ban Debate, 1954–60* (New York, 1978), 1–21.
86 See CC(54)23rd Conclusions, item 1, 31 March 1954, CAB 128/27; Young, *Churchill's Last Campaign*, 256–7.
87 See Divine, *Blowing*, 21; entry for 6 April 1954, Shuckburgh, *Diaries*, 160.
88 Churchill letter to Eisenhower, 9 March 1954, in Peter Boyle (ed.), *The Churchill-Eisenhower Correspondence, 1953–1955* (Chapel Hill, 1990), 122–4.
89 Brook minute for Churchill, 'Hydrogen Bomb,' 9 March 1954, CAB 301/173.
90 Entry for 25 November 1954, in Harold Macmillan, *Tides of Fortune, 1945–1955* (London, 1969), 567.
91 See Moore, *Royal Navy and Nuclear Weapons*, 99–101.
92 Arnold, *Britain and the H-Bomb*, 37–52.
93 See Young, *Churchill's Last Campaign*, 255–60; Baylis, *Ambiguity and Deterrence*, 178–9.
94 See GEN 464/1st Meeting, 13 April 1954, CAB 130/101.
95 Cherwell minute for Churchill, 5 May 1954, PREM 11/797.
96 *Hansard*, House of Commons (HC) debates, vol 537, col 1898, 1 March 1955.
97 Penney letter to Brook, 21 April 1954, CAB 301/173.
98 See DP(54)6, 'United Kingdom Defence Policy,' memorandum by the Chiefs of Staff, 1 June 1954, CAB 134/808.
99 For an excellent account see Peter Hennessy, *The Secret State: Whitehall and the Cold War* (London, 2003), 49–58.
100 See Confidential Annex, DP(54)3rd Meeting, 16 June 1954; and also DP(54)4th Meeting, item 4, 24 June 1954, CAB 134/808. For ministerial protests, see entry for 7 July 1954, Peter Catterall (ed.), *The Macmillan Diaries: The Cabinet Years, 1950–1957* (London, 2003), 327–8. Harold Macmillan had thought the decision 'too grave to be taken by 3 or 4 ministers, without informing the others.'.
101 CC(54) 47th Meeting, item 5, 7 July 1954, CAB 128/27.
102 CC(54) 48th Meeting, item 2, 8 July 1954, CAB 128/27.
103 See Lord Penney and V. H. B. Macklen, 'William Richard Joseph Cook,' *Biographical Memoirs of Fellows of the Royal Society*, 1988, 34, 45–61; 'Sir William Cook: Hydrogen bombs and nuclear reactors,' obituary, *The Times*, 19 September 1987; Arnold, *Britain and the H-Bomb*, 59, 77–82, 152–3, 224.
104 Cmd 9391, *Statement on Defence: 1955*, paragraphs 1, 4–5, 18–9 and 25, February 1955.
105 *Hansard*, HC, vol 537, cols 1896–7, 1 March 1955.
106 *Hansard*, HC, vol 537, col 1905, 1 March 1955.
107 Group Captain S. W. B. Menaul minute for Assistant Chief of Air Staff

(Operations), CMS 1721/50/7414, 24 August 1954, covering draft 'Command Directive to Air Marshal Sir George H. Mills,' AIR 2/15917.
108 C(54)329, paragraph 32, 'Defence Policy,' note by the Prime Minister, 3 November 1954, CAB 129/71.
109 See D'Isle draft letter for Macmillan, 23 March 1955, and attached memorandum 'The Size of the V-Bomber Force,' DEFE 11/101; extracts are also quoted in Baylis, *Ambiguity and Deterrence*, 187.
110 *Hansard*, HC, vol 537, col 1899, 1 March 1955.
111 Air Marshal Sir George Mills letter to Air Vice-Marshal L. F. Sinclair, BC/TS 81101, 13 April 1955, AIR 2/15917.
112 Ibid.
113 Draft Directive to C-in-C Bomber Command, attached to ibid.
114 Command Directive to Air Marshal Sir George H. Mills, 31 May 1955, AIR 2/15917.
115 See Wynn, *RAF Nuclear Deterrent Forces*, 373–5.
116 See Aubrey Jones minute for Sandys, 12 October 1957, DEFE 13/193.
117 See Baylis, *Ambiguity and Deterrence*, 279–82.
118 Air Ministry note for Minister of Defence, 24 January 1957, AIR 2/14712, as quoted in ibid, 282.
119 See Philip Zielger, *Mountbatten: The Official Biography* (London, 1985), 560; Ken Young, 'The Royal Navy's Polaris Lobby, 1955–62,' *Journal of Strategic Studies*, 25, 3, 2002, 56–86; Moore, *Royal Navy and Nuclear Weapons*, 153–6.
120 See J. E. Moore (ed.), *The Impact of Polaris: The Origins of Britain's Seaborne Nuclear Deterrent* (Huddersfield, 1999), 13–24; Graham Spinardi, *From Polaris to Trident: The Development of US Fleet Ballistic Missile Technology* (New York, 1994), 21–57; Robert J. Watson, *History of the Office of the Secretary of Defense, Volume IV: Into the Missile Age, 1956–1960* (Washington, 1997), 159–63, 179, 374–9.
121 COS(S)(55) 5th Meeting, 15 June 1955, DEFE 8/52. See also Baylis, *Ambiguity and Deterrence*, 185–8.
122 See D'Isle draft letter for Macmillan, 23 March 1955, and attached memorandum 'The Size of the V-Bomber Force,' DEFE 11/101.
123 JP(55)67(Final), 'Long Term Defence Programme,' report by the Joint Planning Staff, 20 July 1955, DEFE 6/30.
124 MISC/M(55)69, 'Long Term Defence Programme,' minutes of a meeting held at the Ministry of Defence, 12 July 1955, DEFE 7/963.
125 Maudling letter to Lloyd, 30 August 1955, DEFE 7/964.
126 D'Isle letter to Lloyd, 8 September 1955, DEFE 7/964.
127 Confidential Annex to COS(56)70th Meeting, item 5, 17 July 1956, DEFE 32/5.
128 ACAS(I) minute for ACAS(Ops), ACAS(I)/6/54, 12 January 1955; 'Co-ordination with US of plans for the Use of Strategic Bomber Force in War: Brief Notes of a Meeting in VCAS's Room at 2.30 – Tuesday, 25th January 1955,' AIR 20/12508.
129 COS(56)451, 'Co-ordination of USAF and RAF Nuclear Strike Plans,' note by the Chief of the Air Staff, 31 December 1956, DEFE 32/5, and in AIR 20/12508. See Wynn, *RAF Nuclear Deterrent Forces*, 254–5, and for the direction of US nuclear strike planning in this period see Watson, *Into the Missile Age*, 473–7.
130 Confidential Annex to COS(57)3rd Meeting, item 7, 8 January 1957, DEFE 4/94.
131 See Harold Macmillan, *Riding the Storm, 1956–1959* (London, 1971), 244.
132 Entry for 29 October 1954, Macmillan, *Tides of Fortune*, 560.
133 See Howard, *Central Organisation of Defence*, 8–9; Ziegler, *Mountbatten*, 562; Baylis, *Ambiguity and Deterrence*, 207–8.

60 *The making of a deterrent force*

134 See Colin Gordon, 'Duncan Sandys and the Independent Nuclear Deterrent,' in Ian Beckett and John Gooch (eds), *Politicians and Defence: Studies in the Formulation of British Defence Policy, 1845–1970* (Manchester, 1981), 132–53.
135 Johnson, *Defence by Ministry*, 54–6.
136 See Baylis, *Ambiguity and Deterrence*, 243–4, on the Cabinet Secretary's continuing criticisms during 1957 of the lack of coordination in overall defence policy.
137 The minutes of the Defence Board between 1958 and 1964 can be found in DEFE 30/3 and DEFE 30/4.
138 Cmnd 476, *Central Organisation for Defence*, July 1958; Howard, *Central Organisation of Defence*, 10–11.
139 Cmd 124, *Defence: Outline of Future Policy*, paragraph 15, April 1957. On the Sandys White Paper see Michael Dockrill, *British Defence since 1945* (London, 1988), 65–71; French, *Army, Empire, and Cold War*, 159–71; Navias, *Nuclear Weapons and British Strategic Planning*, 1–4, 134–87.
140 Clark, *Nuclear Diplomacy and the Special Relationship*, 7; and see Martin S. Navias, '"Vested Interests and Vanished Dreams": Duncan Sandys, the Chiefs of Staff and the 1957 White Paper,' in Paul Smith (ed.), *Government and the Armed Forces in Britain, 1856–1990* (London, 1996), 217–34.
141 D(57)2nd meeting, 27 February 1957, CAB 131/18.
142 Confidential Annex to COS(56)4th Meeting, item 3, 10 January 1956, DEFE 32/5.
143 COS(57)34, 'Long Term Defence Policy,' memorandum by the Chiefs of Staff, 5 February 1957, DEFE 5/73.
144 *Hansard*, HC, vol 568, col 1761, 16 April 1957; also quoted in Clark, *Nuclear Diplomacy and the Special Relationship*, 15.
145 Arnold, *Britain and the H-Bomb*, 140–50.
146 Williams minute for Sandys, 22 October 1957, DEFE 13/193.
147 See Aubrey Jones minute for Sandys, 15 October 1957, DEFE 13/193; and see material in AVIA 92/25.
148 See Clark, *Nuclear Diplomacy and the Special Relationship*, 157–75.
149 See Sandys explanation to his senior colleagues at GEN 567, 23 January 1957, CAB 130/122; Sandys letter to Charles E. Wilson, 30 January 1957; Wilson letter to Sandys, 1 February 1957, AIR 20/12508; also Wynn, *RAF Nuclear Deterrent Forces*, 257–60.
150 See Wynn, *RAF Nuclear Deterrent Forces*, 275–6.
151 See COS(57)42nd Meeting, item 3, 20 May 1957, DEFE 4/97; COS(57)224, 'Strategic Target Policy for Bomber Command,' memorandum by the Chiefs of Staff, 16 October 1957, AIR 8/2201; also Wynn, *RAF Nuclear Deterrent Forces*, 271–3.
152 See DCAS minute for CAS, 'Co-ordination of Strategic Plans with SAC: Memorandum of Understanding,' June 1957, and attached draft minute for COS Committee, AIR 20/12508.
153 See GEN 570/2, 'Strategic Bomber Force,' memorandum by the Minister of Defence, 27 May 1957; GEN 570/2nd Meeting, 30 May 1957, CAB 130/122; D(57)15, 'Strategic Bomber Force,' memorandum by the Minister of Defence, 26 July 1957; D(57) 7th Meeting, 2 August 1957, CAB 131/18.
154 'Soviet Target Systems and the Ability of the Western Powers to Attack Them,' Annex to COS(57)224, 'Strategic Target Policy for Bomber Command,' memorandum by the Chiefs of Staff, 16 October 1957, AIR 8/2201; and see also R. C. Kent memorandum, 23 May 1957, AIR 2/14699, as quoted in Navias, *Nuclear Weapons and British Strategic Planning*, 207–8.
155 Confidential Annex to COS(57)72nd Meeting, item 5, 23 September 1957, DEFE 4/100.

156 Confidential Annex to COS(57)78th Meeting, item 3, 15 October 1957, DEFE 4/100.
157 COS(57)224, 'Strategic Target Policy for Bomber Command,' memorandum by the Chiefs of Staff, 16 October 1957, AIR 8/2201.
158 This was certainly Dickson's assumption, see Confidential Annex to COS(57)72nd Meeting, item 5, 23 September 1957, DEFE 4/100.
159 Dickson minute for First Sea Lord, CIGS, and CAS, 'Bomber Command – Strategic Target Policy,' WFD/256, 20 November 1957, AIR 8/2201; and see also Wynn, *RAF Nuclear Deterrent Forces*, 261.
160 See Wynn, *RAF Nuclear Deterrent Forces*, 276.
161 See Air Vice-Marshal R. B. Lees minute for PS to CAS, 'Strategic Target Policy for Bomber Command,' and attached draft report, 30 April 1958; COS(58)148, 'Co-ordination of Anglo/American Nuclear Strike Plans,' memorandum by the Chiefs of Staff, 5 June 1958, AIR 8/2201; Air Chief Marshal Harry Broadhurst letter to the Under Secretary of State for Air, 25 June 1958, AIR 20/12508.
162 See 'Bomber Command/Strategic Air Command Co-ordination,' summary of Bomber Command presentation, 11 July 1958, AIR 8/2201.
163 OR 1139, 'Medium Range Ballistic Missile System,' 8 August 1955, AIR 2/13206, and see Wynn, *RAF Nuclear Deterrent Forces*, 373–4.

2 The rise of ballistic missile defence

Early years: the British and American experience

From soon after the first German V-2 rockets began to reach their British targets in September 1944, scientists, engineers and defence planners had turned their collective attentions to the problem of defence against ballistic missile attack. At its most basic level the problem was reducible to the tasks of detecting and tracking an incoming missile, and devising a means of interception so that the missile and its payload were destroyed, neutralised or somehow deflected from its target. Techniques of radar acquisition of V-2s in early stages of flight from their launch sites was quickly developed, but methods of intercepting such a high velocity object proved elusive. Existing means of air defence such as fighter aircraft and conventional anti-aircraft artillery were simply unable successfully to engage a missile target. Attempts to destroy V-2s by a massed barrage of anti-aircraft fire as they approached the end of their flight had been studied but typically regarded as impracticable given the huge volume of ammunition that would have to be expended and the low chances of an interception. Direct air attack against V-2 launching points or storage and production sites, or their capture by Allied ground forces, were the only means open to removing this new threat to the cities, ports or military installations lying within missile range. In the immediate post-war years preventing an adversary gaining bases close enough to launch short-range rocket attacks, as the Germans had done from the Low Countries, was considered the surest means to prevent a repeat of the experience of V-2 bombardment. With countering a still-putative missile attack against the UK hence rendered impractical, British air defence planners focused their efforts on the growing threat from the Soviet long-range air force.[1]

In the United States, where resources tended to be more plentiful, interest in the potential for missile defence, again prompted by examination of the V-2 experience, was present at an early stage. The end of the war had given the Allies an insight into the highly advanced state of German experimentation and designs in rocketry, where plans had even been concocted to construct much longer-range missiles than the V-2 which could have been capable of reaching the continental United States. Several key German rocket scientists eventually found their way to the US after 1945, and provided invaluable assistance to the fledgling American missile programme; the Soviet Union's exploitation of German personnel, knowledge and techniques was even more extensive, and a modified version of a V-2 was test-fired as early as October 1947.[2]

Although the long-range bomber aircraft remained for the time being the prime means to deliver an attack against targets within the homeland of an enemy, the ballistic missile, when rocket motors were made efficient and reliable enough and guidance systems perfected, was already being discussed as the strategic weapon of the future. The addition of nuclear warheads, where improvements in design would eventually make them light enough to be carried by ballistic missiles, made a means of countering this impending threat appear all the more important. As early as July 1945, recommendations were being received from the US military authorities that research and development into schemes of defence against missiles such as the V-2 should be initiated, and in March 1946 the first contracts for studies into the area were let. The most important of these was for 'Project Wizard', which began by examining the feasibility of developing a missile that could engage and destroy another object travelling at 4,000 miles per hour at altitudes between 60,000 and 500,000 feet; over subsequent years the work of Project Wizard would extend into some of most basic problems of missile defence.

During the 1950s the US Army adopted the mantle of responsibility for providing air defence from the ground for the United States, with work proceeding on several projects for guided missiles which could counter the threat of bomber aircraft or air-breathing missiles. The entire Army programme, which could trace its origins to studies which were begun in the final months of the war, was given the umbrella name 'Nike'; by the end of the 1950s, the Nike-Hercules, a nuclear-tipped air defence missile, had entered service in an anti-aircraft role. Defence against ballistic missiles was, however, an altogether more challenging task, and in March 1955 the Army asked Bell Laboratories to look ahead to the air defence requirements of the next decade through a study known as Nike II. In a sign of the rivalry that was already developing between the Army and the US Air Force over missile defence, the latter service also approached Bell at this time for a study of ABM systems. Bell issued a comprehensive report on the problem at the end of 1955 which covered such fundamental issues as the optimum point on a missile's trajectory for interception, the need for defending radars to discriminate between real warheads and any decoys which might have been included in a payload, and the crucial role played by high-powered long-range radars in a defensive system. From the Army's Nike II studies emerged the design concept for a new Nike-Zeus missile, intended for intercept in the highest part of the earth's atmosphere with a nuclear warhead.[3]

The Nike-Zeus system began development in November 1956, but its subsequent testing programme was marked by repeated failures. Meanwhile, the Air Force, a comparative latecomer to the ballistic missile defence field, had taken forward the earlier Project Wizard studies with several industrial contractors, but these had led to a series of sceptical conclusions, and in particular technical doubts that the Army's Nike-Zeus would be able to deal with missiles equipped with even the most primitive penetration aids and decoys. More fundamentally, the basic Air Force philosophy was that the nation's resources were better spent on improving offensive capabilities rather than propagating a 'Maginot Line' mentality which encouraged the view that an ABM defence could be made wholly effective.[4]

As we saw above, in Britain defence against the more readily apparent threat of aircraft attack had been given initial emphasis, not least as intelligence assessments in the late 1940s pointed to the improbability that the Russians would be capable of developing rockets able to deliver nuclear warheads for at least another decade. In both their 1947 and 1950 reports to the Minister of Defence on future defence research policy, the MoD's Defence Research Policy Committee had recommended that no research and development effort should be given over to the problem of defence against V-2 type rockets.[5] When a member of the Committee raised the need to allocate research effort into new radar for air defence against the threat of V-2 style attacks in May 1949, for example, the DRPC's then-Chairman, Sir Henry Tizard, dismissed it with the comment that 'so far as he was aware, no possible solution to the problem of intercepting long range rockets was in sight. That being so, there was clearly no point in including a requirement in the programme at present.'[6] By mid-1952, however, the DRPC's Guided Weapons Sub-committee had identified an anti-missile missile as one of several 'possible needs' for future research and development, but the subject still had a low priority.[7]

In their June 1952 paper on Defence Policy and Global Strategy the COS had painted a bleak picture of the UK's vulnerability in the nuclear age, but also noted that the problem was reciprocal. The Air Defence Committee, they reported, had examined the problem over the previous year and that it was now

> clear that there is in the foreseeable future no effective defence against atomic air attack. This conclusion carries the gravest implications for the United Kingdom. But if the United Kingdom, with its great experience, its technical skill, and its highly developed communication system, is unable to devise an effective defence for such a small area, the task is all the more difficult for the Soviet Union. Russia's vast size and relatively undeveloped communications have obvious advantages from the point of view of security against land invasion, but for air defence against attacks that can come in from every point of the compass they present her with an almost insoluble problem.[8]

An Anglo-American technical conference held in February 1953 to discuss and share knowledge about air defence underlined the advanced radar and data processing technologies that would be required to detect and then track incoming missile threats and guide defending interceptors within close enough proximity for a successful engagement. Even if a defensive system could be devised it was generally concluded that adding to attacking missile numbers was an easy and sure way to overcome it.[9] One report compiled in October 1953 by the Controller of Guided Weapons and Electronics (CGWL) at the Ministry of Supply wanted it stressed, 'that in general we are pessimistic about any possibility of creating a defence against ballistic rockets which could be regarded as adequate in the context of the atomic, or still less the thermonuclear, warhead where an attrition defence is of almost no value. This does not invalidate the need for continuing research on the problem, but it is particularly desired to avoid giving any impression that any solution can be seen in the light of our present knowledge.'[10]

Nevertheless, as rapid progress with indigenous Soviet missile development began to be observed during 1953–54, the challenge of tracking and destroying fast moving missiles was not one that could be simply ignored by UK air defence planners.[11] For example, a February 1953 report from the Chief Scientist at the Ministry of Supply on the technical problems involved with an active defence against V-2 type rockets armed with atomic warheads recognised the 'extreme difficulty' of finding solutions, but found that there was 'no one technical factor which ruled out the possibility of a defence system against a V.2 weapon.' It accordingly recommended that a start be made on a programme of work on radar techniques which could be used to determine the 'reflecting characteristics' of rockets, guidance systems for defending missiles, and warheads which might be used in a defensive weapon.[12] In view of the growing and serious threat to the UK from ballistic missile attack, the DRPC staff, moreover, was unhappy with the negative conclusions of the October 1953 paper by the CGWL cited above, and called for more urgent and positive action.[13]

By March 1954 the DRPC now considered that defence against ballistic rockets was a pressing requirement.

> 'There has been no effort at all in this country directed to the development of ballistic rockets,' the Committee advised, 'and scarcely any to devising any means of defence. It is vital that the highest priority be given to a detailed technical assessment of the possibilities of both offence and defence and that research is started into any technique which may contribute to a solution of an ultimate defence [sic].[14]

In early 1954 the Ministry of Supply therefore placed a study contract with English Electric and the Marconi Wireless Telegraph Company for design of an early warning radar and a defensive missile system respectively; the resulting report, eventually produced in July 1955, yielded a potential system which would use existing but improved radar technology to track incoming threats, and an interceptor missile armed with a nuclear warhead, with a range of about 55 miles and putative engagement height of 70,000 feet. Several more years of basic work to study the problem would be required, it was estimated, and in any case the Air Staff calculated that the economic costs of providing a defence would be enormous, while an attacker could increase the offensive threat at much less expense.[15]

Indeed, in line with earlier assessments, many of the studies from this period were pessimistic that any successful solution to the difficulties of ABM defence could be found, especially as in the context of defence of the UK only a small number of warheads penetrating a defensive screen would be enough to inflict such a high degree of damage as to render the whole subject moot.[16] Small-scale research efforts into methods of defence nevertheless continued, while work on long-range early warning radar systems which might be able to detect missile attack began to receive new emphasis, not least so that Britain's own strategic nuclear force of V-bombers could be dispersed before being caught at their main airbases by a surprise Soviet strike. In February 1955 the Air Ministry took the step of issuing to the Ministry of Supply an Air Staff Target – OR/1135 – which outlined the future need for an active air defence system against ballistic missiles and called for fuller investigation of the problem. The most immediate major nuclear threat to the UK itself, moreover, was still reckoned to come from the Soviet long-range air force; the threat from large numbers of Soviet Medium Range Ballistic Missiles (MRBMs) was thought some years away. It was generally acknowledged (mirroring the attitude of the US Air Force) that the prime means to prevent such an attack remained possessing the means to retaliate, and it was for this reason that the DRPC continued to assign the highest priority to the development of Blue Streak.

A note of guarded optimism was sounded in early 1956 following a tripartite conference on defence against ballistic missiles held in London between US, British and Canadian officials. Serving as the UK Chairman of the meeting, Sir Frederick Brundrett, the then-Chief Scientist at the MoD, found that long-range ballistic missiles could be detected with present radar technology, and that there were no 'insurmountable difficulties' in the design of a defensive missile system, although further studies would be needed. On the other hand 'lack of knowledge of the design and vulnerability of the target missile and of diversionary systems which might be employed made it very difficult to assess the performance of a complete defensive system.'[17] That same month, the Air Ministry were concluding (in a view concurred with by the COS) that although an ABM system seemed technically feasible, 'formidable difficulties' still lay in the way of its development and that the immediate focus of attention should be directed toward adequate means of early warning of ballistic missile attack. By 1962, 'and probably until at least 1965', the principal threat to the UK was still predicted to come from the manned bomber, while intelligence on Russian capabilities and intentions in the ballistic missile field remained parlous.[18]

Over the course of the next year, as it became apparent that Britain's economic circumstances would mandate cuts to defence spending, the chance that ballistic missile defence would receive any substantial allocation of research and development funding became even more remote. At the start of October 1956, Robert Cockburn, CGWL at the Ministry of Supply, presented a paper to the DRPC which attempted to summarise the findings of the past three years of work. The general picture, Cockburn explained, was that, as long as small nuclear warheads were available, it was possible to conceive of a defence against long-range ballistic rockets 'on the basis of extensions of existing techniques of guidance and little more than existing radar techniques. Thus it was possible to say that there were no technical reasons why interception and destruction of a missile was impossible.' But there still existed many uncertainties over where the best point of interception lay (above or below the atmosphere) and there would be 'great operational problems. It was possible to conceive a defensive system,' Cockburn thought, 'but not one that would cover all the possibilities of surprise or saturation which existed in practice.' Further issues were the financial costs involved, and the need to test the system in peacetime. There was consequently 'great difficulty' in 'taking a balanced view between excessive optimism and the desirability of carrying out all the essential research before being committed to a particular line of development.' It would, for example, be a waste of time attempting to issue of design specification for a missile when the radar problems of ABM defence had not been adequately examined.[19]

Nevertheless, Brundrett remained impressed with the need to pursue more work in the area, and the DRPC he chaired recommended the funding of further research. In October 1956 Brundrett was informing the COS that the latest findings coming out of the Ministry of Supply (which had built on the English Electric and Marconi work) 'leave me in no doubt that detection, interception and destruction of a ballistic missile is technically feasible and that against a limited threat, an active defence system can be conceived. But at least five years must elapse before such a defence could be specified in any detail.'[20]

The stress of the Sandys review of 1957 on the primacy of the deterrent, however, meant that any measures of air defence that were then under consideration were subordinated to the requirement to protect the V-force from pre-emptive air and missile attack, rather than devoted to any general scheme to protect population centres. During the course of the review the COS had endorsed the opinion of the JPS that there was no foreseeable effective defence of the UK against nuclear bombardment and that the focus of air defence should be on the protection of the deterrent itself.[21] The Defence White Paper of April 1957 had accordingly declaimed that 'there is at present no means of providing adequate protection for the people of the country' against the consequences of nuclear attack.[22]

By this time an additional and important rationale for work on studying the possibilities of missile defence had begun to emerge: equipped with knowledge of the problems involved British officials would have a better idea of whether the Soviet Union would eventually be able to develop ABM defences, and, equally significantly, could gain insight into how modifications to attacking missiles could help to overcome such defensive efforts. During early work on the Blue Streak programme, the Royal Radar Establishment (RRE) at Malvern had carried out some fundamental small-scale research work on warhead echoing areas, while the Royal Aircraft Establishment (RAE) at Farnborough had undertaken studies on possible decoys for use in the Blue Streak warhead re-entry system. Forms of decoys for ballistic missiles were the subject of an April 1957 paper from the Guided Weapons Department at RAE which found them to be 'just feasible' but probably requiring a 'major effort' before becoming 'a practical operational system', while their effectiveness was still difficult to evaluate.[23] Spare capacity for the incorporation of possible countermeasures to Soviet defences was noted by the Defence Board in October 1958 as an important feature of Blue Streak, giving it certain advantages over alternative delivery systems then being discussed.[24] Defending the Blue Streak programme against its growing number of critics, the Minister of Supply had told the House of Commons in February 1959 that given that ABM systems were no longer inconceivable, 'it was not too early now to take counter-measures. This meant the insertion in a missile of jamming equipment able to embarrass any defence.' Despite its other disadvantages, such as slow preparation time, a powerful liquid-fuelled missile such as Blue Streak could carry the extra weight further than its newer solid-fuel equivalents.[25]

Basic research and testing in such key areas as re-entry vehicle (RV) design and re-entry phenomena was facilitated by use of the Black Knight launcher system, a proving rocket which had begun development in 1956 as a smaller 'lead in' to the full-scale Blue Streak project. First flights of Black Knight were conducted in 1958 at the Woomera rocket range in Australia. Meanwhile, decoy work at RAE had stepped up a gear in early 1959 as designs were mooted which might be incorporated in the Blue Streak re-entry system; such work, it was noted, should be done in parallel with that on the warhead, 'in order to influence it where necessary. The aim should be to provide a cloud of decoys bracketing the drag and echoing area characteristics of the warhead, the two parameters not being correlated.' A ten-mile radius decoy cloud was envisaged, with spacing of about two miles between objects, 'so that a hit on an adjacent decoy will not destroy the warhead.'[26] By April 1959 the design of a decoy to match Blue Streak's RV was in hand, and planning for experimental trials work to evaluate the radar-echoing properties of decoys using Black Knight was also progressing.[27] The decoy stowage plan for Blue Streak was to have about 30 of them mounted in a bay behind the warhead.[28]

By the spring of 1960, one retrospective summary noted, considerable progress had been made with penetration aid techniques. The radar echoing area of the Blue Streak RV had been minimised by careful design of shape and use of surface-skin materials, so that 'only the highest power and most sensitive radars would have had any chance of seeing the re-entry head at all.'

Indeed, there was the prospect during the next round of Blue Streak trials of having no radar available which would even be capable of doing the necessary tracking. Very small and lightweight decoys had also been designed – at least on paper – to match the radar-echoing properties of the RV, as well as its dynamic characteristics as they began to re-enter the atmosphere. By the time the differences between real warheads and decoys began to become evident to defending radar (and as lighter-weight decoys began to burn up), there would be very little time (perhaps only 30 seconds) before the real warhead would reach its impact point, making a successful interception by any defender extremely difficult. Noise jammers – as the Minister of Supply previously hinted – had also been worked on, as a method to confuse the ability of enemy radars to accurately track a cloud of decoys with a warhead hidden within.[29]

In the aftermath of the publication of the Sandys Defence White Paper in 1957, the Air Ministry was keen to pursue an ambitious programme of research and development into the whole area of ballistic missile defence. Faced with the objection that the problems of radar detection and tracking of warheads and decoys had to be tackled before any design of a defensive missile could be attempted, Air Ministry officials tended to reply that a step-by-step approach had to be taken, and that the first challenge was countering the threat of single missiles which had no penetration aids.[30] They had support from Brundrett, who in August 1957 can be found advising the Minister of Defence: 'Two years ago we had absolutely no conception how any form of defence against the ballistic missile could be achieved. During the past two years that position has radically changed and we can now see quite clearly the lines of development we should follow which might lead to a reasonably effective defence of small targets against a ballistic missile threat.'[31] It was for this reason that the Chief Scientist advocated proceeding 'as rapidly as is scientifically justified with research into defence against ballistic missiles.'[32]

Nevertheless, the majority of assessments covering the prospects for ABM defence during the late 1950s remained pessimistic, given the known capacity for an offensive missile designer to include increasingly sophisticated penetration aids in their payload package. For example, Cockburn delivered a paper on the radar requirements of ballistic missile defence to the DRPC in September 1957 which underlined the difficulties which the use of decoys would present to any defender. Cockburn was a singularly appropriate defence scientist to cover the topic: during the war he had played a major role in devising techniques for disorienting enemy radar systems, including the idea of releasing bundles of small metallic strips – known as 'window' – to mask the flight path of Bomber Command formations over Germany.[33] The latter innovation, adopted and refined by the Americans with the use of numerous fine metal wires and purpose-built dispensing systems, and now called 'chaff', was soon seen as a useful penetration aid by the designers of offensive ballistic missiles. In the simplest techniques, Cockburn's DRPC paper explained, the main body of an attacking missile could be broken up in ballistic flight after warhead separation in order to confuse defensive radars by creating a cloud of objects, such as motors and guidance packages, perhaps spread over a tube of ten miles diameter and travelling along the same trajectory as the actual warhead. Additional, expressly-designed artificial decoys, as were then under study for Blue Streak, created even more difficult problems of tracking and radar discrimination for radar systems. Atmosphere sorting of decoys from warheads would help to mitigate the problem – as lighter decoys would burn up as they began to re-enter or change their radar signatures – but gave defensive missiles far less time to be launched and to make a successful interception. 'The operational value of an active defence will be limited by the effect of decoys, whether "natural" [i.e. from missile parts and debris] or "artificial",' he had advised. 'Inability to identify the warhead from surrounding decoys may make active defence virtually impossible, and until this problem is solved, it is not possible to undertake the design of a defensive missile.'[34]

The late 1950s also witnessed a much deeper and more extensive exchange of Anglo-American views on the subject of ABM defence. This development was a by-product of the very real improvement that was witnessed in Anglo-American relations following Macmillan's accession to the premiership in January 1957. Steps to repair the rupture caused by the Suez crisis had been taken at the Bermuda meeting between Eisenhower and Macmillan in March, where among other things, agreement in principle was reached for the deployment of 60 US Thor IRBMs to the UK. The two leaders had a long-standing and friendly relationship that had its origins in the Mediterranean theatre during the Second World War, where Eisenhower had commanded Anglo-American forces from the Allied Force Headquarters in Algiers where Macmillan had operated as British Minister Resident. Despite their determination to move closer, nevertheless, progress over negotiating the details of the arrangements for basing of Thor remained slow, and the two governments still differed over some aspects of Cold War strategy (including, for example, in the Far East).

It took the shock of the Soviet launch of the Sputnik earth satellite in early October 1957, however, to propel an anxious US administration into offering to place the relationship with the UK on an entirely new footing. With the threat from the Soviet Union – underlined by Moscow's apparent technological prowess – now appearing so much more formidable, close allied support seemed more than ever necessary to many key officials. At the end of the month, Macmillan held important meetings with the American President in Washington that helped to foster a new spirit of cooperation, and included American acceptance that the principle of 'interdependence' might operate in specific areas of defence research and development, allowing the pooling of resources and ideas.[35] As the next chapter will detail, the most significant agreement Macmillan secured from these talks was a commitment from Eisenhower to work toward the restoration of the full and frank Anglo-American nuclear collaboration that had been severed in 1946 by the

McMahon Act, a process which was eventually crowned in July 1958 with the conclusion of the 'Agreement on the Uses of Atomic Energy for Mutual Defence Purposes'.

But even before this breakthrough, in follow-up meetings between US and British officials held after Macmillan's visit to Washington, it proved possible at the end of 1957 to reach quick agreement to establish a regular pattern of technical cooperation in the more general defence field.[36] This found practical manifestation, and with additional Canadian participation, in the form of a Tripartite Technical Cooperation programme, where in numerous sub-groups defence scientists and engineers could meet to discuss (non-nuclear) topics including such varied matters as guided weapons, aircraft engines, chemical and biological weapons defence, electronic warfare, and sonar and radar systems.[37]

During 1958 rudimentary exchanges began on issues connected to ABM defence between UK, US and Canadian officials on the programme's Sub-Group F, including how radars could discriminate between real warheads, decoys and missile debris. But it was soon obvious that the Americans were proving reluctant to divulge the full scope and detail of their active work in the missile defence field. The third meeting of the Sub-Group, held in Washington in late October 1958, had seen officials discuss elements of the Nike-Zeus missile system. Target tracking which would enable decoy sorting was still evidently a major issue; the American proposals were described in the UK report of the talks as 'extremely fluid at the present time and nobody has any idea whether a practicable scheme can be worked out. Hope is largely placed on discrimination by "radar signatures" outside the atmosphere.' There was no claim made by the Americans that their system would 'necessarily be effective. It depends entirely on the solution of the decoy sorting problem.'[38]

The Sub-Group's meetings were only scheduled at six monthly intervals, so the process of information exchange could hardly be considered continuous. It was also apparent from these encounters, as the DRPC was informed, that while the Americans were described as 'extremely forthcoming with information', at this stage they did not seem in favour of a joint project, and would prefer that the UK pursue its own studies and ideas.[39] Thus, basic questions still had to be tackled by British defence scientists very much alone and without the data from an extensive programme of flight testing of missiles and re-entry systems there was a limit to how far indigenous research work could go.[40]

There also continued to be little high-level political appetite to embark upon major expenditure on active measures of ballistic missile defence. When the future nuclear programme was the subject of ministerial discussion during the summer of 1958, the Prime Minister wanted his officials to know that there was a need to 'avoid a confusion' over the resources that could be devoted to the air defence of the UK. 'There was a danger,' Macmillan had said, 'lest the defence of the deterrent should lead to undue expenditure in seeking to develop and produce an "anti-missile missile" which, if only because of the pace of scientific advance, could not be expected to protect the United Kingdom from successful attack by nuclear weapons of one sort or another. It was, perhaps, in this field that economies should especially be sought.'[41] In October 1958, the MoD's DRPC produced a report on air defence which found that an adequate defence against ballistic missile attack was unlikely to surface in practical form for at least another ten years, though it was noted the Americans were planning to deploy an initial system by 1963. As far as the Committee was concerned, 'we could not, within our own resources, carry the load involved in the development of a complete system.' A joint approach with the Americans was therefore seen as the most advisable course for the future.[42]

In fulfilment of the latter brief, the Ministry of Supply came forward with a another paper at the very end of 1958 which proposed a modest research programme on ballistic missile defence which took into account knowledge of the US work in the field. The intention was to produce results from experiments with radar equipment which could contribute to a joint Anglo-American programme of work. From experience with Blue Streak it had been found that a 'complicated threat of a warhead accompanied by 20–30 decoys could be achieved by the USSR in the early 1960s.' The lethal effects of defensive nuclear explosions, particularly when it came to their radiation aspects, was an area where knowledge was still notably lacking, but in most British studies a lethal radius of 500–1,000 feet was assumed. This meant that accurate tracking and interception of incoming objects – and sorting between real warheads and decoys – remained a critical issue for the defence. As the fundamental problem of an active defence system was widely regarded as that of decoy discrimination, the Ministry's proposals would focus on developing a new type of discriminating radar within the next five years, and to conduct basic research into electronically scanning aerial systems, as mechanical scanning was seen as such a limiting factor in radar early warning and tracking systems. Research into types of high-acceleration missile, for lower altitude interception, was also proposed. Total extra-mural costs (i.e. those involving contracts with industry) would be £11.5 million over five years, £750,000 having already been allocated for the 1959/60 period. Such basic research was considered necessary so that value of any US defensive system that was eventually produced could be properly assessed, but also because it would help in assessment of 'possible Russian ABM systems and hence to modify our own ballistic [missile] programme to counter any defence which might arise.'[43]

The DRPC, at a meeting held in late January 1959, decided to approve the first of these areas of work, examining a new type of discrimination radar, but wanted reconsideration of the other proposals. The Committee's main concerns were over the costs of the programme and the diversion of scarce highly-skilled staff from other projects that would be involved. As Cockburn put it, 'opinions on this subject varied from those who thought that any project we undertook would be impossibly expensive, to those who said that it was vital and must be undertaken at all costs.' Supporting the Ministry of

Supply, Brundrett called the subject 'the most important defence problem of our time and we must establish, as soon as possible, if the chances of an effective ABM defence were promising enough for us to devote money and effort to such an end. If it was possible then we could not afford to be out of it.'[44]

As it emerged, however, the prime goal of the committee was in fact to reduce the effort devoted to that which would provide standing with the Americans. There was no inclination to promote any possibility of an independent UK programme in the ABM field; in March 1959, the DRPC confirmed that a decision on electronically scanned aerial systems would be postponed for another year, while expenditure of £2.5 million over the next four years was approved for basic work at RAE on the possible designs for new high-speed missiles.[45]

By the late 1950s study of the problem of ballistic missile defence was only one of the many – and by no means the most important – preoccupations of a troubled Ministry of Supply. Throughout the decade it had held responsibility for the supply of all strategic raw materials, military equipment and military aircraft, as well as atomic weapons and guided missiles, making it a significant Whitehall ministry in spending terms (though the Minister of Supply was not a member of the full Cabinet, he attended the Defence Committee); total expenditure on defence research and development was running at about £220 million per annum by 1960/61, £160 million of which was spent in industry and the remaining £60 million in the government-administered research establishments.[46]

The MoS's leading role in military research, development and procurement gave it control over a wide array of such government research facilities, including the Royal Aircraft Establishment at Farnborough, which supervised and carried out work on the design and development of missiles and other guided weapons (including, as we have seen, the Blue Streak IRBM). With a large central staff of experienced and expert officials housed in Shell-Mex House on the Strand, the Ministry also played a central role in controlling the process by which nuclear weapons were developed and produced, issuing the requirements of the services in the form of contracts to AWRE as and when necessary. It had, however, few friends in Whitehall, and its cause was not helped by the numbers of expensive, profligate and delayed defence equipment projects which it had initiated and was charged with overseeing, most obviously in the military aircraft field. Parliamentary criticism of the failings of the defence equipment programme had gathered strength by the late 1950s, and some argued that the MoS was an unnecessary middle tier between the services, the research and development establishments, and industry. Under Treasury pressure, in May 1958 a wide-ranging inquiry was launched by Lord Hailsham, the Minister of Science, into the whole subject of the government's management and control of research and development; the committee of experts given the task, under the chairmanship of Sir Claude Gibb, soon fastened its attention on the defence programme.[47]

One solution might have been to centralise control of R & D at the Ministry of Defence, but with a unified Ministry of Defence yet to be realised, and the central defence staff still relatively small, there was no question yet of transferring responsibility for the large-scale and complex arena of defence procurement. Administrative reform eventually came in October 1959 when the MoS was revamped, with many of its traditional 'supply' functions returned to the separate service departments. The MoS was, however, given extra responsibilities for civil aviation, and accordingly re-named the Ministry of Aviation (MoA). In the military field, moreover, it continued to oversee aircraft, guided missiles, radar and electronic equipment; it also maintained its special role in the nuclear field, with a Director of Atomic Weapons Development continuing to place warhead orders with Aldermaston through the Atomic Energy Authority. A key position within the new Ministry of Aviation from which many these activities were led, including in the nuclear field, remained the Controller of Guided Weapons and Electronics – CGWL – a holdover from the 'Controllerate' system used in the now defunct MoS.[48]

The Ministry of Supply's problems were mirrored within the MoD by the reputation of the DRPC, on which several MoS officials sat along with the deputy chiefs of army, navy and air staffs, the chief scientists of the three services, and a Treasury representative, and which was supposed to approve and then monitor its research and development programmes. Taking over from Brundrett as Chief Scientific Adviser (CSA) at the MoD in January 1960, Sir Solly Zuckerman later wrote that 'despite its name', the DRPC which he now had to chair had very little influence over 'policy' as such. The basic function of the Committee, as far as Zuckerman could see, was to set 'an order of financial priority for the R & D needed to satisfy "operational requirements" which the Services put up separately – ostensibly in the implementation of a coherent defence policy.' It therefore became a 'gentlemanly forum' for inter-service competition, while it also had a 'notional responsibility' for keeping defence R & D projects under review but was evidently incapable of such an immense brief. Shortly after taking over as CSA, Zuckerman was warned by the Prime Minister that defence R & D was 'difficult to control.' Macmillan had used a 'piscatorial analogy', where 'small fry … grow into sprats, and the sprats into herrings. If they are likely to be cancelled, kill them when they are no bigger than sprats, he advised.'[49]

During the 1960s Zuckerman would try to change aspects of the system to achieve a greater degree of control over the process by overhauling the DRPC. Indeed, before he had taken over as CSA Zuckerman had been accorded a very close view of the problem when in January 1959 he was drafted in to take over the government's review of the entire R & D effort after the premature death of Sir Claude Gibb. Zuckerman's first findings and recommendations as they related to the defence R & D field were presented in December 1960, and considered by the Cabinet's Defence Committee the following month.[50] The full-scale Report of the Committee on the Management and Control and Research and Development, or Gibb-Zuckerman

Report, was eventually published in July 1961 and made many recommendations for more effective project management and oversight procedures in the defence field and for reform of the DRPC (an ironic twist considering that Zuckerman now chaired the committee his own report had brought under criticism). But implementing new procedures would not be easy, and until a unified Ministry of Defence was created, where service autonomy was reduced, many of the basic problems of the system would continue to prove intractable.

The vulnerability issue

Basic research into the radiation output of nuclear explosions, particularly when occurring at very high altitude and even above the earth's atmosphere, had begun to enter a new phase during the late 1950s. The application of the results to air defence and ABM systems was a subject that soon started to be examined more seriously by those few defence scientists who enjoyed access to the carefully controlled and sensitive knowledge being generated from nuclear test programmes. In the UK, physicists at Aldermaston, working through older data, began to discern in early 1956 that fission warheads – including the types which were used as the first stage in thermonuclear weapons – were vulnerable to the effects of the radiation produced by a nuclear explosion occurring nearby. Plutonium-fuelled nuclear cores were particularly susceptible to the neutron radiation given off by such a defensive blast. The implications were startling and wide-ranging: if the Russians were aware of the phenomenon, defensive weapons could be designed which would neutralise incoming British warheads. Similarly, the large 'miss' distances involved offered Western ABM designers the hope that they too could employ a new 'kill mechanism' – as the jargon put it – that would obviate the need for precise accuracy of interception. Intensive efforts were subsequently made to examine the problem further and to make fission warheads which were immune to what AWRE called the R1 effect. Indeed, as the official historian of the British hydrogen bomb programme has detailed, testing of immune primaries formed an important part of the later stages of the Grapple series of British thermonuclear tests carried out in 1957–58.[51]

Similarly, during the extensive series of atmospheric tests carried out by the United States in the Pacific during 1958 which were collectively known as 'Hardtack', three shots were specifically designed to record and examine the radiation output from high altitude explosions (of which there was no previous US experience).[52] In a presentation for members of the US Atomic Energy Commission (AEC) – the government agency that since 1947 had controlled and overseen all military and civilian nuclear programmes in the United States – one Department of Defense official explained the purpose of the high altitude tests as being 'to provide information in three major categories; (1) weapons effects data for anti-ICBM missiles (2) data on neutron fluxes at high altitudes, and (3) the ability to detect nuclear detonations at high altitudes.'⁵³ In December 1957, having been informed by American officials about the aims of the series, Penney reported in excited tones to the Atomic Energy Sub-committee of the DRPC that the 'high altitude measurements were of the greatest interest.' The largest bursts planned by the Americans were 'fairly obviously' directed toward 'an anti-missile application.' Penney even thought that a test at a height of 100 miles might be a possibility:

> At such heights novel and startling effects were likely to appear; the flash would only last for a matter of micro-seconds; the energy would depend on the yield/mass ratio of the weapon and could on this account vary from thousands to hundreds of electron-volts. According to the yield mass ratio such energy could either heat up the whole of a missile to a few thousands of degrees centigrade in a matter of micro-seconds or heat up the skin layers and cause destruction by mechanical failures. It must be emphasised that this was a completely new field and this was thinking some ten years ahead. The Americans would tell us some of results, but not all and perhaps some study of these matters ought to be undertaken.⁵⁴

The first of the high-altitude tests, 'Yucca', had been a kiloton-yield balloon-carried shot fired at 85,000 feet above the earth in April 1958, but some important instrumentation had failed to activate, leaving results disappointing.

However, two further high-yield tests, both with warheads launched by Redstone rockets, provided results that proved crucial for further research into the possibilities of ABM defence. 'Teak' was a 3.8 megaton shot staged on 1 August 1958 at about 250,000 feet (or 77 kilometres) above Johnston Island in the central Pacific; 'Orange' was fired 11 days later at about 140,000 feet (or 43 kilometres), and registered a similar yield. One retrospective analysis of the 1958 high-altitude tests that has been declassified noted that they had produced the finding that the two key radiations which could be useful against an ICBM attack above 250,000 feet were neutron and X-ray. Neutrons could render a nuclear warhead inoperable by raising the temperature of the fissile material within its core, but X-rays worked by creating structural failures in the materials making up the surface skin of missiles or re-entry vehicles. This structural failure, it was explained, was 'caused by the following sequence of events: (1) The X-rays penetrate the missile [or re-entry vehicle] wall by a short distance. (2) The energy dissipated within the thin outer layer by the X-rays, as they are absorbed, serves to raise this layer to an extremely high temperature and pressure. (3) The pressure is sufficiently high to cause the thin layer of metal vapor to expand explosively, imparting a large impulse to the wall. (4) The wall is forced inward at high velocity and may fail if the yield point of the material is surpassed.' It was this violent X-ray impulse or shock, transferred to within the body of whatever object that was encountered, which caused most concern to weapon designers. There was an obvious application to attacking re-entry vehicles with defensive warheads optimised for the production of X-rays, but the 'extremely large destructive range' of this particular form of radiation meant it was a method that could also be used to 'blow away' a swarm of decoys designed to conceal a real warhead, and to attack the warhead at the same time. Below 250,000 feet, where X-rays were absorbed quickly by the atmosphere, the most effective kill mechanism against re-entry vehicles designed to resist blast effects was thought to be neutron radiation from defensive warheads.[55]

Knowledge about such effects was still in its relative infancy, however, and defence scientists who studied such phenomena maintained that the kill mechanisms which could be used by ABM warheads – and the techniques and materials that could be used to counter them – required fuller investigation and more testing (leading to fears from some that the test moratorium maintained by the United States and Soviet Union after October 1958 could result in significant gaps in knowledge essential to national defence). Exchanges with the UK about such findings could only be conveyed under the terms of the 1958 agreement covering nuclear weapons, not in the forum of the Tripartite Technical Cooperation programme. In July 1959 the first such extensive exchange took place under the provisions of the 1958 agreement between US and UK weapons scientists on nuclear effects, with meetings lasting two weeks in total. A few months later, further talks were held between Ministry of Aviation and Air Ministry officials and their AEC and Department of Defense counterparts dealing with some of the nuclear vulnerability aspects of ABM defence. As Brundrett informed the DRPC

> It was clear from this meeting that there were no nuclear kill mechanisms that had not been considered by the UK previously and that US and UK thoughts on kill radii were in accord. This meeting recommended an intense study of the decoy problem and the blast kill mechanism at lower altitudes, and suggested that this work be co-ordinated by Sub-Group F. Because the nuclear kill mechanisms, as applied to specific design features of warheads, cannot be widely discussed and cannot be discussed at all with the Canadians, the forum for discussion arranged on the nuclear side remains in being, but will only meet if new evidence shows a need for further discussion.[56]

In a further sign of the closeness of the technical cooperation that was starting to develop in the field, British representatives were invited to a comprehensive Department of Defense review of the US ABM programme in August 1959, while relevant papers were handed over to RRE and RAE.[57]

By this stage, the United States had made significant strides in its work on ballistic missile defence. One additional spur to the US ABM programme were the political ramifications of the Soviet Sputnik launch in October 1957, and the debate that ensued following the subsequent production of the Gaither Report. During the summer of 1957 the Eisenhower administration had begun to examine the merits of protecting the US population from nuclear attack through a large-scale shelter programme. In the search for advice on the relative value of 'active' as against 'passive' forms of defence it appointed an independent high-level panel under the chairmanship of H. Rowan Gaither, who led the board of directors of the Ford Foundation, to study the problem.

Taking its remit much further than had been anticipated and gathering advice from many experts in the defence community and academia, the Gaither Committee analysed the whole subject of US strategic vulnerability. The huge shock of Sputnik, which provided a graphic demonstration of the advances made by Soviet missile technology, and how a nuclear payload might be delivered directly to the American homeland, helped to focus the work of the panel. Included within its final report, produced in November 1957, were many alarmist conclusions – which quickly leaked to members of Congress concerned over national security – and its recommendations included an injunction to develop missile defences at an early date to protect SAC bases and eventually critical US urban areas (all measures which could only be implemented at huge extra cost). Both the United States and the Soviet Union, the Gaither Report had noted, were likely to have developed some methods of anti-ballistic missile defence by the mid-1960s. Although privately sceptical about the extent of the Soviet missile threat and concerned to keep a check on defence spending, President Eisenhower felt compelled to inject new momentum into programmes designed to protect against surprise missile attack.[58]

Heightened concerns over strategic vulnerability in the aftermath of Sputnik were manifested in fresh efforts to reduce the damaging inter-service rivalries that had been such a feature of the US ABM programme. In January 1958, the US Secretary of Defense, Neil H. McElroy, issued an important directive intended to demarcate areas of responsibility in an attempt to address the problem. The Army was told to carry on with its development efforts with the Nike-Zeus missile programme, with associated tracking and guidance radars, 'as a matter of urgency, concentrating on system development that will demonstrate the feasibility of achieving an effective, active AICBM [anti-intercontinental ballistic missile] system in an electronic counter measure and decoy environment.' The Air Force was given the main role for long-range early warning radar systems, and the communication links that would allow integration with the Army's Nike-Zeus system.[59]

McElroy's initiative also came in the context of a major reform of the US Department of Defense, which had the basic goal of centralising control over the proliferation of military research and development projects that had occurred during the Eisenhower years. As a further step forward in this area, in February 1958 McElroy had brought into being the Advanced Research Projects Agency (ARPA) which, among many other tasks, soon assumed the central responsibility for coordinating and directing all US ABM programmes.[60] The new Agency quickly inaugurated 'Project Defender', a new set of studies with the goal of looking beyond Nike-Zeus – which was designed for shorter-range interception in the upper part of the atmosphere – to the whole field of possible future approaches to the problems of ballistic missile defence.[61]

A subsequent Defense Reorganization Act, passed in August 1958, heralded the creation of a new position of Director of Defense Research and Engineering (DDRE) within an office of the same name, which was to stand third in the hierarchy of the whole Department, just below the Secretary of Defense and his deputy. After some delay in finding a suitable candidate, its first occupant, taking up his duties in March 1959, was Herbert F. York, who over the previous year had been chief scientist at ARPA, and before that the director of the AEC's Lawrence Livermore Nuclear Laboratory in California.[62] DDRE would serve as the Secretary's main adviser on scientific and technical matters, and supervise and/or control all research and engineering activities within the DoD's purview, with ARPA also falling under his considerable remit by the end of 1959. In October 1959, British officials in Washington on the Joint Services Mission were already commenting that 'the extent to which the hand of Dr York appears firmly behind most of the technical decisions taken in the Department of Defense is quite remarkable.'[63] The final charter for DDRE's roles also included scientific collaboration with other countries, a stipulation which meant the occupant of the post was to play a key part in the nuclear relationship with the UK over many years.[64]

Having won primary responsibility for ABM defence from the Air Force, after 1958 the Army lobbied hard for additional funding for its troubled Nike-Zeus programme so that deployment could occur as early as 1962. Support came from Congressional advocates of ballistic missile defence who pushed the administration to allocate extra resources to prepare for production, even though testing and evaluation were far from complete. The Air Force, piqued at the position, continued with some basic research of its own and was keen to criticise the Army's decision to commit to a missile design when so many aspects of the defensive problem, and the options open to an attacker, remained to be investigated. There were mounting concerns, in particular, that Nike-Zeus could be overcome by the simple expedient of placing multiple warheads on offensive missiles, while its radar had a very limited discrimination capability and might be blinded by the effects of its own defensive nuclear explosions.

Officials in the Department of Defense and elsewhere in government shared much of this Air Force scepticism over the effectiveness of the Army's preferred system, and baulked at the huge costs associated with a full-scale production programme for Nike-Zeus (with some estimates for the eventual bill put at around $15 billion). In March 1959, for example, a panel led by the President's science adviser on defence in the missile age queried whether Nike-Zeus could be made effective before 1964 at the earliest. Instead, other measures to protect deterrent forces and bases, such as rapid dispersal, improvements in warning times of attack, and the hardening of bomber and missile bases were seen as more cost-effective. The first Zeus missile was finally test-fired on 26 August 1959, but suffered serious technical problems soon after launch. While research and development funds continued to flow in large amounts into US ABM programmes during the final years of the Eisenhower administration – the defense budget for the financial year 1961, drawn up by US officials at the end of 1959, included $287 million for Nike-Zeus alone – money for actual production continued to be denied.[65] The Eisenhower administration remained wary of the technical problems, high deployment costs, and dubious effectiveness of ABM defence.[66]

In the UK, by July 1960 the Ministry of Aviation had reached the similar conclusion that the prospect of developing a defence against ballistic missiles that was 'operationally feasible and effective against multiple attack' was 'extremely small at present, and that it will remain so for a substantial number of years.' In view of the importance of the field, there was no inclination to abandon research entirely, however, and continuing work on radar decoy discrimination techniques, and use of the Black Knight rocket as a test vehicle to study re-entry phenomena was recommended. Nevertheless, almost total reliance on the US for knowledge and research work on ABM systems – where the Americans were obviously devoting considerable efforts – would have to be accepted in the future. A principal aim of the UK programme was therefore to build up enough 'technical capital' so that the Americans might be interested, and contacts with them could be maintained.[67] The DRPC was content to follow these recommendations, and, considering the need to find savings in the MoA budget, agreed to curtail further basic work at RAE on possible high-speed interceptor missiles.[68]

The Treasury's opposition to any substantial expenditure on ABM defence meant that MoA officials, and those at the Royal Radar Establishment at Malvern, had to be content with a three year radar research programme costing not more than £1.78 million (while an RRE project to develop a new type of decoy discrimination radar had had to be cancelled at the start of the year).[69] Once the major breakthroughs of 1958 in Anglo-American defence cooperation had been achieved – with the Macmillan Government publicly extolling the virtues of Anglo-American interdependence in the defence field – there was a marked tendency thereafter to depend on US sources of information about the latest developments in ABM defence from its own extensive research programme; a small UK effort was kept going primarily in order to attract American interest and promote the benefits of exchanges concerning the developing technology.

The emergence of a Soviet ABM programme

As in the West, Soviet interest in the possibilities of defence against the threat from ballistic missile attack seems to have been apparent from the soon after the end of the war. Development of surface-to-air missile (SAM) systems, designed for use against aircraft, was a key precursor to later ABM work, and testing of anti-aircraft missiles, derived from German wartime experiments, began in 1948. The following year saw orders issued for the construction of a SAM system for the defence of Moscow. First tests of a complete SAM system, with both a guided interceptor missile and target tracking radar, were held in May 1953, and the S-25 launcher system (designated SA-1 in the West) was commissioned for service two years later. By the end of the 1950s, Soviet air defence forces were fielding the much improved S-75 (SA-2) system.[70] After their return home in the early 1950s, German scientists and engineers initially captured by the Russians in 1945, or sent to the Soviet Union from the occupied zone in Germany in 1946, and then exploited for their technical knowledge in the defence and industrial fields, also reported that ballistic missile defence had been a field of Soviet interest. Theoretical studies into possible ABM systems were reportedly underway at the Soviet Ministry of Defence between 1948 and 1951, at the same time as work on guidance systems for ballistic missiles was being undertaken.

A further significant step was taken in early 1954 when, following representations to the top level political leadership from senior military figures, Design Bureau 1 of the Main Special Machine-Building Directorate of the USSR Council of Ministers, which had been heading SAM development since 1950, was given the job of investigating the practicality of creating an ABM defence. A positive appraisal from the resulting report in August 1954 led to the formation, in late 1955, of Special Design Bureau 30 (SKB-30) of Design Bureau 1, under Gregory Vasylovych Kisunko.

Kisunko was to become the key scientific figure in the history of the Soviet ABM programme until his replacement in the early 1970s. After a short period of further work, Kisunko was ready to begin testing of an experimental system, known as System A. In August 1956 authorisation was given to begin building work in earnest on a new special test range in and around Sary Shagan, a village on the Western shores of Lake Balkhash in Kazakstan, and about 1,000 nautical miles to the east of the principal Soviet missile testing range at Kaputsin Yar. Extensive tests at Sary Shagan using interceptor missiles with conventional warheads guided by ground-based radar, it appears, began in October 1957. The interceptor missile used was the V-1000, developed by Special Design Bureau 2 under the direction of Peter Grushin.[71]

The first extensive and positive mention of the possibilities of missile defence appeared in a Soviet military journal in July 1957 where it was claimed that 'work on the development of a means of defence against ballistic missiles is being conducted no less intensively than the development of the [offensive] missiles themselves.' In a speech to military students at a Moscow academy in November 1957 the Soviet Defence Minister, Marshal Rodion Y. Malinovsky, identified missile defence as an area which should receive attention in their training and alluded to the 'painstaking work' needed to achieve success.[72] A government decree issued in April 1958 ordered that designs for an ABM system which could defend Moscow should be drawn up, and by the following year an improved performance specification for what was called System A-35 was issued. Unlike the kind of missile tests then being conducted at Sary Shagan, this called for the interception of the multiple re-entry vehicles of a number of ballistic missiles outside the earth's atmosphere. During 1960 Kisunko set to work on the design of the A-35 System, his main focus on the complex issues of coordinating early warning, tracking and missile guidance radars, missile control, and overall system integration, with an enhanced position within Design Bureau 1.[73]

Several authors have attempted to chart the evolution of Soviet ABM policies during these crucial formative years and the strategic background which informed the policy choices being adopted. The Soviet programme for the development of medium and long-range ballistic missiles that was built up during the 1950s was clearly accompanied by the imperative to carry out basic research into possible countermeasures. Such an effort was also consistent with a Soviet preoccupation with air defence – whether in the form of surface-to-air missiles, anti-aircraft artillery, or modern interceptor aircraft – which was discernible throughout this whole period. Indeed, Soviet air defence forces were organised into an independent service after 1948 referred to as PVO Strany (Home Air Defence Force), with its own fighter aircraft, anti-aircraft artillery, early warning organisation, and surface-to-air missile systems. In 1955, PVO Strany was accorded equal status with the other branches of the armed forces; the creation of a separate service gave ABM advocates an autonomous base from which to argue for more resources from within the Soviet military bureaucracy.

In general terms, Soviet military thinking during the latter half of the 1950s emphasised large-scale use of nuclear weapons to defeat the enemy, protect the homeland, and preserve the state. Nuclear weapons, it was assumed, would be used by both sides at the outbreak of major war, and many Soviet observers were convinced that the US leadership was ready to contemplate a pre-emptive air atomic offensive while it still held overwhelming strategic superiority: the Eisenhower administration's embrace of 'massive retaliation' after 1954 was seen very much in this light. Correspondingly, Soviet nuclear planning seems to have placed a premium on hitting the enemy's nuclear forces before they had a chance to be employed. Surviving and 'winning' a nuclear exchange with the United States, where Soviet society and its political and military leadership was still able to function, necessarily entailed, as well as strategic rocket forces, the development of means to defend population centres from enemy missile attack.[74]

At the top political level, Nikita Khrushchev, who by 1956 had clearly emerged as the dominant figure within the post-Stalin collective leadership, placed a high priority on the development of sophisticated military technology as a way to both showcase the achievements of Soviet science to a global audience, and reinforce an impression of burgeoning military strength, an increasing preoccupation as the US nuclear stockpile grew at an exponential rate and fears of Western aggressive intentions remained unabated. The prestige conferred by the Sputnik breakthrough in 1957, and the anxieties this induced in the West about Soviet missile capabilities, was an obvious sign that technological leaps could offer significant political benefits. There was also the basic point that the United States had begun to press ahead with ABM research and development from the mid-1950s, and could not be allowed to open up a decisive lead in this latest dimension of the nuclear arms race; American experiments with the Nike-Zeus system were watched and discussed by Soviet military commentators and their general tone was optimistic that the obvious difficulties of constructing an effective defence could be overcome.

As well as admitting the exaggerated claims made for its effectiveness, Khrushchev's own retrospective description of the ABM programme was that it was a 'very costly luxury and an extremely complex task', but he appears to have viewed it as essential complement to an offensive ballistic missile force.[75] Asked in September 1961 by the renowned and well-informed *New York Times* correspondent, C. L. Sulzberger, whether Russia had 'any guaranteed defense against western weapons – such as an antimissile missile with a neutron warhead?', Khrushchev replied in guarded yet revealing terms:

> You are intruding on the most secret ground of any country and there is not a leading statesman who would disclose to you everything that he has, all the more so in such tense times ... I can only tell you that at the same time we told our scientists and engineers to develop intercontinental rockets we told another group to work out means to combat such rockets. We expressed our great satisfaction with the work of the experts who produced the ICBM. At the same time, we remain very satisfied with the work of those who produced the means for combating such rockets.[76]

During the late 1950s and early 1960s Soviet military journals featured many articles on the topic of ballistic missile defence, while it was also a subject whose treatment was influenced by the internal power struggles between the party and the military establishment, and within the military establishment itself.[77]

In January 1960 Khrushchev signalled a number of very important changes to Soviet defence policy when he announced in a speech to a session of the Supreme Soviet that the overall size of the armed forces would be reduced, with a greater emphasis being placed on their nuclear and missile components. Investment in nuclear systems henceforth increased, and the Soviet leader's infatuation with advances in missile technology continued, even while the Soviet economy struggled to grow and living standards atrophied. It was Khrushchev's basic conviction that if general war were to breakout between the Soviet Union and the West it would be dominated by the strikes of long-range nuclear missiles against each other's territory, a view he articulated in a number of articles and speeches from 1960 onwards.[78]

The Soviet defence establishment was by no means happy with such departures from previous assumptions – and the budget cuts that went with them – and over the next few years Khrushchev had to compromise, coming to acknowledge the role of large standing military forces and all branches of the armed forces; at the same time, the primacy of the strategic rocket forces (which after December 1959 were organised into a separate service) and the vital importance of the short initial period of a nuclear exchange was universally understood. Such tensions between Khrushchev and the military would ultimately have longer term political consequences for the former when – bereft of powerful allies – he was successfully removed from the Communist Party leadership in October 1964.[79]

Soviet interest in ABM development, and the major investment in resources and infrastructure that were going into the area, were obviously noted in the West, and formed a topic of major concern for the intelligence communities in both the United States and Britain. Construction of new buildings and military installations at Sary Shagan was first reported in February 1957, and later in the year ballistic missile firings were being detected from the extensive test range at Kapustin Yar into an impact area lying about 70 miles west of the village. Over the next few years, it was estimated that over 100 medium-range missiles were fired into the area, in what was evidently a large-scale anti-missile testing programme. Intelligence information on the Soviet ABM programme was, nevertheless, sparse, despite it being seen as an important area of interest; at such long ranges, telemetry recordings of missile launchings from Sary Shagan itself were difficult to obtain, while the initial focus of the U-2 photo-reconnaissance overflights of Soviet territory begun in the summer of 1956 was, understandably, on the status of the ICBM programme.[80]

From the early 1950s onwards, high-level American policymakers were periodically furnished with National Intelligence Estimates (NIEs), authoritative documents which attempted to summarise the consensus opinion held by the plethora of groups and agencies which made up the US intelligence community on major topics of importance for national security.[81] The March 1957 NIE dealing with Soviet guided missile capabilities, described the current state of intelligence in the area as 'deficient'. All the NIE could offer was a forecast that guided missiles adapted for use as defence against ICBMs could probably be produced at some stage between 1963 and 1966 but the characteristics of such a missile system could not be estimated with any confidence.[82] The following year's NIE was almost equally thin, noting that 'We have little evidence indicating either Soviet priority or technical approach to an anti-ballistic missile system.' A 'first operational capability' for a missile system of 'limited effectiveness' against ICBMs was again seen as achievable during the 1963–66 time period, but a 'considerable Soviet electronic development program' extending for many more years was viewed as necessary before a fully effective system could be deployed.[83]

One of the items on the list of the 'ten most wanted' areas of information on the Soviet missile programme, compiled by the CIA's Office of Scientific Intelligence at the start of the 1959, was the likely first date of deployment of an ABM system.[84] President Eisenhower's reluctance to sanction an extensive series of U-2 overflights during the second half of 1958 and much of 1959, for fear of the diplomatic consequences if an aircraft was downed over Soviet territory, was another factor contributing to the opaque intelligence picture.[85] In November 1959, the latest NIE dealing with Soviet guided missile capabilities again had to admit to a 'paucity of positive intelligence on Soviet missile and space programs'. As a result stress had had to be placed on estimated Soviet military requirements, Soviet capabilities in related areas, and extrapolation from US experience. When it came to air defence – once more, 'in the absence of evidence, but considering Soviet technical capabilities and probable needs' – it was estimated that 'in 1963–1966 the Soviets will have available an antiballistic missile system with undetermined capability against ICBMs, IRBMs, submarine-launched, and air-launched ballistic missiles.'[86]

Assessments produced by the UK intelligence community during this period reflected the prevailing view that Soviet air defences would not be adequate, at least for the next few years, to provide any kind of effective counter to large scale air or missile attack; there was, it was admitted, no 'direct knowledge' of current and future research and development programmes in the air defence area.[87] On the more specific subject of ABM defences, beyond the basic conclusion that a great deal of effort was being expended in the area, there was again much uncertainty in evidence over what stage Soviet work had reached. Some saw the growth of Russian offensive nuclear missile capabilities as inevitably leading to a vigorous search for the means also of defence against a similar threat. 'It is generally agreed that the efficacy of the deterrent depends entirely on the Russians believing that any war with the West will mean the destruction of their homeland,' one MoD official observed in January 1958. 'We do not know how far ahead of us the Russians are in the missile field and in particular in developing an anti-missile defence (in the first instance, perhaps, against IRBMs), but I have no doubt that the Russians will allocate to this research the highest priority. If the Russians solve this problem before us, our offensive deterrent will be valueless, and since we would have no defence against Russian IRBMs, we would be entirely at their mercy.'[88]

As noted above, interception of the telemetry signals from Soviet missiles when under test was a common but uneven practice by the late 1950s, but interpretation of the information gathered was by no means straightforward.[89] A February 1960 paper from the Joint Intelligence Committee which examined Soviet air defence capabilities over the next five year period, could only offer the vague and general conclusion that there were then 'no positive indications of Soviet progress in the sphere of defence against ballistic missiles but it is considered that they will have taken active measures to develop such a system.' It was believed that the individual components of such an ABM system would be deployed when they became available, and that 'by the end of 1964 a limited active system of defence against simple ballistic missiles could be deployed for a very small number of important targets.'[90]

An intelligence breakthrough of sorts occurred with the information generated from a U-2 reconnaissance flight (mission 4155, or less prosaically, Operation 'Square Deal') conducted on 9 April 1960, the last successful U-2 overflight of the Soviet Union before the aircraft piloted by Francis Gary Powers was famously shot down a month later by an SA-2 missile over Sverdlovsk. This produced evidence of what were called by one CIA photoanalyst 'numerous guided-missile associated activities', who went on to describe the imagery collected as 'the most provocative and possibly the most productive results' from any U-2 coverage thus far. The scope and complexity of the installations observed at Sary Shagan suggested that analysis of the bounty gathered by 'Square Deal' would be a major task and problem for the US intelligence community.[91]

Overhead photography of the Sary Sagan area, according to a later NIE, had revealed a large and sprawling complex of facilities extending westwards from Lake Balkhash for about 125 nautical miles, with a north-south width of about 65 nautical miles, and at 8,000 square miles making it about the size of Wales. Housing accommodation for about 20,000 people was identified, along with over 20 electronics and communications installations. Various radars were observed, including a very long 900-foot building with a sloping west face and antennae located near the edge of the lake. Launching sites both for modified SA-2 SAMs and larger guided missiles were identified and it was noted that much construction work was still underway at the whole site (not least on the 900-foot long radar installation).[92]

The new picture of Soviet ABM progress presented by the U-2 overflight was reflected in one of the final NIEs produced for the Eisenhower administration in December 1960 which looked at Soviet military capabilities over the next five years. While there was at present no defence capability against any kind of ballistic missile attack, there was now what was called 'firm evidence' that the Soviet Union had 'extensive, high priority research and development programs in the fields of warning and defense against such missiles. It is almost certain that the Soviets are developing a static antimissile system. Considering their progress to date, their technical capabilities, and the advantages to them of an early deployment, we estimate that in 1963–1966 the Soviets will probably begin at least limited deployment of an antimissile missile system of undetermined effectiveness.'[93]

The more guarded language of previous estimates was gradually superseded by a far more categorical forecast. More detail was provided by an NIE issued in April 1961 on Soviet guided missile capabilities. Given the large number of missile firings into the test area that had taken place over the previous three years, the US intelligence community assumed that the Sary Shagan facilities were designed to 'investigate phenomena associated with mid-course and terminal phases of the trajectories of these missiles.' Such testing was seen as directed toward 'a terminal intercept system', using a multi-stage solid-propellant boosted missile probably armed with a nuclear warhead. It was thought that two of the nuclear devices included in the Soviet test series in 1958 could have had a possible anti-missile use, but there was no evidence of any pre-moratorium testing having been done at very high altitudes, which would yield basic data on the effects of such explosions on missiles and their guidance systems. Even without such data, nevertheless, it was not believed that deployment of a nuclear warhead for ABM use would be precluded. There were still many areas of Soviet ABM development that remained opaque. The role of the different radars that had been seen at Sary Shagan was not known, and the fact that the range was evidently being used for a variety of purposes, and was not confined just to ABM testing, did not help interpretation of the technical evidence.[94]

Meanwhile, and as Western analysts attempted to piece together the elements of the Soviet ABM programme, Kisunko's experiments at Sary Shagan with his initial System A had finally borne fruit. On 4 March 1961 a notable milestone was achieved with the successful intercept in the upper atmosphere (at a height of about 25 kilometres, or 15 miles) of a simulated re-entry vehicle from an SS-4 IRBM by a V-1000 missile armed with a conventional high-explosive warhead dispensing thousands of small metal balls in an explosive shower.[95] However, Soviet designers were already aware that the techniques used in the V-1000 intercept would be wholly inadequate when it came to facing a larger number of faster-moving targets arriving simultaneously. For one, the V-1000 was not agile enough to be effective, if at all, against anything other than the slower threat presented by IRBMs. A new, much more powerful interceptor, dubbed the A-350, capable of longer-range exo-atmosphere intercept, and able to carry a nuclear warhead, was instead earmarked for use with Kisunko's more advanced System A-35 intended for initial deployment around Moscow (the A-350 was another product of Grushin's Special Design Bureau 2).[96]

As we shall see, the resumption of atmosphere nuclear testing by the Soviet Union in September 1961 allowed further investigation of the effects of nuclear explosions at very high altitudes on ABM radars and defensive systems, giving confidence that the design concept for System A-35 was viable. Following these experiments, the Soviet leadership appears to have taken a decision at around the time of the 22nd Congress of the Communist Party in October 1961 to devote substantial resources to ABM development; Malinovsky announced to the Congress, during a review of the condition of the armed forces, that the problem of 'the destruction of missiles in flight has been successfully solved.' No weapon was specified but it was generally assumed in the West, where Malinovsky's comments were widely reported, that this was a direct reference to recent tests of an anti-missile missile.[97]

The effectiveness of any Soviet ABM defence would also be dependent on the provision of an adequate long-range early warning system. It was soon deduced by US observers that the large 900-foot long antenna structure at Sary Shagan identified by overhead reconnaissance during 1960 was designed for just such a task. Called the 'Dnestr-M' by the Russians, but dubbed 'Hen House' in the West, its signals were first picked up when they were reflected from the ionised cloud from a Soviet nuclear test explosion in 1962. In January 1964, US electronic intelligence analysts began to use a special technique – 'moon bounce', where Soviet radar signals were collected and analysed after having been reflected off the moon back to receiving stations in the US itself – in order to monitor the performance of Hen House. Their conclusion was that Hen House was a very high-powered and sophisticated ballistic missile early warning radar. Its unusually low frequency signals (for a long-range radar system) also suggested it was configured for use in an exo-atmosphere ABM engagement.[98] Following testing at Sary Shagan, variants of Hen House began to be constructed during 1963 at two sites aligned along the 'corridors' along which ICBMs launched from the United States would approach European Russia on their shortest flight paths: one was at Olenegorsk at Murmansk in northern Russia, the other at Skrunda near Riga in Latvia.

By this time, Kisunko's ambitious plans for System A-35 had received examination and high-level approval by a governmental commission convened in the autumn of 1962. Kisunko's original System A had relied for overall control on a new and powerful radar, the Dunay-2 (codenamed 'Hen Roost' in the West), which had been installed at Sary Shagan for experimental purposes in 1959, but it was understood that a longer-range improvement would be needed for System A-35. Construction of this massive – and highly conspicuous – radar, the Dunay-3 (or 'Dog House' as it became known in the West) began at a site about 35 miles south west of Moscow in 1963. Kisunko's early plans had called for a ring of 32 ABM installations around the Soviet capital (many of them positioned at existing SA-1 SAM sites). Each of the ABM installations would also have a target tracking and missile guidance radar, and eight A-350 missiles armed with conventional warheads.

As with much of the history surrounding Soviet-era ABM development and deployment, information remains fragmentary and sometimes inconsistent, but it appears that in 1963–64 important aspects of the A-35 system were modified. The A-350 interceptor was now to be equipped with a high-yield nuclear warhead, while the number of ABM installations planned for the Moscow area was reduced to 16 (giving an anticipated total of 128 A-350 interceptors when the system was fully deployed). The goal of the system was to permit six to eight simultaneous intercepts of incoming missiles, but (as with the US Nike-Zeus development) its capacity to cope with threats which included decoys or multiple warheads was negligible. Moreover, and as we shall see, deployment of System A-35 around Moscow proved a slow and protracted process, indicating doubts about its ultimate utility, not least as US offensive missile systems increased in numbers and sophistication; indeed, a full-scale version of the system, intended for testing purposes, was only finally assembled at Sary Shagan in 1967.[99]

By the time of President John F. Kennedy's inauguration in January 1961, nevertheless, it was evident that the Soviet Union was engaged in an extensive and ambitious programme of research and development concerned with ballistic missile defence. To Western intelligence analysts, there were even signs that portions of a first generation system could soon be ready for operational deployment. The April 1961 NIE already referred to above conveyed the belief that 'the Soviets are well advanced in a program to collect basic data, conduct technical investigations, and test antimissile system components. Antimissile tests and integrated systems tests may have occurred in late 1960 or early 1961.' If great urgency was attached by the Soviet leadership to an early deployment, an option was open to begin construction of operational sites and production of components before all the system's technical problems had been fully resolved. Among the biggest of those problems would be that of 'achieving the flexibility and discrimination to cope with the numerous, widely dispersed strategic missiles of various types and ranges which the West will possess within a few years, including types with sophisticated nosecones and penetration aids.' As in December 1960, the NIE speculated that a first generation system, which would lack any great discrimination capability against missiles equipped with decoys, could be deployed at some point between 1963 and 1966 assuming the Soviet leadership was prepared to take the 'high risks' involved in starting production before full system tests had been completed. Given the trend of Soviet development and testing, and the priority ABM defence had been accorded, it seemed reasonable to assume that even such a limited system would be deployed as an interim measure in an attempt to protect 'a few critical areas'. Deployment of an ABM system, whatever its limitations, was likely to be regarded by Soviet leaders as holding 'great political impact and as weighing significantly in the world balance of forces.'[100]

The United States, for its part, had also been investing heavily in ABM technology, and pressures within the military establishment, with support from some members of Congress, had grown during the closing phases of the Eisenhower administration for the placing of pre-production orders for long lead items required for an early Nike-Zeus deployment. What was clear to all observers was that the assumption common at the beginning of the 1950s that it was impossible to devise the means to provide for some degree of defence against the threat of ballistic missile attack no longer held good. Assured retaliation, a concept which stood at the heart of deterrence theory and was seen by many as an essential element in maintaining strategic stability between East and West, was potentially undermined as a result. To be sure, improvements in the numbers, design and performance of offensive ballistic missiles could serve to mitigate the impact of ABM defences. The addition of penetration aids, including the use of decoys, was one obvious way to achieve this effect. As we shall see, in time other innovations, including the advent of multiple warheads on single missiles, and the development of increasingly elaborate dispensing and guidance systems, would also threaten to overwhelm the earlier forms of ballistic missile defence system. Indeed, during the 1960s it was apparent that a technological imperative was emerging as an important driver of the nuclear arms race, where a technical development or innovation in one area would generate the need to find a countermeasure in another.

For political leaders struggling to meet the needs of their domestic constituencies for both physical security and economic and social well-being, the demands of this race on national resources were becoming a persistent headache. Even in the United States, whose post-war economy dwarfed its main competitors and whose industry led the world in aeronautics, electronics and computing, the costs of developing and producing a nationwide ABM system was often seen as prohibitive by government. In an altogether weaker economic position, British ministers were to decide during the 1950s that there was no question of becoming a full participant in the ABM race and that reliance would have to be placed on the United States for advice and assistance in this field. Moreover, by the end of the decade, as we shall see, the costs of maintaining an indigenous strategic nuclear force – underlined by the Blue Streak experience – were coming to be questioned by many.

During the 1945–47 period, when the Attlee Government had taken the crucial decisions to inaugurate a national nuclear programme, ministers had seen Britain as standing very much alone in facing the dangers and uncertainties of the post-war world, where Soviet power straddled Eastern and Central Europe, and the United States remained undecided over the degree of commitment it was prepared to offer to the weakened states of Western Europe. By the late 1950s the strategic situation seemed very much different. Now Washington presided over a NATO Alliance which had successfully integrated the Federal Republic of Germany into its structures in 1955, Western Europe's economies had not only recovered from the war but were on the road to new levels of prosperity (underpinned by the formation of the European Economic Community in 1957), and following the Suez crisis, a new level of intimacy had been established in Anglo-American relations by the Macmillan Government. Why then persist with the high costs and demands of staying in the strategic nuclear club – which were only likely to rise over the coming decade – when reliance could instead be placed on the overwhelming strength of US strategic nuclear forces to provide the source of Western deterrent power? To understand how this fundamental issue was understood and confronted by the British governments of the period, and why the maintenance of an independent deterrent capability was still accorded such a high priority, we now need to examine both the nature of the Anglo-American nuclear relationship that developed after 1958 and the strategic and political context within which deterrent policy was formulated.

Notes

1 Stocker, *Britain and Ballistic Missile Defence*, 20–33; Lewis, *Changing Direction*, 276–84.
2 See David Holloway, *The Soviet Union and the Arms Race*, 2nd ed (New Haven, 1984), 21–3.
3 Donald R. Baucom, *The Origins of SDI, 1944–1983* (Lawrence, KS, 1992), 4–7;

Ernest J. Yanarella, *The Missile Defense Controversy: Technology in Search of a Mission,* rev ed (Lexington, 2002), 27–8.
4 Yanarella, *Missile Defense Controversy,* 32–5.
5 See DRP/M(53)3, 10 February 1953, item 2, DEFE 10/39.
6 DRP(49)9th Meeting, item 6, 31 May 1949, DEFE 10/37.
7 See Stocker, *Britain and Ballistic Missile Defence,* 63–5.
8 D(52)26, 'Defence Policy and Global Strategy,' paragraph 12, report by the Chiefs of Staff, 17 June 1952, CAB 131/12.
9 Stocker, *Britain and Ballistic Missile Defence,* 66–7.
10 DRP/P(53)50, 'Long Range Ballistic Rockets,' note by CGWL, Ministry of Supply, 28 October 1953, DEFE 10/32.
11 Stocker, *Britain and Ballistic Missile Defence,* 46–7; and see also Benjamin Cole, 'British Technical Intelligence and the Soviet Intermediate Range Ballistic Missile Threat, 1952–60,' *Intelligence and National Security,* 14, 2, summer 1999, 70–93.
12 DRP/P(53)9, 'Defence Against the V.2,' memorandum by the Chief Scientist, Ministry of Supply, 2 February 1953, DEFE 10/32.
13 DRP/P(53)54, 'Comments by the DRP Staff on GGWL's Paper on Long Range Ballistic Rockets,' note by the Chairman DPRS (William Cook), 9 November 1953, DEFE 10/32.
14 DRP/P(54)10, 'DRPC Review,' note by the Chairman of the DRP Staff, p13, 10 March 1954, DEFE 10/33, and see Stocker, *Britain and Ballistic Missile Defence,* 68.
15 Ibid, 68–72.
16 See, for example, the major report of the Air Defence Committee Working Party, AD(55)2, 7 January 1955, 'Air Defence of the United Kingdom, 1960–1970,' note by the Joint Secretaries, issued as DRP/P(55)2, 11 January 1955, DEFE 10/34.
17 See Stocker, *Britain and Ballistic Missile Defence,* 74, and DRP/P(57)10, 'Defence Against Ballistic Missiles,' note by Deputy Chief of the Air Staff, 21 March 1957, DEFE 10/276.
18 'Long Term Defence Review – Role of Fighter Command,' note by the Air Ministry, Annex III to COS(56)81, 'Long Term Defence Review,' note by the Secretary, 22 February 1956, DEFE 5/65.
19 See DRP/M(56)11, item 3, 9 October 1956, DEFE 10/40. The original report was 'Defence Against Ballistic Missiles,' Annex to DRP/P(56)40, 'Radar Research for Defence against Ballistic Missiles,' note by Ministry of Supply, 13 September 1956, DEFE 10/35.
20 COS(56)379, 'Soviet Ballistic Missile Threat,' note by Sir Frederick Brundrett, 12 October 1956, DEFE 5/71. The COS endorsed Brundrett's conclusions, see COS(56)108th Meeting, item 20, 1 November 1956, DEFE 4/91. Brundrett was basing his views on 'Defence Against Ballistic Missiles,' Annex to DRP/P(56)40, 'Radar Research for Defence against Ballistic Missiles,' note by Ministry of Supply, 13 September 1956, DEFE 10/35.
21 See JP(57)8(Final), 'Long Term Defence Policy,' report by the Joint Planning Staff, 24 January 1957, and Confidential Annex to COS(57)8th Meeting, item 4, 29 January 1957, DEFE 4/94; COS(57)34, 'Long Term Defence Policy,' memorandum by the COS, 5 February 1957, DEFE 5/73. See also DRP/P(57)10, 'Defence Against Ballistic Missiles,' note by Deputy Chief of the Air Staff, 21 March 1957, DEFE 10/276.
22 Cmd 124, *Defence: Outline of Future Policy,* paragraph 12, April 1957.
23 'A Preliminary Survey of Ballistic Missile Decoy Systems,' GW/S.1000/DAB, 1 April 1957, AVIA 13/1283.
24 See DB/C(58)3rd mtg, 20 October 1958, DEFE 30/3.

25 See 'Seeking Defence Against Nuclear Missiles: Joint Research in Progress with United States,' *The Times*, 27 February 1959.
26 'Decoys – Notes on a Meeting, 17th February 1959'; 'Decoys – Meeting at RAE on 20th March 1959, AVIA 13/1283.
27 E. C. Cornford (head of Guided Weapons Department) minute, 'Investigation of Ballistic Missile Re-entry Heads and Decoys,' 13 April 1959, AVIA 13/1283.
28 'Minutes of a meeting held at RAE GW Department on 30th September 1959 to discuss with RRE and Marconi's WT Co representative the problem of ABM decoy discrimination at re-entry,' AVIA 13/1283.
29 See Cornford minute for Zuckerman, 'Protective Measures Against ABM Defences,' 18 January 1962, DEFE 19/115.
30 See DRP/P(57)20, 'Defence Against Ballistic Missiles,' note by the Air Ministry, 17 June 1957, DEFE 7/699.
31 Brundrett minute for Sandys, 'Possibility of Defence Against the Ballistic Missile,' FB/319/57, 1 August 1957, DEFE 7/970.
32 Brundrett minute for Sandys, 'Air Defence – To Be Or Not To Be?' FB/367/57, 25 September 1957, DEFE 7/970.
33 See Overy, *Bombing War*, 332.
34 DRP/P(57)33, 'Defence Against Ballistic Missiles,' note by CGWL, 18 September 1957, and attached annex, DEFE 10/276.
35 See Harold Macmillan, *Riding the Storm, 1956–1959* (London, 1971), 320–22.
36 See Arnold, *Britain and the H-Bomb*, 198–201.
37 See, for example, DRP/P(57)48, 'Report of US-UK-Canada Technical Committee,' note by Secretaries, with attached 'Report of Subcommittee "F" on Defence Against Ballistic Missiles,' 23 December 1957, DEFE 10/276.
38 DRP/P(58)85, 'Ballistic Missile Defence,' note by Chairman, 13 November 1958, and Appendix A, 'Report on Third Meeting of Sub-Group F,' DEFE 10/279.
39 See extract from DRP/M(58)15th Meeting, 16 December 1958, DEFE 7/699.
40 Moore, *Nuclear Illusion, Nuclear Reality*, 34; Stocker, *Britain and Ballistic Missile Defence*, 81.
41 Note for the record of informal meeting held on 18 August 1958 between Macmillan, Sir Edwin Plowden, Sir Norman Brook, and Frederick A. Bishop, 25 August 1958, PREM 11/2275.
42 DRP/P(58)82, 'Guided Weapons for Air Defence,' note by the Chairman, 22 October 1958, DEFE 10/279.
43 DRP/P(59)1, 'Defence Against Ballistic Missiles,' note by the Joint Secretaries, 13 January 1959, and attached note by the Ministry of Supply, 30 December 1958, DEFE 10/356.
44 DRP/M(59)1, item 2, 27 January 1959, DEFE 10/355.
45 See DRP/P(59)23, 'Research on Defence Against Ballistic Missiles,' note by CGWL, 5 March 1959, DEFE 10/356; DRP/M(59)4, item 4, 10 March 1959, DEFE 10/355.
46 The figures come from D(60)63, 'The Defence Research and Development Programme,' note by the Minister of Defence, 20 December 1960, CAB 131/24.
47 See Solly Zuckerman, *Monkeys, Men and Missiles: An Autobiography, 1946–88* (London, 1988), 160–3, 198.
48 See William P. Snyder, *The Politics of British Defence Policy, 1945–1962* (Columbus, OH, 1964), 142–6; Moore, *Nuclear Illusion, Nuclear Reality*, 19–20.
49 Zuckerman, *Monkeys, Men and Missiles*, 194–6.
50 D(60)64, 'Control of the Research and Development Programme,' memorandum by the Minister of Defence, 20 December 1960, and attached MR(60)37(Final), 'The Control of Defence Research and Development,' memorandum by the Committee on the Management of Research, 20 December

1960, CAB 131/24; D(61)1st Meeting, item 5, 18 January 1961, CAB 131/25. See also Defence Board minutes, DB(61) 1st Conclusions, item 1, 19 January 1961, DEFE 30/4.
51 See Arnold, *Britain and the H-Bomb*, 176–8.
52 On Hardtack see Richard G. Hewlett and Jack M. Holl, *Atoms for Peace and War, 1953–1961: Eisenhower and the Atomic Energy Commission* (Berkeley, 1989), 477–88, 540–51.
53 Minutes of 114th Conference between AEC and Military Liaison Committee, 25 October 1957, box 181, Record Group 326, National Archives and Records Administration, College Park, Maryland; also available at OpenNet, US Department of Energy website.
54 DRP(AES)/M(57)6, 17 December 1957, AVIA 65/1116.
55 See 'Operation Hardtack: Technical Summary of Military Effects Programs 1–9,' report by Headquarters Field Command, Defense Atomic Support Agency, 23 September 1959 (declassified 23 February 1999); Report of the Commander Task Group 7–1, 29 May 1959 (declassified 27 August 1986); Guide to US Atmospheric Nuclear Weapon Effects Data, Technical Report DASIAC SR-92-007, Defense Nuclear Agency, December 1993, available at OpenNet, US Department of Energy website.
56 DRP/P(59)116, 'US/UK/Canada Technical Co-operation,' note by the Chairman, 11 November 1959, DEFE 10/357.
57 DRP/P(59)107, note by the Joint Secretaries, 29 October 1959, British Joint Services Mission (Ministry of Supply Staff) Newsletter No 27, p21–3, 1 October 1959, DEFE 10/357.
58 See David L. Snead, *The Gaither Committee, Eisenhower, and the Cold War* (Columbus, 1999), 101–2, 122–3, 146–7; Watson, *Into the Missile Age*, 136–41.
59 Yanarella, *Missile Defense Controversy*, 26.
60 See Watson, *Into the Missile Age*, 187–9, 361–2.
61 Yanarella, *Missile Defense Controversy*, 38–42.
62 See Herbert F. York, *Arms and the Physicist* (Woodbury, NY, 1995), 12–4.
63 DRP/P(59)107, British Joint Services Mission (Ministry of Supply Staff) Newsletter No 27, p2, 1 October 1959, DEFE 10/357.
64 See Watson, *Into the Missile Age*, 286–8.
65 See Baucom, *Origins of SDI*, 12–5, 20; Watson, *Into the Missile Age*, 379–82.
66 See Lawrence S. Kaplan, Ronald D. Landa, Edward J. Drea, *History of the Office of the Secretary of Defense, Volume V: The McNamara Ascendancy, 1961–1965* (Washington, DC, 2006), 60; also York, *Arms and the Physicist*, 38–40.
67 See DRP/P(60)62, 'Defence Against Ballistic Missiles,' note by Ministry of Aviation, 20 July 1960, DEFE 10/382.
68 See DRP/M(60)10, item 2, 26 July 1960, DEFE 10/355.
69 See, for example, RAE Guided Weapons Department paper, 'Some Current thoughts on the Defence of the UK against Ballistic Missiles,' W/S.1235/WRBH, 29 September 1959, AVIA 65/1869.
70 See Pavel Podvig (ed.), *Russian Strategic Nuclear Forces* (Cambridge, MA, 2001), 402–5; Christoph Bluth, *Soviet Strategic Arms Policy Before SALT* (Cambridge, 1992), 199.
71 Victor Gobarev, 'The early development of Russia's ballistic missile defense system,' *Journal of Slavic Military Studies*, 14, 2, 2001, 29–48, especially 30–33; Holloway, *Stalin and the Bomb*, 324–5, and especially n.37, 438; Bluth, *Soviet Strategic Arms Policy*, 200; Podvig, *Russian Strategic Nuclear Forces*, 412–3; Steven J. Zaloga, *The Kremlin's Nuclear Sword: The Rise and Fall of Russia's Strategic Nuclear Forces, 1945–2000* (Washington, 2002), 19–20.
72 See Jennifer G. Mathers, '"A fly in outer space": Soviet ballistic missile defence

during the Khrushchev period,' *Journal of Strategic Studies*, 21, 2, June 1998, 31–59, especially 48 for the quotations.
73 Podvig, *Russian Strategic Nuclear Forces*, 413.
74 See Holloway, *Soviet Union and the Arms Race*, 35–8, 44; Bluth, *Soviet Strategic Arms Policy*, 99–100; Jennifer G. Mathers, *The Russian Nuclear Shield from Stalin to Yeltsin* (London, 2000), 4, 9–16, 24–8.
75 See Mathers, '"A fly in outer space",' 34, 37.
76 Diary entry for 5 September 1961, C. L. Sulzberger, *The Last of the Giants* (New York, 1970), 789–90; on Khrushchev's exaggerated claims and use of ABM defence for political effect, see Mathers, *Russian Nuclear Shield*, 21.
77 See the discussion in Bluth, *Soviet Strategic Arms Policy*, 202–6.
78 See Mathers, '"A fly in outer space",' 42–3.
79 See, for example Holloway, *Soviet Union and the Arms Race*, 38–9, 157; Bluth, *Soviet Strategic Arms Policy*, 100–101, 134–42; William Taubman, *Khrushchev: The Man and His Era* (London, 2003), 379–81.
80 See Lawrence Freedman, *US Intelligence and the Soviet Strategic Threat*, 2nd ed (London, 1986), 87.
81 For the NIE process see Freedman, *US Intelligence*, 30–43.
82 NIE 11–5–57, 'Soviet Capabilities and Probable Programs in the Guided Missile Field,' 12 March 1957, Missile Gap collection, CIA Freedom of Information electronic reading room (at www.cia.gov/library/readingroom/historical-collections).
83 NIE 11–5–58, 'Soviet Capabilities in Guided Missile and Space Vehicles,' 19 August 1958, Missile Gap collection, CIA Freedom of Information electronic reading room.
84 Memorandum for the Chairman of the Guided Missiles and Astronautics Intelligence Committee from the Chief, Guided Missile Division, Office of Scientific Intelligence, CIA, 6 January 1959, Missile Gap collection, CIA Freedom of Information electronic reading room. For the bureaucratic context see Freedman, *US Intelligence*, 35.
85 Gregory W. Pedlow and Donald E. Welzenbach, *The Central Intelligence Agency and Overhead Reconnaissance: The U-2 and Oxcart Programs, 1954–1974* (History Staff, Central Intelligence Agency, Washington DC, 1992), 159 and passim (declassified 25 June 2013).
86 NIE 11–5–59, 'Soviet Capabilities in Guided Missiles and Space Vehicles,' 3 November 1959, *Foreign Relations of the United States, 1958–1960, Volume III: National Security Policy; Arms Control and Disarmament* (Washington, 1996), 325–30.
87 See, for example, JIC(59)4 (Final)(Revise), 'Soviet Strategy in Global War up to the end of 1963,' 20 January 1959; JIC(59)8(Final), 'The Air Defence of the Soviet Union up to 1963,' 9 February 1959, CAB 158/35.
88 L. G. Wilson minute for First Sea Lord, 'The Effect on Soviet Policy of the Attainment by the USSR of Nuclear Sufficiency,' 16 January 1958, DEFE 24/11.
89 For references to telemetry interception see, for example, JIC(59)29(Final), 'Soviet Research and Development up to the end of 1958,' 25 May 1959, CAB 158/36.
90 JIC(60)8 (Final), 'The Air Defence of the Soviet Union up to 1964,' 24 February 1960, CAB 158/39.
91 See Pedlow and Welzenbach, *Central Intelligence Agency and Overhead Reconnaissance*, 168–9, including a map of mission 4155; and the imagery report at ODE 4155, 16 April 1960, Missile Gap collection, CIA Freedom of Information electronic reading room. See also Freedman, *Soviet Strategic Threat*, 87.
92 See NIE 11–5–61, 'Soviet Technical Capabilities in Guided Missiles and Space Vehicles,' 25 April 1961, Missile Gap collection, CIA Freedom of Information

electronic reading room. This NIE includes early overhead imagery of the installations at Sary Shagan.
93 NIE 11–4–60, 'Main Trends in Soviet Capabilities and Policies, 1960–1965,' 1 December 1960, Missile Gap collection, CIA Freedom of Information electronic reading room.
94 See NIE 11–5–61, 'Soviet Technical Capabilities in Guided Missiles and Space Vehicles,' 25 April 1961, Missile Gap collection, CIA Freedom of Information electronic reading room.
95 Zaloga, *Kremlin's Nuclear Sword*, 98–9.
96 Gobarev, 'The early development of Russia's ballistic missile defense system,' 36.
97 'Russian Reports Solving Rocket Defense Problem,' 24 October 1961, *New York Times*; 'Rockets in Flight "Can be Destroyed",' *The Times*, 24 October 1961; and see Mathers, '"A fly in outer space",' 40.
98 Frank Eliot, 'Moon Bounce Elint,' *Studies in Intelligence*, 11, 2, Spring 1967, 59–65; and Edward Tauss, 'Foretesting a Soviet ABM System,' *Studies in Intelligence*, 12, 3, Winter 1968, 21–6, CIA Freedom of Information electronic reading room.
99 See Podvig, *Russian Strategic Nuclear Forces*, 414.
100 NIE 11–5–61, 'Soviet Technical Capabilities in Guided Missiles and Space Vehicles,' 25 April 1961, Missile Gap collection, CIA Freedom of Information electronic reading room; and see also NIE 11–3–61, 'Sino-Soviet Air Defense Capabilities Through Mid-1966,' 11 July 1961, *Foreign Relations of the United States, 1961–1963, Volume VIII: National Security Policy* (Washington, 1996), 116–7.

3 In the shadow of Sputnik
The nuclear sufficiency debate and the restoration of Anglo-American nuclear collaboration, March 1957–February 1959

A declaration of common purpose

Once Macmillan had become Prime Minister in January 1957, as we have seen, he made repairing and then maintaining close Anglo-American relations the principal aim of his foreign policy. The humiliation of the Suez crisis at the end of the previous year, when a run on sterling helped to push the government into agreeing a ceasefire and the withdrawal of British forces, had underlined the frailty of Britain's international economic position and the dangers of falling out of step with the United States. It was easy to dismiss the Soviet threats made in early November 1956 to intervene with force in the region, if Britain's invasion of Egypt continued, as empty bluster ('in what position would Britain have found herself had it been attacked by more powerful states possessing all types of modern weapons of destruction?' Moscow radio had asked).[1] Few believed that the Soviet leadership was prepared to start a general war for the sake of Nasser's Egypt, and the Russian military was incapable of such long-range power projection. Yet the suggestion that the UK could be a thermonuclear target, and the crude attempt at nuclear intimidation that it represented, served as a sobering and uncomfortable reminder of the dangers that could face powers which became isolated and when US assistance could not be taken for granted.

The late 1950s, it should be remembered, was a period laced with Western perceptions of growing Soviet technological, scientific and nuclear strength. The Soviet Union had carried out the test of a hydrogen bomb (with an estimated yield of 1.6 megatons) dropped from an aircraft in November 1955, while its medium and long-range air force was steadily increasing in numbers and delivery capability.[2] Medium-range missiles able to hit targets in Western Europe were also being developed, and the first launch of an Intercontinental Ballistic Missile (ICBM) in August 1957 provided graphic demonstration of burgeoning Soviet prowess in some of the most advanced aspects of military science. The dramatic psychological effects of the Sputnik satellite launch, using an ICBM booster, in October of the same year, underlined the point and brought home to Western policymakers that they could not take their previously assumed technological superiority for granted.

All this had added to a new sense of US vulnerability, where the United States might itself be subject to devastating nuclear attack, either in reprisal for US use of nuclear weapons in the event of Soviet aggression in Europe, or through a disabling first strike launched by the new long-range weapons in the Russian arsenal. This had been one of the alarming conclusions of the Gaither Report of November 1957, commissioned by President Eisenhower to investigate the problems of civil defence, but which had taken on a much wider remit. In the event a shrewd Eisenhower had been unwilling to adopt wholesale the major steps of preparedness and boosts to defence spending which were advocated, being convinced that the panel had overdrawn the extent of the Soviet threat. Although still in its infancy, US overhead reconnaissance of the Soviet Union was beginning to reveal that Moscow's long-range nuclear capabilities were far less formidable than had first been supposed, and that the West still had an overwhelming numerical lead in terms of strategic nuclear delivery systems.[3]

Nevertheless, many commentators were convinced that it was only a matter of time before Soviet nuclear capabilities would be developed to the level that in the event of a general nuclear exchange American population centres would be subject to devastation. In such circumstances, many asked, how credible was it to believe that US policymakers would be prepared to risk their own cities by initiating the use nuclear weapons for the sake of defending portions of Western Europe, especially if a European conflict in the first instance was to remain limited to the conventional level? Even if fighting were to involve the employment of 'tactical' nuclear weapons against military targets close to the battlefront, or into the deeper support areas behind the clashing ground forces of NATO and the Warsaw Pact, there would be every incentive, in such estimations, to avoid a further escalation to the use of strategic nuclear weapons. But it was the Soviet fear of such escalation that, in the view of many European observers, constituted the most important factor deterring war from breaking out in the first place. The potential 'decoupling' of US strategic nuclear forces from the defence of Western Europe, and the threat it posed to the overall credibility of the Western deterrent, became the central strategic problem facing the Western Alliance in the latter half of the 1950s and was to be a constant preoccupation for Western political leaders over the next two and half decades.

For British policymakers working in the post-Suez climate there were divided attitudes as to whether Britain's growing strategic nuclear force should be considered merely an adjunct to US nuclear capabilities, or whether it should have the ability to operate in an independent fashion. There were also basic questions as to what the latter concept of 'independence' entailed. Did it involve the ability of the British force, when acting alone, to inflict a particular level of damage on the Soviet Union, and should such damage be of an overwhelming character or simply sufficient – however this could be judged – to deter Soviet aggression? Or was 'independence' rooted more in the practicalities of exclusively national operation and control? In this sense, were British political leaders free and able to order the force to be used as and when they saw fit, and to what extent was (or could) the force be reliant on outside sources of supply or assistance – whether in the form of delivery systems, or information and knowledge? When faced with the emergence of a substantial Soviet nuclear capability, it seemed logical to conduct nuclear planning in concert with the United States, so that the two nuclear forces could complement one another. This approach also promised to offer access to American nuclear thinking and even the possibility of gaining influence over US policy.

However, to many the Suez crisis of 1956 had demonstrated that US and British interests did not always and necessarily coincide. Washington could not be relied upon in all circumstances to support London, even when vital UK national interests were perceived to be at stake. Although US leaders placed rhetorical emphasis on the strength of the US nuclear guarantee to Western Europe, the emergence of a significant Soviet strategic nuclear force raised doubts about the long-term inviolability of the guarantee. A nationally-controlled nuclear force could off-set such doubts and concerns, it was argued, by providing the means to retaliate if the UK itself, or its most vital interests, were threatened. The paradox of British strategic nuclear policy, as the V-bombers began to enter service in greater numbers in the latter part of the 1950s, was that the striving for national independence in this field was seen primarily as a means to secure a condition of closer nuclear collaboration with the United States which when achieved might itself have the consequence of eroding the original conception of independence.

Certainly for Macmillan the nuclear build-up over the previous few years could now finally reap its dividend, while he increasingly saw Britain's strategic nuclear capability as securing a political 'voice' on the world stage when some of the other indicators of UK international power were in decline. Although far from oblivious to the pressures – both internal and external – which were building for the withdrawal from formal empire, the new Prime Minister had no intention of relinquishing a world role. In this sense, sticking closely alongside Washington was essential if Britain's global aspirations were to be fulfilled and upheld.

A good start to the process of mending the breach represented by Suez was made at the productive meetings held between Macmillan and Eisenhower on Bermuda in March 1957 (the two leaders, it must be remembered, had worked very effectively together in the Mediterranean during the Second World War, when Macmillan had served as the British Minister Resident at Eisenhower's Allied Force Headquarters in Algiers). At Bermuda a greater measure of understanding was found regarding the Middle East, the Americans demonstrating heightened concern that Communist gains could follow if radical Arab nationalism served to destabilise pro-Western regimes, and Macmillan proved receptive in principle to US proposals to site IRBMs at British bases in what proved to be the high-level genesis of the eventual Thor deployment.⁴ Much of the detail on a formal agreement over IRBM deployment still had to be negotiated, but the understanding reached at Bermuda – where the government proved publicly willing to offer a base for the only US ballistic missile then capable of reaching Soviet targets, and when the Americans needed such forward locations in Europe to reassure its NATO allies and to counteract perceptions of growing Soviet nuclear strength – was symbolic of the change that had occurred in the relationship.

It had been widely assumed that the development of a thermonuclear capability by the United Kingdom would be an essential precondition for securing a new degree of nuclear cooperation with the United States. Only by demonstrating their own proficiency and knowledge in this advanced field, it was believed, could the UK's nuclear scientists and engineers qualify for access to US information and experience. As we saw earlier, the first test in the Grapple series was fired on 15 May 1957 when the Short Granite device was dropped from a Valiant bomber and exploded at about 8,000 feet over Malden Island in the Central Pacific. Although at around 300 kilotons its yield was lower than many had hoped, Sir William Penney was satisfied that it had achieved its goal of testing the principles of radiation implosion – the critical process by which the energy from a fission explosion could be harnessed to produce thermonuclear reactions in a secondary element to a bomb.⁵

There was, nevertheless, concern in Downing Street that the comparatively low yield obtained might reduce its wider impact and so this, along with another test of the initial Granite design, was only judged a partial success. As a result, in the summer of 1957 Macmillan gave verbal instructions to Brundrett and Sir Edwin Plowden, the Chairman of the AEA, that the disappointing yields obtained in the Grapple series to date should have the highest possible security classification to prevent dissemination much beyond AWRE itself. Several years later, Sir Norman Brook recalled that, 'the 1957 tests showed that, although we had made a hydrogen bomb work, we had not made one in the megaton range; and that was, at least in part, the reason why special secrecy was attached to them at the time.'⁶

Despite the promising initial results of the Grapple series – at least from a technical angle – there were few signs that the door of the American nuclear cupboard was about to be unlocked. Although the McMahon Act of 1946 had been superseded by a new US Atomic Energy Act passed by Congress in August 1954, its spirit lived on in the tight legal restrictions which were still in place when it came to the transfer of sensitive nuclear knowledge. Members of Congress remained wary of British security standards and the dangers that a liberal approach to exchanges would encourage nuclear proliferation in other powers. Party considerations also came into play: Eisenhower led a Republican administration but he faced Democrat majorities in both houses of Congress, with leadership of the JCAE therefore held in the hands of the Democratic Party. Meanwhile negotiations over the British basing of US IRBMs had begun to stall during the summer of 1957 as differences arose over the financing of the deployment and the control procedures which would be introduced to govern the operation of the missiles.[7]

The shock of the Sputnik launch in early October provided the necessary impetus which persuaded President Eisenhower and his closest advisers that some dramatic new measures were required to bolster Western solidarity in the face of a widespread perception that the East-West strategic and psychological balance had shifted. In the immediate aftermath of the launch, Macmillan moved quickly to suggest to Eisenhower that the West should make more concerted efforts to pool its resources to meet the latest threat, mentioning fields for potential collaboration such as nuclear weapons and ballistic missile research, economic warfare and counter propaganda.[8]

More conscious now of its vulnerability to direct Soviet attack, the US administration now seemed receptive to these approaches from its closest ally for a greater degree of cooperation in the Cold War. Macmillan's subsequent visit to Washington from 23–25 October 1957 produced several major breakthroughs which served to move the Anglo-American relationship onto an entirely new footing. In his own estimation, the Prime Minister found the Americans had been shaken by recent developments, and were now keen to adopt the idea of 'interdependence' in order to meet what was seen as the new Soviet challenge. On Eisenhower's suggestion two ad hoc working groups were formed from some of the senior US and British officials present at this meeting to examine how greater measures of cooperation could be achieved in both the nuclear field and more general area of defence research and development (the first group was led on the British side by Plowden, and the second by Sir Richard Powell, Permanent Under Secretary at the MoD).

The President, with keen support from Dulles, was also clear that he was prepared to push through changes to US atomic energy legislation which would allow Britain access to previously denied areas of US nuclear information. It was this change in American attitudes and practice which the Prime Minister called 'the great prize' toward which he had been working; recalling his immense sense of relief, Macmillan later wrote, 'We could now proceed with our work in the atomic field and remain a nuclear power without the appalling waste of effort involved in slowly arriving by our own efforts at the point of development which our American allies had already reached.'[9]

Having long been frustrated by the legal constraints in the area, Eisenhower himself was very much in favour of a full exchange of nuclear information, and instructed AEC officials – some of whom were reluctant to undertake so drastic a change in practice – to be as cooperative as possible when dealing with the British. Indeed, one of the President's main preoccupations was to use the Sputnik shock as a means to persuade sceptics on the Congressional JCAE that a more forthcoming approach with Britain was advisable and necessary.[10] Macmillan's entreaties were rewarded by the issuing of a public 'Declaration of Common Purpose' following the Washington conference, where it was pledged that the President would approach Congress to amend atomic energy legislation to allow 'close and fruitful collaboration' between the UK and US in the nuclear field, as well as with 'other friendly countries.'[11]

After his return Powell told the Chiefs of Staff that the atmosphere during the visit 'could not have been better', and that the agreements reached were 'only a first step and it remained to be seen to what extent really close cooperation could be achieved at lower levels in the Pentagon. In this respect we should probably need to tread carefully and not try to do too much at once. Nevertheless, there was no doubt of the desire on the part of those at the top to co-operate with us.' Moreover, he thought 'the United States clearly welcomed the fact that they would no longer be in exclusive possession of the deterrent. They hoped to impress on their allies that nuclear weapons were held in trust for the alliance to which they belonged rather than as an instrument of national power.'[12]

The prospects for greater Anglo-American nuclear collaboration were enhanced the following month when in the Grapple X test, this time conducted off Christmas Island, British scientists detonated a new design of thermonuclear weapon which registered a yield of 1.8 megatons. Much larger than previous British tests, and witnessed by US observers in the Pacific, it underlined the progress that British weapon scientists at AWRE had made and the benefits that could accrue from closer cooperation.[13] Meanwhile a technical committee of UK and US experts had continued to study the possibilities of cooperation and, after Plowden and Powell had returned to Washington several times to oversee the process, delivered their interim reports to the President and Prime Minister in December 1957.[14]

The report on general defence R & D cooperation in the weapons field resulted – with additional Canadian participation – in the creation of the Tripartite Technical Cooperation Programme noted in the previous chapter. The working group on nuclear cooperation had to overcome certain reservations on the part of the AEC, but it too came forward with a set of recommendations involving a wide-ranging exchange of information covering the design of nuclear warheads and delivery systems, and making clear this would require changes in US law. In January 1958, US officials began the exacting task of persuading the JCAE to agree to a series of amendments to the Atomic Energy Act of 1954 which would allow a bilateral agreement with the UK to be concluded.[15]

It seems clear in retrospect that the Eisenhower administration saw the restoration of close Anglo-American cooperation during 1957 as the start of a process which would see much closer defence ties established with the other members of the Western Alliance. The most pressing requirement here was to give additional substance to the US nuclear guarantee to Western Europe and to offer the means to certain NATO members to defend themselves with the most modern weapons available. Although not involving the complete transfer of US nuclear weapons to European allies – a step which was ruled out by US atomic energy legislation and which raised sensitive issues of inter-alliance politics (not least when it came to the provision of a nuclear capability to the emergent armed forces of the Federal Republic of Germany) – the administration showed an increasing willingness during 1957 to supply nuclear-capable weapons systems to its NATO partners and to offer rapid access to US warheads if war should come.

This line of thinking was finally to bear fruit in December 1957 during the meeting of the North Atlantic Council in Paris, when John Foster Dulles, the US Secretary of State, proposed the establishment of a NATO atomic stockpile (where formal custody of warheads would still be maintained by the United States), and offered to deploy US IRBMs to those NATO members who were willing to accept them under terms to be negotiated. Such deployments would also represent a significant enhancement of US nuclear potential capable of reaching Soviet targets at a time when the US was still in the process of developing an operational ICBM. The atomic stockpile proposal was the most obvious manifestation of Eisenhower's favoured policy of 'nuclear sharing' within the Alliance, and this was complemented by offers during 1958 to assist European members in a cooperative programme to develop and produce a second generation IRBM for NATO's own defensive needs in Europe.[16] For the moment the US administration's whole approach offered British policymakers the long-sought opportunity to re-establish the close nuclear links with the United States that had been severed in 1946 by the McMahon Act. But over the next few years, as Washington began to refine their ideas about the command and control of nuclear forces assigned and allocated to NATO (such as the IRBM deployments offered in late 1957), and tried to invest greater authority in the position of SACEUR, a threat to the long-term future of an independent British nuclear deterrent, under exclusively national control, was to become apparent.

A question of priorities

The Prime Minister had told the Defence Committee in July 1957 that the provision of the UK strategic deterrent

> must have the first call on our resources. Second priority must be given to maintaining adequate forces to carry-out our world-wide commitments and to prevent small-scale hostilities developing into major wars. Lowest priority should be given to the various means of waging global war should the deterrent fail to prevent its outbreak.[17]

This line of thinking encapsulated the essence of the Sandys Defence White Paper and provided the initial framework for a policy which would eventually result in major reductions in conventional military capabilities. It was not, however, a set of priorities which was to be accepted without a further struggle amongst British defence officials, and division between the services, particularly as the subject of 'nuclear sufficiency' began to be addressed with ever-more frequency from the end of 1957 onwards.

The immediate cause for what was to prove the most serious rift amongst the Chiefs of Staff since the onset of the Cold War was the production by the JIC of a paper on the effects on Soviet policy of nuclear sufficiency, a condition at first defined as one where the Soviet Union had 'sufficient nuclear warheads and delivery systems to allocate to the targets in the West which she would wish to destroy in global war' (though this was soon modified to the simpler idea of when the Soviet Union had the capability of launching a devastating nuclear attack against the United States). The JIC had anticipated that this state of affairs could arrive as early as 1962 as Soviet nuclear strength was gradually built up. The chief concern of defence planners was that the Soviet leadership might come to believe that US willingness to commit its nuclear forces to the defence of Europe, or to resist aggressive Soviet moves in other theatres such as the Middle or Far East, would be undermined by the knowledge that their own cities were now vulnerable to retaliation; in such a situation the Soviet leadership might be prepared to embark upon bolder moves to expand Communist influence.

The JIC view, in fact, was relatively sanguine: Soviet aims and methods in the Cold War were unlikely to change despite the new strategic equation, and aversion to war would be just as pronounced as before. At the same time it was predicted that the Soviet leadership would be given a psychological boost, as they would calculate that the West would be less likely to initiate a nuclear attack since this would lead to devastating retaliation. It was therefore probable that Soviet policy would become 'more thrusting', although care would still be taken not to encroach on vital Western interests and Soviet leaders would be aware that the United States would be very sensitive to threats that could further undermine their position. It was even suggested in the JIC paper that with their much increased nuclear arsenal, the Soviet leaders 'will be so conscious of the horrors of nuclear warfare and of the fact that a nuclear war would result in the annihilation of both sides that they will never permit a nuclear war to start, let alone be themselves the first to launch a nuclear attack.' As a result, 'in circumstances of extreme tension, in which war looked probable, they would not fail to withdraw or climb down from whatever position they had got themselves into.' However, using this analysis of possible Soviet behaviour as a basis for planning was ultimately considered 'unwise' such were the continuing possibilities of miscalculation when Western and Soviet interests clashed.[18]

In parallel with the work of the JIC, the COS's own Joint Planning Staff had been asked towards the end of 1957 to examine whether any revision of the strategic concept of the West was warranted by the arrival of nuclear sufficiency. Concluding that the validity of the Western nuclear deterrent remained unimpaired even when both sides in the Cold War had the capacity to destroy each other, the Joint Planners reported in January 1958 that the new conditions underlined even further the importance of preventing war from occurring in the first place. It therefore became even more vital to demonstrate the will and determination of the West to use its nuclear forces if necessary. This could best be assured, it was argued, by keeping the deterrent under the control of the US and Britain. In the opinion of the JPS, the three main considerations that would dictate UK policy in the new era that was soon to arrive would be:

a   To remain a nuclear power and by doing so to exercise a major independent influence in the councils of the world, in particular, with the United States.
b   To ensure as far as possible the continued involvement of the United States in a deterrent policy based on the threat of nuclear attack on the Soviet homeland.
c   To mitigate as far as possible the consequences of an American isolationist policy.

Limited war, in Europe or elsewhere, involving vital Russian or Western interests, was also felt unlikely to occur, while in any case economic factors ruled out the provision by the European members of NATO of sufficient forces to defeat those which could be deployed by the Soviet Union and its Warsaw Pact allies in such engagements. Conventional forces to fight in 'global war' should have the lowest priority in UK defence policy, it was maintained, and the stress should still be on steps to increase the credibility and effectiveness of the nuclear deterrent.[19]

Some members of the COS were not, however, content with these conclusions. Admiral Mountbatten, the First Sea Lord, had already begun during 1957 to re-articulate the Navy's interest in the conventional phase of warfare that might precede an exchange of nuclear weapons. Similarly, for the Chief of the Imperial General Staff (CIGS), Field Marshal Sir Gerald Templer, nuclear sufficiency created the conditions for greater fluidity and instability in the Cold War as the use of nuclear weapons by the West – which would result in mutual devastation – only held credibility in situations where truly vital interests were at stake and where there were no alternative responses available. The Soviet Union, he predicted, would soon

> press her present aggression against the West ceaselessly and with greater freedom, secure in the thought that she herself can now fully 'deter' the West, except in matters which threaten its very existence. It follows to my mind that we shall be faced with an increasing number of local situations due to Soviet political, economic, subversive and military actions – in fact with an increasing number of limited or minor wars.

Templer feared that the rising costs of the deterrent, if allowed to go unchecked, would reduce the resources available for the conventional forces needed for cold or limited war tasks: 'The bluff of the Deterrent acquires credibility only if we show that we are buttressing it by conventional forces to deal with aggression round the periphery where the use of the Deterrent is out of the question.' Templer, moreover, disagreed that the UK contribution to the Western deterrent had to be 'independent', while its size 'must be closely regulated so as to keep a proper balance between it and the conventional forces required under the new conditions.'[20]

During February 1958 COS discussion of the JPS paper on the effect of nuclear sufficiency, and the injection of Templer's forthright dissent, revealed the gulf that had opened up within the Committee. While Boyle, the Chief of the Air Staff, was prepared to accept the Joint Planners' report as it stood, Mountbatten now swung firmly behind the CIGS, stating that he 'had never agreed that the current Government policy on the deterrent would necessarily remain valid after nuclear sufficiency had been reached. It was necessary to examine what would be the effect on the credibility of the deterrent under a condition of nuclear sufficiency.' Templer reiterated his basic point that once nuclear parity was reached the deterrent could only be effective 'in certain areas vital to one side or the other. If we relied on it elsewhere then in the event of a threat to a non-vital area we should have no middle course open to us between inaction and total war.' Moreover, Templer 'did not believe that an independent United Kingdom deterrent would ever be used against Russia unless the United States supported us.' Concurring with the CIGS's call for a proper examination of the balance between spending on conventional and nuclear forces, Mountbatten argued that the deterrent only had value for as long as it was believed by the Russians that it would be used. If there was Soviet aggression against eastern Turkey, for example, he thought that under current conditions the United States would undoubtedly use its nuclear air power to defend its NATO ally, but in a few years time, when American cities could be 'devastated' by a Soviet retaliatory strike, he doubted the Russians would believe the US would intervene in such a fashion.

The CAS, however, disagreed. For Boyle, possession of 'an independent share' of the deterrent forced the Russians to take greater account of the UK, and this would also be the case under a state of nuclear sufficiency. Costs of the deterrent, he continued, would actually fall once manned bombers were replaced with cheaper and easier to maintain ballistic missiles. He would not oppose an exercise to examine how the defence budget was divided between the different categories as Templer had proposed, but felt that 'if the time came when we could not afford both deterrent and conventional forces he doubted whether it would be possible for us to make any worthwhile defence effort at all.' The Chairman of the COS, Air Chief Marshal Sir William Dickson, was left to conclude the discussion with the thought that 'if a war began between the major powers even if it started with conventional weapons only, he failed to see how it could be prevented from turning into a global nuclear conflict,' and to invite the War Office and Admiralty to propose amendments to the JPS paper that had proved so contentious.[21] Mountbatten subsequently told Dickson that the idea the nuclear deterrent would remain valid throughout the period of nuclear sufficiency was a 'dangerous doctrine', and his views now stood 'totally at variance with those of the CAS.'[22]

In the middle of this widening dispute, the appearance of the annual Defence White Paper in February 1958 gave an opportunity for the growing circle of defence commentators and academic observers to unpick the language which revealed the Macmillan Government's paradoxical approach to the deterrent. In a world 'poised between the hope of total peace and the fear of total war' the White Paper argued that the balance of arms between a mutually antagonistic West and Soviet Union was the principal way that peace was being maintained. Reassurance was offered that a large-scale conflict could be prevented, 'for another generation or more through the balancing fears of mutual annihilation. In fact there is no reason why this should not go on almost indefinitely. But that would indeed be a mournful prospect.' Some way to halt the remorseless drive of the arms race, it was observed, had to be found, which hence made 'comprehensive' disarmament the final objective of policy. In the meantime, however, collective measures of defence through the alliance systems of the Western powers were crucial to preserving security. 'The democratic Western nations will never start a war against Russia,' it was proclaimed. 'But it must be well understood that, if Russia were to launch a major attack on them, even with conventional weapons only, they would have to hit back with strategic nuclear weapons.' In what was intended as a reflection of the latest statement of NATO military posture, MC 14/2, adopted by NATO's Military Committee in May 1957, the White Paper explained that the Alliance's strategy was 'based on the frank recognition that a full-scale Soviet attack could not be repelled without resort to a massive nuclear bombardment of the sources of power in Russia. In that event, the role of the allied defence forces in Europe would be to hold the front for the time needed to allow the effects of the nuclear counter-offensive to make themselves felt.'[23]

There thus had to be no flinching when it came to the West's readiness to use its nuclear strength if attacked, even if Soviet aggression was only conventional. Here, the nuclear offensive that would be unleashed would depend above all 'upon the strength and constant readiness of the American Strategic Air Command, with its bases all round the world and its vast supply of megaton bombs.' But that Britain would play a role in NATO's nuclear effort was ever-more apparent: with deliveries of 'megaton bombs' to the RAF having begun, and already holding 'a substantial and growing stockpile of kiloton weapons,' it was asserted that the UK was 'now making an increasingly significant contribution to the Western nuclear deterrent.' Just a few paragraphs later, the White Paper ventured that although the UK's nuclear forces could not be compared to those of the United States, when 'fully equipped with megaton weapons, the British bomber force will in itself constitute a formidable deterrent.'[24]

Aspirations for an independent nuclear capability were, therefore, still mixed in the government's official thinking with the commitment of British nuclear forces to a combined Western deterrent policy. The maintenance of those nuclear forces – which were called 'the decisive factor in preventing major war' – did not mean however that the need for conventional military capabilities could be ignored, and the White Paper reminded its readers that in addition to Britain's commitment of forces to NATO in Central Europe, over 100,000 service personnel remained based in the Middle and Far East.[25] Yet there was no discussion in the White Paper of the balance or priorities that would be established between the nuclear and conventional components of the defence budget. Some seasoned commentators, such as Anthony Buzzard, criticised the White Paper for ignoring the looming issue of nuclear sufficiency and continued to press for an alternative doctrine of 'graduated deterrence' where conventional military strength would be augmented so that the moment when a resort to nuclear weapons was made could be postponed for as long as possible.[26]

Although still very much in favour of retaining an independent nuclear deterrent, the leadership of the Labour Party also assailed the government for its excessive stress on thermonuclear weapons and the unwillingness of Sandys to specify when Communist aggression, wherever it might occur, would be substantial enough to trigger a nuclear response.[27] By maintaining the precepts associated with 'massive retaliation' it was alleged that the government was neglecting the even more pressing need to build-up Alliance conventional forces to meet Communist conventional preponderance (under the 1957 White Paper policies, which included the end of national service, the strength of the Rhine Army, it should be noted, was planned to reduce from a high of 77,000 in the mid-1950s to 44,000 by 1963, within an overall Army manpower ceiling of 165,000, while the cuts also entailed halving the tactical air power deployed on the Continent in support of NATO's central European front).[28]

Sandys was alerted in mid-February to the rift between the Chiefs of Staff over the implications of nuclear sufficiency, just as the White Paper was going to press. Dickson informed him there was 'a considerable divergence of opinion on the fundamental question of the validity of the deterrent in the future, or rather the British contribution to it', and asked for more time for the Committee to clarify its views on the problem. Templer and Mountbatten were, nevertheless, keen that Sandys should take cognisance of their opinions before the Commons debate on the White Paper. Boyle was, by contrast, adamant that the deterrent would remain valid for the foreseeable future and did not want to see a reconsideration of priorities. As for Dickson, navigating the uncomfortable and novel waters of acting as the first chair of the COS, he expressed agreement with Boyle, but only 'on the assumption that the allocation of resources for defence will be sufficient to provide for our contribution to the deterrent as well as for the conventional forces needed to meet our future overseas commitments.'[29]

This, of course, was the nub of the issue. Apart from such fence-sitting, Dickson was in no constitutional position to provide a considered and unitary voice from the COS Committee to the Minister of Defence or the government as a whole since the service heads still had the right to represent their independent and separate views. Under the pressure of an ever-tightening defence budget, with the cutbacks associated with the Sandys White Paper of the previous year only now beginning to be absorbed, the Chiefs found themselves embroiled in their biggest and most prolonged argument over strategic policy since the end of the war.

Forming the future nuclear programme

The dissent from the government's established position that came from Mountbatten and Templer was not founded on any fundamental opposition to Britain's possession of nuclear weapons. Indeed, both even saw a need for tactical nuclear weapons to equip the Navy and Army to prepare them to fight the limited wars of the future. However, some critics of the government's defence policy were prone to ask why it was necessary to make a contribution to the Western deterrent at all, when by the late 1950s US nuclear forces were capable of striking almost every important target in the Soviet bloc with high-yield weapons. One answer to this question was to fall back on the belief that a British contribution confirmed its seat at the top table of international diplomacy, and allowed for the injection of a more influential British voice in the deliberations of the US administration.

This kind of view was held quite firmly by the Prime Minister, at least for the initial part of his premiership. During his whistle-stop tour of Commonwealth countries at the start of 1958, Macmillan spoke to a meeting of British officials and diplomats in Singapore where he laid out, in typically grandiose style, his own conception of Britain's position. Although Britain certainly acknowledged the material supremacy of the United States and Soviet Union in the post-war world, the Prime Minister intoned, she had still decided 'to remain a great power.'

> It would have been possible for us to step back, after the Second World War, into a simpler position; to relax our grip over many more of our overseas positions; and to consolidate on a much narrower front so as to live more easily within our post-war means. We had chosen instead to try to hold on wherever we could – and we were now in the position of a great land-owner who, faced with high taxation and heavy death duties, declined to give up the old house even though he had to close some of the wings and cut down some of the trees.

Britain, had also, the Prime Minister highlighted, decided to become a nuclear power, even though the demands this brought on resources had been 'prodigious' and it now seemed doubtful, because of the accelerating pace of nuclear technology, whether 'we should be able to persist in unlimited competition with the Soviet Union in nuclear development.' But the decisions to proceed with British production of atomic and hydrogen bombs had, in Macmillan's estimation, 'enabled us to continue to speak with the United States on level terms in the formulation of world policy, and it was arguable that they had so far paid a useful dividend.' But now, looking ahead, Macmillan saw opportunities for lightening Britain's nuclear burdens through access to US assistance and know-how, and even 'a coordinated programme of weapons production.'[30] A month later he had a similar message for a wider public audience; when asked during a television interview why Britain needed the hydrogen bomb when the Americans already had it, he referred to the UK's role as a nuclear pioneer and his belief it was a 'good thing we should have an independent contribution to the deterrent ... [it] gives us a better position in the world, it gives us a better position with respect to the United States. It puts us where we ought to be, in the position of a Great Power. The fact that we have it makes the United States pay a greater regard to our point of view, and that is of great importance.'[31]

Yet the size of Britain's contribution to the deterrent strength of the West was very far from settled throughout this period. How one approached this question was strongly influenced by the meaning that was attached to the term 'independence' as well as the demands on resources made by an expanding nuclear programme, not least as Aldermaston's ingenuity was combined with service ambitions to include a welter of different nuclear weapons into their operational requirements for new equipment. The concerns exhibited by some of the Chiefs of Staff about the expenditure demanded by the deterrent, it was apparent, were also mirrored by high-level political interest over where the trends in technological development were heading.

Soon after the publication of the 1958 Defence White Paper, Macmillan had held a meeting with Plowden, where he had made evident the need for a better idea of future planning in the nuclear weapons field, including costs, relationships to the availability of fissile material, the development of delivery systems, and possible changes in US atomic energy legislation. With Plowden's assistance, Downing Street officials composed a minute for despatch to Sandys which highlighted the 'need for a clear picture of what we are doing and what we should aim to do in the whole field of nuclear armaments.' The Prime Minister hoped that such a comprehensive survey would assist the Defence Committee in deciding which projects should have priority and 'to what extent we should apply the principle of interdependence in the field of nuclear weapons.'[32]

Over the course of the next two months, Downing Street was supplied by officials close to Sandys with what were variously described as 'black market advance' or 'strictly under the counter' copies of the proposals being prepared by Brundrett and the COS for the Minister of Defence in response to Macmillan's directive. In what can only be called a very expansive programme, they involved as a 'bare minimum essential requirement' the production by 1970 of 200 megaton warheads 'for all purposes', and 1,475 'defensive and tactical warheads of assorted kinds' in the kiloton-yield range. The total cost of assembling a national stockpile of this character by 1970 was put at £650 million. The megaton-range warheads were intended for a variety of weapons, including 'free-falling bombs, powered guided bombs, ballistic missiles and anti-ballistic missiles.' The last-mentioned potential weapon system was included in anticipation that Anglo-American interdependence would lead to a cooperative or even joint ABM programme, where the UK would provide 'background radar equipment' and the Americans a suitable weapon (not least as there was no item in the R & D programme directed toward production of an anti-ballistic missile). Tactical warheads included, amongst other requirements, 200 for RAF and Royal Navy aircraft, 200 for anti-submarine work, and 800 for use with surface-to-air guided weapons. Plans were in hand to increase future supplies of fissile material to meet the needs of such a build-up, but these would involve adjustments to the civil reactor programme and possible approaches to the Americans to see if they were prepared to make-up a shortfall in domestic supplies of uranium 235. As far as nuclear assistance from the United States went, there had already been warnings that the changes to US atomic energy legislation promised by the White House would not allow a completely free transfer of US warhead design information, while there would clearly be no provision for the outright supply of complete US warheads to the UK.[33]

Original drafts of the MoD paper had provided little detail on estimated costs of the warhead programme, or the particular delivery systems which were to carry the anticipated weapons. Downing Street officials were quick to express their dissatisfaction at the quality of the information that was being made available. This omission can hardly be judged surprising as MoD officials had long struggled to produce accurate internal estimates for the cost of the overall deterrent programme. A major problem here was that they were reliant on figures obtained from the Ministry of Supply (with its responsibilities for oversight of the development and production of weapons) and the Air Ministry. One minute from this period warned that the figures being compiled were 'highly tentative', while those for research and development and production of delivery systems had been provided mainly by the MoS 'many of them under protest and with the greatest reluctance, on the grounds that neither the specifications nor experience were such as to make anything approaching an accurate estimate possible.' The Air Ministry, in turn, had proved unwilling to work with MoS officials on assembling figures for areas such as the Blue Streak programme and 'regarded the possibility of providing anything approaching a reasonable estimate as so remote as to decide they could not co-operate, except after an approach at a high level. The result is that some of the estimates are really nothing more than guess work.' In the case of Blue Streak figures, the conjecture involved was significant enough to undermine the validity of many of the final totals.[34]

When in mid-May 1958 Sandys eventually sent the Prime Minister a copy of the paper – with more detail on costs, as had been requested – Plowden was again on hand to offer advice on the technical issues it raised, particularly over implications for the supplies of fissile material.[35] As well as providing additional financial estimates (although as one of Sandys' MoD officials privately confessed to his Minister, these were 'worked out here without advice from the Ministry of Supply and the Air Ministry'), the paper also included mention of the major nuclear weapons systems which were then under development.[36]

The list of projects included by the Minister of Defence inevitably resembled a long shopping list of items. The total of megaton-range warheads envisaged by the end of 1963 was 100, with an anticipated 15 being produced every year thereafter; this was described as 'just sufficient to provide us with a modest element of deterrent power of our own, and, in due course, with a limited number of anti-missile missiles.' Even though such an ABM might not prove feasible, it seemed clear, the paper contended, that it would need a megaton warhead, while enquiries had been made of the Americans to see if a joint project was possible. A stockpile of 350 kiloton-range warheads was planned by the end of 1963 with a further 140 being produced on an annual basis until 1970.

In his covering comments, Sandys had argued that on the assumption that Britain wished to 'possess some element of independent nuclear deterrent power,' and that the Americans would not be willing to supply 'without strings' the megaton-yield weapons it was estimated were needed, then there was 'no option' but to go ahead with the development and production of the array of bombs, warheads and missiles that he had specified. It was admitted that the costs of the programme were 'difficult to calculate with certainty', although a rough estimate of about £140 million per annum (or about ten per cent of the defence budget) over the next five years was offered, but there was little scope for relaxation in requirements even after the completion of the initial programme in 1963. Sandys asked for additional plants to permit increased supplies of fissile material, an approach to the Americans about provision of U-235, and that development of the nuclear weapons listed in his paper should continue.[37]

The numbers of warheads which featured within the MoD's requirements had been mentioned in Defence Committee papers the previous summer, but the Prime Minister's official advisers evidently baulked at what was now being recommended.[38] Frederick Bishop, one of Macmillan's most able Private Secretaries, immediately fastened onto the possibility of reductions in the programme for megaton warheads, kiloton warheads, new plans for underground silo-basing for Blue Streak, and the proposed short-range rocket for Army use ('Blue Water').[39] There was a certain degree of surprise, if not incredulity, exhibited by the Cabinet Secretary that the MoD considered the figure of 200 megaton weapons (100 for offensive and 100 for defensive purposes in the original versions of its paper) 'a modest element of nuclear deterrent power'.

Sir Norman Brook, along with Bishop, wanted to draw the Prime Minister's attention to the preoccupation with the notion of independence which was contained within the paper, and which carried the clear assumption that the UK should plan to fight the Soviet Union without American support. It was known in the Cabinet Office that the MoD had made 'an assessment of the weapons required by having regard to the number of Russian cities with populations of 100,000 and over,' and that this led to such high numbers of large warheads. But if a different concept of deterrent power was used, one which was more 'in order to establish our position with our Allies and the Commonwealth,' and which was designed to ensure 'that the Americans will not act without consulting us,' then a much lower figure could be sufficient. Questions were raised over the figure of 100 warheads for defensive weapons, and the fact that the light-weight high-yield design which would have to be used in an anti-missile missile was still beyond British means and know-how. Sandys had assumed, moreover, that the option of asking the Americans to sell Thor IRBMs to the UK for use with a British warhead was not viable because Thor's range (1,500 miles, as opposed to over 2,000 miles for Blue Streak) meant it could threaten a fewer number of large Russian cities – 40 per cent instead of 70 per cent of the total – and so was seen as inadequate as an 'independent' deterrent.

Brook and Bishop, however, thought that the kinds of benchmarks used in the MoD's paper were irrelevant for determining the size of a deterrent which should rightly be thought of in diplomatic rather than military terms. They also wondered in any case whether the Russians would have such an accurate gauge of Thor's range, or in any case be in a position to disregard such an element of British-controlled deterrent power. In addition, officials were concerned that the many hundreds of kiloton-yield weapons planned for the next five years were designed for use in limited wars where British forces might be engaged without US assistance, yet there was no settled government policy on whether Britain should ever fight alone in this manner. 'Could Defence Ministers,' it was asked, 'say in which areas of the world, where there are British interests, it would be politically possible to use kiloton weapons?'

Also concealed were the high costs of certain weapons systems which would have to deliver the warheads planned in the MoD programme, most notably Blue Streak, for which total costs of development and production (including the provision of underground silos) could range between £480 million and £580 million.[40] Reservations came from within the AEA itself at what was being proposed by the MoD. One of its most senior figures, Sir William Strath, wrote to Bishop querying whether Blue Streak was necessary in the light of current strategy. Strath saw British policy as being 'to develop a British deterrent so that we shall not be entirely dependent on the Americans but will have a deterrent of our own. But a partial deterrent is enough. We do not envisage actually fighting wars with Russia on our own. All the political advantage we require can be obtained with the partial deterrent which we should still have without the Blue Streak.'[41]

The MoD's May 1958 paper, offering an expansive outline of the future nuclear warhead programme had, it was recognised, been prepared before any agreement on nuclear cooperation with the Americans had been concluded, and was necessarily based on a purely national conception of nuclear development. At the same time, given the claims for the benefits which nuclear interdependence might confer, it must have been received by Macmillan and his officials with a certain irony. The imminent restoration of nuclear collaboration with the United States had several aims and implications as far as British officials were concerned, but for the Prime Minister one of its benefits was supposed to be the potential to reduce expenditure on the nuclear programme now that US technological advances might be available for adoption. One immediate result might be the opportunity to suspend further UK atmospheric nuclear tests in the Pacific, which were beginning to provoke domestic and some international criticism. In early March 1958, for example, Macmillan had met Sandys, Powell, Plowden, Brundrett and Air Marshal Dickson to consider the schedule for the next phase of the testing programme. The meeting took the opportunity to discuss what would be the position if US atomic energy legislation was relaxed to allow the passage of weapons information and fissile material to the UK, and found there could be no justification for continuing with British testing if the necessary US data was made available.[42]

On 5 June 1958 Macmillan held an important gathering with the Cabinet Secretary and other senior Downing Street officials to discuss how to respond to the MoD's proposals for the weapons programme. Over the MoD's figures for megaton warheads, Macmillan said he

> thought it would be a mistake to try to assess our requirements on the basis of our waging total war independently. *What we had to do was to have a sufficiently effective quantum of deterrent to enable this country to influence the course of events and great power negotiations. If, for example, the requirement of warheads had been reached by having regard to the number of big Russian cities then that was wrong* [emphasis added]. Any argument that one type of weapon would enable us to reach something under 50% of these cities whereas another type of weapon would enable us to reach some 75% seemed to him to be unsound [in a reference to whether a Thor purchase might be preferable to development and production of Blue Streak]. The number of warheads we needed must be a matter of judgment. His own personal view might be that 50 would be the right order of magnitude. What was important was that our contribution to the deterrent must be entirely under our own control. We must have unfettered right over our deterrent weapons. It was this which would ensure our full rights as a voting member of the Nuclear Club.

Macmillan also considered that the Americans should be approached for advice over anti-missile technology, but he remained doubtful that it would ever be possible to deploy an entirely effective defence, especially when only a few warheads reaching British targets would be enough to do grievous damage. If ministers were to decide the shape and size of the future nuclear programme, Macmillan stressed, then they would first have to consider the 'political issue' of the pattern of warfare that the UK might have to face in the years to come: 'it was no good producing a whole battery of expensive weapons with nuclear warheads if we were only going to feel able to use them in, say, Borneo.'

The Prime Minister envisaged future wars taking four possible forms. The first was 'total war', which Macmillan called 'the war that must never happen.' It would only occur if the deterrent had failed, while 'we would never contemplate waging it ourselves, but ... we must have a sufficient and independent deterrent to enable our counsels to be heard in the world.' A second type of war would be an 'alliance war,' where Britain fulfilled its treaty obligations as a member of NATO, SEATO or the Baghdad Pact. Some participants in such wars might feel that kiloton weapons could be used without escalation into a total war, but it seemed to the Prime Minister that this was an unrealistic prospect and that an all-out exchange would surely follow. Next were 'joint Anglo-American operations' such as the soon to occur UK and US interventions in Jordan and Lebanon, where Britain had to show it was willing to make an effective contribution alongside its crucial ally. Finally there came 'quasi-police operations' in the colonial or ex-colonial world where the UK would be operating on its own. The question then was what weapons were needed for this array of possible conflicts? An issue also to be faced, Macmillan noted, was whether the MoD's nuclear requirements were affordable, while they would have to be measured against their likely scenarios for use. This kind of analysis might leave the UK nuclear programme restricted simply to its independent contribution to the Western deterrent. Nevertheless, Macmillan did not feel ready yet to go all the way along such a controversial path, not least because of relations with the Americans: 'We could not let them think that we were prepared to do nothing ourselves and [were] content to rely for weapons on them even by purchase.' It was important to know what weapons the Americans were prepared to make available to the UK and what might be provided in return. 'It was beyond dispute that the Americans would expect us to continue to carry out weapon research and development in some fields at any rate,' Macmillan thought, and so 'We must not give up entirely.'[43]

Securing the great prize

Much then would hinge on how nuclear cooperation with the United States was to develop now that President Eisenhower had made his commitment to push for amendments to US atomic energy legislation. Overcoming considerable initial differences, the successful conclusion in February 1958 of an agreement for the basing in Britain of Thor IRBMs under 'dual key' arrangements, whereby the weapons could not be launched without the joint agreement of both governments, had been an encouraging augury. The Thor Agreement boosted confidence that a formal understanding could eventually be reached which would allow for the broader and deeper nuclear collaboration that both Macmillan and Eisenhower had thought was necessary. Important progress had meanwhile also been made in discussions between the Royal Navy and the US Navy over the provision of nuclear submarine reactor technology, with the Americans coming to the view that the British should simply be allowed to purchase a US model outright for use in their own programme.

British officials were particularly anxious to reach an early agreement over nuclear collaboration as at the end of March 1958 a unilateral announcement came from Moscow that the Soviet Union would immediately be suspending all atmosphere nuclear testing. Significant domestic political pressure was soon built-up on the Macmillan Government to follow suit. But the full series of Grapple tests in the Pacific was not yet complete, and British scientists and officials were keen to carry out several further experiments which they knew were of interest to the Americans.[44]

Once Grapple was finished, however, it would be difficult to resist renewed calls for test suspension – indeed international negotiations to that end were soon expected – after which Aldermaston might find itself dependent on the still-to-be established ties with the Americans for the most advanced ideas on weapons design. London's anxieties were not eased by the intermittent reports they received of the protracted process whereby US officials attempted to gain Congressional agreement to the necessary amendments to US atomic energy legislation for an Anglo-American agreement to be concluded. When finally, at the end of May, the amendments were reported out of the Joint Committee on Atomic Energy by US legislators in favourable terms, Macmillan felt ready to ask Eisenhower if a British team could come to Washington in order to start detailed negotiations for a bilateral agreement on nuclear cooperation (any earlier initiation of the talks, US administration officials had warned London, might have prejudiced the JCAE's deliberations by indicating that its agreement to the amendments was taken for granted).[45]

Plowden, Brundrett and Penney arrived in the American capital in early June, before final Congressional approval for the amendments had been obtained, in what was to become a carefully timed sequence of events. There were evidently several sticking points in the negotiations that followed, and British officials were conscious of the reservations held by the Atomic Energy Commission and some elements within the Defense Department over establishing such a candid exchange.[46] A further visit from Macmillan to the US capital in the middle of the month helped to bolster the confidence of the British negotiating team, while British officials had to bargain the release of commercially sensitive information about the UK's civil nuclear power programme, where a technological lead over the Americans was still enjoyed, against openness in the military area. One complicating point was removed when Macmillan decided to defer a request to the administration for supplies of uranium 235, a measure which had prompted some Congressional resistance.[47]

As the negotiations in Washington neared their conclusion in mid-June, Plowden informed the Prime Minister that he was satisfied that the areas defined in the draft agreement for exchanges of information about weapons were 'broad enough to cover our requirements; everything will depend on the spirit in which the Agreement is implemented.' Moreover, he had received every indication that the Americans intended to carry out the Agreement's provisions in as cooperative fashion as possible.[48] The amendments to US atomic energy legislation were finally voted through by Congress on 30 June but not before one other significant manoeuvre had had to be employed. Some members of Congress had wanted reassurance on whether US assistance to the UK would help the British to build the kind of substantial stockpile of weapons that would help to augment Western nuclear strength. In order to allay such concerns, General Herbert B. Loper (the important American official who chaired the Military Liaison Committee which served as the key conduit between the Department of Defense and the civilian AEC) was informally told by a member of the British negotiating party – in all probability Brundrett – about the warhead numbers that were contained in the MoD's proposals for the future nuclear programme (even though they had not yet received collective ministerial approval), and the necessary reassurances were subsequently conveyed.

The way having now been made clear, on 3 July 1958 the 'Agreement on the Uses of Atomic Energy for Mutual Defence Purposes' (hereafter the Mutual Defence Agreement, or MDA) was signed by Dulles and Lord Hood, the British (diplomatic) Minister at the Washington Embassy.[49] The MDA was to form the bedrock of the subsequent Anglo-American nuclear relationship. Under its all-important Article II information could be exchanged in a wide range of areas, including evaluation of potential enemy capabilities in the nuclear field, development of compatible weapons systems, and 'classified information concerning atomic weapons as necessary to improve the recipient's atomic weapon design, development and fabrication capability.' This did not mean, however, that the relevant US authorities or agencies, such as the nuclear weapons laboratories under the control of the AEC, were free to transfer whatever information they pleased. In fact, such transfers were still tightly controlled by the provisions of the amended 1954 US Atomic Energy Act. The US legislation now stipulated that a presidential determination had to be made that any nations receiving transfers of such sensitive information could make 'substantial and material contributions to the mutual defense and security', while for information regarding the actual design and development of nuclear weapons there was an additional requirement that a receiving nation had to have already made 'substantial progress in the development of atomic weapons.' This form of wording was also written into the preamble and Article I of the MDA.

The JCAE, which had inserted the 'substantial progress' clause into the AEC's original draft language of the amendments, was also keen to amplify how this should be interpreted, stipulating that it was 'intended that the cooperating nation must have achieved considerably more than a mere theoretical knowledge of atomic-weapon design, or the testing of a limited number of atomic weapons. It is intended that the cooperating nation must have achieved a capability on its own of fabricating a variety of atomic weapons, and constructed the necessary facilities, including weapons research and development laboratories, weapon-manufacturing facilities, a weapon-testing station, and trained personnel to operate each of these facilities.'[50] In practice, the 'substantial progress' clause was generally taken to mean that a state needed to have developed a thermonuclear weapons capability, as the UK had demonstrated with its Grapple series (and which, in theory, could qualify other allies, such as France, which eventually came to develop a similar proficiency).

Presidential determinations, presented to the White House for approval by the AEC or Department of Defense, had to be issued on a regular basis to underpin the exchange with the UK, but they were also subject to scrutiny by the JCAE, which had the task of ensuring that they conformed to the terms of the amended 1954 Act. In addition, and of immense significance for the UK submarine programme, the MDA's Article III gave permission for the sale to the UK of a complete US nuclear submarine reactor, along with design and manufacturing information and enough uranium 235 to provide the reactor fuel for a decade.

The first intensive exchanges between senior scientific officials from Britain and the US under the terms of the MDA took place towards the end of August 1958 in Washington, and another highly productive meeting occurred the following month at the Sandia laboratories in Albuquerque, New Mexico. After a hesitant beginning, the August exchanges had seen several different weapon design ideas discussed and served to convince the American participants that they would be able to benefit from the relationship established under the Agreement.[51] When American views were brought to Macmillan's attention by Brundrett, Penney and Cook (who had all been present during the August talks), the Prime Minister noted in his diary with satisfaction, 'In some respects we are as far, and even further, advanced in the art than our American friends. They thought interchange of information would be all *give*.' Afterwards Macmillan wrote to Plowden,

> it is clear that the Americans were amazed to learn how much we already know and that this was a major factor in convincing them that we could be trusted with more information than they probably intended originally to give us. I hope that these discussions will be only the first of a series, in which Anglo-American co-operation in this field will become progressively closer.[52]

The 1958 Agreement certainly stands as one of the most remarkable examples of pooling of sensitive national security information by two sovereign states, and has rightly been seen as one of the fundamental pillars of the post-war

Anglo-American relationship. Its implementation allowed enduring bonds to be formed between whole groups of British and American nuclear scientists and engineers. But it must also be recognised that arrangements for collaboration under the MDA were by no means uniformly straightforward. The Americans remained reticent over some of their more advanced weapon designs (particularly in the ABM field), and conservative elements of the US bureaucracy had to be reminded on a regular basis that the injunction for an atmosphere of openness, allowing a full and frank exchange of information, came directly from the White House.[53]

Defence spending and the future of Blue Streak

During the summer of 1958 the debate over the impact of nuclear sufficiency continued unabated. In May Mountbatten had tried to draw the Foreign Office into the argument by raising the issue with Sir Patrick Dean, the senior official who was the Superintending Under Secretary overseeing the Permanent Under-Secretary's Department (PUSD) and who also chaired the Joint Intelligence Committee. The First Sea Lord was to find little support from Dean, however, who felt that because the vital interests of both the United States and the Soviet Union were engaged in Europe, it was a region where nuclear escalation was almost certain to result from any form of armed conflict involving the two powers. As the Soviet leadership probably shared this appraisal, this also made it a region where Russian aggression was least likely to occur. Even when it came to the Middle East and Asia, Dean thought that the West's possession of tactical nuclear weapons, as long as they were prepared to use them against local aggression, would place the onus for any escalation on the Soviet side, making the strategic deterrent to all-out war once more effective.[54]

In July 1958, Dean elaborated on his views after being sent a paper on nuclear sufficiency written by the Vice Chief of Naval Staff. Feeling that the purported effects of nuclear sufficiency on the East-West confrontation had been somewhat overdrawn, Dean argued that as long as the West showed determination and resolve, and was prepared to use nuclear weapons when vital interests were threatened, then the credibility of the deterrent, at least in Soviet eyes, could be preserved. There were strong political reasons why the United States remained committed to the defence of Western Europe. The Americans, to a

> far greater extent than we do, see themselves engaged in a struggle for world power against the forces of darkness. But even if we doubt whether a future United States Government would deliberately countenance the use of nuclear weapons to repel a large scale conventional attack in, say, Europe, the Russians are most unlikely to take the calculated risk of trying it out. Moreover, the increasing deployment of tactical nuclear weapons in the forward areas will surely increase the efficacy

of the deterrent, even though the old policy of massive retaliation may have been losing its credibility.

This did not mean that Dean supported the Air Ministry's overwhelming emphasis on the deterrent. Indeed, the Foreign Office was concerned that a correct balance should be found between conventional and nuclear forces, so that Britain's overseas interests could be protected and alliance obligations fulfilled. He certainly could see no merit in the contention that Britain needed a large arsenal of kiloton weapons for fighting limited wars when there was no intention of taking part in such conflicts without US support.

Whether economies could be found in the nuclear programme would, in Dean's view, depend greatly on the American attitude toward the recently concluded MDA. 'My own view,' he conjectured, 'is that the Americans are beginning to take the concept of Anglo-US interdependence seriously and that, if we play our cards well, we can count on considerable help, and savings, in planning our own offensive programme.' The picture would, however, only become clearer, he felt, in a few months time, when spending on the nuclear programme might be recalibrated, and a proper attempt to find a balance between the conventional and nuclear fields undertaken.[55] Dean's relaxed views about the effects of nuclear sufficiency were reflected in a formal Foreign Office paper produced the following month from the newly-formed planning section within the PUSD which argued that the United States was unlikely to retreat into a 'fortress America' approach over the coming years, despite steadily increasing Soviet nuclear capabilities.[56]

By June 1958, despite Sandys' desire to discuss the issue with the COS on a collective basis, no accord between the Chiefs appeared within sight. Templer continued to think it 'essential to put the deterrent, the importance of which might well have been exaggerated for political reasons, in the proper focus, with a view to giving a clear appreciation of our future strategy to Ministers.' The CIGS now proposed that each of the Chiefs should meet the Minister of Defence individually and outline their views, while Mountbatten was keen to underline that there were genuine differences of opinion held within the Committee which were not merely a reflection of narrow service interests; he too wanted to lay out the issues in front of Sandys. Mountbatten was obviously reluctant to turn the subject over for ministerial consideration without the Chiefs being able to agree a common position. As he put it: 'Owing to the speculative nature of the problem, it was unlikely that Ministers themselves would be able to reach a solution which was necessarily correct, and the Chiefs of Staff must continue to search for the correct solution.'[57] Believing that further study might produce an acceptable compromise, the service Directors of Plans were asked to look at the issue again. However, this exercise resulted in no narrowing of differences: if anything they now appeared even wider. In early July, each service Director of Plans was forced to deliver a separate report on the problem, the Admiralty and War Office submissions even rejecting the validity of the whole concept of an independent deterrent.[58]

Despite Mountbatten's protestations to the contrary, the protection of service budgets, as the full implications of the 1957 White Paper cuts began to be felt, was the most prominent feature of the arguments witnessed at this time, with intense sparring between the Admiralty and the Air Ministry in particular. For the First Lord of the Admiralty, Lord Selkirk, the conditions of nuclear sufficiency would throw into even starker relief the issue of whether it was appropriate for the UK to attempt to maintain its independent deterrent. He drew a sharp distinction between the argument for making a UK contribution to the Western deterrent as a whole, which was offered primarily for political and prestige reasons, and the argument for an independent deterrent which was in the UK's own defence interests. The demands of the former role always had to be kept in careful balance with the requirement to maintain adequate conventional forces, especially as the effects of the 'nuclear stalemate' became more obvious. When it came to an independent deterrent which could be used separately from that of the US, Selkirk thought there was a case for what he called a 'very critical examination.'

> Of all the major powers the UK is the most vulnerable to nuclear attack. Whatever nuclear damage we could inflict on Russia, Russia would certainly annihilate this country. Is it conceivable that we would ever be prepared to bring down this ruin on ourselves, in a situation where America, who could at least ensure the complete destruction of Russia – but at the cost of her own! – would be assumed to be unwilling to act? Even in the most unlikely case of Congress agreeing that the United States should join us in our suicide pact, how would this help us after our own annihilation? Whether it is conceivable or not, since credibility is essential to a deterrent, can it really be credible to the Russians that we would ever use this weapon unless they were to threaten a direct attack on the UK – and there is no evidence that this is part of their intentions?

Selkirk's objection to the current nuclear programme was that it seemed to be dictating the scale of the defence programme as a whole, and he felt that there was scope to rationalise its size.[59]

But Selkirk soon found his views countered by those of George Ward, the Secretary of State for Air, who thought it 'folly' to assume that the Russians would never threaten the UK with a nuclear attack. Ward considered a militarily significant level of deterrent capability crucial in exerting the necessary political influence over US policy. It could also provide a shield or umbrella which could give Britain the confidence to employ conventional forces in limited wars, such as might occur in the Middle East, or take part in a regional military intervention which Russia opposed.[60]

The arguments over nuclear sufficiency were obviously germane to the consideration that ministers would shortly have to give to the MoD's proposals for the future nuclear programme. As the negotiations in Washington over the MDA had entered their final stages in June 1958, the Prime Minister's officials, with Sir Norman Brook taking the lead, worked on the draft of a paper for the Cabinet's Defence Committee which encapsulated many of the questions and doubts over the MoD's nuclear plans.[61] They did so in an environment where the Treasury was increasingly concerned to find savings in the overall defence budget forecasts for the next financial year. On 7 July, the Chancellor of the Exchequer, Derick Heathcoat Amory, made a submission to the Prime Minister on what he called the 'alarming' upward trends in the MoD's forward costings. Pressing for changes in policy to bring about some reductions, he noticed, in particular, that the nuclear programme was then being examined by Downing Street. Heathcoat Amory saw a powerful case for conducting the exercise 'very critically' with a view to

> cutting out projects which seem likely to come too late to be useful for more than a very short period, or to be very expensive in relation to the additions to our strength which they achieve. This may well involve a greater reliance on American weapons, and the taking of some risks.

He suggested, in the first instance, that Sandys should be asked for his proposals on how to keep defence spending in 1959/60 close to the current year's figure of around £1,465 million.[62]

Anticipating a tough fight with the Treasury, Sandys responded with a defiant set of forecasts for defence expenditure over the next few years which showed the sharp rises to come but that, allowing for growth, remained a near constant percentage of gross national product (at just over seven per cent). Any significant reduction, he warned, could only be achieved 'by major changes in our present policies and commitments.' The examples of such changes he gave included, amongst others, eliminating all the UK's fighter defences, reducing further the strength of the V-force, stopping Blue Streak development, reducing the Rhine Army to a token force, or withdrawing from Hong Kong. He could recommend no such drastic changes.[63]

The Prime Minister's paper on the nuclear weapons programme was presented to his colleagues on the Defence Committee, alongside the MoD's proposals, in mid-July 1958. Economic aspects to the problem, Macmillan wanted it remembered, had to be kept

> to the forefront. It would seem necessary to decide what weapons we want and why, and then to consider whether we can produce them, and if so whether we can afford them.

Before deciding on the size of the nuclear programme, the Prime Minister explained that he wanted to lay out his own views on why he considered that the UK should continue to maintain an independent deterrent. Membership of the 'nuclear club' gave Britain 'the opportunity of exercising our influence in world affairs' and building close relations with the United States. But membership of the club required paying the 'annual subscription' as well as the 'entrance fee' of initial development of an atomic and then thermonuclear capability. The size of the deterrent force was, the Prime Minister confirmed, 'a matter of judgment', but it did not need to be any larger 'than is necessary to fulfil our purpose in maintaining it.' Four reasons were then given for retaining a nuclear capability:

a   To retain our special relation with the United States and, through it, our influence in world affairs and especially our right to have a voice in the final issue of peace or war.
b   To make a definite, though limited, contribution to the total nuclear strength of the West – while recognising that the United States must continue to play the major part in maintaining the balance of nuclear power.
c   To enable us, by threatening to use our independent nuclear power, to secure United States co-operation in a situation in which their interests were less immediately threatened than our own.
d   To make sure that, in a nuclear war, sufficient attention is given to certain Soviet targets which are of greater importance to us than to the United States.

Yet although the Prime Minister spoke of an 'independent' capability, he held no expectation that it would ever be used in a unilateral fashion against the Soviet Union, or as he put it, 'the knowledge that we shall not allow ourselves to become involved in war with the Soviet Union (or indeed in any major war) otherwise than in alliance with the United States, is some guide in deciding the size and nature of our nuclear armament.' He also raised doubts he had already rehearsed over whether UK kiloton-yield weapons were appropriate for the limited war scenarios which could be envisaged, once more running through, as he had in June, the various types of conflict in which Britain might be engaged in the coming years.

Regarding the MoD's idea for the UK production programme of megaton-size weapons for offensive purposes, Macmillan queried the appropriate number for maintaining an independent contribution to the deterrent to total war. In line with his earlier views, the Prime Minister wondered if a stockpile of 50 would, in fact, be enough, 'especially if we bear it in mind that *it is not our purpose to provide a deterrent which would operate to restrain the Soviet Union independently of the superior nuclear strength of the United States* [emphasis added].' He then proceeded to question various other aspects of the weapons programme, including the numbers of free-falling bombs for the V-force, and how long they should be retained; the programme for the Blue Steel stand-off missile (which in its Mark 1 variety had a range of about 100 miles) for equipping the V-bombers from about 1961 onwards; the Blue Streak IRBM, which was proving 'extremely expensive to develop and produce'; and any possible development of an anti-missile missile. The Prime

Minister, following the advice he had received from officials, seemed particularly keen on pursuing the idea of simply supplanting Blue Streak with a purchase of the US Thor system, as long as this could be done under conditions which gave the UK complete control over its firing, and it was able to develop a suitable warhead.[64]

With Macmillan in his usual place in the chair, the Defence Committee met at the end of the July to discuss the long-term programme for the research, development and production of nuclear weapons. As was the Prime Minister's prerogative, the senior ministers present were restricted to the Home Secretary and Lord Privy Seal (R. A. Butler), the Chancellor of the Exchequer (Heathcoat Amory), the Foreign Secretary (Selwyn Lloyd), and the Minister of Defence, with all the Chiefs of Staff, along with Brundrett, also in attendance. The initial debate focused on Macmillan's outline of the general purposes of retaining an independent nuclear capability. There was consensus that this was required 'to retain our special relations with the United States and, as a result, our influence in world affairs, and to make a definite, though limited contribution to the total nuclear strength of the West.' This stance, though involving major expenditure, was perceived to have yielded political rewards, and there was agreement that efforts should be made on a more economical basis to continue the policy. What was called the 'doctrine of interdependence' might, it was conjectured, lead to a renunciation of an independent capability, but it was evident that this position had not yet been reached. Moreover, possession by the UK of effective nuclear forces was an insurance against the withdrawal of US nuclear forces from Europe, and could help to deter the Soviet Union from trying to overrun Western Europe when the US nuclear guarantee had been placed in doubt – not least when the condition of nuclear sufficiency was realised. National control of nuclear strike forces also, it was argued, allowed targets of immediate importance to the survival of the UK to feature in the joint plans drawn up with the US authorities.

There was general agreement by the Committee – in a reflection of Macmillan's views – that megaton weapons would 'only be used in operations in which the United States was also involved.' When the discussion turned to kiloton-yield weapons and their possible use in limited war, the Committee was more impressed with the argument that the reduced size of the armed forces meant they should have available the most effective weapons available to meet potential threats. The 'moral support and approval' of the United States could not be assumed in such future engagements, while a 'tactical nuclear retaliatory capability would enhance the ability of our forces to deter aggression. Moreover, potential aggressors might well in future be armed with nuclear weapons by the Soviet Union. We could not rely on being able to obtain all our requirements from the United States and it would inadvisable, therefore, to take any decisions at this stage which would preclude us from being able to develop our own tactical weapons and nuclear warheads in the future.'

However, immediate savings on the megaton warhead programme would be difficult to achieve since fissile material production – which made up the largest portion of expenditure – could not be adjusted in the short term. As for the means of delivery, it was already acknowledged that a ballistic missile force would be required once the V-bombers had reached the end of their effective life as a strategic deterrent in the mid-1960s. Blue Streak was under development

> But if the United States would be prepared to provide us with ballistic missiles without any restriction on their use it should be possible to reduce the effort at present devoted to the development of a British weapon, although as a matter of long-term policy it might be inadvisable to abandon all work on ballistic missiles in this country. If it was decided to rely on United States ballistic missiles, it would be preferable to seek to obtain stocks of Polaris rather than any further supplies of Thor. Although Polaris was being developed primarily as a submarine weapon it could equally well be used as a mobile weapon on land.

It was noted that the main item of spending on the future nuclear programme was for megaton weapons, where the financial forecasts provided by the MoD were likely to be exceeded. 'The allocation of resources to the nuclear weapon programme should not be out of proportion to the effort devoted to the other means of countering Soviet expansion,' the Committee's discussion ran, mirroring the ongoing debates within the COS over the priority to be accorded the deterrent, while

> the total annual expenditure on overseas information services was less than the annual amount being spent on the development of the British ballistic missile. Moreover, the Chiefs of Staff had emphasised in previous discussions that their support for our contribution to the nuclear deterrent was on the understanding that this contribution would not absorb so much of the total resources set aside for defence as to make it impossible to finance the other forces essential to ensure the cohesion of the Commonwealth and our dependencies and alliances.

Although it had debated the general issues, the Defence Committee had had no time to consider any of the detailed aspects of the MoD's recommendations for the future nuclear programme. When Heathcoat Amory called for reductions in the forecasts for next year's defence budget, he was again met with Sandys' rebuttal that while small scale savings might be found, no significant reductions would be possible without ministers taking major decisions over policy.[65]

Few issues had been settled, but in the aftermath of the meeting, Brook noted for the Prime Minister's benefit, and with some degree of satisfaction, that the Defence Committee seemed to be moving toward 'a healthy scepticism' over the value of Blue Streak.⁶⁶ The provocative mention of a Polaris alternative during the discussion had not been lost on Brundrett at the MoD who wrote to Bishop in order to protest how the subject had been handled, noting 'technical considerations' which had not been brought to the attention of the Committee and the important fact that Polaris could in all probability not be brought into service until 1968 at the earliest.⁶⁷

Brundrett's protest underlined the point that the most likely immediate casualty in the nuclear programme from the pressure induced by a combination of the Prime Minister's July paper for the Defence Committee, and the attempts of the First Sea Lord and CIGS to rebalance the defence programme, was the cancellation of Blue Streak. Moreover, from being one of Blue Streak's strongest advocates during 1957 and the first half of 1958, Sandys had begun to change course, starting to push more firmly for some of the alternatives that the recent agreement over Thor deployment and the conclusion of the MDA appeared to offer. Worried by delays in the Blue Streak programme, in April 1958 Sandys asked his officials whether the main contractor, De Havilland Propellers, could be replaced, and ordered a review of the whole project by a working party of MoD, Ministry of Supply and Air Ministry officials.⁶⁸ The recommendations that followed called for an accelerated programme of development involving additional expenditure of £40–50 million. Calling Blue Streak 'one of the central features in our whole defence project', where the earliest possible deployment was the 'critical factor', Sandys presented these unpalatable conclusions to the Chancellor of the Exchequer on 14 July 1958, only a few days before the Defence Committee meeting detailed above.⁶⁹

By now Sandys was ready to consider alternatives, not least in the wake of the conclusion of the MDA and the potential availability of new forms of US assistance. Sir William Cook, AWRE's outgoing deputy director, wrote to the Minister of Defence in the middle of July to express his dissatisfaction at the results of the Blue Streak review (in which he had participated) and his view that if it was possible to buy Thor missiles 'without political strings' he was 'sure this would be the quickest way of providing a British deterrent of sufficient range to make the threat a real one.' He was also confident that it would be possible to make a suitable UK warhead for Thor if British nuclear testing could be continued, but if test suspension were to occur he hoped that the new arrangements under the MDA would allow enough US information to be transferred which would allow the weight of the UK megaton warhead design to be reduced sufficiently to be used with Thor.⁷⁰

At the first meeting of the MoD's new Defence Board, held at the end of July 1958, Sandys began to waver over the future of Blue Streak. Faced with concerted arguments over the need to find the correct balance in the defence programme, he continued to maintain that unless an independent British nuclear deterrent was to be allowed to lapse a new ballistic missile had to be acquired. But he now also felt that as long as it was under effective British control he saw no necessity for such a new missile to be made in Britain.

There had been recent indications, he told the Board, that the Americans might be willing to provide Thor IRBMs 'without strings' to succeed the V-bomber force along with design information under the MDA to enable a new British lightweight warhead to be produced for the missile, in which case the right course might be to abandon Blue Streak, take up the Thor option as an interim measure, and work with the Americans in developing a new solid-fuel missile of the Polaris type. Over the more general issue of defence spending as a whole, Sandys called on all departments to conduct 'vigorous pruning' consistent with maintaining current policy, with the aim of bringing next year's budget estimates down from £1,538 million to no more than £1,500 million.[71]

A few days later, Sandys brought news of the Defence Board's discussion back to the Cabinet's Defence Committee. Explaining that he now wanted time to pursue the new options, Sandys thought it was less necessary to accelerate the development programme for Blue Streak as he had earlier envisaged. General support was given to this approach and the Minister of Defence was left to prepare figures on the savings that would accrue from Blue Streak cancellation. Resuming its previous discussion, the Defence Committee gave the kiloton warhead requirements put forward in the MoD's plans critical scrutiny, with Sandys now claiming the numbers he had provided were more an 'indication of likely orders of magnitude.' The weapon requirements might, he conjectured, be filled from US sources, but he still maintained that increases would have to be made in fissile material capacity. Discussion in the Committee reflected general unease at the number of kiloton weapon projects that were in the pipeline. 'We should consider again whether disproportionate effort was not being applied to the nuclear programme,' the minutes of the meeting ran, continuing:

> The immediate threat to our interests was one of subversion rather than military aggression, but a very much larger part of our total effort was deployed against the possibility of the latter. Again, the likelihood of major war was much less than that of minor operations, but a large part of our defence expenditure was devoted to preparations for the former. There seemed to be a case for reviewing priorities.

Ministers again looked to the possibility of acquiring weapons from the United States as a way out of their conundrum, but no decisions over modifications to the long-term programme were made.[72]

By late August the Prime Minister had become reconciled to the need for an increase in the UK's productive capacity for fissile material so as to meet the needs of the nuclear programme. He was not, however, convinced about the numbers of megaton weapons required for deterrent purposes – he now mentioned a figure of 100 deployed weapons – and, influenced by his officials, was clearly attracted to the idea of acquiring Thor for use with a British warhead, and with no American 'strings' attached. Over kiloton weapons there continued to be deep reservations regarding the MoD's conception of the UK's role in limited wars, and Macmillan expressed his firm opposition to major expenditure in the ABM field.[73] Moreover, and as we shall see, there remained significant doubts in the Prime Minister's mind over the long-term course of nuclear weapons policy.

The nuclear sufficiency debate resumed and the Thor option

After a lull in August, the COS picked up their cudgels once again at the beginning of September over the issue of nuclear sufficiency. The Chiefs had by now found agreement that over time the United States would exhibit more reluctance to risk the destruction of her own cities in the event of a serious confrontation with the Soviet Union. Indeed, it was probable,

> that Russia would believe that the United States would only risk such destruction for the sake of those interests which were really vital to her and that these would be limited to the territorial integrity of NATO Europe [assuming her own forces were deployed there] and of the North American Continent.

It was also increasingly likely that in the future the Soviet Union would be prepared to undertake more risks and to be, for example, more 'thrusting and forcible' in the Middle and Far East. Limited war forces, suitably equipped with tactical nuclear weapons, therefore would be required to meet such new threats over the years to come. For his part, Templer did not dispute that some strategic nuclear contribution had to be made to the Western Alliance by Britain, but felt that addition of the word 'independent' to that contribution should be resisted, as it gave 'the impression that Her Majesty's Government might wish to use it independently and offensively. He did not believe that any British Government would do this.' The essential requirement, in Templer's opinion, was that there should be unconditional British control over a deterrent which could be used if the UK itself was directly attacked and retaliation was then required.

The argument for a completely independent UK deterrent was again advanced with typical force by the Chief of the Air Staff, Dermot Boyle. Boyle saw an independent deterrent as an important marker of military status, over which 'unfettered' control should be maintained. Future developments in ballistic missile defence meant that the West could even perpetuate its strategic advantage over the Soviet Union. 'The Air Ministry had given much thought to the degree of threatened destruction which would deter Russia from attacking the United Kingdom,' Boyle noted. 'Their present opinion was that the guaranteed destruction of about 30 cities would suffice, but it was not a matter that could be calculated and the ultimate decision would have to be based on political considerations.' A minimum deterrent contribution had to be provided, Boyle asserted, and this could be decided once it had been settled at a political level what level of damage against Russia would constitute an effective level of deterrence. Once this had been determined, and the forces allocated to achieve this, then what was remaining from the defence budget should be given over to spending on conventional capabilities.

Joining the fray at the COS meeting was Mountbatten, who voiced his opinion that in the new conditions of nuclear sufficiency, the United States would be 'immeasurably more reluctant to use nuclear weapons, except in self defence. Even today he was doubtful if they would use them if faced with a *fait accompli* in Formosa or West Berlin.' With limited wars considered more likely under a Soviet strategic nuclear umbrella, Mountbatten favoured providing the extra resources for conventional forces to face such threats and to defend Britain's global interests. In a direct inversion of Boyle's position, he said that once these needs had been met, he hoped there would be 'enough money for a useful contribution to the Western deterrent.' The British contribution must be unfettered in its ultimate control, as both Boyle and Templer had argued, but Mountbatten 'did not consider it vital that it should be independent otherwise, since a degree of interdependence might save a vast amount of money. He did not believe that a British contribution to the Western deterrent would ever be used independently except in self-defence.' Attempting to sum up an inconclusive discussion, with his fellow Chiefs clearly divided, Dickson could merely offer the view that ministers would have to decide the level of destruction that should constitute the minimum level of British contribution to the Western deterrent, and a ruling on this was required before more progress could be made with costing the relative balance to be maintained between conventional and nuclear forces.[74]

As chair of the Committee, Dickson was left with the unenviable task of composing a memorandum which could encapsulate the different viewpoints of his colleagues for presentation to Sandys. After several attempts, and countless amendments from the interested parties, Mountbatten suggested to Dickson that he and Templer should simply write their own paper, and that Boyle should do likewise. Dickson could then provide a covering minute to the two separate submissions. It was of 'real importance,' the First Sea Lord stressed, that Dickson should 'make no attempt to minimise the differences in our views – rather, we feel it is your duty to highlight those differences.'[75] This was, in other words, precisely the kind of argument that the recently published White Paper on the *Central Organisation for Defence* had anticipated, but which the modest reforms to the COS system proposed in response – as was noted in chapter one – were ill-suited to tackle.

A paper was therefore submitted in mid-September under Mountbatten and Templer's names developing their views on the whole issue. It began by arguing that the arrival of nuclear sufficiency made the Western deterrent less credible against threats below the nuclear level, as the United States would hesitate before launching its nuclear weapons when the consequence would be devastation of her own homeland. They also discounted the military rationale for an independent UK strategic nuclear force, which they now saw as taking valuable resources away from conventional defence spending. While accepting the 'political' arguments which could be used to justify the case for a British contribution to the Western deterrent, Mountbatten and Templer expressed their convictions in forthright terms:

> While we accept a political contribution to the Western deterrent we absolutely oppose the concept of an independent UK nuclear deterrent if this means a strategic nuclear stockpile complete with delivery systems entirely under the control of HMG, and fully adequate by itself to inflict unacceptable devastation on Russia.
>
> We do not believe it could be claimed, and indeed it would be completely incredible to the Russians, that an independent UK deterrent would be used against them except in the case of their directly attacking the United Kingdom. If that improbable event comes about, we must rely on the full weight of the Western deterrent as a whole being brought into play. If we cannot rely on the concept of an interdependent Western deterrent for the protection generally of an interest so vital to the West as the security of the United Kingdom, the fabric of the Western alliance must collapse.

All-out nuclear war could still be deterred by the combined nuclear forces of the Western alliance, but the First Sea Lord and CIGS wanted the government to make a commitment to maintaining adequate conventional forces, armed with tactical nuclear weapons as required, to prosecute smaller-scale conflicts. Such forces, they felt, constituted

> the real deterrent, which, if applied effectively, will ensure that situations are controlled promptly so that they do not drift into the dilemma of either our having to put into effect the nuclear sanction and so commit national suicide, or, as the only alternative, letting the world fall progressively under Communist domination.

Consideration should be given, they argued, for a full-scale revision of strategic priorities alongside a detailed and thorough costing of the nuclear programme.[76] Relaying the contents of the paper to Sandys, all Dickson could advise was that there was a 'complete difference of opinion' between Mountbatten and Templer on the one side, and Boyle on the other, with no likelihood of agreement in sight.[77]

With the COS split over some of the most basic aspects of strategic nuclear policy, the Minister of Defence was also struggling to present a clear picture of the future nuclear programme to his ministerial colleagues. Following his *volte face* in the summer, on 10 September Sandys returned to the Defence Committee with the view that it was 'desirable' to reconsider previous plans to continue with Blue Streak development. Reflecting the outcome of the first rounds of exchanges in Washington under the MDA, he could now report that American assurances had been given that information on lightweight megaton warheads for ballistic missiles would be provided to the UK, while it was also possible that American IRBMs could be supplied 'without strings'. Sandys recommended investigation of the possibility of stopping Blue Streak development, and working with the Americans on a more advanced type of IRBM (meaning having a longer range, more room for penetration aids, and solid propellants), perhaps in partnership with other West European countries. A new warhead, based on the latest US information, could be designed for the new IRBM. Any gap in capability which resulted from such a programme could be filled, he conjectured, by developing a longer-range version of Blue Steel for use with the V-bombers, or by arranging a purchase of Thor 'without strings' for which a British warhead could be furnished. Sandys saw his latest proposals as offering in the long term a more advanced weapon than Blue Streak, and keeping the UK in the ballistic missile business while the financial burden was shared more widely. Other ministers were wary of making such a dramatic switch, however, Macmillan wanting the proposals thoroughly explored with the Americans first, with detailed estimates made of net savings, and was obviously concerned that another fresh programme of spending on a new IRBM might follow a decision to cancel Blue Streak.[78]

Immediately after the formal meeting of the Committee, Macmillan held an informal gathering with the Foreign Secretary, Home Secretary, Chancellor of the Exchequer, and Minister of Defence to discuss general defence policy (no defence chiefs or service ministers, in other words, were present). The note of the meeting recorded agreement over the need for 'a fundamental reappraisal of defence expenditure' considering the demands on resources which it was making, and that 'in particular it was becoming increasingly unrealistic to assume that we could afford to pursue the policy of the deterrent indefinitely.' It was argued that any democracy would find it virtually inconceivable to authorise the use of nuclear weapons except in retaliation as there were such massive political inhibitions on first use; in such circumstances, it was asked what 'rational justification' could be found for spending about £300 million per annum on the nuclear deterrent?

The only options if it was decided to go out of the nuclear business, however, were seen as basing policy on finding a comprehensive scheme of disarmament which could offer security, or in undertaking a progressive withdrawal from world affairs. To abandon the deterrent without the safeguards of disarmament could lead the whole system of Western alliances to 'crumble', with the collapse of NATO and a retreat by the United States into isolationism:

> It could perhaps be assumed that the Soviet Government would never dare to launch a nuclear attack on this country unless the United States

had first withdrawn completely from Europe. Our possession of the nuclear deterrent was the surest guarantee that such a position would never arise.

There were other grounds on which the effort and expense of the nuclear programme could be justified: progress in this area was seen as

> of vital importance to the maintenance of high scientific and technological standards in this country. In this field competition was very keen, and we could not afford, in terms of international prestige, to drop out of the running. It was our insistence on a high level of qualitative achievement which maintained the morale of our scientists and reconciled the Chiefs of Staff to quantitative reductions in the Forces which they would otherwise be bound to resist.

Having covered this range of arguments, the small ministerial conclave came to conclusion that it would be 'unwise to abandon the policy of the nuclear deterrent.' At the same time, in view of its rising costs, and the opportunities that the MDA could present, it might be decided that the scale of independent nuclear capacity should be reduced

> and that we should rather seek to create a joint Anglo-American nuclear deterrent on the basis of a partnership to which each country would make an appropriate contribution. There were signs the United States were themselves beginning to realise the dangers of excessive reliance on nuclear power and the importance of maintaining an adequate level of conventional forces. They, too, would soon realise the intolerable burden on national resources which was implicit in a twofold policy of this kind; and they might welcome the conception of a joint effort shared with ourselves.

The question that would then have to be decided was the appropriate British contribution to such a joint effort, and whether it should be determined by the purely economic criteria of what could be afforded, or if what was needed was a more basic reconsideration of politico-military priorities. For the moment, all ministers were prepared to do, however, was discuss possible cuts in the defence budget which reduced the strength of Fighter Command even further, as well as the ambitious programme for surface-to-air guided weapons.[79]

By now the future of Blue Streak was increasingly seen to hinge on the degree of Anglo-American nuclear cooperation and 'interdependence' it would be possible to establish over the coming years. A chance to explore options with the Americans was presented when Sandys visited the United States in late September 1958 for talks with Neil McElroy, the US Secretary of Defense. At their final session together McElroy conveyed the welcome news that the State and Defense Departments, following an earlier request from Sandys, had agreed to provide an assurance that the United States would be prepared to offer Thor (minus its warhead) to the UK with no political restrictions. At the same time, the US Government wanted the proviso added that it still reserved the right to raise with the UK the subject of the future operational control of the missiles (this was, in fact, the same proviso that had been included in the exchange of notes that had accompanied the February 1958 Thor Agreement). The Americans feared, it was explained, that if news of the basic assurance was to leak it could create difficulties with the other European members of NATO, where planning to deploy IRBMs was proceeding on the assumption that operational control and target planning would be vested in SACEUR.

The response of the Minister of Defence was to recall that at the time of the February 1958 Thor Agreement, British opposition to initial American proposals that operational control should lie with SACEUR was based on the fact they regarded the Thor force

> as being an extension of the independent British medium bomber force, which, together with the American Strategic Command, had the task of strategic bombing of targets deep inside Russia, in accordance with the plans agreed by the American Joint Chiefs of Staff and the British Chiefs of Staff. SACEUR's mission, on the other hand, was a tactical one and it was militarily unsound that he should be given responsibilities in the field of strategic bombing.

The same considerations would apply to any purchase of Thor from the United States, which must be available for independent use by Britain if desired. However, despite Sandys' arguments, the Americans insisted that their reservation should be included in the private exchange of notes that would convey the assurance – this was not therefore quite the categorical statement that had been hoped for, but it was enough to convince Sandys that a Thor purchase was a political possibility. Sandys also brought back from his discussions in the United States the conclusion that Polaris could not be 'developed to meet UK requirements', and that instead a new programme of UK work on solid fuel rocket motors would be needed to provide a missile with enough range and payload to provide an adequate long-term substitute for either Blue Streak or Thor.[80]

Sandys used the occasion of the second meeting of the MoD's new Defence Board in mid-October 1958 to try to clarify the future programme of UK ballistic missile development. Despite having heard from the Americans that Thor would be available 'without strings' along with the detailed design of its warhead, Brundrett was emphatic that the 'best way of ensuring the indefinite continuance of an effective independent deterrent would be to continue with Blue Streak.' The option of a Thor purchase was not considered worth pursuing on technical grounds, in his view, as it was judged by the US authorities as only having a 'mechanically sound' life for the next 7–10 years and its above-ground basing made it vulnerable to pre-emptive attack. Brundrett also dismissed the notion of a European missile project as the Americans had stated that anything produced with their help would have to be assigned to SACEUR, meaning it would not constitute an independent deterrent; such a scheme was, in any case, 'most unlikely to materialise.'

The Minister of Defence explained to the Board that his own position after its previous meeting in the summer had been that the best option might be 'to persuade the Americans to let us have Thor without political strings, abandon Blue Streak, and develop in its place a solid fuel intermediate range rocket, possibly based on an American design.' But as the Americans were not going to develop an IRBM to replace Thor, a wholly new and expensive programme of British work on solid fuel rocket technology would be needed for a successor, which might not be ready for deployment even by 1968, when Thor would be considered obsolescent. The First Lord of the Admiralty reported Sandys as saying that solid fuel was 'the wrong medium for outer space rockets and that to turn over from liquid to solid fuel R. and D. in the UK would be just as expensive as the Blue Streak programme. It would also waste the considerable capital resources which have been built up for liquid fuel.' Continuing with Blue Streak development, according to Sandys, might still allow the use of a smaller and lighter American warhead design and 'this would leave room for the incorporation of anti-defensive devices and other improvements.'

The Defence Board's discussion had finished with Sandys 'regretfully' concluding that there was 'no practical alternative' to continuing with Blue Streak development. The First Lord had to admit that the Admiralty's opposition to Blue Streak suffered from their being unable to offer a viable alternative at this stage, not least as Polaris submarines could not be produced to assume the main deterrent role by the mid-1960s. Nevertheless, when discussion was resumed by the Defence Board a few days later, the First Lord pressed for further consideration to be given to a seaborne weapon system as a longer term replacement for the deterrent. In the interim, however, he could see little choice but to continue with Blue Streak, subject to a review in a years' time. Sandys seemed happy to accept this form of compromise.[81]

Compromise was very far from evident when it came to the ongoing disputes amongst the COS over the issue of nuclear sufficiency and how it affected the overall role of the deterrent. At the end of October, the Minister of Defence went to the lengths of convening a special meeting between the principal antagonists designed to at least arrive at the semblance of a common position which could be presented to other departments. Worried about the logjam that was occurring in essential staff work, Dickson hoped that the meeting might serve to provide the ministerial guidance required so that planning staffs could carry out their work under an officially approved policy. The dynamics of the argument were by now affected by the fact that the straight-talking figure of Templer had just retired as CIGS (being replaced by the less combative and more detached figure of General Sir Francis Festing), leaving Mountbatten alone to present the position. The First Sea Lord complained that the Navy and the Army were being reduced 'to the absolute minimum size consistent with continued effectiveness' and that future weapons programmes such as Blue Streak threatened yet more reductions. Boyle, for his part, now maintained that the date nuclear sufficiency might have arrived was more remote than had been supposed, and the development of defensive weapons gave the West discernable advantages. His main plea was that the V-bomber force had already been reduced in size from the Air Staff's preferred strength of 240 aircraft, and the current projected numbers constituted the minimum that would deter Russia from 'launching the nuclear offensive' in a situation where the United States would not agree to retaliate.

Sandys attempted to quash some of the central assumptions that had gained ground during the debate over the effects of nuclear sufficiency on the strategic situation. The United States, the Minister of Defence did not doubt, would support her European NATO allies with 'the full weight' of her nuclear power if it were necessary. 'If America hesitated to act, except in a case where her own territory was directly threatened,' he reasoned,

> the Russians might well over-run Western Europe and subsequently dominate Africa and Asia, at will. South America would, no doubt, adopt a neutralist attitude and North America would find itself isolated in a world dominated by Communism. He was sure that the United States would have the foresight to recognise where her interests lay and would act accordingly.

At the same time, the Minister of Defence considered it

> prudent to examine our own position in case the United States should ever feel that she did not need to intervene in helping to resist some peripheral attack on Western Europe. If such circumstances ever arose, it was inconceivable that Britain would hesitate to use her own nuclear retaliatory power. Britain's resolve to use her strategic nuclear force might have sufficient deterrent effect to make Russia pause and, perhaps, change her mind.

For these reasons, Sandys maintained that retention of an independent British deterrent was 'no less important for the future than it was now.' Mountbatten, however, demurred, flatly saying that the worth of a British deterrent would, in fact, be diminished if the US was to take a more isolated position as 'to use it in retaliation for an attack on Western Europe would surely be to commit national suicide immediately and forego any possibility of a negotiated peace.'

The riposte from Sandys was that if the view was taken that the Americans could not be relied on, then the entire strategic concept under which British defence policy had been operating would have to change as well, not least as Britain's world-wide military commitments had carried the assumption of the existence of an American nuclear umbrella. NATO would be likely to fall apart if such beliefs were to become widespread, and the entire set of national priorities would have to be reassessed. This was not, in the Minister of Defence's opinion, a 'practical proposition', and he saw no reason to lower the current high status that was given to the deterrent in the overall programme. In any case, he continued, cuts in spending on nuclear forces were unlikely to yield major dividends for the rest of the defence budget. Sandys could not give any more specific advice to the COS than had been contained in the past two defence white papers: 'the best we could hope to do was to maintain efficient, highly mobile forces, a reasonable share of the Western nuclear deterrent and the ability to make a fair contribution to our various alliances.' As for the UK independent deterrent itself, he summed up the meeting with the opinion that it could be assumed that it would be launched 'if Britain were attacked, and it would be reasonable to assume that they would be willing to use it also in defence of Western Europe, since Britain could not be defended separately.'[82]

The attempt by Sandys to clear the air and lay out his views, however, was far from ending the matter. After protests from Mountbatten at how the substance of the meeting had been recorded in the minutes, the Minister of Defence agreed that there had been no attempt by those present to reach 'a final answer.' Instead he again deferred the issue by letting Mountbatten know that when the government made final decisions on the maintenance of the British element to the deterrent, including its nature and size, he would issue a directive to guide defence planning. Until that point 'the matter of nuclear sufficiency will remain *sub judice*'.[83]

In fact, despite the hopes of the Minister of Defence that the argument could be moderated it rumbled on during January 1959 as the draft of the annual Defence White Paper came up for discussion at the Defence Board, with objections being raised to its extensive nuclear sections from both the new CIGS, General Festing, as well as from Mountbatten, while the Foreign Office was also uneasy about any public airing in the White Paper of arguments over the credibility of the deterrent. Even though he had assumed the new title of Chief of the Defence Staff (CDS) on 1 January 1959 as a result of the Central Organisation of Defence reforms, Dickson did not have the formal powers, nor was he inclined by temperament, to cut through the controversy.[84] Eventually, to avoid further dispute, Sandys decided to make the 1959 White Paper simply a report on the progress that had been made toward implementing the five year plan outlined in the 1957 White Paper, and to leave out entirely the several paragraphs which had been drafted by his officials which dealt with the British contribution to the Western deterrent.[85]

Blue Streak on borrowed time

All the doubts that had begun to arise over the future nuclear programme during the summer of 1958 reached a climax of sorts in the final two months of the year when the figures for defence expenditure in 1959/60 were under discussion in the Defence Committee. The immediate object of attention was whether to cancel the Blue Streak programme, but lying not far below the surface were some fundamental questions concerning the priority which was to be accorded an independent deterrent, and how the role of such a deterrent was to be understood. The Cabinet Secretary, for one, was far from convinced by the arguments which had emerged from the MoD over the course of the year over the balance between nuclear and conventional forces in the defence budget. Reflecting the anxieties of the Chancellor of the Exchequer, Brook was becoming increasingly concerned that the rising trends in defence expenditure were not being kept in check by a detailed and critical review of the whole programme. He was worried, he told the Prime Minister in early November 1958, 'because we do not seem to be getting to grips with the major areas of policy.'

The papers presented by the Minister of Defence to the Defence Committee tended to be distributed too late for ministers to give them proper consideration, and so compressed that they were unsuitable for 'informed discussion.' Sandys' predilection for missiles over manned bombers Brook found particularly unconvincing, and he was uncomfortable with the sums which were being sunk into weapons designed for 'a global war in Europe' when this was the least likely conflict the UK would confront during the next decade. Bomber forces, in the Cabinet Secretary's opinion, were inherently more flexible and could at least be employed in lower level conflicts in a conventional role. Overall, the Cabinet Secretary had 'an uneasy feeling that the logical foundation of our present defence policy is insecure'; Brook wondered if the differences of opinion which had been opened up between the service ministries over the previous few months when it came to the balance between nuclear and conventional forces had been accurately reflected in the way Sandys had presented the MoD's position to the Defence Committee. The condition of nuclear stalemate between the two main power blocs, in Brook's estimation, opened up the prospect of a proliferation of smaller-scale threats and dangers as the Communists probed for weaknesses beneath this umbrella. 'From the military point of view,' he asked the Prime Minister, 'are we in danger of failing to maintain a sufficiently large conventional strength to deal with the police operations and minor wars in which we are likely to be involved?'[86]

The links between the arguments amongst the COS over nuclear sufficiency and concerns over the costs of the deterrent-related aspects of the defence budget were reflected in the subsequent discussion that took place within the Cabinet's Defence Committee in early November on the seemingly inexorable rise in defence expenditure. Macmillan set the mood by asking whether in view of the gap that was opening between what could be afforded and what the services wanted, certain fundamental assumptions in defence policy should be reappraised. In particular, he wondered whether the loss by the United States of its overwhelming nuclear superiority created a new strategic equation. The decision to develop an independent deterrent had been intended to gain prestige and win influence over the United States, and also with the Commonwealth and Western Europe; Macmillan saw this decision as being vindicated by events, shown in particular by the new intimacy that had been established with the Eisenhower administration over nuclear matters in the course of the year. But now that the condition of nuclear sufficiency was within sight, with the Soviet Union possessing a powerful nuclear force of her own, it remained for consideration 'whether we still needed to take into account the possibility of having to use the nuclear deterrent independently of the United States, or to bring pressure to bear on them when our interests were threatened.'

The Chancellor of the Exchequer contributed to the discussion with his warnings that the rise in defence spending would remove any room for reducing taxation levels, and that major policy changes in the defence field were needed to reverse the upward trends that were predicted. One specific proposal he advanced was that Blue Streak development should be abandoned, even if this involved an end to an independent deterrent capability during the 1960s. Sandys reported to the Committee, however, that after long discussions with the service ministers and his military advisers, he found it difficult to come to any conclusions over what policy should be adopted in conditions of nuclear stalemate. All he could offer was his feeling that continuing with an independent deterrent was the right policy to follow, since giving up an independent capability and simply relying on the Americans could not be justified. Having digested the results of his talks with his US counterpart in September, Sandys now felt that Blue Streak development should continue, mentioning that American information would allow 'important improvements' to be made to the missile (this was probably an allusion to information under the MDA allowing a lighter warhead to be produced, the weight saving giving more scope for an extensive package of penetration aids to be included in the payload).

Subsequent discussion ranged over several aspects of the problem, including the continuing merits of the bomber, the likelihood that Blue Streak costs would increase, the relative gains from switching to a Thor purchase and working on a second generation IRBM, and the advantages of Polaris in terms of mobility if it could be based on British ships or submarines (though it was agreed that any decisions about Polaris would be premature at this stage). The Minister of Defence was also determined to defend the commitment made by the Defence Committee in 1957 to build up to a force of 144 V-bombers, as any attempt to reduce this total to only 104 aircraft as a way to find economies would make relatively little saving, yet lower the damage capability of the force from 40 targets to 23. If pressed to make savings,

Sandys would cut the defence of the deterrent, meaning the fighter aircraft and surface-to-air guided weapons that were allocated for the defence of the V-bomber bases.[87]

It was indicative of the procrastination that featured in so many aspects of defence equipment policy during this period that the meeting reached no definite conclusions. Summing up at several points, Macmillan had merely noted when dealing with the issue of the proper balance in the defence budget, that there was agreement that conventional forces would not be reduced below their current levels and that they should be fully and properly equipped. Regarding the future of Blue Streak he was prepared to defer any irrevocable decisions until further work on the options had been carried out.[88]

Just under two weeks later Sandys returned to the Committee with a paper which rehearsed once again the arguments for why he felt cancellation of Blue Streak would be premature. Blue Streak was described as 'advanced as anything that can be designed with present techniques to meet our operational requirements of range and carrying capacity.' Moreover, improvements to the missile would be possible over the next few years, with the introduction of a lighter warhead, the incorporation of 'devices to counter anti-missile missiles', and the possibility of using new forms of 'storable' liquid fuel. (No mention, it should be noted, was made about the obvious criticism that Blue Streak was vulnerable to pre-emptive attack.) The option of a Thor purchase was seen as having 'serious disadvantages', including a short predicted service life, deficiencies over range and payload which meant that there would be no potential to carry penetration aids, and vulnerability to attack if sited above ground.

Cancelling Blue Streak would leave the UK, it was alleged, in the position of buying an unsatisfactory short-term stop-gap in the form of Thor, and then having to acquire (or even develop) a wholly new second generation IRBM, for which the Americans had already signalled they had no operational requirement. Only two major technical advances in land-based missiles were then seen as in sight: storable liquid fuels, or long-range solid-fuel missiles. Blue Streak could be readily adapted for storable liquid fuel, but the prospects for solid propellants being developed which could offer the same energy, capacity or reliability as liquid did not seem promising. Pinning hopes on a solid-fuel second generation IRBM did not, therefore, appear to be a prudent course, while a new missile project would entail fresh expenditure at least as heavy as for Blue Streak.

A Polaris option had been considered, the Minister of Defence informed his colleagues, and would certainly offer certain 'theoretical advantages' over a land-based missile system:

a   It is fully mobile.
b   It needs no defensive system to protect it.
c   While the enemy might endeavour to shadow the rocket launching

submarines, his information would not be sufficiently accurate and up-to-date to give him confidence that he could immediately locate them and knock them out.

d   The comparative invulnerability of the deterrent gives more time for the taking of political decisions.
e   Once the retaliatory rocket bases were removed out to sea, the Russians would have little to gain by making a surprise attack upon the British Isles.
f   The complete flexibility of the nuclear submarine would enable the pressure of the British nuclear deterrent to be applied in any part of the world.

Given this impressive list, it was hardly surprising that Sandys' paper was forced to concede that if ballistic missile submarines could be developed it was 'quite conceivable' that Britain might decide that this was the best way to make her 'limited contribution' to the Western deterrent: 'In that case, the right course would be to adopt the finished American designs and to buy from the United States as much of the equipment as we could not economically make under licence here.'

However, Polaris was still at an early stage in its conception, its costs were very uncertain, and since each missile warhead would be only half as powerful as Thor's, a far larger number of the former would be needed to achieve the same results (Sandys estimating the requirement at eight submarines with 16 missiles each). As there was no certainty that the Polaris project 'with its immense technical complications' would be brought to successful conclusion, the Minister of Defence did not see how it was then possible to opt for Polaris over Blue Streak. Since putting a temporary halt to Blue Streak in order to see how Polaris progressed was not a practical proposition, all that Sandys was left to recommend was to carry on Blue Streak development while continuing to monitor how Polaris fared.[89]

Just for good measure, the Committee was also presented with a paper which defended the current numbers of V-bombers from any effort at further reductions, the Air Ministry arguing that such a cutback

> would not enable us to maintain our special relationship with the United States or our influence in world affairs. Nor would it enable us to use our independent nuclear power if the Americans were tempted to stand aside in a situation in which their interests were less immediately threatened than our own. Both they and the Russians would have reason to believe that if the Russians threatened nuclear attack we would be bound to yield for lack of means of retaliation.[90]

There was, in other words, no substantive concession offered by the MoD to demands for economy when it came to the programme which underpinned the provision of the strategic nuclear deterrent.

With defence expenditure set to run at over £1,500 million per annum for the next few years, and the ambitious weapons development programmes of the services threatening to break the ceilings that he had tried to establish, the Chancellor of the Exchequer was not impressed with the case for Blue Streak. Finding Sandys far too relaxed over the trends shown by the defence programme, Heathcoat Amory noted for the benefit of his Defence Committee colleagues that, 'All experience seems to show … that:

a   the cost of development, and indeed production, of new weapons is apt to be greatly in excess of the original, or even later, estimates.
b   New requirements will arise, and new discoveries [be] made, which the Services will seek to satisfy. Indeed, some new requirements have been put forward or have come up for examination within the last few weeks alone.

Heathcoat Amory thought that it would be wise to avoid any further commitments on Blue Streak spending while the Polaris possibilities were looked at more closely; in the meantime the V-bomber force and Thor would be sufficient to meet the needs of deterrence. The Chancellor also again tried to question the current planned size of the V-force, wondering whether the Air Staff's estimate that it could successfully attack 30 to 40 Soviet cities out of 131 major centres of industry or population was actually the correct measure, when the aim of the deterrent was more to secure the cooperation of the United States for which a different gauge would be more appropriate.[91]

Along with the Chancellor, the Cabinet Secretary continued to be anxious over the rising costs of the deterrent. For the longer term Brook was attracted by the advantages of Polaris rather than continuing with Blue Streak development. 'Plainly, it would be wasteful to commit ourselves to the Blue Streak project if the sea-based alternative is going to be realisable before the date on which our V-Bomber Force ceases to be an effective means of delivery,' he advised Macmillan before the next meeting of the Defence Committee. 'Can we not postpone committing ourselves finally for a year or two,' he wondered, 'and so gain room for manoeuvre? … The manned bomber may well prove to have a longer life than the Minister of Defence now thinks. And the sea-based deterrent may have a more important role to play. In these circumstances we ought not to put all our eggs into the Blue Streak basket.'[92]

In the Defence Committee itself, Sandys once more made the case that neither Polaris – a system not yet fully proved or whose costs could be predicted – or a possible manned supersonic bomber to replace the V-force would be available in time to fill the gap when the effective life of the current V-force came to an end. Blue Streak, however, would be ready for deployment at the right time and was capable of much further development than Thor, including having the ability to carry penetration aids. Carrying on with Blue Streak development, moreover, did not mean that the option to pursue Polaris could not be followed at some later stage. The Prime Minister nevertheless, continued to express a degree of scepticism over whether to persist with Blue Streak, especially in view of the need for economies to be found.[93]

Yet by the end of December, Sandys had managed to coax sufficient further savings from the services in other areas of the defence budget to stave off immediate calls for Blue Streak cancellation. One of the measures adopted included stretching out the missile's development programme so that it might be ready for operational deployment only in 1967 at the earliest (even though this undermined the Minister of Defence's earlier contention that Blue Streak would be available to fill any perceived gap in the effectiveness of the V-force from about 1965 onwards). Considering the position that had been reached, and almost with a collective sigh of relief, ministers on the Defence Committee agreed that it would be 'unwise' to abandon Blue Streak development until 'further consideration had been given to the form which our deterrent should take from the late 1960s onwards.' Macmillan reflected that 'in reaching this decision ... the Committee faced a choice between taking drastic decisions of policy, particularly on the deterrent, and deferring such decisions for a further period provided that defence expenditure was reduced to a tolerable level by other measures, however unwelcome they might be in certain cases.'[94]

The failure of ministers during 1958 to settle the arguments over Blue Streak's future has been roundly criticised by several observers. Aside from its growing costs, by then the missile was widely recognised as being vulnerable to pre-emptive attack making it of dubious utility for retaliatory purposes. This left it as a 'fire first' weapon, which if it was to be used would have to be unleashed once the Soviet Union was embarked upon a major aggression with conventional forces, before a nuclear attack had been absorbed. But merely to state this premise was to make it seem inconceivable, since such an act would trigger overwhelming retaliatory destruction from the Soviet nuclear forces that would be deployed from the mid-1960s onwards, when Blue Streak was planned for introduction. Inter-service bickering was one reason that the issue was not faced squarely, with the Air Ministry proving a strong advocate for Blue Streak against the calls from the Admiralty for more emphasis to be given to the conventional aspects of the defence budget. Another was that the provision of US information under the MDA after the summer of 1958, which offered AWRE the chance to make a lighter high-yield warhead for Blue Streak, so allowing range to be preserved and weight saving for a package of penetration aids.

A more fundamental political problem was that if the government were to abandon Blue Streak in 1958 there was no discernable alternative that could readily take its place that could be construed as maintaining an 'independent' strategic nuclear capability during the decade that was to follow. Provision of Thor 'without strings' could not be assured (notwithstanding the ostensible outcome of the talks between Sandys and the US Secretary of Defense in September 1958), and it was known the US administration was keen to link the supply of IRBMs to Europe with schemes to place them under SACEUR's control, rather than leave them in national hands (this, after all, had been one of the initial sticking points in negotiating the Thor Agreement in February 1958). In addition, the longevity of Thor was questionable as the Americans were now thinking it would be withdrawn from service by the late 1960s (with no plans for a second generation system), and as a liquid-fuelled land-based missile it suffered from the same drawbacks of vulnerability and slow preparation time as Blue Streak. Another option was Polaris, but the missile was still at the early stages of its development, the Admiralty was ambivalent about the US programme, despite Mountbatten's obvious interest, and its estimated range (at least in its initial form) fell short of the UK requirement.

The government's entire declaratory nuclear policy was built on maintaining a substantial nuclear contribution to the overall Western deterrent, and in domestic political terms the preservation of an independent deterrent was becoming an important lodestar of Conservative Party politics. The Labour Party leadership, for its part, had to contend increasingly with a growing anti-nuclear activism at the party's grass roots, fuelled by the rise of the Campaign for Nuclear Disarmament to national prominence during 1958, and widespread concerns over the effects of nuclear testing. With a general election likely during 1959, there was no incentive for Macmillan or his senior colleagues in the Conservative Party to open up a politically damaging debate over the future of the nuclear deterrent, especially when electoral capital might be drawn from the issue.

One final aspect worthy of mention is the international context of the Cold War. On 10 November 1958, just as the Defence Committee was in the middle of its debates over the future of the deterrent, Khrushchev issued the first of several belligerent statements over the Berlin question, which demanded the Western allies 'demilitarise' their zones in the city, threatened to repudiate the occupation statutes which had underpinned the existence of a Western enclave in the middle of East Germany, and to hand over control of West Berlin access routes to the East German Communist government. This was followed by a call from Moscow for international negotiations to settle the ambiguous status of West Berlin with a six months deadline attached. The subsequent crisis saw East-West tensions rise to fresh heights, as the Western powers considered what military options might be open to them if ground access to West Berlin was denied. With such ominous rumblings in the background – Macmillan going to the lengths of arranging a controversial visit to Moscow in February 1959 in a bid to defuse the atmosphere – it may well have seemed an injudicious time to take decisions which would cast doubt on the credibility of the UK strategic nuclear force.

An impossible to foresee but significant consequence of the debates over the future of Blue Streak in 1958 was that continuing with the programme obviated any need for research and development effort in the area of solid fuel missile propellant technology. If Thor had been adopted as a short-term substitute for Blue Streak it was on the premise that indigenous work on a second generation IRBM – in all probability with solid rather than liquid fuel as a propellant – would be initiated. Instead, UK knowledge of solid propellant technology would henceforth be confined to the relatively small and basic motors used in some surface-to-air and air-to-air guided weapons, rather than in the complex ballistic missile environment. A decade later, when independently-targetable multiple-warhead re-entry systems formed the cutting edge of strategic system design, and where solid-fuel propulsion techniques would be crucial to the dispensing mechanisms employed in the most advanced types of submarine-launched missiles, Britain would be faced with a dearth of domestic experience. This not only limited the choice of development route when embarking upon a Polaris improvement programme in the late 1960s, but caused major difficulties in the mid-1970s when liquid propellants were employed by the Chevaline system's designers to the consternation of Royal Navy submariners deeply concerned over safety.

Taking forward the MDA: opportunities and obligations

The initial meetings with the Americans after the conclusion of the MDA in the summer of 1958 had brought home to British officials a number of uncomfortable dilemmas. The ready provision of weapon design information would certainly meet the UK's requirements for different types of nuclear weapons in the future. The Americans, however, were going to continue with major research programmes across the entire field of weapons and it had to be decided how far the UK would be willing or able to make a contribution to future joint progress. There was, Plowden told the Prime Minister in late November, a 'moral obligation' to make such an effort alongside the Americans, but this would require continuing expenditure on research and development effort, with investment in extra facilities at Aldermaston totalling perhaps £10 million over the next three or four years.[95]

Early the following month, Macmillan met Plowden and Penney to review the progress that had been made in cooperation with the Americans under the MDA, and the implications for the future UK programme. Summarising the conversation, and offering his own further reflections on the issue, the Prime Minister noted that it was now possible to build-up a modern stock of megaton and kiloton weapons derived from US information, and that, in theory, reductions in UK research and development efforts over the coming years could be found by concentrating on the information that had been obtained and to cease to play an active part in more advanced work. However, this was an approach seen as

> full of uncertainties. Quite apart from the fact that we would run the risk of not having weapons which we may really need at some time in the

future (e.g. small–yield tactical weapons and very light weight strategic weapons) we might well fail to obtain an anti-missile defence, if one is ever developed.

The Americans were also likely to be critical if the British effort was seen to contract: 'We have already obtained great benefit from the policy of interdependence in the nuclear weapons field, largely on the understanding that we will continue to go along with them in further research in this field. If we were to fail in this moral obligation,' Macmillan said (in an echo of Plowden's remarks), 'we could not hope to maintain our special relationship with the United States nor the international position which we have won as the third nuclear power.' The Americans had understood that the UK research and development effort would become increasingly integrated with their own; this would give the UK 'a key position, and although the value of it cannot be quantified, past experience shows that it is well nigh essential for us.' In order to maintain the close nuclear relationship that had been established an active UK programme of research would therefore still be required, while nuclear collaboration was seen as underpinning a whole set of British aspirations to move closer to the United States across the entire area of defence policy.[96] Within the Prime Minister's circle of advisers, Bishop was sure that the recommendation to continue nuclear weapons research and development was correct, and informed Brook that this was also Macmillan's view.[97]

In retrospect the Prime Minister's meeting with Plowden and Penney in December 1958 seems crucial for the long-term future of the UK nuclear programme. Even though a great deal of nuclear information began to flow to the UK through the effective operation of the 1958 MDA, this did not necessarily mean that Britain's own efforts to maintain a programme of advanced weapons research and development could be curtailed. Contrary to some expectations, therefore, the arrival of 'interdependence' in the Anglo-American nuclear relationship did not bring wholesale economies at AWRE or in nuclear weapons development more generally.

An active UK programme would be required to sustain the relationship by providing topics, knowledge and practical results for a profitable exchange to take place for both sides while access to US designs and information would open up new streams of research and development activity that would prompt fresh warhead and other related work (including, for example, on safety) and carry through well into the next decade. There is no telling what the rate of expenditure on UK deterrent capabilities would have been without access to US information transferred under the MDA and the subsequent patterns of Anglo–American nuclear cooperation, although extrapolation from the later French experience would suggest spending would have absorbed a much larger proportion of the defence budget (perhaps as much as 30 per cent). However, considering the other demands on defence spending, and Britain's worldwide political and military commitments in the late 1950s and 1960s, there is every reason to believe that without the MDA there would have been stronger calls for a major reconsideration of spending priorities and the possibility that some aspects of nuclear capability would have been discarded or sharply diminished. At the same time, a certain irony attaches to the position that had now been reached. Britain's post-war nuclear programme had often been sustained by the argument that it was necessary in order to restore a close Anglo-American nuclear relationship, but the restoration of collaboration in 1958 itself gave an impetus to a programme that might otherwise have been at greater risk from the Treasury's critical gaze.

On 1 January 1959 the Prime Minister, with just Sandys and Heathcoat Amory in attendance on the ministerial side, but a cast of officials which included Brook, Powell, Dean, Brundrett, Plowden, Makins, Strath and Penney, met to confirm policy regarding the future programme of nuclear research and development. As well as agreeing to approach the Americans for the supply of uranium 235 and 'special nuclear materials' (a reference to tritium and lithium 6, both necessary in the designs of more advanced high-yield warheads, but only available in small amounts in the UK), the meeting heard from Plowden that with the information received under the MDA it would be possible to achieve economies in the nuclear R & D field and to focus on building up a stock of weapons of the latest design. But, he continued, this minimalist approach ran the risk of falling behind in certain areas of weapons technology, while a reduction in research and development at AWRE would incur criticism from the Americans, who expected the UK to play its part in the new exchange arrangements. 'If we did not do so,' he warned, 'it would be impossible to maintain our special relationship with [the Americans] in respect of nuclear weapons and other related defence matters, e.g. rockets.' The assembled ministers agreed that Aldermaston should continue to engage in advanced work in the weapons field.[98]

As a result, during Penney's final months at Aldermaston's helm in the first part of 1959, staff requirements increased as attempts were made to take full advantage of the extra information that was now available from the United States.[99] In February, the Prime Minister, with the agreement of Sandys, resolved to go ahead with an approach to the Americans for nuclear materials so that the MoD's future nuclear needs could be fulfilled; at the same time he authorised that preliminary work toward the construction of a new diffusion plant for the production of uranium 235 (to be co-located with the original diffusion plant at Capenhurst) should begin. When completed in 1966 it was expected that the new plant, when combined with supplies from the US, would be able to meet all the UK's needs for the nuclear weapons programme.[100]

By May 1959 it proved possible to reach final agreement with the Americans over an important amendment to the MDA which involved the bartering of US-produced uranium 235 and tritium for UK plutonium, saving Britain considerable expense and time. The extra clauses also provided for the sale to the UK of the non-nuclear components of atomic weapons, which although little noticed, was a crucial form of US assistance to the UK programme when it came to the engineering and 'weaponisation' of particular warhead designs and their delivery systems.[101] In the event, later reductions in the scale of the weapons programme, along with the re-use of fissile material from dismantled older weapons and supplies of uranium 235 from the United States, meant that additional UK capacity was not required to meet UK needs. In fact, after a period of gradual rundown, in 1964 it was announced by the government that all production of uranium 235 for military purposes at the Capenhurst plant had been brought to an end the previous year.[102]

Meanwhile, the collaborative arrangements that were to become such a central feature of the operation of the MDA began to be firmly established. During the first of what was to become a regular series of 'stocktake' meetings, held in London in April 1959, senior personnel at the UK and US weapons laboratories met to review the operation of the MDA. It was decided here to adopt an earlier American suggestion and to form joint study or working groups (JOWOGs) across a whole range of subjects of mutual interest. Specific ideas and findings could be exchanged in this special forum, and a division of labour for future topics agreed. Fifteen areas were identified for the first set of JOWOGs, but eventually, by the mid-1960s, over 25 different groups had been established, covering such fields as neutron sources, high explosives, implosion mechanisms, materials, non-nuclear components, warhead hardening, and nuclear test detection. Creation of the JOWOGs, chaired by either an American or Briton, and with members drawn from the different national weapons laboratories, served to embed close collaboration under the MDA. Not all of the JOWOGs were active at any one time, and several of the original groups were eventually allowed to lapse as business was either concluded or merged into others. The flexibility of exchange arrangements under the MDA was one of its enduring strengths, and collaboration between the weapons laboratories was also fostered by dozens of visits and ad hoc smaller-scale exchanges. Throughout this formative period relations between British and US officials were warm and amicable, the Americans being generous with their sharing of knowledge and experience and appreciative of British expertise.[103]

Though British nuclear scientists had already designed and helped produce two service-standard nuclear weapons in the kiloton range (first Blue Danube, and then the smaller and lighter Red Beard), and understood the principles behind (and tested) advanced thermonuclear techniques, the nuclear bilateral gave them access to fully-engineered designs of a whole range of new megaton and kiloton yield weapons. Straightforward copying of American warhead designs, however, proved far more complex and problematic than had first been anticipated. Many of the materials, components, and processes used in the assembly of weapons were unique to the United States, and could not easily be replicated. But even more fundamentally, British safety standards and requirements, particularly in the field of conventional explosives, meant that exact copies could not be used. Instead US warhead designs were to be 'Anglicised', or in other words adapted to meet British specifications and production capabilities. Probably the most important gain conferred by access to US information was that it allowed significant economies to be made in the use of fissile material in UK warhead designs.[104]

A further, and as we have seen, anticipated benefit of the MDA experienced at a political level by the Macmillan Government was that with proven US warhead designs now available for adaptation for UK use, the immediate need for further UK atmospheric nuclear testing was removed. This became a point of considerable importance when both the US and Soviet Union began a testing moratorium in October 1958 and entered talks at Geneva aimed at reaching a test ban agreement, since British officials could now press for a joint accord knowing their own requirements had already been met. Indeed, in July 1959 ministers were to decide to suspend all further planning for UK tests whether in the atmosphere, underwater, or underground.[105]

The MDA also gave British defence scientists reason to believe that UK ABM development might also be possible, and contributed to the requirement for warheads for ballistic missile defence included in the MoD's future programme assembled during 1958. Considering the scepticism that was permeating the whole discussion about the possibilities of mounting an effective ballistic missile defence it seems remarkable in retrospect that the MoD was still making substantial provision for such ABM warheads. Brundrett, for example, although admitting in October 1958 to the 'gravest doubts' about 'whether any reasonable approach to an anti-missile defence – for this country anyway – will emerge in less than ten years from today' was still convinced that it was 'scientifically feasible'. A minimum of 300 warheads for ABMs would be required, he felt, to meet British needs, and he 'could not possibly advise against taking a decision which would prevent us deploying a defence against the ballistic missile.'[106]

The Sputnik era saw ideas about Western nuclear strategy enter a period of extended flux. The belief that the Soviet Union would soon be in a position to strike the continental United States with high-yield nuclear weapons heightened the sense of American strategic vulnerability and led to sudden scares such as that over the development of a 'missile gap' in the late 1950s (a gap which later proved to have been imaginary). Along with the advent of long-range intercontinental ballistic missiles, advanced and accurate guidance systems, and miniaturised nuclear warheads, emerged a whole new field of strategic studies and deterrence theory, where calculations of the potential results of a nuclear exchange became critical to evaluating the stability of what the American strategist Albert Wohlstetter called in January 1959 'the delicate balance of terror'.[107]

Khrushchev's propensity to brandish Soviet technological advances in the military field, and his willingness to pressure the West over Berlin after 1958, added to the feeling that US threats of 'massive retaliation' rang hollow when facing limited incursions or minor conflicts where it was Soviet nuclear strength which could act to deter a forceful Western response. Even if American presidents were privately resolved that, at a moment of crisis, they actually would be prepared to use nuclear weapons in the defence of Western Europe, the simple *perception* that there might be any element of uncertainty or hesitation over this basic question – especially in the minds of the Soviet leadership – was enough to introduce tensions into inter-Alliance relationships. The plethora of academic commentary and publications by strategic theorists which dwelt on this problem added to such concerns, as did the increasing volume of discussion in the United States which examined the subject of how a nuclear exchange begun as a result of Soviet aggression in Europe could remain limited in scope (and that such limitation, where US and Soviet cities were spared devastation, was thought a naturally desirable end).[108]

The nuclear sufficiency debate witnessed amongst the Chiefs of Staff during 1958 had touched on many of these contemporary concerns and anxieties. It seemed a misapplication of scarce resources if the priority of defence policy was to build and maintain a strategic nuclear deterrent force becoming less relevant to the threats of lower-level conflicts and limited wars in a coming era of strategic parity. Better, in this view, to invest in the conventional forces that could actually bolster the credibility of the deterrent, be used to fulfil Britain's global military commitments, and if aggression should occur in Europe provide the potential means to avert an immediate resort to nuclear weapons and a consequent devastating cycle of escalation. Yet from the viewpoint of the Foreign Office, for example, studies of nuclear sufficiency could only go so far, such were the imponderables of the reactions of the United States and Soviet Union to any decision over whether to use nuclear weapons. Given the task of peering into the future, Sir Patrick Dean's visceral opinion was that the mere possession of nuclear weapons, at least in the European context, would deter any form of aggression, and that concerns over the changing nuclear balance between the Superpowers were overrated. As regards Soviet attitudes, Dean informed Mountbatten in October 1958 of his belief that, 'Unless their situation had become desperate (e.g. the imminent collapse of their Satellite empire) I doubt if they would take the risk of testing out whether or not the US would retaliate with nuclear weapons in the event of conventional aggression. Moreover, the increasing deployment of tactical nuclear weapons in forward areas [in Central Europe] should increase the efficacy of the deterrent even though the concept of massive retaliation may have lessened in credibility.'[109]

Although they had resulted in no discernible and major change of policy direction, the debates over the future nuclear programme, Blue Streak, and nuclear sufficiency had generated new perspectives on the role of an independent UK strategic nuclear force that were to influence subsequent studies of its size and purpose. The conception of a force able to deter the Soviet

Union in isolation, as the Air Ministry's plans for the V-force implied, was increasingly seen as unrealistic. Britain's national nuclear planning was explicitly retaliatory in nature, suggesting to many that its nuclear forces would be released only once a Soviet nuclear attack had been delivered. In October 1958, the CAS felt in a position to inform Sandys that the current approved numbers for the V-bomber force were the 'minimum which would be expected to inflict enough damage on Russia to have any chance of deterring her from launching the nuclear offensive under circumstances in which she calculated that the United States would not retaliate.'[110]

But was it really credible to believe (and that the Soviet leadership would share such a belief) that the United States would stand aloof from such a war? Even in the lesser case of a Soviet aggression in Central Europe where US strategic nuclear forces remained uncommitted and NATO faced defeat at a conventional (or perhaps theatre nuclear) level, how would or could the UK strategic force be employed in a credible fashion? In that case the role of the UK deterrent had to be seen more in political terms of inter-Alliance relationships, its use in influencing US policy, and in terms of global prestige and influence. But how was it possible to estimate the size and capability of a force that could play such a political role? Many of these issues were swirling around the political and military firmament in the late 1950s as increasing numbers of V-bombers equipped with nuclear weapons began to enter service, but it was when the government turned to considering the long-term future of a deterrent force, and the issue of possible successor systems, that they were to be the subject of intensive and contentious study, as the next chapter will show.

Notes

1 The incident is covered in revealing fashion in Alexander Fursenko and Timothy Naftali, *Khrushchev's Cold War* (New York, 2006), 132–7, and Taubman, *Khrushchev*, 359–60.
2 See David Holloway, 'Soviet Thermonuclear Development,' *International Security*, Winter 1979/80, 4, 3, 192–7; Holloway, *Soviet Union and the Arms Race*, 66.
3 See Freedman, *US Intelligence and the Soviet Strategic Threat*, 67–80.
4 For the Bermuda meeting see Clark, *Nuclear Diplomacy*, 38–45. Tentative ideas for an IRBM deployment to the UK had, in fact, already been mooted when Sandys met the US Secretary of Defense in late January 1957.
5 Arnold, *Britain and the H-Bomb*, 144–5, 222.
6 See Watkinson minute for Macmillan, MO 18/4, 13 February 1961; Brook minute for Bligh, 20 February 1961, PREM 11/3583.
7 See Clark, *Nuclear Diplomacy*, 55–62; for the general background on Anglo-American nuclear relations across this period see Timothy Botti, *The Long Wait: The Forging of the Anglo-American Nuclear Alliance, 1945–1958* (New York, 1984), and Jan Melissen, *The Struggle for Nuclear Partnership: Britain, the United States, and the Making of an Ambiguous Partnership, 1952–1959* (Gronigen, 1993).
8 Washington telegram No 2017 to Foreign Office, 7 October 1957, PREM 11/2554; Macmillan to Eisenhower, T/450/57, 10 October 1957, PREM

11/2329; and see Harold Macmillan, *Riding the Storm, 1956–1959* (London, 1971), 314–7.
9 See ibid, 320–4; and Macmillan diary entry, 24 October 1957, MSS Macmillan dep. d.30, Bodleian Library, Oxford.
10 For the immediate background see Clark, *Nuclear Diplomacy*, 78–86; John Baylis, 'Exchanging Nuclear Secrets: Laying the Foundations of the Anglo-American Nuclear Relationship,' *Diplomatic History*, 25, 1, Winter 2001, 33–61; Baylis, 'The 1958 Anglo-American Mutual Defence Agreement: The Search for Nuclear Interdependence,' *Journal of Strategic Studies*, 31, 3, 2008, 425–66.
11 For the records of the Washington Conference, see PM(W)(57)1st Meeting, 23 October 1959; PM(W)2nd Meeting, 24 October 1957, PREM 11/2329; and see also Macmillan's report to the Cabinet, C(57)271, 'Anglo-American Co-operation,' note by the Prime Minister, 15 November 1957, CAB 129/90.
12 Confidential Annex to COS(57)84th Meeting, item 3, 29 October 1957, DEFE 4/101.
13 Arnold, *Britain and the H-Bomb*, 152, 199.
14 See Foreign Office telegram No 4722 to Washington, 8 November 1957; Washington telegram No 2578 to Foreign Office, 6 December 1957, PREM 11/2554; also Baylis, 'Exchanging,' 45.
15 Ibid, 46–7.
16 For the background see David N. Schwartz, *NATO's Nuclear Dilemmas* (Washington, 1983), 62–81; Watson, *Into the Missile Age*, 506–19; Trachtenberg, *Constructed Peace*, 177–200.
17 D(57)6th Meeting, item 3, 31 July 1957, CAB 131/18.
18 See COS(57)86th Meeting, item 4, 12 November 1957, DEFE 4/101; JIC(57)120(Final)(Revise), 'The Effect on Soviet Policy of the Attainment by the USSR of Nuclear Sufficiency,' report by the Joint Intelligence Committee, 21 January 1958, CAB 158/30. The final version of the report was generated in January 1958, but an initial version was in circulation by the end of 1957. See also COS(58)6th Meeting, item 1, 17 January 1958, DEFE 4/103.
19 JP(57)151(Final), 'The Effect of Nuclear Sufficiency,' report by the Joint Planning Staff, 27 January 1958, DEFE 6/44.
20 COS(58)39, 'The Effects of Nuclear Sufficiency,' note by the Chief of the Imperial General Staff, 13 February 1958, DEFE 5/82.
21 Confidential Annex to COS(58)16th Meeting, item 2, 18 February 1958, DEFE 4/104.
22 Mountbatten minute for Dickson, 'Nuclear Sufficiency,' 19 February 1958, AIR 8/1942.
23 Cmnd 363, *Report on Defence: Britain's Contribution to Peace and Security*, paragraphs 1–13, February 1958. For NATO's military posture see Buteux, *Politics of Nuclear Consultation in NATO*, 2, and also Trachtenberg, *A Constructed Peace*, 188–89, who interprets MC 14/2 – with its new stress on conventional 'shield' forces able to hold up a Soviet ground offensive for several days – as a move away from the 'pure' massive retaliation strategy adopted by the Alliance in 1954. For this view, see also Beatrice Heuser, *NATO, Britain, France and the FRG: Nuclear Strategies and Forces for Europe, 1949–2000* (Basingstoke, 1998), 38–41.
24 *Britain's Contribution to Peace and Security*, paragraphs 28–31.
25 Ibid, paragraphs 38–9.
26 See Freedman, *Evolution of Nuclear Strategy*, 112–3, and John Baylis, 'Anthony Buzzard,' in Baylis and Garnett, *Makers of Nuclear Strategy*, 136–52.
27 See *Hansard*, HC, vol 583, cols 554–681, 27 February 1958; see also Andrew Pierre, *Nuclear Politics: The British Experience with an Independent Strategic Force, 1939–1970* (London, 1972), 163–6.

28 See French, *Army, Empire and Cold War*, 162–4.
29 Dickson minute for Sandys, WFD/M/289, 20 February 1958, DEFE 24/11.
30 Brook minute, 'Record of the final session of the Annual Conference of the Commissioner-General, South East Asia, held at Eden Hall at 9.30am on 19th January 1958,' 20 January 1958, D1051/4G, FO 371/135632.
31 'Prime Minister on need for Hydrogen Bomb,' *The Times*, 24 February 1958.
32 Bishop letter to Plowden, with attached draft directives, 19 March 1958; Plowden letter to Bishop, 20 March 1958; Macmillan minute for Sandys, 'Nuclear Armaments,' M.73/58, 21 March 1958, PREM 11/2275.
33 See Brundrett minute for Sandys, FB/183/58, 31 March 1958, with attached Brundrett memorandum, 'Nuclear Armaments,' FB/182/58, n.d.; Bishop letter to Gibbon, 28 April 1958, PREM 11/2275.
34 D. E. Locke minute, 'Cost of Nuclear Weapons,' 30 April 1958, DEFE 7/2332.
35 See Bishop minute for Brook, 20 May 1958, PREM 11/2275.
36 See R. C. Chilver minute for Sandys, 9 June 1958, DEFE 13/193.
37 'Nuclear Armaments,' memorandum by the Minister of Defence, 22 May 1958, PREM 11/2275. An advance copy was actually sent by Sandys to Macmillan on 16 May; copies of the final revised version, dated 22 May, were also sent to the Foreign Secretary, Chancellor of the Exchequer, and Lord Privy Seal.
38 See D(57)14, 'Fissile Material for Nuclear Weapons,' note by the Secretary of the Cabinet, 27 July 1957, CAB 131/18.
39 Bishop minute for Macmillan, 'Nuclear Weapons,' 21 May 1958, PREM 11/2275.
40 See Brook note for Macmillan, 4 June 1958, and attached paper, 'Nuclear Armaments: Some points for Ministerial Consideration,' 3 June 1958, PREM 11/2275.
41 Strath letter to Bishop, 3 June 1958, PREM 11/2275. By 1960, when Strath was Permanent Secretary at the Ministry of Aviation, his views on Blue Streak cancellation had shifted quite dramatically, see Moore, *Nuclear Illusion, Nuclear Reality*, 50.
42 'Note of a meeting at No 10 Downing Street at 10.15am, Tuesday, March 4, 1958,' DEFE 13/150.
43 See Bishop note, 5 June 1958, PREM 11/2275; and Bligh 'Note for Record,' 12 June 1958, Annex to file 59 Part 4, miscellaneous Cabinet Office papers.
44 See John R. Walker, *British Nuclear Weapons and the Test Ban, 1954–1973* (London, 2010), 57–72.
45 Macmillan telegram for Eisenhower, T/194/58, 29 May 1958, PREM 11/2554.
46 See, for example, Dean letter to Hoyer-Millar, 10 June 1958, ZP23/46G, FO 371/135636.
47 See Simpson, *Independent Nuclear State*, 129–41.
48 Plowden minute for Macmillan, CH(58)73, 18 June 1958, PREM 11/2554.
49 Cmnd 537, *Agreement between the Government of the United Kingdom and Northern Ireland and the Government of the United States of America for cooperation in the Uses of Atomic Energy for Mutual Defence Purposes*, July 1958; and Baylis, 'Exchanging Nuclear Secrets,' 47–9.
50 See Wilfrid L. Kohl, *French Nuclear Diplomacy* (Princeton, 1971), 51.
51 Arnold, *Britain and H-Bomb*, 203–10.
52 See Macmillan, *Riding the Storm*, 565–6.
53 Arnold, *Britain and the H-Bomb*, 209–10.
54 See Mountbatten letter to Dean, 20 May 1958; Dean letter to Mountbatten, 27 May 1958, PUSD records, FCO.
55 Dean letter to Vice Admiral Sir Caspar John, Vice Chief of Naval Staff, 11 July 1958, DEFE 24/11.
56 See SC(58)34 (Revise), 'Nuclear Sufficiency,' 14 August 1958, in DEFE 24/11.

57 Confidential Annex to COS(58)47th Meeting, item 7, 3 June 1958, DEFE 32/6.
58 See JP(58)86(Final), 'The Effect of Nuclear Sufficiency on the Strategy of the United Kingdom and the West,' report by the Directors of Plans, 8 July 1958, AIR 8/1942.
59 Selkirk minute for Sandys, 'Nuclear Sufficiency,' 17 July 1958, DEFE 7/2300.
60 Ward minute for Sandys, 'Nuclear Sufficiency,' 29 July 1958, DEFE 7/2300.
61 See Brook minute for Bishop, 1 July 1958, and attached draft paper, 'Defence Policy: Nuclear Weapons,' PREM 11/2275.
62 DB(58)4, 'Defence Expenditure,' 25 July 1958, copy of a minute of 7 July 1958 from Heathcoat Amory for Macmillan, DEFE 30/1.
63 DB(58)3, 'Defence Expenditure,' 24 July 1958, copy of a minute of 9 July 1958 from Sandys for Macmillan, DEFE 30/1.
64 D(58)33, 'Nuclear Weapons,' memorandum by the Prime Minister, 17 July 1958, CAB 131/20.
65 D(58)15th Meeting, 25 July 1958, CAB 131/19.
66 Brook minute for Macmillan, 29 July 1958, and attached memorandum, 'Nuclear Programme: D(58)32 and 33, Note of Points still to be discussed,' PREM 11/2275.
67 Brundrett letter to Bishop, FB/361/58, 25 July 1958, PREM 11/2275.
68 See MOM/29, Meeting of Minister of Defence with Minister of Supply on April 11th 1958, DEFE 13/193.
69 Sandys minute for Heathcoat Amory, 14 July 1958, DEFE 13/193.
70 Cook letter to Sandys, 15 July 1958, DEFE 13/193.
71 See DB/C(58) 1st Conclusions, 31 July 1958, DEFE 30/3.
72 D(58)16th Meeting, 1 August 1958, CAB 131/19.
73 Note for the record of informal meeting held on 18 August 1958 between Macmillan, Sir Edwin Plowden, Sir Norman Brook, and Frederick A. Bishop, 25 August 1958, PREM 11/2275.
74 Confidential Annex to COS(58)77th Meeting, item 1, 3 September 1958, DEFE 4/111.
75 Mountbatten minute for Dickson, 'Nuclear Sufficiency,' 12 September 1958, AIR 8/1942.
76 Memorandum by Mountbatten and Templer, 'Nuclear Sufficiency,' no date but c. 17 September 1958, DEFE 7/2300. As Templer was unwell during this period there are strong indications that the paper was primarily the work of the First Sea Lord and his staff.
77 Dickson minute for Sandys, 'Nuclear Sufficiency,' WFD/M/430, 18 September 1958, DEFE 7/2300.
78 See D(58)47, 'Ballistic Rockets,' memorandum by the Minister of Defence, 8 September 1958, CAB 131/20; D(58)18th Meeting, 10 September 1958, CAB 131/19.
79 'Defence Policy: record of a meeting held at 3pm on 10 September 1958,' 26 September 1958, CAB 21/3509.
80 Record of Meetings held at the Pentagon and State Department, Washington DC, September 22 to 25, 1958: Meeting on Wednesday, September 24 1958, DEFE 11/360; and see also 'Report on Visit to United States with the Minister of Defence – 21st September 1958 to 5th October 1958,' DEFE 24/11.
81 See DB(58)8, 'Ballistic Rockets,' memorandum by the Chief Scientist, Ministry of Defence, 14 October 1958, DEFE 30/1; DB/C(58) 2nd Conclusions, item 3, 16 October 1958, DEFE 30/3; Selkirk signal to Mountbatten, 171331Z, 17 October 1958, DEFE 24/11; DB/C(58) 3rd Conclusions, item 3, 20 October 1958, DEFE 30/3.
82 MOM/56, Meeting of the Minister of Defence with the Chiefs of Staff on Tuesday, October 28th 1958, DEFE 7/2300, and in DEFE 32/13. See also Zielger, *Mountbatten*, 561.

83 Dickson minute for Mountbatten, 'Nuclear Sufficiency,' WFD/526, 9 December 1958, AIR 8/1942.
84 See Festing letter to Dickson, CIGS/PA/29/34, 'Defence White Paper 1959,' 9 January 1959; Mountbatten memorandum for Secretary COS Committee, 'Defence White Paper – 1959: Nuclear Deterrent Section,' 9 January 1959; Hoyer Millar letter to Powell, 12 January 1959, DEFE 13/165.
85 See Defence Board minutes, DB(59)2nd Conclusions, item 3, 15 January 1959; DB(59)3rd Conclusions, item 3, 23 January 1959, DEFE 30/3.
86 Brook minute for Macmillan, 'Defence Committee,' 4 November 1958, and attached note, 'The Position of the United Kingdom in World Affairs,' PREM 11/2275, and in CAB 21/2972.
87 See D(58)57, 'Ballistic Rockets,' memorandum by the Minister of Defence, 3 November 1958; D(58)24th Meeting, items 1, 2 and 3, 5 November 1958, CAB 131/19.
88 Ibid.
89 D(58)63, 'Ballistic Rockets,' memorandum by the Minister of Defence, 16 November 1958, CAB 131/20.
90 D(58)62, 'Medium Bomber Force,' memorandum by the Minister of Defence, 14 November 1958, and Annex B, 'The V-Bomber Force,' note by the Air Staff, CAB 131/20.
91 D(58)69, 'Defence Expenditure,' memorandum by the Chancellor of the Exchequer, 17 November 1958, CAB 131/20.
92 Brook minute for Macmillan, 'Ballistic Rockets,' 18 November 1958, CAB 21/4438.
93 See D(58)26th Meeting, item 3, 18 November 1958, CAB 131/19.
94 D(58)31st Meeting, 22 December 1958, CAB 131/19. See also Moore, *Nuclear Illusion, Nuclear Reality*, 41–3, for coverage of the debates over Blue Streak cancellation in late 1958.
95 Plowden minute for Macmillan, 'Future Policy in the Field of Nuclear Weapons Research,' CH(58)116, 28 November 1958, PREM 11/2275.
96 See Bishop letter to Plowden, 9 December 1958, and attached draft minutes from Macmillan to Plowden; the latter recycled the essence of the meeting and his support for a policy of continuing collaboration with the Americans in advanced nuclear weapons work in Plowden minute for Macmillan, 'Future Policy in the Field of Nuclear Weapons Research,' CH(58)119, 11 December 1958, all in PREM 11/2275. See also Arnold, *Britain and H-Bomb*, 212–3.
97 Bishop minute for Brook, 12 December 1958, PREM 11/2275.
98 D(59)1, 'Record of a Meeting on Nuclear Materials,' note by the Secretary of the Cabinet, 2 January 1959, CAB 131/21.
99 See Arnold, *Britain and the H-Bomb*, 218–9.
100 D(59)7, 'Record of a Meeting on Nuclear Materials,' note by the Secretary of the Cabinet, 6 February 1959, CAB 131/21.
101 See Simpson, *Independent Nuclear State*, 147–51; and Moore, *Nuclear Illusion, Nuclear Reality*, 84–5, for precise details of the barter arrangements.
102 Simpson, *Independent Nuclear State*, 166.
103 Arnold, *Britain and the H-Bomb*, 214–6.
104 Ibid.
105 See Sandys minute for Macmillan, 'Future Plans for Nuclear Tests,' 23 June 1959, DEFE 13/150; D(59)23, 'Nuclear Tests Policy,' note by the Secretary of the Cabinet, 8 July 1959, covering 'record of a meeting held at 10 Downing Street on Tuesday 7th July 1959 at 12 noon,' CAB 131/22; Macmillan minute for Sandys, 'Future Plans for Nuclear Tests,' M.251/59, 9 July 1959, DEFE 13/150.
106 Brundrett letter to Plowden, FB/446/58, 16 October 1958, PREM 11/2275.

107 See Albert Wohlstetter, 'The Delicate Balance of Terror,' *Foreign Affairs*, 37, 2, January 1959, 211–34.
108 For a contemporary statement of this kind of thinking see Henry Kissinger, *Nuclear Weapons and Foreign Policy* (New York, 1957).
109 Dean letter to Mountbatten, 9 October 1958, PUSD records, FCO.
110 MOM/56, 'Meeting of the Minister of Defence with the Chiefs of Staff, on Tuesday, October 28th, 1958,' DEFE 32/13.

4 Breaking the impasse?
Polaris and future deterrent policy, February 1959–March 1960

The formation of the British Nuclear Deterrent Study Group

The protracted debates over the fate of Blue Streak during 1958 had merely resulted in a decision by the Defence Committee at the end of the year to slow its rate of development, so reducing immediate levels of expenditure, and to review the programme in another 12 months' time. During this stay of execution there would be an opportunity for extended study of the respective merits of different types of deterrent launching systems, in a context where elements in the Admiralty were showing growing interest in the US Polaris programme. It was this process which was to lead in 1959 to the formation within the MoD of the British Nuclear Deterrent Study Group (BNDSG), a body which was to survive until early 1963, and become the setting for significant inter-service differences over the size and form of the most appropriate deterrent capability to succeed the V-force.

Although for many senior Naval officers Polaris was still regarded with great wariness, as a potential threat to plans for new surface ships and attack submarines, in the mid-1950s Admiral Mountbatten, the First Sea Lord, had begun to monitor progress with the US Navy's plans for development of a revolutionary submarine-launched ballistic missile. He was kept in touch with US developments, and given encouragement in his interest with the project, by means of a lively correspondence with his counterpart, the Chief of US Naval Operations, Admiral Arleigh Burke. In May 1958, in one of many supportive gestures, Burke had even offered to accommodate a Royal Navy liaison officer on the staff of the US Navy's Special Projects Office in Washington, which was overseeing Polaris development. By this time, the Earl of Selkirk, the First Lord of the Admiralty, was also exhibiting great enthusiasm toward the idea of how the future Navy could be equipped with ballistic-missile firing nuclear-powered submarines.[1]

In early 1958 Mountbatten took a step forward with the establishment of an Admiralty working party to compare Polaris, to be carried by a force of between six and eight submarines, with Blue Streak and a V-bomber based deterrent. The group, led by the Deputy Chief of the Naval Staff, saw several clear advantages in a submarine-borne deterrent but had been reluctant to push forward their findings, concerned that they would antagonise the Air Ministry and that any decision to adopt of Polaris could lead to calls for precious naval resources to be diverted to an expensive new project. Sandys was nevertheless informed of the report's conclusions in April 1958, leading to sharp differences of opinion between the Admiralty and the Air Ministry over the respective merits of different modes of basing. As Richard Moore has highlighted, Mountbatten was nonetheless keen at this time that the Navy's position in the nuclear sufficiency debate, where it wanted to stress the need for adequate spending on conventional defence, should not be blurred by a campaign to supplant Blue Streak with Polaris.[2]

Several government ministers, moreover, had also become attracted during 1958 by the idea of an invulnerable retaliatory deterrent such as Polaris, and by the end of the year the missile had found additional support from the Cabinet Secretary. Yet it was still very much an unproven weapon, with major uncertainties over the costs which would be involved with a purchase from the United States along with the provision of a wholly new set of nuclear-powered submarines able to carry and launch it. When making his submissions to the Defence Committee in November 1958 over the future of Blue Streak, Sandys had dealt with Polaris in very guarded terms. The possibility of adopting this 'very desirable' missile for the UK inventory had been considered, he had then reported, but it was felt too early in its development 'to stake everything upon it.' There were also other drawbacks to the missile as then conceived: its anticipated warhead yield was much lower than that planned for Blue Streak; as a submarine-launched system it would be less accurate than one that was land-based; and the cost of building perhaps six or eight submarines to accommodate Polaris also has to be taken into account.[3]

By the end of 1958, therefore, an impasse seemed to have been reached, with discussion of Polaris opening up sharp divisions between the Air Ministry and the Admiralty, the former concerned that its headline role of maintaining the strategic deterrent force could eventually be usurped by the senior service. The Defence Committee had finished its debates over the deterrent in December with the thought that Blue Streak should not be cancelled until 'further consideration had been given to the form which our deterrent should take from the late 1960s onwards.' It was the Secretary of State for Air, George Ward, who soon after put forward the idea to Sandys of a 'study of future weapon requirements for the deterrent, both airborne and submarine,' which in turn prompted the Minister to suggest that the COS might discuss the matter at an early meeting of the Defence Board. At the start of 1959 Mountbatten, in order to fulfil this injunction, suggested to the other Chiefs that this fundamental and involved issue might best be addressed by establishing within the Ministry of Defence a small high-level working party to carry out a detailed and technical study of future deterrent systems, under the chairmanship of the Permanent Under Secretary, Sir Richard Powell. In Powell's view, the work might take six months and represented 'the most important single defence policy problem we had to decide.' Powell was also instrumental in deflecting Air Ministry arguments that the matter should revert to the Defence Research Policy Committee (chaired, it should be recalled, by Brundrett, who was one of Blue Streak's strongest partisans) or the Joint Planning Staff, where inter-service rivalries were bound to predominate. Instead, Powell wanted to see a more independent group with about five or six members, which could include scientists, as well as Foreign Office and Treasury officials.[4]

There had been much press speculation during 1958 that the future of Blue Streak was under consideration by the Government. In an attempt to allay concerns and quash speculation, when the Defence White Paper was published in February 1959 Sandys had conducted an (unattributed) press briefing at the MoD where he had made clear his view that Blue Streak was the missile best suited to Britain's needs. He had also used the occasion to question the value of Polaris, asking why it should be assumed that missile-carrying submarines would remain 'undetectable and invulnerable' and pointing to the fact that only a small number of boats could be built owing to their great cost.[5]

Many, however, continued to find the Government's defence policy unconvincing. Remarking on how low-key was mention of the deterrent in the 1959 White Paper compared to that of the previous year, *The Times* sought deeper explanations:

> what is the policy behind the independent British nuclear deterrent? Everything comes back to this. ... Are we still seeking primarily to impress the Americans? If so, then it is at least arguable that our possession of nuclear weapons has won us blueprints for American weapons rather than influence, and that our influence with the Americans comes mainly from such unmilitary sources as our traditions, stability and experience in world affairs. Or are we seeking primarily to deter the Russians? If so, our deterrent is credible as an ultimate safeguard for the British Isles against nuclear attack, but no more credible than America's far bigger strategic nuclear armoury as a deterrent against conventional aggression on the Continent. A threat to commit suicide is not a rational defence policy. The implications of the nuclear stalemate will have to be digested before we can draw up a specification for the deterrent.

Despite such current uncertainties, the newspaper noted that ministers nevertheless had already decided the form the deterrent should take, and were wedded to the Blue Streak programme. The Government's reasons for preferring a static to a mobile system (or a 'Maginot Line strategy' as it was called) should, it was contended, be subjected to close examination by the Opposition.[6]

In the face of much concerted scepticism, Sandys informed the House of Commons in the subsequent defence debate that, after having considered the alternatives, the Government was resolved that the missile's development would continue. Placing a major stress on costs, the Minister had used a mixture of unfortunate metaphors:

> If we could afford to have an assortment of deterrents, if we could afford to have several clubs in the bag, we should certainly like to have a proportion of Polaris and Minuteman [the latest US ICBM under development] missiles in our quiver. ... Because it is always a good thing to have a niblick in case one gets into trouble, although one would not necessarily like to have to do the whole round with it ... [but] we cannot put our money on all the horses, like the Americans can, and we therefore have to back our fancy.

Nevertheless, Sandys continued in cautious fashion, saying that Blue Streak was 'going ahead but we shall, naturally, continue to watch the progress of other developments in America and elsewhere. With the rapid advances of science, which are constantly upsetting earlier assessments, strategic plans and weapon programmes can never be regarded as permanent or immutable. But in the present state of knowledge I am confident that our decision to continue with the development of Blue Streak is the right course, and, in fact, that any other course would involve a wholly unjustifiable gamble.'[7]

Despite the Minister of Defence's efforts, many commentators rightly noted that the project's future was still far from settled. One further factor militating against a static deterrent such as Blue Streak was the associated costs of defending missile sites. It was already costing about £150 million per annum, it was reckoned, to defend the airbases of the V-bombers, and more sophisticated surface-to-air guided missiles with nuclear warheads might eventually have to be provided to guard Blue Streak against Soviet aircraft, or even ballistic missiles. Such an air defence system was thought to be beyond the country's means, and according to *The Times* this only reinforced the arguments for 'an elusive deterrent' distinguished by mobility.[8]

Any MoD study group asked to examine the long-term future of the deterrent would, therefore, certainly have a great deal to consider, and have to venture into contentious areas. In fact, even getting the study group underway proved a protracted process. In March 1959, Powell again discussed the formation of the group with Sandys, who gave the idea his provisional approval, but made clear, repeating concerns he had expressed in January, that it should examine all possible future systems, and not become simply a vehicle for comparing Blue Streak with Polaris. As at the start of the year, Powell envisaged a small study group, reporting through the COS Committee to ministers, and composed of officials, service representatives and 'one or two experts and independent scientists'; its task would be to examine the technical issues connected to the best means of maintaining a British-controlled contribution to the nuclear deterrent in the future.[9] Yet by the end of April 1959 the Minister of Defence had become reluctant to give final sanction to formation of the group, his second thoughts prompted by concerns that the study might itself recommend Blue Streak cancellation, and he told Powell not to take any initiative at the present time.[10]

Matters were soon to move out the Minister of Defence's hands, however, as the long-held ideas entertained by the Cabinet Secretary to undertake a wide-ranging review of Britain's place and future prospects in the world, including coverage of its nuclear role, began to move toward fruition. Sir Norman Brook had mooted such a comprehensive study during the discussions over defence spending in November 1958 (and received Macmillan's authority to update an earlier short report – almost as a taster for what was to come – which dealt with the UK's position in world affairs), but in February 1959 the Cabinet Secretary tried to crystallise his latest thinking in a minute for the Prime Minister.[11]

Referring to the previous year's ministerial discussions over strategic nuclear policy, Brook observed that it had not then been possible to reach any conclusions and hence the defence programme had reflected no fundamental changes in policy. Macmillan was reminded of his own view that it had not been 'a good year in which to take far-reaching decisions'. But Brook was now interested in assembling the material which would assist a new government, arriving in office after the next election, to make such difficult choices over defence policy. In the Cabinet Secretary's view, the last such general review of politico-military policy had been the 1952 COS paper on defence policy and global strategy, but he did not envisage a repeat of that exercise since a new study should address the broader aspects of foreign, colonial and overseas economic policy as well as defence (he doubtless also had in mind the dissension amongst the COS that had been witnessed during 1958 over the issue of the deterrent). A report of this kind would offer invaluable background, he thought, for the government to make decisions over defence policy in about a year's time, adding, 'I doubt whether we shall ever get, in particular, a sensible weapons policy, until we have examined, in this sort of way, some of the great unresolved questions affecting our "global strategy".'[12]

The Prime Minister proved responsive, for on 7 June 1959, in line with Brook's advice, he convened a meeting at Chequers to put in hand a large-scale interdepartmental study of future policy, to be conducted by senior officials from the overseas departments and the Chiefs of Staff. It was to include forecasts of significant economic, diplomatic and military developments and how policy could be 'adapted to enable the United Kingdom to continue to play a significant part in world affairs.' The results were expected to inform the decisions of ministers, of whatever government assumed office after the next election, as they scanned the horizon over the next decade, and to help them match aims to resources, particularly in the defence field.

It was obvious from the June 1959 Chequers meeting that nuclear matters would form an important part of the work. Strong echoes of the COS debates during 1958 over nuclear sufficiency could be heard in the call for examination of the effects of strategic nuclear parity, and anxiety that more Soviet probes and minor encroachments on the Western position could be expected over the next few years. Also expressed was the need to look closely at the whole idea of a British contribution to the Western deterrent and whether it could be expected to pay dividends in the future, especially in an era when UK capabilities were dwarfed by those of the United States and Soviet Union. But the view was also offered that 'having paid the entrance fee to the nuclear club, we could not easily withdraw, more particularly when others, e.g. the French, were likely to join it'.

This was one of the earliest occasions when anxieties over the future development of a French nuclear capability were to seep into official discussions of Britain's own rationale for maintaining its nuclear programme. At Chequers it was also resolved that if it were decided to maintain a British nuclear deterrent over the longer-term then a separate study of its possible size and shape would undoubtedly be required 'at an early date.'[13]

The entire Future Policy study was to be led and coordinated by a Steering Committee under the direction of the Cabinet Secretary.[14] However, the principal working group that supplied papers to Brook's Steering Committee was directed by the ubiquitous figure of Sir Patrick Dean from the Foreign Office, who still served as chairman of the JIC. Dean's working group was in turn made up of a clutch of Whitehall officials with key stakes in defence and overseas policy. It was obvious to those officials engaged with the Future Policy study that the more specialist work carried out by an MoD-led deterrent study group could form an important and valuable component of the overall enterprise. Thus, amongst the conclusions of the June meeting at Chequers had been an invitation for Powell – a member of Brook's Steering Committee – and the Cabinet Secretary to consider the 'question of a separate enquiry into the means of delivery of the British contribution to the nuclear deterrent.'[15]

After some further stalling from Sandys, the British Nuclear Deterrent Study Group was finally established in late July 1959 under Powell's chairmanship (the route to this decision may also have been made easier by Mountbatten, who had been one of the first to suggest such an exercise, succeeding Dickson as Chief of the Defence Staff that same month). Membership of the BNDSG included Brundrett as Chief Scientist at the MoD, the three Vice or Deputy Chiefs of Staff, from the War Office, the Admiralty, and the Air Ministry, and representatives from the Foreign Office (Dean once again), the Treasury, the Ministry of Supply, and the Atomic Energy Authority (in the person of Sir William Cook, the former deputy head of AWRE).[16] Over the next few years, when ministers and senior departmental officials were faced with a difficult issue concerned with the future of the deterrent they would often remit the subject to the BNDSG for examination; its papers and ideas were in turn to form an important background influence on the formulation of policy, and revealed fundamental 'official' attitudes to the role, composition and future of an independent deterrent.

Even as the formation of the BNDSG was being discussed within the MoD in the first few months of 1959, it was recognised that a crucial issue that would serve to guide its deliberations was the required size and purpose of a future deterrent system. This was, however, a subject on which several different views were current. From his vantage point at the Foreign Office, for example, and during the debates over the effects of nuclear sufficiency, Dean had always felt that the value of an independent UK nuclear capability should not be underrated, but that determining the size of that capability remained a difficult judgement. In October 1958 he argued that,

> It must be big enough to ensure that we can make an initial nuclear response if Russia should attack us, however improbable this may seem. It must also be big and varied enough to cause the US to regard it as a useful contribution and to want to share their information with us and to supply our needs (a nuclear programme for prestige reasons, as contemplated by the French, would not satisfy this).[17]

During 1958, under the basic directive covering national nuclear strike planning – COS(57)224 – an accepted damage capability of 50 per cent of 40 Soviet cities gradually emerged from a series of Air Staff calculations which examined the likely effectiveness of an attack launched by the agreed final V-force of 144 aircraft – a number regarded as the minimum that was 'operationally viable' and able to inflict an 'adequate measure of destruction in Russia'. By September 1958, the COS Committee was being told by the Air Ministry that having studied the degree of threatened destruction needed to deter Russia from attacking the UK, it was felt that a lower figure of 30 cities would, in fact, be sufficient (this at a time, it should be remembered, when the Prime Minister had rejected the notion that deterrent capability, and hence megaton warhead numbers, should be related to any specific number of Soviet cities which could be destroyed).[18]

In October 1958 the Air Staff concluded that, allowing for an unserviceability rate of 25 per cent and losses to enemy action, the planned front-line V-bomber strength of 104 Mark 2 and 40 Mark 1 Vulcan and Victor bombers could deliver about 50–60 bombs in their first strike against the 131 large centres of industry and administration that had been identified in the Soviet Union. If the higher figure of 60 bombs was used, and several bombs were used against the larger targets, this implied delivery of 35 bombs against 15 cities with populations over 600,000, and 25 bombs on cities which mostly had over 400,000 people (making 40 cities in total). Casualty estimates from each bomb were put at 135,000 immediately killed and the same number injured, giving a total figure of 8 million killed and 8 million injured from a full-scale Bomber Command strike.[19] These Air Ministry assumptions about the damage capability of the UK strategic nuclear force were projected forward when it came to estimating the numbers of Blue Streak missiles that might eventually be required once the V-force was retired. One senior official estimated in November 1958 that 120 Blue Streak were needed (when current plans called for deployment of 60 missiles) on the grounds that missile reliability would only be about 50 per cent and that 60 megaton warheads would have to be delivered against the 30–40 key city targets in the Soviet Union if the capacity of the current planned size of the V-force was to be matched.[20]

As the formation of the BNDSG began to be considered in early 1959, MoD officials recognised that it would need guidance as to what the future capabilities of the deterrent force should be. It was acknowledged that this did not necessarily have to equate to the damage capability of the planned V-force. Powell was advised by one of his officials:

> It would not be adequate merely to say that the deterrent must continue to have a capability equivalent to that of 144 V-bombers. There is room for argument about how many would get through, their effective range, accuracy, etc; and their capability will be different at different times. It is better to define it in terms of the targets we want to threaten.

There would also have to be an appropriate definition of what constituted an 'independent' deterrent, and here it was suggested that this might be condensed to two propositions, namely when the government had under its sole control nuclear weapons either:

a   that a potential enemy would regard as being capable of doing him more harm than he would consider worth risking in order to achieve his objects; or

b   whose existence would lead a potential enemy to believe that if the weapons were ever to be used against him the risk of their being accompanied by an American nuclear attack would be so great as similarly to deter him from seeking his objects.

The specific capability for any future force suggested to Powell at this time was the ability to destroy at least 50 per cent of the buildings in Moscow, and 75 per cent of the buildings in the 20 largest cities in an area of the Soviet Union extending from the Polish frontier to just beyond the Urals.[21]

Calculations of the damage and destruction that could be inflicted on the Soviet Union by Western strategic nuclear forces were informed during this period by a number of committees and working groups which had been established to study the effects of all-out nuclear war. Since February 1956 a Joint Global War Committee, working under the auspices of the COS, and chaired by Brundrett in his capacity as Chief Scientist, had been meeting irregularly to examine the possible forms a general nuclear war and its outcome might take. Papers for the Committee's consideration were prepared by a small working party with service representation and scientific input.[22]

By October 1957 a first report on its findings had been prepared for the COS, but there was some unhappiness with the slow speed at which the work could be accomplished and some of the assumptions and techniques employed (while the Air Ministry demonstrated its customary aversion to considering the pattern of fighting once deterrence had broken down upon the outbreak of a future war).[23] As the Committee broadened its reach and attempted to peer into the likely nature of conflict in the 1970s, during the summer of 1958 it acquired a temporary and enhanced staff in the shape of the Joint Global War Study Group, allowing it to deepen its range of work.[24]

In April 1959 the COS decided that the Study Group should be put on a more permanent basis (while in December the Study Group was re-styled the Joint Inter-Services Group for the Study of All Out War, with the convenient acronym JIGSAW).[25] Refining the Study Group's broad remit was always somewhat problematic, but its service members tended to focus on methods and outcomes of a nuclear offensive and any defence that might be mounted, leaving the civilian scientists assigned to the group to examine the actual effects of nuclear weapons. In this latter area, a particular focus was on the concept of 'breakdown' damage in a city, a condition which would have been reached when the degree of destruction caused by a nuclear attack, measured in terms of civilian casualties, damage to buildings, basic communications and infrastructure, would render the whole area 'ineffective', leaving the remaining population simply struggling to survive in the appalling conditions that would ensue. A city or region might thereby be made incapable of contributing to the war-fighting or productive capacities of a country as a whole; if enough bombs were delivered then the phenomenon of national breakdown might be created, where the entire national structure collapsed. Much of this work had its origins in studies of the effects of conventional bombing during the Second World War (as during the firestorm that devastated Hamburg in July 1943), and extrapolation from that experience indicated that destroying about one third of the dwellings in a city area would be enough to accomplish the effect. Even when considering only damage caused by blast (and taking no account of the fires that would also be produced), it was obvious that the advent of high-yield thermonuclear weapons took the destructive potential of a nuclear strike to a wholly new level. For most cities with up to a million and a half inhabitants, a single burst of a sufficiently accurate one megaton weapon, it was reckoned, would meet the damage requirement.[26]

In one of the BNDSG's first papers, issued by its small secretariat in July 1959, an effort was made to define the tasks, targets and damage capabilities that were required for a British-controlled contribution to the Western deterrent. One approach, as has been indicated, was simply to take the existing Air Ministry estimates of the capabilities of the planned 144 V-bomber force as the yardstick which must be maintained in the future, which would indicate a capability of delivering successful attacks against between 30 and 40 Soviet cities, out of 131 major centres of industry and administration. But the paper

164 *Breaking the impasse?*

thought that this could hardly be taken as an appropriate guide: the damage capabilities of the V-force were bound to fluctuate over time (not least as Soviet air defences gradually improved during the 1960s), while some targets would need to be allocated to more than a single aircraft. Therefore a better approach was to define the number of targets that should be threatened, with one possibility, for example, being to have a deterrent capable of threatening any target within the Soviet Union between longitude 30 and 70 degrees, or another the ability to 'destroy at least 50% of the buildings in Moscow and in 15 of the 20 largest other cities in that area.'[27]

Such basic questions were reviewed by the BNDSG at its first meeting at the end of July 1959, officials acknowledging the difficult ground it would have to traverse, as well as the relationship between its work – which it saw as primarily technical in nature – and more general questions such as whether any future provision should even be made for a deterrent force once the V-force was judged ineffective. Addressing the paper prepared by the BNDSG secretariat, the Study Group considered that the task of the deterrent was 'to pose such a threat of damage to the Soviet homeland that the Soviet leaders would regard it as an unacceptable price to pay for any attack on this country.' The chosen means were to be attacks against 'area targets such as cities,' where precise accuracy in delivery was not important. In a highly significant step, and despite the debate that had circulated over this crucial issue, it was decided that the existing damage capability of the planned 144 aircraft V-force (i.e. attacks with megaton weapons against 30 to 40 Soviet cities) should be adopted as the criterion for the BNDSG's future work. An additional caveat was that the target set of cities should be in the western areas of the Soviet Union, and include Moscow, Leningrad and Odessa. Officials on the Joint Global War Study Group were then asked to examine in more precise fashion the effects of such a scale of nuclear attack.[28]

By early September the Joint Global War Study Group had produced a report for use by Powell's BNDSG, which was based on attacks against the higher figure of 40 cities taking place in 1970. Total deaths from blast effects were estimated at over seven million, with another 10 million at immediate risk in target cities from fallout from the explosions, and a further 23 million people located in nearby areas subject to 'significant' levels of fallout. But the mathematical methodology of the Study Group led it to conclude that such was dispersal of the Soviet population and its administrative centres that in only two provinces would there be 'general disorganisation', while it also could not be assumed that Soviet governmental machinery would break down.[29] Behind the language of the report, Powell was informally advised by the chair of the Joint Global War Study Group that its casualty estimates should be regarded as very conservative, since little allowance had been made for the full effects of fallout, and none from the large fires that would be caused in urban areas by nuclear bursts (the Study Group had also assumed that the Soviet urban population would be under shelter when an attack happened). The clear inference was that real casualty figures would be of a far higher order.

Powell was also alerted to the point that although the report alluded to, but then dismissed, any direct comparison between the figure of seven million and the roughly 20 million Soviet citizens killed during the Second World War (as was then thought), it did not offer a view on whether such a loss would be enough to constitute a deterrent. It was felt that

> The big unknown factor in any such assessment is the effect on morale of all this damage occurring in a matter of hours, compared with the period of years in which the casualties were suffered during the last war. It is also pertinent to note that this attack would deliver the equivalent of 40 million tons of TNT on the Soviet Union, compared with the figure of just under 3 million tons of high explosive delivered on Germany throughout the whole of the last war.
>
> The level of damage should certainly make the Soviet leaders pause before embarking on any aggression, but whether it would, in fact, deter them from any aggression must surely depend on the prize which they would hope to gain from the aggression. This raises questions about the circumstances in which the British deterrent would need to operate independently, which are perhaps [outside] the terms of reference of this [BND] Study Group.[30]

The lack of a definitive judgement about the effects on Soviet behaviour of a certain number of bombs falling on a particular set of targets and the casualties this would cause, and the report's references to the calculations of the Soviet leadership regarding the aims of any aggression, underscored the importance of a precise definition of what the UK strategic nuclear force was designed to achieve. Was it, in other words, ever expected to operate in a unilateral manner against a Soviet enemy which had decided to focus its aggression against the UK alone, and would such a forty-city capability be sufficient to constitute a unilateral deterrent? It would be these kinds of issues that would have to be addressed by the Cabinet Secretary's Future Policy Study (whose basic papers were prepared and presented by a working group chaired by Sir Patrick Dean – the senior Foreign Office official who also doubled as a member of the BNDSG).

The Future Policy Study and the independent deterrent

The overwhelming victory of the Conservatives at the general election held in October 1959 ensured that it would be Macmillan and his ministers who would consider the eventual results of the Future Policy Study which had been launched during the summer. In the ministerial reshuffle carried out immediately after the election, the Prime Minister chose to move the abrasive Sandys away from the MoD to oversee the break-up of the troubled Ministry of Supply, from which he would help form a new Ministry of Aviation, and where he was expected to clean the Augean stables of the government's military research and development programmes and invigorate the aircraft industry. Sandys' replacement as Minister of Defence was Harold Watkinson, now a little-remembered figure but who at the time presided over several of the most important shifts in post-war strategic nuclear policy. Watkinson was an engineer by training, and, after wartime service in the Royal Naval Volunteer Reserve, had a successful career in business – a 'self-made' man in Macmillan's words – which led him to believe that management techniques could be used to improve government.[31] Moved from the post of Minister of Transport and Civil Aviation which he had held since 1955, it was hoped that he could introduce some streamlined decision-making into an MoD which was still adapting to the reforms to the central organisation of defence introduced in 1958.

Watkinson was also determined to reorganise and improve the mobility of Britain's conventional forces (as the gradual end of national service reduced their numbers), arrive at a coherent approach to the problem of limited war, and move away from the disputatious atmosphere that had accompanied the debates since 1957 over the size and role of the strategic deterrent.[32] In retrospect, it is clear that the displacement of Sandys from the MoD eased the way toward a decision to cancel Blue Streak. At the end of October 1959, Watkinson put down his own thoughts on some of the key decisions that would have to be made over the next few months. These included the difficult issues of deciding on the future of Blue Streak and Polaris, where he professed he would be reliant on the advice of the BNDSG. 'When we examine the report,' he noted, 'we shall also have to cover the question of the excess cost of the present Blue Streak programme, which is a matter that worries the Chancellor very much. I shall also wish to consider the political difficulties of siting Blue Streak in this country, and the vulnerability or otherwise of this weapon to rocket attack.'[33]

Even before the delivery of the BNDSG's initial findings, the new Minister was trying to prepare the ground for possible alternatives. On 8 December 1959, Watkinson held a general discussion with the Prime Minister on defence policy where he expressed the view that

> we should be prepared to go for Polaris. There was everything to be said for a submarine-based deterrent. It might take us some years to get this. We should therefore stretch the V-bombers and Blue Steel Mark I as long as possible. There might be a gap: he was looking into this ... He thought we should not discontinue the development of Blue Streak but should restrict the production to about twenty instead of sixty vehicles. He also thought there were arguments in favour of not deploying Blue Streak in hard sites [i.e. underground missile silos].[34]

About a week later, during a meeting held in Paris with his US counterpart, Thomas S. Gates, Watkinson made the first high-level British approach over the potential availability of Polaris. Gates was informed that the Government was carrying out a high-level review of defence problems 'in the light of increasing Russian capability and American progress in missiles such as Polaris.' Blue Streak deployment might have to be reduced, the Minister said, because of concerns over its vulnerability to Soviet missile attack, and he wanted to gauge US reactions to a 'proposal that the United Kingdom should acquire from the United States Polaris missiles and electronic system[s], and the blueprints for the design of a nuclear submarine to carry Polaris, leaving the United Kingdom to build the submarines and their reactors and to provide the warheads.' Gates thought that the enquiry was a little premature as Polaris was not yet fully tested or in US service, but professed that the US administration would 'probably be quite ready to go so far as they legally could to help,' but adding that the proposal might create trouble with Congress.[35]

Whatever approach was adopted toward deterrent policy by the end of the 1950s was increasingly influenced by the fact that Britain was soon to be joined in the ranks of the nuclear powers by France, establishing a whole new set of strategic and political issues for British governments as they assessed what attitude they should take to the French nuclear programme and how its existence affected perceptions of the UK's own efforts. There was, not least, the emerging issue of whether some degree of Anglo-French nuclear collaboration was possible or desirable, either as a means to establishing an eventual European deterrent force, separate from the United States, of rationalising the nuclear defence efforts of both states, or as a way to secure wider political goals.[36]

As early as October 1945 the first post-war French Provisional Government had established an Atomic Energy Commission – the *Commissariat a l'energie atomique*, or CEA – with the task of developing applications for atomic energy in a variety of different fields, including national defence. A five-year plan for civil and industrial nuclear development and the construction of new plutonium producing reactors was approved by the French National Assembly in 1952, but it was not until two years later, at the end of 1954, that a high level bureaucratic decision seems to have been made to proceed with the first stage of a weapons programme. Soon after, in May 1955, a secret atomic weapons unit, the *Bureau d'etudes generalies*, was formed within the CEA. The Suez crisis intensified French desires to loosen dependence on the United States in particular; by the end of 1956 large strides forward in a national military nuclear programme had been taken and preparations for testing began. With faith in the reliability of the US nuclear guarantee shaken, in May 1957 Maurice Bourges-Maunoury, the French Defence Minister, announced that under 'the new conditions of war, our adversary's possession of a substantial stock of atomic weapons ... require that on the list of studies to be undertaken, the strategic reprisal weapon must have priority...'[37] An official order was given in April 1958 by the Prime Minister, Felix Gaillard, to proceed with the building of an atomic bomb, with a test to take place in the spring of 1960, but as with the Attlee Government's

January 1947 'decision', this was more a ratification of already well-established policy.³⁸

The subsequent collapse of the Fourth Republic and de Gaulle's return to office as Prime Minister in June 1958, and adoption of enhanced powers as President after January 1959, ensured there would be no slackening in the French programme. A nuclear capability was widely seen in France as commensurate with her status as an independent great power, and would give the French military a prestigious role divorced from the debilitating memories and effects of bruising colonial wars in Indochina and Algeria. At the same time, de Gaulle envisioned securing an equal standing within the Western Alliance for France alongside the United States and Britain, and was ready to use France's developing nuclear potential as a political bargaining tool. His increasingly disruptive calls for a greater voice in the decision-making counsels of the West, under the guise of 'tripartism', especially when it came to nuclear issues, was to prove more than just an irritant for Washington and London – a fact underlined in March 1959 when the French Mediterranean Fleet was removed from NATO command structures, and later when objections were raised to the storage of US nuclear weapons at US air bases in France. It was also in March 1959 that the development of the *force de frappe* was given 'absolute priority' by the Defence Council in Paris.³⁹ France's drive for nuclear independence reached its initial goal in February 1960 with the explosion of its first test device in the Sahara; it also looked toward the point when it could introduce into service a modern nuclear-capable aircraft (an aspiration which was finally achieved with the entry into service of the supersonic Mirage IV in October 1964), and was keen to begin design and development of an indigenous IRBM.⁴⁰

The nuclear aspects of the Cabinet Secretary's Future Policy Study could not fail to take into consideration the growing importance of the French programme. For one, any idea of relinquishing a British nuclear capability had to be put beside the obvious efforts that the French were putting into assembling a strategic nuclear force. There was also the increasingly salient point that, in a context where several senior ministers and officials were keen to improve ties with Europe, and even looked toward an eventual bid to enter the European Economic Community (EEC), British nuclear (and ballistic missile) knowledge could be offered to Paris as an incentive for France to show a more cooperative attitude.

But for the moment this avenue appeared closed. In March 1957, during the high-level Anglo-American meeting in Bermuda, a joint paper had been agreed between the US Secretary of State, John Foster Dulles, and the Foreign Secretary, Selwyn Lloyd, which had affirmed both states had an interest in preventing the spread of nuclear weapons technology; that active steps to assist the still-nascent French programme should be avoided; and that close contact over the issue should be maintained between London and Washington.⁴¹

By the end of 1959, however, as the date for the first French test moved closer, the Prime Minister thought that it was time to revisit the issue.

Determined to improve his relations with de Gaulle, which he rightly believed had been strained by the close Anglo-American relationship that had been forged in 1957–58, Macmillan was attracted by the proposition of collaboration, as long as Britain's ties with Washington was not compromised as a result. In early 1960 there was no shortage of overtures from French officials looking for indications of British interest in closer defence cooperation, and when de Gaulle and Macmillan met at Rambouillet in March, the French President made clear he would be receptive to nuclear assistance from Britain.

The Foreign Office, however, remained very cautious, unsure that France would prove a reliable partner or that such an offer would eventually help any future move for Britain to join the EEC. There was also a deep degree of concern over gaining American agreement to any initiative which involved the transfer of nuclear information to France, some of which might have been gained from US sources through exchanges under the MDA. Unscrambling the information, so that British knowledge, derived from independent work carried out before the conclusion of the MDA in 1958, could be differentiated from American, was not considered a viable proposition. Both the MoD and the Foreign Office did not want to see their close nuclear links with the US prejudiced – especially during a period when delicate negotiations over future delivery systems would have to be conducted with Washington – by the pursuit of what could prove to be the blind alley of Anglo-French nuclear collaboration. For the time being at least, the Prime Minister was inclined to agree.[42]

Deterrent policy began to feature in the deliberations of Sir Patrick Dean's Future Policy Study working group in mid-November 1959, to some extent shadowing the discussions of the BNDSG. The working group took as its starting point an MoD paper which asked a whole series of basic questions which went to the core of the decisions that would have to be made over the next few years:

1   Is it our aim to be able, acting independently – i.e. in circumstances where the Americans do not intend to act – to inflict severe nuclear damage on Russia or any other country?
2   If this is our aim, are there any circumstances in which we might act independently, with the Americans clearly holding back? Are the Russians likely to believe in our intention to take independent action and thus be deterred from the action which would provoke it, bearing in mind the inevitable destruction of the United Kingdom which would result?
3   If the UK found it necessary to intervene in an overseas territory – e.g. in the Middle East – in defence of a vital UK interest, and if the Russians threatened action against us if we carried out our intervention, would our possession of nuclear weapons under our own control make any difference to our determination to ignore the Russian threat?

170 *Breaking the impasse?*

4   Is it our aim simply to make a contribution to a combined Western deterrent in which we are associated with the Americans and with our European allies?
5   Should the criteria determining the nature, size and value of the UK contribution to this combined Western deterrent be:
    a   the maintenance of the highest possible degree of influence on US policy?
    b   the maintenance of the best possible standing in the various alliances and associations in which we must participate?
    c   making the Russians feel that an attack on any part of the Western alliance is tantamount to an attack on the USA?
    d   giving us a share in the vital decisions of peace or war?
6   For these purposes should:
    a   the political decision whether or not to use our contribution remain under the control of HMG?
    b   our contribution, both as to warheads and means of delivery (or either) be designed, developed and produced by the UK?[43]

Responsibility for clarifying Foreign Office thinking on these fundamental issues lay with two officials in particular, Peter Ramsbotham and Philip Ziegler (the former was later to rise to become an ambassador in Washington in the mid-1970s, the latter went on to forge a highly successful literary career as a biographer of subjects who included Mountbatten and Harold Wilson).

The Foreign Office's contribution to the debate over the deterrent was to undermine the case for its possible 'independent' role. Firstly, it was noted that the whole assumption behind the argument for an independent deterrent was predicated on the Russians believing that the United States would be unwilling to come to Britain's aid in a situation of dire necessity; as long as the Russians felt that the Americans were committed to help the UK, this would be enough to constitute a deterrent to the Soviet Union attacking Britain in any direct fashion. A second major point was that an independent deterrent, in effect, would only be credible as a defence against a nuclear attack against the UK (rather than any other form of action) as its independent use would lead to a Russian attack that would 'annihilate' Britain. Thirdly, it was for political reasons considered 'almost inconceivable' that the UK would use its nuclear weapons against any enemy except the Russians or the Chinese, and that 'local' use (as, for example, in South East Asia) would only be in conjunction with the Americans; once more the only scenario where independent nuclear use could be envisaged would be under conditions where the United States was 'neutral' and the UK was counter-attacking against a direct Russian nuclear attack against the UK itself.

This line of argument necessarily led to the conclusion that an 'independent' UK deterrent had to be conceived of as a purely retaliatory force, able to inflict 'unacceptable damage' against the Soviet Union only once a Soviet strike against Britain's bomber and missile forces had been absorbed.

An effective UK deterrent in around 1970, it was felt, would therefore have to be based on either airborne or seaborne missiles, as land-based missiles, or bomber aircraft operating from their ground bases, might not be able to muster a sufficiently strong retaliatory blow. In any case, a deterrent judged as effective in 1970 might not be seen in the same light by 1975 or 1980 due to technological developments. 'In particular,' the Foreign Office had observed, 'it seems highly probable that, by 1980, the Russians will have greatly improved their ABM defences. It seems therefore equally probable that, in order to maintain an effective deterrent over the years, the UK would have to spend increasingly vast sums, presumably at the expense of our other activities in defence and even of the welfare State at home.'

Foreign Office officials were not impressed by the 'trigger' argument of having a deterrent that would not on its own deter a Soviet attack, but instead rely on the catalytic effect of drawing the Americans into entering a nuclear exchange they might otherwise have tried to avoid. In such a scenario, it was the Russians who might well be forced to strike at the United States first, fearing that a UK attack was part of a more concerted Western effort. However, as the paper pithily noted, 'this would be of no use to us; we should all be dead.' The actual deterrence of a Russian attack, it was affirmed, was down to the issue of the likelihood of US involvement, and this was a separate issue to the existence of a UK deterrent force. What kept the Americans involved in the defence of the UK, and of Western Europe in general, was not the possibility that an independent UK deterrent force might drag the US into a global war, but Washington's estimation of its own vital security interests.

This did not lead the Foreign Office to advocate a complete abandonment of nuclear capability. In the more nebulous area of prestige, the UK's possession of the ability to help defend itself against attack, and to contribute to the overall Western deterrent was felt an asset

> well worth having. It is one of the factors which lifts us, so to speak, from the ranks of the passive into the ranks of the active participants in the East-West struggle. It is also a constant reminder of our status as a technologically and industrially advanced nation.

An additional point was that, having been in the position of a pioneer in the nuclear field, to renounce any role through an act of unilateral disarmament would look like 'an abdication' and so be damaging to political prestige.

As for relations with the United States, the pursuit of an independent UK capability up to 1958 had certainly yielded benefits in terms of the Eisenhower administration's ability to persuade Congress to amend US atomic energy legislation and allow the restoration of Anglo-American nuclear relations. However, the Foreign Office now considered that Britain had proved her point, and possession of a deterrent force capable of wholly independent action would not, in fact, be necessary to sustain the close working relations

172 *Breaking the impasse?*

over nuclear weapons technology that had been established over the previous 18 months. Regarding the prospect of a European nuclear deterrent emerging over the course of the next decade – and with a clear eye directed at the French nuclear programme – the Foreign Office felt that the existence of an independent UK capability only encouraged those European powers which sought nuclear forces under national control. It was felt it was too early to determine what policy to adopt to the possibility of a European deterrent being established, but it would be easier for the West European powers to either remain content with the current form of the Western deterrent, or subscribe to some form of joint control, if Britain gave up her own aspirations for complete nuclear independence.

In the final analysis, the issue of whether the UK should absorb the large and increasing costs of maintaining a fully effective and independent deterrent would depend on the future course of US policy toward its international commitments. Here the Foreign Office predicted that the US would not sink into a 'Fortress America' approach but would become more, rather than less, dependent on its links with the remainder of the West. It would therefore be a mistake for the UK to 'run a serious risk of economic overstrain and breakdown by over-insuring against a highly unlikely change in United States policy. On the contrary, the best way to ensure that the Americans do not let us down if the moment comes is to pursue the policy of political, economic and military interdependence as energetically as we can, including interdependence in the sphere of the deterrent itself. It is upon this that the future security of the United Kingdom will depend.'[44]

During its first (and main) discussion of UK deterrent policy, Dean's working group considered both the MoD and Foreign Office papers. One of the group's chief preoccupations was to decide whether, for practical purposes, the UK would ever be in a position where it might use its nuclear capability independent of the Americans. Here the discussion ran:

> Although in theory we might do this if there was a complete split with the United States, the circumstances were so inconceivable as to be ruled out for planning purposes. Similarly, the Russians were unlikely to believe that we should act independently, or that the United States would allow the United Kingdom or Europe to suffer a Russian attack without intervening. American ties with the United Kingdom and the threat to America of a Russian dominated Europe could be expected to bring the Americans to our aid if our continued survival was clearly at stake.

This line of argument (reminiscent of that contained in the Foreign Office paper) hence obviated the need for an independent nuclear capability able to inflict unacceptable damage on the Soviet Union.

Nevertheless, there were still strong reasons voiced as to why it remained preferable to retain some nuclear capability which could be seen as a contribution to a combined Western deterrent (complete nuclear disarmament, it was feared, might precipitate calls for the removal of all US bases from the UK or provide a boost to neutralist sentiment and hopes for avoiding involvement in any conflict with the Soviet Union). In the light of such conclusions, the criteria to determine the future size and shape of the UK deterrent force would have to be

> primarily political in character. Our contribution should help maintain the highest degree of influence on United States policy and the best standing in the various other alliances and associations in which we must participate.

At the same time, such a contribution would have to convince the Russians that 'an attack on any part of the Western alliance was tantamount to an attack on the United States' while also allowing Britain a share in the 'vital decisions of peace and war.' One of the implications of this new stance was that the design, development and production of nuclear weapons and their means of delivery would not have to be confined to the UK itself.[45]

Objections were soon raised by some of the working group's MoD and service representatives to the whole direction of its discussions. There had been too much emphasis on how the strategic nuclear deterrent in practice might be used, rather than the requirements of preventing the outbreak of war through deterrence. It was also felt that not enough attention had been paid to Russian thinking and intentions – they were, after all, the opponents in the Cold War – and too much examination of possible American and allied reactions when speculating over courses of action. The important thing was the doubts that an independent UK capability would sow in Russian minds if there was any question of the United States standing aside in the event of conflict in Europe:

> To say that we would never use the deterrent because it means suicide is ... irrelevant. What matters is that the Russians could not gamble on our not using it in such a situation.

Over forecast costs for the deterrent, the Air Ministry wanted to underline that its estimates of maintaining an independent deterrent over the next decade did not indicate a rise above current levels of expenditure, and even showed that as there would be a fall in the share of the defence budget allocated to the area. Any assumptions about the costs of a future deterrent (made, for example, in the Foreign Office paper) therefore had to be regarded as highly speculative.[46]

An attempt was made to insert some of these caveats into the final draft of Dean's working group report on the deterrent, but the Foreign Office perspective still predominated. In one of its final meetings discussing the differences that had emerged, the working group's minutes recorded – in a conclusion that would have been thoroughly endorsed by Templer and

174 *Breaking the impasse?*

Mountbatten in the prolonged debates over nuclear sufficiency in 1958 – that its members 'generally agreed' that the 'maintenance of a completely home-made deterrent capable, in itself, of inflicting major damage on Russia would be enormously costly and could only be done at the expense of the rest of the defence programme.' The UK effort was already dependent on the Americans 'for information and components and could not replace their contribution without falling too far behind over the next ten years.' Nevertheless, enough nuclear capability had to be retained 'to enable us to secure weapons from the United States with a minimum of strings attached.' Moreover, 'political disadvantages both at home and abroad' would arise from any complete renunciation of the strategic deterrent.[47]

The Future Policy working group's basic paper on UK deterrent policy in the 1960s was circulated to members of the Cabinet Secretary's Steering Committee at the end of November 1959. Dean's covering note was keen to stress that the paper had been difficult to draft because of 'confusion about the meaning of the word "independent", when used as a qualification to "deterrent".' One meaning of the phrase was to describe a nuclear capability that could, with no other assistance, inflict unacceptable damage on an enemy. But another meaning increasingly being adopted was a deterrent which was part of a 'common effort', but over which 'unqualified control' was maintained.[48] In fact, the preferred definition of an 'independent deterrent' offered by the working group was

> where we retained such a measure of control over our deterrent that, in the last resort, we could use it or not use it, alone or in concert with others as we thought fit. It does not mean that we would at all times during the next decade in fact have, on our own, the military capability of inflicting unacceptable damage on Russia nor does it mean that we would on our own design and produce the entire weapons system in this country.[49]

As far as the working group was concerned, Dean maintained, the most important issue still to be resolved 'relates not so much to the abstract concept of "independence" as to the practical problem of what the United Kingdom deterrent is supposed to do, and on what scale it must be maintained for the accomplishment of this task.'

Quickly rejecting any notion of unilateral nuclear disarmament as a viable policy for the UK, as it would be incompatible with membership of the Western Alliance and could well represent the first step on the road to neutralism, Dean explained that the working group had grappled with the two meanings of an 'independent deterrent'. In favour of an independent force capable of inflicting unacceptable damage on the Soviet Union was the point that before taking any aggressive action the Russians would have to take into account the reactions of the UK, as well as those of the United States, so making it more problematic to calculate the risks that such action might involve. Such a force might be necessary as it was clearly conceivable that one day the US might abandon Europe (or the Russians might assume she had), ultimately leaving a UK deterrent, or that held by any other European power, as the only thing standing in the way of a possible Russian invasion of Western Europe. In the political context, renunciation of independent control 'would lead to our complete subservience to American policy', while Britain's standing in its network of alliances would suffer through having nothing else to offer alongside the nuclear capacity of the US.

Yet these arguments could be countered with the view that an 'independent' deterrent lacked credibility, in that the Russians would never believe that the UK would accept the total destruction that would follow any decision to use its nuclear forces in an unilateral fashion (the only exception might be a situation where a US withdrawal from Western Europe opened up the clear chance of an all-out Russian attack, although in such an instance Soviet aims could probably be achieved without such an overt aggression). Moreover, maintaining an independent deterrent would place 'excessive strain' on the UK's resources, when by contrast a combined Western deterrent would be far more economical. Finally, if the UK renounced its independent nuclear capability and showed a readiness to take part in Alliance-based joint nuclear arrangements it would be 'a striking affirmation of our belief in interdependence and the solidity of the Atlantic Alliance,' as well as do much to remove the potential urges of other European states to strive for nuclear forces under their exclusive national control.

The working group tried to cut through these differences by observing that, whatever the abstract definitions adopted, maintaining a deterrent force capable of inflicting unacceptable damage against the Soviet Union over the next decade was going to be 'an enormously expensive business.' Faced with a situation where the UK was expected by its allies to make substantial contributions to Western security in so many other realms, devoting an ever-increasing share of resources to such an effort, to the detriment of the rest of her defence programmes and other overseas activities, was not seen as being in Britain's national interest. Nuclear deterrence was therefore best conceived as an area for joint Western efforts, including over time the French deterrent forces as they were developed. The working group's conclusions were that Anglo-American, and later European, cooperation should be pursued in the areas of future weapons programmes and research (without, however, duplicating American development or production) and in the 'evolution of combined deterrent forces – the attack plan and the mechanics of decision.' Offers of American weapons should not necessarily be refused because complete freedom in their use could not be guaranteed, although 'if we are to continue to secure with a minimum of strings attached, as many US weapons as we want, and can afford to buy, we must continue to make a nuclear contribution in terms both of skill and of power.' Moreover, it was recognised that possession of an independent nuclear capability, including the ability to produce warheads in the UK, was 'a valuable asset in dealing both with our enemies and with our friends and allies. There is no doubt that it increases our bargaining power with the Russians. An open declaration that this would no longer be under British control would come as a shock to many people at home and would damage our prestige abroad.'

The final point made by the report, while delivered in an even tone, was a clear injunction for the need to look critically at the issue of whether it made sense to attempt to maintain an independent nuclear force which was capable on its own of deterring the Soviet Union. If the rationale underpinning the criterion of 'unacceptable damage' was accepted, then the 'size, composition and arrangements for control' of the deterrent would have to be adjusted accordingly over the subsequent decade, but the commitments which this would involve could not then be calculated: 'we cannot tell what the nature or cost of new technical developments will be or what strings the Americans may in the future attach to their products.' However, the alternative and more modest goal of making 'the best contribution we can to the overall Western deterrent' would allow a better measurement to be made of what this might mean in practice. Accordingly, the report suggested that 'we should put our cards on the table', and discuss with the Americans what the most useful UK contribution to a joint Western effort might be, and that, in due course, the Europeans might also be told that 'we visualise our effort as complementary to, rather than independent of, the American.' The effect of this might be to influence other European countries (i.e. France) to look on their own national nuclear efforts 'in a similar light.'[50]

The Future Policy Steering Committee, chaired by Brook, and comprising the Permanent Secretaries of the key overseas departments as well as the Chiefs of Staff, discussed Dean's report in early December 1959. In a reflection of the views he had expressed when the COS had debated the implications of nuclear sufficiency in 1958, Mountbatten, now the CDS, was vocal in supporting the report's contention that the costs of maintaining the deterrent had to be balanced against world-wide military commitments and the requirements they generated for adequate conventional forces. He told the Committee: 'It would be a mistake ... to prescribe a fixed limit for the size of our strategic deterrent, below which it could never be allowed to fall.' The Americans, in particular, he added, were 'nervous', lest the UK reduce its overseas military effort for the sake of building up strategic nuclear forces. The CDS clearly did not rate the credibility of an independent deterrent very highly, wondering if the Russians would believe it would ever be used on its own, except in the event of a direct attack on the UK.

Directly countering Mountbatten's position, however, was Dermot Boyle, the Chief of the Air Staff, who remained wedded to the idea of holding onto a force capable of inflicting unacceptable damage against the Soviet Union. Boyle felt that relinquishing this standard would result in a loss of influence in the world, and challenged the assumption that the future costs required to maintain the existing deterrent capability (consuming, he reckoned, about ten per cent of the overall defence budget) would prove unsustainable. But Boyle's was an isolated opinion. Admiral Sir Charles Lambe, the First Sea Lord, pointed instead to the need for the UK to play a significant role over the next decade in containing communism by devoting more resources to economic aid and global military efforts, and 'he doubted whether we could, in the long run, accept the cost of indefinitely maintaining an independent deterrent. The whole trend of the Future Policy Study was to emphasise the need for us to act in concert with our friends and he felt that we should endeavour to make a significant contribution to the Western deterrent as a whole.'

Similar sentiments were echoed by the PUS at the Foreign Office, Sir Frederick Hoyer Millar. With future means necessarily limited, Hoyer Millar thought that closer cooperation with allies would be the most productive policy, and agreed with Lambe's contention that British strategic nuclear forces were best seen as contributing to the Western deterrent as a whole. Although he did not think that national control over the deterrent should be relinquished, 'We should stand to lose if, by overemphasising the independent deterrent, we were unable to do what was needed and expected of us as a power with world-wide interests.' Giving the MoD's perspective, and also benefiting from his role as chairman of the BNDSG, Powell was more sanguine, seeing no overriding reason to depart from existing policy, and feeling that the strategic weapons systems planned for the next few years were not prohibitively expensive, and would allow significant influence to be maintained over both the Russians and the Americans. Nevertheless, Powell was noticeably agnostic over the actual size of the deterrent force required.

All members of the Steering Committee, in their final set of deliberations, could subscribe to the view that it was essential for the UK to maintain an independent nuclear programme of research and development. Furthermore, they found, in anodyne terms, that 'we should maintain a significant strategic nuclear force in existence, its composition and cost being determined in the light of our resources, our commitments and the world situation generally.' But the choice of priorities between strategic nuclear forces and other military commitments would need 'careful consideration.' In his summing up, Brook ventured (and despite the contrary position of the CAS) that there was overwhelming support amongst Committee members for the view that 'we could not hope to have strategic nuclear forces sufficient to take on Russia on our own.' British thinking would need to become more attuned to making contributions to its various alliances, and less in terms of independent operations, while 'We should consider what the size and nature of the strategic nuclear deterrent should be in order to perpetuate the position of equipoise. In doing so we might have to accept that there would be periods in which the deterrent could not be maintained at full strength except by introducing costly new weapons systems which could only be effective over a limited period.' (The latter was an indirect but very pointed reference to the future of Blue Streak.) The Cabinet Secretary's recommendation, drawing on the dominant opinions in Dean's working group, was that a decision should be taken on what forces could be provided, fully under national control, which would be

178 *Breaking the impasse?*

a 'significant British contribution to the Western deterrent. We might not be able to deter Russia on our own, but we could offer enough to maintain our influence in the Alliance and our world position.'[51]

The BNDSG interim report and the fate of Blue Streak

While the final draft of the Future Policy Study was being readied in the Cabinet Office, the MoD's British Nuclear Deterrent Study Group was busy compiling its own first 'interim' report dealing with the form the deterrent should take in the period up to the early 1970s, Powell finally producing an agreed draft on 23 December 1959 (although its findings were disseminated on the very final day of the year).[52] The report's preamble began by noting that the longer-term methods of maintaining a British-controlled deterrent had necessarily been studied as part of the group's work, and although the main characteristics of any weapons system meeting the requirement had been identified, it had not been possible to arrive at a recommendation for which system would be most effective, and hence this was a subject best left for a subsequent report. The purpose of the interim study was not to examine the rationale that lay behind possession of a strategic deterrent – for this would stray too far into the 'political' realm – but simply to consider how a nuclear capability equal to Bomber Command's planned full-strength force could be maintained as Soviet air defences steadily improved and Soviet capacity to attack British forces at their home bases increased. It was explained that as the Air Staff had established during 1958 that a 144 strong V-bomber force equipped with its megaton weapons could be expected to achieve a damage level of 50 per cent destruction of 40 major Soviet cities, this had become the benchmark adopted by the BNDSG.

Although it had decided to adopt the 40-city criterion as a measure to assess the effectiveness of different future deterrent systems, the study group acknowledged however, 'that nuclear forces with some lesser capability might still be regarded as constituting a significant contribution to the Western deterrent, provided that those forces were large enough to be operationally viable.' But beyond that single comment on alternative damage criteria the interim report did not venture.

Most Soviet cities were seen as requiring a single one megaton warhead to inflict the level of damage determined by the adopted measure, but Moscow and Leningrad, as larger targets, were assigned, respectively, four and two weapons each (giving a total of 44 separate aiming points). The current V-force, however, even when eventually armed after 1962 with the Blue Steel Mk 1 powered bombs then being developed, was expected to suffer over 50 per cent losses when attempting to penetrate the Soviet air defences which it might have to face from about 1965 onwards. Furthermore, by that same time sufficient numbers of Soviet medium and intermediate range ballistic missiles with high-yield warheads were likely to have been deployed to strike at the V-bomber bases so as to catch a significant proportion of the

Breaking the impasse? 179

bomber force on the ground, a threat which dispersal and improved reaction times could mitigate but not remove, and only if sufficient warning was available. Three successors to the V-bomber force armed with Blue Steel Mk 1 were examined in the study group report: an improved, longer-range version of Blue Steel could be developed and produced for use with the force; a new air-launched ballistic missile system, WS 138A (what was to become known as Skybolt), with an even longer-range and then under development in the United States, could be acquired from the Americans and fitted to the V-bombers; and ground-launched ballistic missiles of the Blue Streak type might be deployed.[53]

Subjected to critical analysis, all three options were seen as having certain important drawbacks. Soviet air defences, it was estimated, would be able to counteract an improved Blue Steel Mk 2 by the time of its likely full deployment date in 1966. The only way to respond would be to steadily increase the numbers of V-bombers and Blue Steel weapons, with all the additional cost implications and doubts about credibility this would create. Acquisition of WS 138A seemed a more attractive option, as development costs would be borne largely by the United States, it was being designed for high accuracy with a range of about 1,000 nautical miles, and as a ballistic missile it was considered invulnerable to Soviet defences. But the earliest date the weapon would be available was likely to be 1966, final purchase price was uncertain, and the V-bomber aircraft adapted to carry it would not be sustainable in the front line beyond about 1970 in any case, making the provision of some new airborne launching system essential. With both Blue Steel Mk 2 and WS 138A the vulnerability of the V-bomber bases to pre-emptive attack remained a problematic issue. Work on the third option, the Blue Streak IRBM, was well-advanced, with anticipated expenditure reaching £50 million by the end of the 1959/60 financial year and initial deployment predicted for 1965. However, the further costs of an extensive testing programme, the purchase of 60 missiles, and the construction of underground launching silos could amount to another £465 million.

The main issue tackled by the study group in relation to Blue Streak was its ability to survive an attempted Soviet pre-emptive strike with ballistic missiles. Its conclusion was that without pre-delegation by the political authorities of decision-making to local commanders so that they could launch Blue Streak on radar warning alone, the missile force would be highly vulnerable to a Soviet attack whether sited underground or on the surface (and even if pre-delegation were allowed, the chances of even a small proportion being successfully launched were seen as uncertain against a concerted, sophisticated and large-scale Soviet effort at pre-emption). In any event, the study group did 'not believe that any democratic Government would be prepared to delegate authority in an issue of such appalling magnitude.'

None of the three alternatives were therefore seen, in a technical sense, as capable in all circumstances of inflicting the necessary level of damage against the Soviet Union, and, due to their vulnerability, none 'would have other

180 *Breaking the impasse?*

than a limited retaliatory capacity.' Nevertheless, the point was also made that before undertaking any attempted pre-emptive attack against British strategic nuclear forces alone, the Soviet Union would need to be satisfied that no retaliation could be expected from the United States (and to Sandys, for example, who was still lobbying the case for Blue Streak from his new post as Minister of Aviation, this was a wholly improbable scenario).

In the light of their analysis of the three options, the study group found that from the mid-1960s onwards only a mobile weapons system, involving either an air-launched or sea-launched ballistic missile, 'would give a reasonable assurance of maintaining the target deterrent capability in all circumstances'. As surface ships were too vulnerable to enemy attack, Polaris-equipped nuclear submarines seemed the best sea-launched alternative for a future deterrent system. Polaris was, however, 'as yet unproven', and the Admiralty proposal, if a decision to adopt was taken, involved construction of the submarines in the UK (of which nine would be needed, each carrying 16 missiles), as well as the provision of UK-produced warheads for the missiles. Submarine building could not start before 1965, the first submarine would be commissioned in 1969, and the whole force deployed by about 1974. Total capital costs for the entire programme were estimated at £350 million, with annual running costs of about £13–14 million. An air-launched mobile system would have to be based on the WS 138A ballistic missile, again with warheads provided by the UK, which the existing V-bombers could be adapted to carry. But the earliest the V-bombers could deploy the missiles would be 1966, and their effective life was not seen as being much beyond 1970, meaning that a new long-range and long-endurance aircraft, capable of maintaining standing airborne patrols so as to reduce vulnerability to pre-emptive attack, would have to be developed in the meantime for introduction in the early 1970s. Costs were expected to be 'of the same order' as a Polaris submarine force 'of equivalent striking power.'

The analysis contained in the interim report allowed the Study Group to draw several conclusions. Anticipated development in Soviet air defence capabilities would result in the V-force, even when armed with Blue Steel Mk 1, becoming increasingly ineffective after 1965. It would also be vulnerable to pre-emptive attack while on its airbases, although its ability to hit targets in the Soviet Union could be extended to about 1970 if equipped with WS 138A (the report contained the firm recommendation that plans for Blue Steel Mk 2 should be immediately cancelled).

The Study Group's main finding, however, and the one which had the greatest potential consequence, was that Blue Streak, even when housed in underground silos, was vulnerable to a Soviet pre-emptive missile strike – though it would have to be on a massive scale if it were to eliminate all the missiles in their silos. Blue Streak was therefore deemed as only effective, and so worthy of further development, if a 'fire first' weapon was considered acceptable as a strategic deterrent. In any event, the report recommended that ministers would have to consider whether they saw it as acceptable to rely on

US-supplied delivery systems as a replacement for the current V-bomber/ Blue Steel Mk 1 combination after the mid-1960s. If the answer was yes, it was advised that an approach should be made to the US authorities to either secure WS 138A for use with the V-bombers by 1966, or to obtain from the Americans a number of Polaris submarines by the same date (to fill the gap in capability that would otherwise result if the submarines had to be constructed in the UK). And if suitable arrangements were agreed with the Americans to either of these options, then Blue Streak should be cancelled. In the event that dependence on the Americans was rejected, or negotiations with them proved fruitless, the limitations of Blue Streak would have to be accepted, or cancellation should take place anyway and a gap in capability accepted until national resources could be mobilised to produce a new mobile deterrent system.[54]

The process of compiling the interim report had been marked by familiar inter-service disagreements, with the Admiralty representative on the BNDSG implicitly pressing for the cancellation of the Blue Streak programme (as Richard Moore has stressed, the bulk of Admiralty opinion nevertheless still exhibited little enthusiasm for Polaris at this stage, and opposition to Blue Streak was partly conditioned by the long-held fears it would distort the balance of the defence budget).[55] The RAF's position on the study group had been put forward with vigour by the Vice Chief of the Air Staff, Air Marshal Sir Edmund Hudleston, who felt that insufficient attention had been paid to the Air Staff's contention that any airborne successor to the V-force would not simply be a replacement system, but have far superior characteristics such as long endurance and quicker reaction and dispersal times. Examining a near-final draft of the report, for example, Hudleston wrote to Powell to 'object categorically' to its conclusions, which he saw as expressing a clear preference for a submarine-borne successor system.[56]

Some involved with the Study Group's work found the prolonged effort to demonstrate Blue Streak's vulnerability to be counter-productive as it could expose some of the underlying weaknesses of the arguments for an 'independent' deterrent if it was seen as designed to thwart a direct Soviet nuclear strike. As one MoD official put it, 'I find it extremely difficult to visualise any circumstances in which the Russians would wish to launch a preemptive attack against the United Kingdom alone, whether or not we were acting in concert with the United States.' 'If the report goes forward as it stands,' he continued, 'I should have thought that it would be the finish of our deterrent policy. Ministers would abandon Blue Streak and, after a period spent in toying with the idea of getting the Americans to supply us with the means of acting independently of themselves, would come to the conclusion that the whole operation was too difficult and expensive to be sustained.'[57]

After having been furnished with a copy of the long-anticipated report, Watkinson was told by Powell that his group had not been able to reconcile the conflicting views of its members over the best means of maintaining the deterrent after 1965, 'largely due to political factors' which were outside its terms of reference. These included, for example, whether the adoption of such US systems as WS 138A or Polaris was regarded as politically acceptable. When it came to the issue of Blue Streak's vulnerability to pre-emptive attack, the likelihood that the Soviet Union might mount such an attack on the UK alone was also regarded as a matter for political judgement. Powell's own belief was that, despite its rising costs, the Blue Streak programme should be continued otherwise the concept of a 'British-controlled' contribution to the Western deterrent would have to be supplanted by the 'British operation' of part of the American deterrent force.[58]

The Minister of Defence was, however, of a very different cast of mind, and during December 1959 he had begun to explore some of the alternative options to Blue Streak. At the start of that month he held a conversation with Macmillan in Downing Street where it was said that 'the main argument against Blue Streak was that it could easily be knocked out by the Russians and would only be an effective weapon if we were prepared to fire it first – that is before the first nuclear bomb had actually fallen on the UK.'[59] On 1 January 1960 Watkinson sent a minute to the Prime Minister explaining that a decision over Blue Streak would have to be taken soon and that he was

> much attracted by the concept of a 'mobile' deterrent which is largely indestructible. Blue Streak has been outmoded by the march of events. The Powell report, which I shall shortly circulate, supports this view. It is clear already, therefore, that we cannot justify the present planned deployment of Blue Streak (60 in hard sites). We must either cancel it, or consider a very limited deployment, perhaps allied with its use in space research.[60]

Within the Minister's Private Office, Watkinson's officials had also turned in decisive fashion against continuing with Blue Streak. Richard Chilver, for example, pointed to the new ideas which had been pushed by the Foreign Office and the Treasury within the Future Policy study for 'a greater dependence on the United States in respect of deterrent weapons, apart from their warheads (which we should continue to produce), than has hitherto been regarded as acceptable.' Chilver also mentioned 'more reassuring information about the availability of the WS 138A, in the light of which the Chiefs of Staff are likely to conclude that, on military grounds alone, there is no justification for continuing with the development of Blue Streak.' Any decision about the programme's future would have to be based on the government's basic objectives in nuclear policy, he continued, and 'If we are prepared to be dependent on the Americans, and if we are ready to drop out of the development of large rockets, then clearly the right answer is to cancel Blue Streak at once and operate whatever American weapon system meets our requirements and the Americans are prepared to make available to us.' Considerations of industrial policy, including the effects of cancellation on the firms involved with the project, could not be allowed to outweigh the political and military arguments which were gathering against continuation with development. Watkinson had already determined, Chilver noted, that he could not accept reliance on Blue Streak alone (in whatever size of force) to provide the future form of the deterrent. The inference from this was that once the V-bombers armed with the Blue Steel powered bombs were judged inadequate due to the development of Soviet air defence, 'we should rely either on the WS 138A launched from the V bombers, so long as they last, and later from a new lifting platform, or on Polaris launched from submarines or surface ships.'[61]

Chilver's paper for Watkinson represented not merely his own views, but also those of the new Chief Scientific Adviser (CSA) at the MoD, Sir Solly Zuckerman, who had replaced Brundrett at the start of January 1960. Zuckerman was to occupy the CSA position at the MoD for the next six and a half eventful years before transferring his base in government full-time to the Cabinet Office; he was also to become a figure of immense importance for the future of UK nuclear policy and to the eventual story of the Polaris improvement programme. His career as a government scientist had begun during the Second World War when his renowned expertise in primate physiology had given him an insight into the effects of wounding from modern weaponry, including blast waves from explosions. Research into the effects of high explosives led to a growing interest in gauging the impact of aerial bombing; during the latter stages of the war he served on the staff of Air Chief Marshal Sir Arthur Tedder in the Mediterranean and North West European theatres and began to have a discernible influence over targeting policy. The war years were also important as they brought Zuckerman into contact with Mountbatten when the latter was Chief of Combined Operations, the start of a close association which was to continue to have an influence in the corridors of Whitehall until the latter's departure as CDS in 1965. During the mid-1950s Zuckerman was drawn back into official work on the blast effects of nuclear weapons on human tissue, and in early 1958 was asked to chair the Air Ministry's Strategic Scientific Policy Committee (which also included Sir William Cook from AWRE among its members). Possessed of immense energy, a mind prepared to challenge the orthodox, and a wide range of contacts (many in the United States), and through his experience of serving on various government scientific and advisory boards over the previous few years, Zuckerman had already developed the instincts of an experienced Whitehall operator by the time he arrived at the Ministry of Defence at the start of 1960. But like his patron Mountbatten, now ensconced as Chief of the Defence Staff, he attracted controversy and disapproval, and was distrusted by many of the officials whose views he delighted in undermining.[62]

When he arrived at the MoD Zuckerman had purposely eschewed Brundrett's former title of 'Chief Scientist' to reflect the fact that his conception of the CSA's role was that of a general policy adviser to the Minister of Defence.

He did not wish to be regarded as an individual who necessarily specialised in the technical or scientific aspects of particular aspects of the defence research and development programme, but as someone who had licence to range much wider in their activities. He later recalled that Brundrett had taken a rather narrow view of his responsibilities, confining himself to the task of deciding which weapons systems should be allocated to each of the services, and he 'did not exercise his imagination to any extent in dealing with strategic matters.' Such a narrowing of interests of defence scientists in government service, as well as their isolation from the wider scientific community, did not find favour with the permanent secretaries at the MoD during this period, especially as the trend in the United States was very much the opposite. A decade later he remembered:

> This was the bill of goods which was sold to me when I was persuaded in 1959 to cease being a three-day-a-week amateur in Whitehall, and to come in as Brundrett's successor. Reluctant though I was to give up my independence I did so, and then set about the business of getting a scientific point of view to bear on all aspects of defence – from questions of major strategic policy, through the field of operational requirements, and on to projects and defence research. My status was the same as that of the CDS and Permanent Secretary, and I reported directly to the Minister. In fact there was a reciprocal inter-change on all matters with the PUS and CDS in the service we tended to the Minister.[63]

Indeed, much to the consternation of many senior officials and service officers, a close working relationship soon developed between Zuckerman and Mountbatten.[64] Zuckerman also had excellent personal relations with the Pentagon's first Director of Defense Research and Engineering, Herbert York, and with York's successor Harold Brown. Such was Zuckerman's reputation that he was also made to understand by the Cabinet Secretary soon after his appointment that, as well as his duties at the MoD, he was expected to offer informal scientific advice to Downing Street on matters connected to defence policy and disarmament.[65]

Where Brundrett had been a vociferous supporter of Blue Streak, Zuckerman exhibited profound scepticism. In October 1959 his Air Ministry Strategic Scientific Policy Committee had submitted a report on the maintenance of deterrent systems to the BNDSG. This had argued firmly for an invulnerable deterrent, able to survive a surprise attack by a potential enemy, as an essential aspect of credibility. Even when sited underground, the report made plain, Blue Streak would not meet this requirement. Only a force of long-endurance aircraft, on constant airborne patrol, or missile-firing submarines, could provide the assurance necessary.[66]

The conclusion offered by the report was that Blue Streak could not be regarded as a weapon suitable for retaliatory use, since it could be eliminated by a Soviet first strike with ballistic missiles. By the time he had become

CSA, Zuckerman was finding the whole notion of persevering with a 'fire first' weapon such as Blue Streak quite incredible. To Watkinson, who was beginning to come under heavy pressure from Sandys at the Ministry of Aviation to save the programme (partly for the sake of the defence contractors with a stake in Blue Streak), Zuckerman affirmed that,

> We are contributing to a deterrence system. In a democracy, one cannot conceive of a Government giving the order to fire first. That is why ... no-one in Whitehall believes an order to fire would be given until – as it is usually put – 'a Russian mushroom rose above our heads'. ... As for the idea of our going it alone with our rockets, if the Russians make a stab at Western Germany – and that strikes me as completely unreal – not only is there a [NATO] Supreme Commander and his nuclear force, if the Russians believed we would strike first and yet intended to advance, they would hit us at the same time, and if the Americans thought we would operate independently and against their judgement, so destroying US troops in Europe, they would surely see that our position was sterilised at the start.

Watkinson's decision over the future of Blue Streak, Zuckerman counselled, would be a 'grave one either way.' But he thought the argument was 'overwhelmingly' for cancellation, despite the effect on 'intangibles like national prestige'. The companies engaged in Blue Streak development might well be demoralised if it were abandoned but Zuckerman could not 'think of anything more likely to demoralise our Services than if the advice of the Chiefs of Staff is rejected. To me, the overriding consideration is that your decision does not weaken the Western defence, and that however painful and expensive your decision may seem now, a decision on the same lines would become more painful and more expensive if it were longer deferred.'[67]

By now, as Zuckerman had noted, the COS had also become convinced that the military and strategic case for Blue Streak was unsustainable. Having digested the BNDSG interim report, at the start of February 1960 they recommended cancellation, advising Watkinson that the Americans should be asked for a replacement weapon on condition that it was 'operationally efficient', would be ready for when the UK wanted it, and could be 'procured with no strings attached'. The COS view was that in view of recent positive reports on its progress from the United States, Skybolt (as WS 138A was by now known) should be the weapon that the British aimed to secure. Much on their minds was the need to prolong the life of the V-force 'in which such a great deal of money has already been invested' beyond the mid-1960s. After this, echoing the BNDSG report, it was recognised that a new study would be needed on the form of the deterrent from around 1970 onwards, and whether it was best to look to extend the life of Skybolt, by launching it from a new aircraft platform, or to building a force of Polaris-carrying submarines.[68]

186 *Breaking the impasse?*

Unanimity amongst the COS was helped by the fact that Boyle – a strong advocate for Blue Streak – had been replaced as CAS by Air Chief Marshal Sir Thomas Pike at the start of the year, while under the new plans the RAF retained its prime role as the carrier of the deterrent. US Air Force progress with the Skybolt project had been watched with growing interest by many RAF officers during 1959 (Pike, for example, was a notable enthusiast) and the Americans had offered reassurances that it could be made compatible with the Mark 2 version of the Vulcan. Within the Air Ministry adoption of Skybolt held out the prospect of contending with the Admiralty over the strategic deterrent role during the 1970s, when the case could be made for a new airborne system to replace the aging V-bomber force. Moreover, George Ward, the Secretary of State for Air, another proponent of manned aircraft programmes, returned from a trip to the US in January 1960 ready to press the case for Skybolt, the missile's development having just received full approval from a high-level Pentagon panel.[69]

From the Admiralty's perspective there were still too many doubts over Polaris for a determined push for its acquisition to be made at the start of 1960, while opting for (a relatively inexpensive) Skybolt in the short-term did not preclude a move for Polaris as a successor system to the V-bombers from around 1970 onwards.[70] At one meeting between the COS and Watkinson in March it was agreed that

> The great merit of Skybolt was its comparative cheapness, because we already had the means of carrying the weapon. Polaris was much more expensive, and we would not be in a position to fit it into our own submarines for a considerable time. Nonetheless, a decision to acquire Skybolt now need not prejudice the acquisition of Polaris later, should we consider it desirable to have both types of weapon.[71]

British officials evidently felt that the Eisenhower administration in Washington would be amenable to their future approaches and that Polaris would be treated in the same fashion as Skybolt. Developments over the next 12 months were, however, to show that this was very far from being the case as the Americans sought to address some of the issues of nuclear defence that had begun to open up strains within the North Atlantic Alliance during the late 1950s. The decision to cancel Blue Streak, as the next chapter will begin to illustrate, would necessitate a sharp turn toward the United States for the future supply of nuclear delivery systems, a development which was to generate a whole new host of political and diplomatic complications.

Notes

1 Moore, *Royal Navy and Nuclear Weapons*, 155–6.
2 See Selkirk to Sandys, 21 April 1958; Sandys to Dickson, 24 June 1958, ADM 1/27375; Ward minute for Sandys, 16 December 1958; Selkirk minute for Sandys, 19 December 1958, DEFE 7/2278. See Moore, *Royal Navy and Nuclear Weapons*,

156–8; Moore, *Nuclear Illusion, Nuclear Reality*, 136–7; Clark, *Nuclear Diplomacy*, 285–6.
3 D(58)57, 'Ballistic Rockets,' memorandum by the Minister of Defence, 3 November 1958, CAB 131/19.
4 See Wynn, *RAF Nuclear Deterrent Forces*, 386–7; Confidential Annex to COS(59) 1st Meeting, item 2, 1 January 1959; Confidential Annex to COS(59) 4th Meeting, item 10, 13 January 1959, DEFE 4/115.
5 'Britain to Develop Blue Streak Missile,' *The Times*, 11 February 1959. That it was Sandys who had held the briefing was revealed a year later by *The Times'* defence correspondent.
6 'What Kind of a Deterrent?' *The Times*, 25 February 1959.
7 *Hansard*, HC, vol 600, cols 1138–40, 25 February 1959.
8 'An Elusive Deterrent,' *The Times*, 6 March 1959.
9 See Powell minute for Sandys, RRP/340/59, 23 March 1959; Sandys minute for Powell, 23 March 1959, DEFE 13/617. Powell had not wanted the Vice Chiefs of the Air and Naval Staffs to be members of the Group, as he feared they would be too strongly biased in favour of their service interests, but later modified his views.
10 See McLeod minute for Dickson, 'British Nuclear Deterrent,' RWM/762, 30 April 1959; Dickson minute for Powell, 'Future of the UK Deterrent,' WFD/622, 4 May 1959; Powell minute for Sandys, RRP/542/59, 8 May 1959, DEFE 7/2300.
11 See Brook minute for Macmillan, 'The Position of the United Kingdom in World Affairs,' 4 November 1958, CAB 21/2972; for the earlier June 1958 report of the same title see papers in CAB 130/153.
12 Brook minute for Macmillan, 'Future Policy,' 20 February 1959, PREM 11/2945.
13 See Study of Future Policy: Record of a Meeting held at Chequers, 7 June 1959, CAB 134/1929, and in PREM 11/2945.
14 For the initial meeting of Brook's Steering Committee, see FP(A)(59) 1st Meeting, 30 July 1959, CAB 134/1930.
15 Study of Future Policy: Record of a Meeting held at Chequers, 7 June 1959, CAB 134/1929, and in PREM 11/2945.
16 See L. J. Sabatini minute for Powell, DS 837, 4 June 1959; Admiral Sir Charles Lambe letter to Powell, 16 June 1959; Powell minute for Sir Frederick Hoyar Millar, RRP/708/59, 9 July 1959, DEFE 7/2300. For the first meeting of the group, see BND(SG)(59) 1st Meeting, 27 July 1959, DEFE 10/665.
17 Dean letter to Mountbatten, 9 October 1958, PUSD records, FCO.
18 Confidential Annex to COS(58)77th Meeting, item 1, 3 September 1958, DEFE 4/111.
19 See R. C. Kent minute for R. G. K. May, AUS(A)/5270, 10 October 1958, and attached note, 'The numbers of V-bomber aircraft which will reach their targets,' DEFE 25/18; see also Kent minute for Director of Operations (B & R), 'Deterrent Capacity of the V-Bomber Force,' AUS(A)/3242, 3 November 1961, AIR 2/13712.
20 See Melville letter to Chilver, 'Defence Programme,' 12 November 1958, DEFE 7/2332.
21 R. C. Chilver minute for Powell, 6 January 1959, and attached draft paper, 'The Requirements of the Strategic Deterrent: Political Guidance,' DEFE 7/2278.
22 COS(JGW)(56)1st Meeting, 2 February 1956, DEFE 10/386. In general see Richard Moore, 'A JIGSAW puzzle for operational researchers: British global war studies, 1954–62,' *Journal of Strategic Studies*, 20, 1, June 1997, 75–91; Hennessy, *Secret State*, 141–4. Background papers for the organisation and history of the Joint Global War Committee can be found in CAB 21/4920.

23 COS(JGW)(57)3rd Meeting, 9 October 1957, DEFE 10/386.
24 COS(JGW)(58)2nd Meeting, 11 April 1958, DEFE 10/386; and see Brundrett minute, 'Provision of Staff for Further Joint Global War Studies,' 4 June 1958, DEFE 19/15.
25 See Powell minute for Watkinson, RRP/416/59, 9 April 1959; G. S. Cole minute for COS, 'Establishment of JIGSAW,' COS.491/11/4/60, 11 April 1959, DEFE 19/15; COS(JGW)(59)4th Meeting, 12 June 1959; COS(JGW)(59)8th Meeting, 9 December 1959, DEFE 10/386.
26 COS(JGW)(58)9, 'Civil Studies,' report by the Joint Study Group, 12 December 1958; COS(JGW)(59)3, 'A Preliminary Assessment of Breakdown in Global War,' report by the Joint Global War Study Group, 13 March 1959, DEFE 10/387. For the general concept of 'breakdown' see, for example, Zuckerman, *Monkeys, Men, and Missiles*, 295; Moore, *Nuclear Illusion, Nuclear Reality*, 60.
27 BND(SG)(59)3, 'Task of British Controlled Contribution to Nuclear Deterrent,' note by the Joint Secretaries, 17 July 1959, DEFE 10/665.
28 BND(SG)(59) 1st Meeting, 27 July 1959, DEFE 10/665; COS(JGW)(59)5th Meeting, 20 July 1959, DEFE 10/386; COS(JGW)(SG) 23rd meeting, 6 August 1959, DEFE 10/389.
29 COS(JGW)(59)10(Revised Draft), 'Request by the British Nuclear Deterrent Study Group,' note by the Joint Secretary, 4 September 1959, and attached 'Effects of a Megaton Attack on Forty Soviet Cities,' report by the Joint Global War Study Group, DEFE 10/387.
30 J. M. Wilson minute for Powell, 'British Nuclear Deterrent Study Group,' 18 September 1959, DEFE 7/2300. It is evident that the Joint Global War Study Group adopted a conservative approach and went to some lengths to avoid any reference to the form of a future deterrent, see COS(JGW)(59)6th Meeting, 18 September 1959, DEFE 10/386.
31 See Harold Macmillan, *Pointing the Way, 1959–1961* (London, 1972), 19.
32 See Harold Watkinson, *Turning Points: A Record of Our Times* (London, 1986), 107–8, 112; and also Pierre, *Nuclear Politics*, 169.
33 Watkinson minute for Powell, 28 October 1959, DEFE 25/13.
34 Bligh, 'Note for the record,' 8 December 1959, PREM 11/2945.
35 MM 18/59, 'Record of a Meeting between Mr Harold Watkinson and Mr Thomas Gates, in Paris on Tuesday, 15th December 1959,' DEFE 32/13.
36 For extensive coverage of this subject, see Constantine A. Pagedas, *Anglo-American Strategic Relations and the French Problem, 1960–1963: A Troubled Partnership* (London, 2000).
37 Kohl, *French Nuclear Diplomacy*, 16–44.
38 See Heuser, *NATO, Britain, France and the FRG*, 93–5; Colette Barbier, 'The French decision to develop a military nuclear programme in the 1950s,' *Diplomacy and Statecraft*, 4, 1, 1993, 103–13.
39 Kohl, *French Nuclear Diplomacy*, 61–87.
40 For more background on the French programme see Wolf Mendl, *Deterrence and Persuasion: French Nuclear Armament in the Context of National Policy, 1945–69* (New York, 1970).
41 'Agreed Note on Military Programmes of Fourth Countries,' 23 March 1957, *Foreign Relations of the United States, 1955–1957, Volume XXVII: Western Europe and Canada* (Washington, 1992), 785–93.
42 See Pagedas, *Anglo-American Strategic Relations and the French Problem*, 46–9, 76, 81, 95–7.
43 FP(B)(59)34, 'The Deterrent,' note by the Ministry of Defence, 5 November 1959, CAB 134/1936.
44 FP(B)(59)37, 'United Kingdom Deterrent Policy in 1970,' note by the Joint Secretaries, 7 November 1959, CAB 134/1936.

45 FP(B)(59) 12th Meeting, 12 November 1959, CAB 134/1934.
46 FP(B)(59)40, 'The Deterrent,' note by the Joint Secretaries, and attached Annex I and II, 19 November 1959, CAB 134/1936.
47 FP(B)(59) 15th Meeting, 23 November 1959, CAB 134/1934.
48 FP(A)(59)8, 'United Kingdom Deterrent Policy in 1960–1970,' note by the Chairman of the Working Group, and attached paper, 30 November 1959, CAB 134/1930.
49 FP(B)(59)42, 'The Deterrent,' note by the Joint Secretaries, and attached draft section of Part II, 24 November 1959, CAB 134/1936.
50 FP(A)(59)8, 'United Kingdom Deterrent Policy in 1960–1970,' note by the Chairman of the Working Group, and attached paper, 30 November 1959, CAB 134/1930.
51 FP(A)(59) 7th Meeting, 4 December 1959, CAB 134/1930. Dean's working group was given the task of reworking the Steering Committee's conclusions into language for the final draft of the Future Policy Study report, see FP(B)(59)46, 'Part II,' note by the Joint Secretaries, and attached paper, 15 December 1959, CAB 134/1936.
52 See BND(SG)(59) 13th Meeting, 23 December 1959, DEFE 7/2301.
53 See Wynn, *RAF Nuclear Deterrent Forces*, 394–5; Moore, *Nuclear Illusion, Nuclear Reality*, 43–6; BND(SG)(59)19(Final), 'British Controlled Contribution to the Nuclear Deterrent,' Interim Report by the British Nuclear Deterrent Study Group, 31 December 1959, DEFE 7/1328.
54 Ibid.
55 See, for example, Vice-Admiral L. G. Durlacher minute for Powell, No 040/3B, 14 December 1959, DEFE 7/2216; and Moore, *Nuclear Illusion, Nuclear Reality*, 136–7.
56 See Hudleston minute for Powell, 'BND(SG)(59)18,' VCAS 4543, 16 December 1959, DEFE 7/2301.
57 R. C. Chilver minute for Powell, 7 December 1959, DEFE 7/2301.
58 Powell minute for Watkinson, 'British Nuclear Deterrent Study Group,' RRP/1355/59, 31 December 1959, DEFE 7/2216.
59 Bligh, 'Note for the Record,' 8 December 1959, PREM 11/2945.
60 Watkinson minute for Macmillan, 1 January 1960, PREM 11/2945.
61 Chilver minute for Watkinson, 22 January 1960, DEFE 25/13. See also Mottershead minute for Lawrence-Wilson, 5 January 1960, DEFE 7/1392.
62 For background on Zuckerman see his two volumes of memoirs, *From Apes to Warlords: The Autobiography of Solly Zuckerman, 1904–1946* (London, 1978), and *Monkeys, Men and Missiles*; and also P. L. Krohn, 'Solly Zuckerman, Baron Zuckerman of Burnham Thorpe,' *Biographical Memoirs of Fellows of the Royal Society*, 41, November 1995, 576–598; John Peyton, *Solly Zuckerman: A Scientist Out of the Ordinary* (London, 2001).
63 Zuckerman letter to Sir William Armstrong, SZ/0837, 1 May 1970, DEFE 23/69.
64 On the so-called 'Zuckbatten' axis, see Philip Ziegler, *Mountbatten: The official biography* (London, 1985), 164, 581.
65 See Zuckerman, *Monkeys, Men and Missiles*, 194.
66 See Hudleston minute for Powell, 'The Maintenance of the Deterrent,' 19 October 1959, and attached report, 'The Nuclear Deterrent – 1970 and After,' note by the Air Ministry Strategic Scientific Policy Committee, AMSSPC/P(59)17, 5 October 1959, DEFE 19/11.
67 Zuckerman minute for Watkinson, 19 February 1960, DEFE 25/13.
68 COS(60)28, 'British Controlled Contribution to the Nuclear Deterrent,' memorandum for the Minister of Defence by the Chiefs of Staff, 5 February 1960, DEFE 5/99. Watkinson had expressed himself satisfied with the COS report, see

Playfair minute for Mountbatten, 'British Controlled Contribution to the Nuclear Deterrent,' EWP/112/60, 5 February 1960, DEFE 19/11.
69 See 'Notes of a Meeting held in the Secretary of State's Room on 21st January, 1960,' AIR 19/813; and see Richard Moore, 'Bad Strategy and Bomber Dreams: A New View of the Blue Streak Cancellation,' *Contemporary British History*, 27, 2, 2013, 145–66.
70 For this important point, see Clark, *Nuclear Diplomacy*, 280–84.
71 MM/COS (60) 2nd Meeting, Meeting of the Minister of Defence with the Chiefs of Staff, 24 March 1960, DEFE 32/13.

5 The future nuclear programme and the cancellation of Blue Streak, December 1959–April 1960

The formation of the Nuclear Requirements for Defence Committee

While officials on the British Nuclear Deterrent Study Group had struggled to reconcile their divergent views on the long-term form of the deterrent during 1959, Macmillan and some of his closest ministerial colleagues were considering in critical fashion the entire future nuclear weapons production programme. After a protracted process that had begun in the spring of 1958, and straddled the negotiations that led to the conclusion of the MDA, the Prime Minister had eventually given his interim agreement at the end of that year to the MoD's plans for a wide-ranging programme involving the development and production of new megaton and kiloton-yield warheads. An important part of the rationale behind this decision was the need to keep an active and viable research and development programme at AWRE which would be sufficient to maintain the flow of exchanges that had recently been established under the MDA. The strain on the UK's supplies of fissile material could be alleviated to a large extent by the barter arrangements over nuclear materials which formed part of the revisions to the MDA agreed by London and Washington in May 1959. However, the MoD was conscious that its ambitious production programme and plans over the next ten years had yet to receive ministerial approval. Towards the end of November 1959, Downing Street officials were duly alerted by Brundrett, the outgoing Chief Scientist at the MoD, to the need for a ministerial decision on the nuclear programme.[1]

Although he could see a prima facie case for bringing the matter to the Defence Committee, the Cabinet Secretary was nevertheless uneasy that decisions might be taken on warhead development and production before ministers had considered the results of both the Future Policy Study, and the MoD's examination of future deterrent systems.[2] The Cabinet Secretary's concerns were a manifestation of the common feeling of Downing Street officials that the details of the nuclear warhead programme, including its crucial financial aspects, were often confined to a few key figures in the MoD and AEA. The tendency was for the MoD and the individual services to generate their own understanding of the broad lines of the government's nuclear policy and to translate this into a set of requirements for nuclear weapons which were then issued, via the Ministry of Supply, to the AEA. By the time the Prime Minister, or senior ministers in other departments, became involved in the issue they were simply presented with a list of warhead requirements which threatened to establish the AEA's development and production programme for the next few years even while some of the fundamental aspects of defence policy which were supposed to inform the nuclear programme remained under review and undecided.

During 1959 the need for better coordination of nuclear policy at an official level had become more widely recognised. In August, Sir Roger Makins, Plowden's successor as head of the AEA, wrote to Powell at the MoD suggesting the need for a review of the machinery for inter-departmental coordination of nuclear matters, particularly on the military side. After consultation between Powell, Makins and Brook, the former advanced suggestions for new committees to oversee the development and production of nuclear weapons, as well as the requirements of the services. On 7 December 1959 Powell convened a meeting with AEA, Ministry of Aviation, Treasury and service ministry officials to discuss his ideas for revising the committee structure dealing with matters of policy in this whole area. There was general agreement with the proposal to create an Atomic Weapons Production Committee to review nuclear weapons requirements and to formulate a programme for dealing with them; as the main business of this committee was expected to lie with technical issues, the chair and secretariat were to be provided by the newly-formed Ministry of Aviation (which had recently superseded the old Ministry of Supply, with all its nuclear warhead responsibilities). The meeting also agreed to establish a new high-level committee of officials to be known as the Nuclear Requirements for Defence Committee (NRDC) which was to operate within the Cabinet Office structure of official committees. This was to meet only occasionally and consider major issues of policy connected with the nuclear requirements of the services, but was also expected to take over the functions of coordinating policy over nuclear testing from the Nuclear Tests Policy Committee.

The creation of the NRDC also meant that the residual committee structure dealing with nuclear matters, which had its origins in the early years of the Attlee Government, would be dissolved, since no defence matters would henceforth be referred to the Cabinet Office-run Atomic Energy (Official) Committee, which was to become concerned purely with questions of civil nuclear power, while the largely moribund Atomic Energy (Ministerial) Committee would also be allowed to lapse. As Powell's meeting noted, 'Defence questions [on nuclear subjects] which required reference to Ministers could be put by the Minister of Defence to the Prime Minister for discussion by those concerned.' It was proposed that the NRDC would be chaired by the Permanent Secretary at the MoD, and include representatives from the Treasury, Ministry of Aviation, the separate services, the COS

Committee, the AEA, as well as the Chief Scientific Adviser at the MoD.[3] After some initial qualms, and protracted correspondence in early 1960, the Foreign Office and the Commonwealth Relations Office were also invited to nominate members, and the terms of reference and composition of the NRDC were finally settled.[4] An attempt by Powell's successor as Permanent Under Secretary at the MoD, Sir Edward Playfair, to scupper the formation of the new Committee (preferring either no change at all or purely ad hoc arrangements) was successfully countered by the Cabinet Office in the spring of 1960; one of Brook's deputies, arguing that change had to pushed through, noted that, 'The system under which nuclear policy has been kept largely as a private preserve of a few people in the Ministry of Defence has not worked well.'[5]

These incipient changes to the committee structure surrounding the nuclear weapons programme came too late to have an influence on the immediate need for the MoD to receive ministerial approval for its long-term plans. In mid-December 1959 Watkinson had approached Macmillan again with details of the MoD's proposed programme, arguing that AWRE needed 'rather more formal guidance than in the past', and referring to unease amongst the establishment's highly skilled scientific staff at 'present uncertainties.' The Prime Minister was reminded that in 1958 he had agreed 'in broad principle' to a programme which would by 1970 provide a total stockpile of about 200 megaton and 1,475 kiloton warheads, and that these were the figures that had been supplied to the Americans in order to secure Congressional acquiescence to the extension of nuclear assistance to the UK under the MDA. Subsequent exchanges with the Americans had provided valuable new information that allowed work to commence on a whole series of new British versions of US warhead designs for a variety of roles (including, for example, air defence and anti-submarine operations), including a new range of sub-kiloton weapons for possible Army use. Stockpile numbers for 1970 were now planned as 200 megaton, 850 kiloton, and 1,300 sub-kiloton weapons, all at an estimated cost of £380 million over the next ten years.[6]

The paper's actual author, Brundrett, felt that the programme it itemised was 'absolutely essential if we are to maintain our relations with the United States on the one hand and [have] any intention to regard ourselves as a nuclear power on the other.'[7] Aside from short-term approval for the warhead production programme for the next financial year, the Chancellor of the Exchequer was however unconvinced that any longer term decisions were warranted by ministers. As he informed the Prime Minister: 'Any major decision on the size, and date of completion, of a UK nuclear *stockpile* should presumably have regard to our future policy, when this has been agreed, and to the "delivery systems" shown to be required by the three services for the fulfilment of that policy.'[8] The Prime Minister's own officials, in line with the Cabinet Secretary's earlier reservations, also thought that the MoD was going too far in its proposals, and that more general questions about the future size of the deterrent and the role of nuclear weapons in defence policy should be settled first. In none of the recent reviews of defence policy, Macmillan was informed, had the size and shape of Britain's nuclear forces been considered by ministers. Once the results of the Future Policy Study and the BNDSG's work had been digested, moreover, further time would be required so that any future proposals could be properly discussed with the Americans 'who have recently been suggesting that there may be an element of over-insurance in the Western strategic deterrent.'[9]

On the eve of the small ministerial meeting called to discuss Watkinson's minute, the Minister of Defence nevertheless repeated his call for a decision on Aldermaston's long-term programme which would form

> a definite basis for their research and development work. AWRE are faced with a serious problem since in the absence of a clearly defined programme they were experiencing difficulty in keeping together their highly skilled scientific staff who were becoming uneasy about their future employment. Every month's delay in settling the nuclear weapons programme was liable to cause further losses of skilled staff.

However, meeting with Watkinson and Heathcoat Amory on 31 December to discuss the issue, Macmillan was liable to agree with the Chancellor's opinion that before the Future Policy Study had been properly discussed it would be impossible to agree anything other than short-term requirements in the nuclear field. Only limited endorsement, allowing AWRE to plan for the next 18 months or so, was felt appropriate in the absence of inter-departmental (and especially Treasury) agreement. A production programme for megaton and kiloton warheads in the financial years 1960/61 and 1961/62 was therefore approved by this select group of ministers (including 24 Red Snow warheads for free-falling megaton bombs approved for production in 1960/61, and a further 50 for 1961/62, by when the warhead was also expected to be used in the Blue Steel powered bomb still under development). In addition, the meeting also agreed that development should proceed for a kiloton warhead suitable for a surface-to-air guided weapon, a sub-kiloton warhead planned for Army use, and a new lightweight megaton warhead (this was intended to be an 'Anglicised' version of the US Mark 47 warhead, and was planned for a future mobile deterrent system then under study by the BNDSG), although production of the latter two was not yet authorised.[10]

The Cabinet Secretary had already been troubled in 1958 by the MoD's tendencies to present the nuclear requirements of the services for ministerial consideration with little time for coordination, or evidence that the concerns of other departments had been addressed beforehand (and this in turn was regarded as an outgrowth of the MoD's inability to work closely with either the Air Ministry or the Ministry of Supply on such critical issues). The decision-making process seen in late 1959, where important proposals were presented to ministers for high-level discussion at short notice and before interdepartmental agreement could be reached, was as familiar as it was unsatisfactory.

To Brook, the salience of nuclear issues in ministerial discussion of defence policy, combined with the tendency of the Ministry of Defence to monopolise debate over both the shape of nuclear forces and the technical and financial information that underpinned the future weapons programme, must have made the formation of the NRDC seem particularly warranted. In June 1960 he was finally able to despatch a minute to Macmillan informing him of the changes which had been made in arrangements for inter-departmental consideration of 'the military aspects of nuclear power'. 'The Ministry of Defence,' Brook noted, 'sometimes tend to think that these are matters primarily, if not exclusively, within their own competence, but in fact they often involve points which are of great importance financially and politically, as well as being complex from a technical atomic point of view.' The NRDC, he suggested, would allow departmental positions to be coordinated and advice dispensed before ministers were brought into the equation and issues were presented for discussion at the Cabinet's Defence Committee. Although its chair would be the Permanent Secretary at the MoD, the presence on the NRDC of a Secretary drawn from the Cabinet Office would allow Brook, as he put it for the Prime Minister's benefit, 'to keep an eye on its proceedings and if necessary to inform you personally of any points of particular importance.'[11] It was intended that one of the first pieces of work directed to the NRDC was a review of the nuclear weapons production programme.[12] Over the next six years, in fact, the NRDC was to play a significant role in facilitating the preparation of official proposals for the UK nuclear weapons programme, including test requirements. Yet aspirations that it would help to loosen the MoD's control over the programme, and improve the quality of information (particularly financial) available to other Whitehall departments were to be largely disappointed and calls for further reform to decision-making structures at both a ministerial and official level were to be revived in the mid-1960s.

The reception of the Future Policy Study

During the final months of 1959 there had been some signs of impatience from the Prime Minister over the time which Brook's Future Policy study was taking to complete. One reason for concern was that decisions by ministers over the next annual round of defence spending had to be made by the end of the year, but the larger background to make longer-term choices would not be available for consideration. The Cabinet Secretary, for his part, was keen that there should be time for full discussion of the Study's findings, and did not feel it advisable to do so in relation to any particular figures for defence spending; to Brook the purpose of his work was to set the overall direction for foreign and defence policy for the next decade, and he did not want the process rushed so that short-term decisions on defence spending could be rationalised.[13]

Brook finally delivered his voluminous Future Policy Study report, which was arranged in three parts, to the Prime Minister at the beginning of 1960, and it was subsequently circulated to the Cabinet.[14] Against a background where the struggle between the West and the Communist world was only likely to intensify over the next decade, the report painted a rather bleak picture of the West needing to devote even greater resources to its Cold War efforts merely to maintain the status quo. When it came to strategic nuclear policy, the central problem for the UK was the arrival of a rough strategic parity between the Superpowers. The report observed that a minority view on the Future Policy working group had argued that the ability and determination of the UK 'on its own to threaten Russia' was 'a priceless political asset which should not be thrown away, even if it is considered that we would not in fact, on our own and without the Americans, threaten to use our strategic nuclear force against the Russians in any circumstances except in the last resort against a threat of direct attack on this country.' Underpinning this view was a concern that in the future the United States might choose not to intervene in a European conflict if there was the chance of escalation to a nuclear clash with the Soviet Union, and it was felt 'very important that we should guard, not only against an American defection, but also against a Russian miscalculation – the danger that the Russians might, however misguidedly, think the Americans would not use their nuclear forces except in the event of an attack on the United States itself.'

However, the overwhelming view of most members of the Future Policy Study Group was that the fundamentals of the Anglo-American alliance would be maintained over the next decade, and 'that we should not think in terms of a United Kingdom strategic nuclear force designed to be capable of deterring Russia on its own.' The preferred idea was that British strategic nuclear forces should be seen as 'associated with and complementary to' the main US nuclear forces. In line with the existing Air Ministry plans and BNDSG assumptions, the Future Policy Study noted that by 1962 the UK force would have been built-up to inflict 50 per cent destruction on 40 Russian cities (the report actually mentioned 44 cities, but this appears to have been a slip caused by confusing aiming points for weapons with actual numbers of cities to be targeted). The report explained that

> This, or whatever else may from time to time be judged sufficient to deter the Russians, is the essential criterion for what is normally called an 'independent British nuclear deterrent'. This concept does not mean that it would be necessary to design and produce the entire weapons system in the United Kingdom. Elements, other than the warheads, could be purchased from the United States, provided they were obtained on terms which gave us a measure of control over them such that, in the last resort, we could use them or not use them alone or in concert with others as we thought fit.

But the majority of the group did not think, except in the case of a last resort response to a direct attack against the UK, that there would any circumstances in which strategic nuclear weapons would be used against the Soviet Union separately from the United States.

Instead, what was required was a force which was accepted by the Americans, and other members of the Western Alliance, as a significant contribution to the Western deterrent as a whole. Without this, it was conjectured,

> Our standing in the Alliance would suffer and we should lose a valuable means of influencing American policy in the event of a serious disagreement with them over the importance of a particular Communist threat. In terms of resources and effort, this concept may not necessarily lead to very different results from that of an 'independent deterrent'. In practice, a contribution significant in American eyes must also have significance for the Russians. Nevertheless, the distinction is important.

Such an approach, the report suggested, would allow the UK greater flexibility in determining the composition of its nuclear forces, while retaining the political advantages that they were assumed to confer.[15]

It was not considerations of the size, cost and composition of the deterrent, Brook was keen to stress, which had influenced the view of most of his Committee that the UK force should not be designed so as to face the Soviet Union alone. Rather, the key consideration, in line with every other aspect of the Future Policy Study, was the need to work with allies over the next decade. In a political sense, therefore, the Study had concluded that '*it did not seem feasible that we should act on our own, without the Americans, to threaten the Russians, except directly in the defence of our territory* [emphasis added].' While it had downgraded the military significance of the UK deterrent, the Study's report nevertheless found that it gave Britain political influence within the North Atlantic Alliance.[16]

One other significant influence on this conception of the future size of a UK nuclear force was the concern that devoting too large a share of defence spending to its maintenance would denude other areas of the defence budget and so erode the contribution that Britain could make in the multiple theatres around the world where it held commitments. The report had argued that the deterrent should not be

> so large as to prevent us from deploying adequate resources to meet our other defence responsibilities in cooperation with our allies. We stand to lose if, by investing excessively in the strategic deterrent, we are unable to do what is needed and expected of us as a Power with world-wide interests. In particular we must ensure that a proper balance is struck between the cost of the strategic nuclear deterrent and that of providing adequate and properly equipped forces as a whole.[17]

198   *The cancellation of Blue Streak*

Although assembled before ministers had had an opportunity to digest the contents of the voluminous Future Policy Study, the annual Defence White Paper published in the middle of February 1960 reflected similar ideas. This document, in its familiar bland language, again suggested that the arrival of Watkinson as Minister of Defence had helped restore some of the balance in the official rhetoric surrounding the role of nuclear and conventional forces in defence policy. Nuclear weapons were now described as 'only one component of the deterrent. Because of the need to meet local emergencies which could develop into major conflict, conventionally armed forces are a necessary complement to nuclear armaments.'[18] But the White Paper had no further detail to offer about deterrent policy, merely noting that the aim of research and development in the field was to 'devise a means of delivery that is invulnerable to the opposing defences.' Blue Streak development was 'continuing', the paper stated in somewhat coy fashion, but exclusive reliance on fixed missile sites as a successor to the V-force had not yet been decided and so 'therefore the possibilities of mobile launchers, whether aircraft or submarines, for long-range delivery of nuclear warheads are being investigated.'[19] The press, nevertheless, already had strong indications of the decisions that were imminent; *The Times* even carried a well-sourced story by its defence correspondent on the work of Powell's BNDSG.[20]

A few days after the publication of the White Paper, a small meeting of senior ministers was held on 20 February where the Future Policy Study's majority approach to deterrent capability was endorsed, and the fate of Blue Streak began to be determined. Here it was decided, so Macmillan concluded, that the UK should 'plan to continue as a nuclear power over the next decade or so.' There was general agreement that the purpose of Britain's deterrent should be 'to retain in being, under our ultimate control, a viable force that would be regarded as a significant contribution to the Western deterrent as a whole.' It was also noted that 'in deciding the allocation of resources within the total amount available for defence purposes, due consideration should be given to the importance of well-equipped conventional forces as a means of maintaining our world position.' In other words, the absolute priority that had been accorded the UK strategic nuclear force under the influence of Sandys in 1957–58, and that had caused such controversy amongst the COS, had now been diluted by economic realities and the need to meet the many demands of Britain's global military commitments. Turning to the proposal to cancel Blue Streak, the meeting observed that one option becoming increasingly attractive was to acquire Skybolt, so prolonging the effective life of the V-force until about 1970, and then to look at purchasing Polaris, perhaps in a later version, which when carried on UK nuclear submarines could provide the deterrent from then onwards.

In any event, Watkinson told the meeting that he thought it would be wrong to rely on a fixed-site weapon as a deterrent during the latter half of the coming decade, and favoured some kind of mobile missile instead. The case for continuing with Blue Streak was presented by Sandys, but was counteracted by the Chancellor's view that some reduction in spending plans for the deterrent was needed. Still somewhat equivocating, the Prime Minister nevertheless thought that the best means of delivering the deterrent in the 1970s would be with a mobile system, and in the meantime Skybolt might be available to fill any gap in capability that emerged.[21] A further meeting three days later allowed the Prime Minister to present his own paper formulating the sense of the initial ministerial discussion, and encapsulating the decision to abandon current plans for Blue Streak, although a much reduced missile launcher research programme might still be possible in order to mitigate the impact of cancellation on UK science and technology.[22]

Finally, on 24 February 1960 the full Defence Committee was provided with a copy of Macmillan's memorandum which laid down future policy for the deterrent. There was no question, as far as he was concerned, that 'in order to maintain our influence in world affairs' Britain should, as he put it, 'remain in the nuclear business.' However, the condition of nuclear 'equipoise' that would be reached in the 1960s required new thinking about the size and shape of the UK strategic nuclear force. 'Our purpose should be to maintain a strategic nuclear force which is accepted by the Americans, and by the Alliance as a whole, as a significant contribution to the Western deterrent,' Macmillan had argued. 'Without this, our standing in the Alliance would suffer and we should lose a valuable means of influencing American policy in the event of serious disagreement with them over the importance of a particular Communist threat. This would not mean that we were aiming to provide a force capable by itself of deterring Russia: nevertheless, a United Kingdom contribution, significant in American eyes, would also have significance for the Russians.'

The Prime Minister, therefore, had accepted majority opinion in the Future Policy Study and did not see a military case for a deterrent – informed by a precise criterion of deterrence – which could be used in a unilateral fashion against the Soviet Union. For the coming decade, Macmillan instead suggested that the UK strategic deterrent would have to be 'a viable force in being, under our ultimate control, *which is sufficiently large to accomplish our political purposes* [emphasis added]' and for which British warheads would have to be produced.

The final principle enunciated by the Prime Minister was also important in view of the looming issue of the possible inability of the V-bomber force to penetrate the air defences which the Soviet Union might have deployed by the end of the decade. He told his colleagues that, 'We should accept that there may be periods during which our deterrent will not be maintained at the strength which we are now about to achieve if such a diminished effectiveness could only be avoided by introducing costly new weapons systems which would be effective only for a limited period.'[23] This was, then, an admission that a destruction capability at a particular level was likely to be, in

200 The cancellation of Blue Streak

some point in the future, beyond the UK's limited resources. At the same time, this did not necessarily deal a major blow to deterrent policy if, as Macmillan now proposed, the criteria of effectiveness was measured through American eyes, while he had also affirmed that a nuclear force should be maintained under national control.

The Defence Committee's endorsement of the Prime Minister's new principles on deterrent policy was accompanied by the provisional decision to abandon the development of Blue Streak as a military weapons system, though its future as a space launcher for scientific and technological purposes was still a subject for debate. Decisions about the choice of a mobile weapons system, for use as a deterrent in the 1970s, could be delayed until a later stage.[24] But determining the optimum size of the UK strategic nuclear force was ideally a matter that had to be settled sooner, as it would have important implications for the numbers of Skybolt missiles that would have to be procured from the Americans, warhead production figures, and for the future study of a successor deterrent system.

One approach would simply be to ask the Americans directly what they considered to be an adequate UK contribution to the Western deterrent. At the end of 1959, informal and wide-ranging discussions on global defence problems, the first of their kind for many years, had been instituted in a low key fashion between senior British and US military staffs. At the start of February 1960, Bishop was expressing his hopes that the next round of the talks could include nuclear questions, telling the Cabinet Secretary, 'Discussions on the deterrent with the Americans are a prerequisite to any development or change in our present deterrent policy. We cannot very well take any deterrent policy decisions, or implement them, before we know where we are with the Americans.'[25]

A proposal made in February 1960 was that the next round of the talks should feature a presentation from Air Chief Marshal Mills (now head of the Joint Services Mission in Washington) to the US Joint Chiefs of Staff on the minimum size of the UK deterrent. On reflection, however, this was not thought appropriate because not all were agreed on what levels of damage capability – derived from the Joint Global War Study Group papers of 1959 – should be put forward to the Americans, and because 'the conclusion drawn from it might lead the Americans to ask us why we were embarking upon the production of our own deterrent when it was perfectly clear that they already had more than sufficient to achieve their aim.' Instead, a meeting was held between Sir Patrick Dean from the Foreign Office, Sir Edward Playfair from the MoD, Solly Zuckerman, and Air Chief Marshal Mills. Here it was agreed that the size and form of the deterrent should first be considered by ministers *before* any approach to the Americans was made, and that the first priority was to move ahead with the decision to cancel Blue Streak and secure a replacement, probably in the form of Skybolt. The consensus seemed to be that in view of the awkward negotiations that were to come over the next few months, the broader issue of the future size of the deterrent force was best left for later discussion.[26]

It was not surprising that no consensus could be reached on how the issue of the future minimum size of the deterrent should be presented to the Americans because views on this basic issue remained divided between the different services. At the start of February 1960, Watkinson, assuming that Blue Streak would be cancelled, had asked the COS for their views on the Skybolt requirements for the V-force or the numbers of Polaris submarines and missiles that would be needed to fulfil the new conception of the UK's deterrent capability as envisaged by Brook's Future Policy Study.[27] The confusing result was rival papers from the Admiralty and Air Ministry. The latter continued to take as its yardstick what it claimed was the BNDSG figure of 50 per cent destruction of '44 major Russian cities' (as has been seen, this was an erroneous reflection of the 44 aiming points within 40 cities which featured in detailed target planning). The Navy's paper began with the estimate that nine Polaris submarines (allowing four or five to remain on station at any one time), each carrying 16 missiles, would be needed to meet this BNDSG criterion. However, it then proceeded to seize on the Future Policy Study's notion of a 'significant contribution' to the Western deterrent in order to discuss what a much smaller force of only four Polaris submarines (providing an average of two on station) might accomplish. The assumption throughout the Naval Staff paper was that such a UK Polaris force would operate in conjunction with US strategic nuclear forces, rather than in a unilateral fashion. As a result it looked at deployment options in the northwest Indian Ocean and eastern Mediterranean which might place city targets in the southern part of the Soviet Union within the 1,500 nautical mile range of the Polaris A2 missile destined for US Navy service by 1962, so complementing US target coverage.[28]

Whereas to some eyes the capital costs of a nine-boat Polaris force had been considered high, a four-boat force made the proposition seem far more economical than the Air Force's emerging plans to maintain a continuous airborne alert for a portion of its Skybolt-equipped aircraft. Nevertheless, the COS Committee did not respond warmly to this attempt to query the established criteria (the CAS was advised by the Air Ministry that the Admiralty's paper was 'largely irrelevant' to Watkinson's concerns and 'contains assumptions and conclusions from which you will wish to disassociate yourself', while it was thought that a force of 12 submarines would be required to meet the full BNDSG target criterion).[29] It was considered premature by the COS to put definite views to Watkinson before the BNDSG itself had had time to discuss the problem and arrive at a position. Moreover, as the COS was quick to observe, the BNDSG would still be using the 40-city requirement in its study of future deterrent systems.[30] As yet there had been no ministerial ruling on reducing the criterion, and until one was made the COS were loath to tackle head-on this controversial territory. By moving the issue back to the BNDSG, the COS were merely papering over the significant inter-service

Skybolt and the Camp David meeting

During the course of 1960 British attempts to secure the supply of Skybolt from the Americans, and later an offer of Polaris missiles for a UK successor system, were destined to become entangled with the nuclear sharing arrangements for the Western alliance that the Eisenhower administration was starting to formulate. It was clear to many observers that doubts regarding the credibility of the US strategic guarantee to Europe were becoming widespread by this period. The State Department, moreover, was also showing growing aversion to the development of national nuclear forces, as in the case of France. Such national nuclear programmes were widely perceived as a threat to Alliance cohesion by undermining the central direction of NATO strategy that Washington hoped to maintain, and, even more importantly, providing a potential spur to the aspirations of some Germans – bristling at their second class status within the Alliance – for the possession of an independent nuclear force. By 1960 the US Joint Chiefs of Staff, in contrast to the State Department, was keen to see nuclear assistance given to selected allies, including the French, while the civilian element at the Pentagon tended to vacillate, but wanted to see France adopt a more cooperative attitude in NATO before steps to enhancing its nuclear capabilities were taken.[31] Eisenhower himself swung between his visceral desire to assist close NATO allies who were determined anyway to pursue national nuclear capabilities, his awareness of the Congressional opposition that any initiative to extend nuclear assistance to France might provoke, and his annoyance at de Gaulle's disruptive tendencies.[32]

To compound the whole issue, the US general who filled the influential role of NATO's Supreme Allied Commander Europe, General Lauris Norstad, was becoming increasingly agitated by the developing nuclear balance within his theatre and the need for a military and political commitment which might underpin NATO solidarity. After a considerable period indicating his needs, and following much discussion by the JCS in Washington, in October 1959 Norstad presented his requirement for an unspecified number of Mid- or Medium Range Ballistic Missiles (MRBMs), to be deployed under his command beginning in 1963, as a replacement for some of NATO's increasingly vulnerable nuclear-capable aircraft and in order to counteract the growing threat from Soviet air (and eventually missile) bases which had the capacity to strike at Western Europe. With a range of between 300 and 1,500 nautical miles, land-based MRBMs could be seen as including missiles of the Polaris type, although Norstad was not specific over whether he saw them as manufactured by the Europeans themselves, or supplied directly by the United States. The important point was that a new missile force should be under his control as SACEUR and targeted according to his priorities (Norstad had also expressly chosen to call the missiles 'mid-range', allowing the use of the MRBM acronym, in order to avoid some of the political controversy that had attached itself to the deployment of US IRBMs, such as Thor and Jupiter missiles, in certain NATO countries over the previous two years).[33]

Norstad's scheme was appealing to those elements in the State Department who saw it as a means to foster greater European unity and strength (a goal also held dear by the President), and to deflect both London and Paris from building up their national nuclear capabilities, which were increasingly seen as a drain on resources better devoted to conventional means of defence. In this context, the beginning of French nuclear testing in early 1960 revealed several policy fissures on the US side and generated new tensions in Franco-American relations. Since the conclusion of the MDA in July 1958, French officials had at various times solicited their US counterparts for different forms of technical assistance in the nuclear or ballistic missile fields. There was an implicit assumption in these tentative feelers that once France had demonstrated its nuclear know-how the bilateral Anglo-American nuclear relationship might be opened up to the newest member of the Western nuclear club. Although Eisenhower himself was keen, most of his key advisers were sceptical about extending help to France at this early stage of its nuclear development. Not only would it undercut the growing sentiment in favour of nuclear non-proliferation, and prejudice the multilateral nuclear arrangements for NATO which were now under intense discussion, but such a move would be strongly resisted by the Congressional Joint Committee on Atomic Energy. That Committee took very seriously the 'substantial progress' clause of US atomic energy legislation; it had been British demonstration of their knowledge of thermonuclear warhead development which had eased open the door to US nuclear assistance, and the fission weapons exploded by the French in their initial tests did not yet qualify them for that distinction.[34] By the spring of 1960 US officials were espousing the line that no nuclear assistance, including help with delivery systems, could be offered to France and that Washington's priority was exploring Norstad's proposals for a collective NATO nuclear capability. De Gaulle, however, was unwilling to sacrifice France's independence when it came to control over nuclear delivery systems.[35]

From a very early stage, British officials were unconvinced by the military case for a NATO MRBM force, and alarmed by the extra expenditure it might entail for Alliance members. Even though warheads for the MRBMs were to remain under US custody, there were also underlying concerns that the scheme might be conceived as a way to put nuclear delivery capabilities into French or even German hands (if centralised control mechanisms were not strong enough), and an implicit anxiety that it foreshadowed a less indulgent US attitude to the UK's own possession of a national deterrent force. A major potential problem with any approach to the Americans over provision of either Skybolt or Polaris was that Eisenhower administration officials would make supply conditional on UK participation in a NATO MRBM scheme, or at least defer any commitment to help the UK with delivery systems until the nuclear sharing issue in the Alliance had been settled one way or another. Indeed, both the State and Defense Departments had adopted this position by the time that British officials in Washington had their first discussions over the possible acquisition of Skybolt in mid-March 1960.[36]

Ministers were, however, determined that national control of UK strategic deterrent forces should not be relinquished. Watkinson, for example, was adamant that there should be no question of it even being contemplated that Bomber Command might be placed under SACEUR's control, for use in fulfilling NATO targeting requirements, without a full discussion in the Defence Committee or the Cabinet. While in general agreement, the Foreign Secretary believed that some thought should be given to the longer-term issues being raised about the deterrent in the Future Policy Study. Nevertheless, he felt that in the forthcoming discussions with the Americans over Skybolt, British officials should be 'careful not to imply any willingness on our part to surrender to NATO any real measure of control over the use of British strategic nuclear forces.'[37]

One other issue that was coming to the fore in Anglo-American nuclear relations at this time was the need by the US authorities for advanced berthing facilities in Scotland for its nascent Polaris submarine force. Informal discussions had occurred during 1959 between the US Navy and the Admiralty on this politically sensitive issue, and in January 1960 Gates, the US Secretary of Defense, formally asked Watkinson for permission to station US submarine tendering facilities in the Gare Loch, located in the Clyde estuary.[38]

Considering the time that Washington might take in formulating and then presenting its proposals for the NATO MRBM force, the prospects for a rapid agreement over a replacement for Blue Streak had not seemed encouraging. Yet the pressing American need for a Polaris base in Scotland gave British officials possibilities for short-term bargaining if ministers were prepared to use it. The Cabinet Secretary had spotted this opportunity from an early stage, advising Macmillan in February: 'The Americans are anxious for a base for their Polaris submarines in the Gairloch [sic]. Cannot more use be made of this as the basis for a firm understanding about the early supply to us of Polaris and of two or three of their submarines?'[39] When the Defence Committee approved the first approach to the Americans over the provision of both Skybolt and Polaris on unfettered terms, the head of the British Joint Staff Mission in Washington was instructed to stress that 'we wish our weapons systems to form part of a co-operative effort in developing the total deterrent forces of the West. This co-operation can take many forms; we are, for example, considering the American request that we should make the necessary facilities in Scotland available for some of their own Polaris submarines.'[40]

By March 1960, the Prime Minister's evident uncertainty over the position, having read the latest telegrams from the Washington Embassy, was reflected in his advice for Watkinson:

> I am left with the impression that we shall not know for some time whether Skybolt or Polaris will be made available to us without strings ... There is a distinct suggestion that the Americans are going to press for the NATO mid-range ballistic missile, and they may not be prepared to make any progress as regards any other weapons, even in a NATO context, until they have got further with this one.... It seems to me that we are not at the moment in a particularly strong negotiating position. We must not give away any of the cards we may hold. I am thinking particularly of the American request for a Scottish base for their submarines.[41]

As for Norstad's MRBM scheme, senior ministers had already reached the conclusion that it was open to several political, financial and military objections, but they were reluctant to come out with open criticism at this stage, preferring that other members of NATO, most notably the French, make the running against it.[42] Indeed, Watkinson's own thought at this time was that 'we should be prepared to support the MRBM project and to accept our fair share of missiles provided that other NATO countries acted likewise.' But regarding the strategic deterrent 'we must retain our liberty of action, and he would accordingly ask Mr Gates to confirm that the Americans would be prepared to release to us both Skybolt and Polaris.'[43]

The chance for Macmillan to raise the question of the supply of Skybolt or Polaris with Eisenhower personally was soon presented by direct talks between the two leaders which had been arranged hastily for end of March, principally to discuss the latest Soviet proposals for a ban on nuclear testing. In the build-up to the meetings, while the US Defense Department maintained that no agreement on the provision of either system should be made until the NATO MRBM problem had been tackled, the State Department shifted to the line that Skybolt had no direct connection to the subject and could be offered to the UK as long as there was no publicity connecting a deal with the outcome of the talks. On the day that Macmillan arrived in the US capital, the US Secretary of State, Christian Herter, sent a memorandum to Eisenhower which maintained that a bilateral deal with the British over Polaris would not be in order while a scheme for a NATO MRBM force was still under consideration: 'We hope the UK will participate fully in a NATO MRBM program and regard this as important particularly as a means of obtaining French acceptance of the NATO Command arrangements, and of thus minimising the prospect of independent nuclear and strategic weapons programs which could be so politically disruptive to the Alliance.' Nevertheless, Skybolt should be treated 'as a separate matter' as it was intended to prolong the effective life of the existing UK V-bomber force. In view of the intimations that had been received on the British side over the possible linkage with the Scottish base issue, Herter continued that 'it would seem desirable to relate British assurances on US Polaris tender facilities to our assurance of Skybolt.'[44]

Following a personal conversation between Macmillan and the President on 28 March at the latter's Gettysburg farm (and held during a short respite from the formal talks at nearby Camp David) British officials gave their US counterparts a written version of what they felt had transpired between the two men. In this document Macmillan merely expressed his thanks for Eisenhower's willingness to provide 'whatever appears to be the better alternative system, either Skybolt or Polaris or a combination of these.' This was not, however, in accord with the American version of events. State Department officials present at Camp David subsequently crafted a three part memorandum which attempted to summarise the nature of the understanding that had been reached by the two principals during the previous day's conversation. With Eisenhower's approval, the document was handed to the British delegation on 29 March. The memorandum offered an assurance to supply Skybolt, if development was successfully completed; informed the Prime Minister that it 'does not appear appropriate to consider a bilateral understanding on Polaris until the problem of SACEUR's MRBM requirements has been satisfactorily disposed of in NATO'; and ventured that 'the UK would be agreeable in principle to making the necessary arrangements for US Polaris tenders in Scottish ports.' After more consultation between British and US officials, the British produced another memorandum – which was accepted by the President – where gratitude was expressed for Eisenhower's 'willingness to help us when the time comes by enabling us to purchase supplies of Skybolt without warheads or to acquire in addition or substitution a mobile MRBM system [i.e. Polaris] in the light of such decisions as may be reached in the discussions underway in NATO.'[45] No mention was made of the provision of facilities in Scotland for US Polaris submarines in the British documents, although the Prime Minister was later to acknowledge the implicit linkage between the issues, and officials felt satisfied with the outcome of the exchange.[46]

There was some degree of ambiguity over what exactly had been agreed during the Camp David meeting: in American minds, within the same transaction, the Prime Minister had agreed to enter into negotiations in order to establish a US Polaris base in Scotland, and been informed that the US administration would be open to the supply of Skybolt 'without strings'. It had also been explained to the British delegation – as both the State and Defense Departments had recommended – that any later offer of Polaris was dependent on the outcome of the NATO MRBM scheme. What the latter meant in practice was not entirely clear. In the British interpretation, Polaris might still be available for national, independent use and deployment, once the NATO arrangements were settled and a fresh approach to Washington could be made, but to some State Department officials, keen to secure UK participation in a NATO MRBM force, supply of Polaris to the UK had to be linked to any NATO arrangements for the future control of European nuclear forces that might eventually be established (in a scheme which would also bind in French nuclear capabilities, once they had been developed). As Ian Clark has observed, the exchanges of notes at Camp David were more 'the beginning of the process of negotiation rather than the culmination.'[47]

On 1 April 1960, Gates presented the US administration's initial ideas on how to meet SACEUR's MRBM requirements to a gathering of NATO defence ministers in Paris. Two alternative schemes were presented in order to meet Norstad's request for an initial mobile force of 300 missiles (based, it was envisaged, on either flat-bed railway carriages or river barges). One involved individual European members of NATO purchasing Polaris missiles from the United States directly, which would then be assigned to SACEUR's control, while the other would turn production of MRBMs – with technical help from the Americans – over to a European consortium which would again earmark its missiles for NATO.[48]

There were seeds sown here for later misunderstandings: to British officials an approach to Washington over a future Polaris deal – where the missiles could be available under full national control – was still very much on the cards, but the Americans would first have to introduce and sell their ideas for the new MRBM arrangements to their NATO partners. Once this had been done, and political agreement over an MRBM force reached, it might then be possible to re-open the Polaris issue with the British, perhaps looking to supply of the missile as a replacement for Skybolt during the period after 1970. But to the Americans, it was becoming plain that any future UK Polaris force had to be conceived of as forming part of a NATO MRBM scheme, where ideas of national control were superseded by reversion to a supranational authority.

In retrospect it is difficult to overstate the importance of the understanding reached between the Prime Minister and President Eisenhower at their Camp David (and Gettysburg) meeting in March 1960. During a period when US policy was moving very strongly toward the conviction that national nuclear objectives within the NATO Alliance should be subordinated to the eventual goal of joint ownership and control at least of nuclear delivery systems, agreement in principle for the acquisition of a Skybolt replacement for the troubled Blue Streak IRBM had been conceded to the British. Moreover, there were no political restrictions on Skybolt's employment, allowing the Government to maintain the position that the independence of the deterrent – in the sense of ultimate national control over use – had been preserved. Without the Camp David agreement over Skybolt, Macmillan would have been faced with the unpalatable prospect of either announcing the cancellation of Blue Streak when no alternative system for maintaining the credibility of the deterrent after about 1965 could be offered as a substitute (surely a political impossibility given the capital that the Labour Opposition would have made of such a fiasco, and a step which would have thrown the whole future of the deterrent into extreme doubt); continuing to fund Blue Streak at a reduced rate (perhaps with a more limited deployment in mind) while other indigenous missile options were pursued; or conforming to the State Department's initial requirements by linking any deal for the provision of both Skybolt *and* Polaris to the scheme for NATO control of nuclear forces. This latter contingency was precisely a situation the Government wanted to avoid as it too would have undermined the case that had been made for an 'independent' contribution to the Western deterrent over the past few years. Bargaining an offer of facilities in Scotland for US Polaris submarines against the supply of Skybolt and Polaris 'without strings' could have been one way to escape from this conundrum (as the Prime Minister had mooted in March), but as subsequent events would show the Eisenhower administration was not amenable to this kind of deal, at least when it came to Polaris, and might then have looked elsewhere in Western Europe for its submarine facilities.

With the arrival of an agreement over Skybolt at Camp David, the way was clear for the Government to announce the cancellation of Blue Streak. Macmillan met Duncan Sandys for a final discussion about the missile project on 5 April, where the Minister of Aviation agreed that he would no longer press his long opposition to cancellation. There was a valedictory feel about the Prime Minister's comments when he summarised the course of Britain's nuclear policy:

> ... we had manufactured the A-bomb because we had invented it [sic]. That had led to the H-bomb, and at the time that we decided to do it, Blue Streak seemed to be the best method of delivery. Our deterrent policy had so far been successful. We had got a great deal out of it and the effort we had put in was quite incommensurate with the results achieved. The policy had been very successful: it had given us a good diplomatic ground [sic] for 15 years. He thought now it was important to concentrate on mobility and our aim should be to rely much more upon the French in Europe.[49]

As for Watkinson, by this stage he had come to the view that Blue Streak should not be completely abandoned, but gradually run down as some form of space launcher, but as he told Macmillan later that same day his close advisers thought it should be 'stopped forthwith.'[50]

The next day the Defence Committee met to confirm the provisional decision made in February to cancel the development of Blue Streak as a military weapon. As well as noting the advantages presented by the mobility and flexibility of a bomber force, which could also be used in a conventional role, the Committee felt that the outcome of the talks between the Prime Minister and President Eisenhower had been very satisfactory in that the Americans had indicated their willingness to supply Skybolt on unconditional terms. It was ventured that it 'should be possible to reach a similar understanding as regards Polaris (on which, however, no immediate decision was required), when agreement had been reached in NATO on the deployment of Polaris missiles as part of the forces of the Supreme Allied Commander Europe.'[51]

The Government's decision to cancel the Blue Streak project represented a major watershed in the history of UK strategic nuclear policy. As the Labour Opposition highlighted at the time, it removed the immediate possibility of developing and producing an indigenous missile delivery system for the UK's strategic nuclear weapons (although it is worth noting that if deployed Blue Streak would have entered service alongside, rather than completely supplanting, a V-bomber force still equipped with a combination of free-falling bombs and the Blue Steel Mark 1 stand-off missile). Britain's technical capacity for development of long-range ballistic missiles for military purposes effectively came to an end with the decision to cancel Blue Streak, a project which had been portrayed as a key symbol of the UK's will and ability to keep up with the latest defence technology. Delivery system dependence on the United States would henceforth become a key feature of nuclear defence policy, and its implications for the idea of independence the subject of contentious political debate.

The abandonment of Blue Streak also had wider technological consequences as it brought to an end, at least for the time being, the work that had begun at RAE on penetration aids to overcome ABM defences (although work on warhead re-entry phenomena did continue, as we shall see). The decision to cancel had also coincided with acceptance of the Future Policy Study's ideas on the nature of independence. In the eyes of ministers, a future UK nuclear force would have to be make what was repeatedly called an 'independent contribution' to an overall Western deterrent, where national control over the use of the weapons would be maintained, but their value would be gauged as part of the concerted Anglo-American nuclear effort. What this meant in terms of the criteria for a national nuclear capability was not always clear.

Macmillan had staked a great deal on building on the nuclear legacy he had inherited from his predecessors, Attlee, Churchill and Eden, and had been fully supportive of the development of the UK thermonuclear weapon capability that had culminated in the Grapple series of test explosions in 1957–58. The conclusion of the MDA in July 1958 had seemed to cap this policy, as Anglo-American defence relations entered a new phase of intimacy. However, the coming era of ballistic missile delivery systems threatened to make a wholly new set of demands on national resources. It was evident that this kind of nuclear largesse came at a price, and by 1960 ministers were beginning to appreciate that a defence budget that still stood at over seven per cent of Gross National Product might be unsustainable as the economy struggled to compete with its European rivals in world markets. Skybolt was readily accepted as a relatively inexpensive way to prolong the effective life of the V-bombers for a few more years – not least as the Americans were

210 *The cancellation of Blue Streak*

expected to meet the full development costs of the new air-launched missile — and to avoid the political opprobrium that would have greeted any move to cancel Blue Streak when no substitute system could be offered. Yet the longer-term future of the strategic deterrent in the missile age, with the spiralling costs of advanced weapons systems, and when Washington was beginning to set its face against the build-up of national nuclear forces, was still clouded with uncertainty. As Macmillan told de Gaulle at Rambouillet in March 1960, after the French President had affirmed that he would continue with a national nuclear programme 'whatever the cost', the British effort was facing problems in the future: 'We were all right till the late sixties — after that we were not sure what to do.'[52]

Notes

1 Brundrett letter to Bligh, FB/577/59, 25 November 1959, PREM 11/2945.
2 Brook minute for Bligh, 3 December 1959, PREM 11/2945.
3 MISC/M(59)97, 'Committee Structure on Military Aspects of Atomic Energy,' note of a meeting held at the MoD, 7 December 1959, AVIA 65/1771.
4 See J. S. Orme letter to E. G. Cass, 9 December 1959; Bishop letter to Playfair, 15 January 1960, AB 49/13; Playfair letter to Brook, 29 March 1960; ND(60)1, 'Terms of Reference and Composition,' note by the Secretary of the Cabinet, 23 June 1960, CAB 21/5346.
5 Playfair letter to Brook, 29 March 1960; J. S. Orme minute for Bishop, 31 March 1960; Brook letter to Playfair, 9 May 1960, CAB 21/5346.
6 Watkinson minute for Macmillan, 'Nuclear Weapons Programme,' MO 18/3, 17 December 1959, PREM 11/2945.
7 Brundrett letter to Bligh, FB/624/59, 17 December 1959, PREM 11/2945.
8 Heathcoat Amory minute for Macmillan, 29 December 1959, PREM 11/2945.
9 Bishop minute for Macmillan, 'Nuclear Weapons,' 30 December 1959, PREM 11/2945.
10 D(60)1, 'Nuclear Weapons Policy,' note by the Secretary, 1 January 1960: record of a Meeting held on 31 December 1959, CAB 131/23; for the complex process involved with the choice of warhead for Skybolt, see Moore, *Nuclear Illusion, Nuclear Reality*, 118–20.
11 Brook minute for Macmillan, 21 June 1960, PREM 11/2913.
12 See Bishop minute for Macmillan, 'Defence Committee: Future Business,' 30 June 1960, CAB 21/4366.
13 Brook minute for Macmillan, 'Defence Policy,' 13 November 1959, PREM 11/2945.
14 C(60)35, 'Future Policy Study, 1960–70,' note by the Prime Minister, 29 February 1960, CAB 129/100.
15 FP(60)1, 'Future Policy Study, 1960–70,' report by officials, 24 February 1960, CAB 129/100; also in CAB 134/1929.
16 See FP(A)(60) 1st Meeting, 1 January 1960, CAB 134/1931.
17 FP(60)1, 'Future Policy Study, 1960–70,' report by officials, 24 February 1960, CAB 129/100; also in CAB 134/1929.
18 Cmnd 952, *Report on Defence, 1960*, paragraph 3, February 1960.
19 Ibid, paragraph 36.
20 See 'Mobile Launchers Plan for Missiles,' *The Times*, 17 February 1960.
21 D(60)7, 'United Kingdom Deterrent Policy,' note by the Secretary of the Cabinet, 3 March 1960, note of a meeting held on 20 February 1960, CAB 131/23. See

also the Prime Minister's brief, Brook minute for Macmillan, 'Saturday's Meeting on Defence Policy,' 19 February 1960, PREM 11/2945.
22 D(60)8, 'United Kingdom Deterrent Policy,' note by the Secretary of the Cabinet, 3 March 1960, note of a meeting held on 23 February 1960, CAB 131/23; see also Clark, *Nuclear Diplomacy*, 181–2.
23 D(60)2, 'Deterrent Policy,' memorandum by the Prime Minister, 24 February 1960, CAB 131/23.
24 D(60) 1st Meeting, 24 February 1960, CAB 131/23.
25 Bishop telegram for Brook, Track No 245 to Cape Town, 3 February 1960, PREM 11/2945.
26 Secretary, COS Committee minute, 'US/UK Talks: Note for Air Chief Marshal Mills for Use in Discussion with the Minister of Defence on Friday, 12th February,' Annex to COS/207/12/2/60, 12 February 1960, DEFE 32/6.
27 Watkinson minute for Mountbatten, 2 February 1960, ADM 205/202.
28 See Director of Plans memorandum for First Sea Lord, 'Polaris – contribution to the deterrent,' PLANS 49/180, 16 February 1960, ADM 205/202; and COS(60)48, 'Significant Contribution to the Western Deterrent – Polaris,' memorandum by the First Sea Lord, 25 February 1960, DEFE 5/100, and in ADM 205/202.
29 Brief for CAS, 'Significant Contribution to the Western Deterrent – Polaris,' 7 March 1960, AIR 20/10057.
30 Confidential Annex to COS(60)17th Meeting, item 2, 8 March 1960, ADM 205/202.
31 On the Pentagon's position regarding assistance to France see Watson, *Into the Missile Age*, 557, 574–80.
32 On the whole issue of nuclear sharing see Trachtenberg, *Constructed Peace*, 195–200, 204–12.
33 Watson, *Into the Missile Age*, 545–6.
34 See Pagedas, *Anglo-American Strategic Relations and the French Problem*, 69–74.
35 Ibid, 80.
36 Watson, *Into the Missile Age*, 562–3.
37 Watkinson minute for Selwyn Lloyd, 7 March 1960; Lloyd minute for Watkinson, FS/60/20, 10 March 1960, DEFE 11/604.
38 See Watkinson minute for Macmillan, 14 December 1959; Watkinson minute for Carrington, 19 January 1960, PREM 11/2940.
39 Brook minute for Macmillan, 'Saturday's Meeting on Defence Policy,' 19 February 1960, PREM 11/2945.
40 FO telegram No 792 to Washington, 24 February 1960, Appendix B to D(60)1st Meeting, 24 February 1960, CAB 131/23.
41 Macmillan minute for Watkinson, M.76/60, 22 March 1960, CAB 21/4366.
42 D(60)16, 'Preparations for Meeting of NATO Defence Ministers,' note by the Deputy Secretary of the Cabinet, 25 March 1960, note of a meeting held on 25 March 1960, CAB 131/23.
43 MM/COS (60) 2nd Meeting, Meeting of the Minister of Defence with the Chiefs of Staff, 24 March 1960, DEFE 32/13.
44 Herter memorandum for Eisenhower, 27 March 1960, *Foreign Relations of the United States, 1958–1960, volume VII, Part 2: Western Europe* (Washington, 1993), 860–1.
45 See Watson, *Into the Missile Age*, 563–4; memorandum from Eisenhower to Macmillan, 29 March 1960; memorandum from Macmillan to Eisenhower, 29 March 1960, *FRUS, 1958–1960, VII, Part 2*, 863–5; 'Minute from the Prime Minister, handed to President Eisenhower on March 29, 1960,' and Dillon minute for Macmillan, 29 March 1960, CAB 133/243.
46 See Macmillan, *Pointing the Way*, 254.

47 Clark, *Nuclear Diplomacy*, 259.
48 Watson, *Into the Missile Age*, 548–9.
49 Bligh, 'Note for the Record: Blue Streak,' 5 April 1960, PREM 11/2945.
50 See 'Note for the Record,' 5 April 1960, DEFE 13/113.
51 D(60)3rd Meeting, 6 April 1960, CAB 131/23.
52 Diary entry for 13 March 1960, in Macmillan, *Pointing the Way*, 182.

6 Skybolt, Polaris and the control of Western nuclear forces, March 1960–May 1961

The aftermath of Blue Streak cancellation

British officials regarded their new plans to purchase Skybolt missiles for use with the V-bomber force as a stop-gap measure to meet the immediate issue of Blue Streak cancellation. It was widely understood that, as Soviet air defences rapidly gained in strength and capability during the latter half of the decade, Skybolt's credibility would gradually decline, while the V-bomber bases also became increasingly vulnerable to pre-emptive attack. While the RAF nurtured hopes that Skybolt's range could be extended even further, and a new aircraft adopted as a launching platform which was capable of extended airborne patrols (and so would not be caught on the ground), some elements in the Navy doubted that such proposals would suffice. In late April 1960 the Vice Chief of Naval Staff, Admiral Sir Walter Couchman, can be found writing to the US Chief of Naval Operations, to explain that Skybolt would merely represent a 'blood transfusion' to carry the life of the V-bomber force through for another decade or so.[1] The longer-term problem of how to maintain a credible strategic deterrent force beyond about 1970 had still to be addressed.

During the Defence Committee's discussions over the future of Blue Streak in February 1960 ministers had felt it advisable to pursue studies of the relative merits of launching Skybolt from a new, long endurance aircraft or of using Polaris submarines as a successor to the V-force. Picking up this cue, at a COS meeting held at the start of March, Mountbatten took the initiative to reconstitute the British Nuclear Deterrent Study Group (which had only submitted an 'interim' report on the issue in December 1959) in a step subsequently confirmed by Watkinson. Powell's important role as the chair of the BNDSG would be adopted by his successor as Permanent Secretary at the MoD, Sir Edward Playfair, and Brundrett's place on the group taken by Zuckerman as the new CSA. The COS Committee heard that it might be desirable that the Group should base their next phase of work not only around a projected capability which could match the planned scale of attack by the existing V-bomber force, but also on greater or lesser scales of attack (in an echo of issues that had arisen the previous year). But the Committee ultimately decided that the initial study by the Group should be based on a requirement to deliver the same kind of damage potential as the presently planned V-force. Only at a later date, after the COS Committee had examined this report, would it decide whether to ask the BNDSG to look at different levels of damage capability.[2] In other words, the Future Policy Study's recommendations about the optimum size of an independent British 'contribution' to the Western deterrent were to be sidestepped once again.

Throughout this period, the strong inclination of ministers and officials was to keep open the option of an eventual purchase of Polaris from the United States, with the work of the BNDSG helping to inform any eventual choices made. Watkinson, for example, agreed, as he informed the COS, that it was important to preserve the UK's 'liberty of action' over the issue.[3] Indeed, during the debate over the Defence White Paper at the start of March, Watkinson had shared with the House his thinking that

> the problem that faced the Government for the future was what we should do in the closing years of the decade and the early 1970s ... we still had time to make our choice. Much had been learnt from the liquid fuel Blue Streak missile. And he believed that the solid fuel rocket Polaris would in due course be a very formidable mobile addition to the deterrent power of the West.

Though he was prepared to stress the attributes of Skybolt, he was open to receiving the latest American information about Polaris development as well, and promised the House that the Government would make a careful study of the longer term options.[4] When, in mid-April, he informed MPs about the final decision to cancel Blue Streak, Watkinson, even though he called it the best option available, was careful to avoid a categorical commitment to a Skybolt purchase, saying he did not 'rule out further decisions at a later stage on other types of missile'.[5] Indeed, the day before his Commons appearance, Watkinson was instructing the COS that 'the examination of our possible requirements for Polaris firing submarines should continue: the fact that an undertaking had been reached with the United States about Skybolt should not be taken to prejudge this examination.'[6]

At the end of April Watkinson confirmed to the House of Commons that acquiring Skybolt did not rule out Polaris for the longer-term, and that he had asked the Admiralty to 'put in hand an urgent study of the requirements for British-built submarines capable of carrying the Polaris type missile.'[7] Yet, in a situation where the Government had now publicly fastened itself to a purchase of Skybolt, the Admiralty's growing interest in a Polaris-based solution to maintain the UK in the deterrent business in the longer-term – encouraged by contacts forged with the US Navy – was still held in check. Writing to a fellow Naval officer based at the Joint Services Mission in Washington, Couchman explained 'no one here is going to throw away the V-bomber force in 1965 after the millions spent on it, and it is useless for us to "plug" Polaris by high-level presentation for the moment – which would be interpreted as an attempt to jump the [BNDSG's] findings.'[8]

That those findings would take some time to produce was gradually becoming clear. Indeed, there was no sense of urgency behind the BNDSG's work in this period. An initial meeting of the Study Group was held under Playfair's chairmanship in mid-April, and here it was assumed that the Air Ministry would prepare studies of a new airborne system carrying Skybolt, and the Admiralty undertake a similar exercise for establishing a force of Polaris-carrying submarines.[9] However, in June 1960 Playfair decided that the BNDSG should defer its consideration of future options until the negotiations with the Americans for the purchase of Skybolt were complete (and one can almost hear a sigh of relief from the Permanent Secretary that the sniping between the services could be suspended for a while).[10] On one level Playfair's decision had a degree of logic: it would make little sense to undertake extensive work on the provision of options – based on either Skybolt or Polaris – which were entirely dependent on the willingness and ability of the US authorities to supply, when American attitudes, and a formal agreement over Skybolt, were not yet certain. But it also meant that when the BNDSG returned to their long-term task, at the end of 1960, there would be considerable slack to be taken up. Moreover, by then much of the BNDSG's time and focus had been absorbed with the more pressing problem of what alternatives were available if Skybolt should be cancelled by the US authorities.[11]

In a reflection of the views he had expressed during the Defence Committee discussions earlier in the year, the Chancellor remained profoundly unhappy about any commitment to a successor to Blue Streak. On 22 April, for example, he wrote to Watkinson protesting about the possibility that an announcement was about to made concerning the Government's firm intention to buy Skybolt. Heathcoat Amory could see 'great disadvantage' in taking such a decision

> on the spur of the moment, with no examination of the merits of the various alternative courses, and to do so months (perhaps even a year or more) before we need to take a decision ourselves, let alone commit ourselves publicly. It cannot be sound to take a decision of this scale – military, political, financial – in this way. I would have thought that all our recent experience, not least on Blue Streak, illustrates the rapidity of change of technological and military circumstances, the need to be continuously adjusting our plans to meet them, and the desirability of keeping our hands free for as long as we can.

Although Sandys, as Minister of Aviation, was stressing the need to make an announcement in order to demonstrate that the Government was not giving up on the deterrent, the Chancellor thought that people would instead 'draw the opposite conclusion' in that ministers were 'plunging wildly from one weapon to another (which is still, as I understand it, very far from developed, and which surely presents problems of vulnerability), that we are running risks of having to reverse engines again, and that our statements of intentions could not be relied on.'[12]

The fact that with cancellation of the Blue Streak programme the Government seemed to be making a significant retreat from the policy of maintaining an independent deterrent – whatever ministers might say about the supply of Skybolt not being subject to any restrictions over its use – created a whole new set of dilemmas for the Opposition Labour Party. Hugh Gaitskell, the Party's leader, had always believed that the case for having an independent deterrent rested mainly on doubts that the US Government or people would, in a last resort, be prepared to risk the destruction of their own cities for the sake of the defence of Western Europe. There was also a fear, he would argue, that excessive dependence on the Americans 'might force upon us policies with which we did not agree, because we would be in such a weak position to argue with the United States.'[13] But now that 'independence' in the provision of missile hardware no longer seemed within the nation's means, and with many voices calling for a greater emphasis on conventional defence, there seemed strong reasons to re-examine the Party leadership's position.

The beginning of this process came with the parliamentary debates that followed the Government's decision over Blue Streak cancellation. Labour's calls for a full-blown independent inquiry into the project's troubled history were resisted by ministers, spurring the Opposition to move a motion of censure on the issue. The resulting debate in the House of Commons, held in a febrile atmosphere on 27 April 1960, saw ministers castigated for their failure to cancel the project at an earlier stage, especially when there had been plenty of evidence available in 1958 that liquid-fuelled missiles were increasingly seen as outmoded, and that fixed site missiles were too vulnerable.[14]

Although he had previously been firmly committed to the maintenance of an independent nuclear deterrent, George Brown, the shadow Minister of Defence, now argued in the Commons that the gap which might open up in deterrent capability after Blue Streak's cancellation raised the new question of whether, after an interval of a few years, the capability should, in fact, be restored. In a withering critique of the wasted expenditure (put by Labour at £100 million) already incurred on the project, and ministerial performance in general, Harold Wilson, who filled the Shadow Chancellor brief, wondered whether Skybolt would even be available given the vagaries of the development process for ballistic missiles. He pointed to American sources which were already questioning the long-term future of the deterrent, especially as V-bombers on their airbases would be just as vulnerable to pre-emptive attack as Blue Streak. To Wilson, who the previous year had taken over as chair of the Public Accounts Committee, the whole saga was a 'dramatic and expensive illustration of a wider problem, that of Parliamentary control over expenditure on defence.' Wilson wanted a general debate on the issues, 'because what we have seen today … is the end of the independent deterrent. From now on, there is no sense in any defence talk about independence.

From now on the word will have to be "interdependence".' While much of Labour's fire was directed against Sandys for his earlier stubborn advocacy of the Blue Streak project, Wilson was also keen to pin some blame on Macmillan:

> When he became Prime Minister he set out to keep up with his nuclear neighbours. Like so many other pathetic individuals whose sense of social prestige outruns their purse, he is left in the situation at the end of the day of the man who dare not admit that he cannot afford a television set and who knows that he cannot afford it and who just puts up the aerial instead. That is our situation, because without an independent means of delivery, the independent nuclear deterrent [the Prime Minister's] cheap, short cut to national greatness, is an empty illusion.[15]

Gaitskell, having missed the Commons debate because he was abroad, returned to find that two of his principal colleagues (and rivals), although not supporting the abandonment of Britain's existing nuclear capability, had effectively repudiated the Party's prior stance.[16]

The growing doubts about the future of the independent deterrent helped to change the terms of debate over defence policy within the Labour Party. Defeat at the October 1959 election had already begun to widen splits within the Labour movement as a whole over which direction to move the Party. The strength of voices calling for unilateral nuclear disarmament correspondingly increased, particularly amongst the powerful trades unions. Having previously derided his 'pacifist', 'unilateralist' and 'neutralist' opponents on the left, Gaitskell was compelled to issue a new statement of party policy in July 1960 which, while maintaining that NATO membership was vital to Britain's security, advocated an undertaking by the West never to be the first to use the hydrogen bomb, negotiations for a test ban, opposition to the stationing of Thor in the UK, and a defence policy which aimed to reduce Britain's dependence on nuclear weapons. The Blue Streak episode, in this view, had revealed that Britain could not maintain an independent nuclear force, and that reliance would have to be placed on the United States to provide the overall Western deterrent.

At the Party's annual conference held at Scarborough in October 1960 a resolution calling for unilateral nuclear disarmament, backed by several large unions (whose leaders were unhappy with Gaitskell's leadership), was carried by a narrow majority despite Gaitskell's impassioned speech in defence of his belief in deterrence (based, as he argued, on 'balanced judgement' not principle). Such conference resolutions were not binding on the parliamentary party, but calls for Britain to renounce its nuclear weapons were by now widespread on the left, while opinion polls showed high levels of support for a formal ban on nuclear testing among the public at large.[17] Gaitskell spent the next few months, with the help of the newly-formed ginger group, the Campaign for Democratic Socialism, weaving together a new coalition of factions that could help to win majority union backing for NATO membership (since many saw unilateralism as implying withdrawal from the Alliance) and acceptance of the US nuclear umbrella. The Labour Party's subsequent and reformulated statement of defence policy, nevertheless, accepted the position that Britain 'should cease the attempt to remain an independent nuclear power', and it was this approach that restored a semblance of unity at the October 1961 Blackpool conference, where the previous year's endorsement of unilateral nuclear disarmament was effectively overturned.[18]

Polaris and the NATO MRBM scheme

All commentators in the debates over the independence of the deterrent held after the cancellation of Blue Streak recognised the significance of an American offer of Skybolt 'without strings' for the credibility of the Government's position. The day before the Commons held its late April debate over Labour's motion of censure, Macmillan had confirmed, when asked about the terms on which Skybolt would be provided during Prime Minister's Questions, that the 'missile will be entirely in our control'.[19] It had been noted in the press, however, that when it came to US assurances about the potential sale of Polaris, Washington was anxious to deploy Polaris under Norstad's MRBM scheme, and the line adopted by State Department spokesmen was that the provision of the missile would 'necessarily have to be considered in the light of NATO discussions.' Therefore, if Skybolt were to fail, plans for maintaining the independence of the deterrent would inevitably be compromised unless the Government could find a way to persuade the Eisenhower administration to shift its position.[20]

Given the domestic political circumstances it is not surprising to find the Prime Minister anxious to move ahead with a formal agreement over Skybolt as soon as possible. A provisional order for 100 Skybolt missiles, Macmillan thought, would be a strong signal of intent to the US authorities and help to prevent too much prevarication over options. As he told Watkinson, 'We must not be straddled between Polaris and Skybolt and getting neither one nor the other.'[21] Although this proposal elicited further objections from the Chancellor, who wanted to look at the comparable costs of the alternatives, the Minister of Defence shared Macmillan's anxieties. Watkinson hoped to dispel any impression that there were second thoughts about Skybolt, not least as the Minister of Defence thought there were 'powerful forces in the Polaris lobby that would like to get this project cancelled.' It was 'very necessary at the moment to show the British public and our allies that we are determined to maintain a British contribution to the Western nuclear deterrent forces.' This could best be done through Skybolt, and Watkinson therefore agreed that the Americans should be told of a British requirement for about 100 of the missiles, and encouraged to begin negotiations for a formal agreement to underpin an eventual sale. Over the American request for facilities to berth and tender their new Polaris submarines in Scotland at the Gare

Loch, Watkinson advised that a publishable understanding with the US would be needed over control of the submarines which used them, 'and we may possibly want to make this part of a wider deal, for example, over a Polaris-carrying submarine force of our own.' The Minister of Defence even envisaged making the Gare Loch a 'joint Polaris base in which we should gradually increase our role.'[22]

In March 1960 Macmillan had felt that the tactic of bargaining Polaris facilities in Scotland against the provision of Skybolt 'without strings' might not be particularly effective, but an understanding had nevertheless been reached with Eisenhower at Camp David. Now, however, Watkinson was keen to extract a further and much more extensive concession from the Americans during the detailed negotiations over the use of the Gare Loch. The Minister may have had in mind the domestic political criticism that the Government would have to incur for concluding what would have to be a public understanding over the basing of US submarines in Scotland as an argument for why a joint Anglo-American enterprise would be more acceptable, but it was always unlikely that Washington would prove responsive to such a negotiating ploy.[23]

Indeed the chances of bringing about any basic change in US attitudes toward the supply of Polaris at this time, except under the terms of a scheme which placed the missiles under the control of SACEUR, were remote. As we have seen, in London however there were strong doubts about the wisdom or viability of the whole NATO MRBM scheme: as well as the complex problems of command and control, and the underlying political point that creation of a force might serve to whet German nuclear ambitions rather than dampen them, its formation would inevitably entail a new and unwelcome financial commitment. Private British reservations were, nevertheless, muted because of their pressing concerns over securing a Skybolt agreement and keeping open their Polaris options. The MoD view, as Watkinson's conveyed it to the Prime Minister, was that the best tactics over MRBMs for NATO were to 'play it long.' If the Americans continued to push forward their ideas, he believed 'we must protect ourselves as best we can without getting drawn into open disagreement. Although I think we ought to play some small part in the project if there is one, we must resist being forced to subscribe large forces to something whose military priority we regard as questionable and which is politically dangerous...' If pressed by Eisenhower to stipulate more precisely the British position, Watkinson advised the Prime Minister to respond with a series of further questions about control of the force, and the crucial decision to use:

> Will it be feasible, if SACEUR is given missiles with megaton heads capable of travelling 1,500 miles, to avoid discussion in NATO of how he gets his orders? Will not the outcome be a decision that all members of the North Atlantic Council must agree before the weapons can be used? Would not that be to proclaim to the Russians that the missiles

were unlikely to be used until it was too late? Are these not weapons for fighting an all-out war, rather than preventing one? Our impression is that the Americans have not thought this through.[24]

The problem with this reserved position was that it conveyed a mixed message to Washington. Such ambiguity might give leeway for the Americans to convince themselves that the British would ultimately fall in with their plans (and so help, for example, to convince the recalcitrant French that they too should consider joining the scheme for the supply of MRBMs). As one of the Prime Minister's Private Secretaries ruefully admitted, although ministers and the COS had never liked the NATO scheme very much, in the spring of 1960 'the general feeling was that we should not take a lead against this American idea, if only because to do so might prejudice our own plans for getting Skybolt, and perhaps Polaris as well, without strings.'[25]

It was hardly a propitious time to open up further divisions within the North Atlantic Alliance. The middle of May 1960 had witnessed the collapse of the Paris four-power summit meeting, when Khrushchev had refused to continue a constructive dialogue with Washington until President Eisenhower delivered an apology for the reconnaissance overflights of the Soviet Union that had been exposed to such international fanfare by the shooting down of a U-2 aircraft and the capture of its pilot at the start of the month. The relative thaw in the Cold War that had been seen since the latter part of 1959 was now replaced by a new degree of tension as the prospects for a nuclear test ban agreement receded and the US and the Soviet Union intensified their rivalry in Asia, Africa and the Middle East. The collapse of the summit represented a particularly low point for the Prime Minister: he had invested much in trying to abate Cold War tensions, and his pleas to Eisenhower to show a little more flexibility in how he responded to Khrushchev's complaints and bluster had fallen on deaf ears. To some observers the whole episode revealed Britain's limited capacity to influence the direct nature of the relationship between Washington and Moscow, and the need for Britain to find a place as the leader of a more powerful collective grouping of Western European states which could carry more weight in international affairs generally.

In late May, with the Minister of Defence shortly due to travel to Washington where he was to meet Gates, the US Defense Secretary, in order to agree a memorandum of understanding which would underpin the sale of Skybolt, Watkinson saw Mountbatten, Zuckerman and Playfair to coordinate his position. Here it was recognised that 'the primary importance of Polaris in present circumstances was that it constituted the only chance of maintaining a British contribution to the deterrent from 1965 onwards if Skybolt failed.' When the Americans asked about UK attitudes to Polaris, the line for Watkinson to take would be that the Government was interested in the missile, 'but because the Americans were not ready to discuss this, we had not yet got to grips with it. We hoped that it might be possible to come to some arrangement during the course of the discussions about the use by the United States of the Gareloch.' If the Americans raised the subject of SACEUR's MRBM plan, the Minister was advised to say that 'we would enter into NATO discussions on it.'[26]

Soon after this the Defence Committee examined SACEUR's scheme for an MRBM force, Watkinson telling his colleagues that it held no political or military attractions for the UK, but it was difficult to argue against the logical military requirement that had been made for the capability. He recommended taking advantage of French opposition to the proposals, which might allow British representatives to avoid voicing their open objections, at least in the immediate future.[27] The priority for the Government was to secure an agreement to supply Skybolt from the US authorities while sidestepping any attempt to link this deal to the provision of Polaris submarine facilities for the Americans in Scotland (not least as this could not then be used to extract further concessions over supply of Polaris to the UK).

These negotiating threads became further entangled in early June 1960 when Watkinson met Gates in Washington. The US Defense Secretary was keen to secure early UK agreement to the basing of Polaris submarines in Scotland, but Watkinson emphasised the political problems this would create, noting that if the project were presented as a joint Anglo-American effort this might help overcome some of the domestic objections that were likely.[28] For Watkinson, however, the principal business of his meetings was to finalise the memorandum of understanding which was to secure the eventual sale of Skybolt, once development of the missile had been completed. Needing to specify approximate numbers for an initial UK production order, the Minister of Defence, taking up Macmillan's earlier suggestion, had offered the figure of about 100 missiles (although he later informed the Cabinet that he envisaged that 144 would be required, as well as extras for spares and test firings).

Gates and Watkinson also discussed US ideas for SACEUR's MRBM programme, where both men acknowledged the political implications of the scheme and that it needed to be handled 'with great care.' It was significant that they agreed it was 'desirable that any Polaris proposal should be handled as a NATO programme. Bilateral arrangements could cause serious problems.' French participation in the MRBM scheme was seen as important, but if this could not be secured, 'the US and UK should agree to examine the question of pushing ahead with the programme with the co-operation of other NATO nations, hoping that the French would come into the programme at a later date.' As a British contribution to the programme, the possible construction by the UK of two Polaris submarines was mentioned, with the missiles and associated support facilities being supplied by the Americans (though warheads would be provided by the UK); this arrangement would also, the Minister of Defence argued, make the provision of facilities for US Polaris submarines at Gare Loch more acceptable to domestic public opinion, as they could be presented as part of a joint Anglo-American Polaris base.[29]

In his subsequent report to Macmillan, Watkinson admitted that the Americans had been 'rather troublesome about what they could fairly claim was a commitment that we had made to support some kind of European MRBM scheme with or without the French.' The formula that the Minister of Defence had eventually concocted provided for British backing for a 'very limited' NATO force of about 50 Polaris missiles subject to French participation, which would allow the UK to begin building Polaris submarines to US design which could then be allocated to a NATO force, while the Gare Loch base could go ahead as a joint project. The Minister of Defence had confessed to being 'very worried about this European MRBM business. It is also obvious from my visit over there that we ought to be in both the air-launched and undersea-launched missile business if we are going to exert a continuing influence on the Americans.'[30]

The Watkinson-Gates talks triggered a flurry of British concerns over both the direction of US policy in the few months that remained before the presidential elections in November, and the impression the Americans might have gained of UK attitudes. While in Washington, Watkinson had managed to convey the idea that the British were sympathetic to Norstad's MRBM scheme, despite the fact that the official position remained one of reserve. The Minister of Defence had compounded the problem by effectively agreeing that a British approach over Polaris could not be disentangled from the NATO MRBM scheme, when the Prime Minister and his senior advisers had assumed that the Camp David understandings of March had succeeded in keeping the issues separate for the foreseeable future. What also made British officials increasingly uncomfortable was the fact that the Americans had now assumed the firm position that the provision of Skybolt was in return for establishment of the Scottish facilities for Polaris. It was certainly the case that the two understandings had been reached during the same set of talks in Camp David, but there was no explicit linkage, and at this stage the British preferred to decouple the two subjects, leaving themselves greater latitude for how the Scottish base issue, with all the domestic political sensitivities it raised, was handled.[31]

Frederick Bishop, one of Macmillan's Principal Private Secretaries, noted with disapproval that the Minister of Defence's talks in Washington had managed to entangle the Polaris issue with the project for a NATO MRBM force. This also raised in turn larger problems about the future of the deterrent:

> It may well be true that we cannot hope that, in their remaining few months, the present American Administration should re-examine their nuclear defence policy. We should undoubtedly do so ourselves without delay, since we shall need six or nine months to think the matter out before a new American Administration takes over. The fundamental question is – what form should the deterrent take in conditions of nuclear equipoise? Ought it not to be primarily retaliatory? We ought to make sure that the answer to this is not prejudiced by the spread of nuclear weapons, particularly by the addition of quasi-strategic weapons to the so-called tactical nuclear weapons already at SACEUR's disposal.

Hazarding a prediction (that turned out to be accurate), Bishop noted that the Democratic Party hopeful, Senator John F. Kennedy, was giving policy speeches calling for the Alliance to build up its conventional forces, and that a new administration might begin to take strong initiatives to limit the proliferation of nuclear weapons and reduce the chances of escalation resulting from the outbreak of fighting in Europe.[32]

In overall terms, Macmillan was anxious about the speed with which talk of a European MRBM scheme was moving forward, without any deeper consideration of the numerous political issues that it raised. Downing Street officials were also troubled that the Americans now seemed to be suggesting that Britain would have to build its own Polaris submarines, where only a short time before there had been indications from US officials they might be leased or bought from the Americans, and so be made available in much quicker time so that the provision of facilities at the Gare Loch could be presented as a joint venture from an early stage of its operation. As Philip de Zulueta, the Prime Minister's Principal Private Secretary for foreign affairs, put it, '…this arrangement does not seem a very good bargain from our point of view.' He informed Macmillan that while in Washington the Minister of Defence had seemed to assume that the Government was in favour of NATO having an MRBM force, and that Watkinson had spoken in terms of a 'commitment' made to support such a scheme 'with or without the French.' But as far as de Zulueta could see, 'the only "commitment" which I have found was a statement in NATO to the effect that we would consider favourably the general idea of a NATO MRBM scheme. But if the French oppose it, there can be no such scheme.'[33]

From the middle of June and into July the Prime Minister conducted a largely unsatisfactory correspondence with Eisenhower where he attempted to secure a number of concessions and attach conditions in return for the provision of base facilities in Scotland for the docking and tendering of US Polaris submarines. Macmillan was certainly animated by the domestic political criticism and security concerns that were raised by the prospect of an American nuclear base located so close to such a major population centre as Glasgow, but he was also minded (at least initially) to use the few bargaining tools he had in order the secure a UK Polaris option for the future.[34] It was soon apparent from the exchanges that the US administration was reluctant to meet the Government's domestic political needs. Eisenhower's assumption, moreover, that agreement in principle had been reached between the two leaders in March that the facilities would be provided was an immediate cause of contention, Macmillan observing on the relevant section of one presidential letter: 'I did not repeat not agree to this at Camp David.'[35]

Regarding the NATO MRBM issue, the Prime Minister had tried to convey British reservations to Eisenhower in guarded form. Macmillan had noted that there was much uncertainty, largely due to French attitudes, over whether the scheme would take effective shape, but if it did 'what we might do in the way of Polaris in the future as well as what we are trying to do with Skybolt puts a pretty heavy strain on our resources, and we could hardly make much of a separate contribution to the European system. But if we go in for Polaris, we might make our contribution through that.'[36] But the Prime Minister's requests that the Americans reconsider the site of the base, assent to British ideas over dual control of the firing of any US Polaris missiles using Scottish facilities even when operating outside territorial waters, and provide an option for UK purchase or domestic construction of Polaris submarines so that a Scottish base could be projected as a joint venture for public consumption, were all rejected by the President.[37]

Indeed, on the very last issue, Eisenhower was insistent that 'a bilateral arrangement with the UK on Polaris missiles outside the NATO framework could jeopardise favourable consideration of the NATO MRBM program.' Moreover, he supported the initial talks that had been conducted between Gates and Watkinson 'along the lines that the acquisition of Polaris submarine missile systems by the UK should constitute a British contribution to the NATO MRBM program. Such a procedure would avoid serious NATO repercussions and also meet your need for a cooperative Polaris submarine undertaking.'[38] Regarding Eisenhower's initial and curt rebuff to Macmillan's list of conditions, de Zulueta was left 'rather distressed' by the tone and was keen for the Prime Minister to 're-establish the position. Of course the Administration is dying and the President's influence will steadily decrease from now on.' It would help the transition to a new administration, de Zulueta advised (in a perspective that reflected the new strains that had emerged concurrent with the collapse of the Paris summit meeting), if Eisenhower's time in office ended on a high note for Anglo-American relations, but he thought it would be 'difficult to keep cordial and intimate relations' going for the final six months of the presidency. Although keen not to take any hasty action, one possibility that had occurred to de Zulueta was that 'it may be necessary to recognise that our "special relationship" with the United States is not worth much in real terms even with President Eisenhower so that we had better start reinforcing ourselves vis-à-vis the Americans by an independent policy with someone else, i.e. the French.'[39]

When informed in late July of the lack of progress in the negotiations that was by now evident, the Cabinet was still ready to agree in principle to the US request for base facilities, but on the understanding that ministers would seek firmer assurances over the control of any US missiles which were based in Scotland.[40] By this stage, the Prime Minister was in full blown retreat over any ideas that a UK Polaris option could be linked to the provision of Scottish facilities. 'We have looked again at the timing,' he informed Eisenhower, 'and we have now decided that, even if you were willing, we could not hope to have Polaris submarines in operation until considerably nearer 1970, for technical and financial reasons. So the question of the relation between our Polaris submarines and the NATO MRBM project does not arise. The latter will be discussed on its merits in NATO.'[41]

By early July 1960 it was apparent that Downing Street officials were keen for the Prime Minister to indicate to the White House the depth of British unease over the whole NATO MRBM scheme so that the Americans could be disabused of any false notions they might have of the extent of potential British involvement. Mountbatten, also, was of the opinion, as Bishop put it, 'that we should begin to come clean with the Americans on these nuclear defence problems, and I think his view is pretty widely shared.'[42]

There was, indeed, a palpable sense of annoyance in Downing Street that the scheme had been allowed to run so far without the MoD subjecting its wider implications to close analysis, or raising any substantive objections. One concern coming to the fore were doubts that the provision of MRBMs to SACEUR – with their range of several hundred miles and warheads of upwards of several hundred kilotons in yield – could be related to the 'tactical' environment of a land battle in Central Europe where the Warsaw Pact had subjected NATO forces to attack. In other words, MRBMs – such as Polaris – were, in effect, 'strategic' weapons, whose use would signify that any intention to limit a ground war in Europe had vanished. Once such weapons were unleashed they would, in effect, signal that a strategic nuclear exchange had begun (leading to questions over whether this was the kind of force that should really be in SACEUR's hands, especially as once NATO governments had authorised him to declare so-called R-hour, he would be allowed to implement his atomic strike plans without political control).[43] To Bishop, the MoD's attitude to the MRBM scheme, having at last been forced to confront the issue, had been 'quite amazing':

> They now admit that the project is an extremely dangerous one, both in relation to the maintenance of the NATO alliance, and (what is even more important) in relation to world peace. It is not really good enough to describe this as being 'wise after the event'. The NATO MRBM project is not a new development. We have been well aware of it for a considerable time, and in any case the same arguments applied to earlier projects resulting in the equipment of NATO forces with long-range nuclear and so-called tactical weapons. The development of NATO strategy over the last six years has (as the Ministry of Defence now admit) been wrong.
>
> What amazes me is this. First, there is not the slightest explanation or expression of contrition for this lamentable state of affairs, either from the Ministry of Defence or from the Chiefs of Staff. Second, if one were in a motor car and had taken the wrong turning and were now heading for the edge of a cliff, the obvious course would be to stop the car and go into reverse. The attitude of the Ministry of Defence in the present case is to apply the brake gently, so that we shall still go over the cliff though perhaps more slowly.

Bishop was understandably anxious that representations should be made to the US administration in Washington, so that the Americans did not read the wrong conclusions into British attitudes.[44]

On the other hand, the great difficulty of coming out too vociferously against the NATO MRBM scheme was that the American reaction might be to deny Polaris altogether to the UK, and so prejudice the possibility of keeping a Polaris option in the event that Skybolt encountered insuperable development problems. Another unwelcome possibility was that, frustrated with the recalcitrance of London and Paris, the Americans might attempt to arrive at a bilateral deal with the Germans over the control of nuclear forces. As a result de Zulueta recommended that British officials should probe SACEUR on the political problems for the Alliance raised by his MRBM scheme, question the military utility of a land-based mobile Polaris force (as was then envisaged), and suggest joint Anglo-US or NATO staff studies on the whole problem of deterrence policy. In short, the best course seemed to be to play for time until after the next US presidential election when a new administration would takeover in Washington, the possibilities of trading the Scottish facilities for US concessions over a UK Polaris option could again be explored, and further study had been given to organising a genuinely European element to a NATO deterrent force (perhaps through some close Anglo-French alignment). To all this, the Prime Minister registered his approval.[45]

In order to coordinate views, Macmillan met Selwyn Lloyd, the Foreign Secretary, along with Watkinson on 7 July to discuss policy toward the NATO MRBM scheme (they were joined on the official side by Playfair, Zuckerman, Mountbatten, and Sir Patrick Dean from the Foreign Office). The Prime Minister alluded to a recent MoD report that had suggested the MRBM project was

> fundamentally ill-advised and carried with it implications of grave concern for the whole concept of the North Atlantic Alliance. It was now thought that the provision of missiles of the range and yield proposed by SACEUR (whose headquarters had recently indicated that there were plans for the use of nuclear warheads up to half a megaton against distant targets) would largely invalidate the distinction between the Western deterrent which was under the undivided control of the United States and United Kingdom Governments and the [conventional] shield forces of the Alliance. It was suggested that the NATO deployment of such weapons in the considerable numbers proposed by SACEUR (300 in 1963 and ultimately up to 1,000) would be altogether excessive as a means of enforcing a pause in the event of any aggression against Continental members of the Alliance and would be likely to exacerbate the danger of full-scale nuclear war.

Clearly implying that he agreed with this analysis, Macmillan noted the very serious political and strategic issues raised by Norstad's proposals. Not the least problematic was German involvement in any MRBM scheme, which might result in the stationing of long-range missiles on German soil, a step which would not only be very provocative to the Soviet Union, but arouse the opposition of British public opinion. A basic difficulty was that SACEUR did not recognise the distinctions that ministers were determined to maintain between the tactical use of nuclear weapons on the Central European battlefield, and the release of strategic nuclear forces controlled by the US and British Governments. The problem was to convince the Americans that the MRBM scheme raised a whole series of profound objections without appearing to be adamantly opposed, and so incurring US disfavour.[46]

The emergence of the Multilateral Force (MLF) proposal and the Holy Loch agreement

The terms of the inter-Alliance debate were soon, however, to shift in a new direction. During the summer of 1960, the Eisenhower administration began to reformulate its approach to the nuclear sharing problem, and to reconsider the Gates proposals made in April on the provision of MRBMs to NATO's European members. One of the principal reasons for this change of tack was that State Department officials had come privately to share some of the concerns also entertained by their British counterparts that Norstad's scheme could become the vehicle by which a West German government might acquire some measure of access to a nuclear capability – and one which could hit targets far removed from the immediate zone of any fighting that might be taking place on German territory between the forces of NATO and the Warsaw Pact. Whatever might be agreed in theory about 'assignment' of nuclear forces to NATO, or 'control' of MRBMs by SACEUR, under the Gates proposals they would still have to be either manufactured by the Europeans themselves or (the clear American preference at the start of the year) acquired by national governments from the United States and positioned in different European countries, including the Federal Republic of Germany. Again, the United States would retain notional custody over warheads (as provided under US laws), but in practice the arrangements here were loose, and ready access could become available under the NATO atomic stockpile plan first promulgated in December 1957.[47] How to avoid a German 'finger on the nuclear trigger', without offending Bonn's sensibilities or engaging in blatant and discriminatory treatment between different NATO members, was to become a perennial and deep-seated issue for US and British leaders and officials, and be the source of major inter-Alliance tensions, over the next few years.

At the beginning of 1960, Robert R. Bowie, a former head of the State Department's Policy Planning Staff, had been recalled from his academic post at Harvard University to undertake a comprehensive review of the problems faced by the North Atlantic Alliance, including its nuclear arrangements, during the decade that lay ahead. Bowie began work after being confirmed in his appointment by the President in April, solicited advice from experts and serving officials, and delivered his important and influential report to the US Secretary of State, Christian Herter, on 21 August 1960.

In the face of growing Soviet nuclear strength, Bowie placed a major onus on an increase in NATO's conventional capabilities so that the 'shield' forces available in central Europe came near to SACEUR's expressed target of 30 divisions. At the same time it was necessary to instil confidence that nuclear weapons would be used in the event of a massive and sustained Soviet attack on Western Europe, and to give the Europeans a sense they had a share in such crucial decisions. An immediate start could be made by 'assigning' several US Polaris submarines with American crews to SACEUR. But recognising that national physical control of nuclear capabilities by the European members of NATO seemed to lie at the root of the sharing problem, Bowie recommended the subsequent development of a genuinely multinational force, under a clear centralised authority, where withdrawal of units for national purposes would be ruled out. The device he chose to achieve this difficult object was to propose a sea-based 'multilateral' NATO Polaris force, consisting of either ships or submarines (helping to remove any features of national territoriality), and manned by mixed crews from different NATO countries, all operating under SACEUR. Warheads for the force would still be held under US custody in peacetime, but would be released under pre-arranged procedures and agreed circumstances (such as a large-scale Soviet nuclear attack). In perhaps the most controversial part of the scheme, a high degree of delegation would be accorded to SACEUR so that a US veto was not seen, in practice, to operate.

In this way NATO was to have its own powerful deterrent force – easing concerns about the willingness of Washington to use its strategic nuclear weapons in defence of Western Europe – and which could even form the nucleus of a European deterrent. Separate national nuclear capabilities or aspirations had no place in Bowie's scheme and would eventually be absorbed under the umbrella of the new multilateral force (MLF). Creation of the MLF, it was maintained, would help to check trends toward the proliferation of nuclear weapons.[48] When Bowie saw Eisenhower to explain his plan he was categorical that 'the national programs being carried forward are very bad and are having a divisive effect.' Although he thought that de Gaulle would be unlikely to accept the proposals, Eisenhower embraced Bowie's ideas on the nuclear arrangements of the Alliance with enthusiasm, commenting that 'if the Europeans are not willing to accept the idea of collective defense by multiple rather than national forces, the whole NATO concept will fall apart.'[49]

The US administration's acceptance of Bowie's ideas for an MLF was a wholly unwelcome development as far as British officials were concerned, even though it signalled that Norstad's original MRBM scheme was no longer a front-runner. The Americans were not ready to offer a system such as Polaris, which would extend Britain's national nuclear capabilities for another generation, until the whole issue of NATO's nuclear arrangements had first been tackled by its members. Any prospect that the provision of Polaris facilities in Scotland for the Americans could be used to lever concessions had by now evaporated. As the head of the British Joint Services Mission in Washington reported in August to Playfair, the PUS at the MoD, '... it is now absolutely clear that the Americans will allow no announcement that they will help us in any way with Polaris or the Launching Submarines until the SACEUR MRBM problem is finished with. Indeed, I very much doubt if they will agree to help us with information over and above what we are getting now.'[50] One of Watkinson's closest officials, Richard Chilver, was even more pessimistic. 'It is very unlikely that the Americans will allow the UK to buy whatever strategic weapon system they may introduce themselves in the 1970s,' he told the Minister of Defence at the end of August. 'Their primary reason for agreeing to sell the UK Skybolt was to clinch the Government's decision to drop Blue Streak. The British Nuclear Deterrent Study Group will be reviewing what the possibilities are for developing during the 1960s a British weapon system for the 1970s, but it is not likely to appear a very attractive proposition. It would have to be put in hand fairly soon to be ready in time.'[51]

A formal Anglo-American agreement providing for the purchase of Skybolt, once it had finished development, was finally signed on 23 September 1960. In the weeks leading up to the agreement, the Americans had proved reluctant to commit to signing until the issue of their Polaris facilities in Scotland was resolved. The fact that negotiations over the terms under which Skybolt would be provided, and exchanges with the Americans over their Polaris facilities in Scotland – which were now to be located at the Holy Loch, rather than the Gare Loch – had been going on in tandem now created an inevitable connection between the two understandings.[52] The British Ambassador in Washington, Sir Harold Caccia, reported at the start of September that one senior State Department official had told him that 'the Skybolt agreement was to all intents and purposes ready for signature and it would be good for our relations as a whole in the defence field if there was not too wide a gap in time between the conclusion of the two arrangements. They both concerned the deterrent and had their origin in Camp David. Although he did not attempt to argue that there was any legal connexion between the two, it is quite clear that the State Department as well as the Pentagon would consider that we had not acted in entire good faith if we took the one and boggled at the other.'[53]

In the last stages of the negotiations with Washington over the Holy Loch facilities, the British authorities had finally decided to drop any idea that when an agreement was publicly announced it should be accompanied by an American offer for the UK to buy or build its own Polaris submarines, since any such British Polaris force would have to be attached to the NATO MRBM scheme.[54] The Cabinet was informed in similar terms when told in mid-September that an agreement over a Polaris base in Scotland had been reached.[55]

This was very far from meaning that the Government has lost interest in Polaris, however. Indeed, Polaris was still regarded as an essential fallback if Skybolt should not eventually appear. There were already several indications that this unhappy outcome might be a strong possibility. Zuckerman had received frequent warnings from his American contacts regarding progress with the project over the previous few months. In September, with conclusion of the formal Skybolt agreement in Washington imminent, he passed on the news to Watkinson that 'formidable' technical problems still had to be overcome, particularly with the missile's innovative guidance system, and that, if badly delayed, the project could even be dropped altogether from the overall US programme. He recommended that in any future references to progress it should be said that things were going 'as expected' rather than 'as planned'.[56] Watkinson minuted his agreement, adding 'we must "play down" Skybolt. My statement "it is not the touchstone of British Defence Policy" is the theme. We must keep ourselves in the position where we can provide alternative means of delivering the nuclear deterrent if Skybolt fails.'[57]

It was Zuckerman's warnings which prompted Watkinson to impress upon the Prime Minister how President Eisenhower had to be made to understand that the Holy Loch arrangements had caused the Government domestic political difficulties, and that there was a clear link to the supply of Skybolt (a link which British officials had, only a few months before, been keen to play down or deny altogether):

> we regard the whole transaction on [sic] a reciprocal arrangement, in accordance with what was agreed at Camp David. It is important that the Americans should recognise that if Skybolt should meet with serious trouble and have to be abandoned they would have a moral obligation to help us to overcome, in one way or another, the difficulties which this would cause for us. After all they have got the Holy Loch and we certainly have not got Skybolt for some years yet. This would give us the necessary standing to re-open the Polaris submarine question or take any other action that seemed necessary if Skybolt fails.[58]

It was also significant that the BNDSG began to re-start its work in earnest in September 1960, with an emphasis on UK-based alternatives if Skybolt should not materialise.[59] All this became even more apposite when the following month Watkinson was warned by the US Deputy Secretary of Defense that the Skybolt programme was in 'real trouble', with development costs running much higher than expected.[60] Despite reassurances that the project was not facing imminent cancellation, Zuckerman was sent to Washington to probe the attitude of Gates and other senior US officials.[61] The pessimistic report he delivered on his return spurred Macmillan to send a message of concern to Eisenhower, who replied in mollifying terms that the understandings about Skybolt remained firm.[62]

It must have been galling to British officials that fresh and real doubts about Skybolt's prospects were emerging just at the point when the Holy Loch agreement was made public. Although the substance of the story had already been revealed two weeks earlier by *The Times*, the Prime Minister finally announced to the House of Commons on 1 November 1960 that facilities would be provided for US Polaris submarines in Scotland.[63] Much criticism followed, and there were awkward questions from MPs over the degree of UK control over the launching of US missiles wherever they might be. In the exchanges between US and British officials before the announcement, although the Americans had readily conceded that when it came to launching Polaris from within territorial waters this would be 'a matter of joint decision between the two governments', they were not happy that a decision to use the missiles outside such waters would be limited in any way. Reluctantly Macmillan had agreed that the UK would have to rely on the 'general understandings and close relationships' that existed with the US when it came to control of the US Polaris missiles using Scottish facilities, while Washington understood that its assurances on the issue were to remain private. In the event, the Prime Minister had responded to questioning in the House by saying that he was 'perfectly satisfied' that use of Polaris would be subject to 'the fullest possible previous consultation' with the United States, phrasing which caused some degree of annoyance at the Pentagon, although Eisenhower was relatively unperturbed.[64]

Having paid the immediate domestic political price for agreeing to the Scottish facilities, ministers were obviously doubly concerned that the other side of the implicit bargain made at Camp David – the eventual supply of Skybolt missiles – should be fulfilled by the Americans. Nevertheless, Watkinson felt that it was important to have a plan for what to say in public if recent US doubts over Skybolt were to leak to the press at this volatile time. As he told the Prime Minister, 'From the start, we have foreseen it as a possibility and for that reason, you and I have been at pains never to say we were certain of Skybolt.' However, he did not advise going all out for Polaris at the present juncture as a new administration would first have to take up office in the New Year, and to pursue Polaris would 'only be to proclaim that we were at the mercy of the Americans.' In any case, Watkinson doubted that Washington would be ready to offer Polaris 'for our national use until the plan for a NATO Polaris scheme has succeeded or failed, and perhaps not even then.'[65] The British attitude, the Minister of Defence felt, should be to continue to show interest in Polaris, but remain wedded to the understanding over Skybolt, not least as any slackening in British enthusiasm for the latter project could aid the cause of those in the Pentagon who might be considering cancellation.

Meanwhile, in mid-October 1960, the Eisenhower administration had given formal indication to British officials in Washington over how its new ideas about meeting Norstad's needs for an MRBM capability had developed since the spring. Following the lead of the Bowie report, it was now suggested that a permanent MRBM force could be formed under SACEUR, initially involving the assignment of five US Polaris submarines with 80 missiles to NATO by the end of 1963, which could not be withdrawn without the consent of the North Atlantic Council. Targeting was to be decided by SACEUR in coordination with SAC and Bomber Command, but SACEUR was also to have delegated authority to use his MRBMs if NATO was subject to Soviet nuclear attack. To match this US commitment, the other NATO governments would be expected to provide on a collective basis another 100 MRBMs during the course of 1964. The Americans thought that this latter force should be organised on the basis of multilateral ownership, finance and control, with mixed-manning (involving international crews) where feasible. A seaborne MRBM force was now felt to be preferable as it avoided the political complications of land basing, and surface ships to carry the missiles were considered a cheaper option than submarines. A NATO stockpile of nuclear warheads, kept under US custody in peacetime and subject to an American veto, would also be created to equip the new missile force.[66]

By this time the view of the Prime Minister's closest advisers was that a constructive response would have to be delivered to Washington, as the MRBM project was clearly not going to just die away. Amongst some Foreign Office officials, moreover, and in the wake of the Future Policy Study, opposition to the whole concept of an independent deterrent was beginning to gather adherents, fuelled by the developing feeling that it would be more realistic to offer a future Polaris-based force to NATO on a permanent basis than to continue with the expensive and provocative business of preserving 'independence'. During the BNDSG's discussions during 1960 the Foreign Office had been keen on pursuing Polaris options, even though it was known this might involve some curtailment of totally independent national control.[67] There were also voices at the Cabinet Office and within Downing Street which were calling for a fundamental reappraisal. Accordingly, Bishop advised Macmillan that although the US MRBM plan could not be accepted as presently conceived, a more serious attempt to cooperate had to be made. The objective, shared with the Americans, would be to offer nuclear reassurance to the European members of NATO: 'Officials believe that the time has now come when we should be ready to consider transferring some part of our independent nuclear capability into NATO. This, I feel sure, is the way our policy is bound to develop. It may be that the time has already passed when we might have voluntarily taken a step of this sort with some hope of securing special political advantage from it, e.g., by way of some political rapprochement with the French Government. It is now necessary that we should be ready to do this for the wider purposes of the alliance.'[68]

Nevertheless, when ministers met at the end of October 1960 to consider the American proposals numerous objections were raised. The assignment of such a large force was described by Watkinson as 'not justified on military grounds', while mixed crewing of surface ships was also judged 'impracticable'. There was deep anxiety over the idea that authority to fire nuclear weapons would be delegated to a military commander such as SACEUR. Watkinson was, however, ready to examine whatever practical alternatives were advanced. Ministers agreed that giving SACEUR delegated authority over nuclear use was 'totally unacceptable', while the costs of the scheme were also seen as prohibitive. Despite this, Macmillan felt it was important not to discourage the Americans in their political aims, which the Government certainly shared. While British criticisms of the American scheme should certainly be raised, a willingness to explore different options should also be displayed, including the assignment to NATO of some part of the British nuclear force.[69]

The official British reaction to the latest US proposals for providing SACEUR with an MRBM force was delivered to Herter by Lord Home, the Foreign Secretary, at the start of November 1960. Herter was to be informed, Home told the British Ambassador in Washington, that the British Government understood that American objectives in proposing the force included giving the European members of NATO a feeling that they had a greater share in the deterrent, reassuring them that the United States remained committed to the defence of Western Europe, and preventing the development of additional national nuclear weapons programmes, especially by the Federal Republic of Germany. These were all aims, Home affirmed, which London shared. Despite its view that the American initiative had great potential 'provided it is launched on the right lines', the Government however did not feel that the current scheme had been given sufficient study from the political angle in that it had to be made acceptable to the European member states, and their publics. A difficult sticking point here was pictured as de Gaulle's policy of building up an independent French strategic nuclear force, and his hostility to any notion of international command of such forces.

But of even more immediate significance were deep reservations over giving SACEUR what looked like unbridled control of his own long-range nuclear forces which might be used in reply to any nuclear attack on the NATO area. It was this delegation of authority that Home found particularly disturbing, as a SACEUR response with MRBMs would almost certainly trigger a general nuclear exchange. Furthermore, investing SACEUR, as a NATO officer, with greater delegated authority over the stockpile of warheads for his MRBM force was likely to be widely viewed as a form of dissemination of nuclear capability which would cause unease in many quarters. Finally, British opinion would have great difficulties accepting what could be seen as a proposal giving the Germans a share in the control of nuclear weapons, even though the ultimate US aim was to frustrate any German future intention to develop a national programme of nuclear development.

The Government would much prefer instead that physical control of American weapons systems and warheads should remain with the US authorities, even though they should be considered clearly and strongly committed to NATO. In a reference to the initial American offer of five Polaris submarines, Home suggested to Herter that the appearance of NATO cooperation and control over such dedicated US weapons could be achieved (in a prescient forecast for what, six years later and under rather different circumstances, would be styled the NATO Nuclear Planning Group), by the formation of 'a small group of national representatives (e.g. the Standing Group powers plus the Secretary General, or the Standing Group powers plus two rotating members plus the Secretary General) who would have secret information about the armaments and deployment of the force and would be kept informed of any changes, so that they could assure member countries that the force in fact remains available and ready for use in case of any attack in Europe.' Again in a foretaste of the debates that were to ensue two years later over the provision of Polaris to the UK, Home moved on to consider the tensions between allocating a dedicated nuclear force to NATO and retaining independent control over its use:

> If the permanent [NATO MRBM] force comes into being, or if a wider range of nuclear weapons were to be included in the scheme, the same sort of committee system could be used for general supervision. One day, perhaps, we may reach a state of affairs where member nations will be willing to place forces permanently and irrevocably under international command and control. But this is hard doctrine today. It seems to me that we are more likely to obtain contributions to the permanent force on the basis of 'assignment' (in the current NATO sense) to a NATO force under SACEUR, with supervision by a committee ... but retaining the ultimate national control. On such a basis it might be possible for the United Kingdom, for example, to put a useful contribution into the pool.

But as it stood, the Foreign Secretary affirmed that the United Kingdom could make no specific contribution to the scheme as currently conceived by Washington.[70]

The victory of John F. Kennedy in the presidential election held on 8 November 1960 gave the Government valuable breathing space. It was recognised that the outgoing Republican administration was unlikely to make any attempt to tie the hands of its Democratic successor. That said, the same interlinked problems of SACEUR's MRBM requirement, the maintenance of the US nuclear guarantee to Western Europe, and the debate over nuclear arrangements within NATO (and lying behind this, the presumption that the Federal Republic of Germany was unhappy with its status within the Alliance) had not disappeared and further ideas from Washington as to how to tackle them could be expected. Macmillan wanted to warn the US authorities that any proposals for a NATO MRBM force would have to be given a thorough technical examination and considered by the Cabinet before any affirmative British response could be given, beyond showing a willingness to engage in further discussion of the problem.[71]

Indeed, the North Atlantic Council, meeting in Paris on 16 December, was given a formal American presentation by Herter of the idea that NATO should consider creating a permanent MRBM force along the lines suggested to the British in October, including the mixed-manning and joint control of its European seaborne component, although the controversial arrangements for authority over its use were made less explicit. The scheme aimed, as the Americans informed British officials, to 'counteract suspicions that the US might become increasingly unwilling to risk nuclear devastation in defence of European countries; and to discourage the development of independent national nuclear forces.'[72] Once again British scepticism was tempered by the belief that simple opposition to such US proposals would not be the best approach, or as Watkinson expressed it, 'a purely negative attitude, although quite possible, may not be in our best interests if we want to get our way in NATO.'[73]

The immediate British reaction was therefore to welcome discussion of the proposals, but also to launch a call for a far wider study of the purpose, control and deployment of nuclear weapons in support of the Alliance so that NATO's nuclear requirements could be properly determined. Such a study would inevitably take time and – so British officials hoped – provide further opportunities for other objections to the latest American proposals to gain traction amongst other Alliance members. This device ultimately led to the production of an elaborate series of questions about NATO's possible employment of nuclear weapons by Frank Mottershead, an MoD official who had been studying such issues since the autumn. They were presented to Britain's Alliance partners in early 1961 and served to prolong discussion about some of the basic principles of NATO nuclear strategy during the initial months while the Kennedy administration settled into office and began its own new studies into US policy towards the North Atlantic Alliance.

The future nuclear programme and Skybolt prospects

The uncertainties that surrounded matters of high-level nuclear policy during this period, and the pressures to make economies in this area, were illustrated once more when the MoD's assumptions for the future nuclear programme came up for ministerial discussion towards the end of 1960. In October 1960, the Prime Minister had convened an important summit on defence policy for ministers and officials at Chequers, where the COS's requirements for Britain's limited war forces began to be measured against overseas commitments and responsibilities with a view to seeing if reductions and rationalisation was possible (Macmillan's own view was that preparations for Britain's involvement in potential limited wars in South East Asia and the Middle East were far too extensive). During the summer, as part of the ministerial reshuffle which had taken Lord Home to the Foreign Office and saw Sandys moved from the Ministry of Aviation to takeover Home's previous post as Commonwealth Relations Secretary, Peter Thorneycroft, a strong pro-European who had resigned as Chancellor in January 1958 over Macmillan's refusal to cutback on public spending, was brought back into the Cabinet to fill Sandys' now vacant position at Aviation. As part of the overall search for savings in defence, by October Thorneycroft was keen to examine the scope for a reduction in the nuclear weapons programme.[74]

Thorneycroft's subsequent paper contained drastic suggestions for halving the UK's strategic nuclear strike potential, and for stopping all work on tactical nuclear weapons, thereby achieving considerable reductions in spending over the next decade.[75] Obviously disturbed by such interventions, Watkinson wanted the whole subject of possible deep cuts to the nuclear programme dealt with by closely-held ministerial correspondence and kept away from regular departmental machinery, and even from the Chiefs of Staff (mainly for fear of politically embarrassing leaks). Thorneycroft's paper, Watkinson reminded the Prime Minister, could only be implemented with a major change of policy, and if its proposals were to be considered it would have to be alongside a re-examination of Britain's entire nuclear strategy, and should also be seen in the context of NATO's nuclear development. Underlining the fact that he had spent a large part of the previous year thinking through the problem of how much to spend on the deterrent, Watkinson explained that his own view was that

> We must limit the nuclear element in the defence programme to what is absolutely essential for our purpose; otherwise we cannot fulfil our world-wide responsibilities to deter limited war or equip our new all-regular forces on the scales which they must have if their reduced numbers are to be compensated for. This does not mean, however ... that we can or should abdicate our position as a nuclear power and destroy the immense capacity which we have built up, both in technical manpower and industrial know-how. Apart from the effect on the Russians, to do so would ... so weaken our bargaining position with the Americans, and possibly with other allies, that we should find ourselves relegated to a position where, with the limitations which we have imposed on the size of our forces, we could really only make a negligible contribution to world affairs. The question, therefore, is ... not one of deciding whether or not we remain a military nuclear power, but what proportion of the defence budget is spent to this end and what means of delivery we select to carry British-made nuclear devices of one kind or another. This problem must be seen against a background of a world that will soon attain nuclear sufficiency and in which the balance of nuclear power will probably be fairly equally poised between the Communists and the free world.

Halving Britain's contribution to the Western deterrent, as Thorneycroft had suggested, would, Watkinson argued, undermine its validity. As long as the proportion of the defence budget spent on the strategic nuclear deterrent was kept at about 10 per cent, Watkinson thought this 'the minimum that we dare to justify our position as a nuclear power.' The Minister of Defence concluded his submission with the assertion that 'our objective in general defence policy should be to present a front of calm and confident decision. Any report that we were questioning the whole basis of our nuclear strategy would be immensely damaging, at home and abroad.'[76]

Cabinet Office officials tended to agree with Watkinson's analysis and preferred to wait until the more general deliberations over defence policy – and in particular the problem of limited war capabilities, where tactical nuclear weapons might be needed – had been concluded before recommending any collective ministerial discussion of the nuclear programme as a whole.[77] The Cabinet Secretary was not altogether happy that the further study of nuclear weapons systems should be undertaken once again within the MoD, and without being informed by the broader framework of policy that the Government had been considering throughout the year, but he did not think it wise to add more delay to the work.[78] Watkinson was instead encouraged by the Prime Minister to prepare a paper offering a comprehensive picture of the entire programme for development and production of nuclear weapons, taking into account the Future Policy Report of February 1960, which gave guidance on the strategic deterrent, and the more recent decisions over limited war forces made at Chequers. In downbeat terms, Watkinson replied to the effect that a MoD review of its nuclear requirements could probably not be completed until the spring, once issues concerning NATO were clearer, and the new US administration had assumed office.[79]

When the Prime Minister then asked about the rate of expenditure on the programme over the intervening period, he was told by the Minister of Defence that for the 1960/61 financial year about £5½ million a month was devoted to research, development and production of nuclear warheads, with most of the costs absorbed by AWRE and the fissile material programme. 'We can do nothing to alter the cost of either of these elements in the short run,' he maintained. 'Cuts in the costs of AWRE are irreversible, in the sense that it means disbanding skilled staff; and to do this without knowing exactly what we want our future programme to be would mean cutting blind.' Although Watkinson professed to be keen to produce a detailed study as soon as possible, sufficient time had to be accorded to give the exercise some proper substance. Nevertheless, the Prime Minister asked that at least an 'interim' report might be available for ministers by the end of January.[80]

The propensity for the MoD to delay the review for as long as possible made the Cabinet Secretary, for one, feel uneasy. Surely, Brook argued, it made more sense to decide on an approach to the UK programme before entering into discussions with a new administration in Washington? Once again Brook complained that although 'much of [the review] can be classified as weapons policy, it turns to some extent on strategic assumptions which the Ministry of Defence ought not to be left to formulate on their own. Much of this is in the "politico-military" field; and in this I am not altogether happy at the thought of leaving the Ministry of Defence in the lead.'[81] What seems surprising in retrospect is that no provision was made to use the new official machinery of the Nuclear Requirements for Defence Committee – introduced, it should be recalled, to ensure adequate inter-departmental coordination in the formulation and presentation of the nuclear weapons needs of the services – to oversee the nuclear review that ministers had called for in the autumn.

When the Minister of Defence finally produced a report on the MoD's future requirements, on 20 February 1961, it was unsurprisingly in the nature of a 'holding paper' (of the interim variety suggested by Macmillan) and not the comprehensive review of a long-term programme and its costs that had first been anticipated in November.[82] The paper acknowledged that in 1960 ministers had accepted the Future Policy Study's recommendation that the size of the independent deterrent should be related to what the Americans would accept as a significant contribution to the Western deterrent 'and which would therefore also have significance for the Russians', but that this was called a 'matter of judgment, not calculation. A force which was only a small fraction of the size of the American deterrent (the size of which is rising) could still be regarded as significant if it could do very great injury to Russia.' By 1962/63, it was noted, there would be 144 Victors and Vulcans in service, 48 equipped with Blue Steel Mark 1 and the rest free-falling bombs. Once the first Skybolt missiles were delivered, plans were in place to cut these numbers to 96 aircraft, consisting of 72 Vulcan Mark 2s, each carrying two Skybolts, and 24 Victors Mark 2s, each with one Blue Steel. 'Forces of this size,' the Minister of Defence pronounced, 'would enable us to hit about one-tenth of the Russian targets the Americans could hit in 1963. I believe these plans are about right.' A new lightweight megaton warhead for Skybolt would be required, but starting UK work on adapting an American-model warhead (such as the new Mark 59) would not be possible until the Americans had settled on their own design of re-entry vehicle for the missile. No long term programme for a new megaton warhead was therefore specified, and all the paper requested was that ministers agree present plans for the strategic deterrent force, the production of 50 more Red Snow warheads in 1962/63, and that there should be a critical examination of the number of lightweight megaton weapons that would be needed in the light of future Red Snow production and the number of Skybolts eventually acquired.

When it came to the programme for tactical nuclear weapons, Watkinson's paper admitted that comprehensive proposals were difficult to compile while doctrine on their employment and use remained in flux, but production of large numbers of kiloton and sub-kiloton weapons to equip British forces was finally ruled out (in January 1960, it should be recalled, the MoD's proposed programme had involved accumulating a stockpile of 850 kiloton and 1,300 sub-kiloton weapons over the next decade). 'We should not plan to provide enough [tactical] warheads to fight a nuclear war,' it was now argued. 'If the doctrine prevails that large numbers ought to be held available, we should have to arrange for the Americans to provide them. We should also exclude the possibility of our wanting to use large numbers of kiloton or sub-kiloton weapons in wars in which America is not involved.' Complete dependence on the Americans for this category of weapons was, nevertheless, to be avoided and so development of a small kiloton warhead (known as Tony) should continue. A further paper on the whole subject was promised.[83] A meeting at Admiralty House of a select group of senior ministers was arranged to be held on 14 March in order to discuss Watkinson's paper, but for unrecorded reasons it never seems to have been convened.[84]

Several points emerge from consideration of the MoD's plans for the nuclear programme at the start of 1961. In the realm of tactical nuclear weapons, the growing scepticism amongst ministers (not least Macmillan himself) that British forces would ever be faced with protracted periods of 'limited war' where they would fight without US support appears to have been translated into a much reduced requirement for kiloton and sub-kiloton weapons. Indeed, in 1962, when it returned to the subject, the Defence Committee would finally decide that the development and production of tactical weapons should be sharply curtailed.

In the realm of strategic nuclear forces, and the size of the UK deterrent, however, there was little evidence of any adaptation to the new guidelines that had been endorsed during ministerial consideration of the Future Policy Study in February 1960. Although there was acknowledgement of the position that Americans perceptions of the size of the deterrent should act as a yardstick there is no indication that this influenced how the capabilities of the V-force were in fact viewed. Instead, during 1961 Watkinson seems to have simply taken the anticipated strength of the Skybolt-era V-force and pronounced that 'these plans are about right.' There were of course few incentives for such a searching re-examination, certainly as far as the Air Ministry was concerned. But it should also be stressed that British officials were perennially reluctant to discuss the sensitive issue of the optimum size of the UK 'independent' deterrent force with their US counterparts – as recommended by the Future Policy study (in February 1960, for example, Playfair, Dean and Zuckerman had vetoed the proposal to raise the matter through the vehicle of the high-level informal staff talks that had recently been initiated).

Indeed, as far as ministers and officials were concerned, the Anglo-American discussions during 1960 over Skybolt, Polaris and a possible MRBM force for NATO had revealed just how opposed many Americans were becoming to the whole idea of independent, national nuclear forces held in West European hands. An approach to the Americans in order to ascertain their opinion on the ideal size of the UK deterrent might elicit the unwelcome answer that instead of planning for continuation of its national capability the Government should work toward pooling their resources in the Alliance, or even opt out of the nuclear business altogether. There was every sign, moreover, that officials in the new Kennedy administration were even more sceptical about the value of national nuclear forces, and indeed saw them as an obstacle to their aspirations to improve Alliance cohesion and curb tendencies toward nuclear proliferation.

This made the issue of a possible Skybolt cancellation all the more problematic, as a Polaris purchase on similar terms seemed more than ever unlikely. By the end of November 1960, and after the presidential election, Watkinson can be found re-iterating the point to Macmillan, advising that the Americans would not allow the UK to purchase Polaris unless it was linked to the scheme to provide SACEUR with an MRBM force, but this would 'not give us the control over the weapon system that we need. We should need to be able to purchase outright and without strings.' But if Skybolt were denied to the UK by a US decision to cancel, then the Minister of Defence was more optimistic that a subsequent American sense of obligation might make it possible to detach negotiations for a Polaris replacement from the NATO MRBM scheme.[85] Were the Americans to decide to cancel before Kennedy took office in January, Macmillan thought that the 'strongest possible representations' would have to be made to Eisenhower as the 'present Administration have a heavy moral commitment to us over this.'[86] The Prime Minister wondered in his diary 'are the Americans going to let us down and what can we do?'[87] On his way to the December North Atlantic Council meeting in Paris, Gates met Watkinson in London and told him that there were growing doubts about the cost effectiveness of Skybolt, and confirmed reports that it had been decided to slow down the rate of spend on the project.[88] In the face of such an uncertain picture, Watkinson had to inform the Prime Minister that Skybolt could not be relied on 'as a certain and necessary resource.'[89]

Nevertheless, the basic fact that Skybolt had been preserved, despite the evident desire of the Eisenhower administration to reduce the high rates of US defence spending predicted over the next few years, gave some heart to British officials. Anxieties in London were also quelled during March 1961 when the new US Defense Secretary, Robert McNamara, after a programme review, approved an appropriation for $50 million in order to continue Skybolt development during the next financial year. When Watkinson met McNamara in Washington for the first time during that same month, moreover, the latter affirmed that the Kennedy administration would adhere to the various agreements made during the previous year to supply Skybolt to the UK. After the Minister of Defence had expressed his feeling that it was important to have 'consultative machinery' in being if there were any changes envisaged by the US in the programme, one of McNamara's officials had offered an assurance 'that the last thing the US would dream of was taking unilateral action in the matter.' Watkinson came away from these meetings with the impression that

> the Americans attach great importance to the maintenance of the strategic nuclear deterrent. Whilst they accept that there may be an

approaching balance in numbers of megatons, they believe that by modernising and diversifying means of delivery, the West could maintain a satisfactory deterrent and one that could increasingly achieve a second strike capability. They accept us as junior partners in this enterprise but they are obviously not willing to share it with anyone else.

McNamara and his Pentagon advisers did not seem enthusiastic about the scheme for a SACEUR MRBM force put forward by the previous administration, and their tendency was to look to the Europeans to make their own proposals on the future nuclear arrangements of the Alliance. On nuclear assistance to France, the administration was described as 'clearly not willing, because it does not think it would serve any useful purpose,' to offer any help in de Gaulle's drive to create a *force de frappe*, but felt there was little that could be done to dissuade the French from their current policy.[90]

Macmillan, Kennedy and the 'grand design'

The prospect of a new administration in Washington had prompted the Prime Minister to form a working group of officials who could survey the whole complex of issues which were beginning to arise in Anglo-American relations, transatlantic relations more broadly, and Britain's attitude to the evident success of the EEC (when it was also becoming clear that Washington was very keen on the UK eventually acceding to the Community as a step which would enhance Western European unity and strength). Led by what he later called 'that fatal itch for composition which is the outcome of a classical education', Macmillan's own contribution to the process was a long memorandum, assembled at the very end of 1960 and in the first days of the new year, which his Private Office (mischievously) labelled a 'Grand Design' for dealing with the economic, political and defence problems of the West. Its overriding theme was the need for greater Western unity in meeting the rising Communist global challenge. But it also brought out Macmillan's anxieties over the position in which Britain now found itself, dependent on the United States in many fields, but not a part of the dynamic economic grouping that was changing the political terrain of Western Europe ('the Six' of the EEC), and instead a leader of the far weaker European Free Trade Association ('the Seven' of EFTA). In the opening section of the paper he noted 'the narrow knife-edge on which our own economy is balanced [and] the difficult task of changing the Empire into a Commonwealth ... the uncertainty about our relations [with] the new economic, and perhaps political, state which is being created by the Six countries of continental Western Europe; and the uncertainty of American policies towards us – treated now as just another country, now as an ally in a special and unique category.' 'However bold a face it may suit us to put on the situation,' Macmillan wrote, 'exclusion from the strongest economic group in the civilised world *must* injure us. It must also injure the world, because economic exclusion must in the long run force us into military isolationism and political neutralism.'

The key to moving closer to the EEC lay in French attitudes, Macmillan reasoned, and so, 'We ought therefore to make a supreme effort to reach a settlement while de Gaulle is in power in France,' not least as the French President shared with Britain a confederal conception of the Community's political evolution, rather than one based on federalist principles. Some concessions to de Gaulle's previous demands over full political consultation on a tripartite basis with Britain and the United States over matters of global strategy, and help in the nuclear field, lay at the root of the conundrum being articulated by the Prime Minister. Macmillan asked:

> Can what *we* want and what *de Gaulle* wants be brought into harmony? Is there a basis for a deal?
>
> Britain wants to join the European concern; France wants to join the Anglo-American concern. Can terms be arranged? Would de Gaulle be ready to withdraw the French veto which alone prevents a settlement of Europe's economic problem in return for politico-military arrangements which he would accept as recognition of France as a first-class world Power? What he would want is something on Tripartitism [sic] and something on the nuclear. Are there offers that we could afford to make? And could we persuade the Americans to agree?

Following various suggestions for how France could be more fully integrated into Anglo-American discussions, the Prime Minister turned to de Gaulle's 'vital' nuclear ambitions. Macmillan wondered whether de Gaulle could be given access to British technology or even weapons on terms which would be publicly defensible and acceptable to Washington: 'At first this seems hopeless. But since I think it is the one thing which will persuade de Gaulle to reach a European settlement – not merely in the economic field of Sixes and Sevens (which is vital), but in the general association of the British, with other Governments, in a Confederal system – I think it is worth serious examination.' Macmillan viewed the legal impediment of US atomic energy legislation as of limited relevance, not least as France now had a demonstrable 'nuclear capacity': 'My experience of Americans – in private as in public affairs – is this. If they *want* to do a thing, they find a way round. If they *don't*, the laws offer an insuperable obstacle.' However, would a more acceptable way to give satisfaction to the French be for Britain and France, Macmillan asked rhetorically, to 'form a nuclear force – sharing the cost, production, etc. – as European trustees for NATO? Could we devise a formula for joint political control?' If this were not possible then at least new procedures for joint consultation over nuclear use could be examined; the French force would therefore be 'nominally' independent but subject to some restraint. The first stage would be to present a workable plan to the new US administration and gauge reactions; Macmillan thought that if such a deal could secure closer

French cooperation, and the harmonisation of relations between the EEC and EFTA (and implying British entry into the former), Kennedy might be interested.[91]

While the Prime Minister's mind, encouraged by some of his Downing Street officials, was turning to some kind of grand bargain involving the sharing of nuclear responsibilities and knowledge with France, and thereby broadening, with Washington's blessing, the bilateral framework of cooperation that had been established under the MDA of 1958 into a tripartite system of collaboration that might bridge transatlantic differences, the Foreign Office position stood at some variance. The tendency here was to discount as unrealistic any chance that the new US administration could be persuaded to either extend nuclear assistance to France, or acquiesce in a British attempt to offer the French nuclear 'know-how' gained under the terms of the MDA, or long-range guided missile technology associated with the remnants of the Blue Streak programme. It was widely appreciated that Kennedy administration officials were even more sceptical about the diffusion of nuclear weapons systems to other states than their Republican predecessors. Although US officials seemed content to maintain the close nuclear relations underpinned by the MDA of 1958, there had been occasional hints from the State Department that Britain's possession of a nuclear capability was a hindrance in efforts to check the spread of nuclear weapons and technology.

Keen not to prejudice close transatlantic ties, by early 1961 Foreign Office officials were prepared to advocate cooperation with ideas to place a proportion of Britain's nuclear capability under the collective control of a NATO nuclear force; with question marks continuing to hover over Skybolt's future, there was even a disposition to consider again Polaris options where the UK nuclear deterrent 'was allocated or entrusted to NATO.'[92] The Cabinet Secretary was told by one of Home's closest Foreign Office advisers that Britain had a strong interest to prevent the further spread of national nuclear capabilities, and that in order to set the right example, 'What we have to do is to work for a NATO system into which it would be possible for us to place the whole of our nuclear force'.[93] Assignment of UK nuclear forces to NATO was seen within the Foreign Office – in an echo of the attitudes that had prevailed at the time of the Future Policy study in 1959 – as carrying an overwhelming logic as it was

> virtually inconceivable that the United Kingdom would want to use its nuclear deterrent except in circumstances where the rest of NATO were equally engaged. Provided the Americans were of the same mind as us, the attitude of the other NATO countries would anyhow be of little importance. And finally, if this country were in some way attacked directly without the other NATO powers being involved, then it would still be possible for us to use these missiles in self defence. The subsequent holocaust would be such that our Allies would hardly find time to reproach us.

The chief problem with such a scheme was increasingly seen as how it could be sold to public opinion at home, in view of the apparent loss of 'independence' involved.[94]

This position was not, however, appreciated by Downing Street which hoped to bargain Britain's nuclear capabilities for a prize more far-reaching than the dubious utility of playing a leading role in the formation of a NATO multinational MRBM force, even if this should enjoy the enthusiastic support of Washington. Whatever course was adopted, the conclusion to be drawn from much of this official thinking, as Brook noted in one minute for the Prime Minister, was that, however much the Air Ministry might not like it, 'on purely *military* grounds there is no great need for us to maintain, over the years ahead, an independent British contribution to the strategic nuclear deterrent of the West.' Even on political grounds, Brook also saw the value of an independent deterrent as diminishing over the next few years: 'Though it has paid handsome dividends up to date, it is now a wasting asset. For the moment, however, it is *still* a valuable asset.' The conclusion of the official studies commissioned by the Prime Minister was that it should be 're-invested' before its value was lost altogether. The options seemed to be:

> (i) putting our strategic nuclear force under the control of NATO and concentrating our efforts on strengthening the Alliance, or (ii) offering to place that force under some form of Anglo-French control, thus conceding some sort of special position to France ... it might be as well to recognise that, putting it crudely, the choice is between (i) stepping down to the same level as France, or (ii) trying to help France to rise up to the level of our own special position. If the alternatives are put that way, it is obvious that the second will be more palatable to France. It may also be more palatable to British public opinion. If we are seen to be stepping down to the position of a European Power – entering into political and economic association with Europe on terms of equality and, in addition, bringing our independent nuclear strength entirely under NATO control – we may seem to be surrendering too much of our 'special relationship' with the United States and our special position as leader of the Commonwealth, which are the main marks of our standing as a world Power.

The second option was clearly seen as preferable to the Cabinet Secretary but it could serve to alienate the other European members of NATO and prove unacceptable to the Americans.[95]

Macmillan met his senior ministerial colleagues at Chequers over the weekend of 21–22 January to discuss the whole complex of issues that his memorandum raised, as well as the studies carried out by the Cabinet Secretary and his officials. The Minister of Defence subsequently produced a memorandum which attempted to encapsulate what had been discussed on nuclear matters, including the principles which should inform the approaches the Government took toward such matters. These included that there should be 'no attempt to limit the ultimate power of the President of the US to initiate the use of American strategic nuclear weapons on his sole authority: this would remain the main deterrent to Communist aggression.' As the French were clearly determined to develop a national nuclear capability, to seek to prevent this would be 'fruitless'. It should be accepted that France would achieve 'equal nuclear status' with the UK, while the US, UK and (eventually) France would have to accept that 'their possession of nuclear weapons brought special responsibilities towards one another and towards other countries of the West, and that they should accept such measures of control and consultation as would, first, maintain and strengthen the deterrent to aggression; secondly, reassure the countries who might be involved in nuclear war that unnecessary risks of starting it were not taken.' Furthermore, the West, including France, should continue to press for an agreement to end all nuclear testing, while all countries with a nuclear capability should 'undertake not to give any help to any other countries to enable them to develop nuclear capacity.' In order to further the principles outlined at Chequers, it was envisaged that a public declaration could be made by the Government which subscribed to the idea of allocating all the UK's nuclear weapons 'so far as necessary for the purposes of NATO, under such system of control as may be agreed by the Alliance; and meanwhile the use of these weapons, for these purposes, will be subject to the joint agreement of the UK and French [and US] Governments.'[96] In January 1961, it is clear, there were significant voices within the government which were prepared to see a move away from the public nuclear posture that unilateral use of the deterrent should be reserved as an option.

The Prime Minister had a chance to explore some of his ideas in very tentative fashion when he met the French President for a weekend of informal talks at Rambouillet in late January. For de Gaulle, as he conveyed in typical forthright style, discussion of a NATO nuclear force, or multinational control systems, was no substitute for addressing his central political concerns over what he saw as US domination of the structures of the Western Alliance. Schemes of integration of nuclear forces would not check German ambitions: 'it was not integration which prevented the Germans from acting on their own but their political will. If they wanted to leave the alliance integration would not stop them ... the idea of a NATO nuclear force had no reality. The nuclear forces were American and the Americans would use them or not as they wished.' Macmillan raised the 'paradoxical' position that 'in England many people were frightened that the Americans would use their nuclear power rashly whereas in Europe people feared that they would not use it at all.' Perhaps, he conjectured, it would be possible to devise arrangements whereby the United States, Britain and France became 'trustees of nuclear weapons for the Free World. Possibly some part of the *force de frappe* need not be under NATO command and there could be a system of allocation together with tripartite arrangements on consultation.' There was no question of proceeding with such ideas, the Prime Minister however made clear, without the acquiescence of the new administration in Washington.[97] Macmillan came away from Rambouillet encouraged that he might have made some progress. He wrote in his diary that de Gaulle had seemed 'genuinely attracted by my themes – Europe to be united, politically and economically; but France and Great Britain to be something more than European Powers, and to be so recognised by the United States. I think everything now depends on (a) whether we really can put forward a formula for Sixes and Sevens which both the Commonwealth and British Agriculture will wear, (b) whether the Americans can be got to accept France's nuclear achievements and ambitions.'[98]

Opinion in the Foreign Office remained more sceptical. Having digested the Prime Minister's 'Grand Design' memorandum, a cautious Home wrote to Macmillan to offer advice on how Kennedy should be approached when they held their first meetings. The Foreign Secretary offered the view that 'on such questions as the emergence of further nuclear powers, de Gaulle's tripartite aspirations and NATO strategy, I do not think it would be wise to urge that the French should be given satisfaction or that some tripartite nuclear trusteeship should be established unless, at the same time, you are prepared to say that Britain is ready to contribute what she can towards solving these problems. This means, in effect, saying that we would be willing to consider putting at least some of our own nuclear capacity into some common NATO arrangement (the nature of which would of course have to be carefully worked out) as a means of bringing French and any other national nuclear forces under similar discipline.'[99]

The Foreign Office's readings of the deep reservations harboured in Washington over any promotion of France's nuclear ambitions were entirely warranted. There were, in addition, signs that US officials were increasingly concerned with the incipient tensions brought to the North Atlantic Alliance by the special nuclear relations that obtained between the United States and Britain. In early February 1961, Kennedy had asked the former US Secretary of State, Dean Acheson, to lead a working group which would examine the problems faced by NATO and make recommendations for the new administration to consider. The document that was subsequently produced was discussed by the NSC at the end of March and issued by the President as an approved statement of administration policy on 21 April. Its principal stress was on bolstering the conventional forces deployed by the Alliance, but also among the many measures suggested were the commitment of five Polaris submarines specifically to NATO as a demonstration of the US nuclear guarantee to the Alliance. Deployment and targeting of the missiles was to be worked out jointly by NATO staffs led by SACEUR and the US military authorities (this, it will be recalled, had formed one of the initial recommendations made by Herter, the outgoing Secretary of State, to the North Atlantic Council in December 1960). The British, it was suggested, should also be urged to make a similar commitment of its strategic nuclear forces to NATO.

The most arresting part of the NSC paper's 'nuclear' aspects read: 'Over the long run, it would be desirable if the British decided to phase out of the nuclear deterrent business. If the development of Skybolt is not warranted for US purposes alone, the US should not prolong the life of the V-bomber force by this or other means.'[100] In October 1961, having been informed by Glenn T. Seaborg, the head of the Atomic Energy Commission, that the British had made a request to include a device in an upcoming US series of underground nuclear tests, Dean Rusk, the US Secretary of State, replied that although there were no technical objections to the proposal he should remind Seaborg about the policy approved by the NSC in April. The administration, Rusk thought, should do nothing to perpetuate the UK nuclear programme, 'since their activity in this field is a standing goad to the French. I believe that we should move to fulfil this policy. I doubt, however, that the present British request is the occasion for this.'[101] The basic conviction of many members of the State Department was that the existence of an independent UK strategic nuclear force acted as encouragement for the French and Germans to aspire to the same type of capability and status, and impeded Washington's attempts to find multilateral solutions to NATO's nuclear dilemmas. How far the White House was prepared to act on this belief had yet to be seen.

In early April 1961 Macmillan, accompanied by the Foreign Secretary, arrived in the US capital for his first extensive round of talks with the new US President. The two men had already held a short meeting at Key West in Florida, at the end of March, to discuss the crisis in Laos, where Western intervention was being considered to avert further Communist gains in the civil war that had erupted at the end of the previous year. They had immediately established a good rapport, sharing conservative and cautious instincts regarding the dangers of escalation in a setting where the stakes did not seem vital. During their Washington discussions they were to focus, among other things, on the problems faced by the North Atlantic Alliance, not least how to accommodate de Gaulle's demands for equality of treatment. It was reported that the future of Britain's nuclear deterrent would also be discussed, and that although the US administration had no plans to press the British to scrap their V-bomber force, there was hope that conventional defence efforts would be prioritised over any attempt to maintain an independent nuclear deterrent beyond Britain's existing capability.[102]

The question of attitudes to the French nuclear programme was in fact first broached during a preliminary round of talks between Rusk and Home, where the former offered the view that the US Government was 'very reluctant to encourage France to develop a national nuclear capability.' Rusk

> hoped that France and the other European countries in NATO would, in concert, discuss how a joint European nuclear capacity could be developed within the NATO context, in a way that would meet their national requirements. The United States would not be willing to give help to France alone and not to other NATO countries. They would

wish therefore to discourage the French from pursuing their *force de frappe*; they would hope to rely on the increasing economic burdens involved in such an enterprise, and, if possible, some form of nuclear combination in NATO which would also take care of the German problem. If the United Kingdom could place its nuclear capacity within NATO, this might contribute significantly to the objective.

Home thought the idea could be considered, but doubted it would work in dissuading de Gaulle from his chosen path as long as technical assistance was denied to France. Again, however, Rusk affirmed that the US could not discriminate in favour of France when it came to nuclear help, and asked the question: 'Would not a collective nuclear arrangement in NATO be a better answer to the German problem than merely assisting France in securing a special position for herself?'[103]

During the subsequent encounter between Macmillan and Kennedy on the morning of 5 April, both leaders were treated to a presentation by Acheson on NATO military policy, based on the comprehensive report he was compiling on the future of Alliance. A first priority had to be put on the build-up of conventional forces, Acheson had stressed, and the desire to give SACEUR the means to hold-up a Soviet attack without immediately having to resort to nuclear use. Regarding nuclear weapons, Acheson wanted to see clearer reassurances that the President would, in fact, order a release of nuclear weapons if NATO were attacked by Soviet nuclear forces, or if SACEUR faced a conventional attack which could not be held. But the circumstances which should dictate nuclear use should be drawn up by the allies with US involvement, and tight control would be retained over US nuclear forces. The Prime Minister sought to turn the discussion to his preferred subject, saying the 'present *malaise* resulted from the feelings of the French and others that their position was in some way inferior to the Anglo-Saxons. One possibility might be that the United Kingdom should offer to share its national nuclear capability with its Allies. Another might be to let the French develop theirs. ... The pride of General de Gaulle and other determined men in Europe demanded that they should have some fuller control over the nuclear strength of the West. They could not tolerate a position in which their future was decided by others. They were determined to put Europe back on the map.' The Prime Minister thought that 'tinkering' with the nuclear forces available to SACEUR was not nearly enough. When Kennedy asked if the French would only be satisfied if they had a national nuclear capability, Macmillan sidestepped the question by replying that once they had that capacity they then might be prepared to look at 'pooling' arrangements.[104]

Reconvening after lunch, Macmillan and Kennedy again heard from Acheson. The former Secretary of State showed no reticence in recommending against giving any nuclear help to France, which would soon begin to appreciate the high costs of an indigenous programme. Developing the means of delivery of nuclear weapons, in particular, was very expensive, and the French might eventually be driven to seek assistance from the Germans. But, as Acheson warned, the 'dilemma was that, if we helped the French, the Germans would insist on equal treatment. If we did not and the French persisted, they could only succeed by calling in the Germans. In either event the Germans would acquire nuclear power. Such a development would be very dangerous. It was not desired by Dr Adenauer.' Having spelt out his alarming prognosis, Acheson's recommendation was formation of a NATO nuclear force from the existing US and UK nuclear capability based in Europe, perhaps with the addition of some ICBMs, and in which France might have a share of the control arrangements. Although he greeted them politely, Macmillan was evidently sceptical of Acheson's opinions.[105]

During a private, informal discussion with the President the following afternoon, Macmillan (disregarding the more hesitant line contained in his Foreign Office brief) had a chance once more to lay out his ideas for the 'Grand Design' and that he wanted 'to treat the whole problem as a single exercise and get French agreement to all the points in my programme ... it was most important not to give the French anything unless they took the whole; for they would pocket any advantage and say no more about it.' Kennedy could see few problems in satisfying de Gaulle over his calls for tripartism, and envisaged an offer of regular six monthly meetings. When discussion turned to Acheson's proposals, Macmillan ventured that they would not 'go far enough to satisfy de Gaulle. If we could somehow or other get him an independent nuclear force, however small, we should be able to persuade him to put it back into "trusteeship", as we could probably do with the British, and as perhaps the Americans might also do for some part of their forces. ... I said perhaps we could study whether he had the power, as President, to allow the British to give either warheads or nuclear information to the French.' The President, Macmillan recorded, thought that this should certainly be studied.[106]

Before he left the United States, Macmillan delivered a speech at the Massachusetts Institute of Technology in Boston where he made a strong call for Western unity but also defended the existence of an independent nuclear deterrent. While Britain had often fought as part of an alliance in its past history, he asserted, 'we have always been ready in the last resort to fight alone ... Our determination to make our own contribution was in a sense instinctive. And perhaps with the Atlantic Ocean between us it has been no bad thing for the people of Europe to see that at least one nuclear member of NATO shares the nuclear power with you.' With an eye on the French programme, the Prime Minister also saw it is as important that there should not be 'wasteful duplication' of efforts in the Alliance, and that a proper nuclear partnership had to be found which could prevent the 'uncontrolled extension of nuclear manufacture' and create a 'sense of real unity which would follow a new agreement with our allies.'[107] Three weeks later, towards the end of April 1961, Macmillan developed this theme in another speech to the Scottish

Conservatives in Ayr where he talked of the US and British deterrents being 'held in trust' for the 'free world':

> We have now seriously to consider how to exercise this trust with due regard to the feelings of our allies. It may be ... that the road lies along the concept of transforming the trusteeship into a partnership. But not yet. Nothing could be more foolish for Britain at this critical moment than unilaterally and gratuitously to throw away the weapon which gives us a voice and an authority in determining these great issues.[108]

Meanwhile, as if to confound the Prime Minister's public hopes, the French Defence Minister was telling Watkinson in private that, while not ruling out tripartite collaboration in the nuclear field, 'French plans for an independent nuclear striking force were in no sense negotiable. Those who imagined that they were a sort of blackmail and would be abandoned in return for concessions by France's allies were completely mistaken.'[109]

Kennedy was due to see de Gaulle for their first substantive meetings in early June and had been keen to solicit Macmillan's advice before his trip to Paris. This provided the Prime Minister with a further opportunity to present some of the central ideas of his 'Grand Design'. At the end of April, shortly after the Cabinet had heard the case for a formal (but conditional) approach to join the EEC, Macmillan wrote to the President enclosing a document he called the 'Memorandum' where he laid out the arguments he would take if he found himself in Kennedy's place. Referring to his Boston speech, Macmillan stressed the need to 'rally the forces of the West and make ourselves more effective in all fields ... To this end I believe that we should be ready to go a long way to meet de Gaulle in certain fields of interest to him.' The 'Memorandum' itself again spoke of encouraging France, as it developed a nuclear programme, to conceive of it 'not so much to create an *independent* nuclear capacity, but rather to make a contribution as a Great Power to the Western deterrent as a whole. This is increasingly the British view of their nuclear capacity.' Macmillan suggested that the three Western nuclear powers could enter into an agreement to consult before nuclear weapons were used, and to make joint arrangements for selection and allocation of targets. If these arrangements were concluded, then the United States (with possible British involvement) might give France several different types of nuclear assistance, whether in the form of technical knowhow or even the provision of warheads.[110]

In this particular area of advice, however, Macmillan was to find the US administration profoundly unreceptive. McGeorge Bundy, Kennedy's Special Assistant for National Security Affairs, let the British Ambassador in Washington know that although the importance of the issue was appreciated it was likely that the President would have the 'greatest difficulty' over any such proposal. The 'limiting factors' mentioned by Bundy included Congressional opposition to sharing nuclear information with the French, scepticism that ultimately the French would prove willing to go through with the high costs of translating their first step of a test explosion into a fully-fledged independent delivery capability, and doubts that nuclear knowledge could be given to the French but denied to other NATO allies (particularly the Germans). There was also the point that if ever de Gaulle were to be persuaded to make a 'commitment' of nuclear forces to NATO, there would be questions about how reliable he would prove in seeing it through.[111]

Indeed, whatever his personal views, the President was subject to strong advice from both his Secretary of State, Dean Rusk, and Rusk's Under Secretary (and one of the leading 'Europeanists' in the State Department), George Ball, that nuclear assistance should not be granted to France, and that any proposals relating to French nuclear capability had to be handled within a NATO framework. On 8 May Kennedy delivered a formal and considered reply to Macmillan's ideas which explained that after careful review he had come to the 'conclusion that it would be undesirable to assist France's efforts to create a nuclear weapons capability. I am most anxious that no erroneous impressions get abroad regarding future US policy in this respect, lest they create unwarranted French expectations and serious divisions in NATO. If we were to help France acquire a nuclear weapons capability, this could not fail to have a major effect on German attitudes. The fact that the Germans are not now tempted to join or imitate the French program is due, in small part, to US opposition to Nth country programs [i.e. those aimed at expanding the number of existing nuclear powers] and to the uncertain prospects of the French (or any other) program in the absence of US aid.' The approach of the US administration would be to try to respond to French concerns over the nuclear arrangements of the Alliance, rather than to assist their national programme. Measures which might be adopted included more intimate political consultation with France, sharing knowledge of, and even control, over the US nuclear capability deployed in Europe, and committing more US and UK nuclear forces to NATO command. 'We have in mind committing a number of US Polaris submarines to NATO,' the President continued. 'I hope that, as we do, you will be able to give serious consideration to committing UK strategic nuclear forces in the UK to NATO. I welcome the indication in your memorandum that you increasingly view the British nuclear capability as being designed to make a contribution to the Western deterrent as a whole.'[112]

The direction of US policy became somewhat clearer nine days later when Kennedy delivered a speech to the Canadian Parliament in Ottawa on policy toward NATO where he mirrored some of the ideas contained in the Herter proposals in December 1960. Noting that US nuclear weapons would continue to be available for the defence of the North Atlantic Treaty area, and that they should be kept 'under close and flexible political control that meets the needs of all NATO countries', the President reinforced this message by pledging to commit to the NATO command five – and subsequently still more – Polaris atomic-missile submarines, which are defensive weapons, subject to any agreed NATO guidelines on their control and use, and response to the needs of all members but still credible in an emergency. Beyond this, we look to the possibility of establishing a NATO sea-borne force, which would be truly multi-lateral in ownership and control, if this should be desired and found feasible by our Allies, once NATO's non-nuclear goals have been achieved.[113]

This apparent commitment to the MLF concept so favoured by the Eisenhower administration in its closing months, and as first proposed in the previous summer's Bowie report, was always more tenuous that it seemed. For one, there were many inter-departmental doubts (not least within the Department of Defense) about the viability of any such multilateral scheme. The only European member of NATO to give a positive welcome to the revival of the MLF proposal in May 1961 was the Federal Republic of Germany. This was a double-edged sword as it provided extra arguments to those members of the State Department who saw the MLF as a way to contain Germany's nuclear ambitions, but was an indicator to others that such proposals only encouraged Bonn to press for more concessions at the potential cost of disruption to Alliance unity. It also added to anxieties over the control arrangements that were introduced for any eventual NATO MLF.[114]

The strong conditions that were attached to the MLF proposals that Kennedy had outlined in Ottawa also demonstrated that the White House's priorities, at least for the moment, lay elsewhere. The President himself, along with McNamara, was most concerned that the Europeans do more in the area of building up their conventional military forces, and there was a great deal of scepticism over the military utility of such unwieldy nuclear arrangements. Indeed, the whole thrust of McNamara and his new team of advisers was to emphasise the importance of the central direction of nuclear forces by the United States, ensuring that effective command and control was maintained if they ever had to be used. That such an awful eventuality might be moving nearer was, moreover, underlined in June 1961 by the crisis atmosphere in US-Soviet relations brought about by the fractious summit meeting held between Kennedy and Khrushchev in Vienna, and the Soviet leader's decision to renew his demands (and ultimatum) over the status of Berlin. All attentions were now focused on how the new administration in Washington would respond to such fresh Soviet pressures, and what degree of solidarity could be maintained within the North Atlantic Alliance. Interest in pursuing the complicated inter-Alliance negotiations required to move Kennedy's Ottawa proposals forward quickly fell away during the remainder of a tense year.

The rebuff represented by Kennedy's letter of 8 May also put a stop, at least temporarily, to the Prime Minister's hopes to forge a nuclear understanding with de Gaulle which could be reconciled with the requirements of the Anglo-American relationship. The President's message nevertheless elicited a reply from Macmillan which stressed his scepticism that Washington's own overtures to de Gaulle, based as they were on working to reform the existing structures of NATO, were likely to succeed. As Macmillan put it, '… I rather fear that he may withhold his full cooperation until he gets some satisfaction for his nuclear ambitions. In any case, even if de Gaulle were to prove more cooperative, there would still be the problem of the nth country [i.e. Germany] to deal with, because I do not suppose that he would go so far as to abandon his own nuclear programme.' The Prime Minister acknowledged the danger that nuclear assistance to France could encourage others to ask for similar help, but the 'only alternative' was to 'find some means of persuading de Gaulle to forgo his ambitions for complete independence in this field – and thus discourage other countries from pressing for this. In my judgment this might be done by giving him a formula about consultation and control which would satisfy his honour and in which he could join.' Having restated his basic convictions on nuclear relations with France, Macmillan picked up on the reference to Britain's own strategic nuclear capability in Kennedy's letter, and made the point, 'so that there will be no misunderstanding', that he was 'very doubtful about "committing" strategic nuclear forces "to NATO command" or giving SACEUR a strategic nuclear force of his own.' This was 'a very big question' which Macmillan hoped that Kennedy would not choose to pursue when he next met de Gaulle.[115]

Clearly feeling that the Prime Minister would get nowhere with Kennedy if he persevered with his present lines of argument, the Foreign Secretary was anxious to put forward his own alternative scheme (primarily of interest here because it prefigured some of the arrangements later adopted for the control of Alliance nuclear forces). Home argued, in an echo of the proposition he had floated in November 1960, that there had to be at least some degree of commitment or pooling of UK nuclear forces in a NATO arrangement, but this could be of a looser kind than some schemes which had been mooted. Forces could be earmarked for 'assignment' to NATO command only in time of war, and there would not necessarily have to be a joint command structure for them. A commitment of forces could also be 'conditional – e.g. subject to national emergency or requirement elsewhere.' There could also be a '"nuclear trusteeship group" consisting of NATO powers which either possess nuclear weapons or allow them on their territory (i.e. United States, United Kingdom, France, Canada, Germany, Italy, Turkey). This group could be responsible, in the name of the Alliance as a whole, for supervising the arrangement.' The UK, Home suggested, could declare that it was willing to consider 'the whole of its nuclear forces as held "in trust" for the free world', and that Britain should be ready to take part in a nuclear trusteeship group as he had outlined.[116]

Watkinson was less convinced by now that such a concrete proposal was warranted. His own conviction was that de Gaulle desired 'equality as a nuclear power.' This did not mean that he advocated the provision of nuclear information to France, but that the 'status symbol' of holding a nuclear capacity should be granted the French President. If this were forthcoming 'we might get him to do what we want with regard to the Sixes and Sevens and the revitalising of NATO. The Minister of Defence feared that turning the UK's strategic capability over to some NATO body was 'not a solution' and would not influence de Gaulle; Watkinson added, in pointed fashion, 'nor do I believe at home we could stand such an abrupt reversal of long declared policy without encouraging the Left Wing of the Opposition and the Campaign for Nuclear Disarmament to a point where it would become a real factor on the political scene.'[117] Macmillan responded with a minute which expressed his agreement with Watkinson's analysis, finding that 'a formula which gave our strategic nuclear capacity to NATO would not influence President de Gaulle, and would therefore not succeed in solving the problem of the emergence of further independent nuclear powers.'[118]

Shortly after these ministerial exchanges, Kennedy had his summit meeting with Khrushchev in Vienna, where the Soviet leader had renewed his threat to turn over control of the access routes to West Berlin to the East German authorities if a negotiated solution to the status of the city was not found. The revival of the Berlin crisis shifted collective Western attentions to the problem of how to meet the latest Soviet challenge without either making damaging concessions (which might unravel the NATO Alliance, and give further encouragement to Khrushchev) or by insisting on access rights through the use of force if necessary, thereby sparking a military clash which could quickly escalate into a wider and disastrous conflagration in central Europe. For ministers in the Macmillan Government another major preoccupation during the summer was the launching of a bid not to merely achieve some kind of closer association between EFTA and the EEC, but to join the Community as full members. To that end, on 21 July 1961 the Cabinet endorsed Britain's first application, with the Prime Minister announcing the decision to the House of Commons at the end of the same month. A combination of events meant that the 'Grand Design' that Macmillan had drawn up at the start of the year could not be pushed forward in the simultaneous fashion he had first hoped. It remained to be seen whether the interplay between its different components, of which revisions to nuclear policy formed a part, would prove crucial to the success of the whole scheme.

Notes

1. Admiral Sir Walter T. Couchman letter to Admiral Arleigh Burke, No 383, 26 April 1960, ADM 1/27389.
2. See Confidential Annex to COS(60)15th Meeting, item 7, 1 March 1960, DEFE 4/125; Mountbatten minute for Watkinson, 'The British Nuclear Deterrent,' 3 March 1960; Watkinson minute for Playfair, 7 March 1960, DEFE 13/617.
3. MM/COS(60)2nd Meeting, 'Meeting of the Minister of Defence with the Chiefs of Staff on Thursday, 24th March, 1960,' DEFE 32/13.
4. See 'Britain Well Equipped with Nuclear Arms,' *The Times*, 1 March 1960.

5 See *Hansard*, HC, vol 621, cols 1265–75, 13 April 1960.
6 MM/COS(60)4th Meeting, 'Meeting of the Minister of Defence with the Chiefs of Staff on Tuesday, 12th April, 1960,' DEFE 32/13.
7 *Hansard*, HC, vol 622, col 244, 27 April 1960.
8 Couchman letter to Vice-Admiral Sir Geoffrey Thistleton-Smith, No 384, 26 April 1960, ADM 205/202.
9 BND(SG)(60)3, 'Programme of Work,' Note by the Chairman, 12 April 1960; BND(SG)(60) 1st Meeting, 13 April 1960, DEFE 10/665.
10 E. W. Playfair letter to Dean, EWP/560/60, 10 June 1960; P.E. Ramsbotham minute, 7 September 1960, PUSD records, FCO.
11 See Moore, *Nuclear Illusion, Nuclear Reality*, 76.
12 Heathcoat Amory minute for Watkinson, 22 April 1960, DEFE 13/195.
13 See 'Interest mounts over Blue Streak debate,' *The Times*, 25 April 1960.
14 See *Hansard*, HC, vol 622, cols 221–3, 27 April 1960.
15 Ibid, cols 327–30.
16 For nuclear issues in the Labour movement at this time see Richard Taylor, *Against the Bomb: The British Peace Movement, 1958–1965* (Oxford, 1988), 291–8; Pierre, *Nuclear Politics*, 201–6; Ben Pimlott, *Harold Wilson* (London, 1992), 234–5; Philip Ziegler, *Wilson: The Authorized Life of Lord Wilson of Rievaulx* (London, 1993), 123–5; Len Scott, 'Labour and the Bomb: The First 80 Years,' *International Affairs*, 82, 4, 2006, 685–700.
17 See Pimlott, *Wilson*, 238–9; Austen Morgan, *Harold Wilson* (London, 1992), 224–8.
18 Taylor, *Against the Bomb*, 299–305.
19 See 'House of Commons,' *The Times*, 27 April 1960.
20 See 'Deterrent After Blue Streak,' *The Times*, 25 April 1960.
21 Macmillan minute for Watkinson, 'Skybolt', M.150/60, 10 May 1960, DEFE 13/195.
22 Watkinson minute for Macmillan, 12 May 1960.
23 See Moore, *Nuclear Illusion, Nuclear Reality*, 66.
24 Watkinson minute for Macmillan, 12 May 1960, DEFE 13/195.
25 Bishop minute for Macmillan, 'Mid-Range Ballistic Missiles,' 24 May 1960, PREM 11/3713.
26 MM.20/60, Record of a meeting between the Minister of Defence and Departmental Officials on 23 May 1960, DEFE 11/155.
27 D(60)5th Meeting, item 1, 25 May 1960, CAB 131/23.
28 MM.23/60, Record of a Meeting between Gates and Watkinson, 1 June 1960, PREM 11/2940.
29 See MM.24/60, Record of a Meeting between Gates and Watkinson, 6 June 1960, PREM 11/2940; and 'Skybolt: Memorandum of Understanding,' 6 June 1960, and attached Ministry of Defence record of conversation, 'Medium Range Ballistic Missiles for NATO,' 9 June 1960, PREM 11/3261; see also Watkinson's report to the Cabinet, C(60)97, 'Skybolt,' note by the Minister of Defence, 20 June 1960, CAB 129/101. For the American version of the talks see Watson, *Into the Missile Age*, 565–6.
30 Watkinson minute for Macmillan, 7 June 1960, PREM 11/3261.
31 See C(60)98, 'Polaris,' memorandum by the Minister of Defence, 20 June 1960, CAB 129/101.
32 Bishop minute for Macmillan, 22 June 1960, PREM 11/2940.
33 See de Zulueta minute for Macmillan, 10 June 1960; 'Minutes of a Meeting at Birch Grove House at 2 pm on Monday, June 13, 1960,' PREM 11/3261; on the express link between the two issues, see Washington telegram No 1639 to FO, 17 August 1960, CAB 21/4073/1.
34 See Macmillan, *Pointing the Way*, 254–5.

35 See Macmillan message to Eisenhower, contained in Foreign Office telegram No 2682 to Washington, 15 June 1960; Eisenhower message to Macmillan, 20 June 1960; de Zulueta letter to Ian Samuel, 21 June 1960, PREM 11/2940.
36 Macmillan message to Eisenhower, T/373/60, contained in Foreign Office telegram No 2827 to Washington, 24 June 1960, PREM 11/2940.
37 For a summary of the American side to the exchanges see Watson, *Into the Missile Age*, 566–7.
38 Eisenhower letter to Macmillan, 15 July 1960, PREM 11/2940.
39 De Zulueta minute for Macmillan, 1 July 1960, PREM 11/2940.
40 See CC(60)48th Conclusions, 28 July 1960, CAB 128/34.
41 Macmillan message to Eisenhower, T.436/60, 30 July 1960, PREM 11/2940.
42 Bishop minute for Macmillan, 'Polaris,' 22 July 1960, and attached draft message for Eisenhower, CAB 21/4073/1.
43 See, for example, Confidential Annex to COS(60)68th Meeting, item 5, 1 November 1960, DEFE 32/6.
44 Bishop note for Macmillan, 'NATO MRBM,' 7 July 1960, PREM 11/3713.
45 De Zulueta minute for Macmillan, 4 July 1960, with Macmillan annotation 'this puts the points admirably', 4 July 1960, PREM 11/3713.
46 D(60)31, 'Medium Range Ballistic Missiles,' note by the Deputy Secretary of the Cabinet, 8 July 1960, Minutes of a Meeting held on 7 July 1960, CAB 131/24.
47 See, for example, Trachtenberg, *Constructed Peace*, 194–6; Eric Schlosser, *Command and Control* (New York, 2013), 255–62.
48 There are numerous sources on the background and origins of the MLF scheme. See, for example, David N. Schwartz, *NATO's Nuclear Dilemmas* (Washington, 1983), 82–5; Trachtenberg, *Constructed Peace*, 212–5; Watson, *Into the Missile Age*, 553–6, 580–2.
49 See memorandum of conference with President Eisenhower, 16 August 1960, *Foreign Relations of the United States, 1958–1960, Volume VII, Part 1: Western European Integration and Security; Canada* (Washington, 1993), 611–4.
50 Air Chief Marshal Sir George Mills letter to Playfair, 26 August 1960, CAB 21/4073/1.
51 Chilver minute for Watkinson, 'Defence Policy,' 29 August 1960, DEFE 13/113.
52 Inter-service discussions in late July 1960 had led to agreement that Holy Loch would be a better location for the US base, see Watson, *Into the Missile Age*, 567.
53 Washington telegram No 1720 to Foreign Office, 1 September 1960, PREM 11/2941.
54 See J. S. Orme minute for Brook, 2 September 1960, CAB 21/4073/1; Bishop minute for Macmillan, 'Facilities for United States Submarines in Scotland,' 14 September 1960, PREM 11/2941.
55 C(60)123, 'Facilities for United States Submarines in Scotland,' memorandum by the Secretary of State for Foreign Affairs and the Minister of Defence, 13 September 1960, CAB 129/102.
56 Zuckerman minute for Watkinson, SZ/653/60, 22 September 1960, DEFE 13/195.
57 Watkinson minute, 27 September 1960, DEFE 13/195.
58 Watkinson minute for Macmillan, 23 September 1960, PREM 11/3261.
59 See material in DEFE 7/2302.
60 See Watkinson minute for Macmillan, 21 October 1960, and attached MM: 46/60 record of a meeting between Watkinson and James Douglas, 21 October 1960, PREM 11/3261.
61 See Zuckerman, *Monkeys, Men and Missiles*, 240–1.
62 See Watson, *Into the Missile Age*, 569–70.

63 See 'Scottish Base for Polaris Submarines: Agreement with US Likely,' *The Times*, 17 October 1960.
64 See Foreign Office telegram No 5250 to Washington, 26 October 1960, containing Macmillan message for Eisenhower, T.660/60, 26 October 1960; Watkinson minute for Macmillan, 27 October 1960; Eisenhower letter to Macmillan, T.663/60, 27 October 1960, PREM 11/2941. See also Watson, *Into the Missile Age*, 569.
65 Watkinson minute for Macmillan, 4 November 1960, PREM 11/3261.
66 UK Delegation NATO, Paris telegram No 252 to FO, 7 October 1960, CAB 21/4073/1; Hood letter to Shuckburgh, 17 October 1960; Bishop minute for Bligh, 'NATO MRBMs,' 24 October 1960, CAB 21/4540.
67 P.E. Ramsbotham minute, 7 September 1960, PUSD records, FCO.
68 Bishop minute for Macmillan, 'NATO MRBM,' 27 October 1960, PREM 11/3714.
69 GEN 724/1st Meeting, 28 October 1960, CAB 130/175.
70 Foreign Office telegram No 5372 to Washington, 2 November 1960, CAB 21/4073/2.
71 See GEN 724/2nd Meeting, 30 November 1960, CAB 130/175.
72 MM: 54/60, Record of a Meeting between Watkinson and Gates, 12 December 1960; FO telegram No 442 Guidance, 17 December 1960, PREM 11/3714. A full text of Herter's statement is contained in 'Long-Range Planning: Statement by Secretary of State Herter to the Council in Ministerial Session on 16th December 1960,' C-M(60)141, 16 December 1960, in CAB 21/4540.
73 Watkinson minute for Macmillan, 'NATO Policy,' 8 December 1960, PREM 11/3714.
74 See D(60)10th Meeting, item 5, 16 and 17 October 1960, CAB 131/23.
75 Thorneycroft minute for Macmillan, 3 November 1960, and attached paper, 'The Nuclear Weapons Programme,' AB/303/01, PREM 11/3724.
76 Watkinson minute for Macmillan, 7 November 1960, PREM 11/3724.
77 See W. Geraghty minute for Bishop, 'Nuclear weapons production programme,' 8 November 1960, Cabinet Office file 59 Part 4.
78 Brook minute for Macmillan, 10 November 1960, Cabinet Office file 59 Part 4.
79 Macmillan minute for Thorneycroft, 11 November 1960; Watkinson minute for Macmillan, 1 December 1960, PREM 11/3724.
80 See Watkinson minute for Macmillan, 7 December 1960; Macmillan minute for Watkinson, M/426/60, 7 December 1960, PREM 11/3724.
81 Brook minute for Bishop, 12 December 1960, Cabinet Office file 59 Part 4.
82 See Watkinson minute for Macmillan, 20 February 1961; Geraghty minute for Robertson, 'Nuclear Weapons Programme,' 21 February 1961, Cabinet Office file 59 Part 4.
83 'The Nuclear Warhead Programme,' MO 18/3, memorandum by the Minister of Defence, 20 February 1961, file 59 Part 4, Cabinet Office; Geraghty minute for Macmillan, 'Nuclear Warhead Programme (MO 18/3),' 13 March 1961, PREM 11/3724. See also Moore, *Nuclear Illusion, Nuclear Reality*, 121.
84 'The Nuclear Warhead Programme,' meeting to be held at Admiralty House on 14 March 1961 at 12 noon: Agendum, note by Bishop and Geraghty, 10 March 1961, file 59 Part 4, Cabinet Office.
85 Watkinson minute for Macmillan, 23 November 1960, and attached paper 'Skybolt,' note by the Minister of Defence, PREM 11/3261.
86 Macmillan minute for Watkinson, 'Skybolt,' 1 December 1960, PREM 11/3261.
87 Macmillan diary entry, 1 December 1960, dep. c. 21/1, Macmillan papers, Bodleian Library.
88 See Watson, *Into the Missile Age*, 570.

89 Watkinson minute for Macmillan, 12 December 1960, PUSD records, FCO.
90 See Washington telegram No 727 to FO, 21 March 1961, PREM 11/3261; MM:20/61, Note by Watkinson of discussions with McNamara and DoD officials, 21 March 1961; MM:21/61, Note of a Discussion in Office of the Director, Defense Research and Engineering, DoD, 21 March 1961, DEFE 11/155.
91 Macmillan memorandum, '29 December 1960 to 3 January 1961', PREM 11/3325; for the background see Macmillan, *Pointing the Way*, 312–3, 323–6.
92 Hoyer Millar minute, 23 January 1961, PUSD records, FCO.
93 Shuckburgh letter to Brook, 26 December 1960, PREM 11/3325, and as quoted in Clark, *Nuclear Diplomacy*, 308.
94 Foreign Office memorandum (drafted by Ramsbotham) for Home, 'Skybolt and the Independent Deterrent,' 20 January 1961, PUSD records, FCO.
95 Brook minute for Macmillan, 'Chequers – 21st-22nd January,' PREM 11/3325.
96 MoD memorandum, 'Political Control of the Nuclear Power of the West,' 23 January 1961, DEFE 7/2127 and in CAB 21/4536.
97 Record of a conversation between President de Gaulle and the Prime Minister in the Marble Room at Rambouillet at 2.30pm, 28 January 1961, PREM 11/3322. See also Pagedas, *Anglo-American Strategic Relations*, 122–3.
98 Macmillan diary entry, 29 January 1961, quoted in *Pointing the Way*, 327.
99 Home minute for Macmillan, 'The Prime Minister's Meeting with Mr Kennedy,' PM/61/29, 23 February 1961, PREM 11/3326.
100 Policy Directive: NATO and the Atlantic Nations, 20 April 1961, *Foreign Relations of the United States, 1961–1963, volume XIII: West Europe and Canada* (Washington, 1994), 289. For further background, see Douglas Brinkley, *Dean Acheson: The Cold War Years, 1953–71* (New Haven, 1992), 117–24.
101 See Glenn T. Seaborg, *Kennedy, Khrushchev, and the Test Ban* (Berkeley, 1981), 109.
102 See 'White House Talks on Finance and NATO,' *The Times*, 6 April 1961.
103 'Talks between Lord Home and Mr Rusk at Lunch on 4th April 1961,' CAB 133/297.
104 'Record of a Meeting held at the White House on Wednesday, 5th April 1961, at 11am,' CAB 133/297.
105 'Record of a Meeting held at the White House on Wednesday, 5th April 1961, at 3.15pm,' CAB 133/297.
106 'Continuation of the Prime Minister's Note on his Conversation with President Kennedy on Thursday 6th April at 2.45pm, 1961,' PREM 11/3780; this note is also reproduced in almost identical terms in Macmillan, *Pointing the Way*, 351. See also Pagedas, *Anglo-American Strategic Relations*, 144–9.
107 'Mr Macmillan Calls for Wider Unity: Nuclear Partnership as Basis of Alliance,' *The Times*, 7 April 1961.
108 See 'Prime Minister Suggests A Nuclear Partnership: Deterrent Held in Trust by Britain and US for the Free World,' *The Times*, 24 April 1961.
109 Record of a meeting, 13 April 1961, FO 371/161231, as quoted in Pagedas, *Anglo-American Strategic Relations*, 151.
110 Macmillan letter to Kennedy, T.247/61, 28 April 1961, and attached 'Memorandum' with 'Annex III: Nuclear,' PREM 11/3319. See Macmillan's own account of the episode in *Pointing the Way*, 354–5.
111 Washington telegram No 1159 to Foreign Office, T.259/61, 4 May 1961, PREM 11/3319.
112 Kennedy letter to Macmillan, T.261A/61, 8 May 1961, PREM 11/3319.
113 Address before the Canadian Parliament in Ottawa, 17 May 1961, *Public Papers of the Presidents: John F. Kennedy, 1961* (Washington, 1962), 385.
114 See Lawrence S. Kaplan, Ronald D. Landa, and Edward J. Drea, *History of the*

Office of the Secretary of Defense, Volume V: The McNamara Ascendancy, 1961–1965 (Washington, 2006), 389–90.
115 Foreign Office telegram No 3383 to Washington, 15 May 1961, containing Macmillan letter to Kennedy, T.272/61, 15 May 1961, PREM 11/3311.
116 Home memorandum for Macmillan, FS/61/64, 24 May 1961, PREM 11/3311.
117 Watkinson minute for Macmillan, 25 May 1961, PREM 11/3311.
118 Macmillan minute for Watkinson, 'Europe and the Nuclear Problem,' M/171/61, 29 May 1961, PREM 11/3311.

7 An arms race intensifies
ABM defence, nuclear testing and the criteria of deterrence, January 1961–January 1962

Anglo-American views on ballistic missile defence at the start of the Kennedy era

Allegations of neglect in defence preparedness had been one of the major battlegrounds of the 1960 presidential election campaign, with the Democratic Party's candidate, Senator John F. Kennedy, critical of the incumbent Republican administration for its parsimony when it came to levels of spending. According to Kennedy, the late 1950s had been the 'locust years', when defence budgets had atrophied, and the Soviet Union had been able to open a 'missile gap' with the United States. Building on the critique that had featured in such investigations as the Gaither Report, Kennedy warned about the vulnerability of the homeland to missile attack. Accordingly, Kennedy's arrival in office saw the initiation of a large-scale build-up in strategic nuclear forces. Most notably, this involved an acceleration of development and production of the Minuteman ICBM, improvements in the responsiveness and alert status of SAC's bomber force (with older aircraft retired), and an increase in the numbers of Polaris missile submarines from that planned by the previous administration. In many respects, the submarine launched ballistic missile would become the favoured strategic weapons system for every subsequent US administration, guaranteeing a retaliatory response in the event of Soviet nuclear attack, and avoiding some of the political complications inherent in the domestic or overseas basing of nuclear-armed aircraft or land-based missiles. In early 1961, the Kennedy administration included extra funding to increase the planned number of Polaris submarines in the US Fleet from 19 to 29, and at the end of the following year this figure was increased again to 41 boats, which would eventually give the United States a total deployed strength of 656 SLBMs.[1] The overall expansion in military spending was overseen by the dynamic figure of Robert McNamara, who endeavoured to shake up the Pentagon through a more rigorous approach to budgeting and cost-benefit analysis. Alarmed by some of the lax controls that existed over how nuclear weapons would actually be used if war should occur, McNamara also put major new effort and investment into command and control systems.[2] The admission – first made in an unguarded comment by McNamara to reporters in February 1961 – that the 'missile gap' was in fact a myth, and that the United States still enjoyed a substantial lead in strategic nuclear capability, was not accompanied by any slackening in the administration's determination to entrench US superiority.[3]

One area, however, where McNamara was not convinced that a major boost to spending could be justified was ballistic missile defence. The final years of the Eisenhower administration had witnessed many technical problems with the development of the Nike-Zeus ABM system, concerns over the high costs of the programme, and much scepticism about whether ballistic missile defence could be made effective, particularly when an attacking force had the ability to incorporate decoys in its missile payloads. This sceptical attitude was carried over into the new administration, with a marked reluctance to fund preproduction items in anticipation of eventual deployment. Amid inter-service disagreements over the future of Nike-Zeus, in January 1961 McNamara asked Herbert York, still filling the key role of Director of Defense Research and Engineering at the Pentagon, to undertake a 'complete reassessment' of ABM work to date. York estimated that by the end of the 1961 financial year, $2.4 billion would have been spent on Nike-Zeus, without any real prospect then or in the future of the system affording an effective defence of American cities. Even more telling perhaps was York's simple conclusion that the Soviet Union would merely have to improve the capabilities of its offensive missiles to counteract the deployment of an American ABM system.[4] Although funding for Nike-Zeus development was eventually preserved in the administration's first defence budget proposals presented to Congress in March 1961 – the Army again having lobbied hard for limited production and deployment – there were clearly signs that the ABM programme would be subject to further critical scrutiny, particularly in an environment where the administration's stress was still on building up offensive missile forces and conventional capabilities.[5] McNamara, in fact, was quite explicit in Congressional testimony that Nike-Zeus had technical and operating problems, and he was not yet prepared to authorise production and deployment. Indeed, he looked toward further studies which could suggest a new system with more advanced capabilities.[6]

Amongst the US military, nevertheless, there was widespread concern in the early 1960s over the signs that the Soviet Union was engaged in an extensive programme of ABM development and testing. One of the reasons the US Joint Chiefs of Staff were opposed to a fresh commitment to a voluntary moratorium on nuclear testing in the first year of the Kennedy administration was that they believed the United States was in danger of falling behind in several key areas of nuclear knowledge with ABM applications. During 1961, the US Defense Atomic Support Agency, which since 1959 had responsibility for overseeing the US stockpile of weapons on behalf of the DoD, had begun to issue reports which summarised the results of the high-altitude nuclear tests conducted in 1958 that had formed part of the Hardtack series in the Pacific, including information on radiation effects and neutron flux. By then most US agencies had come to see neutron heating as the main kill mechanism that could be used against enemy warheads, but work was also beginning to be sponsored on the effects of X-rays on various materials used on the outside shells of the US re-entry vehicles that housed those warheads. The initial idea was that X-rays could divert a re-entry vehicle (RV) from its intended target, even when explosions took place a considerable distance away in environment above the earth's atmosphere, but more dramatic effects were also being observed on the entire structure of the RV when subjected to the shock of encountering 'high temperature' X-rays.

In April 1961, the JCS informed McNamara that the US lacked 'practical and authoritative data regarding the phenomenon of neutron-flux and X-rays outside the atmosphere.' They were especially concerned that Soviet scientists had moved forward in developing 'a pure fusion weapon emitting very high intensities of neutrons,' where the blast and thermal effects of the nuclear explosion were minimised and the energy produced took the form of radiation. Such weapons had the capacity 'of generating at very long distances a neutron-flux in adjacent nuclear and thermonuclear weapons, particularly in space or the higher atmosphere.' The JCS continued:

> The Nike-Zeus, and presumably the anti-ICBM weapons which intelligence sources indicate are being developed by the USSR, depend among other effects on neutron-flux to 'kill', i.e. render impotent, the warhead of the incoming ballistic missile against which the anti-missile is directed. If the Soviets have developed, or could develop by surreptitious and undetectable testing, an efficient pure fusion weapon which could 'kill' enemy missile warheads at a considerable range, there could result a very high degradation to the credible nuclear deterrent posture of the United States. [...] the United States has very little practical data on the intensities of instant radiation produced by fission or fusion explosions in rarefied atmosphere or space. The Orange and Teak shots in the US nuclear testing program [of 1958] just prior to the current moratorium on nuclear testing provided inadequate data for a full evaluation of this effect at very high altitudes. Additional technical information concerning intensities of radiation at very high altitudes might show that X-rays have a much greater lethal radius for 'killing' missile warheads than neutrons. If this were to be the case, we would want to take measures to protect our own warheads and, at the same time, exploit this effect in our own anti-ICBM capability.[7]

The JCS were alluding here to the growing knowledge on the part of weapons' designers that the explosion of a high-yield nuclear warhead above the atmosphere (in a so-called 'exo-atmosphere' environment, or heights above about 250,000 feet, or about 80 kilometres) released a large part of its energy, by some reckoning about 75 per cent, in the form of X-rays which could travel very large distances through the vacuum of space. As the effect of such X-rays on the outer skin of a re-entry vehicle could be so damaging it was realised that 'X-ray kill' could become the dominant mechanism by which a long-range ABM interceptor could overcome the difficulty of achieving an accurate and precise interception of an RV moving at very high speed on a ballistic flight path through space. Improving the design of ABM warheads, moreover, so that they emitted 'high temperature' or 'hot' X-rays, could also be a method of enhancing this effect.

The incorporation of decoys by an offensive missile designer would not provide a ready solution to the X-ray kill problem as one ABM warhead, detonated in the middle of a 'cloud' of indistinguishable incoming warheads and decoys, could neutralise an entire missile payload. Radar discrimination between 'real' offensive warheads and decoys, formerly a major problem for an ABM defence system, might therefore not be required for a successful engagement, as the 'kill' distances of a high temperature ABM warhead might be so big that accurate discrimination was unnecessary. To some, therefore, advances in the field of ABM warhead design, meant that the economics and practicality of an effective ABM defence, previously regarded as a powerful argument against widespread deployment, represented a less insuperable impediment.

The other development in ABM technology during the early 1960s which was set to change appreciations of whether a successful area defence could be deployed was the introduction of high capacity, high power, phased array radars. These replaced the slow physical and mechanical movement of radar antennae with a method whereby beams of radio pulses were emitted by an antennae with a number of fixed faces, all controlled at great speed by computer. A phased array radar could first acquire, and then track simultaneously a very large number of objects deployed from an attacking missile at long range. Picking up an offensive missile payload just as it emerged over the radar horizon, it would be possible for computers to predict trajectories and impact points, so only objects which would eventually arrive at a defended target need be engaged by defensive missiles. Arising from work on Project Defender – the series of studies into techniques of ABM defence commissioned by the Advanced Research Projects Agency in 1958 – the first US phased array radar using a computer to steer its beams was constructed towards the end of 1960, and was quickly demonstrating the utility of this new technology.[8] The Dunay-3 battle management radar that began to be observed in 1963 at Kubinka, about 35 miles south west of Moscow (and was mentioned in chapter two), was also of this phased array type and formed a central component in the Soviet A-35 ABM system.

Such technical developments were still, nevertheless, in their infancy or shrouded in secrecy. British assessments of the possibilities of an effective ABM defence from this period, for example, were still marked by strong doubts. In late 1960, as it turned to looking at the merits of either an airborne platform or submarine-based successor to the V-bomber force for the 1970s, the British Nuclear Deterrent Study Group had established a technical sub-committee, which convened under Sir Solly Zuckerman's chairmanship as CSA at the MoD, in order to appraise the different systems. As part of its remit, Zuckerman's sub-committee asked for a study on the different countermeasures to ballistic missiles that could be developed in the period after 1970.[9]

The subsequent Ministry of Aviation (MoA) report produced in response, concluded in January 1961 that, 'No defence system which has been proposed against ballistic missile attack has, as yet, been proved on examination to be technically and economically worthwhile.' Any active defence, the report noted, would have to pinpoint the present and predicted trajectories of individual missiles; discriminate between warheads and possible decoys or missile debris; and launch an intercepting missile to destroy an incoming warhead. Though in principle intercepting and destroying enemy warheads was achievable with present technology, the addition of decoys complicated the defensive problem so much that constructing a reliable ABM system was considered uneconomic. 'With small weight penalty,' the report noted, 'the ballistic missile designer can eject decoys which resemble the warhead down to burst altitude, making it well-nigh impossible for the defence to pick out the dangerous object.' Though originally conceived as working in a non-decoy environment, the American Nike Zeus ABM system, it was observed, now attempted to use radar discrimination techniques to overcome the decoy problem, with interception of incoming warheads during the re-entry phase by a high-speed ground guided missile armed with its own nuclear warhead. However, due to the difficulties of achieving fast and accurate radar discrimination, Nike Zeus was described as operating on only a research basis at the US ballistic missile test ranges in the Pacific. It was considered unlikely, therefore, that an effective defensive system could be developed during the 1970s, especially as many possible counter-measures had not yet been exploited by ballistic missile designers.

While it was possible to conceive of different methods of radar discrimination, it was contended they could be countered by minor changes in decoy design or method of warhead ejection. Outside the earth's atmosphere it was thought that discrimination techniques 'hold out little hope', as in this environment the missile designer was 'free to use decoys of almost any shape, size or distribution since there is little or no restriction on design. Alternatively he can, for this period of the flight, modify the shape and size of the warhead so as to match decoy characteristics.' Another defensive tactic might be to use the device of a large megaton-yield warhead burst above the earth's atmosphere, and then observe by radar the reactions of incoming objects on the missile flight path, but, 'Studies of these effects, and the instruments to observe them, do not hold out much hope, [and] at most such action will sweep away some of the light decoys and hence reduce the numbers to be tackled later.' Discrimination inside the atmosphere, after re-entry, was seen as easier (not least as warheads and decoys would respond to the forces encountered on re-entry in different ways). However, reaction times from defensive missiles would have to be much shorter, particularly if an intercept was to occur at a reasonably high altitude so that the explosion of a defensive nuclear warhead did not cause damage on the ground. It was also likely that a great many targets would have to be tracked simultaneously by such a short-range system, involving major complexity and expense. In general terms, the cost to the attacker of increasing the number or sophistication of their missiles was regarded as less than would have to be incurred by a defender in devising an effective ABM system. For the future, offensive ballistic missile designers could exploit, as well as decoys, electronic or infra-red jamming, while 'no defensive system has yet been conceived which would be effective against ballistic missiles employing these penetration techniques which are already either available or practical.'[10] That the Ministry of Aviation should come down with such a sceptical response over the possibilities of ABM defence is perhaps not surprising considering the work its officials had already carried out in the decoy field for Blue Streak in the late 1950s.

Accepting the MoA report wholesale, the BNDSG's technical subcommittee considered that given the profound problems associated with the multiple tracking and interception of incoming targets, as well as the capacity to deploy numerous decoys aboard ballistic missiles, a basic advantage would always lie with the attacker.[11] The view of the Director General of Guided Weapons at the MoA, as he remarked in one letter to the MoD, was that, 'whereas in the strictest technical and scientific sense a defence against decoyed BMs [ballistic missiles] is conceivable, operationally it is not on within the next couple of decades.'[12] Informed by these kinds of findings, the BNDSG's work in examining the requirements for a successor system proceeded during 1961–62 with little regard for the problems of ballistic missile defence.

The resumption of atmosphere nuclear testing and ballistic missile defence

During the early summer of 1961 President Kennedy continued to resist calls from within the Department of Defense and from the JCS that nuclear testing by the United States should be resumed, while the newly formed Arms Control and Disarmament Agency attempted to formulate proposals which might help to break the logjam of negotiations at Geneva in the Eighteen Nation Disarmament Committee, where efforts to arrive at an agreement to ban all testing were still ongoing. Among the arguments used by the advocates of resumption included the point that testing would help to determine the lethal range for the kill radii of ABM warheads against ballistic missile re-entry vehicles. 'Knowledge of this kind,' one DoD paper prepared in May ran, 'is important both in examining US possibilities for defense against ballistic missile attack, and in deciding how our ballistic missile attacks (including the nature of the re-entry vehicle, degree of saturation, and the necessary separation between warheads) must be planned if the Soviets should begin to deploy an [ABM] system of their own.'[13] It was also the case that testing might help the weapons laboratories to produce smaller and lighter thermonuclear warheads. This would then allow ballistic missile designers to incorporate decoys in their missile payloads, to 'harden' warheads with new materials against the radiation effects of nuclear explosions, or simply to pack a larger number of warheads into the delivery system of a single missile, giving an attacker the option of saturating an enemy missile defence system.

For McNamara and his civilian advisers at the Pentagon, such as Harold Brown, who had taken York's place as Director of Defense Research Engineering in the spring of 1961, the argument that testing would help to improve the versatility and performance of the US ballistic missile threat to the Soviet Union tended to carry more weight than a justification for resumption that rested on developing new ABM technologies. In one meeting of officials in late May, McNamara remarked on the 'strong evidence that the Soviets were working vigorously on anti-ICBM weapons' and that 'the Polaris and Minuteman missiles could be improved by further testing and that decoys could then be used more extensively.' Brown agreed with the view that 'it was extremely difficult to meet a strong, sophisticated and decoyed attack.'[14]

With Cold War tensions running very high due to the crisis over Berlin, on 1 September 1961 the moratorium on nuclear testing which had been established in 1958 was finally broken by the Soviet Union when it began a new round of atmospheric experiments, featuring a wide variety of different explosive yields and types of warhead.[15] Two weeks later the United States began its own programme of underground tests in Nevada, but Kennedy was reluctant to proceed to atmosphere testing unless evidence of Russian advances in military capability produced by its new test series could be firmly established. In Britain, Zuckerman was quick to offer his appraisal of the military significance of the new Russian tests in a note to the Prime Minister delivered soon after they had begun, and made reference to their possible use in acquiring information for ABM defence (though, in what was to become a constant refrain, Zuckerman himself – informed also by his exposure to the issue on the BNDSG technical subcommittee – doubted the feasibility of ballistic missile defence given the costs and complexities involved).[16]

The relevance of the new Soviet tests for an ABM system was seemingly confirmed on 6 October by Joe 98, a test which had an estimated yield of 200 kilotons and which was burst at a height of between 20 and 40 miles (or 32 and 64 kilometres). The yield and altitude persuaded Western observers that it might be consistent with a warhead designed for ABM use. But probably of even greater interest were two very high altitude 'effects' tests carried out a few weeks later (and the first such tests detected in the Soviet Union). Both tests involved pairs of missiles fired from the Russian ICBM test range at Kapustin Yar, with two minute intervals between them, toward the ABM research establishment at Sary Shagan. Held on 21 October, the first test, Joe 105, involved a low yield warhead (perhaps 5 kilotons) bursting at a height of about 160 miles (or 257 kilometres), while the second missile passed through the area of the explosion. Two more intercept missiles from Sary Shagan were also thought to have been fired at the general area. A second test explosion of another low yield warhead, Joe 109, this time at a height of 80 miles (or about 130 kilometres), was carried out on 27 October, with similar missile firing activity in the area. All these shots, and their associated patterns of missile firings, were believed to have given the Russians valuable data on the behaviour of high altitude nuclear bursts and their effects on radar tracking, information which had an obvious application to an ABM system.[17] It was at the same time as these events, and probably in response to official confirmation from the Department of Defense that the US still had a substantial lead in overall strategic nuclear capabilities, that Marshal Malinovsky, the Soviet Defence Minister, made his announcement to the 22nd Congress of the Communist Party that the Soviet Union had solved the problem of destroying missiles in flight.[18]

It was already believed by Western observers there had been about 20 firings of Soviet defensive missiles from Sary Shagan intended to intercept an incoming offensive missile outside the atmosphere, but up to that point none of these ABM-related tests had used a nuclear warhead; it appeared now that an ABM interceptor was being tested and tracked through the radiation environment created by an exo-atmospheric nuclear explosion. The chief source of information on the Soviet nuclear programme available to the UK Government during this period came from the Atomic Energy Intelligence Division of the Directorate of Scientific Intelligence, which was part of the Joint Intelligence Bureau (quite distinct from the JIC, the latter organisation sat within the Ministry of Defence and specialised in acquiring economic, technical and scientific intelligence).[19] Archibald Potts, the head of atomic energy intelligence at the JIB, believed that the high altitude tests had allowed the Russians to monitor the output of X-rays and neutron radiation from their warheads, and observe their effects on missile and radar systems. 'As an explanation of the second ballistic missile following the nuclear burst,' Zuckerman noted after being briefed by Potts about the October tests, 'his own view was that the Russians were worried lest a nuclear warhead fired at one incoming missile might produce a radio-active cloud which would black-out their own defences against a second incoming missile.'[20]

The October 1961 tests also served to prompt the Ministry of Aviation to form a fresh working party 'to consider and give their views on the potential merits of systems of ABM defence.'[21] The Royal Radar Establishment provided a chair for the group in the person of W. H. Penley, and representatives from RAE, AWRE, Ferranti and Marconi were included. Revisiting the assessment given in the MoA's January 1961 paper on ABM systems, the working party saw no reason to change earlier views, finding in its eventual March 1962 report that, 'No new destruction mechanism has been postulated which, against a well designed offensive warhead, could achieve a sufficiently large lethal radius to significantly ease the problem of discrimination.' Although the Russians were not yet thought to have experimented with using decoys in their own ballistic missile payloads, they provided an obvious avenue to thwart any attempt at an ABM defence. Miss distances of several hundred feet were seen as inevitable given the high velocity of the incoming target, and the vagaries of radar performance and intercepting missile guidance. Use of a one megaton warhead in an ABM interceptor could generate lethal blast and heat effects out to about 1,000 feet at heights of 50,000 feet and below, but was likely to cause general damage at ground level if the burst was too low. At higher altitudes the effects of X-rays and neutron radiation predominated and gave a larger lethal radius. However, damage mechanisms 'resulting from the absorption of X-rays by the missile skin' were viewed as 'uncertain'; some missile materials could be vulnerable at several miles distance from a one-megaton explosion, but there was simply 'no evidence to show that this order of vulnerability obtains for the complete range of permissible materials.' As the damaging effects of X-rays were 'insufficiently understood', they were not given further consideration. At very high altitudes, the neutron effects from a one megaton explosion could be lethal out to 2,000 feet.

From this knowledge base, the Penley working party concluded that 'high altitude interception may be desirable when a nuclear defensive weapon is used against a ballistic warhead well strengthened to survive blast (and certainly so if the more optimistic estimates of X-ray damage are valid).' Nevertheless, it was thought that there could be 'serious blackout effects' on defending radars if nuclear weapons were used during attempted interceptions. The Americans continued to work on their Nike-Zeus ABM system, and it was now said to have 'a reasonable capability' against an Atlas-type ICBM fitted with primitive penetration aids, but this was considered 'more a criticism of the decoy designs rather than a commendation of the Nike-Zeus system.' A limited deployment of Nike-Zeus was now thought possible, but the working party saw the only valid technical reason for this was 'to force the Russians to employ decoys and raise doubts as to how sophisticated these might be to achieve effective penetration of the defence. Even these reactions are likely to cost the Russians only a small fraction of the cost of Nike-Zeus deployment.'

Turning to evidence of Russian ABM development, the working party reported that it was believed that an ABM firing programme may have begun in late 1960 or early 1961, and that the testing regime might even be more advanced than the US programme for Nike-Zeus. Considering the public statements from Soviet leaders, it was believed that a reasonable miss distance to ballistic missile targets had been shown in Russian tests. Although Russian capabilities could be comparable to the US Nike-Zeus system 'more evidence is urgently required'. There was speculation that the Russians might be working on a system designed to deal with the existing generation of ballistic missiles without decoys, and would then try to improve it at a later date. 'It is certainly true also,' the report continued, 'that the present generation of US and British missiles have little scope for decoy deployment and furthermore might be vulnerable to a defensive nuclear burst at much greater distances than we are considering in this report.' It was therefore felt 'logical' that the Russians would consider that deploying on a limited basis 'a non-discriminating, or partially discriminating, defensive system' would be 'worthwhile against existing US ballistic missiles and against many of the missiles which will be in Service with the Western Powers during the next 5 to 10 years.'

Overall, the Penley report, as it soon became known, reaffirmed earlier views that there was no technically straightforward and economically acceptable way of defending against ballistic missiles 'using a high standard of warhead engineering and decoys which should become available in the near future.' It was, moreover, thought doubtful that the Russian ABM system then under development would be 'of great use against hardened warheads using decoys.' The report rendered the advice that 'all future US and UK designs of ballistic missiles should incorporate these features otherwise the balance of the deterrent is likely to be severely upset.'[22]

The resumption of atmosphere nuclear testing by the Soviet Union in 1961 had created overwhelming pressure within the Kennedy administration to embark on a new series of US tests. A prime reason given by the proponents of this course of action was the need to experiment with ABM warheads (for which atmospheric tests would be needed) and reduce the weight of American warhead designs, combined with anxieties that the Russians were gaining a lead in knowledge of nuclear effects. The President finally acceded to requests from the Department of Defense and AEC to proceed with preparations for a resumption of atmosphere nuclear testing, on the assumption that final approval would be given, at the end of November 1961.[23]

Encountering criticism from its own public opinion, which was concerned about the health and environmental impact of atmosphere testing, and convinced an American resumption would serve to exacerbate Cold War tensions, the Macmillan Government tried to persuade the Americans to desist while negotiations at Geneva were given a chance to agree a verifiable and comprehensive ban on all nuclear tests, or at least arrange for another moratorium. Nevertheless, AWRE also saw the initiation of US underground testing in Nevada as a valuable opportunity to gauge the performance of some of its new warhead design ideas, including one (Super Octopus, which employed a novel implosion system) that might have an applicability as a primary for Skybolt. In November 1961, following lower level enquiries, Macmillan formally asked Kennedy if a British test could be accommodated in the US series, while presenting underground testing as the preferable alternative to an atmospheric programme.[24] Agreement from the President was forthcoming, and logistical arrangements for the movement of the components of the British warhead to the United States, along with 15–20 AWRE staff to supervise the test, were quickly made. The first ever British underground shot – 'Pampas' – was duly fired on 1 March 1962 at the

Nevada testing ground, indicating that Anglo-American nuclear links under the 1958 MDA were very much alive and well; Sir Roger Makins, the head of the AEA, for example, reported to Macmillan that US AEC officials had been very helpful and cooperative with planning and execution, while the test had demonstrated ideas which the Americans had found of interest.[25]

The obvious advantage of underground testing was its low visibility, and that its environmental impact could be sharply contained, but it was not a technique that could precisely replicate the environment where ABM warheads would be employed. Pressure for resumption of the more politically contentious atmosphere testing from the military and technical community were not likely to relent. The Government's dilemmas were heightened by the fact the Kennedy administration wanted to use the remote British possession of Christmas Island in the Pacific, which had been the scene for some the UK's Grapple series of hydrogen bomb tests in 1957–58, as a base for their next atmospheric series, opening up London to further criticism if it unconditionally acceded to US plans and requests. While Macmillan and other senior ministers were clear that the American request could not be refused, it was felt imperative that the resumption of Western testing should be accompanied by a fresh diplomatic initiative on disarmament or moves toward a complete test ban. When the US request for use of Christmas Island was made in November 1961, it was explained to British officials that the main aim of the tests was related to development of ABM systems, and the measures that could be used in offensive missiles to counteract them.[26]

With Macmillan due to meet Kennedy on Bermuda at the end of December, where the American request to use Christmas Island was certain to feature during the talks, there ensued a debate amongst British officials on justifications for the resumption of US testing which reflected the differences of opinion that existed about the possibilities of mounting a successful ABM defence. The chief protagonists in the argument were Zuckerman and Sir William Penney. The latter had left his position as head of AWRE in 1959, and by 1961 had been elevated to become deputy head of the UK Atomic Energy Authority, from where he continued to offer his unique authority and advice to the Government on nuclear weapons matters.[27]

Having been central in the creation of a testing culture and its practice at Aldermaston, Penney was more inclined to sympathise with the arguments of the American weapons scientists, with whom he still had many contacts, and was not prepared to discount the need to develop new ABM warheads. It was, however, the Nuclear Requirements for Defence Committee, an interdepartmental body of senior officials (established in 1960 under MoD chairmanship to advise and make recommendations to ministers on matters concerning the UK nuclear weapons programme) that delivered the preliminary opinion that the Americans had yet to make a clear-cut military, as opposed to technical, case which could be used to justify resumption. 'While three tests carried out at high altitude may have provided useful weapon effects information which could have strategic significance in the future,' the

Committee concluded in December, 'no one has suggested that anything learned by the Russians from their recent series of tests will shift the strategic balance of nuclear power in favour of the Soviet Union over the next few years.'[28] Influenced by the sceptical views of Jerome Wiesner, President Kennedy's own chief science adviser, and also by his knowledge of the technical appreciation carried out by the MoA, Zuckerman could also see few merits in the contention that testing was required for ABM purposes, and believed that the moves to develop ABM systems would simply fuel a new phase in a destabilising arms race between the US and Soviet Union.[29]

In the build-up to the Bermuda summit, Zuckerman had informed the Prime Minister of his doubts that a convincing argument had been made for resumption. One of the points mentioned by Zuckerman was that even if the Russians were to make advances in ABM defence, they could still be saturated 'with masses of small weapons or by means of decoys.'[30] In conversation with the Prime Minister's senior officials, Penney, however, demurred. 'The whole question is whether the Russians can develop an anti-missile missile,' he was keen to stress. Referring to the Russian experiments at Sary Shagan in October 1961, Penney argued that 'Some of their recent tests were extremely sophisticated, involving several missiles in the air at once, one of them carrying a nuclear warhead.' While he thought that the Russians still had a long way to go, there was a chance – even if only a hundred or a thousand to one – that they could succeed in discovering the key to a successful ABM defence. It was on this basis that Penney thought that renewed testing could be justified on military – as opposed to purely technical – grounds, as a Russian breakthrough over ABM could affect the overall balance of power.[31]

Zuckerman, nonetheless, maintained that though an ABM defence was technically possible on paper, and could be used to defend isolated targets, in economic terms it was impossible to conceive of such a system allowing coverage of an entire country. Elements of an ABM system could be deployed as a form of bluff, however, in order to compel an opponent to adopt expensive counter-measures. These latter techniques could include attempts to saturate a defence with sheer numbers of missiles; the incorporation of decoys; and the use of electronic counter-measures (including blacking out defending radars with high altitude nuclear explosions). However, Zuckerman was not convinced that any such steps were actually necessary, calling them 'extremely fanciful in the light of what we know. None of our authorities believes that it would be possible to devise an effective defence system against ballistic missiles.' The knowledgeable Americans whom Zuckerman had spoken with about the subject, such as Harold Brown, all concurred with this final point, while there would always, he reiterated, be ways to improve an attacking force of missiles to enable it to overcome an ABM defence.[32]

At their conference held on Bermuda, Kennedy and Macmillan discussed the merits of resuming testing and how it could be best publicly presented. Technical advice at the meeting was provided for the British delegation by

Penney and on the American side by Glenn Seaborg, the Chairman of the US Atomic Energy Commission. During the session at Bermuda on nuclear testing on 21 December Penney and Seaborg had both pointed to the military significance of the recent Russian tests, the former again referring to their relative sophistication 'involving high altitude nuclear explosions and several missiles in the air at once,' while 'the site of some of these particular tests had already been reported by intelligence sources as being the centre of an anti-missile experimental station. This development gave grounds for apprehension ... It was necessary to decide whether [the] risk of giving the Russians a start in anti-missile defence was acceptable.'

Primed by Zuckerman, the Prime Minister preferred to dwell on the problems of perfecting an ABM defence, suggesting to the meeting that 'the difficulty with an anti-missile defence was that to be really valuable it had to be at least 90 per cent efficient and of course the question of decoys had to be considered. In trying to develop such a defence system thousands of millions of dollars would be spent and even then the result would be in doubt.'[33] According to the US record of the talks, Macmillan then proceeded to discuss 'at some length the terrifying prospects of an indefinitely conducted and enormously expensive arms race in this field. If all of these talented people go on about their business, more and more and bigger and bigger bombs would be piled up and if even one of these new bombs should go off, it would burn up all of France. On and on, the two great powers would go.' Britain, Macmillan said, would however '"probably drop out". We have of course an absolute justification for going on with it, because of what the other man [sic] is doing. But as we are now, we are even. Neither side has a defence nor will have one for many years.' Although he could see there were some arguments in favour of a resumption of testing, the Prime Minister wanted to see 'a great new effort to break the cycle of the arms race.' Voicing his concern over the utter devastation that only a few hydrogen bombs would bring to the UK, Macmillan noted for Kennedy's benefit that 'a very large part of the early wave of the Western strategic forces' were based in Britain, and that '"Every time you lift the phone, Mr President, I think that you are about to say that you are going to go, and I always wonder what I would answer."'[34] 'It was terrifying and wrong,' the British record had the Prime Minister saying, 'that such vast resources should be devoted to these weapons of destruction. Each side was making this effort because it was frightened of the other.'[35]

But as far as Kennedy was concerned, the experience of negotiating with the Russians over the previous few months had been 'discouraging': 'He quite agreed the Soviet edge, if any, was not decisive now, but he was also agreed with Sir William Penney that the problem was what would happen in 1964 if we did not continue and the Soviets did. We could not get taken twice [in a reference to Khrushchev's surprise resumption of testing in September 1961]. Therefore, we ought to go ahead and prepare to test, and test, if there was no great progress in other fields ... there was one and only one serious issue, the balance of missile/anti-missile capabilities.' Asked about the availability of

British facilities, Macmillan managed to reserve his positon over the use of Christmas Island, but indicated that British agreement would probably be forthcoming if the Americans consented to another major effort to re-start negotiations for a complete test ban before atmosphere testing was resumed.[36]

A number of conflicting instincts were evidently at work with the Prime Minister at this time. In his diary, he recorded the feeling that the Russian tests were 'rather alarming.' We know that they are working very hard on an '"anti-missile" missile. They have built a town of 20,000 people wholly devoted to scientific work in this sphere.'[37] Loyalty to the Anglo-American alliance was also a consideration: Macmillan was convinced that he had already established an encouraging degree of understanding with the new US President, and did not want to prejudice this relationship by a refusal to act in step with Washington. But he also had domestic and international criticism of nuclear testing to consider, and his own alarm at anything that could add to the already tense state of East-West relations, and fuel even further the galloping nuclear arms race.

In London, Macmillan's ministerial colleagues were understandably keen to explore the technical and military reasons why the American tests might be required. At the start of January 1962 the Cabinet accordingly considered a paper from the Prime Minister dealing with the arguments over testing (but which clearly carried Penney's imprint). This maintained that while the Soviet Union had 'not drawn ahead of the West in nuclear knowledge ... the lead which the West had previously enjoyed had disappeared.' An immediate halt to further testing would probably hold in place the strategic balance, but the recent Russian experiments with ABM systems could eventually have the effect of giving them 'a significant advantage in the anti-missile field.' Admittedly the discussions at Bermuda had highlighted the point that the difficulties of developing an effective ABM defence were 'enormous. To be really effective such a system would have to be able to destroy over 90 per cent of any attacking missiles. This would be extremely difficult in any case, but the task of the defenders could be made even harder if attacking missiles had decoys in them. In addition it is possible that very large explosions at high altitudes might further complicate the defence by interrupting radar and radio systems.' However, even though the technical experts considered the chance of an effective defence 'extremely remote' it was felt that

> the stakes were so high and the resources available to the Soviet Union and United States were so great that it was impossible to entirely discount the possibility that such a defensive system might eventually be developed. Moreover, if one side or the other made significant progress in this field, even if it fell short of a completely effective system, or if they could plausibly claim to have done so, the balance of the deterrent might be decisively upset. Consequently, in the absence of an adequately controlled ban on nuclear tests, neither the West nor the Soviet Union could afford to renounce the effort necessary to try to make progress in this field.

Kennedy and his advisers had also explained that the proposed tests had as their purpose measurement of the effects of high altitude explosions on 'missiles carrying nuclear warheads and on radar and radio communications; tests of existing warheads which might pave the way for weight reductions; and other tests of various advanced designs also with the aim of reducing weight.' Reductions in weight would, it was explained, allow 'decoys and other electronic devices' to be carried. 'All the proposed tests,' the Cabinet were told, 'are therefore directly related to the possibilities of developing or defeating an anti-missile system. It would be hard to argue that these are not "necessary in order to maintain the balance of the deterrent". The threat is not immediate but may become so even by 1964.'[38]

The first two Cabinet meetings of the year were both held on 3 January 1962. During the morning Macmillan gave a personal review of the Bermuda meeting with Kennedy, and of how the issue of nuclear testing now lay. Referring to the paper that had just been distributed, the Prime Minister thought the recent Russian series had given them 'valuable results,' and even that they had 'drawn level'. They were clearly 'going for anti-missile defence' and reductions in warhead weight were certainly of major significance in this context.[39]

Later that day, the Cabinet re-convened to hear directly from Penney the reasons that could be used to justify a resumption of Western testing. Analysis of the recent Russian test series, Penney informed ministers, had shown some of them were directly related to development of an 'anti-missile missile.' Alluding to the October 1961 experiments at Sary Shagan, Penney mentioned that a special cause of anxiety had been (as the Cabinet Secretary's notes recorded) 'three missile explosions at once at various heights – one with n. warhead – various directions. Clearly 1st attempt at anti-missile experiment: one fired from their anti-missile research station.' According to the Cabinet Secretary's record of the meeting, Penney was evidently torn. He informed ministers that an anti-missile system was 'as nearly impossible as anything I have seen,' while the additions of decoys and dummies would make the defender's problems 'even worse.' Although the UK could not afford to contemplate such a programme, both the American and Russians were both devoting major resources to ABM research and development, and in view of the huge efforts now being made Penney did not feel confident enough to conclude an effective defence was completely impossible. With an active Soviet programme, he could not see how the United States would refrain from work in the area, and 'the work of the scientists and technicians in the United States would be bound to lose momentum if they were unable to test the results of their research.' 'If I were an American,' Penney felt, 'I fear I would have to advise [the] President to go on. The US will test, whether they get Xmas [Island] or not.' The new US test series would be designed, in part, to study the effect of high altitude nuclear explosions on missiles, but also to look at ways to reduce warhead size and weight so that penetration aids could be added. But even if missile defence was judged to be practical, Penney saw no possibility that either the United States or Soviet Union could deploy an effective system in less than ten years.[40]

Believing there was no real alternative other than to agree to the American request to use the Christmas Island facilities, and give public backing to any final US decision to begin testing again, the Prime Minister, with the Cabinet's endorsement, nevertheless also tied this with a proposal to Kennedy that another diplomatic initiative be taken.[41] Still reluctant to resume testing in any case, Kennedy was willing to explore how to make progress in disarmament negotiations with the Soviet Union, but at the same time wanted to avoid any direct linkage between his final decision over testing (and hence use of the British facilities) and the talks shortly to start again in Geneva. In early February 1962, Kennedy and Macmillan accordingly addressed a joint appeal to Khrushchev for intensified negotiations, with the direct involvement of the foreign ministers of the United States, Soviet Union and Great Britain. Soon after, the Prime Minister appeared in the House of Commons to announce that on the basis of the military and scientific arguments he accepted the need to prepare for a resumption of US atmosphere testing, and had agreed to the American request to use Christmas Island for a limited and specified programme of tests. Included in his remarks was a reference to Russian claims that at the time of their tests the previous autumn they had 'solved the problems of destroying ballistic missiles in flight.'[42] In the event, Soviet resistance to the idea that a control system of international monitoring and inspections should be a part of any agreement to prohibit testing helped to frustrate progress at Geneva, and on 2 March 1962 President Kennedy gave a sombre speech which announced his decision that US atmosphere testing in the Pacific would be resumed in the latter part of the following month.[43]

The development of US–Soviet competition over ABM systems

The debates over whether to resume atmosphere nuclear testing had served to bring to the fore sharp variations in assessments of the prospects for ABM defence. Meeting in mid-January 1962, Penney and Zuckerman continued to disagree over the need for the Americans to conduct another series of atmosphere tests, Zuckerman again stressing that a defensive system could be easily drenched by decoys, or electronic countermeasures to confuse radar systems, making the military case for resumption of testing on ABM grounds less than compelling. Penney preferred to point to the obvious effort being poured into the ABM area by the Soviet Union and the United States, and though the chances of success were small, it was impossible to predict what might be achieved in the field over the next two decades. Seeing no way to avoid a resumption of testing and a continuing effort to keep pace with technological developments, Penney felt, so Zuckerman recorded, that 'we were somehow caught up in this incredible competition, and that it was impossible to see how we could opt out short of some real progress being made in the field of disarmament.'⁴⁴

For his own part, and from the additional information he gathered from the Ministry of Aviation during this period on the penetration aid measures that had been developed for Blue Streak, Zuckerman was even more convinced of the ultimate futility of ABM defence. Similarly, for Sir Robert Cockburn, now Chief Scientist at the MoA, the inherent advantages of the ballistic missile, and the extra scope that existed for incorporating penetration aids, meant that 'although the West could not ignore Russian programmes indefinitely there seems at present no compelling technical reason for starting atmospheric tests forthwith.'⁴⁵ As far as Cockburn was concerned (reflecting a view which he had consistently held since serving as CGWL at the Ministry of Supply between 1956 and 1959):

> it would always be possible to incorporate features in the attacking missile to outwit any defence system conceivable within the extrapolation of existing knowledge. In the last resort, the offence would have advantage over the defence through the simple processes of surprise and saturation. It was impossible to imagine that even the USSR with its enormous defence effort, could provide a defence against ballistic missiles for more than a limited number of key targets. This would leave the rest of Russia open to the threat of attack, at the same time as the defences of the key targets could, themselves, be overwhelmed by increasing the scale of potential attack.⁴⁶

At the end of January, Zuckerman again conveyed his strong doubts, this time in a minute to the Minister of Defence which questioned the justification given for the new US test series as being necessary to observe the effects of high altitude nuclear explosions as they might apply to ABM systems.⁴⁷

It is important to note, moreover, that within the US scientific community influential voices – many holding senior advisory positions to the US defence establishment – had already begun to emerge which questioned whether an effective ABM system, particularly if it was intended for large-scale area defence, would ever be possible. Among the most important of these early sceptics was Hans Bethe, professor of physics at Cornell University, who had played an influential role in the development of the hydrogen bomb, but was now preoccupied with the steps that could be taken to curb the arms race. Bethe was increasingly concerned that the development of ABM warheads was becoming used as a rationale for the continuation of nuclear testing. At the beginning of January 1962, Bethe began to dismiss the chances of an effective ABM defence in speeches as 'virtually hopeless' as an attacker could saturate any defensive system with numerous decoys. His own approach was based on the requirements of stable deterrence, where each side would possess invulnerable retaliatory forces, and be able to negotiate arms control agreements from this base.⁴⁸

In February Zuckerman visited the United States again to probe his American contacts, where he met Seaborg, Wiesner, and Harold Brown. The inference that Zuckerman drew from his conversations was that no specific and new information could be used to justify the resumption of atmosphere testing, while Brown had repeated his earlier opinion over the unlikelihood that it would ever be possible to devise an effective ABM system that would provide a defence for such dispersed targets as cities. 'In American eyes,' Zuckerman reported, 'the essential justification for tests now is that they cannot stand back and restrain their weapons laboratories, even though they could not see how the balance of strategic power was going to be affected.'[49]

The Kennedy administration's decisions over whether to proceed with deployment of an ABM system also reflected doubts over the viability of ballistic missile defence. At the end of 1961, despite intensive lobbying from the Army, the President again decided to defer a decision on deployment of Nike-Zeus. Congress nevertheless eventually appropriated another $274 million for continued testing of the system (out of a total ABM budget of $384 million), in line with administration requests to keep the programme moving forward during 1962–63.[50] McNamara himself continued to exhibit a familiar level of scepticism over the prospects for ballistic missile defence, testifying before Congress in March 1962, for example, that no amount of money would give Nike-Zeus the ability to offer a really effective nationwide defence against the Soviet ICBM threat. To some observers it seemed that the administration was prepared to see Nike-Zeus reduced to a research and development programme which would allow more knowledge to be acquired about re-entry phenomena and radar discrimination techniques.[51]

Alongside the administration's evolving approach to the funding of ABM defence, McNamara's Pentagon began to take a much more determined approach to the promotion of penetration aids within the US offensive ballistic missile force. There was no provision for the incorporation of such devices and methods in the first generation Minuteman and Polaris missiles, but McNamara decided to increase expenditure on research and development of penetration aids from $20 million in the 1961 financial year to $35 million for 1962.[52] A contract was awarded to Lockheed in November 1961 to develop a penetration aid kit for the Mark 1 re-entry system used with the single-warhead Polaris A2 missile, and flight testing of what was called the PX-1 package took place during 1962 (A2s having themselves become operational in June of the same year).[53] In early 1962, the Defence Research Staff at the British Embassy in Washington reported that the Kaman Aircraft Corporation had begun to study the susceptibility of the Polaris Re-entry Body (REB – the US Navy used 're-entry body' rather than 're-entry vehicle', which was the term favoured by the US Air Force) to 'countermeasures in its terminal phase. Emphasis has been placed on studies of its vulnerability to soft X-ray damage and neutron induced heating, and the benefits to be associated with possible methods of reducing its vulnerability have been evaluated.'[54]

Under the 1958 MDA, an Anglo-American Joint Working Group – JOWOG 19 – was established in the spring of 1962 to examine warhead hardening techniques against the effects of 'neutrons, fragments and shock loading (from blast and X-ray pulses)', though its remit soon expanded to encompass re-entry vehicle vulnerability as well. Discussion within the JOWOG at its first meetings at the Lawrence Livermore Laboratory in April was confined almost wholly to looking at the vulnerability of UK warhead designs at various ranges from nuclear explosions. The topic of X-rays was explored, but – as one of the British representatives present noted – 'as we have not done any work on this we were unable to contribute anything of value to the discussion.' From what the Americans said, there was obviously a great deal of experimental work still to be done in the whole area. The ranges of warhead vulnerability to X-ray effects from a one megaton explosion were mentioned as being about 20 kms, though there was optimism this could be substantially reduced by the addition of protective materials to re-entry vehicles. The general impression was that the Americans were taking the whole subject of vulnerability very seriously, whereas British studies had not gone much further than looking at blast effects on Skybolt during warhead re-entry.[55] The last full meeting of the JOWOG was, however, convened in late October 1962, and after that session, though several British papers were sent to the Americans, none were received in return; the UK representative on the JOWOG, nevertheless, felt it was important to keep it going 'as it gives us an entry into the US thinking on vulnerability and missile systems, including decoys.'[56]

Meanwhile, the Americans, as part of the atmospheric nuclear testing series under the codename 'Dominic' that had begun in the Pacific in April 1962, were continuing with experiments to investigate the radiation output of warheads exploded high above the earth's atmosphere. Probably the most significant of these tests for ABM purposes occurred on 9 July. 'Starfish Prime' was a 1.4 megaton burst staged at a height of 400 kilometres, or about 250 miles (so far higher than the Orange and Teak tests of August 1958). The electromagnetic pulse from Starfish Prime disrupted radio communications and electrical circuits over very long distances, and extra knowledge of X-ray and neutron fluxes at high altitude were gained. The test was also important for suggesting ways in which a high altitude nuclear explosion could be used to 'blackout' defensive radars. Several further lower yield tests at high altitude were conducted in the autumn, but these proved to be the last American atmospheric nuclear tests as the following summer saw the conclusion of the Partial Test Ban Treaty between the United States, the Soviet Union and Britain.

As US weapons designers began to acquire a better understanding of the potential of ABM warheads to neutralise incoming ballistic missiles, and of the tactics that might be used to defeat such a defence, the Soviet Union's own ABM efforts served as an extra spur for such basic work to continue. During 1961 the construction of installations which could have had an ABM role was first detected near Leningrad, but work on them stopped in 1962, and they began to be dismantled the following year prompting American assessments that whatever system had been envisaged was now considered too ineffective to be worth introducing into service. It seems that some construction work for installation of the A-35 system also began around Moscow in late 1962, but the system itself went through several different modifications as its various components were developed, tested, and redesigned once more. Nevertheless, this preliminary work on a Moscow system was detected and noted by Western intelligence analysts who saw it as the basis for a more extensive deployment. By early 1963, McNamara was informing Congress in closed testimony that US planning assumptions were that a limited system around Moscow might be deployed by mid-1968.[57]

Given the evidence that was starting to appear indicating Soviet intentions to bring into service an operational ABM system, the Kennedy administration faced considerable difficulties in fending off calls for a more extensive US ABM programme, with early deployment of Nike-Zeus still thought necessary by some. Just before he assumed the chairmanship of the JCS, one of Kennedy's leading military advisers, General Maxwell Taylor, warned the President in August 1962 that recent intelligence indicated it was probable that deployment of an ABM system in the Soviet Union may already have begun. Taylor wrote that

> Whatever we may think or say about the effectiveness of this ABM the Soviets probably feel that it will pay for its cost in giving some degree of protection to Russian cities and in gaining prestige abroad and morale at home. The Soviets probably hope by these efforts to move from the present strategic situation where the US holds the balance of nuclear superiority largely through manned bombers with neither side having an acceptable missile defense, to one where the US offensive strength against military targets is neutralized by an invulnerable Russian missile force on land and sea and the homeland defenses are significantly better than those of the US. The 'balance of terror' then would be tipped in favor of the USSR.

It was essential, Taylor thought, that the United States keep up with the Soviet Union in the ABM race that then seemed imminent, and he therefore pushed for Nike-Zeus deployment.[58]

The psychological dimension to the state of ABM development between the Superpowers had already been underlined when on 16 July 1962 Khrushchev met several US newspaper editors in the Kremlin. Here he took the chance to boast that the Soviet Union had an anti-missile missile that could hit 'a fly in outer space.' US officials provided background briefings in response that tried to cast doubt on such claims, arguing that an effective system would still have to overcome many problems.[59] Three days later a graphic demonstration of the advances being made in ABM technology was given when the re-entry vehicle from an Atlas ICBM launched from Vandenberg Air Force Base in California was intercepted by a Zeus ABM high over the Kwajalein test site in the Pacific. The inert warhead of the Zeus passed within two kilometres of the Atlas RV, showing that long-range accurate interception of fast-moving bodies in space was now within reach.[60]

The British Defence Staff in Washington reported that the interception had in fact been a second attempt, the first having failed, while the Americans were initially unwilling to divulge any more information about the event than had been given in the official press release. It was felt that as the Army were beginning to consider Nike-Zeus as capable of operational deployment, security restrictions concerning its capabilities had grown tighter. 'It can be safely assumed that there were no decoys present to avoid complicating what was, after all, an initial experiment,' the staff newsletter observed in a sceptical tone, 'but the future of Nike-Zeus largely hinges on the extent to which the system can be relied upon to discriminate between decoys and actual warheads.'[61] McNamara issued a statement to accompany announcement of the successful intercept, explaining that such testing programmes were designed to explore 'the capabilities and limitations' of anti-missile systems, and that, 'Concurrently and in a coordinated fashion, the US have been carrying out a program to insure that our missiles will penetrate anti-missile systems which might be encountered. These programmes give us confidence that our missiles would be able to penetrate any such systems which have been developed by anyone.'[62]

McNamara's publicly proclaimed confidence in the penetration aids that could be incorporated in the designs of US ICBMs and SLBMs was a reflection of the progress that had been made since the beginning of the administration in this critical area of technology. A high-level appraisal of Soviet and US strategic missile programmes presented to President Kennedy in August 1962 affirmed that US penetration aid programmes would probably allow the US to maintain an advantage over Soviet ABM capabilities at least through to the middle of the 1960s. Initial decoy capabilities for Polaris A2 were anticipated for early 1963 and for the Air Force's Minuteman ICBM in late 1964. 'Our advanced ballistic missile re-entry system research program,' it predicted, 'will provide basic technology from which to design new re-entry systems for any of our ballistic missile programs over the longer term.' There remained, nevertheless, 'many complex technical problems and, partly owing to our payload capacities, some difficult compromises between warhead and penetration packages.'[63]

The US Navy's Special Projects Office, along with Lockheed, was however already working on the design and development of a new and more advanced Polaris A3 missile which was intended to offer much longer range – 2,500 nautical miles – than its predecessors. It also introduced a major innovation for missile design with the Mark 2 re-entry system, where, after nose cone ejection, three re-entry bodies, and the warheads within, were tilted out to an angle on their base frame, dispensed by small short-burn solid rocket motors from the top of the missile's second stage, spun for additional accuracy, and delivered to their target in a claw-like cluster. The effect of the three W-58 warheads, each with a yield of 200 kilotons, exploding over a single target would be analogous to a one megaton blast, fulfilling the Navy's objectives for the A3 system's damage potential against a large urban-industrial area. The triple REB configuration also gave the system, it was assumed, some capability to penetrate an ABM defence modelled on the performance of the Nike-Zeus system. The explosion of a single nuclear warhead carried by an ABM interceptor with an equivalent yield to that carried by a Zeus missile (about 20 kilotons), it was believed, would not have sufficient kill radius to neutralise more than one warhead within the incoming cluster dispensed by the A3 system.

Flight testing of the A3, which ran from July 1962 to August 1964, with its complex re-entry system, new guidance system, and much finer tolerances – where weight was sacrificed for range, and higher temperatures produced by more energetic propellants than in previous variants – was not without its problems. First operational deployment, nevertheless, eventually took place on the USS *Daniel Webster* in September 1964.[64] By that same year, the US research and development budget for penetration aids was in the region of $200 million (for example, a new suite of decoys for Polaris A3, PX-2, was tested at this time but never introduced). In the competition between the designers of ABM defensive systems and offensive ballistic missiles, McNamara clearly thought that the latter would continue to have the upper hand and that investment in offensive capabilities was more cost effective than an uncertain and technically demanding defence.

At the height of the Cuban missile crisis Marshal Rodion Malinovsky, the Soviet Defence Minister, was reported to have boasted of Soviet prowess in the ABM realm, saying that 'complexes of numerous means for defence of the country against an enemy missile-nuclear attack have been designed and manufactured.' In fact, a further series of three Soviet high altitude nuclear tests with a probable ABM application took place on 22 October, 28 October, and 1 November 1962. The tests bore comparison with those conducted the previous autumn, in that they each involved three sets of missiles, fired at intervals of a few minutes apart, being launched from the Kaspustin Yar range. The first of the three missiles would explode at high altitude (the highest test altitude being about 160 nautical miles) above Sary Shagan, presumably to enable its effect on the proceeding pair to be monitored. The highest of the yields recorded was just below two megatons. However, no known exo-atmospheric ABM interceptions were believed to have taken place in Soviet tests, although intercepts up to an altitude of about 150,000 feet had been detected.[65]

The Americans had also continued with an enhanced testing programme during the latter half of 1962 for their Nike-Zeus ABM system with mixed results. Recognising the prohibitively high costs of protecting the major centres of US population and the impossibility of providing a completely full-proof protective screen, McNamara had again signalled as loudly as possible in late 1962 (and in the face of objections from a majority of the JCS) that any discussion of procurement or deployment was premature. In November 1962 he had informed Kennedy that over the past year the United States had 'gained a much broader understanding of the problems of ballistic missile defense, the level of defense that may be achieved, and the characteristics of the most effective system.'[66] Nike-Zeus was already seen as of limited value in the more sophisticated offensive missile environment likely to be encountered in the late 1960s and early 1970s, where decoys would be employed. Instead, several alternatives or modifications to Nike-Zeus had been proposed, with McNamara favouring an improved system – known as Nike-X – which used a new high acceleration short-range interceptor missile called Sprint (which would help overcome the discrimination problem by intercepting warheads at a lower altitude), together with a new phased array radar capable of multiple target acquisition and tracking. Development of the old Zeus missile would continue in the meantime, and would eventually become the Spartan interceptor designed for an exo-atmosphere interception, so giving the whole Nike-X system a two-layer level of defence.[67]

Sprint provided Nike-X with a so-called 'terminal' defence capability, where an interception would take place in the endo-atmosphere (perhaps at a height of 20 to 30 miles), once atmospheric sorting of decoys and chaff had taken place. A terminal component to the defensive system was felt to be particularly appropriate for the protection of missile sites and silos, or command and control centres (what were known as 'hard point' targets, as they could only be eliminated by a direct or near-direct hit), and due to US administration statements this, rather than area defence of large urban areas, where the defender's problems were far greater, was assumed to be the direction where the Americans were going. McNamara himself believed that substantial expenditure on ABM development remained necessary, even if the probability of deployment remained low. Within his own office were several officials who believed that a deployment decision was only likely to provoke the Soviet Union into developing its own penetration aids programme for its growing ICBM force, to increase the numbers of its offensive missiles, and to use larger yield warheads. It was noted, moreover, that the costs of the American penetration aids programme was much lower (perhaps only one fifth) of that devoted to ballistic missile defence; the 'economic advantage', as the President was informed, 'is definitely in favor of the offense.'[68]

Despite increasing pressures from within the administration and from the service chiefs to move ahead with plans for deployment in late 1962, budgetary authority therefore remained limited to ABM development only, with the President content to follow McNamara's recommendations.[69] On 12 December 1962, the US Defense Department announced that another successful anti-ICBM interception had occurred over the Pacific involving the Nike-Zeus system, with one of the two missiles launched reaching 'well within lethal radius' of its target.[70] Nevertheless, the President moved swiftly to scotch any expectation that this might presage a decision on pre-production or even deployment. During a televised interview with several network reporters, partly intended to prepare the public for his upcoming budget proposals, Kennedy stressed the frightening power of the offensive nuclear forces available to both the United States and the Soviet Union. Mentioning Khrushchev's earlier claims to US journalists that the Soviet Union could hit a fly in the sky with its defensive rockets, the President was keen to dispel any idea that a real defence against the threat was possible, saying

> He might hit a fly, but whether he could hit a thousand flies with decoys – you see every missile that comes might have four or five missiles [sic] in it, or would appear to be missiles, and the radar screen has to pick those out and hit them going thousands of miles an hour and select which one is the real missile and which are the decoys when there might be hundreds of objects coming through the air. What you are trying to do is shoot a bullet with a bullet. Now if you have a thousand bullets coming at you, that is a terribly difficult task which we have not mastered yet, and I don't think he has. The offensive has the advantage.

In view of its high costs, and the likelihood of countermeasures being developed, the President could see no value in the United States deploying an ABM system until it was proven to be effective.[71] Kennedy's comments represented a graphic foretaste of the efforts made over many subsequent years by the designers of offensive missile systems to outwit and confuse ABM defences.

British perspectives on ABM defence

Growing interest in the potential for ABM defence raised the issue of whether future work on defensive systems, and on methods of overcoming them, should be pursued in the British government's own defence research establishments. When the Penley working party was set up in late 1961, one senior Ministry of Aviation official, the Director General of Ballistic Missiles, found that its remit suggested that the need for research and development into methods of improving re-entry vehicle design and decoy systems – neglected after Blue Streak cancellation in 1960 – should be re-examined so that missile vulnerability to ABM defence could be reduced. Though RRE continued to look into radar discrimination issues, and re-entry phenomena were the concern of the team working on the Black Knight launcher (a smaller-scale rocket than Blue Streak, developed as a test-bed for the latter's technology), he saw the need for 'a definite programme to develop new types of decoy and to study, by actual experimental work on both model and full-scale, the associated problems of re-entry head design, ejection mechanisms etc.' Some of this kind of work, begun under Blue Streak, had been continued in low key at RAE, but no definite new proposals had since been put forward. Coupled with this was the idea of designing an alternative UK re-entry vehicle for the Skybolt air-launched ballistic missile, as the current US design was regarded as vulnerable. The latter scheme was seen as appropriate work for the new Weapons Department that had just been formed at RAE.[72]

Some very small-scale and speculative work was indeed carried out during the autumn of 1961 on possible decoys for Skybolt by RAE.[73] One senior Ministry of Aviation official was keen to emphasise that 'the whole field of design of low vulnerability re-entry heads and matched decoys is one that was pioneered in the UK in our work on Blue Streak, and even though Skybolt is an American vehicle the UK would have a most valuable contribution to make'.[74]

Appearing in March 1962, the Penley report itself had recommended that work in the field of ballistic missile defence ('a relatively inexpensive UK research programme, integrated with those of America and Canada') should continue, despite its unpromising prospects, as its results would 'indicate the necessary features of an offensive weapon to survive any possible defence.' The priority areas for a research programme were discrimination techniques and re-entry phenomena at high altitude, for which the Black Knight proving rocket could be used. Associated with such work could be studies and tests of decoy design. Further investigation of destruction mechanisms might follow, not least as 'present evidence suggests … that work in this field will lead to changes in designs of our offensive warheads to provide adequate hardening.'[75]

By the time of Blue Streak's cancellation in 1960, in fact, a productive testing programme using Black Knight, focusing on re-entry phenomena, under the codename 'Gaslight', was already well underway at the Woomera rocket range in Australia. Its results were interesting enough to catch the attention of the American authorities, and during 1961 the Black Knight programme attracted offers of financial support from the US Advanced Research Projects Agency (amounting to about $2 million) for sophisticated range and monitoring instrumentation; this joint study of re-entry phenomenon acquired the new codename 'Dazzle'.[76]

Continuing work in the area, it was thought, was one way for the UK to hold onto the skills necessary for designing re-entry vehicles and decoy systems, as well as to understand the issues surrounding discrimination between warheads and decoys. Contributing to American knowledge through such schemes as Dazzle also gave UK scientists access to some aspects of recent US work in the field. ARPA, for example, offered reports on re-entry physics to RAE as a part of the cooperative programme. But the supply of information was not always unconstrained from the US side. Although British representatives were allowed to attend meetings of the Anti-Missile Research Advisory Council held in San Diego at the end of April 1962, they were not given access to many of the sessions, some of which covered sensitive topics related to the penetration of ballistic missile defences.[77]

The British had been looking forward to the next meeting of Sub-Group F under the Tripartite Technical Cooperation Programme, which was hosted by the RRE at Malvern in October 1962. However, the limit of how far the Americans were prepared to go in divulging their technical and scientific knowledge was made apparent from such gatherings. At Malvern, the leader of the US delegation had explained that re-entry data on US operational re-entry vehicles and associated penetration aids could not be shared with the British or Canadians, though data from model testing could.[78] Such exchanges suggested to British officials that an indigenous research programme would be required if the UK was to develop its own knowledge of the techniques of ABM defence and the methods that could be used to overcome them.

The Penley report had also called for a new onus to be placed on intelligence gathering in the ABM field, especially as the Russians appeared to be in the process of developing a deployable system.[79] Soviet military capabilities in general were, of course, a prime area of interest for the British intelligence community, and where developments in guided missiles and rocketry attracted special attention. During the early 1960s, the deployment of steadily rising numbers of Intermediate and Medium Range Ballistic Missiles – covering ranges between 650 and 2,000 nautical miles – at sites in the western part of the Soviet Union, was an obvious cause of major concern to defence planners and intelligence analysts, not least as it drastically reduced the warning time of nuclear attack on the UK home base (and so could conceivably catch the V-bomber force on the ground before it could be launched in retaliation), and increased the sheer numbers of nuclear warheads that could be targeted at Britain. Alongside this had to be considered evidence that Soviet ICBM numbers were also increasing. In an effort to improve their collation and evaluation of such evidence, in the summer of 1961 the Joint Intelligence Committee decided to establish a Missile Threat Coordination Sub-Committee, serviced by its own inter-service working party, which would keep under review information on guided missiles of all types held or being developed by the Soviet bloc countries, or any others 'whose policies may affect British interests,' and report to its parent body at periodic intervals.[80]

Collating the initial set of findings from its new Sub-Committee, the JIC issued a brief paper in March 1962 which attempted to sum up the Soviet missile threat over the next few years. The only comment offered on ABM development was that the Russians were expected to create a ballistic missile early warning system, and 'after 1963, a limited active system of defence against ballistic missiles ... could be deployed to provide a measure of protection for a very small number of important targets.' Included in the conclusion of the report was the comment that despite the increase in defensive capability forecast over the next few years, the Soviet Union was still 'likely to be threatened by a degree of retaliatory destruction ... which it will consider unacceptable.'[81]

In the more detailed paper from the Missile Threat Coordination Sub-Committee that had underpinned these conclusions, was contained the stronger statement that there was 'firm evidence that the USSR is pursuing an extensive high priority programme for the development of ballistic missile defences.' Construction of test facilities at Sary Shagan was first thought to have begun in 1956, but as yet there was no evidence that the Russians were staging tests that involved decoy discrimination techniques. If the Russians did deploy a simple ABM system after 1963 it was estimated it would be designed to intercept during the terminal stages of an offensive missile's flight and would have 'an extremely low capability against decoy-masked ballistic missile nose-cones,' though it was thought 'probable' that work on discrimination was being carried out.[82] A more categorical assessment was made by the Assistant Chief of the Air Staff (Intelligence) in February 1962, when he responded to a query from the Secretary of State for Air about Soviet ABM development with a summary of the latest intelligence. It was claimed that

> Evidence now available indicates that the Soviets are well into the field development phase of an ABM system and that weapon evaluation probably started in 1961. If a decision to deploy has already been taken the Soviets would be in a position to deploy elements of an ABM defence by the end of 1963. Such a system would be limited to the partial defence of one target, say Moscow, but it would have little decoy discrimination capability and the interception would take place in the terminal part of a missile's flight probably at a height which would not be greater than 80,000 feet.

A more sophisticated system giving more comprehensive cover to a larger number of targets could be deployed, it was believed, by 1967, and though it would have greater discrimination capability, it would still be designed to intercept within the atmosphere. The report concluded that it would not be until 'well into the 1970s' before the Soviet Union would have developed advanced early warning and target tracking equipment and techniques to allow for mid-trajectory interception of targets, outside the earth's atmosphere.[83]

In the spring of 1963, the MoD's Long Term Study Group – as the original JIGSAW group had now become – submitted the latest synopsis of views on anti-ICBM defence, and particularly its technical feasibility, following a request from Zuckerman. It repeated the familiar point that though it was conceivable for defensive missiles to intercept and destroy incoming warheads, once effective decoys were introduced the problems for the defender multiplied so quickly that 'no worthwhile' defensive system had yet been devised for interception during the re-entry phase. Intercepting a missile during its boost phase, and before it had had a chance to disperse either warheads or decoys, was also a very exacting task, requiring very early detection of a launch, and directing a defensive missile to the launch area in perhaps only two or three minutes. Mid-course interception was another possibility, but here there seemed to be major problems for discriminating between warheads and decoys, as the effects of atmosphere re-entry had not yet acted to filter incoming decoys.[84] British assessments of the effectiveness of ABM defensive systems, in other words, mirrored the judgements of those sceptics within the US defence science community who believed that improvements to the penetration performance of attacking ballistic missiles could always be made which would allow a defence to be overcome.

The BNDSG and the criteria of deterrence

The potential for the Soviet Union to deploy an effective ballistic missile defence was one of the factors which had to be taken into consideration by the British Nuclear Deterrent Study Group's technical sub-committee, which since late 1960, and under Zuckerman's guidance, had been examining the pros and cons of different forms of successor system to the V-force.[85] As the latter process was carried out, familiar struggles between the Admiralty and Air Ministry continued over the various merits, drawbacks and costs attached to a submarine or airborne carrier for the next generation of deterrent. A major source of contention in the debates that ensued concerned the criterion of deterrence, amounting to 50 per cent destruction of 40 Soviet cities, that still served to inform the BNDSG's requirements for a deterrent system in the future. In order to meet this standard, the Air Ministry's working assumption during 1961 was that by the mid-1960s the existing strategic nuclear deterrent force would have to comprise 72 Vulcan Mark 2 bombers, armed with two Skybolt missiles each, supported by up to 32 Victor Mark 2 aircraft carrying the Blue Steel stand-off missile. The figure of 72 Vuclans with two Skybolts had simply been derived from halving the older approved V-bomber force level of 144 aircraft, carrying one megaton-yield free fall bomb each. The obvious drawback to such a force was its vulnerability to pre-emptive attack on the ground, even if techniques of rapid airfield dispersal were practised in time of war. Over the longer term, and looking beyond about 1970, the prospect of metal fatigue in the V-force meant the aircraft would eventually have to be replaced.[86]

Formulated during the course of 1961, the Air Ministry's proposals for the deterrent after about 1970 involved replacing the V-bombers with a version of the VC10 long-range transport and tanker aircraft which was already in an advanced stage of development, adapted to carry four or even six improved Skybolt missiles, with a portion of the force on constant airborne patrol. This was an operational posture which it was recognised would be very expensive to maintain but which would be necessary if arguments about the vulnerability of a bomber force tied to fixed bases were to be overcome.

The Air Ministry's calculations of the size of its putative VC10 force was based on meeting the same 40 city criterion as the V-bomber force was expected to fulfil. Some, however, questioned whether this would be an appropriate measure in the future. In January 1961, the Chief of the Air Staff had told the Air Council, with the Secretary of State for Air in attendance, that though the precise figure was 'a matter of judgement', he thought the 40-city criterion 'seemed about right.' The Scientific Adviser to the Air Ministry, however, wondered if this might be 'excessive', as 'unless for some reason Russia was desperate, a much smaller threat would surely suffice to deter her from deliberate aggression.' The retort of the Permanent Secretary at the Air Ministry, Sir Maurice Dean, was that it was wise to aim high as 'any safety margin it contained might well be taken up in the event by shortfalls in performance,' perhaps through the unserviceability of equipment. The Air Council's conclusion was that 50 per cent destruction of 40 Russian cities was a valid measurement of the necessary deterrent capability of a UK strategic nuclear force.[87] From the Ministry of Aviation, Sir Robert Cockburn (a BNDSG member) also wondered if the scale of the deterrent threat should be reappraised in view of 'the excessive counter-threat which could be brought to bear on us', and 'our relatively modest military stature overseas.' It would also be worth considering, Cockburn felt, 'whether we have any hope with inferior resources of sustaining such a damaging threat against the Russian heartland as her defences improve ... should we be seeking some alternative target system more compatible with our stature and therefore more politically viable?'[88]

After much delay, Zuckerman's technical sub-committee submitted its final report on the issues involved in late July 1961. Despite the best efforts of the Air Ministry, the overall effect of the report was to accord a submarine-based Polaris force several advantages over an aircraft on constant air patrol equipped with a longer-range version of the existing design of Skybolt missile. Although the sub-committee had employed the 40 city criterion to determine the size and character of capability that was required for a future force, at an early stage the report acknowledged that its adoption of this benchmark was merely 'convenient'. A less-powerful deterrent, it was suggested, could also be conceived and still be regarded as constituting 'a significant contribution to the Western Deterrent, provided those forces are large enough to be operationally viable.' The sub-committee thought that more study into the existing criteria of deterrence should be undertaken. Development of a practical defence against ballistic missiles would, it was noted, require the addition of counter-measures to re-entry vehicles, perhaps involving the reduction of their radar-echoing area, or the use of decoys in missile payloads.

Following the earlier advice from the Ministry of Aviation, the limitations of ABM defence were stressed by the sub-committee. Although it was admitted that interception of an attacking missile was possible, there was considered to be

> no economic solution in sight to the problem of discriminating a warhead from the accompanying cloud of matched and unmatched decoys of a

sophisticated ballistic missile. Other countermeasures to assist penetration are available to the ballistic missile designer and have not yet been exploited. There is nothing to indicate that in 1970–80 [sic] he will not be able to maintain the economic and technical advantage which he now possesses over the defence.

As for the main topic of the paper, it simply drew together the known advantages and drawbacks to a submarine-based missile force, or one relying on airborne carriers on continuous patrol.[89]

Although the inference from this was that submarines were ultimately preferable, no positive recommendations were made in the report's conclusions. Admiralty officials were left ruefully to remark that though the balance of the report 'was clearly in favour of Polaris submarines ... the conclusion was shirked.' There was nevertheless a conviction that firm decisions were needed soon on a successor, and that any predilection to delay more action should be resisted; or as one Admiralty official advised: '... if there is any pretence of approaching this question fairly and with open minds, the question should be discussed now. If a decision to provide a Polaris fleet in succession to Skybolt in V-bombers is ever to be taken, it is in fact none too soon to start making firm plans this year.'[90]

The sub-committee's inferred preference for Polaris, moreover, was fully in accord with the Foreign Office's own reading of the potential vulnerabilities of an airborne deterrent during the 1970s. But acceptance of the sub-committee's views carried the necessary political corollary that purchase of Polaris from the Americans would entail some form of nuclear sharing within NATO. Crucially, it also undercut the case for acquiring Skybolt, since its effective operational life would only last for the five years between 1965 and 1970, after which a Polaris force could be available.[91]

As for the Minister of Defence, Watkinson was wary about the costs of the whole enterprise. Doubting whether it would be in the capacity of British industry to produce a new home-grown missile, he could see no other option than buying another US delivery system. Although understanding the operational advantages of Polaris, it would be expensive to introduce and he seems initially to have been drawn to the VC10 option championed by the Air Ministry. Of one thing Watkinson was certain, despite the pressures on defence spending: '... I see nothing at the moment that will cause us to leave this field. I am very opposed to our so doing, except as part of a very large package deal on disarmament or on some general rationalisation of the Western Deterrent. It is time, therefore, that we charted our future course.'[92]

The outgoing chairman of the BNDSG, Sir Edward Playfair, predicted that receipt of Zuckerman's sub-committee report would lead to a 'bloodletting or steam-discharging second reading debate.'[93] Regarding the timescale for a decision over a successor system, the advice given in September 1961 to the incoming Permanent Under Secretary at the MoD, Sir Robert Scott, was that if we think that Skybolt will take care of our needs until about 1970, and if we think that the system we should use in the 70s (if any) should be an American-designed one, then we can leave the subject alone for a couple of years at least. If, however, we have doubts about Skybolt, or if we want to follow it with a weapon which is *not* American designed, decisions are needed earlier.[94]

Presenting his first paper to the BNDSG as its new chairman, Scott noted that it would in essence say that 'we should not change or hedge our plans about depending on Skybolt for the coming decade; that we should not embark on designing a system of our own for the 1970s; and that we should be in no hurry about deciding what American system we should try to obtain for the 1970s.'[95]

Given the lack of urgency, and despite the Admiralty's frustration, it is therefore not surprising to find that it took until November 1961 for the BNDSG to convene only its second meeting of the year, where it gathered to discuss the technical sub-committee's findings. Here it was acknowledged that it would be politically impossible for the Government to backtrack on its commitment to Skybolt, especially as the US administration had recently affirmed its intention to continue with the project and progress with the missile's development appeared to be satisfactory. Attempting to sidestep the objections of the Vice Chief of the Air Staff to any clear-cut endorsement of Polaris as the best next generation deterrent system, Scott observed that a paper might go to ministers which, mirroring the approach of the sub-committee, simply presented the 'facts of the situation', rather than offer any recommendations.[96]

Nevertheless, having discussed the matter with Watkinson further during the autumn, by December Scott was resolved that he would draft his own paper in an attempt to break the evident log-jam between the Air Ministry and Admiralty, and that (in a departure from the BNDSG's original terms of reference) this final paper should address the basic political and strategic arguments which were used to justify the UK's possession of a deterrent force.[97] Again Watkinson, however, could see no case for early decisions, telling Scott,

> it is clearly in our interest to contribute to the nuclear deterrent if we can. Only by doing so can we stay in close relations with [the] USA in this vital field, which because it must include means of delivery, gives us also some insight into rocketry and space. But we must pay the minimum subscription to stay in the club. This means that we must use what we have got as far as possible and buy the remainder from the USA. I agree we cannot make the missile. We have the V bombers; we must be sure whether they are valid until 1968/9/70. As successors we are bound to have to make a fairly substantial investment in VC 10s or similar aircraft for RAF Transport Command. If these are economic carriers for Skybolt

then a V Bomber/VC 10 solution might be cheapest way of staying in the club … [but] I do not believe we can decide which to go for until we see whether Skybolt really works (about 12 months?) If it does, I think we are probably obliged to buy it. If we buy it, probably it has a longer life than the V bombers [i.e. mounted on VC 10s].[98]

Admiralty impatience at this state of affairs was meanwhile growing. In mid-December, Lord Carrington, the First Lord of the Admiralty, tried to prompt Watkinson toward more decisive action with a minute arguing that, although the Navy had been working on the 'hybrid' concept for a nuclear submarine which combined a hunter/killer capability with the ability to launch Polaris missiles, on his reading of the technical sub-committee's report, a force of 16-missile, single-purpose Polaris boats was

> militarily the best solution. It is the nearest approach yet devised to an invulnerable and therefore 'inevitable' second strike weapon system, with the mobility to pose a threat against any country in the world, and the minimum likelihood of its ever being used by mistake. The [new] Polaris A3 missile will have great technical advantages, especially in its range of 2,500 miles and its payload that will accommodate a megaton warhead [sic – actually three 200 kiloton warheads] and decoys too.

Carrington also wondered whether, in view of the heavy financial costs of maintaining the deterrent, the BNDSG 40 city criterion 'should itself be challenged as arbitrary and unnecessarily large. It can be argued that the military and political objectives for which we maintain this capability could just as surely be achieved with half that deterrent power.' If the criteria were lowered, Carrington saw the best system as a force of four 16-missile submarines, which he saw as the smallest that was operationally viable, and which would be able to inflict 'at least' 65 per cent damage on 20 Russian cities. Including warheads, missiles and supporting naval facilities, the whole force could be delivered, he estimated, for the sum of £218 million.[99]

Judgements over the required level of damage to Soviet targets were, it was plain, becoming fundamental to the disputes between the Air Ministry and the Admiralty over the future form of the deterrent. As Watkinson had observed, one of the attractions of the concept of an airborne nuclear force was that it relied on an aircraft that was already part of the RAF's plans, and could use Skybolt (or a later version of the same missile). The initial capital costs for assembling an airborne force would be lower than that of the large numbers of Polaris submarines that would need to be built in order to meet a 40 city criterion (while such an extensive ballistic missile-carrying submarine-building programme would also potentially disrupt the Navy's plans to introduce a new force of nuclear-powered hunter-killer submarines, hence the Admiralty's interest in the hybrid concept). In one paper of January 1962 prepared by the Treasury on the basis of information from both the Air Ministry and Admiralty, to achieve the capability of 50 per cent destruction of 40 Soviet cities with an airborne deterrent would involve 45 Skybolt missiles, each armed with a half megaton warhead, arriving on target. If each aircraft could carry six missiles, and allowing for the possibility of missile malfunction, this would in turn require a force of 12–13 VC10s to be on constant airborne patrol. The demands of constant patrolling meant that an overall force of 36 VC10s was envisaged, equipped with 160 missiles and 91 warheads. However, to achieve the same capability with a submarine force, where 42 Polaris A2 missiles each with a single one megaton warhead were needed on target, would take four boats on constant alert and ready to fire. Allowing for the need for refits and refurbishments, it was calculated that the overall force would have to be eight submarines, with 128 missiles and 128 warheads. In overall terms, and due to its higher running costs, the estimate for an airborne system from the period 1964/65 up to 1979/80 was put at £1,480 million, while that of a seaborne system was somewhat lower at £1,230 million.[100]

The main financial weak spot in the Air Ministry's scheme was therefore perceived to be the high costs of maintaining a VC10 permanent air alert force, with many more personnel required to operate the aircraft and maintain their bases. The advantage the Air Ministry held was the lower unit cost of a VC10 carrier as opposed to a Polaris submarine, and it was this issue that was to play a vitally important role in the debate over deterrent capability that eventually took place within the BNDSG. The Air Ministry was patently unhappy with the way the Navy had arrived at a minimum figure of eight submarines for its Polaris force, while the Air Ministry had been working to a more precise BNDSG target list, with the 'firm expectation' of inflicting 50 per cent damage on all 40 cities it had targeted, 'including the largest cities in Russia.' If the Admiralty had to reach the same goal, they would, it was maintained, need nine submarines, or as many as 13 if the yield of the Polaris warhead was lower than expected.[101]

In the event, the Air Ministry used the Admiralty's methods of assigning warheads to targets as a way to reduce their total requirement for aircraft (down from 36 to 27), and hence running costs, but they were still undercut by the Polaris force's long-term overall costs. The whole issue was muddied further by the First Sea Lord's enthusiasm for a force of smaller hybrid hunter-killer Polaris submarines, which would lower overall costs, but 'at the expense of a substantial reduction in the damage levels of our deterrent.' The Air Ministry could see a danger that 'the Admiralty's cut price deterrent may have exercised a fatal attraction in certain quarters.' One official complained that 'if we are to conduct a Dutch auction in deterrence the Air Ministry is preparing a similar bid, and it should not be assumed that the Admiralty enjoy a monopoly of this sort of tactics.' As it transpired, the idea of some members of the Air Staff to submit their own proposals for a 'cut price rival' to the hunter-killer Polaris idea was deferred, as the CAS was keen that the issue should be 'played as long as possible on the basis that there can be no question of departing from the currently accepted criteria of what constitutes a valid deterrent without reference to the Chiefs of Staff.'[102]

By the end of 1961, having studied some of the preliminary costings that were being attached both to future airborne and seaborne deterrent systems, Scott had become convinced that generating a force designed to meet the old 40 city criterion would prove prohibitively expensive. It would also expose the MoD's plans for a next generation system to unwelcome Treasury criticism, and could even open up a political debate over whether the Government should try to preserve a deterrent capability during the 1970s. Scott was, moreover, now more inclined to see the advantages in Polaris as an invulnerable, second strike weapon. His attempts to summarise his views and reach consensus within the BNDSG were by this stage thwarted by consistent Air Ministry objections.[103]

It was in this context, and in an attempt to open up the sorts of options that Carrington had suggested, that Scott decided in early January 1962 that a formal study should be made of the damage criteria of deterrence. It was a source of wonder to some that this kind of work had not been carried out before. As one MoD official confessed in a minute to the JIC Secretary (and future Cabinet Secretary), John Hunt, 'We in this Department are not very clear where this [40 city] criteria of damage came from, and we do not know whether it was ever submitted to the JIC for judgment or for approval. You may be able to enlighten us.' Aside from this, it was now felt necessary for the JIC to see whether this was still the right level of deterrence to aim for. 'My feeling is,' the MoD official continued, 'that during the last year we have come to regard earlier estimates of what was necessary as probably too large; and that this is not simply a rationalisation based on the need to save money, but a real change of opinion caused by the growing realisation of just what damage a megaton attack would really mean. This, however, is private speculation, and is no basis for the work of the Study Group. What we need, and what Sir Robert has asked me to request from you, is the JIC's estimate of the level of deterrence which it would be prudent for the BNDSG to take as a basis for their discussions.'[104]

It was also of significance that Sir Hugh Stephenson, the then JIC Chairman, was also the Foreign Office representative on the BNDSG. After discussion between Scott and Stephenson, terms of reference for a study were issued to the members of the Joint Intelligence Staff on 11 January 1962. They were asked to examine a) whether a strike force capable of 'knocking out the 40 largest cities in the USSR' would inflict a level of retaliatory damage sufficient to deter Soviet leaders 'from action against the vital interests of the UK'; and b) would such a capability directed against 20 Soviet cities be enough, and c) if both questions were answered positively, what would be the minimum number of cities to be knocked out for the deterrent to be sufficient.[105] When Stephenson gave an outline of the proposed study to his JIC colleagues he added that,

It might be argued that for a nuclear war to start without the United States becoming involved was inconceivable but, by the 1970s, this (though unlikely) was by no means impossible. It would therefore be necessary for the JIC's examination of the problem to be made on the assumption that the United States would not be involved. Similarly, it would be necessary to assume that the Soviet leaders would believe that we would in fact in certain circumstances order a nuclear attack, even though this would result in the virtual annihilation of the whole of the UK. The paper would be a difficult one to prepare both on account of its hypothetical nature and the absence of precise intelligence on which to work. Nevertheless a realistic and objective appreciation of the nature of Soviet thinking on this matter would be of great value to Ministers and the JIC were perhaps in a better position to estimate this than any other body.

There were immediate objections, however, one JIC member finding that the questions posed were 'unanswerable' unless they were related to specific circumstances. The subject was best approached, in fact, from the perspective of looking at what any Russian leader might hope to gain from offensive action:

it was necessary to ask what conceivable Russian purpose (other than the defence of the USSR) could possibly justify in their eyes the destruction of even one city. Even the present Berlin situation must be preferable for the Russians to one city being wiped out. They were not so materialistic as to disregard the appalling loss of life in a large city, nor so foolish as to disregard the devastating effect on their public opinion. It was therefore misleading to try to rationalise the effect of a deterrent. It was even unrealistic to try to calculate the circumstances in which nuclear war might deliberately be started, since we had always appreciated that it would almost certainly be started only by mistake or by accident.

Further discussion in the Committee yielded the view that though it might seem unlikely that the UK would decide to launch an independent nuclear strike against the Soviet Union, 'there might be a point at which our vital interests and our national honour was at stake to such an extent that there seemed no alternative.' In an effort to overcome some of the reservations that had been expressed, Stephenson suggested that the Joint Intelligence Staff should be allowed to add 'riders' to its work, mentioning such qualifications and caveats.[106]

The Joint Intelligence Staff had only a week to carry out their exacting task. They relied, it is apparent, on the large amount of data that had been gathered by the JIB on the make-up of cities, economic activity, critical infrastructure, and demographic patterns in the Soviet Union, and converted this into a mathematical scale to try to assign value to particular targets. Initially, it is apparent, the Staff also tried to define more closely the circumstances in which a UK nuclear strike might be delivered. A first draft of their work did not find favour within the Air Ministry who did not like the methodology involved and its neglect of psychological factors, which it was believed could lead to the conclusions of the study being 'dangerously misleading'.[107] The Staff, nevertheless, continued to refine their draft despite such objections, and on 23 January the JIC gave its stamp of approval to their efforts, issuing the final report as JIC(62)10.

This important JIC report argued that the only practical approach to the problem of assessing what would constitute unacceptable damage in Soviet eyes was to look at how the Soviet Union would stand after a UK nuclear attack in relation to the United States, and perhaps China as well. This was rationalised on the grounds that Russian leaders would 'clearly be unwilling to accept such a degree of damage from the United Kingdom as would severely reduce the Soviet Union's economic and military strength in its struggle to overtake the United States and dominate the world.' Using their JIB information, the JIC report gave a points score to each Soviet city with a population of more than 50,000. One point was given to a city for every increment of 50,000 population, and additional points were added according to whether a city was a particular administrative centre for a region or district, was a centre of economic control, was the home of a major military headquarters, or served as an important telecommunications hub. From the 40 major cities in the Soviet Union subjected to this crude quantitative analysis, was generated a grand total of 888 points. The report made the observation that the top five cities out of the 40 city list between them accounted for 335 points out of this grand total, and Moscow alone registered 136 points. This reasoning led the JIC report to conclude that the destruction of the Soviet Union's 40 largest cities would be 'quite unacceptable' to the Russians, that the destruction of 20 major cities would be 'an unacceptable blow at [the] Soviet long-term economy and would seriously weaken the immediate Soviet military potential.' To the final question they had been posed, of what would be the minimum number of cities that would represent an acceptable deterrent, the JIC confessed 'We cannot give a clear cut answer.' However, using the same statistical methods, their key conclusion was that 'it would not be unreasonable to say that the Soviet leaders would consider that the certain destruction of their five largest cities would put them at an unacceptable disadvantage in relation to the United States.'[108]

The 'rider' that was added to the JIC report explained that its work had been driven by a quantitative approach, and had not, for example, 'discussed psychological, technical, or political considerations affecting the credibility or size of the deterrent, nor have we taken account of questions of vulnerability and operational viability.'[109] The latter subjects were certainly relevant to the BNDSG's debates over the form the deterrent should take in the 1970s, but the psychological or political arguments which might affect perceptions of the credibility and size of the deterrent force had obvious applicability to the level of threat which it might have to present. The inference from such remarks was that if a wider study taking such factors into account had been undertaken, then the results could well have been different (the form of words employed was actually proposed by the Air Ministry, which suggests its officials believed such a wider study would have propounded a higher threshold of damage). It was the Air Ministry's interventions that resulted in the JIC report being couched in such overtly tentative terms. As one minute for the Chair of the JIC put it, 'You will appreciate I am sure that the Air Ministry do not hold there to be anything sacrosanct about the "40 city concept" but if a statement is to be made which might be interpreted as lending support to a "5 city concept" then the Air Ministry do feel that such a statement should be rather carefully qualified.' The attempts of early drafts of the report to define the conditions under which the UK might use its deterrent force in an independent and unilateral fashion were also successfully vetoed, and it was made abundantly clear that the Air Ministry had considerable objections to the basic premise of the exercise, one revised draft of the report being met with the response: 'the whole essence of deterrent philosophy is such that neither we nor the Soviet leaders can predict the precise circumstances in which we might be prepared to use our nuclear strike forces in isolation. To attempt to rationalise the deterrent confuses rather than illuminates the issues involved.'[110]

All this hardly amounted to fulfilling the initial injunction from Stephenson to the JIC that their paper should convey 'a realistic and objective appreciation of the nature of Soviet thinking on this matter'. The shortcomings of the final product were clearly recognised by the JIC Secretary. The Committee 'not altogether surprisingly', Hunt noted, 'found the greatest difficulty in writing this paper since it is very difficult to conceive a situation to fit the assumptions and it is only in relation to a specific aim that one can say what degree of damage would be a worthwhile price for the Russians to pay.' The result was, as Hunt acknowledged, that the lowest five cities benchmark was 'hedged round with reservations.' 'In so far as a purely mathematical assessment can be of value,' Hunt ventured, 'the Report is not unreasonably argued and may be of some help to the British Nuclear Deterrent Study Group (in providing a philosophical argument for a small deterrent).' Nevertheless, Hunt felt that the report would be 'misleading to the general reader' and so did not consider that it should be forwarded to ministers. This was a view with which the then Cabinet Secretary, Sir Norman Brook, concurred.[111]

The tentative conclusions of JIC(62)10 did not have an immediate impact on the formulation of strategic nuclear policy. The report was, after all, commissioned with the intention of helping to inform the BNDSG's work on the minimum size of a UK deterrent force which could be introduced during the 1970s. It did not, for example, play any substantive role in the discussions between ministers and officials which took place during the course of 1962 over the immediate numbers of Skybolt missiles and warheads that should be ordered for the V-force for deployment in the latter half of the decade. Here, debate centred on a reduction in the base line for calculations of the damage capability of the V-bomber/Skybolt force from Bomber Command's 40 city criterion to an arbitrarily-determined lower figure. Indeed, it was the mid-range standard of 20 cities, conveyed in the JIC study's original terms of reference, which tended to be taken as a reasonable estimate of what the Russians would regard as unacceptable damage.

Nevertheless, it should be recognised that JIC(62)10 represented the first time that the subject of the criteria of deterrence had been studied in a systematic manner, where an attempt had been made to assess what the Soviet leadership would consider 'unacceptable damage' rather than taking the existing strategic nuclear capability as a starting point. Nevertheless, its methodology, as many of those involved in the process at the time recognised, was driven by a questionable quantitative analysis of target 'value' and it took no account of numerous other factors. Moreover, by postulating a retaliatory attack against the five largest Soviet cities, with Moscow at the top of the target list, it was directing the UK strategic nuclear force against those areas of the Soviet Union which could be accorded some degree of protection by the deployment of an effective ABM defensive system (the signs of which were only gradually to become apparent during the remainder of 1962). This inherent dilemma in targeting policy was not yet obvious to British nuclear planners who by the end of the year were to be faced with a much greater threat to the preservation of an independent deterrent from the US decision to cancel the Skybolt programme. Before considering the major shift in course that this development engendered, however, we must first return to the debates over the future of the deterrent that occurred amongst ministers and officials during 1962 and their relationship to the evolving views of the Kennedy administration toward the possession of national nuclear forces by its NATO allies.

Notes

1 See, in general, Desmond Ball, *Politics and Force Levels: The Strategic Missile Program of the Kennedy Administration* (1980).
2 See Schlosser, *Command and Control*, 255–7, 265.
3 See Kaplan, et al., *McNamara Ascendancy*, 298–302; and for this issue in general see Christopher A. Preble, *Kennedy and the Missile Gap* (DeKalb, 2004).
4 Kaplan, et al., *McNamara Ascendancy*, 60–63; for York's reservations see also, 'US Expert Doubts Full ICBM Defence,' *New York Times*, 17 February 1961.
5 See McNamara letter to President Kennedy, 20 February 1961, and attached 'Memorandum on Review of FY 1961 and FY 1962 Military Programs and Budgets,' *Foreign Relations of the United States, 1961–1963, Volume VIII: National Security Policy* (Washington, 1996), 41.
6 See Yanarella, *Missile Defense Controversy*, 61–72.
7 Memorandum from the Joint Chiefs of Staff for McNamara, 8 April 1961, *FRUS, 1961–1963, Volume VII: Arms Control and Disarmament* (Washington, 1995), 38–41.

8 See Baucom, *Origins of SDI*, 16–7, 19–20.
9 See BND(SG)(60)17, 'A Weapons System for the Later Period: Proposal for an Independent Technical Study,' 21 November 1960; BND(SG)(60) 5th Meeting, 18 November 1960, DEFE 10/665.
10 Ministry of Aviation report, 'Active Defence Against Strategic Missiles in the Period 1970/80,' W5/11A6, 18 January 1961, AVIA 65/1781.
11 The report was adopted as BND(TSC)(61)3, 18 January 1961, AVIA 65/1869; see also Moore, *Nuclear Illusion, Nuclear Reality*, 129.
12 J. E. Serby letter to A. G. Touch, 17 July 1961, AVIA 65/1869.
13 Memorandum by McNamara for the NSC, 15 May 1961, *FRUS, 1961–1963, VII*, 62.
14 Memorandum of conversation: Meeting of Committee of Principals on Nuclear Test Negotiations, 23 May 1961, ibid, 74.
15 See Freedman, *Soviet Strategic Threat*, 87; Podvig, *Russian Strategic Nuclear Forces*, 450.
16 See Zuckerman minute for Macmillan, SZ/859/61, 6 September 1961; and de Zulueta note for Zuckerman, 12 September 1961, PREM 11/3582.
17 DSI Special Report No 44, 'Missile Considerations of 1961 Series Soviet Nuclear Tests,' December 1961, PUSD records, FCO; JIC(62)24, 'Soviet Nuclear Weapons Progress,' 27 February 1962, CAB 158/100; NIE 11–2A-62, 'The Soviet Atomic Energy Program,' 16 May 1962, CIA Freedom of Information electronic reading room; DSTI report, 'The Soviet Anti-Missile Missile Programme: Outline Intelligence Report from Inception to March 1966,' D/DSTI/127/4, 31 March 1966, LSW/1344/01 Part 2, MoD records; NIE 11–11–66, 'Impact of a Threshold Test Ban Treaty on Soviet Military Programs,' 25 May 1966, Intelligence File, Lyndon B. Johnson Library (LBJL).
18 'Russian Reports Solving Rocket Defense Problem,' 24 October 1961, *New York Times*; 'Rockets in Flight "Can be Destroyed",' *The Times*, 24 October 1961.
19 For the organisation of UK scientific and atomic intelligence, see Michael Goodman, *Spying on the Nuclear Bear: Anglo-American Intelligence and the Soviet Bomb* (Stanford, 2007), 186–9.
20 See 'Agreed record of a conversation with Mr A. Potts of the Joint Intelligence Bureau on Thursday, the 15th January 1962;' and 'Agreed record of a conversation with Dr R. C. Knight of the Joint Intelligence Bureau (expert on ballistic missiles) on Monday, the 22nd January 1962', DEFE 19/115.
21 See Sir Steuart Mitchell (Controller of Guided Weapons and Electronics) minute, 'ABM Defence,' GQ/1/05, 25 October 1961; W. H. Penley letter to Mitchell, 'ABM Defence,' W5/11A6/WHP, 31 October 1961, AVIA 65/1781.
22 'ABM Defence Systems: Report of M of A Working Party,' March 1962, AVIA 65/1781.
23 See editorial note, *FRUS, 1961–1963, VII*, 250–51; and Glenn T. Seaborg, *Kennedy, Khrushchev and the Test Ban* (Berkeley, 1981), 124.
24 Makins minute for Scott, CH(61)156, 'Project Pampas,' 1 December 1961, AB 49/14.
25 Makins minute for Macmillan, CH(62)19, 2 March 1962, CAB 21/4755; and see also Walker, *British Nuclear Weapons and the Test Ban, 1954–1973* (Farnham, 2010), 104–5; 220–225; Moore, *Nuclear Illusion, Nuclear Reality*, 152–3.
26 See Makins minute for Brook, CH(61)150, 7 November 1961, and enclosed note for the record, PREM 11/3246; see also Seaborg, *Kennedy, Khrushchev and the Test Ban*, 116–9.
27 See 'William George Penney,' by Lord Sherfield, *Biographical Memoirs of Fellows of the Royal Society*, 1994, 39, 282–302.

28 See ND(61)6(Final), 'Anglo-American Nuclear Tests: Brief for the Prime Minister,' Note by the Secretaries, 15 December 1961; and ND(61)3rd Meeting, 12 December 1961, CAB 134/2238.
29 See Zuckerman, *Monkeys, Men and Missiles*, 316–8.
30 See Zuckerman minute for Macmillan, SZ/1198/61, 15 December 1961, PREM 11/3782.
31 De Zulueta minute for Macmillan, 18 December 1961, PREM 11/3246.
32 Zuckerman minute for Macmillan, SZ/1214/61, 19 December 1961, PREM 11/3246.
33 'Record of a Meeting held in Government House, Bermuda, on Thursday, 21st December 1961, at 5.15pm,' PREM 11/3782. See also Macmillan's own account in Harold Macmillan, *At the End of the Day, 1961–1963* (London, 1973), 145–6.
34 Memorandum of conversation pertaining to nuclear matters, 21 December 1961, *FRUS, 1961–1963, VII*, 272–8.
35 'Record of a Meeting held in Government House, Bermuda, on Thursday, 21st December 1961, at 5.15pm,' PREM 11/3782.
36 Memorandum of conversation pertaining to nuclear matters, 21 December 1961, *FRUS, 1961–1963, VII*, 272–8.
37 Macmillan diary entry, 23 December 1961, Macmillan papers, Bodleian Library; and see Macmillan, *At the End of the Day*, 146.
38 C(62)1, 'Use of Christmas Island for United States Nuclear Tests,' memorandum by the Prime Minister, 1 January 1962, CAB 129/108. See also Macmillan, *At the End of the Day*, 151–2.
39 CC(62) 1st Conclusions, item 3, 3 January 1962, CAB 128/36; CC 1(62), 3rd January 1962, CAB 195/20.
40 CC(62) 2nd Conclusions, item 1, 3 January 1962, CAB 128/36; CC 2(62), 3rd January 1962, CAB 195/20.
41 See Macmillan, *At the End of the Day*, 152–6.
42 Ibid, 167.
43 For an excellent analysis of this whole episode, see Kendrick Oliver, *Kennedy, Macmillan and the Nuclear Test-Ban Debate, 1961–63* (Basingstoke, 1998), 58–86.
44 'Record of a conversation with Sir William Penney on Wednesday, the 17th January 1962,' DEFE 19/115.
45 See Cornford minute for Zuckerman, 'Protective Measures Against ABM Defences,' 18 January 1962; and Cockburn minute for Zuckerman, 'Nuclear Tests,' CS/163, 24 January 1962, DEFE 19/115.
46 'Agreed record of a conversation with Sir Robert Cockburn on Friday, the 19th January 1962, regarding the significance of resuming nuclear tests in the atmosphere and ballistic missile defence,' DEFE 19/115.
47 Zuckerman minute for Watkinson, 30 January 1962, DEFE 19/115.
48 'Spot Check Urged as Arms Solution: Professor's Idea for Ending Impasse Said to Interest Key Soviet Scientists,' *New York Times*, 6 January 1962.
49 Zuckerman letter to de Zulueta, SZ/193/62, 23 February 1962, PREM 11/3719.
50 See, for example, Ewell memorandum of daily White House Staff meeting, 11 December 1961, *FRUS, 1961–1963, VIII*, 227, note 5; Harold Brown Oral History interview, pp. 43–4, 6 May 1964, John F. Kennedy Library (JFKL); Kaplan, et al., *McNamara Ascendancy*, 90.
51 See Yanarella, *Missile Defense Controversy*, 81.
52 See, for example, McNamara's remarks on penetration aids in 'Statement of Secretary of Defense Robert S. McNamara before the Senate Committee on Armed Services, Tuesday, April 4, 1961,' p14, *Declassified Documents Reference System*, 234801.

53 See Spinardi, *From Polaris to Trident*, 66.
54 DRP/P(62)32, British Defence Staffs (Defence Research Staff) Newsletter No 37, pp. 31–3, 1 April 1962, DEFE 10/490.
55 H. R. Hulme minute, 'JOWOG 19 (First Meeting),' AVIS 156(R), 14 June 1962, ES 13/74.
56 Hulme minute, 'JOWOG 19, Draft Brief for 1963 Stocktake,' J19/63/1, 22 April 1963, ES 13/74.
57 See Freedman, *US Intelligence and the Soviet Strategic Threat*, 86–8, 91.
58 Taylor memorandum for Kennedy, 23 August 1962, *FRUS, 1961–1963, VIII*, 380.
59 'Khrushchev Says Missile Can "Hit a Fly" in Space,' *New York Times*, 17 July 1962.
60 Baucom, *Origins of SDI*, 19.
61 DRP/P(63)13, British Defence Staffs (Defence Research Staff) Newsletter No 39, pp. 19–20, 1 October 1962, DEFE 10/454.
62 See 'Nike Zeus Intercepts a Missile Fired from US Over Pacific,' *New York Times*, 20 July 1962.
63 'Specific Problem Areas for US Defense Policy,' annex to memorandum for Kennedy, c. 23 August 1962, *FRUS, 1961–1963, VIII*, 373.
64 See Spinardi, *From Polaris to Trident*, 68–72.
65 NIE 11–2–63, 'The Soviet Atomic Energy Program,' 2 July 1963, National Secuirty File, Files of Charles E. Johnson, box 30, LBJL; NIE 11–11–66, 'Impact of a Threshold Test Ban Treaty on Soviet Military Programs,' 25 May 1966, Intelligence File, LBJL; Macklen minute for Cook, 'Nuclear Weapon Policy,' VHBM/250/67, 3 November 1967, DEFE 25/107.
66 See Kaplan et al., *McNamara Ascendancy*, 124–5; draft memorandum from McNamara for Kennedy, 20 November 1962, *FRUS, 1961–1963, VIII*, 392–3.
67 Baucom, *Origins of SDI*, 19.
68 Draft memorandum from McNamara for Kennedy, 20 November 1962, *FRUS, 1961–1963, VIII*, 397.
69 Memorandum for the record, 23 November 1962, *FRUS, 1961–1963, VIII*, 415–6.
70 'Nike Intercepts Atlas in Flight,' *New York Times*, 13 December 1962.
71 Television and radio interview, 17 December 1962, *The Public Papers of the Presidents: John F. Kennedy, 1962* (Washington, DC, 1964), 896–7; Tom Wicker, 'President Says Cuba Prevented a Soviet Accord,' *New York Times*, 20 December 1962; Kaplan, et al., *McNamara Ascendancy*, 128.
72 W. H. Stephens letter to Mitchell, 'a-BM,' BS/2/01, 6 November 1961, AVIA 65/1781.
73 G. S. Green memorandum, 'Decoys for Skybolt,' 30 October 1961, AVIA 65/1869.
74 E. C. Cornford minute for Zuckerman, 'BNDSG and Skybolt,' 407/101/24/IV, 16 November 1961, DEFE 19/87.
75 'ABM Defence Systems: Report of M of A Working Party,' March 1962, AVIA 65/1781.
76 See DRP/P(62)2, 'US-UK-Canadian Technical Co-operation,' note by the Joint Secretaries, 11 January 1962, DEFE 10/490.
77 DRP/P(62)64, British Defence Staffs (Defence Research Staff) Newsletter No 38, p24, 1 July 1962, DEFE 10/491.
78 DRP/P(62)86, 'US-UK-Canadian Technical Co-operation,' note by the Joint Secretaries, 10 December 1962, DEFE 10/491.
79 'ABM Defence Systems: Report of M of A Working Party,' March 1962, AVIA 65/1781.

80 See CAB 182/11 for material on the formation of the Sub-Committee in 1961, and for terms of reference see JIC(61)52, and JIC(62)106, 20 November 1962, CAB 158/47.
81 JIC(62)28(Final), 'The Soviet Missile Threat up to the end of 1966 as on 1st February 1962,' 20 March 1962, CAB 158/45.
82 JIC(61)66(Final Revise), 'Report No 1 on the Soviet Bloc Missile Threat up to the end of 1966,' 16 March 1962, CAB 158/99.
83 C. D. Tomalin minute for PS to S of S, 'Soviet ABM Development,' ACSA(I)/110/62, 23 February 1962, AIR 19/999.
84 SG(63)6, 'Synopsis of Views on anti-ICBM Defence,' Report No 5/63, 29 March 1963, DEFE 19/21, and in DEFE 10/526, and DEFE 10/543.
85 For the sub-committee's terms of reference, see Zuckerman letter to Hanbury-Brown, SZ/963/60, 1 December 1960, DEFE 19/87.
86 Air Council, Conclusions of Meeting, 2(61), 23 January 1961, AIR 8/2311.
87 Air Council, Conclusions of Meeting, 2(61), 23 January 1961, AIR 8/2311.
88 Cockburn letter to Zuckerman, CS/299, 7 March 1961, DEFE 19/87.
89 BND(TSC)(61)15 (Final), 'British Controlled Contribution to the Nuclear Deterrent,' report by the Technical Sub-Committee, 27 July 1961, DEFE 13/617.
90 K. T. Nash minute for Deputy Chief of the Naval Staff, 'British Nuclear Deterrent Study Group: BND(SG)(61)3,' 24 October 1961, ADM 1/31023.
91 Ramsbotham minute, 'British Nuclear Deterrent Study Group,' 18 August 1961, PUSD records, FCO.
92 Watkinson minute for Scott, 20 June 1961, DEFE 13/311.
93 Playfair minute for Zuckerman, 'BND(SG),' EWP/776/61, 27 July 1961, DEFE 19/87.
94 Chilver minute for Scott, 'British Nuclear Deterrent Study Group,' 8 September 1961, DEFE 19/87.
95 Scott minute for Durlacher, 'British Nuclear Deterrent Study Group,' RHS/102/61, 16 October 1961, DEFE 19/87.
96 BND(SG)(61)2nd Meeting, 29 November 1961, PUSD records, FCO.
97 See 'Note for the record', 18 October 1961; Scott minute for Watkinson, RHS/256/61, 4 December 1961, DEFE 13/617; BND(SG)(61) 3rd Meeting, 18 December 1961, PUSD records, FCO.
98 Watkinson minute for Scott, 7 December 1961, DEFE 13/617.
99 Carrington minute for Watkinson, 18 December 1961, ADM 1/31023.
100 See draft Treasury report on BNDSG Costings, annexes B and C, enclosed with A. D. Peck minute to H. L. Lawrence-Wilson, 11 January 1962, AIR 2/13712.
101 See J. Henderson minute for B. T. Price, 'BNDSG', Science 2/955, and enclosed 'VC 10/Skybolt and Submarine/Polaris Force Requirement,' 15 January 1962; Henderson minute for Butler, 'BNDSG', 16 January 1962; R. C. Kent minute for PS (R. F. Butler) to CAS, 'BNDSG', AUS(A)/5775, 12 January 1962, AIR 2/13712.
102 Kent minute for PS (R. F. Butler) to CAS, 'BNDSG,' AUS(A)/5726, 10 January 1962; R. F. Butler minute for Kent, 'BNDSG,' CAS.130, 12 January 1962, AIR 2/13712; Kent letter to H. L. Lawrence-Wilson, 11 January 1962, DEFE 7/2143.
103 See BND(SG)(61)6, 15 December 1961, 'British Nuclear Deterrent Study Group,' draft memorandum by the Chairman and related material in AIR 19/998.
104 B. T. Price minute for Hunt, BTP/7/62, 9 January 1962, CAB 163/22.
105 JIC(62)10(Terms of Reference), 'The United Kingdom Nuclear Deterrent,' 11 January 1962, CAB 158/45.
106 Confidential Annex to JIC(62)2nd mtg, 11 January 1962, CAB 159/37.

302 *An arms race intensifies*

107 Confidential Annex to JIC(62)4th mtg, 18 January 1962, CAB 159/37.
108 JIC(62)5th mtg, 22 January 1962, CAB 159/37; JIC(62)10(Final), 23 January 1962, 'The United Kingdom Nuclear Deterrent,' CAB 158/45.
109 Ibid.
110 Air Vice Marshal Alick Foord-Kelcey (Assistant Chief of Air Staff (Intelligence)) minute for Sir Hugh Stephenson, 'The United Kingdom Nuclear Deterrent,' ACAS(I)/16/62, 22 January 1962, CAB 163/22.
111 See Hunt minute for J. M. Robertson, JIC/167/62, 'The United Kingdom Nuclear Deterrent,' 23 January 1962, with annotations, CAB 163/22.

8 Revising the criteria, January–May 1962

'Strategy for the Sixties' and the future of the deterrent

While the BNDSG continued its contentious deliberations over which type of deterrent system would best suit Britain's requirements in the 1970s, the government's overall policy towards the long-term future of the independent nuclear deterrent was a subject of continuing uncertainty during the early months of 1962. In his fresh review of future foreign and defence policy, launched in September 1961 with the specific aim of examining what commitments should be maintained over the coming decade, the Prime Minister had clearly been anticipating, in view of the pressure from the Chancellor for cuts to defence spending, a wide-ranging discussion on the future of the deterrent.[1] As an initial step before the launch of a general review of defence and overseas commitments, in January 1962 the COS came forward with a major statement on future strategy, force structure and size, for military operations in circumstances short of global war, in a paper given the title 'Strategy in the Sixties'. This seemed to allow little margin for savings as it envisaged no substantial scaling back of Britain's extensive world-wide defence commitments over the coming decade. The assumption used in the paper was also that an independent contribution to the strategic nuclear forces of the West would be maintained throughout the 1960s at planned levels of expenditure; however, it was anticipated that the position over the deterrent would be reviewed 'in 1962 when the future of Skybolt should be more precisely known.'[2]

Indeed, awareness of the rising costs attached to pursuing the latest trends in nuclear and missile technology made many in government doubt whether a home-produced deterrent system would be a viable proposition over the longer term; such concerns also carried an implication that perhaps no provision for a successor system in the 1970s should even be made. In January 1962, when the Cabinet's Defence Committee discussed 'Strategy in the Sixties', ministers had voiced the telling point that in future estimates of defence spending

> No provision had been made for research, development or production for the purpose of maintaining our independent contribution to the

strategic deterrent when the system based on manned bombers using Skybolt came to the end of its useful life. The cost and complexity of strategic weapons was becoming so great that it might in any case prove impracticable for us to provide a successor to Skybolt: we might have to rely on the purchase of US equipment and weapons. It might perhaps be our best policy to make the most effective political use of our possession of a strategic nuclear capacity within the next 10 years. *For the present, plans should be based on the assumption that there would be no increased expenditure for a new generation deterrent; if at a later stage it became necessary to revise this policy, the allocation of defence finance in general would need to be reconsidered* [emphasis added].

This position was very much in accord with the Prime Minister's personal view. Summing up the meeting's discussion, Macmillan had noted that effort in the nuclear field should be concentrated on

maintaining the effectiveness of a system based on Skybolt for as long after 1970 as possible and no plans should be based at present on the assumption that we should provide for ourselves a further generation of strategic nuclear weapons. It would, however, be open to Ministers to reconsider the question at any time in the next two years.[3]

Macmillan and his colleagues could clearly see that for the UK to produce its own successor system to Skybolt – a project which would involve a new ballistic missile – might be too great a strain on a defence budget which was proving very difficult to control. Left open was the question of whether this would necessarily mean, in the long term, turning to the US for provision of a replacement weapon, but this too would be costly and might encounter political obstacles.

The COS's approach to meeting Britain's worldwide defence commitments during the 1960s called for maintenance of modern conventional forces able to operate far from their home base, combined with the provision of a Strategic Reserve capable of rapid deployment overseas. Coming on top of the NATO commitment to the Central Front in Europe, the rising costs of sophisticated military equipment, and preserving the strategic deterrent, it was clear that there would be no relaxation of the demands placed on the defence budget in the decade ahead.[4] Withdrawal from formal empire, whether in Africa, the Middle East or South East Asia, it was increasingly clear, did not signal any immediate dividend when it came to reductions in Britain's global Cold War defence commitments, with independence arrangements often accompanied by the signing of defence agreements and the maintenance of strategically located bases.

It was against this background that by the end of January 1962 debates within the BNDSG had reached an impasse, with a failure to reach agreement over whether a submarine-based Polaris system, or a new aircraft (such as the VC10) equipped with Skybolt missiles, would prove a better deterrent once the V-bombers had moved out of front line service in the 1970s. One member of the Group, Sir William Cook from the Atomic Energy Authority, thought that apart from the Air Ministry representative (the Vice Chief of the Air Staff, Air Marshal Sir Edmund Hudleston) all of its members were in favour of moving to Polaris, but its work had been frustrated by the Government's continuing commitment to base the deterrent on Skybolt.[5] The costings exercise conducted in late 1961 had, moreover, shown no great overall difference between the alternatives: a submarine force would involve greater initial capital costs than an airborne deterrent, but the eventual running costs of the former would be less than the latter, not least as maintaining a constant airborne alert with sufficient force – essential to ensure invulnerability – would be a very expensive proposition. Indeed, *all* the options looked beyond the nation's means if the current 40 city criterion, used as a yardstick in national nuclear planning, were to be maintained.

From this basic fact, the chair of the BNDSG, Sir Robert Scott, drew the conclusion that the existing criterion would have to be lowered, but it also opened up the possibility for arguing that the credibility of the existing V-force could be prolonged into the 1970s, making early decisions on a successor system less urgent. Within the Air Ministry, the basic attitude was that any moves to reduce the criterion should be resisted. Even though different criteria of deterrence might allow the high costs of maintaining an airborne alert force of VC10 aircraft to be lowered, to Air Ministry officials it would also provide powerful substance to the contention that a submarine force would be an affordable alternative because fewer boats might have to be built (so reducing the initial capital costs of a successor system). But a flat opposition to lowering the damage capability of the UK force was not necessarily seen by all as good tactics. When he first learnt of the Admiralty's concept for a force of hybrid submarines which could meet a 20 city criterion, one senior official remarked that,

> We are not in a strong position to oppose this approach. We are parties to the evolution of a defence strategy whose cost leaves no margin for re-equipping the V-force. What level of threatened damage would really deter Russia is a matter of opinion – unless we argue that a reduced deterrent would not be worth having at all. This would be too dangerous, since there are numbers of people in the discussion who would jump at such a conclusion.

The difficulty for the Air Ministry was in offering any constructive alternatives, and the preference of most officials and senior airmen was to press for a delay in considering the whole matter, not least to allow development and purchase of Skybolt to move a stage further forward.[6]

Armed with the JIC's new conclusions concerning lowering the level of damage which the deterrent might inflict on the Soviet Union, towards the end of January Scott circulated to the members of the BNDSG a revised draft note for the Minister of Defence which attempted to summarise the conclusions reached by his group. Following the assumption adopted in JIC(62)10, Scott agreed with the notion that in order to constitute a valid deterrent, its damage capability would merely have to be enough to alter in significant terms the balance of power between the United States and Soviet Union after an attack had been delivered. As a result he now spoke of the figure of 20 cities as being a sufficient level. This new approach found favour in the Foreign Office, but officials there also referred to the 'basic impossibility' of arriving at any particular figure for cities destroyed, shown by the way the JIC staff had reduced the damage criterion from 40 cities to 20, and then even further to five. An earlier draft of the JIC report, it was observed in revealing fashion, had contained the statement 'it could well be argued that the certain loss of even one major Soviet city (especially Moscow) would be enough to deter the Soviet Union.' Though the 'one city' option had been dropped from the final JIC paper, to one Foreign Office official this showed 'how completely this is a matter of guesswork based on a hazy impression of Russian psychology.' It was on this basis that it was suggested that Scott's proposal to reduce the criterion from 40 to 20 cities was too conservative. Better instead, it was argued, was to regard 20 as a maximum target, and that the 'best option is that we go on satisfactorily with quite a lot less ... From the Foreign Office point of view the less cities we try to destroy the less cost will be involved and the more money will be available for other objects. It is therefore in our interests to pitch the target figure as low as possible.'[7]

Sir Hugh Stephenson, the Foreign Office Chairman of the JIC, described the subsequent BNDSG meeting held on 24 January, and which considered Scott's new conclusions, as 'interminable', with 'the Air Ministry fighting a battle on every point.'[8] With the JIC having just endorsed a new approach to the criterion, Stephenson had told the meeting that the questions put to his Committee had been 'exceedingly difficult to answer.' Sticking closely to their terms of reference, there had been no scope for the JIC to examine the 'psychological, technical and political considerations affecting the credibility and the size of the deterrent, nor questions of vulnerability and operational viability had been taken into account.' Scott nevertheless interjected that he had found the JIC's report 'useful', only for Hudleston to criticise the narrow focus of the JIC paper, arguing that it was 'dangerous to try to reach too precise a solution ... the 40 cities assumption was not sacrosanct but it represented a reasonable objective with some allowance for fluctuations.' Hudleston argued that it was important to remember that the Russians had 'demonstrated a remarkable capacity to sustain heavy damage and casualties in war and yet to continue operations.' In order to reinforce his point, he tabled his own paper which noted that according to the Air Staff's calculations, the Vulcan force armed with Skybolt could 'render ineffective' 38½ million people in the Soviet Union, or 30 per cent of the urban population. Statistics of the damage and huge loss of life suffered by the Soviet Union during the

Second World War were then cited in order to reinforce the contention that the Soviet state and people were capable of great resilience. Given the historical precedent, halving of the current damage capability of the nuclear force was regarded by Hudleston's paper as 'highly questionable', while on the other hand preserving the ability to 'put out of action 38½ million Russians should be sufficient to convince Russia that the game was not worth the candle. But half the level of damage *might* be an acceptable price even granted that they rated the effectiveness of the attacking force correctly. The smaller the force the more liable they would be to underrate its power.'

The meeting as a whole was not impressed by these contentions. For one, the level of damage was considered a political matter, and was not something for the Government's military advisers to decide. There was also a 'necessary distinction' to draw between the kind of capability which would deter Russian action, and the kind which was designed to bring about its complete subjugation and surrender. It was also argued that any amount of further study of the problem of appropriate criteria was unlikely to yield an answer which everyone would accept, and what the JIC had produced was considered to be

> good enough. There must always be a wide margin of error in such assessments and personal judgment would always play a large part. The best course would be to refer the matter to Ministers for decision now and thereafter, on the basis of their decision, to proceed to a more detailed examination of how the assumed level of damage could be achieved.

In fact, amid the BNDSG's discussion over how to proceed, was a strong current of feeling that the existing 40 city criterion had been arrived at in an ad hoc fashion and applied to a period of the Cold War that was rapidly disappearing. Its selection, it was noted in significant fashion, 'had been influenced intuitively by the fact that the West at that time had a nuclear superiority. Now there was a balance of forces and this must affect the way in which we looked at the problem of the deterrent.' Such was this tide of scepticism, and bolstered by the JIC's recent work, Scott now felt confident enough to recommend that a 10 city criterion would be 'an ample margin' (when, as was observed above, his original draft note for the Minister of Defence had actually offered the higher figure of 20).[9]

The failure of the BNDSG to reach an agreed and unanimous position led to Scott submitting his own personal Chairman's report to the Minister of Defence at the beginning of February 1962, which noted the dissenting views of the Vice Chief of the Air Staff, and directed Watkinson to the crucial issue of the level of damage that a UK strategic nuclear force should be capable of inflicting. Referring in pointed fashion to the recent discussion in the Defence Committee, where the Prime Minister had given his view that no plans should be made on the assumption that another generation of strategic nuclear weapon would follow the effective end of Skybolt's life in the early

308 *Revising the criteria*

1970s, Scott nevertheless assumed that the work of the Study Group should continue as ministers would want to see all the options that were open to them. Of all the various starting points that could be adopted to begin an enquiry into a successor system – the operational merits of various weapons systems, availability, cost, or expected lifespan – Scott preferred to begin by looking at the damage criterion that had to be met, but this was above all 'an issue of political judgment.' The present 'working assumption' of 50 per cent destruction of 40 Russian cities was 'an arbitrary choice,' geared to the planned capacity of the V-bomber force. Scott explained that the JIC, having been asked to examine the subject of level of damage, and after noting all the caveats attached to its conclusions, had arrived at the five cities formula. 'Such is the importance of this issue to the validity of the deterrent,' Scott wrote, 'to present planning, to the life of the V Bomber force, to the date when the Government must take decisions on a successor system, to the choice of that system, and to manpower and expenditure during the sixties, that I do not believe that we can continue our work without a decision.' His own BNDSG had reached no agreed verdict on the issue, but Scott himself felt that for the purposes of deterrence (and so not to actually bring about the defeat or submission of the Soviet Union in war),

> the elimination of ten Russian cities – the five largest and five other major cities out of the next thirty largest – would be more than enough. This is the working assumption I ask the Government to accept. Though in my view it gives (in the context of damage) an ample margin of credibility to the British deterrent, it is a major reduction on the present working assumption.

Once a decision was made on the criterion to be adopted, Scott anticipated another round of work by the BNDSG which would then examine its implications for current plans for prolonging the life of the V-bomber force, and future options for successor systems.[10]

Included as background alongside Scott's personal submission was a BNDSG paper laying out a summary of the Group's analysis of the problems faced in maintaining an effective deterrent system into the 1970s. Aside from its familiar reiteration of the unresolved differences within the Study Group over the merits and drawbacks of a Polaris submarine-based future deterrent system or one launched from an airborne platform, it was mainly noteworthy for the basic arguments it contained over whether a policy of retaining a deterrent through the period should be followed at all. An often stated political argument advanced for the deterrent, it suggested, was that 'Britain is, and must remain, a nation to be taken into account in any calculations of major war, and that she cannot hope to retain this position without an effective strategic nuclear capability.' But while this undoubtedly held good for a direct attack on the UK in a general war, the paper observed, 'the case is less easy to argue convincingly for other circumstances.' Despite this reservation, 'there remains an intuitive feeling that our value as a military ally, even in limited war, might be lessened if our friends did not know that in the last resort we had a nuclear capability with which to deter their enemies.' A deterrent which was independent of the United States also had advantages in increasing Russian difficulties in gauging allied reactions, while in political terms it gave the UK a major role in disarmament talks and the ability 'to exert influence with the Americans which might otherwise be difficult to achieve.'

But on the other side of the ledger, the BNDSG had found, stood 'powerful reasons for questioning whether continued expenditure on a costly deterrent is entirely advantageous to this country.' Alliance relationships should form the core of Britain's defence policy, in this view, and it made no sense to duplicate the nuclear capabilities of others when a more valued contribution could be offered with non-nuclear forces. Britain's possession of nuclear weapons, it was sometimes held, was also liable to lead other countries to follow suit. After weighing these arguments, the paper noted that the future was 'highly uncertain. The course of prudence is to retain this capability, if we can afford to, even if we are not sure what its function is to be – at least up to the time (which had not yet come) when it is obvious that it has become a costly and unproductive luxury.' Having ventured into this thorny debate, the BNDSG paper pulled back by explaining it would make the assumption that a strategic nuclear capability should be maintained, primarily because it held out 'the prospect of a bigger say in our destiny than any other form of military power could give us,' and despite the fact that the government would surely try to limit its size to the 'minimum necessary to justify our claim to be a nuclear power, and even though they realise that this deterrent may not turn out to be either independent or non-European when the time comes.'[11]

Appended to Scott's report was yet another dissenting note from the VCAS, registering his conviction that any change in the level of damage expected of the strategic nuclear force was profoundly mistaken. For the benefit of the Minister of Defence, Hudleston once again rehearsed his criticisms of the narrow approach taken by the recent JIC paper on the subject, and his concerns that, in an age of nuclear parity, the Russians might gamble that the Americans would stay out of a conflict which began in Europe if intervention would lead to global war. But if UK nuclear capability gave it the potential to 'put out of action 30–40 million Russians ... [this] should be sufficient to convince Russia that the game was not worth the candle. But half the level of damage might or might not.' Reprising the statistics of the awful degree of destruction that had been inflicted on the Soviet Union during the Second World War, Hudleston sought to persuade the Minister of Defence that Russia could absorb tremendous punishment but still recover.

> 'Even within the framework of the limited approach adopted by the JIC to the problem,' Hudleston had contended, 'it is fallacious to assume that

the damage to a relatively small number of cities, even if it severely reduced the Soviet Union's economic strength in its struggle to overtake the United States, would necessarily weigh very much with the Russians. Economically they are behind the United States anyway. They might be content to drop further behind for a short period of time if it would enable them to eliminate America's allies in circumstances in which they reckoned the Americans regarded those allies as expendable. But since the Russian bomber and missile bases would not be situated in cities however many we attacked, there is no reason why the nuclear balance of power between Russia and the United States would be upset at all.

Hudleston finished his missive by pointing out the possibility that influence with the United States would be lost when it was noticed that the UK's nuclear striking power had suffered a diminution, and that while the 40 cities figure was not set in stone, it represented 'a reasonable objective having regard to fluctuations in the actual level of damage which might be achieved from time to time according to the current state of development of Russian defences – including possibly anti-missile defences.'[12]

Foreign Office officials found Hudleston's dissenting paper 'very unconvincing,' calling its use of Second World War analogies in order to show the kind of damage the Soviet leadership might be prepared to suffer in order to achieve their expansionist goals 'patently false. Clearly there is no resemblance between voluntarily accepting the destruction of ten of their largest cities and absorbing – admittedly immense – damage over a long period of war which they were unable to avoid without surrender and without having any third power (or fourth if you count China) in a position to profit by their weakness.'[13]

Scott's note to Watkinson reflected his appreciation that in view of the pressures that were unfolding for the defence budget, and the earlier conclusions of the Defence Committee, the best approach in political terms was to defer any immediate decisions over the most suitable successor system, and instead to focus on how to extend the credible life of the V-bomber force. Reducing the damage criteria would open the prospect of a Skybolt-equipped V-force still being considered credible through to the mid-1970s, so easing the Government's dilemmas over the need to make a decision over a replacement system. From within the Foreign Office there was much support for Scott's contention that the existing criteria could be safely lowered, one official finding:

> Certainly de Gaulle believes that France's position and influence as a nuclear power need not be dependent on the certainty of destroying such a large number of Russian cities. Nor do I believe that the American attitude will be influenced one way or the other by the number of Russian cities we believe we can eliminate. They can eliminate them all themselves without our help; but it is our contribution to their deterrent, the fact that

we share the odium with them of being a nuclear power and of testing weapons, and our contribution in the technical field, which count.[14]

But whether any of these last points 'counted' with the Americans was, in fact, increasingly debatable by 1962 in the face of Washington's growing preoccupation with the need for centralised control over the Western deterrent, and its efforts to reverse the trends toward nuclear proliferation that were becoming more apparent.

The Kennedy administration and the independent deterrent

In December 1961, Sir David Ormsby Gore, who two months before had taken up his post as Ambassador in Washington, wrote to the Foreign Secretary, Lord Home, 'As you know, the Americans fear at least as much as we do the spread of nuclear weapons to further individual countries, and here they have Germany particularly in mind.' In the light of such considerations, the Ambassador wondered whether it was not the time to re-examine the Government's own long-term intentions in the nuclear field, asking, 'For how much longer do we really believe that we can preserve an independent nuclear deterrent? If we try to do so, I imagine it will mean we intend to rely in time entirely on United States manufactured means of delivery. If this is the case, we shall gradually put the Americans in a very difficult position because they will come under increasing pressure to give other countries equivalent help.' Although it was probably not the moment to make any dramatic public announcements, Ormsby Gore wondered if Kennedy should be given some indication of

> how we see these matters developing in the future and if we could say that we had it in mind at some suitable moment to make the gesture of giving up a purely national nuclear potential in order to help over the nth power problem with Germany particularly in mind, and also as a mark of confidence in the United States' commitment to the defence of the free world. I suggest this on the assumption that no-one really believes we can maintain a purely British deterrent that makes economic and military sense for very much longer and that if we continue with our policy for purely prestige reasons, thereby encouraging the French and Germans to follow suit, then far from increasing our influence with the United States Government it will in the end prove to be a positive handicap in our relationship with the United States.[15]

It would be easy to dismiss the Ambassador's views as unrepresentative of wider official opinion, but within the space of a month, as noted above, members of the Cabinet's Defence Committee were to voice doubts over how long Britain could remain in the nuclear game.

In the immediate future, however, the credibility of the deterrent still relied on the supply of Skybolt missiles to Bomber Command's V-force in the mid-1960s, a fact which underlined the uncomfortable point that dependence on the United States for delivery systems could render such long-term problems moot. Indeed, in January 1962, the head of the British Defence Staff in Washington was writing to Scott to remind him that the arguments over the various merits of different successor systems in his BNDSG were likely to be 'completely overshadowed' by the wider issue of 'whether the Americans will ever be willing to let us have any weapon after Skybolt without its having unacceptable strings attached.' The consensus among the Embassy staff was that purchase of a US successor system could not be taken for granted, and all discerned a great reluctance in Washington to provide one unless it was closely tied to NATO.[16]

American reservations concerning the stress that continued to be placed by the Government on the 'independent' nuclear aspects of British defence policy were made manifest only a few weeks later when in mid-February the annual Defence White Paper was published. The White Paper had noted how much the overall strategic landscape had altered from that which had existed in 1957. Both sides in the Cold War now had the ability 'to inflict upon the other a degree of devastation which has never before in human history been either possible or imaginable.' Mutual destruction was seen as the likeliest outcome of an armed conflict which involved the vital interests of the protagonists, and it was argued that this 'truth must increasingly condition the attitude of powers to the use of force as an instrument of policy, for Governments can no longer choose to have either a full-scale conventional war or a limited war without risking the use of nuclear weapons.' There was, nevertheless, hope that the deterrent effect of the overwhelming power of nuclear weapons, and the maintenance of a balance of forces between East and West, would hold the peace 'until disarmament provides a more lasting solution.'[17]

In order to deter the range of threats which were present, the White Paper continued, 'carefully balanced forces' had to be maintained, both conventional and nuclear, but as the Government did not believe that a major war could continue for long without nuclear weapons being used it was 'the prevention of war' that was considered 'vital rather than preparations for long drawn out conventional war.'[18] Within this picture, the government believed British strategic nuclear deterrent remained a 'significant' contribution to Western strength, and (in a telling passage) was

> by itself enough to make a potential aggressor fear that our retaliation would inflict destruction beyond any level which he would be prepared to tolerate. Moreover, it adds considerably to the flexibility and dispersal of the total nuclear forces available to the West and thus to their retaliatory power. The efficacy of our deterrent will therefore be maintained throughout the 1960s by using our V-bombers and fitting them with stand-off weapons, Blue Steel in the first instance and later Skybolt.[19]

The White House had serious reservations over the tone of the White Paper. The administration's boost to US spending on conventional defence and its overall contribution to NATO during 1961 (reflecting its new stance of flexible response, and partly spurred by the Berlin crisis), had not been matched by its European allies. This was the cause of much frustration to US officials, and at the December 1961 NATO ministerial meeting in Paris, McNamara had chosen to highlight the 'glaring weaknesses' which were present in the Alliance's ground forces, with 'deficiencies ... so extensive that both initial and sustained combat effectiveness are inadequate to meet NATO's needs.'[20]

It was in this general context that when given an advance version of the contents of the Defence White Paper by Ormsby Gore, President Kennedy reacted by despatching a strongly worded letter to Macmillan on 16 February 1962 which expressed deep concern over the whole substance and tenor of British defence policy. Particular objection was made to the lack of any indication that a greater build-up of British conventional forces on the European continent was planned, or that there was a need to encourage more efforts by other NATO allies in this area. The President also, however, wanted to 'express special concern about the statement that the United Kingdom would continue to maintain throughout the 1960s its independent nuclear deterrent.' Alluding to the major reappraisal of NATO's nuclear policies which was then in train, and the pressures building up for independent nuclear capabilities (including in Germany), Kennedy thought that such a 'flat statement may well have the effect of convincing de Gaulle of the rightness of his course ... [and] hasten the day when Germany will pursue a national program.' Public statements, he remonstrated, should take into account such considerations, adding 'we ourselves are prepared to be as forthcoming as possible to meet our objective of finding a NATO solution to head off independent national aspirations.' Wanting to soften the critical nature of the whole message, Kennedy concluded that his comments on British defence policy were delivered

> with reluctance. Yet I have felt an obligation to speak candidly because of our deep concern about the summary [of the White Paper] we have seen ... In some measure, my comments have related to the substance of your defense policy, but it may be that to some extent our concerns may be met as much by the way in which you state the matter as by the substance of what you do.
>
> I have written with great candor – first, because of the deep concern which we feel here over the possible impact of the White Paper, if we understand it right – but second, because of my confidence that you will not misunderstand this wholly private communication. I could not raise a matter of this sort in this way with any other man – at the head of any other country – and I am sure you know I do so only because we can both be confident of our continuing partnership.[21]

314 *Revising the criteria*

This was a remarkably forthright message, representing an attempt to intervene in the normal processes of UK defence policymaking, but also underscored the irritation that Washington felt with the state of affairs.

Macmillan chose to reply in defensive fashion, expressing his appreciation that the President felt able to write to him 'in this frank way. It may be unusual but it is really helpful. After all I am not a General.' The government's upcoming statement on defence to the House of Commons, Macmillan stressed, was going to be softer on the presentational side than the language used in the White Paper. The British nuclear contribution would throughout be set out against the background of the West's deterrent as a whole. Moreover, while British possession of a force of V-bombers during the 1960s was a fact which could not be ignored, this did not 'in itself rule out a completely different organisation of the Western deterrent.' So as not to cause any misunderstanding, the Prime Minister added that he did not, however, believe it would be possible

> to devise a 'NATO' deterrent. All this comes back to the question of command and veto over the use of nuclear weapons. I know that I may be wrong about this and that an elaborate formula may be found, and, of course, we will play our full part in examining the possibilities. In any case, the major decision must rest with you. Our contribution, important though it is, is relatively small. But I have never been persuaded that its existence necessarily encourages the French and the Germans to try to develop their own independent nuclear capacity; they will be moved or deterred by quite other factors. Indeed, I think one can argue quite plausibly that the existence of the British nuclear force gives some comfort both to those Europeans who fear that the United States might, in the last resort, shrink from using the nuclear deterrent for the defence of Europe, and to those who, contrariwise, are worried lest America might use it too precipitately.

There were advantages for the United States, Macmillan suggested, in being able to share nuclear responsibilities. Having thought deeply through the issues, the Prime Minister felt that in the absence of concrete measures of disarmament it would not ultimately be possible to prevent other powers from acquiring their own nuclear capabilities, however crude these might prove to be.[22]

Such arguments made few impressions in Washington, where US officials were keen to see a greater share of European resources devoted to conventional defence, wanted to centralise control of nuclear forces, and were anxious over possible German nuclear aspirations. The views of the Kennedy administration were also important in bolstering Labour's objections to maintenance of an 'independent' nuclear deterrent. After visiting Washington, in early March, Harold Wilson, now handling the shadow Foreign Secretary brief, reported to the House of Commons that 'there is not one person in authority there who thinks that our nuclear deterrent adds one iota to the strength and credibility of the Western deterrent.'[23] For the Macmillan Government, however, the role of the deterrent was increasingly seen in political terms, as the negotiations for Common Market entry began a final and difficult phase during the spring of 1962. To Philip de Zulueta, the Prime Minister's Principal Private Secretary for Foreign Affairs, it made no sense to consider discarding the 'independent' nuclear deterrent at the point when the alternatives seemed to be either complete dependence on the United States, or an uncertain prospect of a 'European' deterrent, perhaps organised around an Anglo-French core effort once Britain had become a full member of the European Community. Moreover, the recent tenor of US policy did not give him grounds for confidence that Washington would be forthcoming with more nuclear help: 'We have refused to bribe the French to let us into the Common Market [with offers of nuclear collaboration] so as not to jeopardise this special relationship which we may now find quite useless.'[24] As in the previous year, the Prime Minister, for his part, still remained attracted to the notion of a nuclear understanding with de Gaulle which might look toward the creation of an Anglo-French force in the 1970s – but only once the UK was safely within the Community.[25]

Skybolt and the defence budget

Meanwhile, the impasse within the BNDSG over the size and nature of deterrent capability required during the 1970s had, inadvertently, provided a pretext for a reconsideration of the capability and hence size of the currently planned V-bomber force. The Minister of Defence had received Sir Robert Scott's views on lowering the damage criterion required by a successor nuclear force at the same time in February 1962 as he was grappling with mounting demands on the defence budget. Writing to Scott in response to his personal submission, Watkinson asserted that although he had some sympathy with the VCAS's views about retaining a 40 city criteria, he had to take a different perspective: 'It is not what we would like to do but what we can afford to do.' Anticipating a bruising struggle with the Treasury over the defence budget costings, beginning in May when the next five years of spending was under review, Watkinson saw his only option as to examine a reduction in the deterrent's anticipated damage capability, leading to a reconsideration of the numbers of Skybolt missiles and warheads needed to equip the V-force. 'I am sure,' Watkinson told the Permanent Under Secretary (in wording which laid the ghost of Sandys' 1957 White Paper to rest), 'if we have to choose between reductions in manpower and primary equipment, and the reduction of the present target levels, we shall have to choose the latter.' Scott was therefore asked by the Minister of Defence to look at cutting the current damage level by a third or a half, and then seeing what would be the minimum number of Skybolt and Blue Steel missiles, together with their warheads, required to meet these new targets. He also wanted a critical examination made of further nuclear weapons research and development. 'I must make it plain,' Watkinson stressed, 'that I am asking for this work to be done not on the grounds of strategy and tactics but on the basis that we may be forced into it for budgetary reasons.' In the meantime, Watkinson saw no need to pursue further work looking at successor systems until the operational possibilities of Skybolt had been fully assessed – a ruling which effectively suspended the activities of the BNDSG for the time being.[26]

Reflecting the position as reported by Scott, the Minister of Defence then approached Macmillan with a minute which suggested a study of the consequences of a reduction in the damage capability of the strategic nuclear force from the existing level of 40 Russian cities to ten. Watkinson himself, so he informed the Prime Minister, thought that the figure of ten, which had been arrived at in a similarly arbitrary fashion to that of forty, was too low, but he was equally sure that 40 was too high. A change in the damage level would, Watkinson highlighted, have to receive political endorsement, but it would allow savings to be made in the defence budget which might otherwise have to be found in manpower or equipment, 'provided we were certain that our contribution to the strategic deterrent still remained valid.'[27] The Minister of Defence's minute, it should be noted, coincided with the arrival from Washington of President Kennedy's strong criticism of the just-published Defence White Paper, which the American saw as neglecting any emphasis on Britain's conventional contribution to NATO.

Support for change in the level of damage came from the Foreign Secretary, who considered that there were two main aspects to whether such a reduction was judged to be 'politically acceptable'. The first was whether it would be viewed as an 'effective contribution to the deterrent' by the Russians; the recent JIC study was cited by Lord Home as evidence that a much lower threshold would still be credible. Home observed that

> The figure of ten cities seems to me a sensible compromise between the acceptable minimum propounded by the Joint Intelligence Committee and the present, inflated figure of forty cities, which was, I believe, taken as a criterion for a British deterrent capable of deterring Russia from attacking vital British interests even though the Americans might not be with us.

The second aspect was whether any revised level met the criterion set out by Macmillan himself in early 1960 of how the British contribution appeared in American eyes. Here the Foreign Secretary's argument came close to undermining the case for using any kind of city-based criterion of destruction at all. The Americans, Home conjectured, would not be impressed by any particular number of Russian cities that could be eliminated, as they could accomplish all they needed without British help. 'It is our contribution to their deterrent,' he continued (and recycling the same language used by his officials earlier in the year), 'the fact that we share with them the odium of being a nuclear power and of testing weapons and our contribution to the technical field which count.' When the two measures he had enumerated were considered satisfied, the Foreign Secretary argued, 'then the important thing is that we should not waste a penny more than is absolutely necessary on our Strategic Nuclear Deterrent.'[28]

A similar observation was made by Sir Norman Brook, the Cabinet Secretary, who was ready to venture even further than Home. The BNDSG's work had proceeded on the assumption that the criteria of deterrence should be measured according to what degree of damage would be enough to deter the Soviet Union from 'attacking vital British interests', Brook had noted. But this had been calculated on the assumption that the UK would be acting alone, and Brook was keen to remind the Prime Minister that policy was actually 'not to have an independent deterrent, but to make an independent contribution to the Western deterrent.' This was the line that Macmillan himself had laid down to the Defence Committee in February 1960, following the recommendations of the Cabinet Secretary's Future Policy Study, and Brook wanted to stress that it still held good in 1962. As Home had also maintained, the crucial point for the Cabinet Secretary – as it had been in 1960 – was whether the contribution made by a UK force would be enough to impress the Americans. Brook also wanted to see work done on the political advantages that would be derived for the UK's possession of a strategic deterrent force in the 1970s, in view of the enormous costs likely to be involved and the fact that its military significance was likely to be much diminished. For his part, the Cabinet Secretary clearly felt that the political benefits of remaining a nuclear power of the leading rank would not compensate for the economic drain it would impose.[29]

The Cabinet Secretary's feelings about the long-term future of the deterrent were mirrored within some quarters of the Foreign Office. One member of the Permanent Under Secretary's Department closely involved in nuclear matters as head of the Planning Section, Peter Ramsbotham, believed even if the Americans could be persuaded to supply another generation of weapons as a successor to Skybolt, there would be a heavy political price to pay in return (perhaps through having to pool the UK deterrent in multilateral arrangements of some kind), and the costs would be huge. 'Although the Air Ministry will not agree,' Ramsbotham advised, 'there is a very strong case against continuing with an independent British contribution to the strategic deterrent into the 1970s.' If this position were accepted, then, Ramsbotham continued, it might make sense to derive some benefit from sharing Britain's existing nuclear capability with its allies:

> At the moment there is little incentive for us to make what would undoubtedly be a political sacrifice, since nothing is likely to deflect General de Gaulle from his chosen course. But HM Embassy Paris are reporting that many of his subordinates are horrified by the cost of the

French nuclear effort and are well aware of its political hazards. When General de Gaulle disappears from the political scene, we should be ready to offer to relinquish our present 'independent' control over our V Bombers and to accept alternative arrangements which could divert the French from developing their own 'independent' force and thus prevent the Germans from following suit.[30]

Foreign Office attitudes were undoubtedly influenced by their unease over the whole tenor of the Kennedy administration when it came to discussion of the existence of 'independent' deterrents and how they might encourage the phenomenon of nuclear proliferation.

The Prime Minister met Home, Watkinson, Scott, Stephenson, and the Cabinet Secretary on 7 March 1962 in order to discuss the issue of reducing the 40-city criterion to perhaps ten. Uppermost in ministerial minds, as we have seen, was the need for a ruling to settle the number of Blue Steel and Skybolt missiles which would be needed to equip the V-bomber force through to the end of the decade. One of Macmillan's Private Secretaries, Tim Bligh, wondered in fact whether the BNDSG should now be asked to study a range of different numbers, perhaps including 15 or 20 cities, so that the costs of different levels of deterrence could be brought out more clearly.[31] Informing the meeting that the 40-city criterion was one which had 'grown up' and which 'was not a matter which had been reached as a result of a conscious decision,' Watkinson explained he now felt it was necessary to 'try and reach some considered view on what the V-bomber force should aim to do.' When the Prime Minister asked if the Americans should be told of any such revision, Watkinson replied in the negative: 'The first thing was to try to get our plans worked out and then to see what was involved before deciding whether to accept a new deterrent target.' As a first step in the process, Watkinson proposed that the BNDSG should look at a 15-city criterion, the whole matter to come back for later ministerial decision, a proposal to which the Prime Minister was agreeable.[32]

The subsequent report from the BNDSG, produced in early April, was derived from an Air Ministry study of the revised squadron patterns of a V-bomber force equipped with Skybolt – part of which was to be on airborne alert – under the new criterion that was proposed.[33] When it met to discuss the Air Ministry study, the BNDSG had noted how problematic it was to maintain a portion of the V-force, even with a reduced criterion, on continuous airborne alert from the mid-1960s onwards, while fatigue on airframes, considering the many of thousands of hours spent in the air, was an additional difficulty (some estimates putting 1972/73 as the end of effective service life). The extent of the Air Ministry's unhappiness with the whole exercise, and the cost cutting which was obviously driving it, was shown when the Vice Chief of the Staff objected to a suggestion that new figures be revised to include only eight aircraft on airborne alert as this would tend to give the impression that this was an operationally acceptable alternative. If there was not enough money to finance an adequate deterrent force ... the Air Staff would prefer to be allocated an arbitrary sum and told to do their best within it rather than be told to plan on the basis of a concept which was not operationally viable.

Nevertheless, the Air Ministry were invited by the BNDSG to reconsider the margins they had built into their figures, with a forward costing for a V-force equipped with 128 Skybolts, and another with a drastically reduced total of only 70 missiles. At the same time, as a counterpart to this exercise, the Admiralty were asked to generate, for comparison, their own estimates for a hybrid submarine force (where its boats were equipped with Polaris, but were also be capable of fulfilling a hunter/killer role), operating according to a 15-city criterion.[34]

Air Ministry officials were not alone in their alarm at the implications of the new costings exercises which the BNDSG had set in train. The new Skybolt warhead numbers which a revised and much-reduced programme would involve also caused concern at the AEA for the effect they would have on the skilled workforce at Aldermaston. Changes to assumptions about tactical warhead numbers made in 1961, and the reuse of fissile material from retired older weapons, already meant that production of uranium 235 at the Capenhurst plant would cease in 1963, and the enrichment facilities at the site would be forced to close, with the potential loss of 3,000 jobs. Once the requirements of the Skybolt warhead programme were met, weapons development work needed at AWRE would scale down rapidly after 1964, so that by 1967/68 it would be 'at a level of a post design service in support of the nuclear weapons held by the Services.' Staff numbers could be cut by 50 per cent if a minimum capability was desired. There had been, Sir Roger Makins, the Chairman of the AEA, reminded Scott, ministerial statements which had given general assurances over the continuing employment of workers at Aldermaston, and from 1964 onwards 'the Authority will have the difficult problem of running down the staff to match the declining load or of re-deploying them on other work. There is no prospect of finding civil work to match the run-down.' Makins also warned, nevertheless, that it would be 'impossible' for the AEA to provide post-design support to the services for the nuclear stockpile 'without an appropriate research and development programme.' Such a programme would also need to take into consideration the need to maintain an adequate amount of work to sustain Anglo-American collaboration under the MDA (including a continuing programme of underground nuclear testing, such as the Skybolt warhead-related Pampas test of March 1962). A reduction in the military programme, Makins warned, 'will lead to a fall in the level and character of our joint collaboration with the United States in the nuclear field.'[35]

During May 1962, the BNDSG struggled to arrive at firm conclusions over the effects of a reduction in the criterion. Based on Air Ministry calculations, the original plan to meet a 40-city criterion had been to buy a total of 170 Skybolt missiles, and to equip them with 158 warheads. Working on the new 15-city criterion suggested by the Minister of Defence, the BNDSG had eventually plumped for an allocation of 128 Skybolts and 112 warheads to be deployed across a total front-line strength of 72 Vulcan Mark 2 aircraft (allowing 12–13 aircraft, each carrying two Skybolts, to be kept on continuous airborne alert). This kind of force, it was believed, would be able to destroy 50 per cent of between ten and fifteen Soviet cities. However, Watkinson demurred, finding this alternative still too costly considering the other calls on defence spending over the next few years. He instead proposed to cut the Skybolt purchase to 100 missiles, for which 90 warheads were to be furnished.[36] Facing a stand-off with the Secretary of State for Air, Julian Amery (who refused to accept the lower numbers suggested by the MoD), Watkinson told the Defence Committee on 6 June that even with his proposed reductions in the overall scale of the nuclear programme 'there would still be a need for severe retrenchment in other parts of the Defence programme if the Defence budget were to be brought within acceptable limits of cost.'[37] By July, following another inconclusive Defence Committee meeting, Watkinson and Amery reached an uneasy compromise, where the totals of 100 Skybolt missiles and 90 warheads was accepted for the time being, while the Air Ministry looked for economies in the running of the Vulcan/Skybolt force which would possibly allow for more missile purchases to be made in the future.[38] According to Air Staff calculations, however, the Minister of Defence's preferred total of 100 missiles would only give a Vulcan force on airborne alert the ability to threaten between seven and ten Russian cities, reducing the deterrent criterion in arbitrary fashion yet further, and to below what Amery had considered an acceptable level.[39]

Dealing with France

As the British Government was trying to come to terms with the costs and compromises associated with maintaining a strategic nuclear capability, the French seemed determined to press ahead almost irrespective of the budgetary consequences. In March 1962, the Embassy in Paris reported that,

> The programme for the production of entirely French nuclear weapons is to continue despite the enormous expenditure that is involved. The cost of the programme is always falsely represented in the budget: the true figures of over-expenditure might shock even the critics who have drawn attention to it. Whether the French will ever be able to create a nuclear weapons system which by any standards could be thought of being up-to-date or useful out of their own resources is open to question.[40]

In July 1962 the French government even managed to defeat possible parliamentary censure of its decision to fund out of the general defence budget a portion of the massively increased forecast costs for building the Pierrelatte plant in south east France for the production of U-235 (an important step if France were to move toward thermonuclear development).[41]

During the spring of 1962, occasioned by press speculation over the possibility that the United States might consider assisting the French nuclear programme (with missile technology, if not with weapons themselves) some of the fractious debate within the Kennedy administration over nuclear policy towards the Atlantic Alliance reached a climax. Advocates of extending nuclear assistance to France, many located in the Defense Department, had maintained that such an offer would allow France to devote more resources to conventional defence spending and help persuade de Gaulle to commit a portion of his nuclear force to NATO control. However, Kennedy's visceral conviction that de Gaulle could not be trusted – rooted above all in fundamental differences over the proper US role in Western Europe – combined with State Department arguments over the need to devise mechanisms to curb nuclear proliferation (with a clear eye on Germany), were to prove stronger. At a meeting held on 16 April 1962, the provision of nuclear assistance to France was ruled out for the time being, and it was decided that the State Department would renew its push for the European members of NATO to form a multilateral MRBM force with US support. At this gathering McNamara diluted the Pentagon's previous position by voicing his belief that nuclear help would not serve to change de Gaulle's attitudes, but at the same time there was nothing that could stop the French developing a nuclear delivery capability and so some forms of assistance might make sense. Rusk, however, was adamant that this would only lead to divisive calls from other Alliance members for similar treatment when they encountered the heavy costs of a nuclear programme:

> in effect we should be reducing the price of entry into the nuclear field. [His] view was that we should instead seek a way to reduce our special nuclear relation to the British. The re-establishing of such nuclear sharing with the British in 1958 had been a mistake.

Kennedy concurred with the State Department's opposition to nuclear assistance to France, feeling it was 'wrong to move on this matter now.' Regarding the MRBM proposals, McNamara was extremely doubtful of their military necessity, but accepted that policy in this area had to move forward for political reasons.[42]

The State Department's success in gaining White House backing for a fresh attempt to sell the idea of a multilateral MRBM force to the European allies of the United States came at a particularly bad time for Macmillan and his senior officials. De Gaulle's attitude was considered essential to the success of Britain's bid to enter the EEC, and the French President was known to be adamantly opposed to the whole MRBM scheme. If London was now expected by Washington to offer support for a NATO-controlled nuclear force, this could place Britain in the difficult position of having to align against de Gaulle on one of the most sensitive issues of French external policy. Moreover, subscribing a future UK nuclear force to an MRBM scheme would probably put paid to any notion of using the idea of a collaborative Anglo-French nuclear effort, held 'in trust' for Europe (but free of US control), as a bargaining chip in the EEC negotiations with France.

The Prime Minister was due to see Kennedy once again for a brief series of talks in Washington at the end of April 1962, where Berlin, nuclear testing, and the need to bolster the conventional forces of NATO would figure heavily on the agenda. In the light of the President's critical message in February, British officials also anticipated that the subject of the independent nuclear deterrent might be brought up while Macmillan was in Washington. This was certainly on some American minds: McGeorge Bundy, Kennedy's Special Assistant for National Security Affairs, noted a few days before Macmillan's arrival that,

> We want the British in Europe, and we do not really see much point in the separate British nuclear deterrent, beyond our existing Skybolt commitment; we would much rather have British efforts go into conventional weapons and have the British join with the rest of NATO in accepting a single US-dominated NATO force.[43]

The defensive brief supplied by the MoD for the Washington talks rehearsed a familiar set of arguments for the maintenance of an independent UK strategic nuclear force. The point was made that although it was dwarfed by the US nuclear forces which could be brought to bear in attack against the Soviet Union, Bomber Command's force of Vulcans and Victors, from their forward bases, would form part of the initial wave of any Allied strike, diversifying and so complicating the air defence problem faced by the Russians. It was argued, moreover, that since the Soviet Union 'might doubt the will of the United States Government to use nuclear weapons in defence of a purely European interest,' the UK's possession of strategic forces under its sole national control, which could inflict extensive damage on a Soviet aggressor, contributed to the effectiveness of the overall Western deterrent. Any savings which might result from giving up such a strategic nuclear capability were also unlikely to find their way back into improved conventional forces (there would still be a requirement, for example, to maintain a V-bomber force in the conventional bombing role). The British nuclear force, in sum, was seen as providing good value for the extra degree of deterrence it provided, and the influence in world affairs it offered, while the MoD saw no reason why its existence encouraged the French or Germans to develop independent nuclear forces of their own. There seemed no grounds, according to this analysis, for establishing any new organisational arrangements for the Western deterrent.[44]

But this was not how the Prime Minister could afford to consider things. For one, as the Foreign Office was well aware, US agitation for a change to the nuclear organisation of the NATO Alliance was unlikely to relent over the coming months. But even more immediately, and as noted above, Macmillan was interested in returning to some of the notions of Anglo-French nuclear partnership he had included in his Grand Design memorandum at the start of 1961. There were particular reasons why a new initiative of this kind held attractions: by the spring of 1962 the negotiations in Brussels between the six members of the EEC and British officials over the terms for UK entry to the Community had become stalled, and French intransigence was perceived to be one of the causes of the deadlock. Press speculation that a deal involving Anglo-French nuclear collaboration could be one way the negotiations could be brought to a successful conclusion was becoming more widespread. On 10 April, Edward Heath, the Lord Privy Seal, and the minister overseeing the detailed negotiations for British entry, made a speech to the Council of the Western European Union where he spoke in novel terms of the government's readiness to discuss an eventual political union with the existing six members, and that such a union would inevitably develop a defence dimension. But he had also stressed that any European common point of view or policy on defence 'should be directly related to the Atlantic Alliance … The new Europe will be a great power, standing not alone but as an equal partner in the Atlantic Alliance, retaining its traditional ties overseas and fully conscious of its growing obligations towards the rest of the free world.'[45]

From the MoD, Watkinson was also attracted to the possibilities of Anglo-French collaboration, which he saw as the best means to restrain German nuclear ambitions. Two days after the Heath speech he told the Prime Minister he was in favour of Britain

> offering to join with France in a nuclear trusteeship over strategic weapons for NATO Europe … Now that it is clear that any use of nuclear weapons would bring a devastating retaliation on American cities as well as on Europe, the European NATO nations might well feel happier if there was an element of the strategic deterrent under European control.

Rather than drive the French down the path of a purely national development of nuclear weapons by denying them help, the Minister of Defence felt that a share in UK manufacturing capacity could be provided, while the combined force that was eventually produced could be targeted together, 'fully integrated from an operational point of view', and

> firmly committed to NATO. One could, however, maintain the concept of an 'independent' British or French deterrent by reserving the right of each Government to withdraw its forces and employ them on a purely national basis.[46]

De Zulueta was also drawn to Watkinson's proposals, which he also thought should extend to helping the French acquire thermonuclear weapons, 'either by providing them with information or by manufacturing the finished product on their behalf.' There would also be need for agreement to a joint study on a delivery system which could be introduced in the 1970s.[47]

In private, Macmillan was in sympathy with the idea of some form of nuclear offer to de Gaulle, and in April, for example, he mentioned the future possibilities of joint manufacture of nuclear weapons to the outgoing French Ambassador.[48] Nevertheless, de Gaulle seemed cool to such suggestions, believing that the British would not be able to offer cooperation without American approval, and because he was unwilling to dilute – through possible pooling arrangements – any aspect of French nuclear independence.[49] On 19 April, as part of preparations for his forthcoming visit to Washington, Macmillan convened a meeting at Chequers with the Foreign Secretary, as well as Brook and Sir Harold Caccia, the PUS at the Foreign Office. Their main topic of conversation was how to handle the issue of the UK deterrent if it should arise during the talks with Kennedy. Macmillan explained that he would follow the same line as he intended to employ when he next saw de Gaulle, by noting that the V-bomber force would remain a valid deterrent 'until the mid-1970s', but that 'having regard to the problem of other powers seeking a nuclear capacity and the feelings of European countries about their total dependence on the United States in nuclear defence,' he recognised

> that we may want to make some use of the force in the general interest as the basis for some communal, probably European, defence system. Various alternative ideas are open to us including, for example, assigning the force to NATO (SACEUR), offering to form some joint Anglo-French nuclear force or offering to form some broader European system within NATO.

None of these ideas were for the immediate future, as they would probably be disruptive to current arrangements, or were not practical politics (such as a European nuclear force, which could not begin to be realised until Britain was a member of the European Community), but Macmillan was ready to tell Kennedy that after Britain had joined, he thought the Community would 'have its own views and interests in the defence field.' Within this context, and reviving the proposal he had put forward in early 1961, the Prime Minister considered that Britain and France might devise a scheme to place their nuclear capabilities 'in trust', serving the defence interests of the Community within the Atlantic Alliance. Such notions were 'vague and undeveloped', Macmillan admitted, and presented some major difficulties – such as the reluctance of either government to surrender independent control of their own nuclear forces – but he was clear that the 'basic idea is that, when the enlarged European Community exists, the nuclear capability of the two members which have such a capability should somehow be given a European label, without withdrawing it from NATO.'[50]

The concept of placing British and French nuclear forces 'in trust', perhaps with coordinated command and control procedures and a common approach to targeting, did not, however, represent a concrete proposal to offer all-out technical assistance to the French nuclear programme. In Washington, US officials, while keen that Britain should join the Community as soon as possible, had wondered if Macmillan might be tempted to make an offer of such nuclear cooperation in the technical field to de Gaulle in order to reduce French resistance to British membership. It was not a gambit, however, which found any support within the administration. Bundy, for example, noted for Kennedy's benefit that 'there is nothing for us in any possible British notion that the UK might pay its entrance fee to the Common Market by providing nuclear assistance to the French. In such a case the British would be appeasing the French with our secrets, and no good would come of it for Europe or for us.'[51] Senior British officials who accompanied the Prime Minister on his trip to Washington in late April reported that Rusk, Bundy and George Ball had asked them whether any overtures from the French regarding nuclear cooperation were expected 'as their price for letting us into the Common Market.' When the reply was offered that such a proposal was not expected, and would in any event by rejected on the British side, Rusk expressed relief, saying that it would have created problems for Washington if a bargain of this sort was floated. The United States, Rusk had confirmed, was determined not to help France with nuclear weapons technology either directly, or through the UK.[52]

In the event, when the Prime Minister's party held its discussions over Western defence with senior members of the US administration in Washington at the end of April, they were not pressed in any concerted manner on the future of the independent deterrent. However, Kennedy did point out to his visitors that his administration had a somewhat different position on the need to build up the conventional strength of the Alliance than that exhibited by Britain. Macmillan responded in robust fashion that

> it was vital to the security of the West that the credibility of the nuclear deterrent should be maintained. It was specially important that we should avoid defining in advance the circumstances in which the deterrent would be invoked. It was essential that the Soviet Government should be left in uncertainty on this. It mattered less that the members of the alliance should be in some intellectual confusion about it: what was important was that the Russians should be left in substantial doubt. Above all, we must avoid giving the Russians the impression that we should in the event be afraid to use our nuclear strength.

Kennedy, however, doubted that this kind of approach would be applicable over a situation such as over Berlin, where it might be the West which had to initiate action if access were blocked. This allusion to the need for more non-nuclear military options gave the Prime Minister a chance to observe that he was 'disturbed' by the recent arguments he had seen over the potential that a conflict beginning in Europe could be confined to the conventional level, and that this was an important reason to build-up the conventional strength of the Alliance. 'Two conventional wars had been fought in Europe in the present century,' he noted dryly, 'and neither of them had been a pleasant experience.' This did not mean, he went on to stress, that he did not accept there should be adequate conventional forces to ensure a pause before a recourse to the use of nuclear weapons, and he observed that steps were being taken to this end, but there was no mistaking the tenor of the Prime Minister's remarks and his reluctance to downplay the ultimate sanction of a nuclear response to Soviet aggression. When Macmillan discussed the future of French defence policy and de Gaulle's nuclear programme with McNamara, he suggested that there would have to be readjustments to British defence policy if Britain managed to join the EEC. 'This would throw up the nuclear problem,' Macmillan had said, and, 'It might be that some European nuclear deterrent force ought to be formed in which the British contribution could merge. However, this was all in the future.' McNamara, for his part, voiced his concerns over 'the drive for military power, including nuclear power, which the Germans were beginning to make.'[53]

The Prime Minister also had a deeper private talk with Kennedy about the subject of French readiness to receive nuclear information (in this case from the United States). It would be possible to ask Congress to allow such a transfer of information to take place, as had occurred with the agreement reached with the UK in 1958, but Kennedy did not feel it would be popular and would expend political capital. Asked for his opinion about such a proposition, Macmillan was reserved, saying that it would depend on what was received in exchange and that 'the matter might be left for the moment just to see whether the British are able to negotiate reasonable terms for their entry into the Common Market, and consequently to see after this what would be the European attitude, including that of the French, towards the reorganisation of NATO.' Macmillan thought that an immediate transfer of US nuclear information would 'not now produce results. I would be quite frank and say that the idea of an Anglo-French nuclear contribution to NATO might one day be a good thing, and I would not be precluded from dangling this carrot before de Gaulle's eyes; but it would be a mistake to come to an agreement now. He would merely take and pay nothing for it.' Kennedy agreed wholeheartedly with the Prime Minister's views, adding that while the Pentagon was keen on the idea of extending nuclear assistance 'he was against it and was prepared to hold out.'[54]

The Kennedy administration's evolving attitudes regarding nuclear strategy and the role of independent national nuclear forces was given expression only a few days after the Prime Minister had left Washington, when on 5 May 1962 McNamara addressed a closed meeting of NATO defence ministers in

Athens. In this highly significant speech, which it is worth quoting from at length, the US Defense Secretary explained that the United States had

> come to the conclusion that to the extent feasible basic military strategy in general nuclear war should be approached in much the same way that more conventional military operations had been regarded in the past. That is to say, our principal military objectives, in the event of a nuclear war stemming from a major attack on the Alliance, should be the destruction of the enemy's military forces while attempting to preserve the fabric as well as the integrity of allied society. Specifically, our studies indicate that a strategy which targets nuclear forces only against cities or a mixture of civil and military targets has serious limitations for the purposes of deterrence and for the conduct of general nuclear war.

Current overwhelming US nuclear superiority over the Soviet Union, both in numerical and technological terms, he continued, offered the option of destroying a large portion of Soviet nuclear forces while still holding substantial US forces in reserve which could be used against Soviet urban-industrial areas if necessary. Although it was uncertain whether the Russians would reciprocate by adopting similar 'damage limiting' strategies, and so reduce the horrendous casualty toll of a general nuclear exchange between the Superpowers by a marginal level, McNamara believed they would have 'very strong incentives' to do so. Whatever the case, the current administration had clearly decided that a counterforce approach to targeting, made possible by improvements in the design and accuracy of nuclear weapons, held the prospect of prevailing in the event of nuclear war while limiting civilian casualties to the maximum degree possible.

McNamara made clear that the United States intended to maintain its existing levels of superiority over the Soviet Union, and planned to improve the survivability and control of its nuclear forces. The emphasis was on 'unity of planning, executive authority, and central direction' so that responses to enemy action could be properly coordinated, especially in relation to

> retaliatory attacks against him. There must not be competing and conflicting strategies in the conduct of nuclear war. We are convinced that a general nuclear war target system is indivisible and if nuclear war should occur, our best hope lies in conducting a centrally controlled campaign against all of the enemy's vital nuclear capabilities. Doing this means carefully choosing targets, pre-planning strikes, coordinating attacks, and assessing results, as well as allocating and directing follow-on attacks from the center. These call, in our view, for a greater degree of Alliance participation in formulating nuclear policies and consulting on the appropriate occasions for using these weapons. Beyond this, it is essential that we centralize the decision to use our nuclear weapons to the greatest extent possible. We would all find it intolerable to contemplate having only a

part of the strategic force launched in isolation from our main striking power.

Underlining the point further, McNamara stressed the dangers if a portion of the Alliance's nuclear force was used in an uncoordinated fashion to launch a retaliatory attack against Soviet military targets, so 'endangering all of us', and that 'equally intolerable' would be 'one segment of the Alliance force attacking urban industrial areas while, with the bulk of our forces, we were succeeding in destroying most of the enemy's nuclear capabilities. Such a failure in coordination might lead to the destruction of our hostages – the Soviet cities – just at a time at which our strategy of coercing the Soviets into stopping their aggression was on the verge of success. Failure to achieve central control of NATO nuclear forces would mean running the risk of bringing down on us the catastrophe which we most urgently wish to avoid.' The analysis carried out by his staff in the Department of Defense, McNamara intoned,

> suggest rather strongly that relatively weak nuclear forces with enemy cities as their targets are not likely to be adequate to perform the function of deterrence. In a world of threats, crises, and possibly even accidents, such a posture appears more likely to deter its owner from standing firm under pressure than to inhibit a potential aggressor. If it is small, and perhaps vulnerable on the ground or in the air, or inaccurate, it enables a major antagonist to take a variety of measures to counter it. Indeed, if a major antagonist came to believe there was a substantial likelihood of it being used independently, this force would be inviting a pre-emptive first strike against it. In the event of war, the use of such a force against the cities of a major nuclear power would be tantamount to suicide, whereas its employment against significant military targets would have a negligible effect on the outcome of the conflict. In short, then, weak nuclear capabilities, operating independently, are expensive, prone to obsolescence, and lacking in credibility as a deterrent.

Having outlined his thinking on desirable nuclear strategy, McNamara was keen to tell his audience that owing to its 'non-nuclear deficiencies' there was a 'high probability' it would be the NATO Alliance which would have to take the momentous decision to be first to use nuclear weapons in the event of a major Soviet conventional attack in Europe. Moreover, despite the US nuclear superiority he had just described, such a decision would be made in the knowledge that the 'consequences would be catastrophic for all of us.' The US administration, McNamara confirmed, was ready to accept its share of this enormous responsibility, and would 'fulfil our pledge' of the nuclear guarantee to Western Europe, but admitted he would be 'less than candid if I pretended to you that the United States regards this as a desirable prospect or believes that the Alliance should depend solely on our nuclear power to deter the Soviet Union from actions not involving a massive commitment of Soviet force ... in our view, the threat of general war should constitute only one of several weapons in our arsenal and one to be used with prudence.' The Defense Secretary then proceeded to exhort his NATO colleagues to do more in the realm of conventional defence spending so that the Alliance's formal goal of a well-equipped and supplied 30 division ground force deployment along the central European front could be achieved.[55]

Immediately after McNamara's weighty contribution, Rusk reiterated to other NATO ministers the need to enhance NATO's conventional 'shield' forces, and offered the State Department's latest thinking on the nuclear arrangements of the Alliance. Underlining that the concurrence of its allies would be required if the scheme were to be introduced, Rusk affirmed that the US administration would be willing to investigate the possibility of forming a sea-based MRBM force 'under fully multilateral ownership, control, financing and manning. They would be prepared to facilitate the procurement of MRBMs for an allied NATO force only if it were fully multilateral ... They wanted to avoid the idea that they were trying to ram a particular idea down the throats of allies.' Watkinson responded to all this by noting that an excessive emphasis on conventional defence strength could create the wrong impression by persuading the Russians that the West had lost its willingness to use nuclear weapons. Over MRBMs, he did not accord them the same priority as areas such as the strategic nuclear deterrent or the need to modernise delivery systems. The French Defence Minister, Pierre Messmer, took stronger exception to McNamara's remarks, calling the 'condemnation of small scale national nuclear forces ... a bit premature. A relatively weak nuclear force possessed a deterrent effect which in certain circumstances might be superior to that of a considerably stronger force whose use might be regarded by the enemy as less probable. That was the justification for the independent *forces de frappe*.'[56]

In retrospect it is clear that the theoretical counterforce targeting options which McNamara had outlined in his Athens speech were far ahead of what lay within the capabilities of the US strategic nuclear forces then in existence. The nuclear target planning undertaken by the US military authorities throughout this period, and the philosophy that underpinned it, remained wedded to a large-scale and overwhelming use of nuclear weapons against an extensive list of military, industrial and economic targets in the Soviet Union and the territories it controlled. Indeed, it would not be until the mid-1970s that the kind of selective and discriminating nuclear strikes envisaged by McNamara in 1962 would find their way into such targeting plans (for one, US command, control and communications systems were simply not advanced enough to conduct the kind of extended and discriminating nuclear campaign postulated).

Marc Trachtenberg has cast doubt on whether McNamara and the President ever really believed in such counterforce/no cities options, and that the real function of such pronouncements was political: in attacking the notion of separate national nuclear forces a further marker was delivered that the administration would do nothing to foster German nuclear ambitions.[57] But it was equally the case that such addresses were designed as a reminder that the Alliance had to show more commitment to the build-up of conventional forces if the general nuclear war-fighting strategies that were becoming available to Washington were never to be put into practice. Kennedy had read McNamara's draft speech, put forward his own amendments, and had wanted the Secretary of Defense to 'repeat to the point of boredom that our general war response will come only if our allies are subjected to major attack.'[58] The implication here was that they should therefore make more efforts in the area of conventional defence. McNamara himself was quizzed by British officials on a number of occasions during the remainder of the year about his ideas on nuclear strategy. In September he thought that 'in the conditions of today neither side was likely in fact to resort to counter force strategy. This would become a stronger possibility as Soviet nuclear capacity increased. The United States would welcome the adoption of this strategy as it opened up additional alternatives to total nuclear war. It was relevant to note that the American public believed American forces were inadequate. This was not true and never had been true. So one purpose of advocating a counterforce strategy was to reassure the American public. It was emphatically not the same as a first strike (or surprise) strategy: counterforce strategy was one option out of many.'[59]

Whatever McNamara's reasoning, and his desire to 'educate' America's NATO allies in the finer points of nuclear strategy, his criticisms of small national nuclear forces had a deep and long-lasting resonance. As Macmillan later recalled, the speech 'could hardly have done anything more calculated to upset both his French and his British allies,' while McNamara's 'fervent denunciation of the dangers of the "dissemination of nuclear power" was an ill-disguised attack upon the determination both of Britain and of France to maintain, at any rate in the foreseeable future, their separate, independent nuclear forces.'[60] The worrying point for British observers was that the US Defense Secretary's ill-advised comments coincided with the State Department's renewed interest in promoting the idea of a collective NATO-controlled multilateral nuclear force, or MLF as it was by now more often known, and that this appeared to have presidential backing. In the middle of May, Kennedy was asked at one of his regular news conferences about his attitudes toward independent nuclear forces, and replied: 'We do not believe in a series of national deterrents. We believe that the NATO deterrent, to which the United States had committed itself so heavily, provides very adequate protection. Once you begin, nation after nation, beginning to develop its own deterrent, or rather feeling it's necessary as an element of its independence to develop its own deterrent, it seems to me that you are moving into an increasingly dangerous situation.'[61] The day before the press conference, Bundy had seen Ormsby Gore in order to deliver a verbal message from Kennedy to the

Prime Minister which was intended as a follow-up to their recent private conversation at the White House. 'As I understand it,' the Ambassador wrote to Macmillan, 'you had suggested it might be worth considering whether, in order to satisfy the French, we, the British, might pool our nuclear knowledge with them and that having constituted ourselves nuclear trustees, as it were, of the European half of the Atlantic Alliance, we would then jointly continue to receive American help in the nuclear field. From what the President has said to me since that talk, and Bundy confirmed this, he does not take up an attitude of doctrinaire opposition to such an idea but he does feel, as I think you do, that it would only be worth considering if it would buy something really spectacular like full French cooperation in NATO and elsewhere plus British entry into the European Economic Community. The President's message relayed through Bundy was that he wished you to know that under present circumstances and in view of de Gaulle's inflexible attitude, he could not give American support to any such move. The right moment might come when such a proposal would have value, although it would need extremely careful examination, but the President was quite convinced that this was not such a moment. Evidently he is concerned that you might hint at some such arrangement when you see de Gaulle early next month.'[62]

White House reservations over a nuclear initiative involving France were compounded by the State Department's growing opposition to Britain's independent nuclear status.

Towards the end of May, Rusk received a memorandum from Foy Kohler, the Assistant Secretary for European Affairs at the State Department, which outlined a programme of action regarding the UK independent nuclear capability and the Anglo-American nuclear relationship. Remarking that little had been done to persuade the British to 'phase out' their independent deterrent, as had been advocated in the NSC Policy Directive of April 1961, Kohler now saw the need to bring the matter to a head because of the current UK negotiations over EEC entry, which could raise the undesirable issue of UK nuclear assistance to France, but also because Macmillan had recently signalled his intention to maintain an independent deterrent throughout the 1960s. This British position, Kohler noted, stood at odds with the criticisms of weak national nuclear forces that McNamara had recently put forward during his Athens speech, and was not helpful to US arguments that the conventional strength of the Alliance should be bolstered.

> 'The heart of the matter,' Kohler advised, 'is that we should avoid any actions to increase the degree of our special nuclear relationship with the UK. We should make clear that we are not prepared to extend that relation, notably in regard to creation of a UK Polaris missile force. The British will undoubtedly show a continuing interest in acquiring Polaris or other missile-bearing submarines, as they come closer to the end of

the effective life of the V-bomber force. Even if that life is prolonged through Skybolt, the V-bomber force is a wasting asset ... If the V-bombers are not replaced by a sea-borne missile force, the independent British deterrent will expire, since the British have already decided to phase out land-based Thors by about 1964.

Among the more detailed actions that Kohler thought could be taken was to reconsider the cooperation offered to Britain, particularly in the ballistic missile field, under the Tripartite Technical Cooperation programme; encourage the British to join any MLF that was formed; and disseminate the April 1961 policy line on the UK deterrent throughout the lower levels of the US government bureaucracy. In view of what was to transpire later it was also pertinent that Kohler warned that while the US should explore with the UK the idea of a commitment of their strategic nuclear force to NATO, this should not be done 'until we see how action to this end could be fitted in with the concept of a genuinely multilateral force. We would not want commitment of V-bombers to substitute for full UK participation in the multilateral force or to set a pattern for a multilateral force based on national contingents rather than on units under multilateral ownership, control and manning.'[63]

Kohler's remarks were indicative of a much sharper turn within the Kennedy administration away from automatic support for a UK national deterrent force, and toward a prioritising of multilateral solutions to NATO's nuclear sharing problems. As far as the State Department 'Europeanists', such as George Ball and Walt Rostow, were concerned, once the inconvenience of the Skybolt deal concluded by the Eisenhower administration in 1960 was removed, provision of a successor system to UK could not be in the same terms if the wider policy objectives of the administration were to be met. That such an issue might have to be confronted sooner rather than later was just then becoming apparent to some US officials. Skybolt's initial test firings in the spring of 1962 had been unsuccessful and McNamara was becoming increasingly unhappy with its steadily rising costs. Kennedy's science adviser, Jerome Wiesner, produced a report for the President in April which gave extensive detail on the history of the missile's technical problems, but included the pointed remark that a decision on its cancellation had been avoided by the previous administration on the political grounds that a firm commitment had been made to the UK over its supply.[64] It remained to be seen whether the Kennedy administration would be prepared to risk the damage to Anglo-American relations that would result from discontinuing the programme, and how this might mesh with its growing determination to maintain central direction of the West's nuclear forces.

Notes

1 See 'Our Foreign and Defence Policy for the Future,' memorandum by the Prime Minister, 29 September 1961; FP(61) 2nd Meeting, 10 October 1961, CAB 134/1929.
2 Paragraph 102, COS(62)1, 'Strategy in the Sixties,' report by the Chiefs of Staff Committee, 9 January 1962, DEFE 5/123; and as later presented to the Cabinet, COS(62)49, 'Digest Report on British Strategy in the Sixties,' 31 January 1962, appended to C(62)24, 'Defence Policy' note by the Minister of Defence, 9 February 1962, CAB 129/108.
3 D(62)1st meeting, 12 January 1962, CAB 131/27.
4 See, for example, French, *Army, Empire and Cold War*, 249–51.
5 See Cook letter to Scott, 'Draft Report to the Minister of Defence: BND(SG)(62)1,' 2 February 1962, DEFE 7/2143.
6 See Kent minute for PS to VCAS, 'BNDSG,' AUS(A)/5898, 19 January 1962, AIR 19/998.
7 Ramsbotham minute, 23 January 1962, PUSD records, FCO.
8 Stephenson minute, 24 January 1962, PUSD records, FCO.
9 BND(SG)(62) 1st Meeting, 24 January 1962; and attached note by Hudleston, 'Weight of Attack and Effect on Russia,' 24 January 1962, DEFE 7/2143.
10 Scott minute for Watkinson (circulated as BND(SG)(62)5),'Strategic Deterrent Policy,' RHS/93/62, 6 February 1962, DEFE 13/618, and in AIR 2/13713, and DEFE 7/2143.
11 'Annexe to Sir Robert Scott's Report of 6th February 1962, to the Minister of Defence,' DEFE 13/618.
12 'Appendix to Sir Robert Scott's Report of February 6th 1962 to Minister of Defence: Note by the Vice Chief of the Air Staff,' DEFE 13/618.
13 P. S. Ziegler minute, 8 February 1962, PUSD records, FCO.
14 Ramsbotham minute, 9 February 1962, PUSD records, FCO.
15 Ormsby Gore letter to Home, 13 December 1961, PREM 11/4166. As with other correspondence from Ormsby Gore to the Foreign Secretary, the Prime Minister was shown a copy of this letter.
16 Air Chief Marshal Sir George Mills letter to Scott, 22 January 1962, attached to BND(SG)(62)4, 1 February 1962, DEFE 7/2143.
17 Paragraph 7, Cmnd 1639, *Statement on Defence, 1962: The Next Five Years*, February 1962, and copy in C(62)23, 'Defence White Paper, 1962', note by the Minister of Defence, 9 February 1962, CAB 129/108.
18 Paragraph 9, ibid.
19 Paragraph 13, ibid.
20 See Kaplan et al., *McNamara Ascendancy*, 304–5.
21 Kennedy letter to Macmillan, 16 February 1962, PREM 11/3711; copy also in telegram from Department of State to the Embassy in the United Kingdom, 16 February 1962, *FRUS, 1961–1963, XIII*, 1059–61. See also Schlesinger, *A Thousand Days*, 849.
22 Macmillan to Kennedy, T.79/62, 23 February 1962, PREM 11/4052.
23 *Hansard*, HC, vol 655, cols 228–96, March 1962.
24 De Zulueta minute for Bligh, 27 February 1962, PREM 11/3716.
25 For this general argument see also Pagedas, *Anglo-American Strategic Relations and the French Problem*, 198–9, 203–5.
26 Watkinson minute for Scott, 12 February 1962, DEFE 13/618.
27 Watkinson minute for Macmillan, 'Strategic Deterrent Policy,' 19 February 1962, PREM 11/3716.
28 Home minute for Macmillan, 'Strategic Deterrent Policy,' PM/62/33, 1 March 1962, PREM 11/3716. Foreign Office officials had also discussed Home's

response beforehand with the Cabinet Secretary, see Ramsbotham minute, 'Strategic Deterrent Policy,' 27 February 1962, PUSD records, FCO.
29 Brook minute for Macmillan, 26 February 1962, PREM 11/3716.
30 Ramsbotham minute, 'Strategic Nuclear Deterrent,' 6 March 1962, PUSD records, FCO.
31 Bligh minute for Macmillan, 'Strategic Deterrent Policy,' 7 March 1962, PREM 11/3716.
32 Bligh, 'Note for the Record,' 7 March 1962, PREM 11/3716.
33 BNDSG/P(62)8, 'The Implications of a Change in the Level of Damage Required,' note by the Vice Chief of the Air Staff, 9 April 1962, DEFE 7/2144.
34 BNDSG/M(62)3, 13 April 1962, DEFE 7/2144.
35 See Makins letter to Scott, CH(62)45, 29 May 1962, and attached paper 'Effect on Atomic Energy Authority of the Proposed Revised Warhead Programme,' memorandum by the Atomic Energy Authority, CH(62)47, 29 May 1962, AB 48/194.
36 See D(62)29, 'The Provision of Nuclear Warheads,' memorandum by the Minister of Defence, 1 June 1962; D(62)34, 'The Nuclear Programme,' memorandum by the Secretary of State for Air, 4 June 1962, CAB 131/27; Michael Cary minute for Macmillan, 'Nuclear Warheads,' 5 June 1962, PREM 11/3716.
37 D(62) 10th Meeting, 6 June 1962, CAB 131/27.
38 D(62) 11th Meeting, 9 July 1962, CAB 131/27; Watkinson minute for Macmillan, 13 July 1962, PREM 11/3716. See also material in DEFE 13/409.
39 See D(62)36, 'The Nuclear Programme,' memorandum by the Secretary of State for Air, 4 July 1962, CAB 131/27.
40 Rumbold to Home, 29 March 1962, FO 371/163515, as quoted in Constantine A. Pegadas, 'Harold Macmillan and the 1962 Champs Meeting,' *Diplomacy and Statecraft*, 9, 1, 1998, 226.
41 See Kohl, *French Nuclear Diplomacy*, 193–4, 214.
42 Minutes of meeting, 16 April 1962, *FRUS, 1961–1963, XIII*, 377–80; and see also Kaplan, et al., *McNamara Ascendancy*, 393–6, and Kohl, *French Nuclear Diplomacy*, 211–21.
43 Bundy memorandum for Kennedy, 24 April 1962, *FRUS, 1961–1963, XIII*, 1068.
44 PM(W)(62)4, 'Washington Talks: April 1962: The United Kingdom Contribution to Western Defence,' memorandum by the Ministry of Defence, 11 April 1962, CAB 133/246.
45 See Kohl, *French Nuclear Diplomacy*, 322–3.
46 Watkinson minute for Macmillan, 'Nuclear Weapons,' 12 April 1962, PREM 11/3712.
47 De Zulueta minute for Macmillan, 13 April 1962, PREM 11/3712.
48 See more on such hints and suggestions in April and May 1962 see Pagedas, *Anglo-American Strategic Relations and the French Problem*, 203–4.
49 See Piers Ludlow, *Dealing with Britain: The Six and the First UK Application to the EEC* (Cambridge, 1997), 118.
50 Evelyn Shuckburgh note of conversation, 19 April 1962, DEFE 7/2144, and in DEFE 7/2278.
51 Bundy memorandum for Kennedy, 24 April 1962, *FRUS, 1961–1963, XIII*, 1069.
52 'Note of a conversation at luncheon at the State Department on 28th April 1962,' CAB 133/300.
53 PM(W)(62)2nd Meeting, 'Record of a Meeting held at the White House on Saturday, 28th April 1962 at 3.30pm,' CAB 133/246; 'Record of a conversation in the British Embassy, Washington, on Sunday 29th April 1962, at 11.30am,' CAB 133/300; full records can also be found in PREM 11/3722.

54 'Note by the Prime Minister of his conversation with President Kennedy on the morning of Saturday, April 28, 1962, at the White House,' miscellaneous Cabinet Office papers.
55 McNamara speech to NATO Council, Athens, 5 May 1962, reproduced in Philip Bobbitt, Lawrence Freedman, and Gregory F. Treverton (eds), *US Nuclear Strategy: A Reader* (London, 1989), 205–22; the speech can also be found in 'Ministerial Meetings of the Council of the North Atlantic Treaty Organisation, Athens, May 4–6, 1962: Volume II, Military Questions,' in PREM 11/3722.
56 Ibid.
57 See the persuasive evidence cited by Trachtenberg in his *Constructed Peace*, 315–21.
58 See Kaplan et al., *McNamara Ascendancy*, 305–6. See also Freedman, *Evolution of Nuclear Strategy*, 234–9, 305–7.
59 MoD minute, 'Minister of Defence's Visit to the United States, September 1962: Counter Force Strategy,' 19 September 1962, DEFE 13/323.
60 Macmillan, *At the End of the Day*, 334–5, 341.
61 Presidential news conference, 17 May 1962, *Public Papers of the Presidents: John F. Kennedy, 1962* (Washington, 1963), 402.
62 Ormsby Gore letter to Macmillan, 17 May 1962, PREM 11/3712.
63 Kohler memorandum for Rusk, 24 May 1962, *FRUS, 1961–1963, XIII*, 1073–6.
64 See Kaplan et al., *McNamara Ascendancy*, 378–9.

9 The prelude to Nassau, June–December 1962

The road to the Ann Arbor speech

By the summer of 1962 it was evident that a major preoccupation of the Kennedy administration had become the potential for German nuclear ambitions to destabilise the position in central Europe, particularly once Adenauer had left the political scene. It was the firm conviction of many in the State Department that the formation of a NATO-linked multilateral nuclear force, with German participation in its manning, operation and control, could prevent this from occurring. Despite the professions of officials in Washington that a multilateral force could only be formed from a European initiative, it was clear to British observers that the Americans intended to promote their own ideas on the purpose and composition of such a force to their NATO allies. Yet to British officials there seemed no pressing reason why an MLF was required at this particular juncture, with little immediate discernible pressure for a greater European nuclear role coming, most importantly, from Germany itself. Steps were already being taken to improve procedures for nuclear consultation and information sharing within the NATO Alliance, and between its nuclear and non-nuclear members (indeed this had been one of the achievements, as far as British officials saw it, of the Athens meeting in May 1962).

There seemed every reason in continuing to try to meet European concerns over US readiness to provide nuclear support to the Alliance through this lower-key route. The British position was that an MLF would be 'politically dangerous and unwarrantably expensive'. Although it might create difficulties for Anglo-American relations – US officials had already indicated that they hoped the UK would stay silent rather than try to block the scheme – the inclination of ministers was to press for NATO members to study SACEUR's (debatable) claims for a military requirement for an MRBM force before tackling the political issues that underlay the proposals for the MLF, and then to urge that the alternative of increasing the Alliance's consultative capacities, through the new device of the Nuclear Committee (made up of the permanent representatives to NATO) created at the Athens meeting, should be examined. 'If the Americans want to help us to negotiate our way into Europe,' one Foreign Office telegram opined, 'they must not expect us to take up a position on this important nuclear matter which will only confirm de Gaulle's suspicions that we are incapable of maintaining a point of view independent of the Americans on a matter of vital interest to European defence.'[1] However, and much to British annoyance, it was the political case for a European MLF that was pushed forward in Alliance circles from June 1962 onwards by the zealous US permanent representative to NATO, Thomas K. Finletter, while the military arguments were sidelined. British tactics remained to steer immediate talks between Alliance members back to the military requirement for MRBMs; as Lord Home, the Foreign Secretary, noted, 'If we can play the hand this way the discussions should go on for several months … This process may take the heat out of the subsequent discussion about the multilateral force without our having a head-on clash with the Americans.'[2]

For British policy there also remained the problematic issue of how de Gaulle's profound reservations over Britain joining the European Community could be overcome. The advice of Sir Pierson Dixon, the Ambassador in Paris, was that the French President had definitely decided to exclude Britain, but Macmillan was not yet convinced that de Gaulle had reached any final decision.[3] Thus, when he saw de Gaulle at the Chateau de Champs at the start of June, Macmillan did what he could to persuade the French President that Britain was suitably 'European minded' to become a member. The reasonable tone of the conversations at Champs, and the friendly feelings that were evidently on display between the two leaders gave the Prime Minister enough confidence to write to Kennedy that he thought this all indicated that 'de Gaulle will not offer strong resistance to our entry into the Community. Of course, there will be some hard bargaining still, but the French will see the position in broad political terms.'[4] There was, in fact, scant ground for such optimism, and it was apparent that de Gaulle's fundamental attitudes to British membership had not changed. After the meeting, he informed two senior French figures that he had told Macmillan that British views had 'evolved' and that 'you now understand how it would be in your interest to build Europe. But you are not yet ready to do this, since you remain attached to the world beyond Europe and because the idea of choosing between Europe and America is not yet ripe in your heart … Great Britain is coming towards Europe but it has not yet arrived.'[5]

Macmillan also informed Kennedy that there had been little firm discussion of nuclear matters at Champs, apart from de Gaulle's familiar explanation of why he considered that a small French nuclear force was essential. In the build-up to Champs the Prime Minister had, in fact, broached with Home and Heath, as well as close advisers such as de Zulueta, whether he should suggest the idea of Anglo-French defence collaboration, including future possibilities in the nuclear field. There were acknowledged to be many difficulties in such proposals, and the situation was exacerbated by the current bout of press speculation that an Anglo-French nuclear deal might be in the offing. The Prime Minister had even had to instruct Ormsby Gore to inform Kennedy that there was no validity to the stories and that he had 'no intention of doing anything foolish at Champs.'[6] In the latter half of May, Macmillan was also questioned directly in the House of Commons over whether he was contemplating this kind of bargain, to which he delivered a series of non-committal responses.[7] Knowledge of US disapproval was surely a major inhibitor on what the Prime Minister felt he could say to de Gaulle at Champs, while the Foreign Office was also very cautious about making any clear connections between defence and the final stage of the negotiations to enter the Community.

The British records for the conversations about European defence at Champs show that Macmillan and de Gaulle had skirted around the topic, the latter always (and characteristically) wanting to avoid being placed in the position of *demandeur*. On the second morning of the talks, on 3 June, Macmillan ventured that any future defence arrangements

> should be based upon an Atlantic Alliance. There must be a European organisation allied to the United States. There would be a plan for the defence of Europe. The nuclear power of European countries would be held as part of this European defence … he was convinced that a solid European organisation was the best solution. The Atlantic Alliance would then be an alliance of equals. There would be two pillars of approximately the same strength.[8]

When the Prime Minister asked whether the Germans would ever have nuclear weapons, and after receiving the reply that 'he did not wish them to do so but one day they would,' Macmillan had suggested 'that if a European defence became a reality there might be an arrangement by which Europe, including the Germans, would control its own nuclear deterrent.'[9] Later, de Gaulle claimed that Britain and France thought of their nuclear armaments in similar ways, and that

> If it was possible to make a reality of Europe then there would have to be an Anglo-French plan agreed with others. Such a plan would not exclude NATO although it would not be solely concerned with NATO. A small deterrent force would have to be kept separate if threats were made … It seemed to him that Britain and France were in the same psychological position in this matter and that this was an area in which agreement would be possible. It might be useful if further talks between the two Governments could take place about the future possibilities of cooperation in the political and defence fields.[10]

All this did not represent much advance on Heath's public comments in April, and the Prime Minister had been careful to stress the need to keep any Anglo-French arrangements linked to NATO. Two weeks after the Champs meeting, moreover, the Government's room for manoeuvre appeared to have been further narrowed when Washington's evolving views on the nuclear arrangements of the North Atlantic Alliance were made even more explicit.

The speech that McNamara had delivered in restricted session to NATO ministers in Athens at the start of May had been intended for private consumption, and its multiple, complex themes and ambiguous messages (how, for example, was it possible to reconcile the administration's call for greater spending on conventional arms, with its new enthusiasm for a Western European contribution to an MRBM force, which would carry major financial implications?) would take time digest and for appropriate European responses to be formulated. It was all the more vexing, therefore, when the US Defense Secretary chose to deliver an unclassified version of his remarks, which still contained some of their blunt language, in a commencement address at the University of Michigan in Ann Arbor on 16 June.[11] The repeat of the line that independent nuclear forces were 'dangerous, expensive and prone to obsolescence, and lacking in credibility as a deterrent,' caused particular irritation in London, even though many British officials thought it was a comment aimed specifically at French nuclear policy. Not all were prepared to be so charitable. The defence correspondent of *The Times*, for example, noted that the new American counterforce strategy had as an essential corollary that 'the western nuclear effort must be unified and centrally coordinated. There is no longer room for national nuclear deterrents which, if the enemy believes that they be used independently of the western alliance as a whole, are simply an invitation to the pre-emptive strike … In this context, Britain's V-bomber force is clearly vulnerable, and the projected striking force of General de Gaulle will be even more open to such an attack in the early stages of its development.'[12]

With a damaging story already current in *The New Statesman* alleging that his relations with McNamara had become deeply strained by Britain's approach to conventional defence spending, an exasperated Watkinson minuted the Prime Minister that although he was 'quite sure that [the speech] was not aimed at us but at the French', he thought it was 'awkward and will be used by our critics against us.' The Minister of Defence did not propose to respond publicly and he had instructed his press department 'to do their best to calm it down.' The dilemmas of taking a clear public posture towards the speech's content were plain, but Watkinson's

> personal preference would be to side with the French and to seek to persuade the Americans to accept the French position for what, in fact, it is – that of a small highly inefficient nuclear power. I am sure that the more McNamara or any other American attacks the French deterrent the more it makes the General and those around him absolutely determined to carry on with their current deterrent policy. Do you think it would be any good saying this to the Americans and asking them if they could not

manage to accept what is, after all, the fact? I do not necessarily believe this would encourage the Germans to do the same thing.

It was not going to be easy, Watkinson thought, to 'steer between the two conflicting policies of trying to be in agreement with the Americans and the French, particularly as I can see how much it is in our interests that we should not offend the French at this stage.' With Rusk soon scheduled to arrive in the UK, Watkinson wanted the former to reply to the inevitable press questions 'not that we were the good boys and the French the bad ... but merely that Mr McNamara's statement was on the lines of a policy that he and I had agreed together and one that we were indeed implementing because Bomber Command is targeted and integrated with Strategic Air Command.'[13]

Taking up Watkinson's prompt, the Foreign Secretary signalled to Rusk that the Ann Arbor speech was likely to 'give rise to strong attacks by the [Labour Party] Opposition on our policy of maintaining our contribution to the Western nuclear deterrent. In fact, the Opposition are likely to be elated with this opportunity.' If criticised in the House of Commons, he warned Rusk, ministers 'shall have to hit back and some hard things will have to be said.' Divergences between US and British approaches to deterrent policy might have to be revealed and 'thrashed out' on the floor of the House. There was 'much to be said in our own and American interests for taking the heat out of debates on this issue if possible.'[14] The line the Government chose to propound was that McNamara, with his criticism of independently *operating* nuclear forces, was not referring to the British strategic deterrent as Bomber Command worked according to an agreed and coordinated joint target plan with the US Strategic Air Command. The unattributed briefing material disseminated by the Foreign Office was even more explicit: the strategic role of the V-bomber force 'in support of NATO' was 'fully integrated' with that of the US strategic air force and its 'assigned targets are part of a unified plan.' The UK government had 'never conceived' of the V-force 'as contributing to anything in the nature of a third force'.[15] Nevertheless, critical comment continued, including a BBC television news report and commentary which Watkinson found so tendentious that he felt compelled to write a letter of protest to the BBC's director-general, Hugh Carleton Greene.[16]

Efforts at damage limitation continued. US Department of Defense spokesmen, when questioned in Washington, duly repeated the British official line, and were ready to add that 'control' of the force remained in the hands of the UK.[17] This all represented an unwelcome distraction, however, from the Government's prevailing concerns over how to lower French opposition to British entry into the Community. Hence, Ormsby Gore sought out McNamara in Washington where he explained, as the Ambassador reported, that

> in the coming weeks we would find ourselves in a very delicate situation over our negotiations to enter the Common Market. It was not therefore in our interest to have to point out all the time the differences between

our position over nuclear weapons and that of France. I was afraid that on this occasion his lucidity of mind and clarity of expression had proved something of an embarrassment to us.

McNamara took the point, but had wanted, he claimed, to undertake for the NATO allies 'a process of education' in the realities of the nuclear world and the choices in nuclear strategy that confronted the United States, of which his recent pronouncements had been a key part. At the close of their conversation, McNamara professed that he was 'very sorry for any difficulties' which his Ann Arbor speech had caused, and that he was 'extremely anxious to maintain very good and close relations with the British Government and he hoped that the excitement would soon die down.'[18]

Unfortunately it refused to do so. In the *New York Herald Tribune*, Walter Lippmann produced a column which claimed that the UK force could never be used independently and that the last word on its employment would always lie with President Kennedy. This was story which caught the Prime Minister's eye prompting him to send a curt message to Watkinson: 'As I see it, legally, the President can use the American deterrent *without* my agreement. I can use the British deterrent without his approval. We have a gentleman's agreement to consult each other "if there is time to do so". All that is being said to the contrary is just anti-British propaganda.'[19]

Anti-British propaganda or not, press coverage of McNamara's speech threatened to undo some of the work that ministers had put into the recent European negotiations. Bringing up the close integration of US and UK nuclear planning, rather than the independence of the UK force, was hardly likely to help delicate approaches to the French over how UK membership would affect defence arrangements between the key players within the EEC and helped to undermine the effect that Macmillan had tried to achieve at Champs when he had seen de Gaulle. Just when the requirements of Anglo-French diplomacy seemed to demand that ministers should assert the element of independence in British nuclear policy, the Ann Arbor speech had pushed them into stressing how close to the Americans they still remained.

In fact, Watkinson had already been busy with a further effort to kill the controversy once and for all by giving an interview to the defence correspondent of *The Times* on 22 June, where the position was affirmed that Britain had the 'unchallenged right to use its nuclear force independently or to withhold its use if the Government think it right to do so.' He explained that while Bomber Command's target plans were 'completely integrated' with those of SAC, Britain had the 'political freedom' to withdraw the force for 'national purposes,' but added his opinion that this would make 'no military sense at all in the present state of Anglo-American relations.' Watkinson went on to assure the correspondent – less than accurately – that 'all the implications' of the Ann Arbor speech had been discussed between himself and McNamara before it was made, and that the Government was in full agreement with the 'broad outlines' of US strategic thought. To suggest that

British nuclear targets in the coordinated plans with SAC were 'centres of population' was 'quite wrong', although there 'might well be many cases where it would be difficult to distinguish between military and civilian targets.' American belief in the value of the UK force, Watkinson argued, had been demonstrated by the assurances he had recently received from McNamara that the Skybolt missile was being produced according to plan. Nevertheless, whatever the 'official' British position, *The Times'* correspondent was adamant that the effect of the speech was to bring the British nuclear force 'firmly into the centre of the political scene' and that whether he meant it or not, McNamara's comments on small independent deterrents applied 'as forcibly to the British deterrent as any other.'[20] A day later, goaded by his earlier interview with Ormsby Gore, McNamara issued a statement which clarified that his Ann Arbor remarks referred to the dangers of separate capabilities operating independently. As Bomber Command's aircraft were organised as part of a coordinated Anglo-American force alongside SAC, this clearly did not apply in the UK case, 'although of course their political control remains with the British Government.' He had not been referring to the British force at Ann Arbor, McNamara reiterated, adding that the US 'appreciate[s] the important role' which the British force played in joint strike plans.[21]

From the contents of a personal memorandum that McNamara dispatched to Kennedy on the same day as his Ann Arbor address it is clear that the Defense Secretary did make a clear distinction in how he regarded British and French nuclear policy and their relationship to US interests. In McNamara's view

> Except for several short-lived episodes, such as the abortive Suez affair, British foreign policy for a century has rested on the proposition that it cannot afford a fundamental split with the US. This drawing together has become far more explicit in recent times in view of the over-riding importance the British attach to the American Alliance. The British have accepted the status of junior partner in the firm in exchange for a special relationship which they believe affords them a unique opportunity to influence US policy.

The British had forged their post-war nuclear policy in this political context, and were now reaping the benefits to the revision of US atomic energy legislation in 1958 that permitted the transfer of highly-sensitive US weapons information to the UK authorities. This had allowed the British for 'relatively small expenditure' to gain nuclear warhead technology which on qualitative terms was on a level with American. The advantages of the MDA and its later amendments for the UK were legion: the British could buy from the US or make as much nuclear material as they could afford; there were no restrictions on the size of their technical and scientific nuclear weapons establishment, or the nature of their research programme; or the number and type of nuclear systems they chose to field. Except for data on gaseous diffusion, the UK was 'privy to virtually every US development in the nuclear weapons field. They had the run of almost every US research institution; access to a large part of US intelligence data; and they could, if they chose to do so, construct almost any one of the US weapon designs...'

As for the level of independence that the British were able to enjoy, McNamara felt it would be

> difficult to contend that the US controls the British nuclear program in the sense that we make, or influence, the British to do things to which they really object. Rather, the more reasonable interpretation is that the harmonization of their nuclear policy with that of the US caused them no pain, and that the atomic assistance received from the US has been sheer profit.

At the same time McNamara recognised that the UK had had to play a price for this special nuclear relationship with the US, including accommodating a number of American facilities on UK soil which had created occasional political problems at home, and showing cooperation over several colonial issues. McNamara stressed the different quality of Franco-American to Anglo-American relations, and the way this influenced the nuclear field. 'We lack the long experience of close partnership,' he noted. 'Not only de Gaulle's ideas, but French ideas generally are not easily assimilable [sic] to our ideas.' The French under de Gaulle were 'determined to re-establish a political position they had not had for generations.' France's recent negative attitudes toward NATO and the presence of US nuclear weapons on its soil did not auger well for the future: there was not a 'firm and well-established foundation of mutual confidence and trust which would seem to be essential for an activity so delicate and important as nuclear sharing.' Unlike de Gaulle, the British had been 'willing to live within the nuclear policy favored by the US, and they have done so without having to sign any written commitments to this effect beyond the [1958] arrangement not to retransmit data and atomic materials. On the other hand, there is reason to believe that de Gaulle is unwilling similarly to restrict his policy options whether the pledge would be written or unwritten.' As far as McNamara was concerned, 'the British have not surrendered their independence, however little it may be worth. And the French are no more likely to. Finally, since the US is the great nuclear power, the French have every incentive to seek coordination with us whether or not we assist them rather than the other way around. The problem to be overcome is de Gaulle's sense of pride.'[22]

Less than a week after Ann Arbor, Rusk had talks in Paris with senior French officials. After discussing the latest US position on the MLF with the French Foreign Minister, Maurice Couve de Murville, the conversation turned to how France would organise its nascent nuclear force. Couve said he thought, like the British, it might have combined targeting with the Americans but ultimate independent control. He added, moreover, that 'In the theoretical event of the Continent being overrun by Russian conventional forces and the Americans at that point not having made use of their nuclear arms, he thought it conceivable that the British might then use theirs independently. There was no question of the French force being used independently except in the very last resort.' When asked by Rusk if this meant the *force de frappe* would be used to trigger an American nuclear response, Couve simply replied that 'they would not be so silly.'[23]

Reading an account of Rusk's meeting, Macmillan was irritated that the Americans had again raised their MLF proposals with the French, as well as nuclear issues in general. The Prime Minister's reaction is not surprising. For Macmillan, a successful outcome to the negotiations on EEC entry was now regarded as Britain's overriding objective, but he was anxious that Washington's approach to Alliance matters, including its espousal of the idea of the MLF, could prejudice that goal. At the end of June, Macmillan can be found complaining to Home:

> If we cannot persuade the Americans to keep quiet about the Common Market, I would hope that we could at least impress on Rusk the importance of leaving the nuclear question, and indeed the re-organisation of NATO, until the negotiations with the Six have come to a head. In the nuclear field, we have an independent deterrent and the French are going to get one; these are facts which the Americans cannot alter. There is therefore no point in their going on talking about them; the moment to take stock will come quite soon after our talks with the Six have ended.[24]

Part of the problem was that the Kennedy administration's policy toward the issue was, as the official history of the Office of the Secretary of Defense puts it, in a state of 'disarray', 'proceeding more by drift and instinct than by direction.' The MLF had few supporters in the Department of Defense, and Norstad continued to advance his own agenda, behaving almost in the manner of a semi-independent pro-consul. Kennedy's advisers on Bundy's NSC staff were divided on the issue (with Bundy himself notably lukewarm), and the policy found its strongest adherents amongst the Europeanists at the State Department. For his own part, the President himself seemed prepared to run with the MLF idea in the absence of anything that seemed better, but there were clear limits to the political capital he would be prepared to invest in the scheme if it ran into serious opposition.[25]

Although Rusk was prepared to admit to British officials that German pressures for a nuclear capability had relented since the Athens meeting of the NATO Council, the United States did not want to give the impression to other members of the Alliance that it was indifferent to the MRBM issue. His anxiety above all, as he informed Home at the end of June, was the evidence he saw that 'the Germans would, sooner or later, seek to have a nuclear capacity of their own unless they were offered some alternative arrangement such as the multilateral force.' The US Secretary of State saw a need to move the talks within NATO forward 'with all deliberate speed', and 'he was not asking [the UK] to agree with the American position but simply that we should not frustrate the exercise.' Home's response was to assure Rusk that the British would not try to prevent the issues being discussed in NATO, but he hoped that the political problems, as opposed to the military need for an MRBM force, could be reserved for later discussion.[26]

McNamara's hope that the fuss created by his Ann Arbor speech would soon dissipate was not to be realised. On 26 June, just a few days after the US Defense Secretary's interview with Ormsby Gore, several Labour MPs, reacting in part to the repeated attacks in the past by the Conservatives for their Party's allegedly incoherent approach to Britain's nuclear future, took the opportunity to quiz Macmillan very closely in the House of Commons on where the Government's nuclear policy now stood. The Prime Minister began with the statement that the independent deterrent was

> the creation of successive British Governments of both parties. The British Government of the day is, of course, constitutionally free to determine upon the use of this power. Nevertheless, as a matter of practice, there has been joint planning between the British and American authorities against any future emergency. What may be the ultimate development of European defence is a matter for consideration with changing circumstances.

However, Harold Wilson, for one, was not satisfied, and referred to the fact that as a result of recent pronouncements, both British and American governments seemed to have condemned 'the idea of independent deterrents which are capable of operating independently', and asked for further clarification. Refuting Wilson's interpretation, the Prime Minister ploughed on by saying,

> It is for us to decide what we are to do. We have to recognize – and do recognize – that France is now a nuclear power, and is likely to remain one. There are great problems which can be discussed as to the future. For the present, we have this independent deterrent ... [and] there are very strong reasons for maintaining it, and we intend to do so.

This was not enough, though, to prevent further probing about how the UK force could operate independently when it was 'integrated' with that of the US for planning purposes, and so presumably could not be used without American approval. Again, Macmillan had to try to explain that 'although in practice the targets are discussed and arranged between us', the force itself was under complete national control: 'the sovereignty, the power of control, rests with Her Majesty's Ministers for the time being, and the officers concerned would follow the instructions given to them by the Government of the day.' Sensing the contradictions that seemed to lie within the Prime Minister's argument, Gaitskell then raised the inconsistency between McNamara's

346 *The prelude to Nassau*

recent remarks and the Government's position. All Macmillan could reply was he was 'not responsible for what Mr McNamara may have said' and that there remained strong reasons, as Gaitskell himself had recognised in 1960, for retaining a deterrent under national control.[27] During the summer of 1962, it is apparent, and partly owing to the exigencies of party political considerations as well as the after-effects of the Ann Arbor speech, the Government's rhetorical commitment to maintenance of a strategic nuclear force under independent control showed no signs of diminishing.

Skybolt cancellation and the deterrent gap

Meanwhile, the BNDSG was nearing the end of its long consideration of future options for maintaining a national deterrent force which had become more than ever associated with Conservative defence policy. The Group's efforts would, however, receive overall direction from a new Minister of Defence. Macmillan's ruthless cull of the Cabinet in mid-July 1962 saw Watkinson lose his ministerial office (to his evident surprise and distress), and the arrival of Peter Thorneycroft at the MoD in his place. An experienced politician, with strong pro-European beliefs, over the previous two years Thorneycroft had done his best to drive through economy measures at the Ministry of Aviation and had been an advocate of offering residual missile technology from the Blue Streak programme to France as a way to build stronger Anglo-French defence cooperation (which might eventually develop a nuclear dimension).[28] Thorneycroft evidently believed that the issue of a successor system to the V-force would have to be confronted soon. However, Scott advised the new Minister just after his arrival that a decision over a successor would not have to be taken for another year or two, and that the best solution would ultimately prove to be one based on Polaris submarines. But whether such a system should be entirely independent of American 'control and participation' remained a moot point, and Scott himself thought it worth exploring ideas of a US-UK-French, or NATO deterrent for the longer term future.[29]

By early October 1962, the Permanent Under Secretary felt the need to open the discussion over a successor system with the Minister's Private Office again, not least as speculation about a possible NATO or European-shared deterrent, or of 'rationalising' the UK deterrent with the French, was becoming more widespread, while future capacity at Aldermaston also had to be determined. The first question to be settled was the most basic one of whether the Government wanted to maintain a strategic nuclear deterrent over the long term (the issue that Macmillan had deferred at the Defence Committee meeting in January 1962). Assuming the answer was yes, Scott then argued that:

> we must reconcile ourselves to the certainty that we cannot ourselves devise, construct and maintain a wholly independent system. Do we wish

to join with the Americans, or the French, or with NATO? Whatever the formula for control and whatever system is chosen, large sums will have to be added to the Defence Budget. Are these to be additional to other funds, or will they be provided only at the expense of other items of defence expenditure and if so which commitments are to be dropped?

Anticipating that these questions would be addressed by ministers in the context of another discussion of forward strategy that was just then beginning, Scott nevertheless proffered his own opinion that if the UK entered the EEC as hoped, some measure of cooperation with the French could be discussed before the V-force ceased to be credible, but if these negotiations were to prove fruitless, then the possibility of a NATO force could be examined.[30]

Scott's entreaties appear to have had some effect, as towards the end of October he was asked to reconvene the BNDSG. Under Thorneycroft's instructions, the Group was again to consider the issue of a successor to the V-bomber force, but now in the context of some kind of 'internationally shared' system. It was significant that at the same time the Foreign Office was beginning to come forward with ideas for the creation over the long term, and after British membership of the European Community had been consolidated, of a NATO nuclear force specifically allocated to European defence, and consisting of contributions from the UK, France and the United States.[31]

Certainly by now a major influence on the trajectory of Scott's thinking was the unavoidable assumption that after Skybolt it was unlikely that another US system would be supplied to the UK without political strings attached.[32] Moreover, in its consideration of deterrent criteria, by the autumn the Group seems to have accepted that a 15-city criterion would be sufficient to deter the Soviet Union (even though this lower figure had not yet received explicit ministerial endorsement). At this stage the Admiralty had also worked up a full paper for the BNDSG on the Hybrid concept for Polaris. This envisaged a seven submarine force, with each boat equipped with eight Polaris missiles, and allowing three or four to be kept at sea at any one time. Three such boats would offer a 15-city deterrent, and four a 20-city capability. During peacetime the submarines would be used in a regular hunter/killer role, but in times of tension they would become a force able 'to pose a powerful and fully credible deterrent threat to the Soviet Union.' If orders were placed in 1966, the first boat could be operational by 1970, and the full force by the mid-1970s.[33]

After convening a meeting with Scott, Mountbatten and Zuckerman on the future of the deterrent, at the end of October Thorneycroft was circulating his own thoughts that, *inter alia*, 'Britain could not opt out of the nuclear business in the post-Skybolt era,' but that development costs would probably have to be shared with Europe and/or the United States, and that such additional expenditure on the deterrent would require the MoD's forward estimates of defence spending to be increased.[34] Nevertheless, in the absence of a fundamental political decision over priorities in defence policy, the future of the deterrent – beyond the Government's rhetorical commitment to its maintenance – was still uncertain in the autumn of 1962, with no allowance made in the MoD's long-term costings for a replacement to the V-bomber force.[35]

It was still of course assumed within the Ministry of Defence that the short and medium-term future of the UK's strategic nuclear force was underwritten by the agreement to purchase Skybolt from the United States. Making his first visit to the United States as the new Minister of Defence in mid-September 1962, Thorneycroft had however heard at first hand from McNamara about the steadily rising costs of Skybolt during its prolonged development and testing phase (which had increased by 30 per cent from the previous year's estimate), the total costs of which were now expected to reach $500 million, to which would have to be added production costs of $1.8 billion to meet an initial order of 1,100 missiles. Nevertheless, the US Defence Secretary made no mention of any reconsideration of the merits of continuing with the programme. The Minister of Defence, for his part, was keen to stress that Skybolt occupied for the British Government 'a very special position,' that 'they had no alternative in mind', and 'it would be a major sensation if it failed to arrive.'[36]

The chief preoccupation of both McNamara and President Kennedy during Thorneycroft's visit, however, was on the French nuclear issue and the possibilities of Franco-German nuclear collaboration, with both men said to be 'resentful and distrustful of … French and German intentions.' Thorneycroft was inclined to downplay any such talk of German nuclear ambitions, but Kennedy was irritated enough to warn that if the Germans started work in the nuclear realm which broke their international obligations (under the 1954 Treaty of Paris) not to manufacture nuclear weapons the US might have to reconsider its troop commitments in Europe and 'haul out'. In a further attempt to dispel any lingering doubts following his Ann Arbor speech, McNamara made clear that the United States considered that the British possession of a national deterrent force was of a different character to the French because in the former case 'independent political control coupled with integrated targeting was tolerable to the United States because of basic identity of political outlook and aims and because we understood each other well. These could not be taken for granted by the United States in the case of France.'[37]

The upbeat report with which Thorneycroft returned from Washington (he told the Prime Minister that his reception in the United States could 'not have been more hospitable and the talks could not have been franker') might have been qualified if he had been aware of the State Department's increasingly firm conviction that positive steps should be taken to scale back the extent of Anglo-American nuclear cooperation. Echoing the advice he had received from Kohler earlier in the year, a few days before the Thorneycroft visit Rusk had written to McNamara to remind him of the importance of the April 1961 Policy Directive on the long-term future of the British deterrent. When the current negotiations on British EEC entry were concluded, he explained, it would be necessary to re-examine the special UK–US nuclear relationship, in the context of US desires 'that future European nuclear efforts are based on genuinely multilateral rather than national programs.' Before this exercise was conducted, the Secretary of State believed it was 'of the utmost importance to avoid any actions to expand the relationship. Such actions could seriously prejudice future decisions and developments and make more difficult the working out of sound multilateral arrangements.' Rusk expressed his confidence that McNamara understood that any moves by the UK to acquire Polaris or similar systems as a successor to the V-bomber force were to be avoided, and that 'US decisions relative to Skybolt should be made on the basis solely of US interest in this missile for our own forces.' Maintaining this posture was considered important because the UK was probably considering its future nuclear options once it had entered the EEC and that a European deterrent force would have to be based on missiles rather than manned bombers. Previous British interest in Polaris, it was conjectured, might be revived, in an effort to perpetuate a UK national force which could then be combined with the French under joint arrangements.

Rusk then expressed in the clearest terms possible that Macmillan's conception of a pooled Anglo-French nuclear deterrent, held in trust for Europe, had no support in the State Department: 'Such an arrangement might be termed a European multilateral force, although it would in fact be neither European (since it would discriminate against the Germans) nor multilateral (since it would involve nationally manned and owned forces). By reason of these facts, such an arrangement would be politically divisive and vastly complicate our efforts to hold pressures for a German national program in check.' There was much uncertainty about which direction British thinking on such issues would go, Rusk wanted to emphasise, but US willingness to supply Polaris without tying it to genuinely multilateral arrangements could influence the UK to turn in a direction inimical to the wider goals of US European policy.[38]

Over Skybolt, McNamara had already decided by August 1962 – and before he saw Thorneycroft – that in view of its technical uncertainties and questionable cost effectiveness, more investment in the project was not advisable and that it should be omitted from the administration's defence budget proposals when they were finalised at the end of the year. In late October, after the worst perils of the Cuban Missile Crisis had passed, McNamara and his deputy, Roswell Gilpatric, discussed the likelihood that the annual budget review would probably result in a recommendation to cancel, and resolved that the issue should be decided 'on its merits, without reference to a "commitment" to the British.' US officials were aware that such a decision would create major problems for the British Government, but saw themselves under no formal obligation to supply Skybolt: the formal agreement reached in September 1960 had stipulated that the system would be sold only if it completed necessary development (and the British, it should be recalled, had contributed no funding at all to Skybolt development). It was at this stage that the

Defence Research Staff at the British Embassy in Washington became alert to the 'grave' situation that had now arisen, and Ormsby Gore was informed. The Ambassador's immediate reaction was that it would be difficult to make an official approach, either to the Pentagon or the White House, in advance of a formal decision to end the programme. Nevertheless, by early November, as McNamara put the recommendation to cancel to the Joint Chiefs of Staff, press rumours also began to circulate that the project was under threat, prompting some British defence officials to make further enquiries in Washington.[39]

On 5 November an anxious Thorneycroft sent a message to McNamara, intended to invite a reassuring reply about the status of the project, which referred to an upcoming test of the missile.[40] His hand forced, McNamara convened a meeting on 7 November involving the President, Rusk, Bundy, and Paul Nitze, the Assistant Secretary of Defense for International Security Affairs. Here Kennedy was content with McNamara's recommendation that Skybolt should be cancelled, and the main business of the meeting was in dealing with the fallout. It was recognised that cancellation would represent a serious political blow to Macmillan's Government, and possibly even lead to its fall, an eventuality which no-one wanted to see. Furthermore, the Camp David understandings of March 1960 reached between Eisenhower and Macmillan, and the impression that had been created of Skybolt progress since then, was held to impose a moral obligation on the administration to provide some replacement. The possible provision of Polaris was mentioned by both Bundy and McNamara, but in any event it was acknowledged that the British would have to be informed that cancellation was likely and given time to decide what to propose before the administration made its final recommendation on the defence budget towards the end of the month.[41]

Back in London, Thorneycroft drew the Foreign Secretary's attention to the emerging crisis, recalling that he had told McNamara in September that it would be a 'catastrophe' for the UK if the Skybolt programme was scrapped, and this would have

> the most profound repercussions over the whole field of Anglo-American relations. The implications go wider than defence. Cancellation of Skybolt would have a profoundly disturbing effect upon the attitude to America on the Conservative Back Bench.

Convinced that the Americans could overcome Skybolt's problems if they were prepared to expend the requisite effort, he now asked for Home's support in emphasising to the US administration the 'disastrous' effect on relations of a decision to cancel: 'It would certainly provoke a first-class political crisis in this country.'[42]

On 8 November, Ormsby Gore was summoned to the Pentagon for what proved to be a difficult meeting with the US Defense Secretary. McNamara explained that Skybolt cancellation was under serious consideration, but stressed that no final decision had been reached, and there would be consultation with the UK before it was made. There was no mistaking the Ambassador's subsequent agitation, Ormsby Gore describing abandonment of the programme as 'political dynamite' which would reduce to 'ruins' a major part of British defence policy. People would speculate that this was a means by which the US administration could put pressure on the Government to abandon an independent nuclear deterrent, Ormsby Gore argued, and he proceeded to lay out the serious political consequences that would follow for the Government, and also to the fabric of the Anglo-American relationship if the decision was confirmed. Acknowledging the political considerations, McNamara presented three alternatives, including the idea of the UK continuing the Skybolt project and its development from its own resources; the alternative of the 'Hound Dog' air-to-surface cruise missile (which the US Air Force had introduced as a temporary measure in 1960 before the arrival of Skybolt); and another alternative missile system 'such as Minuteman or Polaris.' The Ambassador expressed his doubts as to whether any of these options would be satisfactory for the Government's purposes.[43]

The following day, by arrangement, McNamara and Thorneycroft spoke on the telephone. Once more McNamara maintained that no final decisions about Skybolt had been taken, and that it was likely to be several more weeks before firm recommendations or decisions emerged. McNamara observed that the technical aspects of the programme could probably be resolved, but his principal concern lay with Skybolt's rising costs, and the delays in timescale that were being experienced. The Minister of Defence could only underline the great political problems that a decision to cancel would bring and that full consultation between the two Governments would be required before any final decision. If Skybolt were to be abandoned, Thorneycroft noted, then 'it would be necessary for the two Governments to consider alternative means of providing the British Government with an independent deterrent but also to ensure that both Governments were fully in line in their public presentation of such a decision.' 'He was at pains to stress,' the report of the telephone conversation recorded, 'the need for any alternative British deterrent – whether Polaris or any other – to have the same degree of independence as Skybolt would have. McNamara took this point.' Once he was fully apprised of the Skybolt situation, and of possible alternatives, McNamara said he was prepared to come to London to discuss the subject more fully with his British opposite number.[44]

Worried by what he had heard, the Minister of Defence took the immediate step of asking for a study of alternative means by which the UK could continue to have an independent deterrent if Skybolt were cancelled. Among the issues that he expected to be addressed was how long the Blue Steel stand-off missile, which had entered service with the V-bomber force earlier in the year, could be continued as a credible deterrent weapon, and within what timescale could British-built Polaris submarines be available.[45] Thorneycroft's own view was that he would be 'prepared to settle for four Polaris submarines here and now without strings, and that we should be put in a position to build our own by 1970.'[46] In response to the Minister's request, Scott held a special meeting of the BNDSG on 14 November to consider the options, although this was done in the face of some opposition from the Air Ministry, which not only disliked the BNDSG itself – as a forum where the RAF's role as the future carrier of the deterrent was challenged – but simply wanted to avoid any discussion of the subject.

The Group's deliberations revealed the seriousness of the position. Anxious officials voiced the opinion that limited-range missiles on manned bombers, such as Hound Dog or Blue Steel, were not considered suitable for the long-term as Soviet air defences would increase in strength and effectiveness during the coming few years (while Blue Steel itself could not be maintained on constant airborne alert, rendering it vulnerable to a pre-emptive strike). The Air Ministry doubted that the TSR-2 advanced strike aircraft then under development, though capable of reaching some targets in the Soviet Union, could provide a viable substitute for Skybolt; in any case TSR-2 was not expected to enter service in any numbers until 1969. Land-based weapons, such as Minuteman, or a new US-developed MRBM (dubbed Missile X), were also deemed unsatisfactory, not least as the vulnerability of fixed-sites had been one of the stated reasons for Blue Streak's cancellation in 1960. Going ahead with Skybolt alone – with the UK taking over development from the Americans – would be too expensive and risky a proposition to entertain, but it was felt that if Britain's insistence that the Skybolt programme should continue were to show signs of weakening, the Americans would be encouraged to push for alternatives, and in that case 'the State Department might press for multilateral solutions.' 'It was desirable that our reaction to any US decision to cancel Skybolt should be as vigorous as possible,' the meeting was told.

> If the Americans did cancel it, we should have a moral claim on them to help us to provide ourselves with an alternative deterrent. One possibility might be for them to let us have Polaris missiles, or even a complete submarine deterrent system, without political strings.

It should be possible for a UK warhead to be produced for Polaris by about 1965/66, it was optimistically predicted, but a hybrid submarine capable of both carrying Polaris and performing hunter/killer duties could not be ready before 1972.

The most troubling aspect to the option of a Polaris replacement, with the submarines built in the UK, therefore, was the 'gap' in deterrent capability that would open up from the mid-1960s when the V-bomber/Blue Steel combination might be unable to penetrate Soviet air defences, and the early 1970s when the first new Polaris boats could be deployed. If it were made available as an alternative, the purchase of complete Polaris submarines from the Americans, along with the missiles themselves and warheads would not only be very costly, but make any such force subject to an American veto (which could be made practical through new electronic locks on warheads – what would later become known as Permissive Action Links), and to multilateral rather than national control. This would clearly spell the end of any claims that Britain would possess an independent deterrent. Summing up the group's conclusions, Scott found that:

a   if a gap was acceptable after our present deterrent system expires (i.e. about 1965), the answer seemed to be Polaris missiles without political strings, with British submarines and warheads; this would not be possible before 1972;
b   if a gap was not acceptable (and the meeting felt that if a gap was allowed to develop, this country would find it impossible to create an independent deterrent again), neither Minuteman nor Missile X seemed likely to fill the bill;
c   it therefore seemed that, if we wanted to maintain an independent deterrent without a gap, there was no alternative to Skybolt.

The meeting resulted in the Ministry of Aviation being asked to see if it was possible to develop a longer-range version of Blue Steel in a short timescale; the Air Ministry to look again at the credible life of the existing V-bomber/ Blue Steel combination; the Admiralty to examine a 'crash' programme for its hybrid submarine concept, and a programme involving the purchase or lease of two Polaris submarines from the Americans; and AWRE to study how quickly a Polaris-type warhead could be produced.[47] The BNDSG, as Scott's summary had recorded, clearly felt that the perception of a gap in deterrent capability that would be opened by Skybolt cancellation was a threat to the entire concept of possession of a national deterrent force and should be filled by whatever expedient means seemed possible.

On 20 November, Macmillan met Home, Thorneycroft and Heath to review the unfolding Skybolt crisis. If the project were cancelled and no suitable alternative could be agreed between London and Washington, Thorneycroft predicted 'disastrous' political consequences for the Government. However, the advice received from Ormsby Gore in Washington was that as the President and McNamara were fully aware of the political implications for the Government, a high-level approach to the US administration was at this stage superfluous. There was a danger, nevertheless, that the news of an American decision to cancel would leak, and so the Americans should be asked to defer this final step until Thorneycroft had had an opportunity to speak in person with McNamara about possible alternatives. Meanwhile, the MoD would work on costings for other options, so that officials would be in a good position to make recommendations at short notice.[48]

Three days later, President Kennedy met McNamara and other senior officials to settle several outstanding details arising from the Department of Defense's draft budget recommendations. Among their conclusions was that

354 *The prelude to Nassau*

Skybolt cancellation should be confirmed 'subject to consultation with the UK on alternatives.'⁴⁹ McNamara now had an opportunity to begin the process of consultation with Thorneycroft that had been promised, but he delayed travelling to Europe – or even exchanging messages with the Minister of Defence – until 11 December. He had hoped to come to London for a brief trip at the end of November, he told Ormsby Gore, but intensive work on the US defense budget had prevented this.⁵⁰ One additional reason for the hiatus may have been that McNamara realised he had not done anything up to that point to disabuse Thorneycroft of the belief that Polaris could be offered as a straight substitute for Skybolt, and so 'without strings'.

In fact, on 24 November, Rusk had written to McNamara to make it plain that the State Department would be adamantly opposed to any such move. Instead, Rusk put forward three alternatives: Britain to continue with Skybolt development and production (with US financial and technical assistance); provision of Hound Dog missiles for use with the V-bomber force; and participation in a sea-based NATO MRBM force, with mixed-manning of surface ships. 'It seems essential,' Rusk had stressed, 'that we make quite clear to the British that there is no possibility of our helping them set up a nationally manned and owned MRBM force.' This State Department approach was based on the critical European reaction that would follow any decision to extend the UK-US nuclear relationship from its current V-bomber phase into the new sphere of MRBMs, and that the US had 'repeatedly emphasised that we would only facilitate MRBM procurement for a force under genuinely multilateral manning and ownership.'⁵¹ What is surprising in retrospect was how little objection was made by McNamara to the State Department's position, as it undercut the comments he had already made concerning Polaris to Thorneycroft, and the implicit suggestion that this could be furnished as a direct replacement for Skybolt.⁵²

By the end of the month, press reports had gathered pace that Skybolt was in serious trouble following the failure of some of its latest tests, and amid widespread doubts over its cost effectiveness at the Pentagon. There was now no escaping the unpalatable choices confronting the Government. Second guessing the work the BNDSG had just set in hand, Scott advised Thorneycroft that it was obvious that the V-bomber/Blue Steel combination, even if the latter could be given improved performance, would cease to be viable after about 1965/66, while TSR-2 could not offer an adequate replacement. There seemed no prospect that British-built Polaris submarines could be ready before the early 1970s, while fixed-base missile sites in the UK were not a credible solution. Proposals for an internationalised force of Polaris submarines, as pushed by Washington, would not be an acceptable alternative to an independent British deterrent. Two choices therefore seemed to remain:

a Accepting a gap of years in which we should have no valid strategic deterrent of our own.

b Persuading the Americans to sell, or rent, us some Polaris submarines with their missiles, complete except for the warheads. (We could probably adapt the Skybolt warhead for Polaris; if this proved impossible it might take as long as five years to produce a new warhead.)

Both options had significant drawbacks, however. Allowing a gap to develop in the credibility of the deterrent in the second half of the 1960s was a hard proposition to entertain, not least as it was 'difficult to see us going out of this business for some years and then coming back in,' while acquiring Polaris submarines from the Americans – if they were even on offer – would underline dependence on the US, be expensive in terms of foreign exchange costs, and deny work to British companies.[53]

The unfortunate interval between the meeting in Washington on 23 November, when Kennedy effectively took the basic decision to cancel, and 11 December, when McNamara finally arrived at Gatwick airport to a crowd of reporters asking about the status of Skybolt, tended to fuel anxieties in British official circles about US intentions, and gave the press ample opportunity to dig further into the story of a potential Anglo-American rift.[54] The atmosphere was not helped by the ill-timed speech given by Dean Acheson, the former US Secretary of State (and sometime adviser on NATO policy to the Kennedy administration), at West Point on 5 December, which alleged that Britain had lost an empire and not yet found a role, and that its attempts to 'play a separate power role' apart from Europe, based on its 'special relationship' with the United States and position as head of a Commonwealth which had no unity, strength or structure, was 'about to be played out.' Although Acheson's unofficial intervention was intended, by his later account, to urge the Government forward, in a supportive fashion, with the negotiations for EEC entry, its effects on popular attitudes and opinion was anything but constructive. An ever-laconic Macmillan noted in his diary that Acheson 'was always a conceited ass, but I don't really think he meant to be offensive.'[55] In fact, the Prime Minister's officials had to persuade him to tone down a fiercely-worded letter of protest he had at first wanted to send to Acheson.[56]

For once, Ormsby Gore's antennae in Washington were not quite attuned to the gravity of the crisis, as he had formed the impression that British needs in the event of Skybolt cancellation would be automatically met by the administration. In early December, the Ambassador wrote to the Prime Minister to reassure him that the consequences for his Government of a decision to cancel were fully appreciated by the White House. The President himself was a

> highly developed political animal and is even more acutely aware [than McNamara] of the political implications. When I last talked to him about Skybolt, he said that if we all came to the conclusion that the weapon was no good or hopelessly extravagant in resources, then the Americans ought to provide us with whatever weapons system suited us, and he

mentioned both Polaris and Minuteman. To be fair, he had not at that time given the matter any detailed thought, but I think it is indicative of the feeling here that there is a strong moral obligation on the Americans to offer us some satisfactory alternative to Skybolt if it is to be abandoned. Above all they are determined not to be accused of using the technical failure of Skybolt in order to bring pressure upon us to abandon our nuclear independence. If, therefore, Skybolt cannot be saved, this is certainly the moment for us to put forward whatever alternative demands we may wish to make.[57]

But there were several factions in the State Department who did indeed see the Skybolt crisis as an occasion where Britain might be persuaded to renounce its independent strategic nuclear force, while the 'strong moral obligation' Ormsby Gore had mentioned was not universally recognised in Washington. More frequently encountered was the legalistic American view that no formal agreement existed between the two governments which compelled them to supply Skybolt under all circumstances, and there was also a degree of annoyance that the British had attached the future of their deterrent so firmly to a weapons system the production of which could not be guaranteed.

The Minister of Defence was now certainly of the view that Skybolt cancellation offered the chance to move to a Polaris deterrent force. By 7 December, when it was clear that McNamara would soon be arriving in London, Thorneycroft (with Scott's advice probably in mind) had formulated the positon he would adopt when he saw the US Defense Secretary.[58] Despite advice from the Ministry of Aviation – which like the MoD, was concerned about the deterrent gap – that Skybolt was technically still a sound project, Thorneycroft did not feel that attempting to persuade the Americans to reconsider cancellation would be good tactics.[59]

Instead, Thorneycroft informed Macmillan that he wanted to ask for the provision of an 'alternative weapon system to suit our conditions and on the same basis as Skybolt, i.e. with no political or other strings or conditions upon the use to which we put our force.' Polaris, in the Minister of Defence's opinion, was the only such suitable alternative, and the Admiralty, he noted, already had outline plans for the construction of a force of hybrid submarines, each carrying eight missiles, which meant that seven boats would be required to meet UK needs. Under an accelerated programme, the first hybrid submarine might be ready as early as 1970, and the whole force deployed by 1974, but as the credibility of the V-bomber force armed with Blue Steel missiles and free fall bombs was likely to 'disappear' after the mid-1960s, it was acknowledged that this would give rise to a gap in the effectiveness of the deterrent. The temporary solution envisaged by Thorneycroft to close this gap was to 'borrow' two or three Polaris submarines from the Americans, with the warheads for its missiles provided by the UK, until the British-built hybrid submarines became available. The Americans, Thorneycroft summed up, should be asked:

a   to re-affirm their support for an independent strategic nuclear deterrent;
b   to undertake to give us options to acquire what we need for this purpose. What this will be requires careful working out with them, but it will include the purchase by us of a number of Polaris missiles with control and navigational equipment; the loan to us of two or three complete Polaris carrying submarines for a period of years until our own submarines are ready; and technical help in assisting us to create, maintain, and operate the force.[60]

The Prime Minister, however, was not entirely convinced that such a forthright approach would yield dividends. His initial instinct, as he told Thorneycroft on 9 December, was to take a 'cagey line', and he felt, according to one of his Private Secretaries that 'the best plan would be to play Skybolt along for another year or eighteen months to avoid political difficulties at home,' although it was 'clearly in our interests to get on to a Polaris deterrent at some stage'.[61]

Meanwhile, on that same day in Washington, Zuckerman had been at the Pentagon for a series of meetings and took the opportunity to see McNamara, who ran through some of the alternative options for the UK if Skybolt were to be cancelled. The last mentioned was Polaris, which Zuckerman recommended as the only option which 'did not appear to suffer from technical or political objections or both.' Although in Zuckerman's view McNamara seemed to want to be as 'helpful' as possible, he did also observe that Polaris could cause 'embarrassment' to the UK in its EEC negotiations.[62]

Meanwhile, the Kennedy administration was beginning to settle its position. Just before he left for his London meeting with Thorneycroft, on 10 December McNamara saw the President, Rusk and Bundy to review a number of issues, including the latest situation regarding Skybolt. McNamara explained that in his talks with Thorneycroft he would

> present the strongest possible case for the technical decision which was anticipated, and he proposed to offer the United Kingdom three alternative means of meeting its requirements. The British could meet the remaining development costs of Skybolt themselves and buy what they wanted for their own use; an adaptation of Hound Dog might be developed and supplied; or there might be UK participation in a multilateral system of some sort.

However, McNamara did not think that the British would be happy with any of these State Department-inspired options, and so he believed that

> we might consider, at some stage in the negotiations ... a proposal to give the British access to a more up-to-date weapons system on the condition that the venture became multilateral if and when a multilateral force was developed. Such a course might conceivably be taken, for example, with Polaris.

Rusk, by contrast, was more inclined at this stage to offer extra assistance to the British to meet the rest of the development costs of Skybolt, so they could still eventually acquire the system. Kennedy indicated his approval for McNamara's line, saying 'that he was not eager to join in a large share of further development costs for a weapon to be supplied only to the British.'[63]

In the event, the manner of McNamara's arrival in the UK on 11 December contributed to the sharp deterioration in relations between London and Washington that was already being witnessed. Responding to the questioning of reporters soon after leaving his aircraft, he delivered a prepared statement which confirmed that Skybolt's recent tests had been failures, that the project was suffering from major technical difficulties, and that its costs were rising. Rather than coming to London for consultation over Skybolt's future, McNamara's press statement (issued against the advice of George Ball of the State Department) in effect gave notice that cancellation had already been decided in Washington.[64] It was hardly the most politic of ways to begin his visit, and the ensuing encounter with Thorneycroft was notably tense (or a 'foregone disaster', in Ball's later apt summary).[65] Reading from a prepared text, McNamara had begun by explaining the reasons why the US administration had reached the conclusion it would have to cancel the project, stressing the technical issues that still had to be overcome with Skybolt's development programme. Recognising the problems this would create for the British Government, McNamara then outlined the three alternatives agreed with the President and the State Department. To Thorneycroft's evident surprise, if not dismay, there was no explicit offer made of Polaris as a Skybolt replacement (especially as Zuckerman had reported that McNamara had talked about a Polaris option two days before in Washington).

Shunning any extensive discussion of the alternatives, Thorneycroft's aggrieved response was to emphasise that an American decision to cancel 'raised political and military implications of the gravest character', and he asked if the United States would be prepared to say publicly that it would do all in its power to help the UK maintain its independent deterrent. McNamara pointed to major investment that had already been made by the American authorities in Skybolt, but also that the whole issue of the independent deterrent raised problems because of Germany, and the UK's application to join the EEC. Thorneycroft moved quickly to reject the Hound Dog offer, as it was seen as merely a slightly improved version of Blue Steel (while the V-bombers themselves would have to be modified at some expense to carry the weapon). Straightforward participation in a multilateral force was seen as politically unacceptable, militarily dubious, and financially prohibitive. This left the option of Britain assuming responsibility for Skybolt development, but as the Americans themselves seemed to have little faith in the system this also was seen as unsatisfactory. For his part, the Minister of Defence thought that the 'best alternative might be Polaris' and asked for US reactions to the idea of purchasing the missile, with the UK manufacturing the submarines and warheads. In the inevitable gap that would open up between the loss of credibility of the V-bombers against Soviet air defences, and when a new UK Polaris force could be generated, Thorneycroft also expressed interest in hiring Polaris submarines with their missile systems from the United States for a few years.

McNamara promised to look at the possibility, but noted the legal obstacles to the UK hiring US submarines, and the heavy costs involved for Britain in building its own Polaris boats. As a further option, McNamara then asked whether the UK would consider contributing Polaris submarines, if they were built, to a NATO multilateral nuclear force. Avoiding a categorical response, Thorneycroft replied that this would have to be examined, but could not be made a condition of the supply of Polaris; he also made clear his feeling that it would be 'impossible' to combine any statement of the US agreement to provide Polaris with a British commitment to join a multilateral force, as 'no-one would believe that the choice had in fact been free. The test of the independence of a nuclear deterrent was whether, like the V-bomber/Skybolt force, it would be operable entirely on its own.' Considering the differences between their positions, all sides agreed that no further progress could be made in the current meeting and discussion moved on.[66]

Aside from McNamara's unwillingness to offer Polaris in the same 'no strings' attached form as Skybolt, perhaps the most disturbing part of the meeting was the manner in which the US Defense Secretary had avoided any commitment to help preserve Britain's independent deterrent. Briefing his fellow permanent secretaries on the talks, Scott noted that McNamara had argued that the decision to review Skybolt's future was not related to any desire to deprive the UK of its independent nuclear deterrent. However, when pressed further by the Minister of Defence, McNamara had admitted that 'personally, he felt unable to come out in public in support of the independent deterrent.'[67] To uncharitable British observers and commentators it appeared that the Kennedy administration had led London up the garden path over Skybolt, and was now prepared to see its closest ally lose the nuclear independence it still prized so highly.

A pre-Christmas meeting between Macmillan and Kennedy was already scheduled for Nassau in the Bahamas (in what officials were coming to see as a regular six-monthly conclaves between the President and Prime Minister), where their main topics of conversation were expected to be the aftermath of the Cuban crisis, Europe, and the situation in South Asia following the recent Sino-Indian border war. But with the Skybolt crisis threatening 'to develop in a very damaging way', Macmillan now predicted 'a great row in both countries' and that the Nassau Conference would witness 'a great battle with President Kennedy' on the issue.[68]

By this stage in their relationship, having traversed together the perils of the Laos and Berlin crises in 1961, tackled the vexed issue of nuclear testing, and had close exchanges during the most recent Cuban missile crisis, it is clear that a good degree of rapport had been established between Macmillan and Kennedy. Despite their differences in age and temperament, both had come to enjoy each other's company, and shared an ironic and detached intelligence. They also had an appreciation of the enormous responsibilities that they both carried, and the domestic and bureaucratic constituencies that often complicated their own clear vision that the way to mitigate international tensions was through the painstaking process of negotiation. Yet it was impossible to ignore that their political and diplomatic priorities did not always coincide, with the nuclear arrangements of the Western Alliance a particular case in point. During the second half of 1962, this disjuncture had become all the more obvious, and was to reach a climax at Nassau. Since June, when at Ann Arbor McNamara had delivered his blanket criticism of independent nuclear forces, operating according to national priorities in a fashion uncoordinated with the main US strategic nuclear forces, there had been a lingering suspicion in London that the Kennedy administration would not be displeased if British policy in this area were to go through a major transformation. It was at Nassau that, it was apparent to anxious officials, Britain's future course of nuclear development was to be determined under less than ideal or auspicious conditions.

Notes

1 Foreign Office telegram No 4309 to Washington, 14 June 1962, and Bligh minute for Macmillan, 'MRBMs for NATO,' 15 June 1962, PREM 11/3715.
2 Home minute for Macmillan, 'MRBMs for NATO,' PM/62/85, 21 June 1962, PREM 11/3715.
3 See Macmillan, *At the End of the Day*, 118–22.
4 Macmillan letter to Kennedy, T.284/62, 5 June 1962, PREM 11/3775.
5 See Ludlow, *Dealing with Britain*, 119–22, with quotation on 121.
6 Macmillan message to Ormsby Gore, 29 May 1962, PREM 11/3712.
7 See Pagedas, *Anglo-American Strategic Relations and the French Problem*, 206.
8 'Record of a meeting at the Chateau de Champs at 10.30am on Sunday, June 3, 1962,' PREM 11/3775.
9 'Extract from a Conversation between the Prime Minister and President de Gaulle which began at 10.30am on Sunday, June 3, 1962,' PREM 11/3775.
10 'Extract from a Conversation between the Prime Minister and President de Gaulle which began at 12.30pm on Sunday, June 3, 1962,' PREM 11/3775. See also Pagedas, *Anglo-American Strategic Relations and the French Problem*, 209–11, where more is read into Macmillan's comments than is warranted considering their speculative and vague nature.
11 See 'Nuclear Weapons in Western Defense: Address by Secretary of Defense Robert S. McNamara, Ann Arbor, June 16, 1962,' in Richard B. Stebbins (ed.), *Documents on American Foreign Relations, 1962* (New York, 1963), 230–36; Deborah Shapley, *Promise and Power: The Life and Times of Robert McNamara* (Boston, 1993), 141–5; and Kaplan, et al., *McNamara Ascendancy*, 308–9.
12 'America Sets Out Nuclear Policy Principles,' *The Times*, 18 June 1962.
13 Watkinson minute for Macmillan, 'Nuclear Weapons,' 18 June 1962, PREM 11/3709. See also Anthony Verrier, 'The Watkinson Scandal,' *New Statesman*, 8 June 1962.

The prelude to Nassau 361

14 Foreign Office telegram No 1637 to Paris, Home personal for Rusk, 19 June 1962, PREM 11/3709.
15 Foreign Office guidance telegram No 245, 'Nuclear Strategy,' 18 June 1962, DEFE 7/2396.
16 Watkinson letter to Greene, 20 June 1962, DEFE 7/2396.
17 'Mr McNamara Not Opposed to British Nuclear Force,' *The Times*, 20 June 1962.
18 Washington telegram No 1656 to Foreign Office, 22 June 1962, PREM 11/3709.
19 Macmillan minute for Watkinson, 'British Deterrent,' M.175/62, 24 June 1962, PREM 11/3709.
20 'Britain's Nuclear Targets Agreed with U.S.: Minister Says Right to Act Alone is Unchallenged,' *The Times*, 23 June 1962.
21 See Washington telegram No 1667 to Foreign Office, 23 June 1962, PREM 11/3709.
22 McNamara memorandum for Kennedy, 'Answers to Eight Questions re European Nuclear Matters,' 16 June 1962, folder 14, box 221, Paul H. Nitze papers, Library of Congress. It seems likely that Nitze was the original author of this paper.
23 Paris telegram No 232 Saving to Foreign Office, 22 June 1962, PREM 11/3709.
24 Macmillan minute for Home, M.168/62, 24 June 1962, PREM 11/3715.
25 See Kaplan, et al., *McNamara Ascendancy*, 397–9.
26 'Record of a Meeting held at the Foreign Office at 11 am on June 25, 1962,' PREM 11/3715.
27 *Hansard*, HC, vol 661, cols 954–60, 26 June 1962; and 'Britain to keep her independent deterrent,' *The Times*, 27 June 1962; see also Kohl, *French Nuclear Diplomacy*, 325.
28 On Thorneycroft's important role in this episode, see Constantine A. Pegadas, 'The Afterlife of Blue Streak: Britain's American Answer to Europe,' *Journal of Strategic Studies*, 18, 2, 1995, 1–24.
29 Scott minute for Thorneycroft, 'Deterrent Policy,' RHS/475/62, 20 July 1962, DEFE 13/618, and in DEFE 7/2236.
30 Scott minute for Thorneycroft, 'Future of the British Nuclear Deterrent,' RHS/641/62, 9 October 1962, DEFE 13/618.
31 See BNDSG/P(62)11, 'Problems of Nuclear Defence,' memorandum by the Foreign Office, 15 October 1962, DEFE 7/2144.
32 BNDSG/M(62)4, 25 October 1962, PUSD records, FCO.
33 See BNDSG/P(62)9, 'Hybrid Submarines,' Note by the Deputy Chief of Naval Staff, 11 October 1962, AIR 2/13715; the paper was discussed at BNDSG/M(62)4, 25 October 1962, PUSD records, FCO.
34 Hockaday, 'Note for the Record,' 30 October 1962, DEFE 13/618.
35 See, for example, COS(62)71st Meeting, 13 November 1962, DEFE 4/149.
36 MoD minute, 'Minister of Defence's Visit to the United States, September 1962: Skybolt,' 19 September 1962, DEFE 13/323.
37 MoD minute, 'Notes on Talks during the Minister of Defence's Visit to the United States, September 1962: Nuclear Problems in Europe,' 19 September 1962; Watkinson minute for Macmillan, 'Visit to the United States 9th to 17th September, 1962,' 18 September 1962, DEFE 13/323.
38 Rusk letter to McNamara, 8 September 1962, *FRUS, 1961–1963*, XIII, 1078–80. Copies of this letter also went to Bundy and Glenn Seaborg at the AEC.
39 See DRS Washington message ZO 315 to MoD London, 31 October 1962; BDS Washington message ZO 324 to MoD London, 5 November 1962, DEFE 19/78; Richard E. Neustadt, *Report to JFK: The Skybolt Crisis in Retrospect* (Ithaca, 1999), 30–37; Schlesinger, *A Thousand Days*, 858.
40 Foreign Office telegram No 7857 to Washington, 5 November 1962 (with Thorneycroft-McNamara message), DEFE 19/78.

41 Kaplan et al., *McNamara Ascendancy*, 379–81.
42 Thorneycroft minute for Home, 'Skybolt,' 8 November 1962, PREM 11/3716.
43 Washington telegram No 2832 to Foreign Office, for Permanent Under Secretary, 8 November 1962, PREM 11/3716.
44 Arthur Hockaday (Thorneycroft's Private Secretary) report for A. C. I. Samuel (Home's Private Secretary), 'Skybolt,' 9 November 1962, PREM 11/3716.
45 Hockaday minute for Scott, 'Skybolt,' 9 November 1962, DEFE 19/78.
46 H. Godfrey, 'Note for the record,' 14 November 1962, DEFE 19/78.
47 Full minutes of the BNDSG meeting on 14 November were not circulated as the officials present did not want the contents of their discussion to be given wider currency. A truncated version appears as BNDSG/M(62)5, 14 November 1962, and a fuller draft is attached to E. H. St.G. Moss minute for Scott, 'BNDSG Minutes,' 20 November 1962, DEFE 7/2145. The principal points were also recorded by a Foreign Office official in attendance; see E. J. W. Barnes minute, 'British Nuclear Deterrent,' 14 November 1962, PUSD records, FCO.
48 See GEN 778/1st Meeting, 20 November 1962, CAB 130/189. For Ormsby Gore's advice see Washington telegram No 2891 to Foreign Office, 18 November 1962, DEFE 19/78.
49 Memorandum for the record: Second Meeting with the President on FY 64 DoD Budget Issues, 23 November 1962, *FRUS, 1961–1963, VIII*, 415.
50 See Washington telegram No 2987 to Foreign Office, 29 November 1962, DEFE 19/78.
51 Rusk letter to McNamara, 24 November 1962, *FRUS, 1961–1963, XIII*, 1086–8.
52 A point made in Kaplan, et al., *McNamara Ascendancy*, 382.
53 Scott minute for Thorneycroft, 'Strategic Nuclear Deterrent,' RHS/780/62, 28 November 1962, DEFE 7/2145 and in DEFE 13/619.
54 See the critical tone regarding McNamara's performance at this stage contained in Kaplan et al., *McNamara Ascendancy*, 381.
55 Macmillan diary entry, 7 December 1962, MS Macmillan dep. d.48, Bodleian Library; see also Macmillan, *At the End of the Day*, 339.
56 See diary entry for 8 December 1962, in Harold Evans, *Downing Street Diary: The Macmillan Years, 1957–1963* (London, 1981), 233.
57 Ormsby Gore letter to Macmillan, 8 December 1962, PREM 11/4229.
58 See, for example, Scott minute for Thorneycroft, 'Skybolt,' RHS/818/62, 7 December 1962, DEFE 13/410.
59 Amery minute for Thorneycroft, 7 December 1962, DEFE 19/78.
60 Thorneycroft minute for Macmillan, 'Skybolt,' 7 December 1962, PREM 11/3716.
61 Bligh, 'Note for the Record,' 'Skybolt,' 9 December 1962, PREM 11/3716.
62 Washington telegram No 3098 to Foreign Office (personal for Minister of Defence from Zuckerman), 9 December 1962, DEFE 19/78.
63 Memorandum of conversation by Bundy, 10 December 1962, National Security File, box 317A, JFKL.
64 See Kaplan et al., *McNamara Ascendancy*, 382.
65 See George W. Ball, *The Past Has Another Pattern: Memoirs* (New York, 1982), 263–4.
66 See MM(62)30, 'Record of a Meeting between the Minister of Defence and the US Secretary of Defense on Tuesday 11th December 1962,' DEFE 7/2145; and see also the analysis offered in de Zulueta letter to Ormsby Gore, 11 December 1962, PREM 11/3716. Zuckerman, who was present alongside Thorneycroft, offered his own account in *Monkeys, Men and Missiles*, 249–52, while Neustadt, *Report to JFK*, 69–76, assembled a full and colourful record of the meeting from contemporary documents and interviews. Schlesinger also provides a version of

the meeting based on Neustadt's original report into the crisis in *A Thousand Days*, 861–2.
67 Meeting of Permanent Secretaries, Confidential Annex to P.S./M(62)27 held on Wednesday, 12th December 1962, DEFE 7/2145.
68 Macmillan diary entry, 11 December 1962, MS Macmillan dep. d.48, Bodleian Library.

10 Securing Polaris
The Nassau negotiations, December 1962–January 1963

From Rambouillet to the Bahamas

As the transatlantic crisis over Skybolt had begun to unfold towards the end of 1962, the COS's Joint Planning Staff had been busy preparing a series of papers examining the future of British strategy. One of the first they compiled – with uncommon timing – presented the military case for maintaining a UK-controlled strategic nuclear capability in the period after 1970. The JPS had not found it difficult to come to the basic conclusion that as there was no foreseeable system that could provide defence against ballistic missiles, the only counter to the threat of direct nuclear attack against the United Kingdom was national possession of the ability to retaliate with nuclear weapons. To form a valid deterrent, the JPS argued, UK strategic nuclear forces had to fulfil three conditions:

a They must be seen to be capable of inflicting more damage on the nuclear power envisaging such bombardment than it could accept as the price of nuclear attack on the United Kingdom.
b They must be seen to be capable of inflicting this damage before, while, or after the United Kingdom was under nuclear bombardment.
c They must be sovereign (independent) in the strictest military sense.

'Credibility' of the deterrent would be assured provided that the force levels capable of inflicting the damage called for under (a) were adequate (the JPS acknowledging this was an area 'in which the political element predominates'), and that the response was 'guaranteed and automatic.' Meeting condition (b) was seen as a military problem, which though feasible, 'cannot, however, be cheap.' The third element of the deterrent – independence – was defined as meaning the final authority for using the strategic nuclear force must be retained by the UK Government.

The paper went on to stipulate that the UK strategic force could certainly be allocated to the military alliances of which Britain was a member. In that sense its 'position need be no different from that of other nuclear or conventional forces which are committed to alliances but which remain in peacetime under United Kingdom control and are available for use if necessary in support of purely national operations.' However, in order for final UK authority over the force to be exercised

> every element of the weapon system should be British owned, manned, maintained, supported, and controlled. Provided that these conditions, which do not specify reliance on British production of the equipment, continue to be fulfilled, United Kingdom strategic nuclear strike forces can be committed to NATO on the same terms as our other forces, and thus avoid any suggestion that we have a 'go it alone' policy. A 'go it alone' capability, however, will remain. There can, therefore, be no question of lack of resolution entering into its operation as a deterrent to attack on the United Kingdom itself, as there can be no doubt that it would be used in revenge.

As for the argument that the UK deterrent was superfluous, in that it merely added to the overwhelming striking power possessed by the United States, the JPS were careful to make clear that it was unwise to rely in all circumstances on the Americans being prepared to act to defend vital British interests. They warned that

> It is by no means certain that British, or indeed European, interests will remain coincidental with those of the United States in the future and the French would appear to be of this same opinion. Even in the past there have been no instances [sic] of the automatic military support of the United States in the conditions leading to the outbreak of wars; indeed sometimes the reverse.

Britain's membership of a world-wide network of military alliances, including NATO, CENTO, and SEATO, was underpinned by its status as a nuclear power. Moreover, possession of a strategic nuclear force conferred political advantages for the UK in its relations with allies, and in what were grandly called the 'counsels of the world'; in the military sphere enhanced cooperation with the United States was also seen as deriving from nuclear status (with strategic warning systems and intelligence on nuclear targeting seen as two examples where this effect was tangible). There was one note of budgetary caution inserted at the end of the paper. Though forces for the prevention of wars, rather than their actual fighting, should have 'a first charge on our resources', it was felt that the 'scale of their provision must be realistic but not so large as to prevent us from deploying adequate resources to meet our other defence responsibilities in cooperation with our Allies.' The final conclusion offered was that there was a 'continuing military requirement for a strategic nuclear capability under our sovereign control both to deter attack on this country and to preserve our world-wide freedom of action.'[1]

There is a certain degree of irony in the fact that the JPS paper was endorsed by the COS on the eve of the Nassau conference, where its strictures about national control of the UK strategic nuclear force were threatened by the Kennedy administration's aversion to the existence of independent European deterrents. Indeed, in a reflection of known US priorities, while agreeing with the paper's fundamental points, the Chiefs noted that its findings would need to be 'considered in the light of mounting political pressure to contribute to some form of multilateral deterrent.' But they also affirmed that any multilateral force which involved mixed manning of units or ships was likely to be 'militarily inefficient', while it would be essential that the UK could, in the last resort, 'extract our contribution for exclusively national purposes.'[2] It was to be just such issues of national control in a situation where UK nuclear forces were committed to the Western Alliance, and how these forces related to the multilateral nuclear arrangements for NATO now promoted by the Americans, that were to form the core of the discussions between the Prime Minister and President Kennedy at Nassau. These were also matters which held an important domestic political resonance for a Conservative Government which since the cancellation of Blue Streak in 1960 had staked out a continuing claim for nuclear independence even though reliance had to be placed on the United States for the provision of nuclear delivery systems.

Indeed, the news that Skybolt was likely to be cancelled came at a very awkward moment in the Macmillan Government's fortunes. There were few signs that the major changes in Cabinet personnel carried out in peremptory fashion by the Prime Minister in July 1962 had led to any boost in popularity. A series of by-elections at the end of November had shown a marked swing against the Conservatives, and Macmillan wrote in his diary that as a result the press had been 'quite hysterical and prophesy a revolt against me in the Parliamentary Party. The only thing to do is to remain calm and go on with our work.'[3] The negotiations over British entry to the EEC, which had begun again in Brussels on 8 October after a summer recess, had made some progress, but their outcome was nonetheless still highly uncertain (with some Conservatives growing concerned over the concessions being made, and Labour also ready to exploit the issue). Acheson's jibe in early December about Britain having lost an empire but not yet having found a role had hit an uncomfortable nerve and sparked a round of angst-ridden commentary in the press over the decline of Britain's international prestige. Now, despite the apparent warmth of the relationship between Macmillan and President Kennedy, Britain's closest ally seemed ready to put the UK out of the strategic nuclear business altogether and to undermine the Government's long-stated policy of maintaining an independent contribution to the Western deterrent. To many it was not just the future of the deterrent that would be at stake during the meeting between Macmillan and Kennedy at Nassau, but the Government's overall credibility.

After McNamara's uncomfortable meeting with Thorneycroft on 11 December there was no sign that the crisis triggered by Skybolt's cancellation could be resolved without a major confrontation between the principals.

McNamara had continued from London on to Paris for a NATO Council meeting where he had repeated the position to the assembled ministers (Thorneycroft included) that the United States was ready to examine 'possible arrangements for a multilateral nuclear force in which NATO allies would share in the actual operation, employment, and support.'[4] On 15 December, a day after this latest presentation of the US position on the MLF, the Minister of Defence had had a private lunch with McNamara in Paris, where the latter seemed to be much more forthcoming than previously over providing a suitable replacement for Skybolt. 'We talked throughout upon the basis that the Americans would offer us Polaris,' Thorneycroft recorded (in a note sent to the Prime Minister), 'though he emphasised that important policy issues would be involved for both our Governments.' Responding to McNamara's queries, Thorneycroft gave him some idea of the size of force the UK would require, and McNamara in turn stressed that the US would be ready to give full support for manufacture of the submarines and training, with resultant reductions in timescale and costs for the British effort. But McNamara also confessed, alluding to the wider European scene, that his 'main concern was Germany. He believed that not now but in two or three years, Germany would want to get into the business of manufacturing nuclears. This was part of the United States' concern over supplying Polaris to us. He did not mind what solution was arrived at with regard to Europe, but wanted one which would help keep Germany out of manufacturing nuclears.' With the financial costs of forming a European MRBM force seeming so prohibitively high, Thorneycroft wanted to discuss the idea of subscribing part of the West's existing nuclear potential to a NATO force (an expedient, as we have seen, which had been floated in British official circles several times since the end of 1960 and which had several adherents in the Foreign Office). Having already considered the possibility, McNamara found it an attractive notion as a starter, and thought it would 'help if in the Polaris deal we and the Americans could look forward to a European force to which we both were prepared to subscribe a part of what we had.' This could then, McNamara suggested, be combined at a later date with a multilateral European MRBM force.[5]

A further crucial prelude to the Bahamas conference was provided by the meeting that Macmillan held a few days beforehand with President de Gaulle at Rambouillet over the weekend of 15/16 December in an effort to persuade him to relax French opposition to British entry into the EEC. By now there was a general sense of pessimism that de Gaulle could be persuaded to change his views, engendered not least by the significant strengthening in his political position at home which had come with the increased representation gained by Gaullist parties and their allies in the elections held for the French National Assembly in November. Moreover, German support for British EEC membership had also grown lukewarm since the summer, a trend which ran parallel with the development of the improvement in Franco-German relations that had been witnessed following Adenauer's state visit in July.[6] By the end of November, the British Ambassador in Paris, Sir Pierson Dixon, was even given to wonder whether the subject of the Brussels negotiations between the Six and the UK over terms of entry should be tackled at all by the Prime Minister when he saw de Gaulle, and that discussions were best confined to general world problems and East-West relations: 'The background remains,' Dixon reported, 'that General de Gaulle does not want the negotiations to succeed, for general political reasons.' On balance, however, it seemed advisable that the Prime Minister should not draw back from the keen stance the Government had adopted toward membership throughout the past year, if nothing else than to widen the gap between France and the other five members.[7]

The Champs meeting in early June had, however, given Macmillan some false confidence that he might be able to persuade de Gaulle that the Government was now sufficiently 'European-minded' to join the Community, where attitudes to defence formed a crucial part of French perceptions. Macmillan's persistent interest in possible Anglo-French nuclear collaboration, it should be emphasised, was predicated on it occurring only once Britain had become a member of the EEC, and that the United States had acquiesced in this new point of departure for British nuclear policy. After Champs, he had instructed Philip de Zulueta (by now the Private Secretary on whose foreign policy advice he had come mainly to rely) to look again at the scope and nature of such collaboration. In line with its previous attitude and mindful of American objections, the Foreign Office, however, was less than enthusiastic over pursuing the subject any further. In mid-July 1962, Home was minuting Macmillan to the effect that there was no urgency over examining Anglo-French nuclear collaboration, and that 'we can afford to delay for a year or two any decision whether to prolong the British strategic deterrent after the end of the V-bomber-Skybolt system'. Moreover, it was

> now clear that there is no question of our having to buy our way into the Common Market by co-operating with de Gaulle in the production of a nuclear deterrent. There is therefore no compelling reason for embarking on a joint programme at present. On the contrary, until we can play our part from inside the Community in the evolution of a European point of view on defence it seems to me prudent not to take any step which might pre-judge its development one way or the other.[8]

Nevertheless, at a meeting held on 20 July with Brook, Makins and de Zulueta, Macmillan had asked that officials continued to pursue a study of what the practical possibilities and difficulties might be in the area, on the assumption that the European negotiations were successful and that the Americans proved acquiescent.[9] Over the next few months, this small group, with eventual assistance from Scott at the Ministry of Defence and Caccia from the Foreign Office, worked on the issue, but on the eve of the Rambouillet meeting had come to the discouraging conclusion that no fruitful possibilities existed primarily because of the French determination to retain complete independence when it came to the provision, control and operation of their strategic nuclear force.[10]

The auguries did not seem good, therefore, when the formal talks with de Gaulle began at Rambouillet on the afternoon of 15 December. Yet still the Prime Minister was prepared to go further on nuclear matters than his more cautious officials had considered advisable. When discussing the general organisation of Western defence, Macmillan stressed his determination to preserve an independent deterrent 'in the sense that it was under the control of United Kingdom Ministers.' As with France, a nuclear force was a 'symbol of independence' and showed that 'the two countries were not just satellites.' At the same time, there had to be joint planning with Allies for the most effective use of these nuclear forces if war should occur. Referring to the problems over Skybolt, the Prime Minister explained how the missile had been looked upon as the key to preserving Britain's independent deterrent, and that the position was now of 'some embarrassment.' If an adequate replacement could not be obtained from the Americans, Macmillan told de Gaulle, Kennedy would be informed that Britain would then have to make her own system, 'whether submarine or aerial', even though this would have a great impact on other areas of the UK's defence effort.[11]

It is apparent that British reactions to McNamara's Ann Arbor speech earlier in the year — when officials had stressed that the V-bomber force was integrated with the US Strategic Air Command, and so should not be included in McNamara's strictures against independent deterrents — still coloured French views of UK nuclear policy. To de Gaulle's criticism that the British nuclear force remained 'linked with' the US, Macmillan responded with the argument that joint targeting with the Americans 'was a perfectly sensible arrangement which was desirable between Allies but did not exclude national plans.' Since 1958 there had been an exchange of nuclear information with the Americans,

> but the British bombers had a British plan as well as a joint plan. This was completely natural and sensible. When France had a nuclear force he hoped that France would put this in the same position. When there were three Western nuclear forces he hoped that there would be a joint operational plan and he would have no objection to considering the possibility also of an Anglo-French plan which would operate supposing that the Americans for some reason deserted the alliance. No doubt France, like Britain, would also at that stage have a plan of her own in case all her Allies ran out.[12]

Venturing into more sensitive areas, the Prime Minister also suggested that nuclear cooperation between Britain and France could open up in the future, and that 'we could do everything short of disclosing secret information which we obtained from the Americans on the warhead itself.' Despite this, and other entreaties, the French President remained unmoved about how he saw the immediate prospects for British entry, which he thought would change the essential character of the EEC as an economic organisation.

However, de Gaulle's fundamental objection, as he subsequently made clear to Macmillan, was that France's ability to dominate decision-making in the Community would be curtailed if Britain, and perhaps others, were to join. In that event, de Gaulle explained in a crucial part of the discussion,

> he foresaw difficulties at Brussels. In the Six as they existed France had some weight and could say no even against the Germans. France could stop policies with which she disagreed because in the Six she had a very strong position. Once the United Kingdom and the Scandinavians and the rest had entered the organisation things would be different.

A stunned Prime Minister could only reply that this was 'a most serious statement' which represented a 'fundamental objection of principle to the British application. If this was really the French Government's view, it should have been put forward at the very start.'[13] As Macmillan remarked in his diary, 'the discussions went about as bad as they could be from the European point of view. The only glimmer of hope lies in the French unwillingness to be held up to all the world as having openly wrecked our entry and having never really tried to negotiate seriously.'[14]

With the Government's European policy facing collapse, its transatlantic ties to the United States were simultaneously going through immense strain. Just before Rambouillet, for example, *The Times* spoke about a special relationship 'on trial.'[15] On 14 December, Macmillan had sent a personal message to Ormsby Gore about the agenda arrangements for the Nassau meeting, saying,

> You will realise what a row Skybolt is causing. We must treat it calmly but there is no use trying to ignore facts ... My difficulty is that if we cannot reach an agreement on a realistic means of maintaining the British independent deterrent, all the other questions may only justify perfunctory discussion, since an agonising reappraisal of all our foreign and defence policy will be required.[16]

The domestic political consequences of the Skybolt imbroglio began to be felt more acutely on 17 December, when, with Thorneycroft fresh from his return from the NATO meeting in Paris and due to appear before the House to explain the latest position, *The Times* carried reports that McGeorge Bundy had given a television interview in Washington where he admitted that Skybolt had become a major issue between the two countries but claimed that the United States did not have a fixed obligation to provide Britain with an alternative system if the missile was cancelled.[17] Offering an outline of his recent talks, and in the face of Opposition ridicule and much unease from

Conservative MPs, the Minister of Defence described to the House the doubts that had begun to emerge over Skybolt, and that he had stressed to McNamara 'the serious consequences for the United Kingdom of a cancellation of this project'. Thorneycroft tried to assure MPs that no final decisions had yet been made and that 'consultation' with the Americans was still continuing; nevertheless, he mentioned that discussions had looked at alternatives to Skybolt, 'of which the most important is Polaris'.

Speaking for the Labour Opposition, George Brown attacked the Government for its failure to heed the warnings that had been issued in the past about the problems with Skybolt. He derided ministers for their continued attachment to a missile which the Americans now regarded as redundant to their needs, finishing with the argument: 'would it not have been better to do what we have consistently urged, which was to face facts as they are, accept that there is now no possibility of us having an independent nuclear deterrent, and base our defence strategy in accordance with the facts and not in accordance with the political hopes of the party opposite?' More hostile questioning followed, some of it from the Government's own backbenchers, who were very unhappy with the way the whole matter had been handled by the US administration (indeed, over 100 Conservative MPs were subsequently to sign a motion exhorting the government to retain the independent deterrent).[18] As *The Times* subsequently put it during the Nassau Conference, '...Mr Macmillan and his Cabinet colleagues know perfectly well that it would be an almost certainly fatal step in party and electoral terms to assent to the abandonment of Britain's independent deterrent.'[19]

In view of the political storm that was starting to engulf the Macmillan Government, the Kennedy administration was coming to the view that something would have to be offered if unwelcome political changes were not to occur in Britain. The President had met with his key advisers on 16 December in order to determine the American approach to the impending conference in the Bahamas. McNamara began by giving a summary of his recent talks with Thorneycroft, noting his refusal to give an assurance that the US was in favour of an independent British nuclear deterrent. Nevertheless (and perhaps mindful of what he had said to Thorneycroft in Paris), he was now ready to recommend, he told the meeting, that the British should be supplied with Polaris, linked 'to the same rules of use and control as those applied to Skybolt...' As could be expected, opposition came from George Ball of the State Department, who noted the wider European political aspects to the issue and that 'a decision in favor of a national force in this range of weapons would change our entire policy and would represent a major political decision.' The President then intervened with a comment which showed his appreciation of the British perspective, saying, 'Looking at it from their point of view, which they do almost better than anybody ... It might well appear to them that since Skybolt was a substitute for Blue Streak, which they had cancelled in reliance on our assurances, we should now provide an alternative.' David Bruce, the US Ambassador to the UK, who had been recalled for consultation, remarked that the whole problem was essentially political, and revolved around the situation which would occur at the end of January when Parliament would return after the holiday season: 'The old question,' Bruce remarked, 'was what would meet the Prime Minister's needs for this hour, and he thought only the Prime Minister could decide this question.' With the tide seemingly turning in Macmillan's favour, McNamara next delivered a strong critique of the MLF proposals, which he said seemed entirely incompatible with the administration's stress on building up NATO's conventional forces: 'it was time,' the Defense Secretary argued, 'to move on to a more realistic arrangement and one which would better serve our interests.'

Kennedy saw that he would have to reach a delicate balance in his forthcoming decisions as it was difficult to reconcile the different strands of US policy. The President noted that there were 'grave' political risks for Macmillan if he was not helped over Skybolt, but also risks to the administration's European policy if he was helped too much. The President was, however, clearly inclined to assist the British, giving his own view that if Polaris was offered 'it must be in the context of our understandings with respect to Skybolt.' Ball immediately made the point that if Polaris was offered to the British and not the French 'we would appear to have intensified our special relationship to the British and our refusal to cooperate with the French.' Further discussion within the group led to the formulation of a proposal which involved an offer to provide Polaris to the UK, but conditional on a British commitment of their eventual Polaris force 'to a multilateral or multinational force in NATO,' and an undertaking to build-up the British conventional forces allocated to NATO. At the same time, underlining the ambiguities that were already emerging due to divided American opinion, the 'terms governing the use of Skybolt would apply also to the use of such Polaris missiles.'[20] That same day the President recorded an interview with several news correspondents (which aired on national television on 17 December) where he virtually confirmed that a decision to cancel Skybolt had already been taken, citing the estimated overall costs of $2.5 billion as a prime reason for his decision.[21]

Nassau: the opening rounds

The Prime Minister's party arrived in Nassau after the long trip from London on 18 December. Accompanying Macmillan on the ministerial side were Home, Thorneycroft, and Duncan Sandys, the Commonwealth Secretary (who was in the party as steps to bolster India were on the conference agenda following the Sino-Indian border war of the previous month). Vital official support for the Prime Minister also came from de Zulueta and Tim Bligh, while Thorneycroft's MoD party included the Permanent Secretary, Sir Robert Scott, the Minister of Defence's Private Secretary, Arthur Hockaday, as well as Zuckerman as CSA. Back at home the Cabinet, chaired by R. A.

Butler, the First Secretary of State, was kept in regular touch with the negotiations. Conspicuous by their absence from the conference, considering that military and strategic matters would be so heavily affected by the outcome of the discussions, were the Chiefs of Staff; their presence, however, would undoubtedly have triggered their American counterparts – the US Joint Chiefs of Staff – to appear, and the principals obviously saw the negotiations at Nassau as essentially political in nature. British naval interests were, however, overseen by Vice Admiral Michael Le Fanu, the Third Sea Lord and Controller of the Navy (and so holding direct responsibilities for ships and equipment), but as he was later to report, 'professional/technical subjects' were hardly discussed at the Conference at all, while there was present no counterpart from the US Navy with whom he could discuss Polaris requirements (such as whether the A2 or A3 variant of the missile would meet British needs).[22]

On the flight to the Bahamas, another member of the British delegation, James Lighthill, the noted mathematician and then Director of the Royal Aircraft Establishment, was available to brief Thorneycroft on the technical state of the Skybolt programme. Influenced also by the upbeat assessment of the Ministry of Aviation, Thorneycroft obviously still felt that the difficulties encountered with the project had not justified cancellation.[23] The MoD brief prepared for the Prime Minister before the conference, for example, asserted that there was 'a very strong case' to press the United States to continue Skybolt development through to completion, but also noted that for Britain to take over the development process would be 'a very high gamble' with serious consequences if it failed. (Lighthill, for his part, thought the 'damning of Skybolt on technical grounds was a trumped-up affair'.)[24]

If Skybolt were to be abandoned, the MoD's brief recommended the alternative of Polaris fired from a submarine platform. 'Britain can construct for herself the hull, the normal submarine fittings, the nuclear propulsion, machinery, and the warheads. But it will take us a great deal of time and money and a very great effort in terms of scientific resources and manpower to construct the actual rockets themselves together with their associated systems. This is why it is essential that we are allowed to acquire from the United States the missiles themselves with their associated control, firing, navigational and launch systems, and also test and training facilities and technical knowledge and assistance.' At this point a force of seven nuclear-powered submarines, each armed with eight Polaris missiles, was envisaged, with the first boat operational 'before the end of the decade' (an annex to the MoD paper also gave a very rough estimate of £335 million to construct the submarines, procure launcher and fire control equipment, and provide warheads for the new force). This would still leave a gap in capability after the mid-1960s when Britain's V-bombers, even when equipped with stand-off missiles such as Blue Steel, would be vulnerable to improvements to Soviet air defences: there would be 'an interval of some years when we could not claim that we had a true strategic deterrent system, which could be counted on to penetrate deep into Russia. We would of course still have our V-Bomber force armed with powerful weapons of types which could inflict vast damage on peripheral and other accessible targets.' But in order to maintain 'continuity in ... strategic deterrent power', the MoD brief suggested the loan or hire of two or three US Polaris submarines with their missiles to cover the deterrent gap. American refusal to supply Polaris 'on the same terms as Skybolt' would create 'a most serious situation' with 'profound consequences for the Atlantic Alliance and for NATO': the President would have to be warned that Britain would dissociate itself from the unilateral US decision to cancel Skybolt, and that without an independent strategic system would refuse to take part in any multilateral nuclear arrangements within the Alliance, partly for reasons of military risk. 'A country that lacks a strategic deterrent system of its own has much less chance of deterring a massive attack on its homeland,' the brief advised. 'It must be exceedingly prudent. It should not take part in a lesser force, not wholly under its own control, when this might invite the destruction of its homeland.' Refusal would also, it was predicted, lead to 'pressures in Britain to review the Holy Loch arrangement and possibly the stationing of American aircraft in this country.'[25]

Alongside his own entourage, Kennedy was joined on his flight from Washington to the Bahamas by the British Ambassador, Sir David Ormsby Gore. Elected as a Conservative MP in 1950, Ormsby Gore had served as a Minister of State at the Foreign Office from 1957 until his appointment as Ambassador in Washington in the autumn of 1961. In that position he had assiduously used his close personal relationship with Kennedy (forged through a friendship which began in 1938 when Kennedy had spent time in London, and then reinforced in the late 1950s when Ormsby Gore's Foreign Office duties often took him to New York), to promote British interests and develop a strong understanding of the basic convictions of the President in key policy areas.[26] It was during the journey to Nassau that Ormsby Gore managed to impress on Kennedy the dire political consequences for the Macmillan Government, and for Anglo-American relations more generally, if a suitable replacement for Skybolt was not found, or the missile project was not continued in some form. It appears that on the flight they devised together a scheme whereby Skybolt development might be continued by the British, with the costs being shared 50/50 between Britain and the United States.[27] But more importantly, Kennedy seems to have begun to appreciate that Macmillan's Conservative Government could be threatened by the crisis, and that a Labour alternative was not something that his administration would welcome. One of the State Department briefing books that came with the President's party to Nassau included extensive analysis of Macmillan's domestic political position, advocated support for the younger and more progressive Conservatives in Britain, and warned of the prospect of a Labour Government 'which would be equivocal on the subject of the EEC, would persist in dangerous illusions regarding East-West relations, would wish to spend more on social welfare and less on defense and would allow the British ship of state either by design or indifference to drift toward the Scandinavian positon of part-participant, part-spectator with regard to the Atlantic community.'[28]

With both leaders now ensconced in close proximity in their respective villas, the President and Prime Minister spent informal time together late on the afternoon of 18 December. According to Arthur Schlesinger's later account, Macmillan had said that he now wanted Polaris as a substitute for Skybolt, pushing back the 50/50 offer that Kennedy and Ormsby Gore had discussed on their flight to Nassau.[29] It was immediately apparent that there would be no quick or easy reconciling of positions. The following morning, as the delegations prepared arguments for their first formal session, Macmillan spoke to his Press Secretary of the chances of a full-scale row, and of his ending the talks if the Americans refused to make concessions (a step, he acknowledged, which offered tempting political advantages).[30] The opening round of talks began with Macmillan laying out, in his familiar grand style, the history of Anglo-American nuclear relations since the war, and the understandings that had been reached with the Eisenhower administration in 1960 over the procurement of Skybolt and the basing of US Polaris submarines at Holy Loch in Scotland. Regarding the more recent concept of a multilateral nuclear force, Macmillan professed some confusion over what it would actually involve: 'Would it be manufactured in Europe and would it belong to those who had manufactured it? Would it be put into some sort of pool?' The Prime Minister admitted that

> Of course it was possible to put national forces into alliances and in planning to work inside that framework. But this did not mean that the national forces passed completely under the authority of the commanding General. The United Kingdom had been used to working within this concept from the days of Marlborough onwards. The national forces were independent as regards ultimate political authority but interdependent for the joint campaign. It would, therefore, be possible to put many British forces into some such an interdependent arrangement on this basis. But until there was a supranational political authority which would exercise juridical control there would have to be interdependence with an ultimate national authority.

As a gesture toward this kind of arrangement, Macmillan then offered to make available to SACEUR 'for planning and tactics' a squadron of V-bombers, as a step which 'would enable the philosophy to be developed in a controlled fashion that nuclear forces were not entirely independent.' The Prime Minister finished his presentation with the warning that differences of opinion between the members of the Western Alliance 'would be as nothing to the difficulties which would follow if the United States seemed to be using the Skybolt decision as a means of forcing Britain out of an independent nuclear capacity.'

Acknowledging the storm that would erupt if it was believed that the Skybolt cancellation decision had been made for political rather than technical reasons, Kennedy responded by repeating the proposal that the US and Britain share equally the future development costs of Skybolt (with the sums involved reckoned at $100 million each), and then order for production however many was desired. The problems with the Skybolt guidance system that had affected its development programme did not, the President suggested, necessarily undermine its role as a deterrent: the presence of only 20 Russian missiles in Cuba during the recent crisis had been enough to deter the United States from taking immediate action, and so, he said, 'How much more would a missile system based on Skybolt deter the Russians even if they thought that the weapon might have the accuracy to fall only in the suburbs and not in the centre of Moscow.'

Yet considering all the strong doubts that had already been sown in public and in private regarding Skybolt's performance and viability (not least by Kennedy's own television performance two days before), and the practical difficulties of the UK being able to 'share' development of a US weapons system, the President's proposal was never likely to be taken seriously. Indeed, Macmillan turned it aside with some disdain, and instead appealed for Polaris as a substitute for Skybolt. Kennedy was reluctant, however, to make such an open-ended offer, and reiterated the administration's aspirations to sponsor a European multilateral nuclear force. Perpetuating the UK national deterrent would increase the sense of exclusion felt by the non-nuclear members of the Alliance and undermine plans for an MLF. The United States, Kennedy was keen to stress, had not been willing to extend nuclear cooperation to France, even though this had been to the detriment of its relations with de Gaulle, because this would only serve to excite nuclear ambitions in Germany. US concerns were focused on what would happen in Germany once the current Chancellor, Konrad Adenauer, left the scene, and this was one reason Washington had supported British entry into the European Community, and developed the idea of the multilateral force. Giving Polaris to the UK would be offering a 'new type of power' compared to Skybolt, and, as the President put it, 'Polaris not only was but manifestly appeared to be different.' Kennedy was also anxious that Anglo-American cooperation over Polaris would

> add further force to all President de Gaulle's arguments, which he used to some effect round Europe, about the United States intentions to dominate Europe. And it would certainly have a further effect on the Germans. It might be possible to overcome these pressures and it might be necessary to face them. But in the United States' view it was not true to say that the supplying of Polaris would make no difference at all. It would represent a change in the British position and would be exploited as such by the French.

Keen to disabuse the Prime Minister of any notion that Polaris might be provided as a straight replacement for Skybolt, Kennedy noted the importance of the longevity issue for how the systems were seen: the latter would simply prolong the life of the V-force to about 1970, while Polaris would 'last from 1968 or 1969 until the Russians had an effective anti-missile missile – say in 1980. To give Polaris to Britain would be a new step and so regarded in Europe.' But the President did say that, 'If we could work out a solution in regard to Polaris which would move Europe away from national deterrents, we would be prepared to consider such a move but it should be in that context.'

A chink of light in this bleak opening round of the talks was provided by the fact that Macmillan had not dismissed the idea of a European multilateral force, while the President had said it might be possible to supply Polaris under certain conditions. Nevertheless, what the latter might entail was broadly suggested when George Ball outlined for the meeting's benefit how the State Department saw the multilateral force as being formed on the basis of mixed nationality crews, with no right of withdrawal for any 'national' contingents which were contributed. German pressures for nuclear weapons were only likely to increase in Ball's opinion, and 'nuclear capacity was a status symbol and the lack of it was a stigma. Germans would not be prepared to be condemned as second-class citizens forever.'

However, keen to quash a supposition which informed American attitudes, the Foreign Secretary gave vent to his own feelings that British acquisition of Polaris would have no effect on French behaviour, as they were resolved, in any case, to follow their own course. Moreover, any disagreement with France over preferential treatment for Britain would be overshadowed by the effect on the Alliance of a serious breach between London and Washington in the nuclear field if a satisfactory solution to the current crisis were not found. And a multilateral force would never be accepted in NATO as France would find its control features incredible, and other members did not to want to see 'a German finger on the trigger.' Home saw the only sensible solution as one where some existing US, British and French nuclear capabilities were placed 'in a NATO framework', with a suitable mechanism for ensuring the smaller non-nuclear countries of the Alliance could be involved. Backing Home's arguments, the Prime Minister thought this kind of scheme the best answer to Germany's grievances. As for a multilateral force, while he would be ready to agree a joint study of its possibilities (as Kennedy had earlier suggested), he did not see how British public opinion would regard a share in it as a substitute for an independent deterrent: 'He was quite clear no one in England would accept the position of there being two nuclear Powers – the United States and Russia – with no other effective nuclear force.'

Much discussion ensued about the possibilities of offering Polaris to France if the missile were to be supplied to the UK. Kennedy spoke of the need for a careful examination of any such proposition, and that 'it might be necessary to abandon the multilateral concept and for the United States and United Kingdom to make an approach to President de Gaulle to see if France would be prepared to join with their two Governments as joint defenders of Europe.' After reaffirming that the earlier American offers of Hound Dog or a share in Skybolt development should be included in any statement that was issued after the Nassau talks had finished, Kennedy then suggested that also included in such a statement were the points that the situation regarding Polaris had been examined

> with great care in view of the many complexities involved. Broadly speaking the United States felt this missile should be considered, so far as other countries were concerned, in a multilateral context. There would need to be talks to determine the constitution of the political authority and military controlling mechanism. The study would have to consider the effect of this idea throughout Europe and it was likely that any offer which they made to Britain would also have to be repeated to France.

By offering an alternative form of deterrent, the intention of the wording, the President explained, was to refute any accusations that the United States had acted in bad faith, and this would prevent the French from saying the US and Britain were still 'locked in a monopoly.' All this, however, was a far cry from the basic British desiderata of a Polaris force which was under unfettered national control: a joint study of the provision of Polaris in a multilateral context would hardly satisfy the Government's domestic political critics.

Having once again rejected the notion of a taking a share in future Skybolt development, Macmillan, recognising there was 'a serious problem here', chose to put the issues in more dramatic form:

> ...what was really at stake was the future of the British independent deterrent and this was not an issue which could be blurred. There were in effect only two possible courses open to the United Kingdom Government. They could either retreat from the field of the nuclear deterrent altogether or they could go on no matter what the cost or the effort required. There were many who would point to the advantage of discontinuing the nuclear deterrent altogether. It would reduce the burden on the economy and would lead to an easier life for the people. But he did not think that when all was said and done this would be the majority view. He was sure that those who felt that the United Kingdom should continue to exercise full responsibilities would not be satisfied with some form of participation in a multilateral force and he thought that it was the people who would take this line who were the staunchest friends of the United States. He was quite prepared to agree that some form of multilateral arrangement should be studied and that as much as possible should be done to help the other NATO allies with information about joint

planning, targeting and so on. But he did not think the United Kingdom should be expected to contribute all their nuclear force to a supranational authority. He agreed that some method must be found of dealing with the German problem but this could be done without necessarily constituting an organisation which would cover the total nuclear deterrent capacity of all the allies.

In pointed fashion, the Prime Minister noted the risks run by the UK in hosting both the US submarine base at Holy Loch in Scotland, and the ballistic missile early warning radar facilities at Fylingdales (due to become operational in 1963), and though there was 'no wish in any way to retreat from these obligations', he wondered if it would be said that Britain was to 'run all the dangers and exercise none of the power.' Macmillan would be prepared, he said, 'to put in [to a multilateral arrangement] all of his part of a Polaris force provided the Queen [sic] had the ultimate power and right to draw back in case of a dire emergency similar to that in 1940.' If the United States decided not to assist the UK with the supply of Polaris as a replacement for Skybolt, this would, Macmillan warned, 'lead inevitably to a deep rift' in Anglo-American relations, and in such a situation 'public opinion could not be controlled.' Not responding in any direct fashion to these entreaties, with their implicit warnings, Kennedy merely reiterated the previous American offers of Hound Dog, a 50–50 share in completion of Skybolt development, or a joint study of the multilateral arrangements under which Polaris could be offered to the UK. After a little more desultory discussion, the first session of the conference broke-up for lunch with the distance between the two delegations apparently remaining as wide as ever.[31]

When they reconvened towards the end of the afternoon, Kennedy presented three US documents for the British to consider. These included a simple statement of the previous American offers, which might be made public, a private memorandum of understanding between the President and Prime Minister, on how a NATO multilateral force might be created from UK and US nuclear forces (including the 'assignment' to such a force of any Polaris missiles supplied to Britain, along with a similar US contribution), and a final paper which suggested a form of words that the British might use if asked whether the UK deterrent was independent. This last document mentioned that the nuclear defence of the Western Alliance was 'indivisible', and avowed the belief of the President and Prime Minister that

> in all ordinary circumstances of crisis or danger, it is this very unity which is our very best protection. Only in the event of dire national emergency – an emergency in which it might be necessary to act alone – an emergency which we cannot envisage and which we must all trust will never occur – would Her Majesty's Government be faced with a decision of utilising such forces on its own – of course after adequate notice to all partners.

Such a formulation, with its heavy caveats and qualifications, was unlikely to be acceptable to the Prime Minister, and the subsequent session of talks showed just how far apart the delegations continued to be.

There was recognition from both Kennedy and Macmillan that a key aspect of how an eventual agreement would be perceived was over how the term 'assigned to NATO' was interpreted, with the Americans favouring a tight definition, and the British a very loose one. Picturing the two countries as poised before a coming world of interdependence, but still retaining a need to control national forces as the mark of sovereignty, Macmillan remarked that there might be little point 'except an emotional one' in having the latter, 'though it was also possible to envisage a situation in which the United Kingdom might wish to use its deterrent force as an instrument of policy. At present this did not seem likely as the Russians were the chief enemy.' However, if he had to 'ask the British people to spend something like £300 million he must be able to say to them that in the last resort there remained to them an element of sovereignty.' It was, for example, conceivable that the UK might want to send some of its force to the Far East, and so away from the NATO area. However, the situation Kennedy was thinking about for when the force could be withdrawn involved some dire national emergency, such as a direct attack on the UK which threatened its national survival. He was also keen to remind Macmillan that the concept of assignment to NATO was essential if the US was to defend itself against accusations of inconsistency through the differing treatment of NATO allies, and especially after McNamara's Ann Arbor speech decrying small national deterrents. Macmillan responded that though he was in favour of putting British Polaris submarines under NATO, any Government must have

> the unquestioned right to use them in a serious national emergency. The situation might arise in the Far East in which the mere presence of British Polaris submarines would ward off a threat to Singapore. He thought it would be possible to find some way of putting them under NATO while preserving this right ... If he was questioned he would much rather not have to say that despite the conditions on which the missiles had been made available he would cheat if he absolutely had to: he would very much rather say honestly and openly that it was understood between the British and the Americans that the British had the ultimate right to control these submarines.

The basic problem, as the Prime Minister observed, was in the meaning of the word 'assignment', and the ultimate right of withdrawal that would be available to the UK.[32]

By the end of the difficult first day of talks, the Minister of Defence, in particular, was extremely pessimistic that any positive outcome to the conference could be achieved. Having studied the draft documents Kennedy had presented, Thorneycroft sent a minute to Macmillan which noted that 'my professional advisers tell me that they can see no method even under the most liberal interpretation of the word "assigned", of being continuously able to pose the deterrent threat in accordance with the policy of Her Majesty's Government and at the same time honour the NATO obligation.' Given the attitudes of the US administration, he would be against 'any attempt to find a formula which glosses over the very deep and wide chasm between us. Even if such a formula could be found it would lead to a series of public disagreements on the interpretation.' In Britain, the accusation would be made that the Government was 'spending vast sums of the taxpayers' money to create a force not under our control in order to subscribe it to NATO.' Thorneycroft now favoured ending the talks and issuing a communiqué explaining that the Americans had withdrawn their support from Skybolt, that UK-led development of the missile was impossible due to the cost and delays involved, but also because of doubts over its ultimate reliability, and that no suitable alternative had been agreed.[33]

While recognising the strength of Thorneycroft's argument, Macmillan's reply stressed that if a break with the Americans was to be made, there would have to be very firm grounds for such a radical step. He felt that the idea of a NATO force might be attractive to some, and that the formula proposed by the Americans to cover withdrawal of Polaris in case of 'dire emergency' was moving toward what was necessary from the national point of view.[34] To Butler in London, presiding over the Cabinet in the Prime Minister's absence, Macmillan conveyed the gloomy news of the first day's proceedings, and that the formula so far suggested by the Americans for 'assignment' meant that Polaris would not be available 'outside the NATO area or play a role in strengthening our foreign policy ... Our feeling is that it would not be tolerable to British public opinion that we should pay about £300 million for a force which would then become, as it were, the property of NATO.' Nevertheless, the Prime Minister still had some grounds for optimism as he felt that 'the Americans do not like the idea of ditching their old friends. Unlike his highbrow advisers, the President is a political animal and senses the dangers ahead.'[35]

Nassau: an agreement is forged

The two delegations reconvened on the morning of 20 December knowing that the outcome of the conference was still in the balance. After recapping his rejection of the previous day's US offers, Macmillan began by admitting that he might have been wrong in picturing Polaris as a straightforward replacement for Skybolt since it had implications 'both in character and in time' which 'marked the beginning of a new phase.' Professing to understand the President's anxieties over French and German reactions, Macmillan presented the key issue as being the organisation of a 'contributory NATO scheme which would not exclude the concept of multilateralism'. He could sympathise, Macmillan continued, with those Americans who wondered why the British felt they needed their own deterrent, and was prepared to admit 'that part of the reason was to keep up with the Joneses. This was a universal and perfectly respectable feeling in the world.' But there was also the point that great nations such as Britain, France and even Germany, regarded nuclear capability as a way to attain authority and independence in the nuclear-armed world of the current international system: apart from the military value of nuclear weapons in war, 'their main value was that they satisfied the instinct of great nations that they should not become clients – not to use the word satellites.'

Finally, Macmillan pictured British control of strategic nuclear forces as necessary to uphold many of its overseas commitments, enabling a defence to be made against any attempt to threaten the UK with nuclear attack: the express example used here was a reference to the threat to unleash Russian rockets following the Anglo-French invasion of Egypt in 1956. Kuwait, where Britain had intervened with military force in 1961 to forestall a possible Iraqi invasion, was also cited as an instance where a vital British interest might have to be defended, but there might be 'an Administration in the United States or powerful commercial interests there or elsewhere who would not mind seeing the British thrown out of Kuwait and the oil wells lost to the West.' In this instance, as over Suez, the possession of the means of nuclear retaliation would allow the Government to neutralise any blustering threats that Khrushchev might make to use nuclear weapons against London if conventional military operations were launched to protect vital British interests overseas.

Regarding the differences in language used by both sides in defining how Polaris might be used independently if supplied to the UK, Macmillan preferred to avoid terms such as only 'in a dire emergency', as this would lead to further difficult questions. It was this matter of language that now constituted the key sticking point of any agreement. Kennedy put the issue very cogently when he maintained that he was

> not now worried about the rights the United Kingdom would have over its Polaris submarines 10 years hence in the event of an emergency. He thought the two sides were agreed on that. He also thought that a decision to provide Polaris submarines to the United Kingdom could be defended as a first step towards the creation of a multilateral force, as a step which was at last being taken after years of talk in order to make a multilateral deterrent a reality. On that basis he thought an agreement could be 'sold' as helpful to the United States, to the United Kingdom and to Europe. But what did worry him and what was still not agreed was what Mr Macmillan would say if he was asked a direct question in Parliament or by the Press 'Is this an independent national deterrent'. This was the key to the whole problem. People must not be able to say that the multilateral aspect of the agreement was no more than a fig leaf.

It was for this reason that the Americans felt compelled to stress the creation of the MLF as being an essential part of any Polaris deal, and to downplay British desires to point to the independence of the deterrent.

Seeking a means to give the Americans something more substantial than a fig leaf, Macmillan next suggested the allocation of part or all of the V-bomber force, along with some US aircraft, into a common NATO pool, with the French also encouraged to contribute, and 'in this way a multilateral force would grow naturally.' Eventually, the UK Polaris submarines would be assigned in a similar fashion. Though liking the idea, Kennedy continued to press the Prime Minister over the central issue of independence. Imagining a press conference where this key question would be posed, Macmillan conjectured that he could say the situation was 'hypothetical', and that the present agreement involved the assignment to NATO of bombers and submarines. If he was then pressed as to what would happen 'if the United States pulled out', he proposed replying that 'all sorts of suppositions were possible but in the last resort the crews of any of Her Majesty's ships would obey national orders. This was true in every force. There were no constitutional means of obliging the officers and men to do otherwise. But all this was only in the last resort.' When Home added that 'the last resort' would mean something that 'threatened the life of the country', Kennedy agreed that this was a suitable definition.

The President asked what Macmillan would say if asked whether the agreement meant that the UK was 'continuing to maintain an independent deterrent', to which the latter replied he would say 'we were maintaining an independent contribution to the Western deterrent'. Wanting to see a draft text of the position that had now been reached, Kennedy responded that 'these were the very words that he had to be so careful about,' and that he was 'worried lest General de Gaulle or someone else might ask whether the same offer was open to France. He thought that he might have to be ready to say that it was.' While he had no difficulty agreeing with Macmillan that nuclear forces under multilateral control could revert to national control in the extreme circumstances of an emergency which threatened national survival – though he would expect to be consulted if the Prime Minister felt compelled to take such a step – Kennedy made clear that his prime concern was with the public presentation of any formal agreement that was made at the conference.[36]

After a short recess, the principals reconvened at noon where they considered a further US redraft of a possible communiqué that could be issued. This again specified the joint aim to develop a 'NATO missile force', where the Polaris missiles to be supplied under an agreement would be 'assigned' to NATO alongside an equivalent US contribution, with an eventual goal of making them part of a NATO multilateral force. The US draft went on to assert that the nuclear defence of the Western alliance was 'indivisible', and that it was the conviction of the President and Prime Minister 'that in all ordinary circumstances of crisis or danger it is this very unity which is the best protection of the West.' Obviously dissatisfied with the text, as it contained so little cover for the British position on ultimate national control, Macmillan ventured that it might not be possible to reach agreement on the terms proposed, saying

> Britain needed some independent deterrent in order to give their [sic] voice a legitimate authority and strength in international councils. Whether the force was committed or assigned or dealt with under some other phrase, in fact it must still be capable of being used when they wished by the British Government. This use would be exercised with the utmost sense of responsibility. *But in the ordinary day-to-day diplomatic life and during periods of international stress people must know that the force could be used when the British Government regarded supreme national interests are involved* [emphasis added]. Unless this principle could be accepted he would prefer to drop the whole idea of the Polaris system and find some other way. He would go a very long way to tie the force to NATO but in the last resort he would have to say that it was as much a part of Her Majesty's Government's forces as were the Brigade of Guards. The point was that if The Queen's Ministers gave orders Her troops would obey. If this great effort was to be made to maintain a British independent force it was to give Britain a standing in the world which her position and history commanded.

If the current text was accepted, Macmillan argued, it would be said that Britain had 'sold out' to American views. He had, however, drawn up his own a paper which attempted to reconcile the position on national control. Though only a relatively small distance now separated the two sides, he contended, 'This was too important a matter for ambivalence and it was no good trying to paper over a disagreement which was serious.' After referring in personal and emotional terms to the persistence of national affiliations at times of great danger or peril – 'When in the 1914 war his battalion had been nearly wiped out, the officers and men had fought not because of the "entente cordiale" but because of their loyalty to their King and country' – Macmillan maintained that the final decisions over nuclear use had to lie with the Government.[37]

Both sides retired to regroup once more. At this stage of the proceedings, Macmillan appears to have furnished Kennedy with a personal memorandum intended to quell some of the President's anxieties. This began by alluding to the series of assurances and agreements, dating back over many years, that had been made between Presidents and Prime Ministers over nuclear consultation procedures, and related these to a situation where the UK would feel compelled to invoke the 'supreme national interests' element of a Polaris deal:

> Recalling his long-standing arrangements first with President Eisenhower and then with President Kennedy by which neither the United States nor

the United Kingdom will use their nuclear force without consultation with the other, the Prime Minister stated in response to a request from the President that in the same spirit he would give as much notice as possible to the President of the United States of any British intention temporarily to withdraw Polaris missiles from their assigned role to other purposes. He also expresses his confidence that his successors will act similarly.[38]

This was a very carefully worded qualification to the essence of any right of withdrawal. While its first part referred explicitly to 'consultation' as underpinning previous Anglo-American understandings over nuclear use, it finished with the weaker assurance to 'give notice' of any intention to withdraw Polaris. But the memorandum also linked the two procedures by referring to the latter provision as being offered 'in the same spirit' as the previous assurances over consultation. Whatever the finer points of the wording, however, the political message the memorandum was intended to convey was clear: in the event that the Government felt that consideration should be given to the independent use of Polaris, there would be a process of consultation with Washington (and this was certainly the way the contents of the memorandum were summarised to his Cabinet colleagues by the Prime Minister).

The feeling of the Prime Minister was that the personal assurance he gave to Kennedy at Nassau underscored the fact that the eventual agreement reached at the conference enshrined the right of withdrawal from NATO. Indeed, he had no objection to it being shown to the French, or being made public.[39] All this suggests that the main scenarios that Macmillan had in mind when he thought of an independent use of Polaris under the conditions of the Nassau agreement were relating to precisely those world-wide global commitments that had been broached with the President, where a UK nuclear force might be a necessary insurance to deter a nuclear threat when British conventional forces took part in military operations, whether in the Far East against a putative Indonesian adversary which was attempting to foil the Malaysia scheme, or in an instance, such as Kuwait, where vital British interests in the Middle East were at stake. Ignored, however, was the more sensitive situation where the United States had held back from the use of nuclear weapons to defend Western Europe, but British ministers and officials felt that national survival was threatened by Soviet aggression and warranted a nuclear response.

Just before Nassau, the COS had identified this kind of eventuality as a key reason why an independent UK strategic nuclear force would be required during the 1970s. Even if, in the last resort, decision-makers in London would be unlikely to sanction the independent use of nuclear weapons against the Soviet Union in an eventuality when the US nuclear guarantee for Western Europe failed to materialise, it was important that Soviet leaders were convinced that the ability and will to execute such independent UK nuclear action existed. This was the 'second centre of decision-making' argument in its starkest form. But to be entirely credible it had to be implicit that the UK was willing to act in defiance of US wishes, for an independent UK nuclear strike was almost certain to trigger a general nuclear exchange between the Superpowers, while the Soviet leadership could never be certain of the national origin of a ballistic missile fired from a submarine. In this context, therefore, the private assurance given to Kennedy actually diluted one of the central aspects of nuclear use by suggesting that the Americans might have a veto power of some kind over independent nuclear action.

By the early afternoon of 20 December, with Kennedy having accepted the need for a 'supreme national interests' clause, agreement on the wording of a conference communiqué was finally reached. The draft text was quickly referred back to the Cabinet in London with the approval of the Prime Minister, Home, Thorneycroft, and Sandys, who all felt it gave the Government what it needed. For the Cabinet's benefit, Macmillan also explained that the formal communiqué would be supplemented by the exchange of personal messages between himself and Kennedy, one of which clarified the full extent of the American Polaris offer, with the inclusion of fire control, launching, guidance and navigation systems for the submarines that would be built, and the other (cited above) which gave the Prime Minister's personal assurance – in the context where supreme national interests were involved – that the UK Polaris force would not be used without prior consultation with Washington. This latter assurance, Macmillan advised his colleagues, 'underlined and strengthened our rights.' If pressed by Parliament on the full extent of the agreements reached in the Bahamas, Macmillan thought that both these documents would eventually have to be made public, but for the moment they were to be treated as private assurances.[40]

Several members of the MoD delegation at Nassau had strong reservations about the deal that was being crafted as they still believed it would tie the UK to NATO arrangements for an MLF. Asked for his opinion by the Prime Minister, Admiral Le Fanu had told him that 'if a force was specifically assigned to a NATO commander, [he] found it hard to see how Her Majesty's Government could exercise effective control if they wished.'[41] Lighthill supplied a memorandum to Thorneycroft on 20 December, intended to strengthen the Prime Minister's resolution, which outlined a possible fall-back position if the conference failed to reach agreement on any substitute for Skybolt. Reductions in warhead weight and improvements in rocket technology, including the development of two-stage systems, he argued, now made it possible to achieve Blue Streak's performance with a far lighter missile. Lighthill envisaged adapting the smaller Black Knight test vehicle with a new second stage so that it could carry a warhead over 1500 miles. This configuration 'would use proven components that started development in 1956', and could be flown after two years of further development, and then deployed on small hardened launch sites. Putting the rough costs of development and flight testing at £50 million, with another £1 million for each missile, including its launch site, Lighthill conjectured that 50 missiles could be produced for about

£100 million. The obvious drawback to such a programme, as with Blue Streak, was the vulnerability of fixed sites to pre-emptive attack, but, as Lighthill argued, it would have 'a compensating advantage of being entirely British in design, construction and control.' Whether the Prime Minister ever looked at this option is unknown, but even if it was mentioned to him by Thorneycroft, it is unlikely that it would have seemed an attractive course, or even a viable fall-back. Polaris was so widely seen as a front-runner to replace Skybolt, that Black Knight would have seemed a very poor substitute, requiring further development, with all the risks involved, and open to the same objections on the grounds of vulnerability as Blue Streak.[42]

Deep concerns over the agreement then being forged were also reflected in a memorandum, composed late in the evening of 20 December by Sir Robert Scott, the Permanent Under Secretary at the MoD, which questioned whether the deal secured basic British requirements. By the morning Scott had managed to persuade Zuckerman to add his signature to the protest (an unusual step, to say the least, as up to then Zuckerman had seemed happy with the agreement being forged). The document in question sought to draw the Prime Minister's attention 'to the very serious risks of the proposed arrangement.' The claim that Polaris was genuinely independent could, they noted, be made

> only with difficultly – the more so as we know that to the President it is a cardinal feature of his policy to deny his allies independent nuclear forces. In fact, we shall be spending vast sums of money in order to make a contribution to a multilateral force the object of which is political rather than military.

They saw the potential deal as constraining Britain's freedom of manoeuvre within NATO, and were by no means certain that the missiles themselves would ultimately be supplied. Conclusion of an agreement along the lines mooted would, they felt, expose Britain to 'grave risks' and place great strains on the Anglo-American relationship in the future.[43] Scott's basic reservation, as he confided to the Prime Minister's Press Secretary, was that 'the agreement would, in effect, put us in the Americans' pocket for the next decade.'[44]

Amongst the Cabinet back in London, there were clearly also ministerial reservations over proceedings in the Bahamas. One concern was over the financial costs involved, as no consideration seemed to have been given by the British delegation to any estimates for the construction of a British Polaris force. Despite the savings that would come from Skybolt cancellation, Reginald Maudling, the Chancellor of the Exchequer, was understandably anxious about the extra expenditure that the whole Polaris project would entail, especially given the strains likely to be placed on the defence budget over the coming years, while American stress on the need to improve the effectiveness of conventional forces in Europe – which US officials also saw as an important aspect of the understandings being reached at Nassau – was also seen as unwelcome. Though the value of an agreement which could secure UK control of an invulnerable and advanced second-strike weapon which was likely to have a long service life was recognised, so too was the 'heavy price' of the financial and other conditions under which it would be supplied.

At the centre of ministerial concerns, however, were those elements of the agreement which touched on the degree of independence that the UK's new Polaris force would be able to exercise. In view of the price that was being paid for the system, the Cabinet wanted their feeling understood that in any final agreement 'the independent role of Her Majesty's Government in the use of nuclear forces must be clearly and unambiguously expressed.' Ministers in London were reassured that the 'supreme national interests' clause inserted by the Prime Minister in the jointly agreed draft statement to be issued after the conference would allow complete national control over use of the deterrent. However, the even-more cautious Cabinet in London preferred that the order of words in the relevant part of the statement be reversed to give extra weight to this interpretation. On this basis, and also offering the Prime Minister their full support in his conduct of the negotiations, the Cabinet endorsed the draft terms early on 21 December.[45]

That same day, employing language that was vague and ambiguous, but that served the interests of both sides in avoiding a failure to compromise, Macmillan and Kennedy finally issued a 'Statement on Nuclear Defence Systems'. Beginning with a brief précis of the negotiations, it noted that the possible provision of Polaris as a replacement for Skybolt 'created an opportunity for the development of new and closer arrangements for the organisation and control of strategic Western defence and that such arrangements in turn could make a major contribution to political cohesion among the nations of the Alliance.' Building on this, the sixth paragraph of the statement mentioned that the Prime Minister had suggested, and the President agreed, that an immediate start could be made 'by subscribing to NATO some part of the forces already in existence.' These might include allocations of the UK's V-bombers, US strategic forces, or tactical nuclear forces based in Europe. 'Such forces,' it was explained, 'would be assigned as part of a NATO nuclear force and targeted in accordance with NATO plans.' Regarding Polaris, the seventh paragraph continued, the two governments had agreed that along with its provision 'must be the development of a multilateral NATO nuclear force in the closest consultation with our NATO allies. They will use their best endeavours to this end.'

The eighth paragraph of the statement outlined in the most general way the crucial framework within which Polaris would be supplied to Britain, and the conditions under which it could actually be used. Polaris missiles, but not their warheads, were to be made available for use in British-built submarines 'on a continuing basis' (a phrase actually suggested by Zuckerman, and used as the legal cover for the later sale of the Trident system to the UK under the same Anglo-American arrangements).[46] The UK would have responsibility for furnishing the nuclear warheads for their Polaris missiles, and the British forces developed under the terms of the statement were to be 'assigned and targeted in the same way' as the NATO nuclear forces mentioned in the sixth paragraph. However, the very next sentence in the statement went on to say that the UK's Polaris force

> and at least equal US forces, would be made available for inclusion in a NATO multilateral nuclear force. The Prime Minister made it clear that except where Her Majesty's Government may decide that supreme national interests are at stake, these British forces will be used for the purposes of international defence of the Western Alliance in all circumstances.[47]

There was an obvious tension between the 'multinational' NATO nuclear force envisaged under paragraph six, and the altogether different multilateral force, or MLF, mentioned in paragraph eight (involving, it might be supposed, a mixed-manned component of a genuinely shared weapons system). Under the confusing terms of the agreement, the UK's Polaris force would be 'assigned' to the multinational force, but could find itself, if suitable arrangements were reached and if such an interpretation were accepted, eventually allocated to the still-putative MLF.[48] The concept of assignment was always recognised to be a somewhat loose and amorphous idea.[49] Some of the practical issues of command, control and targeting were broached during the conference when Admiral Le Fanu was asked if a Polaris submarine 'assigned' to NATO, and targeted according to NATO requirements could be redirected 'to threaten a British target.' 'The idea, obviously enough,' Le Fanu wrote, 'is that if we were in a fracas in Kuwait or some place of no great American or NATO interest, and Khrushchev said "if you don't lay off I'll bash you", we would be in a position to say "we, Britain, will bash you back". My answer to this, which was made to the Prime Minister, was that we could so threaten "British" targets subject to two reservations:

i   response time was not critical, i.e. that response in a matter of hours was the thing, not minutes; and
ii   that if the "NATO" target was at, say, some peripheral point, e.g. Murmansk, and the British boat was stationed 2,500 miles from Murmansk, then, in the nature of things, it would not be able to threaten Moscow.

It was generally accepted that these provisos were acceptable, i.e. that the response time did not greatly matter, and that we could swing it so that the boat was not stationed on the rim of the circle.'[50]

In his personal message to the Queen outlining the agreement that had been reached at Nassau, Macmillan did not shy away from noting the difficulties encountered during the negotiation. Referring to the supreme national interests clause, he stressed that the agreement had preserved 'the ultimate independent position for Your Majesty's Ministers at their sole discretion at critical moments, thus maintaining Your Majesty's Sovereign rights.' Securing the terms of the agreement had been 'a hard and at times almost desperate struggle to maintain the two concepts of interdependence and independence.' However, Macmillan was careful to applaud President Kennedy's 'sense of fairness and willingness to be persuaded by argument and over-rule those of his advisers who were not sympathetic to our views.' McNamara, also, had shown 'moral strength and intellectual integrity of a high order' in his desire to resolve the differences that were on display. Tribute was paid to Lord Home 'with his urbane and resolute character – iron painted to look like wood', and to Thorneycroft and Sandys. As for Ormsby Gore's influence with the US administration, his position was described as 'quite remarkable and he uses his authority with discretion.' Although he was expecting initial press and public reactions to be somewhat critical, Macmillan believed 'we have secured for perhaps a generation, the continuance of Your Majesty's Realm as a nuclear power, with all that this implies and at the same time helped to promote those concepts of interdependence and cooperation on which the survival of the Free World depends.'[51]

Kennedy, for his part, seems to have been genuinely delighted with the understanding reached, having satisfied his closest ally with the generous offer of Polaris, but also laying down a marker for the ultimate creation of an MLF. Moreover, despite the tensions over basic interests that were evident between the principals, the atmosphere at Nassau was genuinely friendly containing, as Ormsby Gore put it to Macmillan, 'the flavour of a close family gathering which has become a feature of your talks with Kennedy.'[52] The chief 'losers' were widely perceived as the US sponsors of multilateral nuclear arrangements for the Western Alliance: James Lighthill had a general impression at the conference that while the US Department of Defense, in the form of McNamara, were ready to go a long way in order to reach agreement, 'the State Department and Mr Bundy were seeking to secure the torpedoing of the UK independent deterrent.'[53]

The Nassau Agreement certainly represented a signal achievement for the Prime Minister and his principal advisers. Though some genuflection had had to be granted to the State Department's MLF adherents, the supreme national interests clause of paragraph eight gave tangible political cover for the Government's claim that the future of an independent nuclear deterrent had been secured, and, on a more practical level, would eventually underpin the allocation of national targeting plans to the Polaris force when it became operational. Conducted in the full glare of publicity, with press speculation over the troubled state of the Anglo-American relationship, resolution of the issues at Nassau had a great deal to do with Kennedy's fundamental desire to give Macmillan what he needed to counter his domestic political critics. At the end of December, the President gave a background press briefing to reporters where he affirmed that the decision to cancel Skybolt was technical and financial, not political, in origin and that the offer of Polaris to the British 'was in keeping with both our technical and moral obligation to them, and I think that the arrangement was made in the best interest of the United States, Britain, and the Alliance, because the British will have their deterrent. It will be independent in moments of great national peril, which is really the only time you consider using nuclear weapons anyway. It will serve as a basis for a multinational or multilateral force.'[54]

Where only a few weeks before Skybolt cancellation appeared to have given an opportunity for critical US voices to push the UK out of the nuclear business (thereby easing some of the inequalities of nuclear status they saw as adding strain to the Western Alliance), there was now the promise of provision of one of the most advanced strategic nuclear weapons systems available. As the BNDSG had concluded earlier in 1962 when peering into the world beyond the V-bomber era, a submarine-based nuclear deterrent system offered major advantages over any other then conceivable, including comparative invulnerability to detection, an assured second-strike, retaliatory capability, and low running costs. On prevailing estimates, Polaris might, with the assistance of Aldermaston's warhead work and the information received from the United States through the 1958 MDA, keep the UK in the strategic nuclear club well into the 1980s. 'Those of us who were there,' Lighthill concluded, 'felt pretty convinced that we had got the best terms available short of breaking off altogether; and certainly the Americans had made major concessions.'[55]

As Ormsby Gore noted, the atmosphere in which the conference took place was generally good. David Bruce, the US Ambassador to the UK who attended as part of the US delegation, wrote in his diary that the 'personal relationships are delightful', but the 'bargaining is tough and realistic.' Seeing Kennedy operating for the first time, Bruce was very impressed by his qualities of personal charm and leadership: 'His mind is acute, quick and comprehensive. He reads papers swiftly, but seems to catch every slip or specious argument. He expresses his thoughts easily, and with polish.' As for Macmillan, he was described as dominating his delegation, and 'almost hesitant at times in speech, at others eloquent, sentimental, and, when he wishes, steely.'[56] The whole gathering had, nevertheless, been draining: 'This meeting,' Macmillan recalled, 'in which the arguments were much more violently contested than in any previous one, was an exhausting experience.' At times the Prime Minister had questioned Kennedy's veracity (he 'makes the facts fit his arguments – or so it often seems' Macmillan wrote in his diary), while in order to prevail over the central issues 'I had to pull out all the stops, adjourn, reconsider; refuse one draft, demand another...'[57] In the Prime Minister's view, the Nassau agreement represented 'a genuine attempt' to reconcile the desire for independence of action, with the reality of interdependence within the Western Alliance for a United Kingdom with limited resources: 'This accepts the facts as they are. But I do not conceal from myself that the whole concept will be much knocked about by controversy at home. The Cabinet ... do not much like it, although they backed us up loyally...' He also, in retrospect, wondered how anyone could doubt the 'reserved power' of the Government, as 'a nuclear weapon is not one which is ever used lightly, whether independently or interdependently. Its use, if ever such a horror came, must result [at] a time when supreme national interests are at stake.'[58]

Yet the impressive aspects of what had been gained at Nassau tended to be overshadowed at the time by commentary which was critical concerning the degree of dependence on the United States that was signified by the agreement. Such unfavourable perspectives were not just confined to the Labour Party, which continued to mock the whole notion of an independent deterrent, but included a wide spectrum of political opinion, not least on the Government's own backbenches.[59] While to Macmillan, the 'mere change from a missile propelled through the air to one fired from beneath the sea was one of technique, not of principle,' this was not how it was perceived by many observers.[60] The mistrust and suspicion of American motives and intentions that had been produced by the cancellation of Skybolt was not quick to dissipate and was fuelled immediately after Nassau by the ill-judged release by the Pentagon of news that the latest test flight of Skybolt, in contrast those held earlier in the year, had in fact been successful (a public relations blunder that induced real anger in President Kennedy).[61]

Despite this ill-judged announcement, Macmillan returned to London convinced that the US administration had been 'determined to kill Skybolt on good general grounds – not merely to annoy us or to drive Great Britain out of the nuclear business. But, of course, they have handled things in such a way as to make many of us very suspicious. Nor do we know what will be the effect of the successful test of Skybolt in American politics.'[62] Wary that various lobbies in Washington might try to reinstate the programme, in the aftermath of Nassau the Prime Minister continued to be alive to the possibility that the Americans might eventually even renege on the deal, or attempt to qualify the terms on which Polaris might be supplied ('I think we must be prepared for some pressure to be put upon us, and coming to a point where we would threaten to tear up the agreement'). He therefore asked his officials to examine – with little profit as it transpired – the practicality of producing a Polaris-type system from British resources alone.[63]

Pronounced scepticism over the Nassau arrangements was also exhibited by some of the Prime Minister's own colleagues. For example, Julian Amery, the Minister of Aviation, sent the Prime Minister a note on 27 December expressing his concerns that while the 'Polaris agreement with the President is no doubt all right on paper,'

> it is reached against the background of a false prospectus on Skybolt and a determined attempt by the Administration to deny Britain a continuing independent deterrent. The saving clause at the end of paragraph 8 was only extracted very grudgingly. It is all very different from the spirit in which the Skybolt agreement was reached with President Eisenhower.

It is difficult to feel complete confidence that the Americans will in fact deliver the missiles. At worst they may find a pretext for not doing so in the failure to build an effective multilateral force. At best we shall find ourselves tied even more closely to them in defence and foreign policy.

The alternative that Amery would like to see considered was development by the UK of a ballistic missile of the Skybolt or Polaris type, preferably in collaboration with France. He also suggested that Macmillan approach de Gaulle with a proposal for joint development of a new missile system, but with full national control of the missiles when they were produced. But this would mean abandoning the Nassau agreement and placing huge strain on Anglo-Americans, so Amery would like to see the proposal to de Gaulle predicated on him dropping opposition to UK entry into the EEC. 'If de Gaulle says "Yes",' Amery concluded, 'we shall be in the Common Market and will have a truly independent deterrent. If de Gaulle says "No" we shall have to stretch our existing deterrent as far as we can and either hope for Polaris or make a new missile entirely on our own.'[64]

Yet elsewhere within the defence establishment, opposition to the Polaris agreement was beginning to dissolve. Even within the Air Ministry, where there had been so much resistance in the past to relinquishing the prime deterrent role to Polaris, it was realised that it was time to move on. As the Deputy Chief of the Air Staff advised Scott at the end of December: 'Most unfortunately Skybolt is gone. Attacking Polaris will not bring it back. I think we must accept that and turn all our energies to building up the Royal Air Force to fill a "limited war" role. We cannot afford to antagonise Ministers upon whose support we must depend for success.'[65]

Nassau: the aftermath

Presenting the final outcome at Nassau to the Cabinet in a two-hour discussion at the beginning of January 1963, Macmillan explored the fundamental reasoning that lay behind the Government's decision to accept a new generation of US nuclear delivery system. 'Should we try to retain [an] independent n[uclear] d[eterrent] at all?' he had asked his colleagues in rhetorical fashion.

> France is trying to acquire one, but for reasons of prestige rather than from conviction of its efficacy. Cost and sophistication are increasing alarmingly; and effectiveness of mere warhead will depend more and more on associated decoy systems, guidance systems, etc. Should we therefore drop out of this race?

But it would not be good for the Western Alliance, the Prime Minister suggested, if only its leading member had control of the advanced scientific know-how associated with nuclear weapons. Moreover, an independent capability would allow the UK 'to react appropriately to a Soviet nuclear threat to this country, even if the United States, for whatever reason, were disinclined to support us'. A Soviet nuclear threat, without an adequate counter, he argued, would render all the UK's conventional military strength ineffective. And without an independent deterrent, Britain would lose all influence over international efforts at arms control. 'Our own [V-bomber] system will endure for another few years,' Macmillan had concluded in pithy style, 'thereafter, since we are in the game now, we had better remain in it.' It was for these reasons that Polaris had been sought at Nassau, despite obvious American reluctance. Though recognising that aspects of the agreement would attract much domestic political criticism, Macmillan felt that the 'supreme national interests' clause secured Britain's crucial right of independent use. At any moment of 'gravest national crisis,' the Prime Minister observed, the use of Polaris 'must rest with HMG and they must be served by men who are The Queen's officers.' The Nassau deal therefore 'represented a realistic compromise, in present circumstances, between independence and interdependence; and if, as might well be the case, the development of a multilateral system proved impossible, our own situation would be unchanged, except in so far as we should have acquired, in Polaris, a more effective weapon than Skybolt.'

Immediate backing for the Prime Minister during the Cabinet meeting came from Thorneycroft and Home. The former acknowledged the strong body of opinion in the country opposing an independent nuclear deterrent, and also the opposite view that the UK should provide one from its own resources. What the Minister of Defence called the Government's current 'compromise' between these two positions was in a 'pretty touchy position', but Polaris represented $800 million of US research and development investment that Britain would be spared, and would prolong the deterrent 'for as far ahead as we need look.' There was no real possibility that the Kennedy administration would go back on the recent deal, and no economically realistic prospect that Britain could provide some alternative system against this unlikely contingency. Supporting Macmillan's rationale for maintaining the deterrent, the Foreign Secretary argued that the UK

> can't ignore [the] risk of being blackmailed by [the] S[oviet] Union and not being supported by [the] US. Nor could we accept [a] position in which France … was [the] only nuclear power in Europe. We must make it clear that our right to use Polaris independently in defence of supreme national interests is valid in any circumstances. Allocation to NATO or [a] multilateral organisation is acceptable (subject to this proviso) and should help to dissuade Germany from developing an independent nuclear power of her own.

About to resume another round of negotiations over EEC entry, Heath, for his part, reminded his colleagues that it would remain the US objective to 'eliminate separate independent n[uclear] d[eterrent].s if possible,' and he therefore considered the idea of a European deterrent important, but for the moment France remained uncooperative, and Germany 'must be denied.' As a result, though Europe had 'almost as great an industrial potential as [the] USA, little progress can be made.' Heath, in fact, wanted Thorneycroft and Amery to give detailed study to the possibilities of eventually moving toward a European deterrent, but there appeared little enthusiasm for this amongst Heath's colleagues.

Although in general terms the Cabinet was prepared to endorse the Prime Minister's position, and praised the successful outcome of the negotiations, several reservations were expressed. The Chancellor of the Exchequer was anxious that Polaris would place even more strains on a defence budget that would have to face savings in the future if its share of Gross National Product was to remain the same. There would be powerful arguments by the end of the 1960s that the deterrent was not fully credible against the Soviet Union, while 'if Polaris is to be [an] additional, and first-charge, burden on our resources, [the] problem of economies will be ever more acute.' Other ministers were wary there should be no watering down of the supreme national interests clause of the agreement when the time came to assign Polaris to NATO, and 'it would be necessary to consider carefully the exact wording of any written undertaking to commit our Polaris weapons to a multilateral force. For the same reason we should avoid any precise definition of the circumstances in which the supreme national interest might require us to withdraw them.' The chief anxiety of both Macmillan and Thorneycroft was that an immediate start should be made to the process of agreeing the precise terms on which Polaris would be supplied, and that design details or even the missiles themselves should be acquired as soon as possible.[66]

One Foreign Office appraisal on the effect of Nassau on the independent nuclear deterrent, compiled by Clive Rose (then a junior official, but to progress in his career into several key roles connected with strategic nuclear issues) recognised the point that the American intention, which had had to be accepted, was that the Polaris force would be

> fully enmeshed in a multilateral force and that the possibility of its independent operation should be reduced to the minimum. The wording of the "escape clause" in paragraph 8 of the Nassau agreement is capable of liberal (British) or restrictive (American) interpretation.

Comfort was taken from the practical point that the submarine crews would be British and the warheads British-made, which meant that the force would respond 'to British orders, even if these conflict with orders received from a NATO source.' But there were also limitations which tended to reduce the capability of independent operation, including the proposal to share US navigational and communications facilities, and the obligation to inform the US Government in advance if the Polaris force was to withdrawn from its

NATO role. The latter implied that 'in the event of US disagreement with our proposal to withdraw the submarines for national purposes, they would have practical means of restraining us.' Although it was unlikely that such circumstances would rise, it was therefore necessary, Rose thought, that it could be seen that Polaris was capable of operating in a national role even in the face of American objections, 'if the claim to independence is to appear credible.' This meant, Rose believed, that the submarines would have to remain wholly British manned, there should be no locks or custodial arrangements for the Polaris warheads themselves, a national system of navigation and communications had to be established, and the force had to be responsive to British command and control.[67]

Rose's observations reflected the fact that the Nassau Agreement contained such innate ambiguity that a final verdict on its effect on Britain's freedom to operate its Polaris deterrent system would have to await its practical implementation, and how plans for the creation of an MLF within NATO would evolve.[68] Nevertheless, amongst many there was a widespread belief that Britain's dependence on Washington for its next generation of nuclear weapons system, and the entangling terms of the deal reached with the Kennedy administration, necessarily diminished the capacity for the UK to bring an independent voice and influence to bear on world affairs. Of course, to Macmillan and his senior ministers, it was precisely in order to secure that 'independent' voice that a strategic nuclear weapons programme was given sanction in the first place, and the supreme national interests clause was the peg on which assertions that Polaris remained under ultimate national control would have to hang. But for partisans of Britain's future course as a power looking to create closer links with its continental European neighbours, the Nassau Agreement, which seemed to encapsulate the precedence accorded to the transatlantic connection with Washington, also had general political drawbacks which were soon to make themselves felt.

One of the major concerns of senior members of the Kennedy administration was that the offer of Polaris made to the UK would increase de Gaulle's sense of exclusion and serve to derail the final stages of the negotiations over Britain's entry to the EEC. At Nassau, Kennedy and Macmillan had in fact given some time to discuss the parameters of a comparable offer of nuclear assistance to France. The President moved quickly to follow up on these ideas, sending a message to de Gaulle on 20 December, as the text of the final Nassau communique was being finalised, conveying what had been agreed and saying he would consider a 'similar' offer to France should this conform with de Gaulle's wishes.[69] After Kennedy had travelled from the Bahamas to his home in Palm Beach in Florida for the Christmas vacation, he briefed the US Ambassador to France, Charles Bohlen (who had also been at Nassau), on how to present the proposition to de Gaulle when he returned to Paris, while on 29 December, still at Palm Beach, the President himself saw Herve Alphand the French Ambassador, to explain his view that Nassau represented a framework for the organisation of Western defence which he hoped that the French would feel inclined to join.⁷⁰ According to British reports of the conversation, Kennedy confirmed that the agreement would give Britain (and France if it took up the same offer) the unequivocal right to use Polaris when it was felt supreme national interests were at stake. The President cited the Suez expedition of 1956, or Britain's Kuwait intervention in 1961, as an example of a situation where the clause might be invoked, and that when 'some action on the part of the British or the French, not directly affecting the United States, led to the Russians threatening either country with missiles, they would be in a position to decide to use their own Polaris missiles against, say, Moscow or Kiev.' The MLF proposals were, in Kennedy's view, 'important to calm the suspicions of the other NATO Powers, in particular Germany, and to give them the feeling that there would be a nuclear force at their disposal and a European finger on its use.' If the three Western nuclear powers could all push forward with an MLF proposal as had been outlined at Nassau, this might also help to prevent the proliferation of nuclear weapons.⁷¹

British officials were also anxious to explore the possibilities of involving France more closely in the Nassau arrangements. At the very end of the year Macmillan met some of his senior ministerial colleagues to review the agreement reached over Polaris, as well as its relationship to the EEC negotiations. Expressing his desire quickly to start detailed discussions in order to give practical effect to the agreement, and almost as if he feared the Americans would soon begin to have second thoughts, Macmillan considered that follow-on talks should be 'kept on a naval and technical level so that political considerations need not be brought in.' Ministers also discussed what approaches might be taken to the French if they took up Kennedy's offer of a Polaris deal. It could be stressed to the French, the Prime Minister remarked, that the 'supreme national interests' clause protected Britain's sovereign rights under the Nassau agreement, but that it was unlikely to be invoked except in 'the most grave of circumstances.' The contingencies that Macmillan had in mind, he noted, were of an Indonesian threat to British interests in North Borneo, where conventional forces had been used in the first instance, but then the Russians, much in the manner of the Suez crisis, had made a nuclear threat against the UK in a very direct fashion. In such an unlikely event, Macmillan felt there would be grounds for withdrawing the UK Polaris force from NATO assignment, so that the Soviet threat could be countered, and British operations not hamstrung. Sounding a more negative note, Heath brought up the point that the whole Polaris agreement tended to signify the UK's dependence on the United States, and that until the missiles were actually in British possession 'we would be at the mercy of the United States Government.' In any event, the overall view of the meeting was that de Gaulle would reject Kennedy's Polaris offer, which would be regarded by de Gaulle as 'a further attempt by the Americans to secure the leadership of Europe,' while accepting American missiles would be seen as undermining French independence.⁷²

It was evident that at this stage the Prime Minister was still absorbed with the idea that Britain could also make its own nuclear approach of some kind to France, perhaps in the warhead field, in the hope this might induce de Gaulle to relax his opposition to British membership of the Community. There was a possibility, Macmillan thought, that de Gaulle had not realised the immense complexity and costs of modern weapons such as Polaris, while 'the latest developments in the field of anti-ballistic missiles made the manufacture of an offensive warhead a very difficult and complicated business.' Indeed, he would welcome the visit of a French delegation to discuss the technicalities involved.[73] From Paris, Dixon had made the same point two days before when responding to his instructions to explain the outcome at Nassau to de Gaulle. Dixon thought that while the concept of joining a NATO MLF would be 'anathema' to de Gaulle, he thought he might be interested in offers of assistance for his own nuclear programme. Any possibility of Anglo-French cooperation over ballistic missiles, for example, might therefore be helpful in the current context.[74]

This was clearly how the Prime Minister viewed matters. After the meeting with his senior colleagues, he had sent a message to Ormsby Gore in Washington which mentioned that at Rambouillet it was his impression that de Gaulle was 'still hesitating between the hegemony of continental Europe which France holds and can keep, and a wider approach which in the old days we used to call tripartitism.' If de Gaulle could be tempted into the latter arrangement as an initial step to the mutilateralism sketched at Nassau, Macmillan wondered if Kennedy would agree to the UK providing the warheads for a Polaris system supplied to France. 'Polaris is not much good to the French as they cannot even make an H-bomb – certainly not a nuclear warhead,' the Prime Minister had signalled. 'But if we agreed to supply the warheads it would be an understanding, though not part of the written agreement, that President de Gaulle should bring the Brussels negotiations to a successful conclusion. He and he alone prevents this.' Instructing Ormsby Gore to broach the idea to Kennedy on a strictly 'secret and personal' basis, Macmillan ventured that 'it sounds rather a crude deal but it is not. It is an attempt to bring off during 1963 what would really be the foundation of a very sound system. Without the French, and that is to say without Europe, I fear that we shall all be forced back on to isolationism of one kind or another.'[75]

Meanwhile, having returned from London, where he had received a personal briefing from the Prime Minister and Foreign Secretary, on 2 January Dixon saw de Gaulle in Paris to explain the British approach at Nassau, and to encourage the French to join the framework which had been established there for nuclear cooperation within the Western Alliance. The hope was expressed to de Gaulle that he might 'go into this very fully with us and the Americans. We also felt that the British and French might be able to help each other.' Under the terms of Nassau, 'subscription of part of the British nuclear capacity to SACEUR really amounted to subscribing it for NATO targeting. We would have our own separate targets for the eventuality of the use of our force for national interests and the ultimate control would rest with the owners.' To all such overtures of involvement with the Nassau scheme, de Gaulle evinced no interest. As France lay in much closer geographical proximity to the Soviet Union, he pronounced, it had to have 'complete control' of its own 'force de dissuasion'. He had nothing but scorn for the idea of multilateralism. Under its cover, he claimed, 'the Americans hoped to rally the support, both military and financial, of the European nations in an organisation which would be commanded by an American General and would in reality be under American control. He was frankly doubtful whether anyone, even ourselves, who subscribed to this idea would in practice be able to withdraw their nuclear contribution for national purposes.' Dixon's account of the meeting had de Gaulle mumbling 'acidly' that he could not understand why Britain, 'with all our tradition ... had not found it possible to tell the Americans that the terms of their offer of nuclear help was unacceptable, and to turn instead to cooperation with European nuclear defence.'[76]

During this distinctly unpromising encounter, Dixon had thought that de Gaulle would pick up his guarded signals that Anglo-French cooperation over warhead work might be a possibility in the future. Nevertheless, according to Dixon's account, de Gaulle had taken

> an extraordinarily over-simplified view of the problems of constructing a nuclear deterrent. If he is aware at all of the immense technical and financial advantages of the Polaris offer, they are completely outweighed in his mind by his aversion to getting tied up with the Americans. He really believes he can build what is required alone, if necessary, though he now probably thinks that we and the Americans are bound to help him on his terms in the end.

In his considered opinion, Dixon was not at all optimistic that an offer of bilateral nuclear cooperation would have any great effect on de Gaulle's attitudes:

> Given his bitter anti-American prejudices I cannot believe that this would tip the balance and lead him to accept the American offer with its basic condition of the multilateral force. Nor do I think, after this latest revelation of his sentiments, that help with nuclear matters would dispose him to facilitate our inclusion in the EEC, since he wants a European community in which we would be acceptable if we were 'European' in the Gaullist sense, not a community in which we remained tied to the United States and over which the Americans would gain a political influence through their new defence policy. His objective, if we offered to cooperate over the warhead, would be to pick our brains and acquire what know-how he could in order to speed up French nuclear progress, the better to pursue an independent policy.[77]

In the meantime Ormsby Gore had reported from Washington in negative fashion on the idea of UK assistance to France over warheads for Polaris, if de

Gaulle chose to take up Kennedy's offer of involvement with the Nassau framework. Though he could see no harm in raising the notion with Kennedy, the Ambassador thought there would be very little enthusiasm for such a scheme in the White House. American help with French warhead development, Kennedy had already reasoned, might be the only way to persuade de Gaulle to cooperate along the lines of Nassau but this, he had told Ormsby Gore over the New Year, would mean a complete reversal of US policy, and 'even if he could overcome his own scruples on this,' it was very doubtful that Congress would approve the proposal. Therefore, it was even less likely that Congress would concur with the passage by the UK to France of warhead information, much of which had been derived from US sources.[78]

By 4 January, Dixon was reporting his own strong conviction that the chance of de Gaulle changing his attitude to British entry by means connected with the Nassau Agreement was 'so slim as not to be worth the lengths to which we would have to go.'[79] That same day newspapers carried reports, released in Paris, that de Gaulle's reply to Kennedy's first message containing his offer to provide Polaris had received a non-committal answer and that the French Government was taking 'a cool view' of the proposals.[80] As one Foreign Office official put it, de Gaulle 'does not want, at any price, a multilateral force which he would regard as dependent on the Americans; nor is he going to agree to British entry into the EEC in return for offers in the field of nuclear weapons.' Therefore, the Foreign Secretary was briefed to advise Macmillan that, while continuing to promote adherence to the Nassau arrangements, specific offers to the French over nuclear weapons should be dropped: 'Our objective should be to convince the Americans and the Five [other EEC members] (particularly the Germans) that we are good Europeans, good allies, and good multilateralists in the spirit of Nassau, and that this cannot be said of General de Gaulle.'[81]

De Gaulle's dramatic press conference on 14 January 1963, where he unceremoniously both rejected any offer of Polaris and announced his intention to block Britain's bid to enter the European Community, finally dissolved whatever remaining hopes Macmillan may have entertained that an overture in the nuclear field could overcome the obstacles to a successful outcome to the Brussels negotiations. Over the Nassau Agreement, the French President noted that it did not meet the principle

> which consists of disposing in our own right of our deterrent force. To turn over our weapons to a multilateral force, under a foreign command, would be contrary to that principle of our defense and our policy. It is true that we too can theoretically retain the ability to take back in our hands, in the supreme hypothesis, our atomic weapons incorporated in the multilateral force. But how could we do it in practice during the unheard of moments of the atomic apocalypse? ... we will adhere to the decision we have made: to construct and, if necessary to employ our atomic force ourselves.[82]

Although de Gaulle would almost have certainly found many other reasons to block Britain's accession to the EEC, the Anglo-American nuclear bond which was consolidated at Nassau gave his objections an easy and tangible target and plausible cover.[83] In the space of a few weeks at the end of 1962 Britain's nuclear future had been radically transformed: decisions over a next generation deterrent system to take the place of the V-force, not expected to be necessary for several more years, had suddenly been forced upon a Conservative Government which had attached its waning political credibility to the continued maintenance of an independent nuclear deterrent. It now remained to be seen whether Nassau's undesirable 'multilateral' commitments could be sidestepped, and practical flesh put on the bones of Washington's agreement to furnish Polaris and assist with the creation of a new submarine force to carry it.

Notes

1 See JP(62)134(Final), 'The United Kingdom Deterrent After 1970,' 3 December 1962, DEFE 6/81.
2 COS(62) 81st Meeting, item 1, 18 December 1962, DEFE 4/150. When endorsed by the COS Committee the JPS paper became COS(62)486, 'The United Kingdom Strategic Nuclear Deterrent after 1970,' 19 December 1962. A copy of this important paper should be located in DEFE 5/132, however, as it was updated and superseded in October 1964, all original copies have been removed from the 1962 volume of COS memoranda. Copies of the final version of COS(62)486 can, nevertheless, still be found in DEFE 7/2236, as well as AIR 2/13715, while an extract appears in PREM 11/3702.
3 Diary entry for 25 November 1962, quoted in Macmillan, *At the End of the Day*, 334.
4 See ibid, 341; and also UK delegation to NATO Paris telegram No 206 to Foreign Office, 15 December 1962, PREM 11/4161.
5 Thorneycroft 'Notes of a Conversation with Mr McNamara,' 15 December 1962, and Hockaday minute for Bligh, 17 December 1962, PUSD records, FCO.
6 See Ludlow, *Dealing with Britain*, 176–8, 196–7.
7 Pierson Dixon letter to Sir Patrick Reilly, 28 November 1962, PREM 11/4230.
8 Home minute for Macmillan, 'Anglo/French Collaboration: Nuclear Submarine/Missile System,' PM/62/97, 13 July 1962, PREM 11/3712. Macmillan's handwritten comment on this message was, 'All this must wait, in my view, for some months.'.
9 See 'Record of a conversation at Admiralty House at 11am on Friday, July 20, 1962,' PREM 11/3712.
10 See de Zulueta minute for Macmillan, 'Rambouillet and Anglo-French Relations in the Nuclear Field,' 7 December 1962, PREM 11/3712.
11 'Record of a conversation at Rambouillet at 3.45pm on Saturday, December 15, 1962,' PREM 11/4230. In his memoirs, Macmillan was more explicit in claiming that he had told de Gaulle he would press Kennedy for Polaris at Nassau, see *At the End of the Day*, 347.
12 'Record of a meeting at the Chateau de Rambouillet at 10am on Sunday, December 16, 1962,' PREM 11/4230.
13 'Record of a conversation at Rambouillet at 12 noon on Sunday, December 16, 1962,' PREM 11/4230.
14 See Macmillan, *At the End of the Day*, 348–53.

15 'Special Relationship on Trial,' *The Times*, 17 December 1962.
16 Foreign Office telegram No 9296 to Washington, personal for Ambassador from Prime Minister, 14 December 1962, PREM 11/4147; and as quoted in Macmillan, *At the End of the Day*, 344.
17 'US Not Obliged to Provide Alternative to Skybolt,' *The Times*, 17 December 1962.
18 *Hansard*, HC, vol 669, cols 893–900, 17 December 1962.
19 'Britain's Nuclear Force in the Balance,' *The Times*, 21 December 1962.
20 Memorandum of conversation by Bundy, 16 December 1962, *FRUS, 1961–1963, XIII*, 1088–91.
21 See 'Review of the World Scene: Television Interview with the President, December 17, 1962,' in Richard P. Stebbins (ed.), *Documents on American Foreign Relations, 1962* (New York, 1963), 49–50, 60.
22 Le Fanu minute, 'Notes on Bahamas Meeting,' 22 December 1962, ADM 1/28839.
23 See, for example, Amery minute for Thorneycroft, 'Skybolt,' 15 December 1962, DEFE 19/78.
24 See Lighthill paper, 'The Bahamas Conference: Report of Attendance as Part of the Ministry of Defence Party,' n.d., AVIA 65/1840.
25 Ministry of Defence memorandum, 'Brief for the Prime Minister's Talks with President Kennedy, December 1962: Skybolt and Polaris,' n.d. (but c. 17 December 1962), ADM 1/28839 and in DEFE 13/410.
26 A good picture of the Kennedy-Ormsby Gore relationship is drawn in Schlesinger, *A Thousand Days*, 423–4.
27 See Neustadt, *Report to JFK*, 88.
28 'Background Paper – Current Political Scene in the United Kingdom,' 13 December 1962, National Security File, box 238, John F. Kennedy Library (JFKL).
29 Schlesinger, *A Thousand Days*, 864.
30 Evans diary entry, 28 December 1962, *Downing Street Diary*, 237.
31 'Record of a Meeting held at Bali-Hai, the Bahamas, at 9.50am on Wednesday, December 19, 1962,' WP2/2/G, FO 371/173292; memorandum of conversation, 19 December 1962, *FRUS, 1961–1963, XIII*, 1091–1101. See also Le Fanu minute, 'Notes on Bahamas Meeting,' 22 December 1962, ADM 1/28839.
32 'Record of a Meeting held at Bali-Hai, the Bahamas, at 4.30pm on Wednesday, December 19, 1962,' WP2/2/G, FO 371/173292.
33 Thorneycroft minute for Macmillan, 19 December 1962, PREM 11/4147. For the Minister's attitudes, see also Lighthill paper, 'The Bahamas Conference: Report of Attendance as Part of the Ministry of Defence Party,' n.d., AVIA 65/1840.
34 Macmillan minute for Thorneycroft, 'Nuclear Forces,' M.339/62, 19 December 1962, PREM 11/4147.
35 Nassau telegram No Codel 13 to Foreign Office, from Prime Minister for First Secretary of State, 20 December 1962, PREM 11/4147.
36 Record of a Meeting held at Bali-Hai, the Bahamas, at 10.30am on Thursday, December 20, 1962,' WP2/2/G, FO 371/173292.
37 Record of a Meeting held at Bali-Hai, the Bahamas, at 12 noon on Thursday, December 20, 1962,' WP2/2/G, FO 371/173292.
38 'Memorandum given by the Prime Minister to President Kennedy,' 20 December 1962, PREM 11/4147.
39 See Foreign Office telegram No 9735 to Washington, 30 December 1962, PREM 11/4147.
40 Nassau telegram No Codel 24 to Foreign Office, 20 December 1962, PREM 11/4147. And see also the Prime Minister's mention of his 'understanding' with

Kennedy that the general content of the messages they exchanged containing the assurances would be made public if he was 'pressed in the House of Commons,' see Bligh minute for Samuel, 31 December 1962, PREM 11/4229.
41 Le Fanu minute, 'Notes on Bahamas Meeting,' 22 December 1962, ADM 1/28839.
42 Lighthill memorandum for Thorneycroft, 'A Possible British Deterrent,' 20 December 1962, Appendix II to 'The Bahamas Conference: Report of Attendance as Part of the Ministry of Defence Party,' n.d., AVIA 65/1840.
43 Scott and Zuckerman memorandum for Thorneycroft, 21 December 1962, DEFE 13/410.
44 Evans diary entry, 28 December 1962, *Downing Street Diary*, 241. For Zuckerman's account of this episode, see *Monkeys, Men and Missiles*, 260–2.
45 CC(62)76th Conclusions, 21 December 1962, CAB 128/36; Foreign Office telegram No Codel 62 to Nassau, from Butler to Macmillan, 21 December 1962, PREM 11/4147.
46 See Zuckerman, *Monkeys, Men and Missiles*, 259.
47 And see the final version, 'Statement on Nuclear Defence Systems, 21 December 1962,' in Cmnd 1915, *Bahamas Meetings, December 1962: Texts of Joint Communiques* (though in this document the final two sentences of paragraph eight, including the 'supreme national interests' clause, were detached and placed in a new paragraph nine, perhaps to emphasise their importance for the preservation of an independent deterrent).
48 For this point see, John Baylis, *Anglo-American Defence Relations, 1939–1984*, 2nd ed (London, 1984), 105.
49 See, for example, C. E. F. Gough minute, 'Polaris Submarines – Assignment to NATO,' 1 January 1963, ADM 1/28839.
50 Le Fanu minute, 'Notes on Bahamas Meeting,' 22 December 1962, ADM 1/28839.
51 Nassau telegram No Codel 44 to Foreign Office, 21 December 1962, PREM 11/4147.
52 Ormsby Gore letter to Macmillan, 28 December 1962, PREM 11/4147.
53 See Lighthill paper, 'The Bahamas Conference: Report of Attendance as Part of the Ministry of Defence Party,' n.d., AVIA 65/1840.
54 Comments by the President at a Background Press Briefing Conference, Palm Beach, December 31, 1962, *Documents on American Foreign Relations, 1962*, 247.
55 See Lighthill paper, 'The Bahamas Conference: Report of Attendance as Part of the Ministry of Defence Party,' n.d., AVIA 65/1840.
56 Bruce diary entry, 19 December 1962, in John W. Young and Raj Roy (eds), *Ambassador to Sixties London: The Diaries of David Bruce, 1961–1969* (Dordrecht, 2009), 87–8.
57 Macmillan, *At the End of the Day*, 360; Macmillan diary entry, 23 December 1962, MS Macmillan dep. d. 48, Bodleian Library.
58 Macmillan diary entry, 23 December 1962, MS Macmillan dep. d. 48, Bodleian Library.
59 See 'Parties Agreed on Need for Early Debate,' *The Times*, 24 December 1962.
60 Macmillan, *At the End of the Day*, 357.
61 Kaplan, et al., *McNamara Ascendancy*, 383–4.
62 Macmillan diary entry, 23 December 1962, MS Macmillan dep. d. 48, Bodleian Library.
63 Macmillan minute, 'Polaris,' M.343/62, 26 December 1962, PREM 11/4412.
64 Untitled Amery note for Macmillan, 27 December 1962, PREM 11/4230.
65 DCAS minute for Scott, 'Polaris,' 28 December 1962, AIR 2/18270.
66 CC(63)2nd Conclusions, 3 January 1963, CAB 128/37; CC(63)2, 3 January 1963, CAB 195/22. See also Macmillan, *At the End of the Day*, 362–3.

67 Clive Rose minute, 'The Nassau Agreement,' and attached draft paper, 4 January 1963, PUSD records, FCO.
68 See, for example, 'Defence and Effect of Polaris,' *The Times*, 8 January 1963.
69 See telegram from the Delegation to the Heads of Government Meeting to the Embassy in France, 20 December 1962, *FRUS, 1961–1963, XIII*, 1112–4.
70 See Schlesinger, *A Thousand Days*, 865–6; Pascaline Winand, *Eisenhower, Kennedy, and the United States of Europe* (London, 1993), 320–3; Neustadt, *Report to JFK*, 97–102.
71 See Paris telegram No 3 to Foreign Office, 2 January 1963, PREM 11/4147.
72 Record of a meeting at Admiralty House, 31 December 1962, PREM 11/4147.
73 Ibid.
74 Paris telegram No 640 to Foreign Office, personal from Dixon for Home, 29 December 1962, PREM 11/4147.
75 Foreign Office telegram No 9736 to Washington, for Ambassador from Prime Minister, 30 December 1962, PREM 11/4147.
76 Paris telegram No 2, and No2 Saving, to Foreign Office, 2 January 1963, PREM 11/4147. For these and subsequent exchanges, see also Pagedas, *Anglo-American Strategic Relations and the French Problem*, 260–2.
77 Paris telegram No 6 to Foreign Office, 3 January 1963, PREM 11/4147.
78 Washington telegram No 7 to Foreign Office, 2 January 1963, PREM 11/4147.
79 Paris telegram No 15 to Foreign Office, 4 January 1963, PREM 11/4147.
80 'Gen. de Gaulle's Polaris Reply Non-Committal,' *The Times*, 4 January 1963.
81 E. J. W. Barnes minute, 'General de Gaulle and the Nassau Agreement,' 7 January 1963, PUSD records, FCO.
82 See Neustadt, *Report to JFK*, 107.
83 See the discussion in Ludlow, *Dealing with Britain*, 206–11.

11 The path to the Polaris sales agreement, January–April 1963

Post-Nassau discussions: force configuration and organisational arrangements

The Anglo-American talks in the Bahamas were conducted with such haste that many crucial issues connected with the formation and operation of a British Polaris force, and its implications for the UK's deterrent posture as a whole, had simply not had time to be properly considered. One obvious area was the size and composition of a force suitable to meet UK requirements. As we have seen, this had been a subject of prolonged debate in the confines of the BNDSG, and had received some ministerial discussion in the first half of 1962 when orders for the number of Skybolt missiles and warheads had to be decided, but estimations of the damage capability of Polaris, and what size of force would be sufficient to meet a specific and agreed national criterion of deterrence, had been absent from the British delegation's deliberations at Nassau.

This can hardly be judged surprising given that Polaris was the only system on the table as a substitute for the discredited Skybolt, but it was evidently a case of putting the cart before the horse, while the question of numbers of submarines and missiles would have obvious implications for the financial implications of the agreement reached. Aside from this there was also the tricky issue of the deterrent 'gap', or the period between when the V-force equipped with Blue Steel and free-falling bombs was no longer seen as a credible deterrent threat to the Soviet Union, and when the first UK Polaris submarines could begin to arrive on station. Just after returning from Nassau, Admiral Le Fanu, the Controller of the Navy, noted that

> 'the Gap' which had loomed so largely in everybody's thinking before the meeting vanished out the windows of Bali Hai [Macmillan's villa, where most of the conference sessions were held]. The independent deterrent issue dominated all, and the question of when Polaris boats came in was never a serious issue – though of course our people had early 1969 in the back of their minds. There was some talk of Blue Steel stretch, but [Thorneycroft] is not disposed to have, as it were, a Mark II

development, but might consider ordering a few more off of the Mark I. It is difficult to convey the atmosphere on this accurately, but somehow or other the gap is being fudged or papered over, or perhaps it doesn't exist in any definitive sense anyway.[1]

After the conference it was quickly recognised that extra interim measures might have to be introduced to enhance the potential of the V-force, but the imperative was clearly to deploy Polaris as soon as possible. The latter requirement also arose since any appreciable gap would raise the question of why any capability was required at all if a period of two or three years passed when the national criteria of deterrence – so recently articulated by the Chiefs of Staff – could not be fulfilled.

In fact, during the second half of January 1963, the subject of the forthcoming deterrent gap was already eliciting probing questions in the House of Commons to Thorneycroft, and receiving coverage in press commentary. In these circumstances the rapid establishment of effective channels of liaison with the US authorities to expedite the start of a UK Polaris programme would prove to be critical. On the final morning of Nassau, Le Fanu had held a meeting with McNamara, where the US Defense Secretary, now that agreement had been reached, was described as 'all keen to force on as hard as he can go', encouraging the British to send a technical mission to Washington in early January. McNamara had also said he wanted the Polaris system to 'cost us as little as possible, so we would have more money to spend on our other defence objectives.' Le Fanu was convinced that McNamara was 'straight and keen to help', and reminded his fellow Sea Lords: 'we are now "in" Polaris in a big way. We are in the big time. The Americans are psychologically ready to go and are expecting urgent action from our side.'[2]

The most immediate problem identified by Le Fanu was to decide whether the UK should build a four boat force, each armed with sixteen Polaris missiles, or to proceed with the Admiralty's original idea of having seven boats, each with eight missiles, and (in hybrid form) capable of fulfilling a hunter-killer role as well. Le Fanu had been told by McNamara at Nassau that he did not see the eight missile Polaris boat as an attractive configuration as more would be paid for every missile on station, while 'tinkering with the 16-missile module [as used in the US Polaris force] meant trouble.' In view of the financial constraints that were likely to arise, Le Fanu felt the Admiralty would be under pressure to adopt the four boat, 16 missile format, contending, 'I am certain that the Prime Minister and the three Ministers at Nassau do not give a damn about anything except getting an "independent deterrent" as quickly and as cheaply as possible.' Thorneycroft, he thought, 'intellectually comprehends the hybrid, but emotionally rejects it', while all were aware that the new commitment to Polaris could put the Navy's plans for a new aircraft carrier and more hunter-killer submarines in jeopardy if costs were not controlled.[3]

Sir Robert Scott's assumption just after Nassau, in fact, was that there would be no special supplement to the defence budget to accommodate the extra costs of building the Polaris force. 'Whilst in the long run a Polaris force should not be an exceptionally heavy continuing burden on the Defence Budget,' the PUS advised Thorneycroft, 'it is undeniable that whilst it is being built up the Defence Budget will be under extraordinarily heavy strain. The full implications of this have yet to be worked out. But there may well be far-reaching implications on the rest of our strategy and deployment.'[4]

At the very end of 1962, Carrington was prompting Thorneycroft to follow-up the Nassau talks with quick despatch of a Navy-led mission to the United States, which could 'explain what type of forces and what timetable HMG have decided upon; negotiate how we are to get the help and guidance we need; present our provisional "shopping list" covering the major items; and work out a draft technical and financial agreement.' In the First Lord's view, two matters had also to be settled soon: firstly, whether to build a four boats, each with sixteen missiles (Carrington's preference) or persevere with the scheme for seven hybrid boats, each with eight missiles; and secondly, the extent to which the missile system's US-designed re-entry bodies and submarine-installed equipment should be produced in the UK. As far as Carrington was concerned, the only way to keep to a tight timetable with the programme was to buy American wherever possible, which meant foregoing opportunities for UK production of any system components.[5]

After discussing the matter with Carrington, Amery and his senior officials, Thorneycroft wrote to the Prime Minister on 7 January to broach the crucial issue of the type of submarine that should be built in order to carry Polaris. He now outlined three options: a force of seven submarines each carrying eight missiles, and capable of operating in a hunter-killer anti-submarine role themselves; and a force of four or five submarines each with sixteen missiles dedicated to the deterrent patrol function. The Minister of Defence thought the last configuration of five submarines would offer the best value for money. Nevertheless, the Treasury disputed this analysis and preferred, on grounds of economy, a force of seven eight-missile submarines, anticipating that the Admiralty would find it easier to absorb the requirement into their existing hunter-killer submarine-building programme.[6]

On 15 January Macmillan and Thorneycroft duly met to consider some of the immediate choices that would have to be made to give effect to the Polaris programme. Among the decisions they reached was that a sixteen missile submarine configuration, rather than a hunter-killer hybrid with eight, was to be preferred (although no specific numbers of boats was mentioned). They also agreed that in order to meet the awkward deterrent gap before Polaris entered service, a new high yield 'lay-down' bomb (where detonation was delayed after landing to allow low-level delivery) for the V-bombers would have to be produced – what later became known as WE-177B – rather than undertake the expensive development of a longer-range Mark 2 version of the Blue Steel stand-off missile.[7]

Now that he had the Prime Minister's approval, Thorneycroft felt able to present his ideas on the size and format of the Polaris force in a formal paper for the Cabinet's Defence Committee. Following some of the ideas that had been exchanged in the first half of 1962, this took as its assumption that the level of deterrent strength necessary 'for national purposes' would be 'the continuous ability at any moment to achieve 50 per cent destruction of between 15 and 20 Russian cities including Moscow and Leningrad.' To fulfil this criteria an average of between 24 and 32 Polaris missiles would have to be available on station to fire; 'in theory', it noted, this could be accomplished with a force of either seven submarines carrying eight missiles each (allowing three boats to remain on constant station), or four submarines carrying 16 missiles each (with two boats on constant station). There were many reasons, the paper argued, why a 16 missile per boat configuration was the better option. The cost in money and manpower for each missile was lower than on an eight missile boat, a four boat force would allow more missiles in total to form part of the UK's armoury, and delivery dates would be earlier. An eight missile boat had the potential to enhance credibility, as it would 'carry the eggs in more baskets', and it could be adapted to take on a hunter-killer role when not needed for deterrent purposes.

However, probably the most powerful argument in favour of the 16-missile per boat pattern – as McNamara had stressed at Nassau – was simply that this conformed with the US model, and American advice was that there could be significant re-design and engineering work if a 16-missile compartment were reconfigured, and reliability problems could be encountered. Maintaining commonality with American systems and practices was, at this early stage, coming to be seen as vital for both early introduction and the operational effectiveness of the Polaris force. Thorneycroft believed that the 'best solution, because the quickest, simplest and in terms of cost effectiveness the cheapest,' was the 16-missile boat option. The actual size of the force, Thorneycroft's paper continued, had to be derived from 'a process of compromise in the light of what we can afford.' A force of four boats, allowing two to be maintained on station at all times, gave the required level of deterrent capability, but no margin against accidents or breakdown. The Minister of Defence was therefore persuaded that five boats would be the optimum number.[8]

The Treasury's inclination, however, was to challenge the assumptions on which deterrent capability, and hence the size of the force, was being built. Referring to the Minister of Defence's contention that the requirement was for 50 per cent destruction of 15–20 cities, one Treasury official noted in pointed (and accurate) fashion his impression that

> this bracket grew up rather by accident. We used to work on the basis of 50% of 40 cities. Then, in March last year, the Prime Minister directed that the implications of a destructive capability of 50% of 15 cities were to be studied. In the course of this, the Admiralty calculated that a fleet

of 7 hybrids could do the job, and would indeed provide a 15–20 city deterrent i.e. a bit more than necessary. There seems to be no reason for arguing backwards from this that the criterion is now 15–20 cities. We might suggest reverting to the original 15 city criterion.

The key point here was that an average of 24 missiles on station would meet a 15-city standard, but this would have to increase to 32 missiles for 20 cities; reducing the criterion would add force to arguments for keeping the final number of boats lower.[9]

Another Treasury official exhibited profound scepticism about such attempts to measure damage capability as a guide to credibility. Pointing to what he called the 'immense amount of scientific and political theorising in Whitehall as to what damage level would constitute a credible deterrent' that had been done over the past few years, he thought the Chancellor of the Exchequer would share his own scepticism. Such studies had been built on the basic premise

> that there could be circumstances in which the USSR would be deterred from pursuing political aims by force or the threat of force solely by the United Kingdom's nuclear striking power. It is, in our view, quite arguable that there never could be such circumstances; and that the only relevant factor in influencing USSR decisions is the striking power of the USA. However that may be, there has been interminable argument as to whether the damage level which the UK alone could inflict should be 50% of 40 Russian cities, including Moscow and Leningrad; or 50% of 5 cities; or 50% of 15 to 20 cities, which is the current hypothesis. This type of debate is inevitably inconclusive and, as many of us would say, not relevant.

In the Treasury's opinion, the crucial point was that the front line strength of the striking force, whether V-bombers or submarines, should not fall below a certain level: it was, in other words, the number of weapons carriers available, and not their damage capability, which should be the primary consideration in what formed a credible force.[10]

The Treasury's reservations over the financial consequences for the defence budget of the Polaris programme envisaged by the MoD and Admiralty were conveyed in a subsequent minute for the Defence Committee submitted by the Chancellor of the Exchequer. The cost of introducing a four boat 16-missile Polaris force up to 1972/73 was now estimated at £314 million, and could be up to £454 million if the Admiralty's initial preference for six 16-missile boats was accepted, while the production of a new high-yield lay down weapon for the V-bomber force, in the effort to fill the deterrent gap after 1965, would add another £27 million to this potential bill. By 1967/68, when capital expenditure on the Polaris programme would reach a peak, and research and development efforts were still intensive, he estimated the additional cost on the defence budget rising to £60 million per annum. It was therefore necessary, Maudling thought, to examine the size of the programme, and the possibility of finding compensating savings elsewhere. Describing the necessary destructive potential of the Polaris force 'a matter for speculation', he believed that the level could be lowered from that presented by Thorneycroft in his own paper. A force of four 16-missile boats or six eight-missile boats would still allow twenty-four missiles to be maintained on station, and Maudling suggested 'this should be quite enough.' Either scheme, the Chancellor suggested, would cost about £75 million less than the Minister of Defence's recommendation for five 16-missile boats.[11]

Macmillan's own briefing from the Cabinet Secretary argued that the most compelling argument for a force of 16-missile boats was that it could be introduced into service earlier, so reducing to a minimum the deterrent gap that would open up after the mid-1960s when the credibility of the V-bombers would be thrown into doubt.[12] At the meeting of the Cabinet's Defence Committee held on 23 January, Thorneycroft emphasised the point that with a larger sixteen-missile boat, not only would American practice be followed, but the cost for each missile on station would be less than the alternative. As a smaller number of boats would offer more missiles on station, a full deterrent capability could also be achieved at an earlier date than with the eight-missile variant, reducing the period of the deterrent gap. While the Committee agreed that 16-missile submarines should be constructed for the UK Polaris force, Thorneycroft had to be content with an initial order for only four boats, which would still, as he acknowledged, be 'enough to maintain an adequate deterrent capability at all times'. A decision over whether to construct a fifth boat could be safely deterred to a later meeting when its advantages would have to be set against the extra cost involved. The Defence Committee also endorsed plans to develop a new high-yield laydown bomb for low-level delivery by the front-line V-force of Vulcans and Victors.[13]

By the time of the Defence Committee's meeting, practical steps to give concrete substance to the Nassau framework were already being taken. On 8 January 1963, a team led by Sir Solly Zuckerman began a preliminary visit to the United States to explore US plans for Polaris, American experience with operating the system and submarines, production issues, what assistance would be available to the prospective UK Polaris programme, and how this might be arranged. Zuckerman's party included Vice Admiral Sir Varyl Begg, the Vice-Chief of Naval Staff, James Mackay, the Deputy Secretary of the Admiralty, and Rear Admiral Hugh S. Mackenzie; they were accompanied by Sir Robert Cockburn and F. J. Doggett from the Ministry of Aviation. The mission was instructed to 'have regard as a prime consideration' the need to 'ensure the independent control and operation of the British Polaris fleet.'[14]

The presence of both senior Naval officers and officials from the MoA on the Zuckerman mission was emblematic of some of the inter-bureaucratic tensions which were already becoming apparent regarding the division of responsibilities for delivering the Polaris programme. Carrington's understandable tendency was to give primacy to Navy-to-Navy contacts in establishing the basis of Anglo-American technical cooperation over construction, operation and maintenance of a nuclear submarine force. But with its experience and expertise in missiles, delivery systems, and warhead work, where it placed contracts with both RAE and AWRE, the Ministry of Aviation was, however, reluctant to relinquish what it saw as its essential role in overseeing significant parts of the Polaris project. Admiral Le Fanu, for one, could see difficulties developing as a result. Immediately after Nassau he recorded his own candid thoughts that

> ... there may be pressures to get the management of this deal into hands other than Navy/Navy ... So I think we have got to move in pretty fast on the line that the Navy are the prime contractors. We must carry the Ministry of Defence with us. The Atomic Energy Authority will have to be associated (though their interest is indirect and their position will require careful handling). Finally the Ministry of Aviation will have to be kept firmly in their place ... the United States Navy would neither understand nor relish working with the Ministry of Aviation [not least as the MoA was seen as having strong ties with the Royal Air Force, offering a possible conduit to the US Navy's inter-service rivals in the US Air Force].[15]

The Admiralty began the process of forming its own Polaris organisation with the appointment, on 31 December 1962, of the then Flag Officer Submarines, Rear Admiral Mackenzie, as Chief Polaris Executive (CPE). Mackenzie would answer to Le Fanu, as the Controller of the Navy, for delivery of the programme, but was granted considerable freedom in assembling the necessary personnel and infrastructure to meet his demanding schedule. Building on recommendations which had first been made in 1960, Mackenzie set about creating a direct counterpart to the US Navy's Special Projects Office. With his formidable personality and energy, Mackenzie would eventually assemble a CPE staff about 500 strong, divided between London and a special new office at Foxhill near Bath, where the headquarters of the Navy's ship design, weapons and logistics groups were located.[16]

Mackenzie was determined to make his CPE organisation the principal liaison channel with the Americans on all matters of Polaris procurement. To the Admiralty this made perfect sense: there was already a substantial history of cooperation between the US and Royal Navies over the possibilities and prospects of a UK Polaris programme, cemented by the establishment in October 1958 of the post of Royal Navy Liaison Officer in the US Navy's Special Projects Office (SPO), while an Admiralty technical mission under Sidney Palmer had assembled invaluable information on the design of US Polaris submarines from American officials in early 1961.[17] Furthermore, Mackenzie had a long personal friendship with Rear Admiral I. J. Galantin, the head of SPO, helping to ensure that the maximum amount of cooperation was achieved, and that the Royal Navy had absolute confidence in the weapons system it would have to operate.[18] Soon after Nassau, Carrington had indicated that he wanted to see the Navy-to-Navy relationship continue and prosper, seeing it as an essential ingredient to the ultimate success of the UK Polaris programme.[19]

A complex and sometimes confusing division of responsibilities between the two principal ministries engaged with the acquisition of Polaris soon, however, emerged. The Minister of Aviation, Julian Amery, was firm during January 1963 in rejecting the Navy's bid to administer the entire programme, and insisted that the MoA should continue to exercise its normal research and development (R & D), and procurement responsibilities in the nuclear field, while meeting the broad requirements of the Admiralty. A senior officer from the Admiralty would, it was therefore agreed, be drafted into the MoA to act as a Polaris Project Officer, with another to be based in Washington who could act as the 'uniformed' MoA liaison to the US authorities.[20] Rear Admiral Frederick Dossor took up his duties within the MoA that same month, his appointment being officially announced at the same time as that of Mackenzie as CPE.[21] Dossor was regarded as the Ministry of Aviation's direct complement to Mackenzie, was represented on CPE's Management Board, and also chaired his own Polaris Management Board at the MoA, which was intended to bring together research establishment representatives (including AWRE and RAE), officials from the Directorate of Atomic Warheads Development in the MoA, and Naval officers from the new CPE organisation. However, when major matters of policy had to be decided between the MoA and the Admiralty, they were put through a higher-level Polaris Interdepartmental Policy Steering Committee (PIPSC). This was a body formed in February 1963, and included representation from the Admiralty (the CPE and Assistant Chief of Naval Staff), Ministry of Defence, Ministry of Aviation, Treasury, Foreign Office, and Atomic Energy Authority. Chaired first by James Mackay, and then later in the year by Sir Clifford Jarrett, Permanent Secretary at the Admiralty, it was charged with keeping under review the programme to provide Polaris missiles to the Navy, to ensure that any interdepartmental problems or issues were quickly resolved, and arrange for the submission to ministers of progress reports.[22]

Although Admiral Mackenzie's CPE organisation had won the right to handle the procurement of the missiles and supporting services from the United States during inter-departmental sparring that took place in January, responsibility for all research, development, and production aspects of the missile's re-entry system (RES) was allocated to the MoA. Under the MoA's ultimate jurisdiction also came design, development, manufacture and procurement of the UK warhead for Polaris. The Admiralty, however, as well as overseeing the submarine parts of the programme, would necessarily take a close interest in the entire Polaris weapons system that they would have to operate and maintain in service, including (sometimes controversially) the 'front end' aspects of the missile which remained within the MoA's formal purview. Since the Navy, through the CPE, was to act as the principal liaison channel with the American authorities on all matters connected with Polaris procurement, it would also have to perform the role of 'agent' for the MoA when it required US equipment or support related to the interface between the missile and its re-entry system.[23]

But to complicate matters even further, information regarding the nuclear warhead side of the Polaris programme was passed under the terms and separate channels of the 1958 MDA, where the principal agents were the weapons laboratories in the United States and AWRE. There was room here for much friction and tension, as warhead matters were inextricably linked with the design and performance of the missile's re-entry system, which in turn could not be artificially divorced from the remainder of the missile system, the latter regarded by the Navy as its recognised realm. Whether questions connected with the RES should be processed through the machinery of the 1958 Agreement (and hence within MoA's jurisdiction), or through Navy-to-Navy channels, between CPE and the US SPO, was not always clear. These intricate issues of jurisdiction, responsibility, and liaison with the US authorities were to reverberate through subsequent years (indeed decades) but they had their origins in decisions made at the very outset of the UK Polaris programme.

The Zuckerman mission and the Polaris surcharge debate

By the middle of January 1963, Zuckerman's initial mission to the United States had returned to the UK having made good progress with fulfilling its fact-finding remit. As well as reporting American advice that a 16-missile submarine was much to be preferred over any other configuration, Zuckerman's report also came down firmly in favour of acquiring the A3 version of the Polaris missile system. The existing Polaris A2 carried a single half-megaton Mark 47 warhead, and had a maximum range of about 1,500 nautical miles, but was nearing the end of its production run and was due to be superseded by the A3, to which the US Navy was fully committed. The newer missile was expected to have a range of up to 2,500 nautical miles, and would carry a payload of three smaller Mark 58 warheads; the latter improvement was expected to give it 'the valuable ability to penetrate the improved enemy anti-missile defences which are likely to come into being in about 1970.' Yet there were risks to outright commitment to an A3 purchase: though due to enter service in August 1964, the missile system was still effectively under development, and in the middle of a difficult trials programme where its new design of rocket motors, and the propellants they used to give it a longer range, were causing teething problems.[24]

One of the considerations influencing the attitudes of Zuckerman's team to the choice of A2 or A3 was the selection of a UK warhead design for the

Polaris system. Having completed work on the UK warhead for Skybolt (the primary for which was successfully tested underground, in a shot dubbed 'Tendrac', on 7 December 1962 at the Nevada test site), and notwithstanding the other work in the pipeline on a tactical warhead to replace the first generation Red Beard bombs, AWRE was, as one MoA official noted, 'at the beginning of a cautious and calculated rundown.' With the arrival of the Nassau Agreement, however, this picture had been dramatically changed, that same official remarking that the rundown 'may have to be reversed rightaway.'[25]

Study within the MoA of possible warhead/re-entry vehicle combinations for Polaris began in early January, though this was still very speculative work considering the limited US information available. The capability of any UK system to overcome Soviet ABM defences which could be deployed by the 1970s was an important factor which entered into these preliminary discussions, where it was acknowledged that space and payload constraints might limit the capacity of whatever RES was chosen to carry penetration aids.[26]

By mid-January, the information brought back by the Zuckerman mission allowed a much clearer understanding of the choices and their implications. The most straightforward option would be to fit the UK's Skybolt warhead, but this would require using the US Mark 1 single-warhead RES which had been developed for use in the A1 and A2 variants of Polaris. The Mark 1 RES, however, was considered to have no real penetration capability against an ABM defence. Furthermore, the extra range offered by the new A3 missile was also regarded as a major attraction. The use of the Skybolt warhead in the A3 missile, however, would require development of a new RES, involving considerable UK re-design and new flight testing (estimated at £30–40 million by the US Navy, with 15 test firings). Space constraints within the front end of the A3, moreover, meant that with this configuration, the amount of penetration capability that could be added to the RES would be 'severely limited' and therefore, as the Admiralty's report on the mission noted, 'the effectiveness of these systems which we can only deploy in the late 60s or early 70s and thus much later than the equivalent US system, needs careful study in the light of likely deployments of USSR anti-ballistic missile defence.'

An alternative route would be to adopt the new US Mark 2 Mod 0 RES which the Americans proposed to use in the triple warhead A3, and to employ a completely new design of UK warhead (although one based on US information). The Americans estimated this would involve much less flight testing (perhaps only five tests of the new RES, at a cost of about £10 million), leaving the UK to develop and test its own warhead. It was also known that the Americans were already working on ideas to improve the penetration capability of the Mark 2 RES, and this might be the model in production by the time the British were ready to make their purchase. Despite the extra expense and complications that might be involved the A3 was expected to be a more viable weapons system in the mid-1970s than the

A2 and the mission's view was that this was the variant that should be adopted.[27]

There was certainly also political impetus behind this technical preference: even before Zuckerman's final report was received, during the meeting between Macmillan and Thorneycroft in mid-January where they decided that a 16-missile submarine was the best option, they also concluded that the 'right course' would be to opt for the A3 version of Polaris (though adding the proviso that A2 might have to be fitted in the first submarine depending on the timetable for A3 development).[28]

Warhead matters came up for discussion when the BNDSG was reconvened by Sir Robert Scott for one final swansong meeting on 21 January in order to take stock of the position after the Zuckerman visit, and to consider what decisions would be needed over the coming months. It was noted by the senior officials present that

> at first sight it would appear possible for us to use a Skybolt warhead on the A3 missile, possibly with a Minuteman re-entry vehicle, and this solution would use less fissile material; it would also rule out any question of a need to carry out a further nuclear test. On the other hand, the proposed US A3 warhead would have greater penetration against sophisticated defences and would thus probably remain credible for longer.

However, a more definite view, including, the BNDSG minutes recorded, 'the question of decoys,' would depend on the accumulation of further information by AWRE, a process which was then just getting underway. It was explained that, over the Nassau Agreement, the Minister of Defence intended that 'once the terms of assignment to NATO had been worked out, all British deterrent forces, including those of the RAF, would be assigned to NATO, while retaining at the same time a national deterrent role for which there would be separate targeting arrangements.'[29]

Full details of the US Mark 47 warhead, used in Polaris A1 and A2, were already known to the UK authorities from exchanges with the Americans under the 1958 MDA, but the new Mark 58 design was still an unknown quantity. However, once a presidential determination to release the latest Polaris warhead information to the UK had been issued, a small team from AWRE, led by the Chief of Warhead Development, John Challens, carried out a low-key visit to the Lawrence Livermore Research Laboratories in the United States from 22–24 January 1963. Here they were shown designs for the Mark 58 (which contained some hardening and shielding against neutron attack), and its new Mark 2 Mod 0 REB. It would be possible, Challens believed, for AWRE to produce a 'Chinese copy' of the Mark 58, with some investment in new engineering equipment, but the design would still need to be passed by the relevant UK safety authorities. One of the pieces of information they picked up was that the Americans were working on a new re-entry system for the A3 which incorporated penetration aids, but there were no more details available.[30]

Parenthetically, the AWRE visit was the cause of some umbrage at the Ministry of Aviation, as despite what was called by one senior official their 'very direct interest in the matter', they had received no notification that the visit was to take place (and this despite the fact that MoA officials had met senior AWRE staff only a few days before to discuss the MoA's view that a technical mission to look at Polaris warhead options was required).[31] Within the MoD, it was recognised that a further technical visit from a combined Admiralty/MoA/AWRE team would be needed before firm recommendations could be made on warhead/REB/missile combinations, and – in a foretaste of dilemmas to come – that 'if we did not go for an exact copy of the American warhead, we might run into certain problems arising from the fact that our assessment of accident risks was sometimes more stringent than that of the Americans. The whole question of the price to be paid for maintaining different standards might need to be reviewed.'[32] The Nuclear Requirements for Defence Committee – the interdepartmental official group established to oversee the overall warhead and testing programme in 1960 – discussed the results of these preliminary assessments in early February, reaching the conclusion that no firm recommendations could be made until more technical information was received from the United States, and a choice made between the different variants of Polaris missile.[33]

Much to the encouragement of the Zuckerman mission, the Americans had also proved very forthcoming with their offers of full technical training and support for the UK Polaris programme. It was suggested by the Americans that all Polaris material and training should be supplied on a Navy-to-Navy basis, with UK orders for equipment and supplies meshing into the US programme, and the US Navy's SPO acting as the UK's 'technical, financial, and management agent'. To advance this scheme, it was proposed that a number of Royal Navy personnel, along with Ministry of Aviation officials, be appointed to work inside SPO in Washington, and that equivalent US appointments should be made in London. Overseeing the whole programme of liaison would be a joint steering group, drawn from both navies, and which could act as the 'supreme technical adviser for the integration of the complete UK ballistic missile system.'[34] The Minister of Aviation's office was informed by Doggett, the senior MoA official in the party, that the US Navy had been 'undoubtedly anxious to co-operate and to make the venture a success. They would like to see the British boats (and missiles) integrated as closely as possible with theirs. They offered for example full support in spares provisioning and stockholding and maintenance and repair facilities. Left to themselves the RN would welcome this. But they recognise that the need for independence will necessitate a measure of separate facilities.'[35]

The fly in the ointment for this otherwise harmonious picture of emerging Anglo-American collaboration was that the team were informed that the British would be expected to pay, 'on a pro rata basis to be negotiated,' a contribution to the research and development costs of the A3 missile (backdated to 1 January 1963), including new equipment which the British might be interested to acquire, should this be the system selected for procurement. As was noted above, the A3 was still in the process of development, with production scheduled to begin in 1964, but the Americans were expected to spend perhaps another $700 million on the missile up to 1968. A contribution to this expensive programme could involve considerable sums of expenditure that had simply not been anticipated in British official circles. Indeed, in his first remarks to the press after returning from Nassau, and in an attempt to sell the deal to sceptical domestic opinion, Macmillan had emphasised that Britain would pay nothing for Polaris development (of which about $800 million had already been spent by the US up to that point) for a weapon that would last 'for a generation.'[36]

As the Americans had not previously indicated that an additional charge would be connected to the purchase of Polaris, there was a degree of shock and consternation felt in London at what was now being mooted. Though in his report on the Zuckerman mission Doggett thought it was 'difficult to deny the reasonableness of seeking from us a contribution to the cost of r. and d.,' at the MoD Thorneycroft was alarmed by the implications.[37] He informed McNamara that at Nassau, as he understood it,

> we were at pains to agree that the Polaris development should be made available to the United Kingdom *on a continuing basis*. My clear understanding was that we were entitled to make use of future R. and D. on the same basis as past work. We have had a fairly rough ride on the Nassau agreement since my return [from the Bahamas], and I have laid some stress on this aspect of the agreement in public. Clearly, we would pay for anything which we might conceivably wish to ask you to do for a United Kingdom requirement only. Clearly, too, we will buy the finished missile with its necessary auxiliary equipment. I am sure however that you will understand that we could not now say that we had decided to make a subscription to United States research and development costs which they would, in any event, have undertaken. We should be open to the criticism, either that we had concealed this vital factor from the public in the published [Nassau] agreement and in our statements on return, or that we had been so incompetent as not to know what it was that we were agreeing to.[38]

Despite this plea, McNamara remained unmoved. He replied to the Minister of Defence with the (accurate) observation that no discussions about such detailed aspects of the agreement had been possible at Nassau, and he was surprised at the attitude the British were now adopting. Congress would not stand for an agreement where the entire costs of the programme were borne by the US alone, and he 'could not believe that we thought it right that we should have no responsibility and no commitment to share on an extremely modest scale in the further development of this vital weapons system.' It was most important, he felt, 'that America's Allies should understand the cost of participating in the nuclear weapons field.' If the British wanted to take advantage of any improvements to the Polaris A3, McNamara reiterated to the British Ambassador, they would have to make a contribution to the R & D programme (the A2, on the other hand, could be purchased at production price). Discussing the relative merits of the A2 and A3 missiles, McNamara had, in addition, noted that 'there was always the danger that with the Soviet development of an anti-missile capability the A2 might become obsolete and incapable of penetrating the Russian defences. If therefore we committed ourselves to it we might find it hard to explain in a few years time why we had embarked upon the expenditure of so much money for a weapon which the Americans were retiring from service.'[39]

Macmillan let Ormsby Gore know of his 'great shock' at the terms which were now being proposed by the Department of Defense, but formulating a response to the American insistence on an R & D contribution presented several dilemmas.[40] The situation was discussed at a meeting between Thorneycroft, Amery, and Carrington on 16 January. It had become apparent, the Minister of Defence explained, that the Americans 'expected the United Kingdom to pay a financial price for the availability of Polaris missiles on a continuing basis in addition to the political price which had been extracted at Nassau in the form of commitment to NATO.' This development was called 'entirely unexpected'; the alternative to outright opposition to the proposal was to seek every advantage from any contribution that was finally made, an option which held some attractions for Thorneycroft who speculated this might aid a future indigenous UK missile programme.[41]

Zuckerman's mission had been followed immediately after by a reciprocal visit to London of an American delegation, led by Paul H. Nitze, the Assistant Secretary for International Security Affairs at the Pentagon, and including Walt W. Rostow, the head of the State Department's Policy Planning Council, and Admiral Galantin, the head of SPO. Chairing the opening meeting of the talks, Zuckerman noted that the issue of a UK R & D contribution would have to be settled in more detailed negotiation, but the British would require full information concerning development projects involving Polaris so that they could decide the extent of their participation. In general terms, Zuckerman stressed the point that 'Anglo/American co-operation in the establishment of a British Polaris Submarine Fleet would provide the largest field of technical co-operation between the two countries since the war.' This development was naturally welcomed, and he felt that in 'two fields in particular which touched upon the vulnerability of the weapons system – anti-submarine detection and anti-ballistic missile systems, it was necessary for the scientists of both sides to work together as closely as possible.' At this early stage, and as they had previously told the Zuckerman team in Washington, the Americans were envisaging organisational arrangements involving the appointment of two project officers from each country to oversee the UK Polaris programme, and 'a Joint Steering Group to meet at regular intervals and give guidance to contractors, etc.'[42]

One of the prime aims of the reciprocal American visit was to start to explore how to put some flesh on the bare bones of the Nassau communiqué. Of immediate contention was the desire of the Americans for a comprehensive published agreement which would spell out both sides' obligations regarding the assignment of nuclear forces to NATO, their joint commitment to creating a multilateral force, and an annex which would detail the terms under which Polaris missiles would be provided to the UK.[43] The annex, the Americans proposed, might include such matters as the missile components to be provided, production and delivery schedules, and payment terms. Significantly, they also suggested that it include a paragraph to the effect that the UK Government would 'benefit as a result of any improvements that might be made in the weapon, and promising supplies on equivalent terms to their own.' The difficulty of having such a comprehensive agreement from the British point of view was that it linked so clearly the supply of Polaris with proposals for the MLF, potentially making progress with the first dependent on steps toward creation of the second (a scheme about which, as we shall see, British officials were less than keen). Nevertheless, some comfort could be drawn from American indications that the initialling of a comprehensive US-UK Polaris sales agreement would not have to wait for the conclusion of multilateral agreements with other NATO members regarding the MLF.[44]

In his own restricted meetings with Nitze, Thorneycroft had tried to strike a more conciliatory note over the R & D issue by saying that at Nassau the British delegation had simply assumed the payment arrangements for Polaris would be the same as for Skybolt, and that there would be no extra contribution, 'except in respect of any developments that might be required for United Kingdom purposes only.' Thorneycroft opined that he was not arguing that the American case was unreasonable, but that the request had come as a shock, and would cause great political embarrassment at home.[45] In the advice he offered the Prime Minister after the meetings with the Americans, Thorneycroft thought that the case for a British R & D contribution would have to be conceded in principle, as there was no prospect of avoiding a payment of some kind, and he did not want progress on the Polaris programme to be held up. Nevertheless, there was still room to manoeuvre when it came to the amount and nature of the contribution, and the Minister of Defence considered that 'we must insist on having the same rights as the American Government in the results of the R & D work to which we contribute.'[46] The feeling in the Treasury was that 'we were extremely lucky to have got away with the Skybolt no-payment formula; the present administration appears to be much hotter on financial points of this kind and there is really no case "on merits" we can deploy against a UK contribution of some kind.'[47]

With a full-scale parliamentary debate on the Nassau Agreement scheduled to take place at the end of January, the political imperative of the Government was to avoid the additional criticism that would flow from any revelation that the financial costs of a Polaris purchase would be much heavier than had been supposed (and the unfavourable comparisons with Skybolt which might also be made). A worried Chief Secretary to the Treasury minuted the Chancellor of the Exchequer, 'The more I think of it the more politically explosive is ... the proposal that we should pay for a share in the R. & D. cost of Polaris.' There was, he thought, 'deep suspicion in the country, and above all in our own Party, of American motives in dropping Skybolt,' and he predicted 'one hell of a row' especially as there had been no mention of the provision at Nassau or in the communiqué issued after the Conference. There were obvious financial objections in agreeing to a potentially open-ended commitment, but the political issues were even more serious: 'All our critics would say that this was yet further evidence of our spineless weakness towards the Americans.'[48]

To compound the Government's problems, the negotiations for EEC entry were just then going through their painful denouement, with de Gaulle having wielded his veto on 14 January; a further round of negotiations in Brussels between the six member states and Britain was due to open on 28 January, but the French had moved that the talks should be brought to an end. The fact that de Gaulle had cited Nassau as one of the principal reasons why he did not consider that Britain – as he pictured it, tied to nuclear dependence on the United States through its purchase of Polaris – was an appropriate state to be a member of the Community, had given the arrangements surrounding the deal an additional degree of domestic political controversy.[49]

A direct appeal from the Prime Minister to President Kennedy was considered the best method to bring about some speedy resolution to the R & D dispute, and before the Government's critics found another issue on which to attack the Government's performance at Nassau. As in the Nassau negotiations themselves, Macmillan chose to impress on Kennedy the domestic political crisis that, he claimed, could be provoked if the Nassau arrangements were now to breakdown over their detailed implementation just at the moment when his Government's European initiative was in the process of being frustrated.

Signalling to Ormsby Gore in Washington on 26 January, Macmillan wanted the President warned that he did

> not see how our Government here could survive the collapse of both policies simultaneously. At a moment when a certain disillusionment with Europe may at least do good to Anglo-American relationships, it would be particularly unfortunate if the British people felt that they were not only being rebuffed by the Europeans but being treated harshly by the United States. The result could be a mood of sullen isolation here which could do no good to any of us.

There was no question, Macmillan asserted, of Britain being willing to make an open-ended contribution by assuming a percentage share of the future

R & D costs of Polaris. Instead, the Prime Minister proposed as a compromise a fixed additional five per cent to the production cost of each missile. This was a formula he thought he could defend in Parliament, and he would say this was 'the price for getting the more advanced missile rather than the one at present developed [i.e. A3 rather than A2].' Macmillan continued:

> Of course, I realise that we cannot have things both ways and that paying a tax of this kind gives us no inherent right to any participation in the R & D programme. However, I will hope that in return we would be given the maximum of information in order to improve our knowledge and ability to handle the weapon and keep it in good repair, as well as share in such rights as accrued to the United States Administration.

For good measure, Macmillan complained to Ormsby Gore in Washington that he still thought this outcome was not in line with what had been agreed at Nassau, and that he was 'very upset by the whole affair.' The same percentage formula, he then suggested, could be applied to any later marks of Polaris missile developed after the A3, as this was how he interpreted the phrase 'on a continuing basis' drawn from paragraph eight of the Nassau Agreement. He also maintained that access to later variants of the missile was fair and reasonable because at Nassau he had come around to agreeing with the American view that Polaris was 'a different kind of animal [to Skybolt] because it would last so long and take us into a different category of weapon extending far beyond the bomber force which is now in our hands.' As a result he had been ready to pay the political price demanded of assignment of the whole force to NATO 'for all ordinary purposes except conditions of supreme national importance.'

He asked the Ambassador to gain assurances from Kennedy that the deal Macmillan had outlined would be the basis on which a detailed financial agreement covering the Polaris sale was made. Otherwise, the Prime Minister warned, he would have to tell the House of Commons that the Nassau arrangements were still provisional pending the successful outcome to financial negotiations. This kind of approach in the forthcoming parliamentary debate could, Macmillan wanted the President warned,

> result in the defeat of the Government with all the consequences which would follow; and in any case will show a most serious disarray of all our forces. Europe is broken in half and if this is to be succeeded by an Anglo-American quarrel – reproaching each other for an agreement at Nassau which is either misleading or ill-thought out – we shall be in a rare fix.[50]

As if to underline the dangers that the rift could present to the Government's position, the story about R & D costs broke in the press at precisely the same time, prompting fresh concerns from the Chancellor.[51]

In one of his characteristically effective interventions as Ambassador, Ormsby Gore saw Kennedy the same day he received Macmillan's message in order to explain the British position. The President appreciated the domestic political point immediately, and after joking that Macmillan's proposal of a five per cent surcharge 'was not the most generous offer he had ever heard of,' he made clear he did not want an 'Anglo-American row' over the issue. In the Ambassador's presence he telephoned McNamara and presented the British formula as the most acceptable way out of the problem of the R & D contribution to the Polaris programme.[52] With the matter settled, both Governments worked to agree a form of words that would convey the essence of the deal, while protecting the President from his own domestic critics who might argue that he was being too generous (thus, for example, the British case was to be presented as a unique one, and not seen as a precedent for any other arms supply agreement Washington might choose to make). In his diary, Macmillan recorded his thoughts that McNamara had been 'very grasping' in the R & D negotiations, and while the five per cent formula was 'not a bad bargain,' the whole episode had caused him several sleepless nights.'[53]

A disgruntled McNamara had to accept the presidential ruling, and he was even more 'put out' (as Ormsby Gore informed the Prime Minister) because he had mistakenly assumed from Kennedy's call that the formula involved calculating five per cent of the R & D costs of the Polaris A3 programme, and then adding this to the production cost of the missiles for the sake of public presentation. The US Defense Secretary did, nevertheless, embellish the deal by arguing that the five per cent surcharge should be applied to the production price of not just the missiles themselves, but the fire control, navigation equipment, and other smaller items, as these formed essential parts of what could be deemed the A3 system as a whole. As it was calculated that this added only about £2 million to the final bill, Ormsby Gore recommended acceptance of McNamara's package, 'in view of the staggeringly good bargain we are getting'. The Ambassador told McNamara – in terms that would later hold some significance – that because of the nature of the agreement 'we would claim no inherent right to any participation in the R & D programme,' and 'in view of the immeasurably small contribution we would be making to the cost, we could not claim any right of ownership in the results of the research.'[54]

What might have occurred if the Nassau arrangements for the supply of a replacement for Skybolt had broken down is far from clear. A UK-devised programme to provide a ballistic missile system by the early 1970s was an option explored in very rudimentary fashion within the Ministry of Aviation after Macmillan had made his original queries just after Nassau about the possibility of a fall-back position. By the middle of January 1963, Amery had come forward with a submission that explained it would be possible for the UK to produce an air-launched ballistic missile of a simpler design than Skybolt in eight or nine years, at a cost of about £175 million, or a submarine-launched ballistic missile similar to Polaris A2 (with a range of

1,550 nautical miles and a 450 kiloton warhead), but including penetration aids, in ten years, and at a cost 'of not less than £200 million.' The figures for the latter option were, it was admitted, highly uncertain, and excluded the submarines which would have to carry the weapon system itself.

> From the point of view of this Ministry,' Amery had stated, 'I would naturally have preferred that we should have decided to develop our own weapon rather than buy American. This would have lessened the complaints of our guided weapons industry faced as it is with the prospect of redundancy. It would also have assured us of control of the production of our deterrent system and so fully guaranteed its independence. Most important of all it would have given us the technological base from which to develop the new weapons systems which will no doubt be needed as and when ... Polaris becomes obsolete.

Though he accepted that progress was now being made with the Americans with the arrangements to acquire Polaris, Amery still thought the possibility of a British project should not be discounted as an insurance against the Prime Minister's earlier fears that negotiations for its purchase might drive the UK 'into a corner.'[55]

Replying on 28 January, and so just after the R & D issue was settled with the Kennedy administration, Thorneycroft acknowledged the work that had gone into the studies, and that they would 'provide a useful starting point for more detailed study should we have to face a go-it-alone situation.' But a British project could not then be contemplated, nor were there immediate grounds for any more detailed study of the problems involved.[56]

The subject of the independence of Britain's future deterrent force formed the central issue of contention in the two-day Commons debate on the Nassau Agreement which began on 30 January. The Prime Minister started proceedings with an account of the background to British nuclear policy leading up to Nassau and offered a long and detailed defence of what had been agreed with President Kennedy, including the five per cent surcharge arrangement which he described as 'generous', and dismissal of any notion that the 'deterrent gap' caused by Skybolt cancellation was of any great significance. Regarding the supreme national interests clause, Macmillan said that such was the terribly destructive nature of nuclear weapons no Government would use them

> lightly to counter a bluff, or to resist a bully. They would only be morally justified in using this immense power to counter a threat in a situation which was of supreme importance to the nation.

Mentioning that both he and Kennedy had recognised the crucial significance of the phrase, he continued that he had therefore offered the further assurance that it would not be invoked without consultation:

> I agreed to bring up to date the moral undertaking which we and the United States already have, that is not to use nuclear weapons anywhere in the world without prior consultation with each other, if circumstances permit ... I therefore gave the President – this is important as to what the American view of the case is – an assurance that should the British Government wish to operate this independent clause I felt sure I and my successors would give the same notice of intention ... the fact that the United States Administration wanted me to give this assurance shows how fully they accept the reality of our independent rights.[57]

To Macmillan, it is clear, the unveiling of his private assurances to Kennedy at Nassau in front of his parliamentary critics added strength to his argument that the right of independent use had genuine substance (as no such assurance would have been necessary if the Americans had not taken the clause seriously), but he seems to have overlooked the fact that this extra provision also represented to some a qualification or caveat that had to be applied to the original terms of the agreement. Winding up his speech, Macmillan also took the opportunity to announce the Government's intention of assigning to NATO the whole of the existing V-bomber force, and later the Polaris submarines when they became available (confirming this was expected to be in 1968), subject to the right to use the UK's nuclear forces independently if supreme national interests were deemed at stake.[58]

The immediate response to Macmillan's speech was delivered by George Brown, who had assumed the acting leadership of the Labour Party following the sudden death of Hugh Gaitskell on 18 January. Brown lambasted the Government's past 'wishful thinking' over Skybolt, and criticised the deal that had been reached over Polaris:

> How can something for which one totally relies on someone else to provide be described as independent, especially when it is never final? No modern rocket ever can be. They go on developing. They go on getting more and more sophisticated and one must stay with the improvements all the time or, sooner or later, be landed with an outdated and useless piece of ironmongery.

The possession of an independent deterrent had not given the Government increased 'influence or strength in the world', but providing adequate conventional defence forces, Brown contended, would.[59]

On the second day of the debate, another leading Labour front-bench spokesman, Patrick Gordon-Walker, as well as criticising the costs involved, commented on the underlying premise of the 'supreme national interests' clause of the Nassau Agreement:

> It is based on distrust of the United States. Yet, to get the weapons and to maintain them and carry out the strategy, we have to have absolute

confidence in the United States. It is barmy, topsy-turvy logic. The truth is that the safety of the United Kingdom from nuclear attack depends upon the Western deterrent, which is effectively 98 per cent in United States hands. This was shown at Suez. Here, if ever, there was a case we had, as the Government thought, a national interest to protect where we were not being backed by the United States and where there was a threat of a nuclear attack by Russia. The whole circumstances occurred. What happened? The United States immediately responded that if we were attacked it would regard that as an attack upon itself.[60]

Some of the strongest rhetorical blows against the Government were landed, however, by Harold Wilson, now filling the role of shadow Foreign Secretary, and ready to further demonstrate his leadership credentials now that Gaitskell (who had always distrusted Wilson) was removed from the scene.

With a political base on the Party's left of centre – Brown, his great rival, coming from the right – Wilson had already emerged as a national figure with formidable intellectual and political skills. An economist by academic training, he had worked in the civil service during the Second World War, and never lost a bureaucrat's love of the techniques of government. After securing election as an MP in the Labour landslide of 1945, Wilson had cut his ministerial teeth as a junior member of Attlee's Government, only to resign in 1951 over the budget cuts to social provision necessitated by the rearmament programme. His driving ambition soon saw him rising through the ranks of the Opposition front bench in the latter 1950s, where he earned a reputation for masterful parliamentary debating and an intimidating eye for detail. He had, as we saw earlier, already spoken out in scornful terms about the Government's attempts to maintain an 'independent' nuclear deterrent – most notably in the Blue Streak cancellation debate in 1960 – and he now saw every opportunity to drive home the message that the Nassau deal was being sold on a false prospectus.

Attacking the 'vain nuclear posturings' of the Government which undercut the necessary contribution that Britain should make to the West's defence, Wilson argued in the Commons that Britain's claim to being an independent nuclear power had ended when Blue Streak was scrapped. 'From that moment,' he said, 'nuclear status for this country became a costly pretence. How can one pretend to have an independent deterrent when one is depending on another nation – a reluctant one at that – to supply one with the means of delivery?' Did the argument for 'pretending' to be an independent nuclear power, Wilson asked, involve the

> right to use it in some private war of our own, independent of the Western alliance, against, perhaps, a non-nuclear nation – another Suez? Have not hon. Members opposite learnt? Have they in mind a war without allies, without the Commonwealth, condemned, as it would be, by world opinion? For my part, I acquit hon. Members opposite of that intention.

Another view might see a UK deterrent as 'an essential ingredient for Western defence', but a Polaris fleet ('perhaps flotilla would be a better word') would make up only a very small proportion of the nuclear forces of the West, and there was 'not a single one of our allies, or anyone else ... who believes that argument, or takes it seriously.' As for the notion British membership of the 'nuclear club' meant that she would be consulted and 'be there when the big decisions are taken', Wilson pointed to the recent Cuban missile crisis as evidence to how illusory was such a belief.

A final argument might be that 'in this world of mutual deterrence we cannot trust our allies; that we must have the means unilaterally of triggering off a nuclear war that will ultimately force the hand of the Americans'. But if this were the argument for an 'independent' UK nuclear force, Wilson would reject it as 'fundamentally immoral – and, indeed, in this tightly-packed, vulnerable island, a prescription for suicide.' Instead, Wilson thought that the principal explanation for attachment to nuclear status was

> simpler – pathetic, perhaps, but not immoral. It is nostalgia. It is striving to relive our imperial greatness. Within the lifetime of older hon. Members we were once top nation, and it is not easy, even at heavy cost in terms of national security, to accept the facts of history, geography and economics. I think that the Prime Minister understands this. Nassau was not a willing agreement between partners; it was a reluctant sop thrown by the Americans to a Prime Minister who knew in his heart that what he was asking had no defence relevance, but who knew that he dare not return and face some of his more atavistic supporters without it.

In contrast to the Government's stance, Wilson explained that Labour considered maintaining an independent nuclear deterrent an inappropriate use of resources which were better deployed in the conventional defence field to fulfil other commitments, not least to NATO. Wilson maintained that,

> Our conventional troops are stretched out dangerously as a tenuous red line all over the world. Their security and their contribution to our still scattered defence effort should count more in the final reckoning than nuclear prestige ... We can, with our limited resources, either pay for the pretence of the nuclear deterrent or honour our commitments in NATO and elsewhere. But we cannot do both.

Mirroring some of the arguments made by the Kennedy administration, Wilson held that an adequate conventional defence of Western Europe might help to slow the process of escalation if conventional fighting were to occur. Finally, Britain's nuclear policy had, he claimed, been damaging to the cause of non-proliferation, by encouraging others to follow the same path.[61]

While it ended with a comfortable victory for the Government over the Opposition's motion of censure, the Commons debate at the end of January was instructive in laying out the respective position of the main parties over nuclear policy. There was already every indication that if Labour were to assume office, the Nassau arrangements would be subjected to a searching reappraisal, while Wilson's barbed critique of ministers again did him no harm amongst his supporters in the parliamentary party: two weeks after the debate Wilson would in fact defeat Brown in the run-off election for the Labour leadership. At the same time, re-examining Nassau did not mean that the Party advocated abandoning the UK's existing strategic nuclear capability as represented by the V-bomber force, a point Brown had been keen to emphasise during the debate.

As for the Conservative Government, Macmillan's performance had helped to pacify some of its more recalcitrant backbenchers. Considering some of the anxieties he had expressed earlier, Macmillan's Press Secretary, for one, was satisfied with how matters had gone, feeling that the Prime Minister's contributions, in particular, had been very effective.[62] Yet having come away from Nassau with an agreement which allowed the Government to claim that independence had been preserved, there would be little domestic political room for manoeuvre when it came to pressures to fulfil all the multilateral aspects of the accord. Moreover, in the period before the election that would have to be held in 1964, Conservative spokesmen – believing it was a popular vote-winner – were inclined to stress the 'independent' aspects to the UK deterrent as a means to attack the Opposition's approach to nuclear issues.

The basic conflict between the Government's domestic political imperative to demonstrate that the Nassau's accord's 'supreme national interests' clause safeguarded Britain's nuclear independence, and the diplomatic need to implement its 'multilateral' or multinational aspects, was to present some difficult dilemmas over the next 18 months. Indeed, with the Nassau arrangements having passed an important parliamentary hurdle, British officials were now keen to move ahead quickly in establishing under NATO command an 'Inter-Allied' nuclear force, as called for by paragraph 6 of the Nassau Agreement, from NATO's existing nuclear capabilities, including, as the Prime Minister had announced, all of Bomber Command's V-force. Three squadrons of the oldest UK-based Valiant Mark 1 V-bombers, amounting to 24 aircraft, and considered surplus to front-line requirements, had, in fact, already been 'assigned' to SACEUR for targeting purposes in 1960–61, but it was anticipated, in the Foreign Office at least, that the new 'Inter-Allied' nuclear force would have more elaborate political control arrangements, and so help to involve the non-nuclear members of the Alliance to a greater extent than hitherto in nuclear planning and consultation.[63]

The device of assigning the entire V-force to SACEUR as part of such a force was also undoubtedly seen in British official circles as a means to deflect some of the criticism that London was reluctant to embrace other important elements of the deal reached between Macmillan and Kennedy in the Bahamas. As the Minister of Defence had privately noted, the assignment of the V-force was to show that 'we have no intention of dragging our feet in

NATO or with our European allies and that we are giving wholehearted support to the idea of the NATO nuclear force, including its multinational component, without waiting for the complex issues of assignment and control to be settled.'[64]

Reactions to the multilateral force proposals

In Washington, however, the 'multinational' parts of the Nassau Agreement were not regarded as of the same level of significance as its 'multilateral' aspects. Indeed, the Bahamas meetings served to inject new political momentum into the State Department's arguments that proposals to form a multilateral force, including a newly created mixed-manned and jointly controlled and financed element, should now be more actively promoted within the North Atlantic Alliance. President Kennedy had convened an important meeting with his senior advisers on 12 January 1963 to discuss implementation of the Nassau arrangements, where it had been decided that, rather than wait for the Europeans to come forward with ideas about how to create an MLF, the US administration would now take more active measures. Rusk felt that, 'With respect to Germany … we must push immediately for discussions in NATO of a multilateral force in order to meet Adenauer's demands for German equality.' After Kennedy told the meeting that US plans for control of the MLF should be developed, McGeorge Bundy interjected that 'it was important that we move promptly so that the British will not slip away from their commitment to a multilateral force. If the British move away from the multilateral concept, the Germans will create major difficulties.'[65]

Despatched on a European tour in order to explain the Nassau Agreement to America's major NATO allies, a few days later George Ball was telling Adenauer that at Nassau 'our first preference had been to have British contribution solely to a multilateral force but that we recognized special problems of the British Govt and had therefore settled on an intermediate position whereby our agreement to supply Polaris to [the] British was tied to their contributing that force to NATO and to supporting US in an effort to create a multilateral force.' When Adenauer had asked about the right of Britain to withdraw its force in the event of a national emergency, Ball had sought to downplay this with the comment that at Nassau, 'Macmillan had recognized that there was little possibility of withdrawal and independent use, but he had public problem of past history and British image of 1940 to deal with.'[66]

In the wake of the Franco–German treaty of cooperation which was signed by de Gaulle and Adenauer on 22 January 1963 (a development which caused some shock and consternation to the Kennedy administration), and which came just a few days after the French veto of Britain's entry to the EEC, the MLF was also increasingly seen as a means to ensure that Bonn clung to Washington's leadership in the Alliance when de Gaulle seemed to be in the business of creating a new centre of gravity within Western Europe. 'Our interest,' the President told a meeting of the NSC the same day the

Franco-German treaty was signed, 'is to strengthen the NATO multilateral force concept, even though de Gaulle is opposed, because a multilateral force will increase our influence in Europe and provide a way to guide NATO and keep it strong. We have to live with de Gaulle. One way to respond is to strengthen NATO and push for a multilateral nuclear force which will weaken de Gaulle's control of the Six.'[67]

By mid-February 1963, senior administration officials had come to some level of agreement that the MLF was best envisaged as being formed by 25 surface ships, each equipped with eight Polaris missiles, carrying crews of mixed nationality, and all to be delivered at a cost of about $5 billion, with the United States footing about a third of the bill.[68] Developing these ideas, and often overlooking some of the practical objections from military observers over how such a force could operate, during the remainder of the year 'Europeanists' in the State Department, with Ball to the forefront, and supported by strong-minded adherents such as Walt Rostow, attempted to push forward negotiations with the interested European members of NATO so that political agreement to its creation could be secured.

As in the latter half of 1962, when American ideas for an MLF had begun to be promoted once again in NATO circles, British officials reacted with scepticism, finding the scheme militarily unnecessary and impracticable, financially unacceptable, and politically dangerous because – despite its avowed intention – an MLF carried for some the potential to awaken dormant German desires for nuclear status which were best left quiescent, or created them where none had existed before. A deeper anxiety was that if an MLF was eventually formed, although the United States might initially retain its veto over the use of the force's nuclear weapons, there would be longer-term pressures from the Germans for the veto to be relinquished, and for 'majority' voting among its members to be allowed. Hence one of the key aims of the MLF – to prevent a German 'finger on the nuclear trigger' – might be in fact be undermined by its very creation. Yet British opposition to the whole MLF concept in early 1963 could not be voiced too openly, especially when the legal, financial and technical arrangements to bring about the supply of Polaris had yet to be finalised with Washington. Thorneycroft had already registered his objections with McNamara to any attempt to use the negotiation over the terms for a Polaris sale to create a connection with implementation of all the other aspects of what had been agreed at Nassau, including the commitment to help create an MLF. As the Minister of Defence put it, 'I can see difficult political consequences and complications if we try to re-write in legal jargon the rather delicately-balanced phrases of the Nassau Agreement.'[69]

The Prime Minister was also very unhappy with the first US drafts of a proposed Polaris sales agreement, which tried to incorporate other aspects of the Nassau accord. When it was suggested that if the Americans could not be dissuaded it might be necessary to compromise in order to secure progress with the Polaris negotiation, he scrawled across the bottom of one memorandum: 'How can the Americans *insist* on altering an agreement to which they have put their signature? If some shyster American lawyers try on that game, I will appeal to the President and/or to the public.'[70]

The detailed negotiations that would underpin Anglo-American agreement for the supply of Polaris missiles to the UK began in earnest on 19 February 1963 with the arrival in Washington of a joint team led by Mackay from the Admiralty, and officials from the Ministry of Aviation and Ministry of Defence. Mackay's group had the task of reaching agreement on the technical and financial aspects of the sale, while the 'political' side to the negotiation was led by Denis Greenhill, the (diplomatic) Minister at the Washington Embassy. One of the first and most significant tasks of the British negotiators was to override the initial American proposal that there should be a 'covering agreement', accompanying the terms of a Polaris sale, the latter to be added as an annex. The comprehensive covering agreement, the State Department had anticipated, would re-state in more explicit form the understandings contained in the ambiguous Nassau Agreement and which could – in theory – be used to link the supply of Polaris to progress with the creation of a NATO multilateral force, about which there already signs that major differences were emerging between London and Washington. Taking his cue from Downing Street, Thorneycroft wrote to Home, just after the negotiating mission departed for the United States, in order to check any Foreign Office inclination toward making concessions on such matters, wanting to make it 'quite clear that the American agreement to supply us with Polaris would be unaffected either by the collapse of NATO or by the failure of NATO, despite our best endeavours, to agree to the constitution of the NATO force to which our V-bombers and later our Polaris submarines are, under the Nassau Agreement, to be assigned. This was my understanding with Mr McNamara at Nassau, and I believe that it should be firmly established at this stage.'[71]

There was therefore some relief in London when towards the end of February, after the first week of 'political' talks in Washington covering the procedure by which Polaris would be supplied, the Americans acceded to the British position that the idea of a general covering agreement recapitulating in more precise language the Nassau arrangements should be dropped. Instead, the detailed terms of the sale itself would form the substance of the inter-governmental document to be negotiated between UK and US officials.[72]

British objections certainly played a role in persuading US officials to adopt this new position, but behind the scenes McNamara was also keen to separate the supply of Polaris to the UK – which he wanted to expedite – and the other aspects of the Nassau Agreement, about which he harboured deep scepticism. The Americans may also have been satisfied, at this stage, with the progress that was made in moving forward ideas to assign national nuclear forces to NATO control, where British officials had been active in making detailed proposals.[73] Nevertheless, Americans officials still hoped to insert a form of words in the sales agreement which would make some link between the supply of Polaris and the other aspects of the Nassau Agreement.[74]

In the event, a very general reference to the Nassau communiqué was included in the agreement's preamble, along with a further statement in its first article that the sales agreement was 'subject to the understandings' about British Polaris submarines referred to in paragraphs 8 and 9 of the communiqué. However, any suggestion that provision of Polaris would be dependent on the implementation of all aspects of the Nassau agreement was scotched by an exchange of letters between Thorneycroft and McNamara, planned to accompany conclusion of the sales agreement, and which committed the United States to supply Polaris irrespective of developments in NATO or progress with the MLF scheme (this was later modified to become an exchange of letters between foreign ministers, as the sales agreement was classed as a high-level inter-governmental document).[75] The Prime Minister's facetious view, as expressed by de Zulueta, was that 'the point should be put simply to McNamara that of course we would stand by the Nassau Agreement but that if NATO did not want a multilateral force or if the Germans joined the Russians, the Italians went Communist and the French went neutral, [and] NATO came to an end, we would like an assurance that the Americans would still sell us the Polaris submarines [sic]. Without such an assurance against these admittedly rather remote contingencies, we would not feel justified in embarking upon vast expenditure.'[76]

As noted above, to the State Department the MLF scheme was, in any case, beginning to make headway during the early spring. A significant step here was the tour of European capitals undertaken between 22 February and 17 March by a senior State Department official, Livingston Merchant, along with a large support staff, in order to sound out opinion toward the MLF in NATO. Although he encountered many queries and several problems were raised, Merchant put a very positive gloss on his mission when he returned, reporting that the Germans had shown definite interest, while the Italians, Belgians and Dutch were also keen to examine the ideas further.[77] Gaining significant currency in Washington was a conviction that the MLF would give Germany 'associate membership' of the nuclear club it desired, some sense of nuclear equality with the UK and France, tie its future ever more firmly to the US-led NATO Alliance, and provide a European arm to the Western deterrent. Without it, more radical German voices might, it was feared, begin to call for nationally-manned and controlled nuclear systems, and future governments, further to the political right, turn toward France, for an example of independent behaviour, and even possible nuclear assistance.

None of this was accepted in British official circles, where German nuclear ambitions were more widely doubted, and if they did exist, it was felt they should not be encouraged. But it was difficult to voice open opposition to the MLF as long as Washington remained enthusiastic, Bonn interested, and as ministers had agreed at Nassau, admittedly in vague terms, to back the scheme. When his touring party had reached London in March, Merchant's ideas for an MLF consisting of a mixed-manned force of surface ships had met with scepticism and hostile questions from British military experts.[78] Greeting Merchant on 12 March, Macmillan had however said that the Government stood by all the clauses in the Nassau Agreement, and that the UK 'would support the American plans for the paragraph 8 force so far as they could.'[79]

The Foreign Office was also cautious about striking an overly negative tone, and the Foreign Secretary, Lord Home, was already indicating he would hope to engage with American ideas rather than appear obstructive. Indeed, US officials were acutely aware that British participation would be essential to the success of any MLF, a point which Kennedy made to the Prime Minister in a message sent after Merchant's return to Washington. All this left Macmillan decidedly unimpressed, informing Home after receiving the presidential correspondence that he interpreted the Nassau Agreement as envisaging an MLF eventually made up of three components. These included the British Polaris force mentioned in paragraph 8 of the communiqué; 'at least equal US forces' as mentioned in paragraph 9; and 'units of mixed nationality to which non-nuclear members of NATO would contribute personnel and resources.' There was no obligation, in the Prime Minister's adamant estimation, that the UK should make any contribution to the third category of units, though this did not mean that 'general sympathy and support' should not be expressed for the concept of the MLF. Precise commitments should, in any event, be avoided until a formal agreement for the supply of Polaris was reached with the Americans.[80]

Nevertheless, the Foreign Secretary could see some of the advantages to be gained from participation in the mixed-manned component of an MLF. As Home explained, if the force were to play a key role in NATO, Britain would clearly want to influence its development, rather than see it 'become a predominantly American-German venture.'[81] 'I do not think there is any chance of the Cabinet or the House of Commons agreeing to any contribution,' Macmillan again reminded Home in March 1963. 'We have had quite enough trouble to defend the immense sum to be spent on our own nuclear force. To spend any more would be political suicide.' He also believed that the Americans had 'unilaterally altered the concept of Nassau', where there was no question that they would contribute to a new mixed-manned force, which was to be formed by the non-nuclear powers in NATO: 'The Cabinet should be informed of what has happened. The Americans have changed their ground and we are under no obligation to follow them. Of course it is true that if we don't take part this force may become an American/German/Italian force, but that is a matter for the Cabinet to discuss. We must not be slid into it without knowing what is happening.'[82]

While agreeing about the need for care, Heath, the Lord Privy Seal, was more alert to the political dangers of an outright refusal, and, when it came to the issue of UK involvement, the 'political advantages for us. The main point is that, if Germany could be tied effectively into an arrangement of this kind, it would frustrate any plans of General de Gaulle to set up a French or Franco-German hegemony in Europe. We should not want the Americans to be in a position to say that this had broken down because we were lukewarm or negative.'[83] From Washington, Ormsby Gore could also see problems if the British were too determined in their opposition.

> 'It would be exceedingly unfortunate to say the least,' he signalled Thorneycroft, 'if it could be plausibly represented that British opposition was the cause of [the MLF's] failure. It is already possible that the scheme will be killed by the continental countries who seem highly sensitive to the cost problems, amongst others. The Americans are only too likely to become aware of these objections without our having to argue on behalf of the Allies. More importantly, the President has agreed to support our initiative on the inter-Allied nuclear force as part of a package in which we support the mixed-manned force. At stake also is American willingness to implement the Polaris Sales Agreement in a truly forthcoming manner ... It seems to me that there is everything to be said for going along with the mixed-manned force as long as the President and McNamara attach major importance to it. Indeed we have no alternative as a result of the Nassau Agreement'.[84]

Kennedy himself, it is crucial to note, exhibited a fundamental scepticism over the MLF throughout its history, and was not willing to make the major political investment required to push forward the scheme, or to surrender ultimate US control over the employment of nuclear weapons (some of the more extreme proponents of the MLF implied or even suggested in their arguments that the US veto over use of nuclear weapons allocated to the force might eventually be relinquished). His basic position was that the Europeans themselves would have to agree any new arrangements for nuclear sharing, and it was not for the United States to force reluctant allies to subscribe to a scheme in which they had no confidence, or whose implementation would create more inter-allied strife. De Gaulle was already trouble enough to contain within the Atlantic Alliance.

On 18 February, for example, just before the departure of the Merchant mission, the President had expressed his 'deep concern' about prospects for the scheme, and gave as his impression 'that the British were not for it; the French were clearly against it; and the Italians did not have a deep-seated interest in it. The Germans reportedly were interested, but once they realised how little they were getting for their money, they might look at it differently.' He had no desire to relax the US veto after an MLF came into being. Despite the efforts of Rusk and Merchant to convince him that a determined attempt to sell the idea had to be made, he 'remained concerned that we might be identifying ourselves too closely with a proposition (MLF) that might be rejected. Rather than take this risk, he thought we might better focus on some version of a multinational force [as stipulated under paragraph

6 of the Nassau agreement], operated through an Executive Committee.'[85] As for McNamara, he held many private doubts over the scheme but 'tacitly supported the MLF while convinced as ever that long-term it would fail,' while the JCS had major reservations over the practicality of mixed-manning of the force (even though this was perhaps its key feature).[86] Yet within the State Department, and marshalled by the still influential figure of the Under-Secretary of State, George Ball, were a group of determined 'Europeanist' officials who remained convinced that the MLF represented the only realistic solution to the political problem of forestalling future German ambitions to acquire independent nuclear status, with all the destabilising effects on the situation in central Europe and relations with the Soviet Union that this was predicted to generate.

Merchant had hoped that preliminary agreements amongst the European contributors to an MLF could be ready by the time of the ministerial NATO gathering scheduled for towards the end of May 1963 in Ottawa. However, the numerous doubts that were already emerging about many of its control, financing and manning features meant this deadline would prove impossible to keep. British opposition, moreover, was to prove one of the main obstacles toward rapid progress being made and, as the next chapter details, steps leading toward the 'assignment' of the V-bomber force to NATO as part of the (paragraph 6) 'multinational' nuclear force stipulated in the ambiguous Nassau Agreement were used by officials to deflect any criticism directed at their reluctance to engage with the proposals for a multilateral force. There was also the wider diplomatic point that the Soviet Union had begun to express alarm about how ideas for new nuclear arrangements within the Alliance which might give Germany a voice in the control of long-range nuclear weapons (this at a time when delicate negotiations with Moscow were still underway over a ban on nuclear testing). The faltering steps along the path toward the creation of an MLF in early 1963 were not, therefore, to hold up the conclusion of a Polaris sales agreement with the UK, and this decoupling of the provisions of Nassau – a considerable, if unheralded, success for British diplomacy – gave some lassitude for basic British objections to the MLF to be made manifest through the tactics of delay.

Penetration aids, the Williams mission, and the conclusion of the Polaris sales agreement

It was well known to the British defence staff in Washington that Polaris A1 and A2 test firings carried out during 1962 had carried penetration aid (or PX) packages in what was obviously the start of an important new development programme (while as we have seen US progress in the whole area was publicly acknowledged by President Kennedy himself at the end of 1962).[87] Moreover, at an early stage of their involvement with the Polaris programme officials from RAE, which had responsibility in the area, were concerned with the ability of the new US Mark 2 Mod 0 Re-entry System, intended for use for Polaris A3, to penetrate a future ABM defensive system. In early 1963, as thoughts began to turn to the acquisition of Polaris, staff at the establishment considered whether a more effective UK-designed REB and re-entry system could be developed, rather than simply adopt the US design. Penetration aids were an early feature of British ideas, not least as it was assumed that, once developed by the Americans, they would be deployed on their Polaris missiles. From a paper produced by Sidney A. Hunwicks, the Director of Atomic Warheads Development (DAWD) at the Ministry of Aviation, there was even the idea that if the A3 missile were acquired instead of the A2, rather than use its triple warhead arrangement, a single warhead of about 200 kilotons – and so of comparable yield to the Mark 58, and adapted from a British-tested device – could be fitted, along with 'ample' decoys (RAE staff had mentioned that they might be able to include up to six decoys in such a new design). This would be an arrangement designed specifically for defence penetration, and, in the words of the DAWD paper, 'presents the only hope of overcoming anti-missile defences as they are expected to develop in the mid-1970s. The fundamental principles are well understood and were under development for Blue Streak.'[88]

By the end of February 1963, following the previous month's experience of AWRE's unilateral Polaris warhead visit to the American Lawrence Livermore laboratory, fresh plans had been laid to despatch to the United States a joint Admiralty/Ministry of Aviation/AWRE technical mission under the leadership of Leslie T. D. Williams, Director General Atomic Weapons at the MoA. The Williams mission was to investigate and report on the Polaris A3 missile and its re-entry system (with the secondary task of gathering information on the A2 variant if problems were being encountered with the A3); its members included Rear Admiral Dossor, John Challens from AWRE, Fred East from the Weapons Department at RAE, and Hunwicks from the MoA. The remit of the Williams mission reflected the fact that despite the preference expressed by Macmillan and Thorneycroft in January, no final choice had yet been made as to which version of the Polaris missile system to procure.

In early March, Carrington sent an anxious minute to Thorneycroft asking that a decision on this crucial matter had to be made very soon if the Polaris programme was to maintain its early momentum. The Admiralty were adamant that the new A3 variant should be adopted by the UK force. Elaborating the reasons for his own strong preference for the A3, Carrington pointed to its longer range, better accuracy, the fact that it would be the standard SLBM in US Navy service, and that, unlike the A2, it would be able to carry penetration aids. The latter, he considered, would 'help to insure against an anti-missile breakthrough and increase confidence in the deterrent'.[89]

Within the MoA, while officials could not disagree with the Navy's enthusiasm for the A3 on operational grounds, they felt obliged to highlight the technical risks attached to an immediate commitment to the newer missile, as it was still undergoing a troublesome development and testing regime. In line with this advice, the Minister of Aviation, Julian Amery, agreed with Thorneycroft that an A3 purchase would be preferable, but added that there were still development problems associated with the new missile. Amery wanted to stress that until the report of the Williams technical mission was received, there was no certainty that the 'warhead and nose cone section problems' could be solved in an acceptable timescale; he therefore made his support for Carrington's recommendation conditional on the outcome of the mission.[90]

It is important to remember that what might be called the shadow of Skybolt hung over and coloured much official thinking during this period. At the MoD, for example, Robert Press, Zuckerman's chief adviser in the CSA's Nuclear Group, believed that the decision should not be rushed. Cancellation of the A3, as in the Skybolt case, would have a major impact on a UK programme if it had been tailored to receive the missile, and basing a quick decision simply on operational and logistical reasons would be 'indefensible'; Press therefore considered that Carrington's recommendations should be 'resisted as premature.'[91]

The Minister of Defence was subsequently advised that although the Admiralty were keen to have an early decision in favour of the A3 in order to simplify their work and planning, and avoid unnecessary delay, there was still important information on the warhead and re-entry system that had to be gathered.[92] Thorneycroft and Carrington finally agreed that the Williams team should express a strong preference for the A3 when in the United States and investigate the system as a first priority, but if difficulties were to arise had to report back to London and seek such information as they needed on the A2.[93]

Some of the information about the RES and warhead that was lacking concerned US plans for the development of penetration aid packages which could be installed on the Polaris A3 missile. Finding suitable language and the requisite legalistic formulas to underpin a Polaris sales agreement had not always been easy, especially considering the restrictions of US atomic energy legislation, but by early March a substantial measure of progress had been made by the US and British negotiating teams in Washington. The Americans had, however, maintained a blunt refusal to discuss or include penetration aid technology under the terms of the sales agreement. 'I decided not to press further against the exclusion of penetration aids,' W. G. Downey, one senior MoA official involved in the talks reported. 'The other side refused to explain the reason for their stand (it seems obvious that they regard it as a hypersensitive area) but I got the impression that the decision was made or endorsed at top level in DOD [Department of Defense]. We have simply reserved our position. We have, of course, argued that it is a whittling away of the Nassau Agreement but further argument at our level at this stage seems quite useless.'[94]

The Williams technical mission visited the United States from 11 to 22 March 1963. It went armed with terms of reference and a set of possible warhead/RES/missile combinations that reflected the wide range of options open to the British at this stage, some of which included the ability to incorporate penetration aids. The operating assumption for AWRE was that whatever UK warhead was chosen would have to avoid the need for further nuclear testing, but believed that the four years research and development time they had before the warhead was scheduled to enter production would be long enough to complete their part of the Polaris programme.[95]

The Williams mission would have been interested to learn about US views on the penetration performance of Polaris, but, in the understated words of its preliminary report, it was 'unfortunate that strict US orders prevented any discussion of the matter.' Indeed, when the Williams team had begun their talks with American representatives at the US Navy's Special Projects Office on 12 March they had at the outset been handed a paper which identified the subjects which were considered off limits. These included penetration aid programmes, except for the fact of their existence and what they could mean for certain weight and range trade-offs, as well as volume restrictions, in the A2 and A3 missile systems; the vulnerabilities of the Mark 1 and Mark 2 re-entry systems in absolute terms; and designs for re-entry systems other than the Mark 1 and Mark 2.[96]

When news of these limitations was received at RAE, James Lighthill was troubled enough to write to Amery, the Minister of Aviation, expressing his concern that information on improving the capability of Polaris REBs to penetrate Russian defences was to be denied to the Williams mission. It was presciently noted that this could have 'a very serious effect' on either 'the credibility of our deterrent on deployment' (as the basic Mark 2 RES might be vulnerable to Russian ABM defences) or 'on the total cost of the Polaris system, since if we become convinced that increased penetration aids are necessary, we may have to develop a completely British re-entry system and perhaps undertake modifications to the missile itself.' It was hoped that Amery could raise the issue at a higher level, with the aim of securing access to US design plans, as 'this country is at present being asked to buy Polaris without any knowledge of whether it can be made effective against Russia's rapidly growing ABM defence system.'[97]

The nature and future deployment patterns of the Soviet ABM system was, as we have seen, still highly uncertain, but as far as the US intelligence community was concerned, the prospect of an operational capability appearing over the next few years had become more likely. In March 1963, for example, the US National Intelligence Estimate on Soviet military capabilities over the next five years predicted that deployment of ABM defences would be the largest military programme undertaken by the Soviet leadership, with several different systems already under development. The Leningrad complex, it was believed, would reach some operational capability during 1963. There was no basis for evaluating its effectiveness but it was doubted it could deal with a threat which contained decoys or other penetration aids. Once a better system was devised a 'vigorous' deployment programme was expected, covering perhaps 20–25 key Soviet cities and taking another five or six years to complete.[98]

Of great interest also was the build-up, from 1963 onwards, of a new set of surface-to-air missile and radar installations along a line stretching from Archangelsk to Riga, that seemed to bisect the 'threat corridor' along which US ICBMs would have to travel in order to reach targets within the Soviet Union. This so-called 'Tallinn Line' – named after the city in Estonia where some of the new construction was first observed – became the subject of heated dispute within the US intelligence community over the next few years, with early suppositions by some analysts that it could be developed to have an ABM capability gradually being challenged by analysts who pointed to the increasing evidence that its prime function was in fact defence against high-speed high-flying aircraft.[99]

To British officials there was every sign that the Americans were beginning to take seriously the Soviet ABM threat. Gathering as much information about implications for Polaris effectiveness soon became an important element of their interchanges with the Americans. Within the MoA, however, it was recognised that the issue of the bar on penetration aid discussion had already been faced before the arrival of the Williams mission, during the negotiations that had taken place over the terms of the formal sales agreement. During these it was said the American delegation responsible for the sales agreement had

> pulled the shutters down and flatly refused to agree to us discussing future penetration aids on the grounds that the Nassau agreement was confined to the Polaris missile as formally authorised for introduction into the US Navy. This agreement did not in their view include the right of enquiry into nebulous future plans. Despite continued pressure they were adamant, and declined to receive a technical mission authorised to discuss future plans for the re-entry bodies and penetration aids.

With the Admiralty restive over any delay or hold-ups in the negotiation, keen that the best available solution should be accepted, and anxious the MoA might be 'rocking the boat', MoA officials felt it was advisable to wait for the Williams mission to deliver its final report, and to decide then, in fact, if the Mark 2 RES was still considered unsatisfactory for UK purposes.[100] In view of the genuine goodwill and cooperative disposition generally shown by US officials, and the US Navy in particular, along with the probability such an attempt would be unsuccessful, there was a marked reluctance to challenge the prohibition on information about penetration aids, despite the fact that some British officials saw it as 'arguably a derogation from the Nassau Agreement'.[101]

Members of the Williams technical mission had nevertheless spent useful time visiting Lockheed Missiles and Space Company (LMSC), the maker of Polaris, at its headquarters in Sunnyvale, California. When they discussed the design of the Mark 2 RES, and how it might be made compatible with different UK warhead options, British officials raised RAE's idea of using a single REB with reduced radar echoing area and adding a number of decoys to the RES. 'A short discussion with Lockheeds was held on these matters,' the final report of the Williams mission noted, 'and although they had little time to consider the problems they suggested that, on the basis of their past experience, a two year development programme followed by a flight demonstration programme of six months would be adequate.' As the trials programme suggested might involve ten to fifteen tests this was thought optimistic. Estimated total costs for such a programme were naturally very tentative, but Lockheed suggested that a figure of $200 million to develop such a British-designed RES 'was of the right order of magnitude.'[102]

The Williams mission began its time in the US supposing that uncertainty over US plans was a key reason why the Americans were proving so reticent over talking about penetration aids. Its members nevertheless returned to the UK reassured that the Americans were committed to bringing the existing form of Polaris A3 into service, and had no intention of discarding the 'triplex' warhead configuration used in its front end. It was for this reason that MoA officials decided at the end of March that Amery should not be informed about the reservations entertained by the Director of RAE over the RES that would be employed with Polaris A3, and the degree of access to US information about penetration aids; indeed the impression gained from early messages from Washington in the MoA was that there were 'grounds for optimism' that US attitudes would soften and that the restrictions against discussions did not appear to be as absolute as first feared.[103] By the end of their time in the United States, though, the members of the mission was less sanguine, and they had been offered no extra information on penetration questions. From what were called 'unintentional lapses of security' on the US side, and an 'incautious display of wall charts,' it had been possible to surmise that production of the existing Mark 2 RES would probably be discontinued by the end of 1965, while there were plans to bring a so-called 'fourth generation' weapon into service by 1967 (and it was thought this was the larger diameter B3 missile which had been touted by the respected US journal *Aviation Week* as a successor to Polaris).[104]

From all this, the Williams mission had, in fact, discerned that the Americans were not altogether happy with the Mark 2 Mod 0 RES, and were developing a Mod 1 variant including penetration aids for use with the A3, 'but no details whatever were released on the devices used', and they were said to be 'severely volume limited' by the amount of space available within the missile nose fairing. Ideas for possible re-entry systems with a better penetration capability than the existing RES had been raised by the British team, but the Americans had resisted being drawn into talking about their own plans or intentions. Nonetheless, the (inaccurate) conclusion reached by the team was that it was 'highly probable that the next generation of weapon is being planned to have a re-entry system which will be quite different from the Mark 2 and which will consist of a single warhead with decoys.'[105] 'It must be pointed out,' the mission's overall interim report stressed, 'that, unless some relaxation of this US ban can be secured, the UK project may be gravely prejudiced, since, even apart from the question of penetration, the presence of this package may affect the functioning of the re-entry system.' Recognising how essential it would be to maintain close liaison, not least if the Americans introduced modifications to their system such as penetration aids, Williams had discussed with Admiral Galantin, the sympathetic head of the US Navy's Special Projects Office, the idea of establishing a joint US/UK working group, 'meeting a few times a year as necessary and consisting of senior specialists directly engaged on the development and manufacture of the warhead', with could supplement the role of the permanent British Royal Navy liaison officer based with SP.

The relatively relaxed view of the Williams mission was qualified by a highly significant paper (seen by the all the top officials at the MoA dealing with guided missile and nuclear matters) which was drawn up in early April 1963 by D. J. Lyons, the head of RAE's Weapons Department. This summarised the latest state of knowledge on the US Polaris programme and how difficult the decisions over the choice of a UK re-entry system could prove to be. It was believed from US Navy comments, Lyons had noted, that a new RES would be introduced to the A3 before it became obsolete, with the emphasis on increasing the missile's penetration ability. However, all the discussions held so far with the Americans had been frustrated by their unwillingness to discuss their future plans for systems beyond the A3, new designs for REBs after the Mark 2 Mod 0, or any information regarding penetration aids. Recalling the document handed out by the American authorities to the Williams mission when it first arrived in the United States which delineated the areas banned for discussion, Lyons remarked that such areas 'unfortunately coincided almost exactly with those the mission most desired to talk about.' Nevertheless, direct questions about the Mark 2 RES had elicited the response from personnel in the Special Projects Office that it was expected to be too vulnerable to ABM defences by 1968 (exactly the point, of course, at which UK Polaris was planned to enter service).

Lyons was evidently concerned by the future Soviet ABM environment, and despite the fact that intelligence information was 'conjectural in date, quality and quantity', was ready to draw inferences from the recent Russian testing programme, and Russian public statements. Alongside the possibility that the widely deployed SA-2 missile system – as seen in the Tallinn Line – could be adapted for an anti-missile role (though it was unlikely to be very effective) he saw 'ominous indications' that a new type of ABM system was being installed near Leningrad. This consisted of radar and control sites, and three launching areas, with the capacity, he reckoned of supporting 90 missiles. 'This may well be the system for high altitude interception we have suspected,' Lyons speculated, '...the degree of discrimination this may have between [war]head and decoys is simply not known, but it would be most unwise to assume that it cannot separate out simple decoys such as "chaff" or light balloons, and somewhat heavier but still imperfectly matched decoys.' Given their heavy investment in air defence, Lyons thought the Russians 'would not boggle' at a very wide deployment of the new system to protect their cities.

From the crude penetration calculations carried out by Lyons, he rated the chances of a single triple warhead missile penetrating this new Leningrad system as very low, even if the Russians committed not more than ten defensive missiles to its attempted interception. On the other hand, a single warhead missile, with 20–30 decoys was given a very good chance of penetration to its target. His conclusion was that the Mark 2 RES should be replaced, and 'fortunately, within the nose fairing of the Polaris A3 there is a fair measure of flexibility for incorporating different re-entry systems and we have made a number of tentative redesigns including one based on a single UK warhead plus decoys.' However, the costs of such a UK programme, Lyons acknowledged, could prove heavy, not least as the Americans would have to play a large role in design and testing. Tentative estimates quoted for a UK RES programme during Zuckerman's January 1963 visit had been in the order of £40 million, and Lyons also quoted Lockheed's recent estimate of $200 million. The consequences of the ban laid on discussion of penetration aids were then elaborated in unmistakable terms:

> It is at this point that we must regret the clamp the US has placed on discussion of the new re-entry systems; we are sure there will be one that would be more credible in the period 1970–80 than the Mk. II, but we cannot tell what it is and whether it will apply to the A3 missile. And above all we don't know what size warhead we would need to make which would fit into this new US system at minimum cost. One thing is almost certain, however, that as the US are stopping production of the Mk 58 warhead for the Mk II triple re-entry system in 1965, any new re-entry system will use a different warhead, and so if we decide initially to use the Mk II system, our special warhead to fit this will not fit any newer developments. Thus we might well have to make yet another new warhead unless we can use the one we already have in development for some other purpose. The time scale here is very important as to have warheads available by 1967/8 we must decide on the warhead this year 1963.

Aside from this, there was always the additional and alarming possibility that the Americans would jump to what Lyons called a '4th generation missile' (i.e. the B3) capable of carrying a much larger payload, and an entirely new RES. This could then leave the British even further behind as, unless the UK switched to the newer missile system in line with the Americans, an improved re-entry system for the A3 would have to be designed by the UK alone, with all the extra costs this would entail. The conclusions offered by Lyons in his paper were stark:

1 The present blank refusal by the US authorities to tell us anything about their future technical plans for the Polaris system is putting impossible difficulties in the way of proper technical planning for our force.
2 The USSR is probably starting deployment of an effective ABM system now; this will only be defeated adequately by saturating its local missile capabilities with a large number of decoys.
3 We consider the Mk. II triple warhead re-entry system will not be credible even at the initial operational date for our submarine force.
4 The British Polaris should have from the start, a credible re-entry body system which should consist of a re-entry head with low [radar] echoing area, accompanied by at least 20–30 matched decoys.
5 The choice of warhead for the British Polaris system depends critically on the design of the re-entry body system, so a decision on this system is urgently required.[106]

Even before a decision over its adoption had been made, therefore, it is apparent that there were serious concerns within RAE, which were disseminated to senior MoA officials, over whether the Mark 2 Mod 0 re-entry system would satisfy the penetration requirements of the UK's small Polaris force.

The case for adopting the A3 variant of Polaris was powerfully reinforced by the interim report of the Williams technical mission, which was delivered at the start of April 1963. It noted that Polaris A2 would stop production in December 1963, leaving the costs of re-opening production lines falling to the UK if it were adopted, a step which would also be very unwelcome to the US Navy. Though the Williams report could not therefore recommend acquiring the A2, it had not escaped British attention that A3 development had been marked by problems with test firings and rocket motor design. The designers of the A3 had given paramount consideration to maximising range, and this had led, Williams observed, to the introduction of several 'unusual features',

> including second-stage guidance and no termination of second stage thrust. All this made the whole front end of the missile unusually sensitive to even very small changes in the system. Weights, layout and centre of gravity must be held within extremely narrow limits in order to avoid upsetting dramatically missile guidance and functioning. Broadly speaking, the design presses harder on present limits of technology than any other US missile.

The implications of this for a UK purchase were that US practice in operating the system would have to be followed as closely as possible, and US components and parts used during in-service maintenance and support. Any UK manufacture of components would also need to follow US standards and specifications. In other words, the very closest collaboration between the two

Navies over the A3 system would be essential if Polaris was to operate in an effective manner, not least as it was virtually inevitable that further design changes and refinements would gradually be introduced by the Americans as they gathered in-service experience.[107]

A key finding of the technical mission was that the Americans were committed to introduce the A3 into service, fitted with the Mark 2 Mod 0 RES and the Mk 58 warhead. 'The nuclear element of that warhead can be closely copied in the UK and it is practically certain that no nuclear testing will be required,' it was advised. 'The UK should therefore now decide to adopt the same type of warhead as is now planned by the US for their A3 missile and make in the UK as close a copy as possible of that part of the warhead which, by law, the US cannot supply.' Yet it was a key concern of the Williams mission that the US could in the future continue to withhold information on the properties of the improved RES for Polaris A3 they were developing. If this were then to be introduced for the A3, the British programme to manufacture a warhead for Polaris could be affected, as it might not prove compatible with the modified US version of the RES with penetration aids. Thus a second recommendation made by the mission was the setting up of the liaison group earlier mooted by Williams and Galantin to ensure compatibility between US development of the Polaris system and British work on the warhead; the group was also seen as a means to 'bring about what is at present denied to us, namely, an exchange of information about penetration aids, since we conceive of this to be of the greatest importance to the RN in the long term.'[108]

By the middle of March 1963, the British team negotiating the terms of a Polaris Sales Agreement (PSA) in the US had completed their work, and were evidently very pleased with the outcome.[109] The fact that penetration aid issues would be excluded from the terms of the PSA was not held important enough to hinder or derail the process. At the start of April, reflecting Admiralty desires to move ahead as swiftly as possible, Carrington advised Thorneycroft (in a minute that also went to the Prime Minister, Foreign Secretary, and Chancellor of the Exchequer) that

> we simply do not have the knowledge to assess how far [the exclusion] would impair the value of the missile to us or how it would affect problems of design and proving of the 'front-end'. But I understand that given only partial knowledge of these devices, which we might hope to get after the agreement is signed, we might well be able to help ourselves out of the difficulty.

As a result, he did not feel it necessary to raise any high-level objections to the exemption of penetration aid information from the PSA. Aside from clearing up a number of legal points and minor amendments, Carrington recommended that the agreement was signed as soon as possible, not least considering the urgency of the programme and the fact that further progress would be held up until it could be concluded.[110]

When the draft PSA was collectively reviewed by interested ministers, Williams was present to sound a note of caution, warning, 'It was essential that every detail of size, weight, and location of centre of gravity in the [UK] re-entry vehicle should be identical with those of the American missile. In order to get these points right we should require the necessary information regarding the American penetration aids.' Nevertheless, on 3 April Thorneycroft passed on his own recommendation to the Prime Minister that, subject to a few minor reservations, the terms of the draft Polaris Sales Agreement be approved, along with its several confidential annexes. Mentioning the work of the Williams mission in passing, Thorneycroft advised Macmillan that it seemed 'reasonably certain' that copies of the American warhead could be made in the UK, and that a suitable RES for the missile could be acquired: 'But the Americans have not yet taken firm decisions in this area [of the RES] and the position therefore contains an element of risk for us, in particular as regards the penetration aids.' However, the Minister of Defence did not feel that the risk was sufficient to hold-up conclusion of the agreement.[111]

Accordingly, the Polaris Sales Agreement was signed in Washington on 6 April 1963 by Dean Rusk, the US Secretary of State, and Ormsby Gore. In the history of post-war Anglo-American nuclear relations the PSA was to prove almost as fundamental as the landmark 1958 MDA by which it has tended to be overshadowed. Affirming that the United States would provide for British purchase, 'Polaris missiles (less warheads), equipment, and supporting services,' the PSA laid out the terms and the organisational arrangements under which the transaction would be accomplished. As had been first proposed from the American side, the two Governments would designate a Project Officer with direct responsibility for managing each Government's activities under the Agreement. Liaison officers would also be embedded in each other's project offices, and a Joint Steering Task Group (JSTG) created, to meet alternately in the US and Britain on a quarterly basis (reduced to three times a year in 1967), with senior project officers and liaison representatives attending (including the American director of the Special Projects Office, and the British CPE). The Agreement stipulated that an array of associated equipment, spares, and ships systems would be offered to the UK, and arrangements put in place for assistance with the training of submarine crews and UK maintenance staff, and for missile test firings at US ranges. However, there were clear restrictions placed on the transfer of design information concerning the Polaris missile itself, with Lockheed, its manufacturer, holding the key position of 'design authority'. There would be close Anglo-American cooperation to ensure 'compatibility of equipment' between the US Polaris submarines and their counterparts being built in the UK, with information about many design features of the former to be transmitted.[112]

The PSA was accompanied by an exchange of confidential minutes and notes (the existence of which was revealed by the Prime Minister to the House of Commons only a few weeks later), providing further clarification and interpretation of some of the language used in the Agreement. In one of the classified minutes, the term 'Polaris missiles (less warheads)' was interpreted to mean

> Polaris missiles ready for deployment minus the atomic weapon, as defined in the [US] Atomic Energy Act of 1954, as amended, and minus any penetration aids. It therefore includes windshield, reentry body (less those parts of the reentry body which constitute part of the atomic weapon), separation devices and ancillary supporting structures.

The minute went on to stress that the supply of information or services in the field of 'atomic weapons, non-nuclear parts of atomic weapons or non-nuclear parts of atomic weapons systems involving [US] Restricted Data' was not covered by the PSA, although it was understood that Anglo-American exchanges in these areas would continue under the terms of the 1958 MDA 'in coordination' with the PSA.[113]

To the satisfaction of the British negotiators, at the same time as the PSA was signed, letters were exchanged which safeguarded the UK's right to be supplied with Polaris even if other parts of the Nassau Agreement remained unfulfilled (so offering an assurance that there would not be repercussions on the provision of Polaris if progress with creating the MLF remained slow, or the scheme had to be abandoned altogether).[114]

Much to the annoyance of Thorneycroft, it was not to be until the end of May 1963 that the Admiralty and Ministry of Aviation, drawing on the interim report of the Williams mission, came forward with their own formal and joint recommendation that the A3 missile should be adopted in the UK Polaris programme.[115] Carrington had included in his submission the point that the Americans were known to be developing a modified RES for the A3, and that if the UK wanted to base its own RES on this US development, information on 'weight, dimensions and certain engineering characteristics of the penetration aids as well as of the other elements which it will employ' would be needed. Though the PSA excluded penetration aids, assurances had been received from the Americans that enough information would be supplied to the UK to enable 'a viable system' to be produced, 'and we believe that through the joint working party which is being established we shall get sufficient information to produce a satisfactory warhead for the A3 missile.' Preparatory work to begin development in the UK of the Mark 58 warhead would now begin, Carrington reported, as well as discussions with the Americans for their plans for re-entry systems so that firm recommendations on the choice of a British RES could be made 'within about six months'.[116]

Copied into this correspondence, the Chief Secretary to the Treasury sounded a note of caution. Though ready to accept the choice of A3 missile, he also raised the

> possibly expensive and dangerous repercussions of any failure to obtain the kind of information we require about American re-entry systems, but

I understand that it is the intention to clear up any doubts on this score as soon as possible. I am sure this is essential.[117]

This reservation did not hold up the process, however, and already perturbed by the delay, Thorneycroft endorsed the Admiralty/MoA position in a minute that went to the Prime Minister on 7 June. Downing Street's assent to the proposal came three days later, marking the official adoption of the Polaris A3 missile system as the chosen weapon system for the strategic nuclear deterrent (though, as we have seen, this had been the assumption at a working level for some time).[118]

As outlined in the PSA, the JSTG was to become the principal forum through which close and effective Anglo-American cooperation in the field of submarine-launched ballistic missiles was secured, while it also served to cement the remarkable relationship that was beginning to develop between the US and Royal Navies. But even before the JSTG was to hold its inaugural meeting in late June 1963, an ancillary body (the 'working party' Carrington had mentioned in the minute quoted above), the Joint Re-entry System Working Group (JRSWG) had met in Washington. Reporting to the JSTG, the JRSWG was assigned the crucial job of ensuring that the interface between the missile and its guidance system, and the British-designed and developed nuclear warhead package ran smoothly. The group was to 'assemble, co-ordinate and consider all relevant data, US and UK, necessary to ensure full compatibility between US and UK produced components of the Re-entry System for the British Polaris Missiles, and between this re-entry system as a whole and the US produced missiles.'[119]

Within the Ministry of Aviation, since the RES and the warhead it housed were considered to be so closely integrated, it was Sidney Hunwicks, the Director of Warhead Development, rather than a Naval officer from the CPE organisation, who initially acted as UK Chairman of the JRSWG, and was responsible for all UK aspects of the design and development of the Polaris RES.[120] The formation of the working group was considered to be crucial by UK officials, as it offered the chance to be kept fully informed of any design changes made to the A3 missile which might affect compatibility with a UK-produced warhead and RES. As Admiral Dossor, the Navy's Polaris Project Officer in the MoA, noted, it could also become a route to bring about 'an exchange of information about penetration aids' since this was believed to be 'of the greatest importance to the RN in the long term.'[121]

Yet, under the restrictions of the PSA, it was soon found that the JRSWG's work was limited by the stipulation that there was to be no discussion of the operational effectiveness of Polaris, its vulnerability to countermeasures, or the penetration aid programme that the Americans were already embarked upon, 'except for the fact of its existence, information on weight and range trade-offs and on volume and weight restrictions for the missile system.' The US would also not undertake any work on penetration aid design for the UK, or other advanced US system components for Polaris.

All that the US officers at the first meeting of the JRSWG, held in mid-June 1963, would say about their ideas for penetration aids for their planned upgrade to the RES for Polaris A3 (the Mark 2 Mod 1) was that the package contemplated for inclusion would not influence the interface between the RES and the rest of the missile, and so would have no impact on the UK Polaris programme.

To Admiral Dossor it almost went without saying that if the British-produced RES for the UK Polaris force were to be ready in time for the first delivery of the submarines, then it would simply have to follow the Mark 2 Mod 0 design being introduced by the US Navy for the A3 missile. He was sure, however, that the RES would need improvement at some stage in its service life, but he was 'equally sure that it will be technically unsound and prohibitively expensive to introduce improvements, actually or potentially involving proof by missile firing trials, independent of USN development policy. We can follow or go along with USN development; we should not take a separate road.' In the meantime, as the subject of penetration aids for Polaris was expressly excluded from the terms of the exchanges allowed under the PSA, he wanted the US naval authorities on the JRSWG to know that the UK intended to work toward full collaboration in this area, once it had been shown that the UK had a worthwhile contribution of ideas and resources to make.[122]

A British ABM research programme, 1962–64

But how was the UK to demonstrate that it had such a 'worthwhile' contribution to make to the complex of issues surrounding ballistic missile defences, especially as early penetration aid work had come to an end with the cancellation of Blue Streak in 1960? The small-scale efforts made by the UK's defence research establishments to continue work connected with the subject, building on the Penley Report's recommendations of early 1962, and encompassed by the Dazzle experiments conducted at the Woomera rocket range in Australia, was one method by which officials hoped the UK might build up some technical capital which might interest the Americans and so open doors which were closed to exchanges over penetration aids. In October 1962, for example, the MoD's Defence Research Policy Committee had considered a paper from the MoA on space and high altitude defence research. Proposals for using the Black Knight proving missile for defence penetration and ABM studies were presented, with the argument that 'present plans for a co-operative research programme with the US Advanced Research Projects Agency are intrinsically of great importance to the mutual understanding of the problems of ballistic missile defence and provide a stimulus to a flow of information of American activities in this field.' It was noted that ARPA had offered to provide a free supply of advanced radar and optical equipment at Woomera, without which the experiments could not be conducted, and a firing programme throughout 1963/64 was planned, while further development of Black Knight, so that larger and faster re-entry heads could be tested, was also being contemplated. Annual costs for the programme were expected to rise to about £1.6 million over the next few years. Though endorsing the current space research programme, however, the DRPC had merely taken note of the MoA's proposals to extend the Black Knight tests.[123]

As far as the Treasury and MoD were concerned, approval to proceed was not yet granted, and officials sought more specific and detailed scrutiny of the MoA's ideas. The Treasury, in particular, was not persuaded with the worth of the Black Knight programme, and balked at the increasing costs involved. After pointing out that the Americans were already reluctant to continue with ABM research and development as the costs were so high, in April 1963 one Treasury official minuted that, 'One cannot escape the suspicion that this work is really being carried on in order to keep a team in being working on a large rocket which could later be developed as the upper stage of a ballistic missile or satellite launcher for space purposes ... This would be remarkably expensive as an insurance, and of course the cost of developing a separate UK launcher would be enormous. But the Ministry of Aviation's reluctance to running down this programme will no doubt be all the stronger for this thought in the background.'[124]

As a result, Treasury and Ministry of Aviation officials met in May 1963 to discuss the future of the programme. Work with Black Knight, the latter explained, was necessary to examine the problems of ABM defence, and might also be 'helpful in the design of the Polaris warhead, if it was necessary to incorporate a decoy without American know-how.' The American Nike-Zeus ABM system was described as 'only a crude first step with propaganda value, and the Americans were unwilling to let us know how much further they had gone in solving the technical problems.' Finally persuaded that a continuation of the existing programme had some value, not least as Black Knight was a useful form of insurance if ever a launcher were needed, Treasury officials gave approval for two more years of funding and the completion of the Dazzle series of experiments, but reserved their position over an extended programme until the matter could be considered by the MoD's DRPC.[125]

An MoA paper justifying an extended Black Knight programme, which would carry the test flights beyond October 1964 when existing authorisation for the Dazzle series was due to come to an end, was submitted to the DRPC in the summer of 1963. A key objective of the new programme was to see whether discrimination between warheads and decoys in mid-course, or during re-entry through the atmosphere, was feasible, and to test the ability to match decoy characteristics with those of real warheads. However, an uprating of Black Knight's performance would be required before this new series of tests could begin, and further development of the launch vehicle would take another two and a half years, with another year to complete the five experiments which were planned (expenditure for the entire programme was estimated at about £1.5 million per annum over the next four years).

Once more an important rationale advanced for the Black Knight high altitude test programme was that it might yield results which were interesting to the Americans. It was noted for the benefit of the DRPC that since the summer of 1962 there had been a 'hardening' of US attitudes toward the release to the UK of US information concerning ballistic missile defence, 'and we can no longer rely on full exchange of such information.' Reference was made to the US attitude at the Malvern Sub Group F meetings in October 1962, but most importantly, the exclusion of information over penetration aids from the terms of the April 1963 PSA.[126]

The programme of work the DRPC had been asked to consider would provide some collateral that could be offered to re-open channels of exchange, while it was also seen as 'the minimum work necessary for the UK to retain the expertise required to make an independent judgment of the effectiveness of the warhead and decoy re-entry systems of any US weapons, such as Polaris, which we may purchase.'[127]

The Treasury, however, remained sceptical and questioned the value of the information which would be derived from the programme. At earlier meetings in May, MoA officials had already, it was pointed out, downplayed the importance of the programme in order to generate an exchange with the Americans, particularly as the Americans appeared to be losing interest after Dazzle was completed, and were conducting their own experiments with decoys. There remained the point that the programme might help determine the effectiveness of the Polaris warhead and possible decoy systems against ABM defences, especially if a UK decoy system was eventually approved. However, to Treasury officials there seemed a 'considerable gap' between the expertise preserved by continuing the Black Knight work, and that required to reach decisions over penetration aids for Polaris or other future missile systems. 'The Black Knight information,' it was conjectured,

> appears to be hardly relevant at all to the questions whether Russia has an anti-ballistic-missile capability (as they claim), whether it is deployed in service, and how effective it can expected to be, which seems to be the key questions in deciding whether to develop decoys for Polaris. And if a decoy is thought to be necessary, the Black Knight information may or may not be any help in determining the characteristics most likely to be effective against a Russian system. £4m would seem a lot to pay for this side-light on the ballistic missile problem; on the other hand, the Polaris system will be so expensive that there is a strong *prima facie* case in favour of anything which may help to make it more effective.

The Treasury conclusion was that an extension to the programme might have to be accepted 'as an adjunct to Polaris' even if there were some very strong doubts over the importance of the eventual findings.[128]

When the DRPC met in August 1963 there was all-round support for the extended programme, with the Controller of the Navy, Admiral Le Fanu, noting its particular applicability to Polaris; the value of the programme, he thought, lay with the fact that the Americans 'would not necessarily continue to supply us with all the information we wanted on penetration and re-entry problems concerning Polaris.'[129] After the COS had added their own endorsement to the proposals, Zuckerman, as DRPC chair, prepared a submission which backed the studies, finding that this was an 'area of work [which] has its importance for Polaris since it is relevant to warhead penetration and re-entry problems on which our agreement with the Americans leaves us much more dependent on their goodwill than on the clear cut rights that we have for the rest of the Polaris system.' Thorneycroft gave his approval in mid-September 1963 for the work to proceed.[130]

However, it was not until December 1963, when the overall level of the MoA's spending on defence projects for 1964/65 had been settled, that Treasury authority was finally granted for the MoA to continue with the extended Black Knight programme, which it was thought would cover flights up to March 1967.[131] A new sequence of six Dazzle experiments, with improved range instrumentation at Woomera, began in August 1964, with the final test in fact taking place in November 1965 before the whole programme was wound up.[132]

Conclusion

The Polaris Sales Agreement represented a major negotiating achievement for British ministers and officials, making possible rapid progress with implementing the Nassau accord's understandings over the supply of Polaris to the UK, the development and manufacture of a submarine force to carry the missiles, and the instigation of extremely close cooperation between the US and Royal Navies over the operation of SLBM systems. Moreover, the payment of only a five per cent surcharge on the costs of each missile and associated equipment to cover the R & D investment by the US authorities in the A3 system was an excellent financial deal. Continuing US logistic and maintenance support for the UK Polaris force under the terms of the PSA would help to ensure that its running costs were kept to low levels (especially when compared to its V-force predecessor). Yet the exclusion of information about penetration aids from the PSA framework was a significant gap in British knowledge of how the Polaris system might be expected to perform against ABM defences, and what plans the Americans had for introducing improvements to the Mark 2 re-entry system. At the MoA there was hope that a deeper level of exchange in this area could be generated by engaging US interest in the Black Knight/Dazzle experiments on warhead re-entry phenomena being conducted in Australia, but the research programme was very modest and there were few indications of any relaxation of official US attitudes in this area over the next few years. By this stage, it is worth noting, US ABM research, and associated development of decoys and other penetration aids, was clearly ahead of anything being worked on at the UK research establishments. One sign of the relative paucity of UK work on ABM problems generally during this period is that when an MoA group was convened in August 1963 to discuss how the Penley report's recommendations for further ABM research had been implemented, a decision was taken not to show the report's contents to the Americans, 'as it revealed the inadequacy and poor state of the art of the British effort in this area.'[133]

Speculation is possible over why the Americans proved so reluctant to share penetration aid information with the UK during this period. This was obviously a very sensitive area of advanced technology, where compromise to an adversary of either technical details or level of capability could, in a worst case, do potential damage to national security. But highly sensitive warhead information, such as the design details of the Mark 58, were routinely and securely passed to the British authorities under the provisions of the MDA, and there is no evidence to suggest that US officials were unduly concerned by British security procedures for handling classified information at this stage of the Cold War. Another interpretation would suggest that improvements to the A3 re-entry system, including addition of penetration aids, would necessarily require new expenditures by the US authorities on R & D. There was undoubtedly a degree of annoyance within the Department of Defense over the bargain that the British had extracted with the five per cent surcharge deal at the end January 1963, and so perhaps a reluctance to once more sacrifice, for no return, knowledge that was acquired at some cost, and for which some later commercial gain (through the provision of penetration aid kits for the UK-acquired Polaris system) might be derived. This interpretation, however, has to be set against signs that even before the five per cent arrangement was finalised, the Americans were becoming reticent over the release of ABM-related information.

Whatever the case, the CPE organisation was not prepared to let reservations over the issue of penetration aids, as expressed within the MoA, hold-up momentum with the demanding timetable for the introduction of Polaris that had been established. Orders for the initial four Polaris submarines were placed on 8 May 1963, for example, with two separate shipbuilders, Vickers-Armstrong at Barrow-in-Furness and Cammell Laird at Birkenhead. Both firms saw a rapid expansion in their workforce and supporting staff as they began their onerous tasks. They were helped by the fact they could base the design of the new submarines on that used for HMS *Valiant*, the Navy's latest nuclear-powered attack submarine, which had just been completed. But this would have to be heavily adapted to accommodate a US-designed missile compartment and fire control system, with all the attendant and major problems of ship-fitting and integration. Manufacturing and introducing the vital nuclear reactors to the new submarines was perhaps the most difficult of the challenges that had to be overcome, for which vital US help was forthcoming in early 1964.[134] As the next chapter will show, however, the speed with which the Admiralty pushed ahead with the introduction of Polaris after the conclusion of the PSA worked against those who were starting to argue that

452 *The path to the Polaris sales agreement*

additional time and resources should be allowed to improve the capabilities of the new missile system – an issue of steadily increasing significance as Soviet ABM development entered an entirely new phase.

Notes

1. Le Fanu minute, 'Notes on Bahamas Meeting,' 22 December 1962, ADM 1/28839.
2. Ibid.
3. Ibid.
4. Scott minute for Thorneycroft, RHS/3/63, 1 January 1963, DEFE 13/619.
5. Carrington minute for Thorneycroft, 'Polaris Submarines,' 31 December 1962, DEFE 13/619 and in AVIA 65/1840.
6. See MM(63)1, Record of a meeting between the Minister of Defence, the First Lord of the Admiralty, and the Minister of Aviation, held on Thursday, 3rd January 1963, DEFE 13/619; Thorneycroft minute for Macmillan, 'Polaris,' 7 January 1963; John Boyd-Carpenter minute for Macmillan, 'Polaris,' 9 January 1963, PREM 11/4148; Maudling minute for Macmillan, 'Polaris,' 9 January 1963, T 225/2548.
7. Bligh, 'Note for the record,' 15 January 1963, PREM 11/4148.
8. D(63)1, 'Polaris Submarines: Size and Number,' memorandum by the Minister of Defence, 15 January 1963, CAB 131/28.
9. A. M. Fraser minute for Dodd and Peck, 'Polaris,' 17 January 1963, T 225/2548.
10. A. D. Peck minute for Caulcott, 'Polaris Submarines: D(63)1,' 17 January 1963, T 225/2548.
11. D(63)6, 'Polaris Submarines,' memorandum by the Chancellor of the Exchequer, 22 January 1963, CAB 131/28.
12. Trend minute for Macmillan, 'Polaris Submarines: Size and Number,' 22 January 1963, PREM 11/4148.
13. D(63)1st Meeting, items 1 and 2, 23 January 1963, CAB 131/28.
14. See Thorneycroft minute for Macmillan, 'Polaris,' 7 January 1963, and attached 'Mission on Nassau Agreement: Terms of Reference,' PREM 11/4148.
15. Le Fanu minute, 'Notes on Bahamas Meeting,' 22 December 1962, ADM 1/28839.
16. See 'Setting up the UK Project,' by Sir Hugh Mackenzie, in in J. E. Moore (ed.), *The Impact of Polaris: The Origins of Britain's Seaborne Nuclear Deterrent* (Huddersfield, 1999), 46–52; and Peter Nailor, *The Nassau Connection: The Organisation and Management of the British Polaris Project* (London, 1988), 9–14, 23–9.
17. See 'Technical Evaluation 1961,' by Sidney John Palmer, in Moore, *Impact of Polaris*, 42–5.
18. See, for example, Carrington minute for Thorneycroft, 31 January 1963, DEFE 7/1752.
19. See, for example, Carrington minute for Thorneycroft, 'Flow of Polaris information from US Navy to Royal Navy,' 9 January 1963, DEFE 13/734.
20. D. L. Haviland minute for Air Marshal Sir Edouard Grundy (Controller Guided Weapons and Electronics – GGWL – at the MoA), 9 January 1963, AVIA 65/1840; and also Le Fanu minute for First Sea Lord, 'Organisation for Polaris – Sitrep by Controller,' 16 January 1963, ADM 1/28839.
21. See 'Two Named for Polaris Posts,' *The Times*, 23 January 1963.
22. The proposal for the PIPSC had first come from the Admiralty, but the MoA was keen that its own prerogatives over the missile system were upheld in how the Committee functioned, see Haviland minute, 29 January 1963, and attached

The path to the Polaris sales agreement 453

draft proposals for Inter-Departmental Policy Steering Committee, AVIA 65/1840; Jarrett letter to Scott, 6 February 1963, and attached terms of reference, AVIA 65/1843; C. M. Rose minute, 'Polaris Interdepartmental Policy Steering Committee,' Z20/23, 14 February 1963; PIPSC/M(63)1, Minutes of the First Meeting, 13 February 1963, Z20/39, FO 371/173516.
23 See Nailor, *Nassau Connection*, 93–6.
24 Admiralty paper, 'Report on Polaris Fact Finding Mission to Washington – January 1963,' 15 January 1963, and Appendix III, 'Missiles,' AVIA 65/1866, and in ADM 1/28987.
25 D. F. Allen minute for US/Air B., 31 December 1962, AVIA 65/1852.
26 See MoA paper, 'Polaris: Re-entry Vehicle and Warhead,' n.d. (but c. early January 1963), AVIA 65/1840.
27 Admiralty paper, 'Report on Polaris Fact Finding Mission to Washington – January 1963,' 15 January 1963, and Appendix III, 'Missiles,' AVIA 65/1866, and in ADM 1/28987.
28 Bligh, 'Note for the record,' 15 January 1963, PREM 11/4148.
29 BNDSG/M(63)1, Minutes of a meeting held on 21 January 1963, DEFE 7/2145.
30 'Warheads for Polaris – AWRE Visit to Livermore 22nd-24th January 1963: Notes on Discussion with Mr Newley and Mr Challens at AWRE on 28th January 1963,' DAWD memorandum, XY/71/06, 1 February 1963, AVIA 65/1852.
31 See L. T. D. Williams minute for DGW, 'AWRE Visit to USA,' XY/71/06, 22 January 1963, AVIA 65/1852.
32 Frank Wood letter to James Mackay, 'Polaris Programme (Technical and Financial Agreement),' 25 January 1963, 2 DM 22/116/02 Part D, Treasury records.
33 ND(63)3, 'Review of Possible Nuclear Warhead Programmes, 1963–69,' note by Atomic Energy Authority, 1 February 1963; ND(63)1st Meeting, 7 February 1963, CAB 134/2240.
34 Admiralty paper, 'Report on Polaris Fact Finding Mission to Washington – January 1963,' 15 January 1963, and Appendix III, 'Missiles,' AVIA 65/1866, and in ADM 1/28987. See also, 'Meeting of 9th January 1963 between Polaris Fact Finding Team and USN Special Projects Office,' ADM 1/28987.
35 F. J. Doggett minute for Private Secretary/Minister, 'Polaris,' 14 January 1963, AVIA 65/1866.
36 See 'Prime Minister Justifies Polaris Choice,' *The Times*, 24 December 1962.
37 F. J. Doggett minute for Private Secretary/Minister, 'Polaris,' 14 January 1963, AVIA 65/1866.
38 Foreign Office telegram No 562 to Washington, 15 January 1963, containing draft message from Thorneycroft to McNamara, DEFE 13/734, and in PREM 11/4148.
39 Washington telegram No 154 to Foreign Office, Ormsby Gore personal to Thorneycroft, 15 January 1963, PREM 11/4148; and see also McNamara letter to Thorneycroft, 16 January 1963, DEFE 13/734.
40 Foreign Office telegram No 581 to Washington, T.26/63, from Prime Minister, 15 January 1963, PREM 11/4148.
41 Note of a meeting held on Wednesday, 16th January 1963, DEFE 13/734.
42 See 'Meeting with Mr Nitze in the Foreign Office, January 17th – 6.00pm,' AVIA 65/1866.
43 M(63)6, 'Nassau Agreement: Visit of American Team to London 17th/18th January 1963: Minutes of the opening conference held in the Ministry of Defence, Storey's Gate, on Thursday, 17th January 1963 at 10.30am,' 24 January 1963, DEFE 13/734.
44 See 'Meeting with Mr Nitze in the Foreign Office, January 17th – 6.00pm,' AVIA 65/1866.

454 *The path to the Polaris sales agreement*

45 Note of a Meeting with the Hon. Paul H. Nitze, held on Thursday, 17th January 1963, DEFE 13/734.
46 Thorneycroft minute for Macmillan, 'Polaris,' 22 January 1963; see also Thorneycroft letter to McNamara, 24 January 1963, where the payment of some contribution to R & D costs was conceded in principle; both in PREM 11/4148.
47 A. D. Peck minute for Mitchell, 'Minister of Defence's Minute of 22nd January,' 23 January 1963, 2 DM 22/116/02 Part D, Treasury records.
48 Boyd-Carpenter minute for Maudling, 24 January 1963, 2 DM 22/116/02 Part D, Treasury records.
49 See Macmillan, *At the End of the Day*, 365–6.
50 Foreign Office telegram No 1117 to Washington, T.51/63, from Prime Minister, 26 January 1963, PREM 11/4148.
51 See, for example, 'Anglo-US Dispute Over Polaris: Britain Asked to Pay for Development Costs,' *The Sunday Telegraph*, 27 January 1963; 'Anglo-US Disagreement on Polaris Costs,' *The Times*, 29 January 1963; and see Maudling minute for Macmillan, 28 January 1963, 2 DM 22/116/02 Part D, Treasury records.
52 Washington telegram No 297 to Foreign Office, personal for Prime Minister from Ormsby Gore, 26 January 1963, PREM 11/4148.
53 Macmillan diary entry for 28 January 1963, Macmillan MS dep. d.49, Bodleian Library. See also Zuckerman's reflections on the episode in his *Monkeys, Men and Missiles*, 267–8.
54 Washington telegram No 312 to Foreign Office, for Prime Minister from Ormsby Gore, T. 65/63, 28 January 1963, PREM 11/4148.
55 Amery minute for Thorneycroft, 15 January 1963, AVIA 65/1840, and in PREM 11/4148.
56 Thorneycroft minute for Amery, 28 January 1963, AVIA 65/1840, and in PREM 11/4148.
57 *Hansard*, HC, vol 670, cols 967–8, 30 January 1963.
58 *Hansard*, HC, vol 670, col 974, 30 January 1963.
59 *Hansard*, HC, vol 670, cols 983–8, 30 January 1963.
60 *Hansard*, HC, vol 670, col 1146, 31 January 1963.
61 *Hansard*, HC, vol 670, cols 1240–46, 31 January 1963.
62 See, for example, Evans diary entry, 3 February 1963, *Downing Street Diary*, 252.
63 For the assignment of Valiants to SACEUR, see Wynn, *RAF Nuclear Deterrent Forces*, 363–72.
64 See Thorneycroft minute for Macmillan, 'NATO Nuclear Force,' 23 January 1963, PREM 11/4148.
65 Memorandum for the record, 12 January 1963, *FRUS, 1961–1963, XIII*, 475–8.
66 Telegram from the Embassy in Germany to the Department of State, 14 January 1963, ibid, 478–82.
67 Remarks of President Kennedy to NSC Meeting, 22 January 1963, ibid, 485.
68 Summary record of NSC Executive Committee meeting, 12 February 1963, ibid, 494–8.
69 Thorneycroft letter to McNamara, 24 January 1963, PREM 11/4148.
70 See Macmillan minute for Home and Thorneycroft, M.33/63, 31 January 1963; Macmillan handwritten comments on Wright letter to Bligh, 'Nassau Agreement,' 15 February 1963; and de Zulueta minute for Wright, 18 February 1963, PREM 11/4149.
71 Thorneycroft minute for Home, 20 February 1963, DEFE 7/2163.
72 See Washington telegram No 606 to Foreign Office, 23 February 1963, PREM 11/4149; and Record of a Meeting held at Admiralty House, 25 February 1963, attached to D(63)9, 'Nassau Agreement,' Note by the Secretary, 26 February 1963, CAB 131/28.

73 See, for example, memorandum from Bundy for McNamara, 11 March 1963, *FRUS, 1961–1963, XIII*, 524.
74 See Washington telegram No 678 to Foreign Office, 3 March 1963, DEFE 7/2163; and W. G. Downey letter to Haviland, 4 March 1963, AVIA 65/1866.
75 See Washington telegram No 758 to Foreign Office, 12 March 1963, PREM 11/4149; Washington telegram No 823 to Foreign Office, 16 March 1963, DEFE 7/2163.
76 De Zulueta 'Note for the Record,' 13 March 1963; Foreign Office telegram No 2701 to Washington, 16 March 1963, PREM 11/4149.
77 See Kaplan, et al., *McNamara Ascendancy*, 405–6.
78 See Donette Murray, *Kennedy, Macmillan and Nuclear Weapons* (London, 1999), 124 and passim.
79 See E. J. W. Barnes minute, 'NATO Nuclear Force,' 16 May 1963, PREM 11/4161.
80 Macmillan minute for Home, M.96/63, 19 March 1963, PREM 11/4150.
81 Home minute for Macmillan, 'NATO Nuclear Force,' PM/63/38, 22 March 1963, PREM 11/4150.
82 Macmillan minute for Home, M.111/63, 23 March 1963, PREM 11/4150.
83 Heath minute for Macmillan, PM/LPS/63/48, 2 April 1963, PREM 11/4150.
84 Washington telegram No 1025 to Foreign Office (personal for Minister of Defence from Ambassador), 2 April 1963, PREM 11/4161.
85 Memorandum of conversation, 18 February 1963, *FRUS, 1961–1963, XIII*, 502–6.
86 See Kaplan, et al., *McNamara Ascendancy*, 407.
87 See DRP/P(63)15, British Navy Staff Washington Quarterly Technical Report No 33, p21, 1 January 1963, DEFE 10/454.
88 S. A. Hunwicks memorandum, 'Warheads and Re-entry bodies for the Polaris Missiles,' DS/65/01, 4 February 1963; Beards minute for Hunwicks, XY/71/06, 7 February 1963; Hunwicks letter to Challens, 12 February 1963, AVIA 65/1852.
89 Carrington minute for Thorneycroft, 'The Choice of Polaris Missile: A2 or A3,' 4 March 1963, DEFE 13/735.
90 Copy of a minute from Amery for Thorneycroft, 7 March 1963, DEFE 13/735.
91 Press minute for Zuckerman, 'The Choice of Polaris Missile: A2 or A3,' RP/121/63, 6 March 1963, DEFE 7/2164.
92 H. L. Lawrence-Wilson minute for Thorneycroft, 'Polaris Missile and Warhead,' 7 March 1963, DEFE 13/735.
93 Thorneycroft minute for Carrington, 'The Choice of Polaris Missile,' 8 March 1963, AVIA 65/1843.
94 W. G. Downey letter to Haviland, 4 March 1963, AVIA 65/1866.
95 See Robert Press minute, 'Polaris Warhead Possibilities,' 7 March 1963, DEFE 13/735.
96 'Memorandum for the record,' 12 March 1963, AVIA 65/1782.
97 Lighthill letter to Amery, 'Polaris,' 13 March 1963, AVIA 65/1843.
98 NIE 11–4–63, 'Soviet Military Capabilities and Policies, 1962–1967,' 22 March 1963, *FRUS, 1961–1963, VIII*, 472, 476. Also available on the CIA's website, at www.foia.cia.gov/document/0000267775.
99 See Freedman, *US Intelligence and the Soviet Strategic Threat*, 91–2.
100 CGWL minute for PS to Minister, 'Polaris,' GQ/1/04, 14 March 1963, and subsequent minutes, AVIA 65/1843.
101 E. M. St. G. Moss minute for Lawrence-Wilson, 'Polaris Sales Agreement,' 22 March 1963, DEFE 7/2163.
102 'Report of a Technical Mission to US on the Polaris Re-Entry System March

11th-22nd, 1963,' XY/411/09, 21 October 1963, Appendix V, 'Application of UK Warheads to Polaris,' AVIA 65/1843.

103 CGWL minute for PS to Minister, 'Polaris,' GQ/1/04, 19 March 1963, AVIA 65/1843.

104 See Defence Research Staff, Washington to MoA, Admiralty, AWRE Aldermaston, TECSU box 481, 21 March 1963, AVIA 65/1843.

105 'Report of a Technical Mission to U.S. on the Polaris Re-Entry System March 11th-22nd, 1963,' XY/411/09, 21 October 1963, Appendix VI, 'Penetration Aids for the Polaris Re-entry System,' AVIA 65/1843.

106 D. J. Lyons memorandum, 'Polaris System and Vulnerability of Re-entry System,' 8 April 1963, AVIA 65/1782, and in AVIA 65/1843.

107 J. E. Serby letter to Mackenzie, 'Polaris,' 1 April 1963, and attached report by L. T. D. Williams, 'Polaris,' XY/407/02, 1 April 1963, DEFE 13/736, and in DEFE 7/2163.

108 J. E. Serby letter to Mackenzie, 'Polaris,' 1 April 1963, and attached report by L. T. D. Williams, 'Polaris,' XY/407/02, 1 April 1963, DEFE 13/736, and in DEFE 7/2163.

109 For the report of the negotiating mission, see J. M. Mackay letter to Frank Wood, 21 March 1963, and attached draft report, 'The Polaris Sales Agreement,' DEFE 7/2163, also in FO 371/173518.

110 Carrington minute for Thorneycroft, 'The Polaris Sales Agreement,' 1 April 1963, DEFE 13/736.

111 See MM(63)6, 'Record of a Meeting between the Minister of Defence, the Lord Privy Seal, the Chief Secretary to the Treasury, the First Lord of the Admiralty, and the Minister of Aviation held on Wednesday, 3rd April 1963,' DEFE 13/736; Thorneycroft minute for Macmillan, 'Polaris Sales Agreement,' 3 April 1963, PREM 11/4150.

112 Cmnd 1995, *Polaris Sales Agreement*, April 1963.

113 Texts can be found in 'Agreed Minutes and Exchanges of Notes in Connection with the Polaris Sales Agreement,' Z20/78/63, CAB 21/6044, and attached to Rusk letter to Ormsby Gore, 6 April 1963, in DEFE 7/2164, and PREM 11/4150.

114 See Thorneycroft minute for Macmillan, 'Polaris Sales Agreement,' paragraph 6, 3 April 1963, DEFE 13/736.

115 One reason for delay was the need for choice of missile and RES to go through the elaborate interdepartmental bureaucracy; for a good example, see PIPSC/M(63)3, Minutes of the Third Meeting held on 24th April 1963, ADM 1/28974.

116 Carrington minute for Thorneycroft, 'The Choice of Polaris Missile,' 29 May 1963, DEFE 13/736.

117 John Boyd-Carpenter minute for Thorneycroft, 6 June 1963, PREM 11/4150.

118 Thorneycroft minute for Macmillan, 'The choice of Polaris missile,' 7 June 1963, PREM 11/4150; Hockaday minute for W. I. Tupman, 14 June 1963, DEFE 13/736.

119 'United States and United Kingdom Polaris Technical Arrangement: Modifications Nos. 1 and 2,' Section 16, pp. 32–7, n.d., DEFE 7/2165.

120 See Polaris Management Board: Minutes of Third Meeting at Ministry of Aviation, Wednesday, 29th April 1964, LSW 738/04 Part A, MoD records.

121 Dossor minute, 'Polaris Management Board,' ZH/9/01, 12 June 1963, file LSW 738/04 Part A, MoD records.

122 See Polaris Management Board: Minutes of Second Meeting at Ministry of Aviation, Friday, 26th July 1963; Dossor minute, 'Polaris – UK Re-entry System,' 13 August 1963, file LSW 738/04 Part A, MoD records.

123 See DRP/P(62)73, 'Military Requirements for Capability in Space Technology,'

note by Ministry of Aviation, 26 September 1962, DEFE 10/491; DRP/M(62)15, item 2, 10 October 1962, DEFE 10/417.
124 A. M. Bailey minute, 'Black Knight,' 22 April 1963, T 225/2124.
125 'Black Knight: Note of a Meeting on 22nd May, 1963'; F. R. Barratt minute for R. Anderson, 'Black Knight,' GP/43/01, 24 May 1963, T 225/2124.
126 See DRP/P(63)58, 'Defence Penetration and Ballistic Missile Defence: Studies using Black Knight,' note by the Ministry of Aviation, 24 July 1963, DEFE 10/455, and in DEFE 7/1390.
127 Ibid.
128 A. M. Bailey minute for Barratt, 'DRP/P(63)58: Black Knight,' 1 August 1963, T 225/2124.
129 DRP/M(63)14, item 4, 14 August 1963, DEFE 10/453.
130 Zuckerman minute for Thorneycroft, 'Defence Penetration and Ballistic Missile Defence Studies using Black Knight,' SZ/791/63, 13 September 1963, DEFE 7/1390.
131 R. A. Clifford letter to Mountfield, 10 January 1964, T 225/2124.
132 For comprehensive coverage of the Black Knight flights see C. N. Hill, *A Vertical Empire: History of the British Rocketry Programme,* 2nd edition (London, 2012), 263–88.
133 'Notes of a Meeting held in Room 101, Castlewood House, on Thursday, 29th August 1963, to discuss ABM Matters and Associated Activities,' AVIA 65/1772.
134 For excellent coverage of these issues, see Hennessy and Jinks, *The Silent Deep,* 227–33.

12 The origins of a Polaris improvement programme

HR 169 and the emergence of the Moscow ABM system

The ABM threat and re-entry system options for Polaris

As technical preparations for the introduction of Polaris missiles into Royal Navy service gathered pace during early 1963 it was apparent that the ability of Polaris to overcome the Soviet ABM environment that could be expected to appear in the 1970s was already an issue that would require attention. The unwillingness of the US authorities to share their ideas and information about improvements to the Polaris A3 missile to enable it to defeat such Soviet defences through the addition of penetration aids (improvements that the Americans were known to be investigating) was a handicap to British officials who were concerned to acquire the best possible re-entry system available. Although the bar on passage of US information on improved re-entry systems had been noted by officials and was known at ministerial level, this had not been a sufficient issue to impede the conclusion of the Polaris Sales Agreement in April 1963, such had been anxieties to press ahead with as much speed as possible. At the same time, the requirement for an improved Polaris re-entry system to cope with the future ABM environment was a feature of British thinking during much of this period when critical choices about the UK programme were being made.

British evaluations of the potential difficulties Polaris might face in reaching its targets were conducted against a background where little hard evidence was available on Russian ABM development or the precise nature of Soviet intentions in the field of ballistic missile defence, beyond the basic fact that an extensive research programme was clearly underway. In July 1963, for example, the JIC produced its latest estimate of Soviet air defence capabilities up to the end of 1967. It reported that large radars consistent with an ABM research and development programme were believed to be installed at the Sary Shagan test facility in Kazakhstan, but there was as yet no evidence of the deployment of a widespread network of ballistic missile early warning radars. A 'probable' ABM system was in the process of being deployed around Leningrad, and might be operational by the end of the year. But it was believed to have limited effectiveness, being designed for 'point defence' (i.e.

short range) use against MRBMs or IRBMs not equipped with decoys. This could, nevertheless, give it some potential against the earlier variants of Polaris, and the Soviet Union was considered likely to continue work on new ABM development.[1] At one meeting held in the summer of 1963 on the ABM issue involving the Prime Minister, several of his senior colleagues, and Sir William Penney, the latter had made the point that while the technical means for providing an ABM defence were far from insoluble, the financial implications of trying to deploy a system to defend large areas of land mass would be 'so formidable that it seemed to him doubtful that either power [The US or Soviet Union] could afford to make more than a token deployment.'[2]

Within the US intelligence community there were major doubts over the stage reached by the Soviet ABM weapons programme. The National Intelligence Estimate produced in July 1963 which examined in more detail Soviet atmosphere nuclear testing carried out in 1961–62 came to the conclusion that though there had been some 'highly sophisticated' ABM experiments involving missiles, the whole programme 'apparently lacked some of the characteristics which would give them detailed information on warhead kill mechanisms and on communications-blackout effects.' One example offered was that no warheads had been detonated near a re-entering missile nose cone.[3] During the sharp debates in Washington over ratification of the Limited Test Ban Treaty in August 1963 (when some sceptical senators had wanted to demonstrate Soviet superiority in the ABM field as a reason why the US should not forego atmosphere nuclear testing), McNamara had allowed his officials to give briefings which included low evaluations of the Leningrad system while he had expressed doubts – in the line with the conclusions of the recent NIE – that the Russians had ever carried out high altitude nuclear tests intended to determine the vulnerability of re-entry vehicles.[4]

Western observers had their first close view of what they assumed was a Soviet ABM in early November 1963 at the annual military parade held in Moscow to celebrate the anniversary of the Bolshevik Revolution, when the Russians displayed what they claimed was a rocket which was capable of being employed against 'any modern means of air-space attack.' Soviet commentators made clear it was this missile (known in an earlier incarnation as the V-1000) that Khrushchev had referred to when he had spoken the previous year of Soviet rockets being able to hit a 'fly in space.'[5] Soon given the NATO designation 'Griffon', US and British analysts were not overly concerned by this development as the missile's observable properties suggested it would have quite limited performance and would have very little utility against the kind of ballistic missiles that the West could field (maximum range was postulated at 100 nautical miles, and maximum altitude only 125,000 feet).[6] The ambiguities of Soviet plans were underlined by the fact that Griffon's appearance coincided with the suspension of all work at the three ABM complexes which had been under construction near Leningrad. In fact, the Griffon missile was soon withdrawn completely from service, leading to speculation the following year that all along its primary task may have been high altitude interception of aircraft, and that any primitive capability against ballistic missiles was probably regarded as a bonus.[7]

On the British side, the principal source of intelligence in Whitehall dealing with Soviet military, technical and scientific developments was still the Joint Intelligence Bureau, a counterpart to the JIC formed in 1947 and operating within the ambit of the MoD (the JIC itself had transferred to the Cabinet Office in 1957). By early 1964, the former head of atomic energy intelligence at the JIB, Archibald Potts, had risen to become its overall Director of Scientific and Technical Intelligence. In the absence of any direct evidence, all that Potts could tell senior MoA officials in one conversation held in February 1964 was that it had to be assumed that ABM engagements would be within the earth's atmosphere, while radars seen deployed to date were described as 'essentially simple.' Despite the dearth of information available, Potts offered the conservative view that 'it would be wise to assume [the Soviet ABM system] to be effective against the Polaris A3 system from mid-1968 onwards.'[8] In the annual JIC review of Soviet Bloc War Potential, a voluminous and distilled catalogue of Soviet military capabilities, issued in early 1964, there was the brief comment that the presumed ABM system being deployed around Leningrad might have some operational capability that same year. It was believed that the system was designed for terminal defence, and was unlikely to have any decoy discrimination capability. The deployment of additional ABM systems 'around other selected high priority targets' was to be expected in the future.[9]

Despite, and indeed, perhaps because of, the uncertainties of this intelligence picture, anxieties at UK technical establishments over the potential for Soviet ABM development to nullify the UK's Polaris threat were increasing during this period. During the summer of 1963 such concerns fed into the work of a new Re-entry System Study Group which was formed under the Chairmanship of F. H. East, the head of the Projects section at RAE's Weapons Department (a task which marked Fred East's first formal involvement with Polaris improvement, an association which was to continue for the next two decades). Though documentation on its work is sparse, the group had two main tasks: consideration of the existing Polaris RES and methods to improve its penetrability; and examination of the possibility of introducing an entirely new and improved RES. The group was made of up of six staff from RAE, including East, and five from AWRE, led by John Challens. Most of its background studies, on possible ballistic missile defences, and the types of decoy that could be used, were carried out by different sections of RAE's Weapons Department, but Challens also noted that AWRE were looking into the design of an improved re-entry body, housing the Polaris warhead, which aimed to reduce its vulnerability to X-rays, neutron radiation, and blast, though this was specifically in the context of threats met in the endo-atmospheric environment.[10]

The work of East's group undoubtedly helped to influence the UK approach to exchanges with the Americans on the Joint Re-entry System

Working Group that had been formed under the provisions of the PSA. At the second session of meetings of the JRSWG in mid-September 1963, British and US representatives convened in London, and at RAE and AWRE. During the talks, the US Chairman gave assurances that the Mark 2 Mod 0 RES, after its introduction with the initial operational deployment of Polaris A3 with the US Navy in 1964, would remain in service for another ten years. Agreement was reached that the UK would need to be kept informed of all modifications or changes planned to the RES, and that these would need to be jointly reviewed before being implemented to avoid incompatibilities with UK warhead work. With the group recognising that the UK was working to a tight timetable which involved producing a warhead/RES recommendation for final decisions by the start of 1964, it was still considered desirable to study other approaches and alternatives which were either simple additions to the RES, or direct developments from its design, and which RAE had felt could increase its effectiveness. The US Navy representatives on the JRSWG were particularly adamant that the UK should not simply settle for the existing Polaris RES, but look at alternatives, with the American Chairman of the meeting rejecting the British assumption that there was too little time to develop other options if the initial deployment target date in 1968 was to be met. Indeed, he went so far as to say if the UK went ahead with the existing system against US advice, the Americans would not be able to support the UK decision. A study of alternative options could be undertaken by Lockheed, the missile designer, in the next two months, he maintained, allowing a proper estimate of development costs and timescale to be made, and for the UK to decide whether the performance benefits of adopting an improved system would outweigh the possible drawbacks in terms of cost and delays. The whole US group shared this opinion, and it was also supported on technical grounds by the UK contingent.

The basic attraction of the proposal was that it might show that it was technically and financially possible to provide a UK RES for Polaris that would be viable for a longer period than the existing US system. But this kind of study, British officials reasoned, might also help to break down US restrictions on discussion of penetration aids. In view of the short timescale involved, the UK Chairman of the JRSWG, Sidney Hunwicks, the Director of Atomic Weapons Development at the Ministry of Aviation, was adamant that planning for the study should immediately commence. It was reported by the US and UK Chairmen that the Group's discussions had taken place in an atmosphere of 'extremely willing and full co-operation.' The one problem area remained the US block on discussions concerning 'plans of, or thoughts on, future development and on the philosophy and techniques of penetration aids,' and this meant that some work would be 'handicapped and restricted.' It was hoped, their joint report concluded, that relief from this restriction could be secured as soon as possible.[11]

When the PIPSC met on 30 September, MoA officials were keen to stress that they were committed to introducing the Polaris RES on time, but the American proposal for a study of alternatives was construed 'as a helpful indication of the way in which a degree of co-operation could be achieved in providing information about penetration aid characteristics.' There was a consensus view that the Americans, in making their suggestion, were trying to be genuinely helpful. Though willing to approve expenditure for the study, the Admiralty were cautious about its potential impact on the overall programme, and hoped that 'no new development programme would be contemplated.'[12] Having attended the meeting as one of the MoD representatives, Press reported to Zuckerman that the MoA position did not mean 'anyone was still hankering to plough a lonely furrow or that that the chances of being forced to do so would be necessarily increased by agreeing to the study.' Indeed, the proposal raised in the JRSWG was believed to be 'an American attempt to help [the] UK in discussing penetration aids even though their proposal had to be stated as unattractively as it was.' The PIPSC had concluded, Press noted, that, 'On the understanding that the study was no more than an attempt to reciprocate good will, buy our way into a useful discussion on penetration aids and that there was no commitment to pursue an independent UK course of re-entry system development, all of those who arrived at the meeting opposing the proposal were prepared to allow it on the basis put forward.'[13] Despite the considerable reservations about how the study might be used to build up pressure for a more extensive programme, and for the additional funding to accompany it, Zuckerman was also prepared to give the idea his approval. In early October he informed Peter Thorneycroft, the Minister of Defence, that, 'While I am by no means persuaded that we need penetration aids, I think it will be difficult to deny the proposition that we would be better off if we did contribute a small sum in order to get US assurance that, whatever proposal we may make, these additions to the warhead [sic] are compatible with the re-entry vehicle.'[14]

In retrospect it seems unlikely that at this stage there was any serious possibility that the basic American RES for Polaris A3 would have been rejected in favour of a British development such were the pressures from above to mount the first Polaris patrols in 1968. The thought of introducing anything other than the existing design of Polaris Mark 2 Mod 0 RES was largely anathema to the Navy. From the Admiralty's point of view the priority was to opt for the most straightforward development, and which was likely to meet its timetable for the Polaris programme as a whole (a timetable, it will be recalled, which was driven by concern over the prospect of a 'deterrent gap' developing after about 1965, but which some regarded as a spurious fear). The Expanded Staff Requirement for the Polaris RES, officially adopted by the Admiralty Board in early October 1963, had skirted over the issue of possible improvement options by simply stating that the RES's characteristics, 'apart from penetration aid capabilities', should be such that the performance of the British Polaris system was not inferior to its US equivalent. It also required the complete RES comply with acceptable safety standards, and that

16 operational standard versions be ready for loading into the first Polaris submarine by mid-May 1968.[15]

Opinion amongst MoA officials was more ambivalent. There was recognition that adoption of the existing US Mark 2 Mod 0 design would allow full use of readily available American information on reliability and safety, as well as overall system performance. But this had to be put beside anxieties of future penetration capability against possible Soviet ABM deployment. Referring to the work that Lockheed would be asked to do at British behest, one senior MoA official noted:

> If the study showed that it was technically and financially practicable to provide a UK re-entry system which would be significantly more effective than the one the Americans are planning to introduce in 1964 and if for one reason or another the Americans were not interested in the system we should clearly have to consider very carefully whether it would be sensible for us to 'go it alone'. I need hardly say that all our inclination would be against ploughing a lone furrow, particularly since we doubt whether a new re-entry system could be developed within our timescale.

Nevertheless, within the MoA it was resolved to go ahead with the study work in order to at least see what options might be available, while it had the added bonus of opening up a channel to the US authorities which might yield more information over their intentions in the field of penetration aids. At the most recent meeting of the JRSWG, it was reported, 'the Americans hinted very strongly that, if we adopted either of the two systems we had in mind, we would in their view be taking the wrong turning and we would be bringing into service in 1968 an out of date 1964 system.' By commissioning their own study of a penetration aid system, MoA officials hoped that further discussion with the Americans might even spark interest in development of a joint system. However, very little was known about US plans, and 'all we have to go on at present are our own suspicions of what lay behind the very strong American pressure that we should carry out a study of alternative re-entry systems.' The significance of the 'American hints and innuendos' was, it was felt, only to be understood once the proposed study had been completed.[16]

It fell to Fred East's Re-entry System Study Group, with the assistance of a US Naval officer from the Special Projects Office, to assemble a specification for a study by Lockheed Missiles and Space Company (at a cost of about $75,000) on RES alternatives, which would also include a development programme, and some cost estimates.[17] A visit was made by MoA and RAE representatives to LMSC's headquarters at Sunnyvale, California, in October 1963, where the specification was amplified. The variants looked at by Lockheed over the next two months included the current Mark 2 Mod 0 RES with the addition of some form of penetration aids; replacing one or two of the REBs in the RES with penetration aids, or a penetration aids vehicle; reorientation of the REBs, to reduce their radar echo; the design of an REB with improved re-entry characteristics (and a lower radar echo) and some decoys; and the replacement of one or two of such modified REBs with a penetration aids vehicle. A variety of different decoy types were also defined for the penetration aid system, with attention given to reducing the possibilities for radar discrimination between decoys and real warheads. Although the final Lockheed report looked at possible designs for decoys and jammers, there was, however, little consideration given to the problems of deployment of the former from the RES, not least due to the awkward design feature of Polaris that its rocket motor did not simply cut out after ejection of the three REBs carried on its second stage, but motored on past the dispensed REBs, creating complex gas dynamic effects on any objects caught in its wake. A Development Cost Plan attached to the report gave LMSC's dollar estimate of how much it would cost to research, develop and produce either the Mark 2 Mod 0 RES with penetration aids of various sorts, or the whole new REB system described in the report (with the former amounting to $71 million, and the latter $209 million). The figures assumed that penetration aid development could be carried out at LMSC on the basis of the Ministry of Aviation providing explicit decoy design information, so that US rules on the non-release to the UK of penetration aid technology could be upheld.[18]

A draft of the study was considered by the JRSWG at its third meeting, held at Sunnyvale in December 1963. After further discussion with Ministry of Aviation officials, a final version of the LMSC report was passed by the US Navy's Special Projects Office to the UK authorities in mid-January 1964. RAE considered that the modifications to the existing Mk 2 Mod 0 RES studied by LMSC 'appear technically sound and would offer some useful increase in penetration performance.'[19] While it had been examined as an option in the LMSC report, the chief conclusion of RAE at this stage was that pursuing a wholly new REB design (of a high beta, or ballistic parameter, type, and so with superior re-entry performance) would be impracticable, as there were likely to be technical, administrative and political delays in development of what would be, in effect, a completely new re-entry system.[20]

Some of the differences in emphasis detectable about how best to move forward over the Polaris RES issue reflected the bureaucratic divisions that were still apparent within the overall programme. By the autumn of 1963, the blurred lines of control and responsibility between the Admiralty and the MoA were beginning to become a cause of concern to senior officials, and suggestions began to be made about how the UK organisation might be streamlined so that it more closely resembled the US Navy's model of a single special projects office. The principal point of management friction concerned the relationship between the CPE, the formidable Admiral Mackenzie, and the Controller of Guided Weapons and Electronics at the MoA, Air Marshal Grundy. Mackenzie complained that the CGWL was not prepared to transfer many of the programme management functions carried out by his subordinate staff to Admiral Dossor, the Naval officer seconded to the MoA as Polaris Project Officer in January 1963. The problem for CGWL was that he retained responsibility for delivering many of the technical aspects to the programme, but if he simply transferred his staff and their functions to the MoA's Polaris Project Officer he would lose the control and direction he felt necessary to fulfil his allotted task. The MoA was simply not organised on a 'project' basis, though some officials in the MoD thought that it should be.[21] It was difficult to ignore the impression that Dossor was simply a vehicle through which Admiralty views could find expression (sometimes unwelcome) at the MoA; at one meeting with the CGWL, for example, Dossor stressed that there was not much margin in time for a decision to include penetration aids in the design of a Polaris RES, while extra missiles for proving a new RES would have to be ordered soon if one were to be developed.[22]

Bureaucratic tensions were also manifest in the belief within the MoA that not all Polaris matters to be discussed with the Americans should necessarily move through Navy-to-Navy channels under the new liaison arrangements established by the PSA. This was mainly because information regarding the nuclear warhead side of the programme was passed under the terms of the 1958 MDA between the weapons laboratories in the United States and AWRE, and this kind of information was crucial to the design and development of the re-entry system for Polaris, rather than the rest of the missile. Whether questions connected with the RES should be processed through the machinery of the 1958 Agreement (and hence lie within the MoA's jurisdiction), or through Navy-to-Navy channels and the designated Polaris Project Officers, was to become a persistent source of tensions on the British side of the programme and to show itself again in 1969–72 as the UK's own Polaris improvement project was launched. In fact, by early 1964 the Admiralty had had to accept the uncomfortable point that some American officials were coming to interpret the PSA in such a narrow manner that almost all questions of the development, purchase of equipment, or exchange of information connected with the RES had to take place under the auspices of the 1958 Agreement.[23]

During this same period it was being argued by the Polaris Project Officer at the MoA that – for administrative convenience reasons alone – it made sense to transfer to the Admiralty responsibility for procuring the missiles themselves from the US authorities. As for the Polaris organisation at the MoA, in February 1964 Admiral Dossor noted that it had been 'set up when nobody had a clear idea about the job to be done. It was an "ad hoc" means of achieving integration of the Admiralty and MoA Polaris activities whilst safeguarding MoA's established position regarding "missile systems".' Though the MoA had 'gone through the motions', as Dossor put it, of setting up a 'project' sub-section linked to the Admiralty's CPE organisation, it 'presently balks at making it effective'. The Admiralty seemed to believe that as the missiles were to be bought direct from US production lines, the MoA, with its jurisdiction over the major areas of UK guided weapons expertise at the research establishments, had no real role, but Dossor thought that

> if Polaris is to be a meaningful independent deterrent in which we invest some £400M, it is essential to have full technical knowledge of the system, its capabilities and limitations, how to use and maintain it and knowledge of hazards special to our circumstances. Much of the expertise for this is available only within the MoA orbit. The MoA cannot abrogate its basic responsibilities, sulking in a corner because 'it was not invented here'.

All this pointed to the need for the MoA to take a more active interest in the weapons system as an integrated whole.[24]

While Admiral Dossor lobbied for an improvement to his precarious position and responsibilities within the MoA, other factions were far from happy that this naval presence at the Ministry was tolerated at all. It seemed in fact, that by early 1964, the preservation of Dossor's position was largely due to the need to maintain goodwill with the Admiralty. 'The fact of the matter,' Grundy, the CGWL, concluded, 'is that the Admiralty and ourselves, having conformed to the American requirements for production and procurement, are landed with a bastard organisation and we might as well put up with our share of it.'[25]

Finally, in February 1964 a new MoA Polaris management scheme was promulgated by Grundy which made Admiral Dossor responsible to him for delivery of the whole of the MoA's contribution to the Polaris programme, and to be the focal point of all liaison with the CPE at the Admiralty; the Director of Atomic Weapons Development (Hunwicks), and the Director of Atomic Weapons Production (S. Chard), would therefore be responsible (and report) to Dossor for the development and supply of the RES/warhead, referring to the Director General Atomic Weapons and Space Activities (Leslie Williams) for technical advice.[26] There were still, nevertheless, many tensions to be overcome, and the Admiralty remained loath to share any sense of responsibility for delivery of the Polaris programme.

The choice of a UK Polaris warhead and re-entry system

An additional factor which pointed toward the Admiralty's preference for a simplified choice of the existing re-entry system for Polaris was the problem faced by this time over the selection of an appropriate warhead design. Initial expectations had been that a direct (or so-called 'Chinese') copy could be made of the US Mark 58 Mod 1 warhead which was intended for the A3 version of Polaris and details of which had been passed to the British authorities in January 1963. However, after careful evaluation, AWRE's Warhead

Safety Coordinating Committee issued a report on the Mark 58 in December 1963 which reached the categorical conclusion that the design did not reach UK safety standards, an appraisal which was confirmed by a separate investigation undertaken by the Ordnance Board soon after. At the start of January 1964, Dr Nyman Levin, the Director of AWRE, informed the MoA of this discouraging news from the WSCC.[27]

With the production of a direct copy of the Mark 58 now ruled out, by early 1964 it was appreciated that a new British-designed primary would probably have to be used in UK Polaris, involving a new round of work at AWRE and perhaps an underground test of the resulting design.[28] There were therefore major concerns within the MoA and Admiralty, most notably from the CPE, Admiral Mackenzie, over the implications for the Polaris timetable of such possible delays, especially as ministers had been told that final decisions over choice of RES and warhead would be taken in early 1964.

Design decisions over the Polaris primary were made in a context where UK knowledge of the vulnerability of warheads and re-entry systems to the effects of ABM explosions was relatively limited (and was an inevitable result of the lack of atmosphere nuclear testing). JOWOG 19, the working group established under the 1958 Agreement to examine vulnerability of warheads and re-entry systems, had held only two meetings, both in 1962. Only kept going by intermittent personal contact between its members, at AWRE there was concern by 1964 that JOWOG 19 had become 'near moribund': it was described as 'staggering along purposelessly and ineffectually', with the UK having little to contribute. Moreover, it was reported that there was some American opposition to its continuance, as there were anxieties that it might become a channel where information on re-entry vehicles in service or development might be communicated. In fact some at AWRE hoped that a British devised modification to the Polaris RES, along the lines suggested by Lockheed, might become a new focus for reviving JOWOG 19 by allowing it to explore warhead hardening techniques.[29]

The UK view tended to be that blast effects, alone or in conjunction with neutron-induced heating of nuclear cores, were the most important damage mechanisms that required further study. But the value of the UK contribution to the exchange, one report from early 1964 noted, was 'much reduced by the absence of any real UK interest in vulnerability.' It was for this reason that 'the most important single topic – the extent to which the nuclear package should be hardened – cannot be effectively discussed by the JOWOG.' The basic problem was that in the US, warhead design was increasingly being integrated with the rest of a missile's re-entry system, as well as being determined by the character of possible defensive ABM systems. Without UK research and development work on either missiles or their re-entry systems, it was difficult to find a focus for UK work in the area.[30]

The final choice of Polaris warhead and RES would have to be made by some of the new MoD machinery for research and development that was introduced as a result of the July 1963 White Paper reforms to the central organisation of defence (detailed in the next chapter).[31] Centralisation of the MoD during 1964 was accompanied by efforts to rationalise the previously disjointed allocation of defence R & D resources, where in Zuckerman's words 'the Services had clearly been operating as though the country could afford almost anything.'[32] The DRPC which had operated since 1947 (in ineffectual and dysfunctional fashion some would argue) was to be abolished. Under the new dispensation, Zuckerman, as Chief Scientific Adviser, would preside over two new bodies, the Defence Research Committee, and the Weapons Development Committee. Reporting to the Secretary of State, the latter was established to resolve some of the inter-service rivalries that had formerly predominated when it came to competing bids for resources to fund equipment programmes, and was supposed to prioritise between different projects as they related to operational requirements.[33] These were to be handed down to the WDC by an Operational Requirements Committee (ORC), which was formed in early 1965, and made responsible to the COS.

By the spring of 1964 Zuckerman also sat at the top of a new MoD Central Scientific Staff, created under the White Paper reforms when the separate service scientific organisations were amalgamated. Beneath him in the new hierarchy were two deputies: Sir William Cook as Chief Adviser (Projects and Research), and Alan Cottrell as Chief Adviser (Studies).[34] Until his retirement from the MoD in 1970, it was Cook who was to exert a powerful influence over how nuclear matters were dealt with at the MoD. As we saw in an earlier chapter, Cook's reputation had been established when deputy director at AWRE, operating in close tandem with Penney, during Aldermaston's 'golden years' in the mid-1950s. He had played an important role in negotiating the MDA with the United States in 1958, giving him a firm understanding of, and commitment to a close Anglo-American nuclear relationship, and at the end of that year had transferred to the Atomic Energy Authority, where he concentrated on the civil nuclear power programme. Cook had collaborated with Zuckerman during 1961 when serving on the BNDSG's Technical Subcommittee, where both men had shown a strong preference for submarine-launched Polaris as the best option for a successor deterrent system, and in 1964 he was brought over to the MoD from the AEA 'as a strong man with experience of large-scale work'.[35] His relations with Zuckerman after arriving at the MoD were not, however, to prove easy. Where Zuckerman began to show an ever-increasing scepticism regarding the future needs of the UK nuclear weapons programme, and the requirements of AWRE, Cook was a firm supporter of Britain retaining the high levels of nuclear expertise and knowledge that Aldermaston's scientists had accumulated by the end of the 1950s.

Nonetheless, such clashes of personality and policy still lay ahead: the most immediate task of the new defence R & D machinery was to make crucial decisions bearing on the future of the Polaris programme. In mid-March

The origins of a Polaris improvement programme 469

1964, an important joint paper from the Ministry of Aviation and the Admiralty dealing with the choice of warhead and RES for Polaris was put forward to the Nuclear Sub-Committee of the MoD's new Weapons Development Committee.[36] This report confirmed that since the design of the primary for the US Mark 58 Mod 1 warhead did not meet British safety standards, the recommended course was to substitute a British primary of the type already under development for use in the new high-yield lay down weapon, WE-177B. Since costs for incorporating a UK primary, or going down the route of modifying the US Mark 58 Mod 1 primary to UK safety standards, were very similar, and the former could be also done within the timescale required with less uncertainty attached, the strong preference for a British primary was not surprising.

Regarding the selection of an RES, the report noted that it was understood the Americans had under development a modified system, the Mark 2 Mod 1, which included penetration aids. While there was little detailed knowledge of the modified US system, British officials had been reassured that even with additional penetration aids there would be no issue of compatibility between this new RES and the existing A3 missile or a UK warhead. It was therefore seen as entirely possible that the Americans would have a new RES in service before the first UK Polaris missiles were even delivered to the Admiralty, leaving the Royal Navy operating a different version of the A3 system than their US counterparts after 1968. Having indicated the dilemma faced, the report provided an opinion on the penetration capability of the Polaris by including a section on Soviet ABM development based on information from the Director of Scientific Intelligence at the JIB, Archie Potts. This noted that the Russians had been very active with ABM experiments over several years, and though acknowledging there was no evidence available on the performance of Russian defences, quoted his advice that 'it would be wise to assume that the defence will have some effectiveness against the Polaris A3 system without decoys at our initial operational date, i.e. mid 1968.' Comparing performance against estimates of the new American Nike-X ABM system, using a short-range Sprint missile, moreover, indicated that a Russian system could have a high probability of successful engagement of a single re-entering REB. As it was 'an essential requirement' for UK Polaris to be a 'credible independent National deterrent' it was considered 'important that each of the limited number of warheads available is given the best chance of reaching its target.' A penetration aid system was the logical countermeasure, and a study would be required to see how one could be made compatible with the US Mark 2 Mod 0 Polaris RES, and what effects on missile range and warhead yield could be anticipated.

The MoA/Admiralty report brought up again the basic problem that the Americans were putting a great deal of effort into penetration aid systems, but had so far refused to share their findings, excluding this as an area of exchange under the PSA. Left with little option but to examine the issue themselves, UK studies had come up with several different possible modifications to the present US RES, including adding a penetration aid package of passive decoys and active jammers, replacing one or two of the REBs on the RES with a larger range of penetration aids, or changing the configuration of the REBs themselves so that they were less susceptible to radar tracking and interception. As we have seen, it was these UK proposals that were examined by Lockheed at the end of 1963, and the report now found that there was 'no reason to doubt that any of the variants could be developed to provide a weapon system including penetration aids to an acceptable standard of safety and reliability.' Straightforward additions of penetration aid packages (with no re-entering decoys) to the standard RES was seen as a comparatively easy process, and if a firm go ahead was given by about mid-1964 it was estimated that this type of modified system could meet the planned in-service date for UK Polaris of 1968, while there would in any case be little difficulty in retrofitting the modification. Based on American advice, a rough estimate of the costs of a penetration aids package scheme was put at £25–35 million, with most engineering development done in the US (though with RAE supervision). Redesigning the REBs, and incorporating re-entering decoys, would entail more expenditure (perhaps £60–80 million of development costs), and reduce the maximum range of the three warhead A3 system to about 2,000 nautical miles. Adoption of these latter, more technically advanced systems was not, however, recommended. Not only would they be 'very costly', but they would make the RES 'unique to the UK'; it was 'doubtful if the proper supporting effort could be found in the UK Establishments'; and they were unlikely to be produced on time for the initial introduction of Polaris in 1968.

As the UK had not done extensive work in the penetration aid field since the cancellation of Blue Steak in 1960, it was thought necessary to undertake a study of the simpler forms of modification, involving passive non re-entering decoys and active jammers, in either a small package added to the Mark 2 Mod 0 RES with its three REBs, or by replacing one or two REBs with a more extensive suite of the same type of penetration aids. A project study of this kind by RAE would enable a better estimate to be made of cost, effort and timescale; most of the work could be done inter-murally, at the Establishment itself, and would involve only between six and nine established members of the scientific civil service, while extra-mural expenditure in industry would be at a maximum cost of £50,000. Carried out 'jointly with the Naval Staff' (as they would have to have a role in determining the performance parameters of a modified system), such a study should be accorded a 'very high priority with the aim of completion by June 1964,' with the obvious aim of allowing decisions to be made about full-scale development so the system might be available as early as 1968. A further consideration, it is clear, was that AWRE and MoA officials believed that only once the British had engaged in some of their own work in this area would they be in a position to broach the idea of cooperation with the Americans and begin to surmount the restrictions of the PSA's stipulation over penetration aids.[37]

In fact, when it had a chance to consider the issue, the Aviation Council at the MoA had been quite bullish over the implications of having to proceed with a penetration aids study largely in the absence of US assistance. American reluctance to be more forthcoming was attributed to their genuine concerns over security, rather than to any political issues, but it was felt 'this was a field in which we were equally as competent as the Americans and there was advantage in our considering different systems from theirs.' The Minister of Aviation, for his part, felt that a penetration aid study as proposed 'seemed eminently worthwhile. If nothing else, it would show what validity could be attached to the existing deterrent system over the next few years.' There might, it was felt, be resistance from the Ministry of Defence, who were prone to underrating the effectiveness of Soviet ABM defences, but if necessary the issue would have to be taken up directly with Thorneycroft.[38]

The conclusion of the joint paper from the MoA and Admiralty was that given the essential need to meet an in-service date of May 1968 for the first 16 Polaris missiles, the US Mark 2 Mod 0 RES would have to be used, with initial orders for components made not later than May 1964. The RES would also have to be fitted with a modified version of the US Mark 58 warhead which used a British-designed primary. But because of possible developments in Soviet ABM defence it was obviously desirable to increase the penetration capability of the RES, and to that end a joint RAE/Naval Staff pilot study should seek to determine the best penetration aid system compatible with the RES, and a suitable Naval Staff requirement would have to be formulated to define the required system performance.[39] Within the MoA the pilot study was indeed felt to be of 'crucial importance' as it could help to assess the effectiveness of the entire Polaris system, where so much money was already being invested.[40] It was also seen as part of a logical process: only once this preliminary study had been completed could a formal staff requirement be formulated, and then a full-scale 'project definition study' be commissioned for an improvement to the existing RES.

The semantics of different stages of development were considered important by some MoA officials, and reflected the bitter experience of many of the large-scale and expensive aircraft and guided missile projects that were felt to have been mistakenly commissioned during the 1950s. There was unease within some quarters that the term 'project study' was used in the papers to go before the WDC's Nuclear Sub-Committee, when this was not the nature of the short exercise being proposed at RAE, particularly as no service requirement had yet been formulated to underpin it. As the study would precede the production of a Naval Staff Requirement, one MoA official preferred to conceive of it as more in the way of an 'Operational Research Study' rather than a 'Project Study' per se. Pre-empting any accusations of being over-pedantic, the official felt compelled to explain that

> The need for these procedures arose from the great waste of public money which occurred – particularly in the area for which the then

Ministry of Supply was responsible – during the 1950s. One of the main reasons for this waste of money was that projects were not sufficiently carefully thought out, or their consequences sufficiently carefully examined, before we became committed to their support. The new procedures are therefore designed to ensure that, if nothing else, the operational requirement is very clearly stated, and the resources needed to meet it carefully examined before public faith is committed. Checkpoints have deliberately been inserted along the route – notably at the beginning of the Project Study and, subsequently, prior to the grant of authority for full development.

Such apparently cumbersome processes inevitably meant that a rapid start to the development process could not be made, but this was 'accepted as part of the price that has to be paid if we are to avoid the mistakes of the past.' The specific procedures which had to be followed in this case, according to the official, were that:

> a policy decision to embark upon a major project involving substantial sums of public money should not be taken until after a detailed plan of development has been drawn up, and the resources needed to carry it through carefully assessed; and that a detailed development plan and realistic estimate of the resources needed to carry it through cannot be prepared until there is a clear statement of what the Service Department wants.[41]

In the case of the study under consideration, the Naval Staff were still coming to terms with the damage potential which would be offered by the Polaris force (indeed, the Cabinet had only just finished the deliberations which resulted in the switch to planning for a five boat force from the four initially conceived in early 1963). One of the fundamental points that had to be resolved was for the Navy to define the penetration capability of Polaris when operating in a national, independent role, but this in turn depended on the ambiguous and shifting relationship between an evolving set of criteria for deterrence (perhaps derived from some of the work of the BNDSG in 1961–62), and the basic assumptions that went into the national retaliatory nuclear strike plan. There is no evidence to suggest, however, that this basic issue was confronted during 1964 when ideas for a UK penetration aid study for Polaris were being mooted.

With Zuckerman in the chair, the Nuclear Sub-Committee of the WDC met on 26 March 1964 to consider the proposals for the RES for the UK Polaris A3 system, as well as to examine the choice of warhead.[42] Conforming to Zuckerman's brief, the Sub-Committee agreed to recommend the adoption of the Mark 2 Mod 0 RES, with a version of the US Mark 58 warhead which incorporated a British-designed primary. Support was also exhibited for RAE to carry out an intra-mural study on fitting penetration

The origins of a Polaris improvement programme 473

aids to the RES, with a financial limit of £50,000 on extra-mural expenditure for associated work in private industry. However, eventual costs of a full penetration aid programme, if they were allowed to go ahead, might be in the order of £25–35 million, and Zuckerman was advised that it was

> difficult to see how additional expenditure of this magnitude can be accommodated during the next five years and it is noteworthy that when Ministers recently agreed to the fifth Polaris submarine they insisted on compensating reductions elsewhere in the defence budget. We could hardly make further cuts of this size within a limited period without deleting some other major projects ... The Committee does not need at this stage to tackle the difficult question of the worthwhileness [sic] of spending large sums of money on possibly doubtful increases in the credibility of the UK's independent deterrent.

There seemed no harm, however, in commissioning the preliminary study, not least as if it were to become public knowledge that US penetration aid technology did not form part of the UK Polaris programme, it could be maintained that steps were, in fact, being taken to maintain the credibility of the deterrent. Therefore, and despite the 'gravest doubts' which were raised by any expenditure in the field, it was considered there would be merit in carrying out the study.[43]

A submission soon followed for Thorneycroft, the Secretary of State for Defence (as he was now titled following the creation of a unified MoD at the start of April 1964), and on 17 April a Polaris penetration aid study was duly authorised under the terms recommended by the WDC's Nuclear Sub-Committee. Thorneycroft had also stipulated that an attempt should be made to persuade the US Government to lift the restrictions that obtained to releasing information to the UK in this field. However, within the Ministry of Aviation, the consensus was against going back to the Americans because of the 'very strong line' they had taken over penetration aids when the PSA had been negotiated. Instead, it was felt it was preferable to complete a UK study of the problem, and then to re-open the question of an approach to the Americans. It would then be possible to discuss proper design proposals with them, and so show the Americans that there was active British work being undertaken which might be of interest. It was felt by officials that the issue was 'entirely a matter of tactics and timing' and moving forward with the penetration aid study before approaching the Americans did not conflict with the Defence Secretary's wishes.[44]

At the beginning of April 1964 Thorneycroft also took a decision approving selection of the US Mark 2 Mod 0 RES with the Mark 58 warhead, adapted by the inclusion of a British primary.[45] By the end of the month information about the choice of warhead had begun to leak into the public domain, and – even though there was little basis for such concerns – speculation was current over potential issues with the compatibility of a UK warhead with the rest of the Polaris system. The immediate cause was a short report in the respected magazine *Flight International* of a reporter's visit to the headquarters of Lockheed where senior members of the Polaris team volunteered the view that fitting British warheads to the missile might well entail some considerable re-engineering of the system and technical difficulties. The director of the Polaris team, A. W. Stevenson, was quoted as saying that British officials were, however, participating closely at every stage of the programme with full exchange of information: 'there are no holds barred, in fact the only way you can tell the difference between their people and ours is the way they pronounce missile.' Everyone at Lockheed, it was reported, believed that the election of a Labour Government would lead to the cancellation of the Polaris order.[46]

At the end of April, awkward questions began to be asked in the House about the topic of the UK warhead for Polaris, including by the Labour defence spokesman, Denis Healey.[47] Background briefing provided by the Ministry of Aviation for the Prime Minister, now Sir Alec Douglas-Home (following Macmillan's departure from Downing Street through ill-health in October 1963), confirmed that arrangements were in hand to ensure that the employment of a British warhead would entail no modifications to the rest of the missile. But it went on to add that 'if the UK were to decide to develop a "penetration capability" for the British missile in order to improve its effectiveness against enemy defences – a question now under study – there might well be some divergence from the American Polaris A3 system if US/UK collaboration in this connection were to be ruled out, as it is under the existing Nassau and Polaris Sales Agreements. However, it is possible that the modification necessary would be quite small and easily accomplished either before or after delivery.'[48]

Labour continued to be ready to capitalise from some of the uncertainty still present. During a party political broadcast aired on 4 May 1964, Healey attacked the Government's record of 'waste' in defence spending, noting also that there was to be heavy investment in Polaris despite questions over whether it would be possible to marry with a British warhead.[49] Douglas-Home tried to clear up some of the confusion over the suitability of a British warhead in the House of Commons a few days later, but this only elicited a critical leader from *The Times* which speculated over the degree of technical skill held by the UK which would allow it to produce a large yield warhead without the benefit of atmosphere testing.[50]

In an attempt to reassure the Prime Minister that the technical choices about warhead and re-entry system were in hand, Zuckerman sent a revealing minute to Downing Street which tackled the 'insinuation' of *The Times* piece, which had suggested that the UK's Polaris warhead 'may not be sufficiently sophisticated.' Purchase of US warheads for Polaris, as raised by some in Parliament as an option, was simply not possible under existing US laws, meaning that Britain was compelled to produce its own warhead. In order to conform to British practices and capabilities a British-designed primary would have to employed, together with a direct copy of a US secondary. But the British-made primary would itself be based on US test experience and knowledge and so there was high confidence in its performance. The issue of that warhead's 'sophistication', Zuckerman continued, was 'somewhat ambiguous.' The UK Polaris warhead could

> well be unsophisticated in comparison with the American in so far as the latter will be furnished with so-called 'penetration aids', designed to off-set the advantages which the Russians might gain from the deployment of an anti-ballistic missile defensive system. We have no plans, as yet, for penetration aids because it is difficult to make out a plain case that such aids are necessary. For example, we do not know whether the Russians are, in fact, deploying an anti-ballistic missile system; what we do know is that whatever system they might deploy would not be able to defend more than a few targets, if that. Furthermore, since we know nothing of the nature of whatever anti-ballistic missile system the Russians might deploy, it is difficult – if not impossible – to design penetration aids for the warheads which would neutralise the Russian defences.

Zuckerman could nevertheless confirm that arrangements had been made to ensure that the British warhead would be entirely compatible with the Polaris A3 missile.[51]

The HR 169 study, May–November 1964: assumptions and conclusions

On 4 May 1964 an important milestone was reached when James Harrison at the Ministry of Aviation wrote to inform all interested officials in the MoA and at RAE that a Polaris penetration aid study had received ministerial approval and was being given the project reference number HR 169; Fred East held his first meeting to launch the study at RAE that same day.[52] The stated purpose of the study was to examine the penetration capability of the current Polaris RES, and methods by which the probability of its warheads reaching their targets could be improved. The study was to be predicated entirely on the use of Polaris in what was called its 'National Independent Second Strike Role', where the enemy was the Soviet Union.[53]

Zuckerman's reference to the dearth of reliable information about Soviet ABM development in the minute quoted above reflected the prevailing view of the intelligence community and was the environment within which studies of penetration aid systems for Polaris would necessarily have to be conducted. Instead of an accurate picture of Soviet capabilities, as through much of this period, defence scientists and weapons engineers had to postulate different levels and types of Soviet ABM development in order to give some context and performance criteria for their work.

Indeed, RAE's evaluation of Soviet ABM defensive capabilities was largely based on extrapolating from what was known of US ABM plans and anticipated effectiveness. The advice received by RAE from the joint intelligence staff was that there was 'not much to choose between the technical capability of East and West.' In other words, advances in US ABM technology and capability had to be seen as a yardstick against which its Soviet equivalent should be measured.[54] On this basis, and the reported performance of the new US radar systems being developed to direct a short-range Sprint missile to accompany the latest Nike-X system, a figure of 70 per cent for lethality of each ABM directed against an incoming missile was used when estimating the effectiveness of a projected Soviet ABM defence. The ABM threat was postulated in terms of an endo-atmosphere terminal defence interceptor, carrying a 10 kiloton warhead.[55] The assumption that informed the analysis contained in the study was that the principal arena for ABM engagement would be high up, or just on the edge of, the earth's atmosphere. One of the main reasons for this was the belief that any defender would want to take full advantage of the effects of 'atmosphere sorting', where re-entering objects, whether REBs, decoys, chaff, or missile debris, would behave differently (or in some cases, such as chaff, burn up completely) as they moved into the final stages of their flight, allowing effective radar discrimination to be obtained and high-speed interceptors launched with greater confidence of success. As the final study report noted, at this stage the only observed Soviet missile which it was assumed could act as an ABM interceptor – though with limited capability – was the Griffon seen displayed in Moscow in November 1963, but this was credited with operating only up to 80,000 feet.[56]

The HR 169 study was carried out under the direction of East's Projects Group within RAE's Weapons Department. Many personnel at RAE were involved, including, as East put it, 'aerodynamicists, ballisticians, re-entry physics experts, radio and radar people including the ECM [Electronic Counter-measures] group, as well as straightforward weapons engineers.' East also reached out for assistance to the Royal Radar Establishment (RRE) at Malvern, and kept in touch with the JIB organisation, for its advice on scientific and technical intelligence.[57] Help also came from AWRE, the Navy Department (as the Admiralty was now known in the newly unified MoD organisation), and the atomic warheads directorate at the Ministry of Aviation, but East had been quite determined at an early stage to establish RAE's overall responsibility for the study, and to fend off any Navy Department attempt to take over the work.[58] The extra-mural support which the study demanded for overall systems work was provided by Elliot Automation Space and Advanced Military Systems (EASAMS) on a contract worth £40,000. The services of Plessey UK were used for 'experimental fabrication and measurement of electronic techniques and decoy design', with a contract for £10,000, while Spembly Company helped with radar echo measurement work, and the General Electric Company offered further support. All these companies were chosen as they had relevant experience and had worked with RAE before.[59]

Initial work was to be carried out on a very tight schedule, officially only lasting from 1 May to 31 July 1964. By September, however, it had been appreciated that RAE had not had sufficient time to cover all aspects of the wide range of issues involved. Within the Ministry of Aviation it was considered that contract extensions for further work were essential, and two of the outside companies employed (Plesseys and EASAMS) should be retained until the end of March 1965. EASAMS would continue to assist RAE with studies of heat transfer, fabrics, flexible ablatives, and chaff, while Plesseys focussed on active jammers. There would be no need to authorise extra spending, however, as the original study had cost less than anticipated, and the surplus could be used to fund the £15,000 cost of the contract extensions for the two companies. The initial results of the HR 169 study, produced in multi-volume form, were issued as RAE Technical Report No 64067 in November 1964.

At an early stage, guidance on what the Polaris system was expected to achieve was sought by RAE from the Navy. The Navy Department's own Polaris Committee duly approved a paper in June 1964 which stipulated that Polaris range could be assumed as between 1,000–2,000 nautical miles, and that 32 missiles should constantly be deployed on station (of which 22 would attain 'on target separation of re-entry bodies'). On this basis, the Navy wanted the study to show the cost in effort and money for a system capable of inflicting major levels of destruction on 7–10 Russian cities, including Moscow and Leningrad, as well as what would be involved with improving this capability, or slightly relaxing it.[60] The damage criterion was described – erroneously – by a later Ministry of Aviation paper, which offered a retrospective appraisal of the HR 169 study, as coming 'from an expressed JIC view of what constitutes a deterrent.' The confusion that tended to obtain in this area was underlined by the comment immediately after that the damage levels were derived from RAF estimates of what would produce 'breakdown' in a city, while the figure of 7–10 cities to be targeted was described as 'an arbitrary number and represents a compromise between the three [actually five] postulated by the JIC and the 20 thought possible with 32 missiles available.' Then again, the view was given that the figures were merely 'expressions of opinion', and it might be that the Navy Department had set their damage levels too high, while in practice RAE had actually looked at a range of different degrees of damage in their studies of penetration performance.[61]

The HR 169 study report gave a picture of a vigorous and wide-ranging Soviet programme of ABM development. The report's authors tended to see the task of basic missile defence against an unimproved, decoy-free force of attacking missiles as relatively straightforward; one of its appendices noted that, 'Against free-falling non-manoeuvring re-entering ballistic missile warheads, American trials and British knowledge of warhead vulnerability indicate that there is no serious problem in obtaining, with a nuclear head, the miss-distance required to give a high probability of a kill.'[62] The Russians, moreover, clearly had a large-scale R & D programme in the ABM field, and had conducted experiments with incoming warheads, while it was suggested that the Soviet programme was 'running at least in parallel with that of the USA.' The reports that a possible ABM system had begun deployment around Leningrad in 1962 could indicate, it was speculated, either that the Russians were ahead of the Americans, or that they were prepared to proceed with deployment of a system which had known limitations.[63]

Whatever the case, the study believed that only two simple forecasts could be made: either that first generation ABM systems were in the process of being deployed (with a later generation hence expected by the 1970s), or that a first generation system would not appear until the late 1960s. From this basic appraisal, three different levels of Soviet ABM defence and rates of deployment by 1973 were postulated in the study. In a favourable case a first generation system would not be available until 1968, and could then only be built up around major cities at the rate of about one a year, so that by 1973 defences around Moscow, Leningrad and three other large cities might be operational. An unfavourable case would give the system seen near Leningrad in 1962 some operational capability, with a second generation being deployed in 1968 at the rate of about two cities a year, so that an advanced system could be defending about ten major cities by 1973. Finally, there was an average or 'expected' case, where advanced systems would be present around Moscow and Leningrad by 1973, with an earlier generation defence for the next ten most important cities.[64]

Considering the targeting requirements that had been set by the Navy, the report saw a real need to deploy a penetration aid system as soon as possible as even the most optimistic assessment of Russian deployment patterns credited the introduction of a first generation system by 1968. The study therefore aimed at providing ideas for a penetration aid system that could be used for early Polaris deployment, during the period 1968–70. Despite the caveats made about lack of information on Soviet ABM defences, the report contained a whole series of nominal penetration calculations that attempted to demonstrate what the introduction of a basic penetration aid system could achieve against different levels of defence. Without any improvement, and against a first generation Soviet defensive system which could be deployed on a wide basis by 1973, the Mark 2 Mod 0 re-entry system was seen as having little chance of inflicting major damage to Moscow even if all the 32 missiles from the two boats assumed to be available were allocated to this one city. However, allocation of the same number of missiles from two boats to Leningrad, assuming that city was also defended, was likely to inflict the required level of destruction. An alternative approach mentioned in the report's penetration calculations was also to target only undefended cities with unimproved missiles. This might allow severe damage to be inflicted on anything between seven and 13 'category B' (i.e. smaller) cities depending on the spread of Soviet defences. However, as this would fall short of the Navy's requirements the study was unable to conclude whether this approach could be said to constitute a valid deterrent.

Countermeasures to Soviet ABM defences were divided into a number of different categories, all of which were designed to frustrate the attempts of radar to discriminate between decoys and real warheads. The first category included the use of passive devices, noise jammers, and active decoys in the Mark 2 Mod 0 re-entry system. A problem here was that the current Polaris REB was not designed to present a low radar echoing area, meaning that decoys designed to match the REB would have to be of an equivalent size (or of a high power in the case of active jammers), which would in turn have weight implications for the RES as a whole. Passive devices examined included 'window', or 'chaff' (the American term which by now had become ubiquitous), consisting of small metallic strips which were dispensed in either large clouds, or smaller clusters in order to surround a particular body in space. This Second World War-era technique of confusing radar, as was noted in chapter two, was still a remarkably effective penetration aid, but the HR 169 report mentioned several of its drawbacks. For one, chaff would burn up rapidly as it began to re-enter the earth's atmosphere, making it useful only during the exo-atmosphere phase of an ABM engagement. But secondly, in order to cover all the possible bands of radar frequency, it was thought that a prohibitive weight of chaff would be required aboard the RES. Chaff also presented peculiar deployment problems which would require solution. Another method considered was the use of so-called passive decoys, designed to resemble REBs in ballistic characteristics or radar echoing area, some of which could be made resilient enough to survive the early stages of re-entry. Noise jammers, and active decoys (which used repeaters to simulate a large radar-echoing area) was also studied, but found wanting in various respects, such as relying to an uncomfortable extent on knowledge of the frequencies employed by enemy radar systems.

A second category of penetration aid was use of precursor blackout tactics. This would involve the detonation of one Polaris warhead or more at perhaps 75,000 feet above the target area, creating a fireball through which radar tracking by the defence would be very difficult. But the relatively small areas that could be screened by such explosions, and the expenditure of warheads the tactic would entail, was given as a reason for precluding blackout tactics from further consideration. In the report's more detailed treatment of the subject, and lost from HR 169's final summary, was the important reservation that 'the "black-and-white" fireball blackout picture, in which the only effect is the opacity of the fireball, could fall short of the truth. Effects on radar might be far more widespread, particularly the degrading of the effectiveness of sophisticated discrimination systems.'[65] As we shall see, the complex topic of blackout effects – on which much theoretical work still had to be done – was to be a persistent and controversial theme of ABM studies, not least as their existence could obviate the need for any more sophisticated penetration aid.

Another approach suggested in the report was to adjust the trajectories of incoming missiles so that their arrival in the target area would be very closely spaced, complicating the task of any defender. A further and related possibility was coordinating the fire from two submarines to achieve the same effect, but this too would require good notice of when firing was to take place so that the necessary calculations and adjustments could be applied (the obvious inference carried in the report was that such carefully calibrated firing tactics might not in practice be feasible given the conditions under which any decision to use the deterrent would actually be taken). The use of a completely redesigned or different REB offering a much smaller radar echoing area was the third main area of change considered by the HR 169 study. This more ambitious development would use techniques which had been developed for the Blue Streak REB, and which the Americans were known to be introducing with the Mark 12 re-entry vehicle, intended for use in the Minuteman ICBM programme. Included in this section, almost as an afterthought, was the idea of redesigning the REB through 'hardening' so that it was 'more resistant to blast, neutrons and X-rays, thus reducing the kill probability for a given miss distance.'[66]

The slender discussion of REB or warhead hardening to withstand the effects of ABM bursts in the HR 169 report was a symptom of the lack of UK data on this whole area, crucial though it was to prove to the whole task of overcoming an ABM defence. The report did feature in one of its appendices a section on the effects of nuclear explosions on the Mk 2 Mod 0 RES. Mentioned here were the different forms of energy emitted from the detonation of an ABM warhead at different altitudes and their effects. It was recognised that the primary thermal radiation that formed about 70 per cent of the total energy yield of an explosion took the form of soft X-rays. Within the earth's atmosphere these very rapidly heated the surrounding air to form a fireball, emitting a blast wave and enormous thermal radiation. Above the earth's atmosphere, with no air molecules to absorb the X-rays, they travelled very long distances and could cause 'damage to the re-entry body at an appreciable distance from the explosion,' while neutron radiation could also be a problem.[67] However, there was no detail in this section of the study on the precise effects of varying yields of ABM warheads on the Polaris RES in the exo-atmosphere environment, a lacuna which reflected the lack of detailed UK information in this sensitive area of nuclear information (it was a subject, nevertheless, which had been investigated during some of the US high altitude nuclear tests staged in the summer of 1962).

The HR 169 study report recommended that an improved RES be developed for Polaris, incorporating all three counter-measures to discrimination, including a tungsten chaff package weighing about 50lbs, about 40 passive inflatable balloon-type decoys (which it was thought would burn up at about 150,000 feet), and four small noise jammers. It was envisaged that chaff packages would be ejected almost immediately after nose cone separation from the motoring Polaris second stage so that accurate radar tracking of REBs was made as difficult as possible; 25 clouds of chaff, each of 20 miles diameter would be distributed along about 60 miles of REB trajectory. The chaff would eventually penetrate to an altitude of about 200,000 feet before slowing and burning up. Noise jammers would supplement the chaff, and be ejected from the second stage in the same way as REBs and chaff dispensers; their task would be to degrade the range and accuracy of enemy radars. The side echoing area of the 40 light decoys would be comparable to the REBs, and there would be a reduced forward echoing area. If Russian defences showed signs of further development, and in particular their radar technology improved, then extra measures would be needed. These could include carrying more chaff, with all the weight problems this would bring, unless one of the three Polaris warheads was replaced by a dedicated penetration aid carrier. The penetration aids considered in the report were expressly designed to counter a 'terminal'-style defensive system, intended to intercept incoming warheads within the earth's atmosphere, using relatively short-range interceptors with small yield warheads. It was assumed that each defending interceptor would be capable of destroying only one offensive warhead, while exo-atmospheric ABM systems, using large yield warheads outside the atmosphere were expressly excluded from the terms of the HR 169 study. Nevertheless, it was suggested that the types of penetration aids examined by the report 'could form part of a system effective against such defences.'

HR 169's summary was filled with understandable caveats about the conclusions that might be drawn from the report. Quantifying the degree of improvement that could be gained by the addition of penetration aids was seen as necessarily speculative, not least as accurate knowledge of the enemy's defensive system was required to assess the effectiveness of an improvement to penetration capability. Nevertheless, the development of decoys was considered to be a profitable route to follow, while knowledge picked up in the JRSWG forum indicated that there were no insuperable problems of compatibility between the existing Polaris RES and a new suite of penetration aids. Some designs for the decoys themselves were featured in an appendix to the report, but it was stressed that these were highly tentative suggestions and 'a major R. and D. programme is required to bring these ideas to a Service standard.' With the proposed suite of new penetration aids, it was estimated that by 1973 against a Soviet first generation defence which was thinly deployed (the most favourable case considered), considerable damage could be inflicted by 32 missiles on Moscow, Leningrad and on another seven undefended large cities. In a situation where an intermediate level of ABM deployment had taken place, where more advanced defences were placed around Moscow and Leningrad only, major damage could still be inflicted on those cities, as well as less severe damage to Kiev, Gorky, and Kharkov. The report included the injunction that, 'If the Naval Staff requirement is to be met in full then it can be argued on the basis of our defence postulations that penetration aids are required in 1968. However, even if it is considered that the effective deterrent does not need to include Moscow and Leningrad as targets then the provision of Penetration Aids is highly desirable by the early 1970s and essential by 1975.'[68]

From information gained from LMSC, it was known that additional weight of almost 500 lb could be carried within the re-entry system without degrading range below the Navy's acceptable minimum range for Polaris of 2,000 nautical miles, or affecting the dynamics of the missile, and the penetration aid kit envisaged by RAE was reckoned to weigh less than 400 lb. If a research and development programme for the proposed system were begun in the first quarter of 1965, it was believed that a 'maximum risk' crash programme, involving ten successful missile firings, could meet the initial Polaris deployment date of 1968. The total cost for providing a penetration aid kit for deployment in 1968 was estimated at £32 million. This sum was broken down into about £6 million of development work with industry in the UK; £0.5 million of intermural work at the Ministry of Aviation's research establishments, including RAE; £20.5 million for costs in the US, including support from Lockheed on interface between penetration aids and the RES and a flight trials programme which entailed the purchase of fifteen Polaris missiles and three Black Knight rounds (assuming that ten successful Polaris firings would be needed to evaluate the system); and some £5 million as a contingency against the cost of US range facilities. A further issue was that a high-level reappraisal of the Black Knight launcher programme would be required so that it met the needs of the anticipated flight trials of penetration aids (since the use of the existing version of Black Knight for the Dazzle physics re-entry experiments at the Australian range facilities was due to end in late 1965). The costs quoted in the report were, it should be noted, seen by RAE as very rough estimates only, with a possible variation of +/− 25 per cent.[69]

The HR 169 study report concluded with the telling observation that against a defended target the current Polaris RES had a low chance of penetration. Intelligence assessments led the authors of the study to believe that the Soviet Union had an extensive ABM research programme, including test interceptions involving missiles armed with nuclear warheads, and that, based on its SAM practice, it was prepared to deploy defensive ABM systems on a large scale. It was therefore considered 'on technical grounds' that there was a 'distinct possibility' that ABM defences would be built-up by the Soviet Union, and that even on a most favourable (for the UK) estimate of deployment rates, a start to this process would be made in 1968, and by 1973 five major cities would be defended. These two factors combined made it necessary to begin a UK penetration aid programme for Polaris, if possible to coincide with the first predicted appearance of Soviet ABM defences in 1968, although 'allowing for development difficulties and delays it would be prudent to plan on introducing a fully developed system(s) not later than 1970.' Provided that a contract go-ahead was given in early 1965, the report believed that a credible penetration aid system could be deployed as early as late 1968 at the estimated cost of £32 million. Over the longer-term, against a more advanced type of ABM defence, further development of a penetration aid programme would undoubtedly be required, however. Moreover, 'the problem of designing penetration aids depends in no small way on the design of the re-entry body. Indeed in an optimum design of re-entry system, the penetration aids and re-entry body designs are completely interdependent. In the face of advanced ABM defences the use of an improved re-entry body, along the lines of [the] Blue Steak re-entry vehicle and the proposed UK Mk 12 REB, with penetration aids to match, might well be the most satisfactory long term solution.'[70]

The HR 169 study featured many of the characteristics common to later studies of Polaris improvement options. In the absence of reliable intelligence on the performance of Soviet ABM systems, a wide range of presumptions had to be employed over the effectiveness and extent of the defensive systems that could be encountered. Western technical knowledge was used as the benchmark which Soviet scientists and engineers were assumed to be capable of reaching. The penetration aids suggested for inclusion in the Polaris re-entry system were derived from some of the residual British knowledge and work that had been carried out on the Blue Streak programme in the late 1950s. An important constraint on any package of penetration aids was determined by the trade-offs that had to be made between weight and range for Polaris, while the design of the Mark 2 Mod 0 REB was not considered ideal for overcoming advanced ABM defences. Finally, both cost and timescale estimates for deployment of an improved RES for Polaris were highly optimistic and reflected a certain technological hubris which flew in the face of British experience with Blue Streak development, where costs had ballooned rapidly from initial forecasts.

The appearance of Galosh and intelligence appreciations of the Moscow system

At the very highest levels of British defence policymaking during this period the ABM issue still tended to be tackled from its effects on the general East-West strategic balance, rather than for how it affected the UK-specific context of how an independent nuclear strike would reach its targets. In October 1964, for example, the COS approved a report from its Defence Planning Staff (as the JPS had now become) on the consequences for strategic policy of likely political, technical, and military developments during the period between 1968 and 1980. Under its technical section, this 'looking glass' paper considered that no general defence against ballistic missiles could be foreseen, and that while it might be possible to offer 'some (but not certain) defence for selected point targets … there is little likelihood of defence against a determined, widespread attack.' Given this finding, it was concluded that both East and West would retain the ability to inflict a devastating nuclear attack on each other at least for the period up to 1980.[71]

This kind of appraisal was, however, far removed from those British officials and scientists concerned with Polaris penetration ability. HR 169 had been predicated on the Admiralty's requirement for a system which could fulfil a set of national target criteria, where the UK Polaris force was operating in isolation. Another fundamental assumption contained within the HR 169 study, moreover, was that the Soviet ABM system in the process of deployment would be of the endo-atmosphere variety, where interception would take place in the terminal stage of an offensive missile's flight as it passed through the upper atmosphere and then descended towards its target. This assumption would soon have to be drastically revised as new information about the direction of Soviet ABM development came forward just as the report's initial findings were being compiled.

On 7 November 1964, at the annual Red Square military parade, a new large four-motor missile, encased by its launching canister, was driven through Moscow. It was described by Russian commentary as being able to destroy enemy missiles 'at great distances' from the defended area.[72] Unlike the smaller and less powerful Griffon seen the year before, this new missile, dubbed 'Galosh' in the West (and the A-350 in the Soviet Union), seemed specifically designed for long-range exo-atmospheric rather than terminal defence. Galosh was an unexpected surprise to Western intelligence analysts, and photographs of the parade, with its tantalising glimpses of the missile, were given immediate and detailed study. Without a clearer view of the missile, however, it was difficult to provide a thoroughly reliable estimate of its performance. Indeed, apart from its protruding nozzles seen at the back of the launch canister, clear views of Galosh would prove very difficult to come by for many years. Initial estimates of its capability were extrapolated from Western experience with missiles of the same dimensions and assumed propulsion systems.

A month after the appearance of Galosh, in December 1964 the annual US National Intelligence Estimate on Soviet air and missile defences gave an opportunity for initial assessment of its characteristics and the implications for the Soviet ABM system. Pointing to articles on ABM defence appearing in classified Soviet military journals from 1961 which stressed the importance of high altitude and long-range intercepts, the NIE was notable for drawing attention to the apparent Soviet belief that exo-atmospheric engagement of attacking missiles in mid-trajectory was the most practical method of defence. The Soviet ABM testing regime at Sary Shagan was still shrouded in some mystery, and there was real uncertainty over whether simulation of ICBM (as opposed to IRBM) intercepts had been attempted. There was, however, no evidence that any tests had been held which used decoys, multiple warheads, or other penetration methods. Preliminary analysis of the photographs taken of the 'missile-in-the-canister' at the November Moscow parade led the NIE to accept it was designed for an ABM role. By initial reckoning, the new missile might be able to carry out intercepts at altitudes of 'a few hundred miles' and ranges of 'several hundred miles' from its launching point, and to carry a large megaton-yield warhead. Galosh's kill mechanism, the NIE conjectured, 'could be designed to take advantage of the exoatmospheric effects of large-yield warheads to destroy incoming nosecones, even though accompanied by penetration aids, i.e. chaff, decoys, etc. in order to reduce the problem of discrimination.' In particular, the 'X-ray pulse of a nuclear burst' was seen as way an ABM warhead could achieve such an interception. One element of Soviet practice that perplexed Western analysts was that they were convinced that no full system tests of an exo-atmosphere type had been undertaken at Sary Shagan. It was believed that such large-scale systems tests would probably be conducted before commitment to an extensive ABM deployment programme was made.[73]

The December 1964 NIE also outlined several developments which indicated that an ABM system for the defence of Moscow was being prepared, and that the overall programme had been modified with the suspension of work at the early ABM complexes first seen around Leningrad in 1962. Building of the very large (over 300 feet high, and 400 feet wide) Dog House radar observed south west of Moscow was presumed to have begun in early 1963. It was thought to be of the phased array type, designed for long-range target acquisition and tracking with an explicit ABM role. In addition, there was new construction activity at the SA-1 SAM missiles sites which formed a large outer ring around Moscow, some of which indicated that new launch positions for an ABM interceptor were being prepared, and that what were called 'electronic facilities' were also being installed. By March 1965, additional detail was available on the work being carried out at the SAM sites, where each was being furnished with a large 110-foot radome – similar to that observed at Sary Shagan in 1961–62 – and two smaller 60-foot radomes, arranged in a triangular pattern: the whole radar complex was soon being referred to as a 'Triad'.[74]

Rounding up its review of the patchy evidence available, the December 1964 NIE concluded that 'we continue to believe that the Soviets may now be deploying ABM defenses at Moscow, but we do not yet understand how the installations we have observed would function as an ABM system.' Not surprisingly, it was found there were still 'critical uncertainties' in US knowledge of the status of Soviet ABM R & D and deployment patterns, with much ambiguity, for example, over the role and purposes of the SAM complexes detected near Tallinn in Estonia.[75] This was once again a reference to the emergence of the so-called Tallinn Line, where deployment of the Griffon missile seems to have begun in 1963 but then stopped soon after. An up-rated version of Griffon, the SA-5 (designated 'Gammon' by NATO) was eventually, from 1966 onwards, to be deployed in large numbers along the arc of SAM sites between Riga and Archangel, leading to renewed speculation in the US intelligence community over whether the system was intended for high-flying aircraft, or was conceived to have some ABM capability.[76]

The NIE was able to offer several general points about the extensive Soviet ABM programme. It was felt that the Soviet Union had 'several years ago probably solved the technical problem of intercepting ballistic targets arriving singly or in small numbers', that from the indications provided by early deployment activity Soviet leaders probably wanted to build ABM defences rapidly when they could, and that while a new interceptor had appeared and new deployment activity seemed to be underway, there were as yet no operational defences against strategic ballistic missiles, although some could be ready within the next two years or so. A major grey area for US intelligence analysts was whether ABM defences would be used to protect a small number of urban-industrial complexes, perhaps even limited to the pilot system being introduced around Moscow, or if a more widespread deployment was envisaged; it might even be the case that the very high costs of large-scale ABM deployment might ultimately outweigh the level of defence that could be offered against the rapidly rising ballistic missile threat from the United States.[77]

The appearance of Galosh had a dramatic impact on Western perceptions of the Soviet ABM threat. Here was an advanced long-range interceptor, capable of carrying a high-yield nuclear warhead high above the earth's atmosphere where it could employ a kill mechanism which did not require a high degree of accuracy. Soviet leaders were also ready to trumpet their recent achievements in the area of ballistic missile defence. In February 1965, Marshal Malinovsky referred to the Soviet Union as having ABMs which were capable of destroying ballistic missiles at great distances from defended installations. A few months later, Leonid Brezhnev, who had assumed the key position of General Secretary of the Communist Party in October 1964 when Khrushchev was removed from power, made reference to recent improvements which had increased the effectiveness of ABM defences. Of even more direct interest to Western intelligence analysts was the appearance of a film on Soviet television in May 1965, called 'Rockets for Peace,' which along with footage of ballistic missile tests and air defence preparedness, showed the launch of what was presented as an ABM interceptor. This had all the signs of being Galosh, and several pictorial representations of the missile were assembled by the CIA's Directorate of Science and Technology from this unexpected but very welcome source.

There were many problems in arriving at an accurate assessment of progress with Soviet development. The sheer size and diversity of the Soviet programme made it difficult to track consistent patterns over time, and it was considered likely that as the Russians made their own evaluations of the offensive threat they were trying to counter, they would make changes and adjustments to their programme, so complicating the task of the intelligence analyst concerned with prediction. It was expected, for example, that some components of an ABM system might well go through advanced development and trials but never ultimately be deployed. One of the most confusing issues was also trying to determine whether testing and development was related to advanced long-range SAM projects, or to an ABM system, as there were many aspects to tracking and interception common to both. From what is now known about the objectives of Soviet ABM designers, their aims were relatively modest. By 1964 the goal of the Moscow system was to simultaneously intercept between six and eight incoming targets from the total of 16 missile sites located in the ring around the capital; there was no capacity for the system to cope with missiles equipped with even the most rudimentary form of penetration aids, or multiple warheads. There was also a deadline date set of 7 November 1967 (the fiftieth anniversary of the Bolshevik revolution) for bringing the new system into operation, although this was not in practice met.[78]

Despite the accumulating evidence of an active Soviet R & D effort, which was now entering into a deployment phase, at the top of the US defence establishment, where McNamara continued to subject all US programmes to a rigorous cost-benefit analysis, scepticism still existed over the efficacy and worth of building ABM defences. It made far more financial sense, as far as the US Defense Secretary and his close advisers could see, to improve the penetration performance of US offensive missiles as a response to Soviet programmes, than to engage in a forlorn attempt to defend America's cities from Soviet missile attack. By November 1963, McNamara had lost all confidence that the original Nike Zeus system had any ability to discriminate between real warheads and decoys and would only continue limited funding to 'provide a technical and organisational base for later decisions,' while no decisions were yet contemplated over whether to proceed beyond the development phase for the next generation Nike-X system.[79]

During 1964–65, influenced by the exponential growth in the striking power and accuracy of US strategic nuclear forces, McNamara had many reasons to doubt whether ABM defence, as opposed to damage-limiting attacks on the Soviet Union's offensive missile capabilities, was the best route to reducing the almost inconceivable domestic casualties and damage that would result from a nuclear exchange. He was also increasingly concerned that building ABM defences, as well as being prohibitively costly, would undermine strategic stability and exacerbate the nuclear arms race, as the Soviet Union would react simply by increasing the numbers of its own offensive systems and warheads as a direct method to overcome whatever shield the United States might try to erect to protect its civilian population. Resisting calls within his own military establishment for the construction of ever greater numbers of ICBMs and SLBMs, McNamara had already come to the view, moreover, that maintaining an invulnerable second strike nuclear capability, able to absorb an initial Soviet attack but still deliver a coordinated, centrally-directed response which would inflict overwhelming damage on the Soviet Union was the best means of deterring any deliberate initiation of general war or a nuclear attack by Moscow. 'Assured destruction' – seen as the best means of preventing the catastrophe of an all-out nuclear war – became the philosophy that underpinned the Pentagon's nuclear war planning from this period onwards.[80]

The UK underground nuclear test programme and the future of AWRE

In the summer of 1963, the US Atomic Energy Commission began to approach the UK Atomic Energy Authority with enquiries over future intentions regarding nuclear testing, and whether a share in US facilities was required over the coming years. The preliminary position taken at the beginning of 1963 by the British technical authorities to base the design of the UK Polaris warhead as far as possible on the US Mark 58 seemed to indicate that no programme of underground testing would be required as long as US knowledge and experience could be utilised. At the MoD it was acknowledged that there was 'no foreseeable need for tests in respect of the nuclear weapons already approved and now being developed for British Service use,' but there was still a need, as far as the AEA was concerned to maintain a high degree of competence in indigenous nuclear weapons technology. This involved, among other things, 'the maintenance of research on nuclear warhead physics, materials and technology at a level necessary to retain the skills and ability to undertake a new project, if it should be required, and to make a useful contribution to Anglo/American collaboration in the nuclear defence field so long as we require and desire that collaboration.'[81]

In view of such considerations, in October 1963 the Nuclear Requirements for Defence Committee, the official inter-departmental committee created in 1960 and chaired by the PUS at the MoD, had considered a memorandum from the AEA which outlined a future experimental warhead testing programme. It was recognised by the Committee that, as the Chairman of the AEA, Sir Roger Makins put it,

> if British scientists were to keep their knowledge up-to-date and continue their present close-co-operation with their United States colleagues, there should be agreement in principle to the continuation of underground testing by the United Kingdom. Meanwhile, the absence of a firm programme was having an unsettling effect on the staff of the Authority's establishments. The areas of the greatest interest for further experimental work included advanced warheads, nearly-clean kiloton devices with only a few per cent fission yield, and the production of nuclear weapons using civil plutonium.

Accordingly, ministerial approval would be sought for a further programme of tests, and AWRE invited to prepare a detailed schedule along with an estimate of the costs involved.[82]

On 28 November 1963, the Prime Minister gave his assent to the MoD's request to agree in principle a continuing programme of underground nuclear testing, with the express aim of maintaining the UK's nuclear weapons technology and close cooperation with the US authorities.[83] AWRE came forward with more detailed proposals the following month, and in January 1964 the Nuclear Requirements for Defence Committee met once again and recommended to ministers a three-year programme of underground tests (nine tests in all, at an estimated cost of £5.9 million), as well as the firing of two low-kiloton shots in 1964 (costing £1.5 million), though a review of the three-year programme would be conducted after the latter two tests had been completed.[84]

Despite some doubts from the Treasury about the manpower and resources still demanded by Aldermaston, and amid the feeling that the AEA were trying to avoid any serious discussion about its future (when it had been anticipated that when work on the Polaris warhead was completed the size of the Establishment would be reduced), at the end of January 1964 the Prime Minister agreed with the recommendations, and planning proceeded for the first kiloton test to take place in Nevada during the summer.[85] By this stage the effects of the Polaris warhead programme, and the new commitment to produce a high yield version of WE 177, on the anticipated rundown of staff at Aldermaston was beginning to be registered. Instead of completion of Skybolt warhead work in 1967, it was now envisaged that it would take until 1969/70 for the new requirements to be met. At that point, as the Director of AWRE explained in April 1964, numbers at Aldermaston would have stabilised at around 6,000, with 4,500 of these engaged in weapons-related work (an increase of 500 staff compared to that planned before Skybolt cancellation, due to higher numbers of warheads to produce and service).[86]

As the AEA had highlighted, an underground testing programme was also seen as necessary in order to keep sustained the flow of exchanges under the 1958 Agreement with the United States. Once the new Polaris warhead moved into service, and the two versions of WE 177 had also been completed, there was no new phase of weapon work on which AWRE could concentrate its talents and energies. Zuckerman had drawn the Prime Minister's attention to the problem in May 1964 when he sent a report on the latest annual 'stocktake' meeting with the Americans, conducted by the heads of the weapons laboratories to review the health and vitality of the exchanges under the 1958 Agreement. While stressing that the atmosphere of the review was 'amiable', collaboration was undoubtedly then good, and that the UK's contribution in nuclear research was obviously welcomed, Zuckerman injected a more worrisome note to his impressions of the meeting. The British party to the talks could not help feeling conscious, much more so than on any previous occasion, that the

> Americans were viewing us rather as poor relations. This seemed as much due to a sense of uncertainty which they appear to be entertaining about the future of British nuclear defence work as to the disparity in the scale of our respective nuclear programmes. This disparity, of course, applies much more in the field of weapon development than in that of basic nuclear research. Here it was fortunate that we could outline to them our extensive research programme. Without this, the review would have been somewhat silly.

It was noticeable that the Americans had tended to talk about collaboration as a way to strengthen Western defences as a whole, rather than being part of a specific Anglo-American relationship. The three year British underground testing programme was certainly appreciated, but the Americans had passed hints that the Nevada testing facilities would not necessarily be available for the period beyond this. Zuckerman's conclusions were sobering: 'in my view, collaboration will hardly develop further, or even continue on its present fruitful scale, unless we show that we are making a substantial contribution to nuclear weapon research aimed at strengthening the nuclear defence of the West. There are signs that American views may be changing as to how our "special relationship" in the nuclear field can best serve this purpose.'[87]

Meanwhile, the UK's underground testing moved forward. Envisaged as the first shot in AWRE's three year experimental programme, and with no explicit connection with the Polaris warhead, 'Cormorant', as it was dubbed by the AEC, was successfully fired on 17 July 1964.[88] In the summer of 1964, concern over the supply and availability of military-grade plutonium led to a decision by the Nuclear Requirements for Defence Committee to substitute the test of a slightly modified primary – though not a new design – for the UK Polaris warhead, which used less plutonium than the American version, in place of the second research test that had been planned in Nevada.[89] Thus, the new second test – 'Courser' – was of a replica of the UK design of the Polaris primary with a reduced amount of plutonium, and went ahead on 25 September, but failed to generate any nuclear yield. The fault was soon traced to the malfunction of American supplied non-nuclear components – neutron generators specifically designed for use in nuclear tests – which meant that no chain reaction was produced in the warhead fissile material. Knowing the cause of the problem, the US authorities (perhaps somewhat chastened) were eager to assist the British with a repeat of the economy test.[90]

But whether a re-run of the Polaris economy test would actually proceed, however, would depend on the course of British electoral politics over the coming weeks and, as it transpired, on the attitude of a new set of ministers to the continuation of nuclear testing. Party political debate over the course of UK nuclear policy had continued unabated during 1964, as the repercussions of the Polaris deal for the whole notion of independence were questioned. Aside from this domestic political context, the control of Western nuclear forces remained a central topic of contention amongst some of the leading NATO allies during the last 18 months of the Conservative Government, and it is with the post-Nassau arguments over the possible creation of a multilateral force that the final chapter of this volume will begin.

Notes

1 JIC(63)49(Final), 'Soviet Air Defence Policy,' 29 July 1963, CAB 158/100.
2 J. C. A. Roper minute, 'Soviet Air Defence Policy,' JIC/660/63, 13 September 1963, CAB 176/126.
3 NIE 11–2–63, 'The Soviet Atomic Energy Program,' 2 July 1963, National Security File, Files of Charles E. Johnson, box 30, LBJL.

4 See John Prados, *The Soviet Estimate: US Intelligence Analysis and Soviet Strategic Forces* (Princeton, 1986), 154–5.
5 See Henry Tanner, 'Soviet Parades "Antimissile Missiles" on 46th Anniversary of Revolution,' *New York Times*, 8 November 1963.
6 See CIA Office of Current Intelligence, 'Special Report: Current Aspects of the Soviet Antiballistic Missile System,' 26 March 1965, CK3100577570, Declassified Documents Reference System (DDRS).
7 See Freedman, *US Intelligence and the Soviet Strategic Threat*, 93.
8 'Notes on a Discussion with Mr. A. Potts, Director of Scientific Intelligence JIB and staff: Information relating to Russian ABM systems with particular reference to Polaris,' 14 February 1964, AVIA 65/1882.
9 JIC(64)3 (Final), 'Soviet Bloc War Potential, 1964–68,' 28 February 1964, CAB 158/51.
10 RAE/AWRE Re-entry System Study Group: Notes on the Third Meeting – 29th August 1963, CWD/10/47, ES 13 box 6, Atomic Weapons Establishment (AWE) archive.
11 'Report of the Chairmen of the Joint US/UK Re-entry System Working Group to the Polaris Project Officers for the Joint Steering Task Group Meeting, 1st – 3rd October 1963,' XY/411/010, 19 September 1963, AVIA 65/1843; circulated as PIPSC/A(63)5A, 27 September 1963, Z20/127, FO 371/173521. See also PIPSC/A(63)5, 'Study of a UK Re-entry System for the Polaris A3 Missile,' note by the Ministry of Aviation, 24 September 1963, Z20/127, FO 371/173521.
12 PIPSC/M(63)5, Minutes of the Fifth Meeting held on 30th September 1963, Z20/129, FO 371/173521.
13 Press minute for Zuckerman, 'Polaris Re-entry System,' RP/371/63, 1 October 1963, DEFE 13/296.
14 Zuckerman minute for Thorneycroft, SZ/835/63, 4 October 1963, DEFE 13/296.
15 See GD 203, 'Expanded Staff Requirement: Polaris Missile – Re-entry System,' 3 October 1963, DS 2/3–32/1, MoD records.
16 R. B. Marshall letter to R. Lewin, D.A. 362/013, 24 September 1963, AVIA 65/1882.
17 RAE/AWRE Re-entry System Study Group: Notes on the fourth meeting – 16th September 1963, file CWD/10/47, ES 13 box 6, AWE archive.
18 See RAE report, 'UK Polaris Re-entry Systems: Comments on the LMSC Study,' LSW/738/03/CWN, 4 February 1964, and Appendix 1, 'A Specification for a Study of the Re-entry System for the Polaris A3 missile,' AVIA 65/1882.
19 See RAE report, 'UK Polaris Re-entry Systems: Comments on the LMSC Study,' LSW/738/03/CWN, 4 February 1964, and Appendix 1, 'A Specification for a Study of the Re-entry System for the Polaris A3 missile,' AVIA 65/1882.
20 Ministry of Aviation memorandum, 'Re-Entry System for UK Polaris Missiles,' 6 February 1964, file LSW 738/04 Part A, MoD records.
21 See Dossor minute for Grundy, 'Polaris – Admiralty/MoA Responsibilities,' 22 October 1963, and attached paper; D. F. Allen minute, 6 December 1963, AVIA 65/1843.
22 'Conclusions of a meeting held by the Controller on 21st January: Polaris RES,' 23 January 1964, AVIA 65/1882.
23 See, for example, Dossor memorandum, 'Polaris Monthly Progress Report, 27th January 1964, No 2,' ZH/37/03, AVIA 65/1843.
24 Dossor minute for Grundy, ZH/18/01, 10 February 1964, AVIA 65/1843.
25 Grundy minute for Secretary, 13 February 1964, AVIA 65/1843.
26 Grundy memorandum, 'Polaris Organisation in the Ministry of Aviation,' DA/360/01B, 19 February 1964, AVIA 65/1843.
27 'Polaris: The WSCC Preliminary Safety Study of the Mk58, Mod 1 warhead,' WSCC/P10B/63, 6 December 1963; Nyman Levin letter to Williams, 'The Choice of Warhead for Polaris,' 1 January 1964, AVIA 65/1882.

28 See Dossor letter to Mackenzie, 'Polaris – RES and Warhead,' 10 January 1964, AVIA 65/1882.
29 AWRE memorandum, 'JOWOG 19,' SB/64/J19, n.d. (but c. March 1964); H. R. Hulme minute for Levin, 'JOWOG 19 (Vulnerability),' CNR/64/28, 3 April 1964, ES 13/74.
30 G. C. Scorgie minute, 'JOWOG 19: Vulnerability,' SB/64/JOWOG 19, 24 February 1964, ES 13/74.
31 See Cmnd 2097, *Central Organisation for Defence*, paragraphs 42–53, July 1963.
32 Zuckerman, *Monkeys, Men and Missiles*, 198.
33 Ibid, 204–6, 358–63; Ewan Broadbent, *The Military and Government: From Macmillan to Heseltine* (London, 1988), 153.
34 See Zuckerman, *Monkeys, Men and Missiles*, 364–5.
35 See Lord Penney and V. H. B. Macklen, 'William Richard Joseph Cook,' *Biographical Memoirs of Fellows of the Royal Society*, 1988, 34, 45–61; 'Sir William Cook: Hydrogen bombs and nuclear reactors,' obituary, *The Times*, 19 September 1987; Arnold, *Britain and the H-Bomb*, 59, 78–9, 152–3, 224.
36 PIPSC/P(64)2, 'The Polaris Re-Entry System,' 13 March 1964, AVIA 65/1843.
37 See PIPSC/M(64)1, Minutes of the Sixth Meeting held at the Admiralty on 13th March 1964, AVIA 65/1843.
38 Aviation Council minutes, Annex to AC/M(64)4, Item 1 of Minutes held on Tuesday, 24th March 1964, AVIA 65/1882.
39 Annex to WDC(NS)/P(64)3, 'The Polaris Re-Entry System,' 12 March 1964, LSW 738/04 Part A, MoD records.
40 See S. A. Hunwicks, 'Brief for WDC(NS) Meeting on Wednesday 25th March 1964,' 20 March 1964, AVIA 65/1882.
41 G. J. Rogers minute for Hunwicks, 'Polaris,' PG/63/01, 26 March 1964, AVIA 65/1843.
42 Unfortunately the central records of the Nuclear Sub-Committee of the WDC do not appear to have survived in the MoD's archives, but it is possible to reconstruct the essential elements of its conclusions from other related sources.
43 E. C. Cornford minute for Zuckerman, 'Briefing for WDC(NS) Meeting,' 24 March 1964, DEFE 19/103.
44 See Hunwicks letter to East, 'HR 169,' XY/412/013, 26 August 1964, quoting from AS/LGW1 letter to Nairne, 8 May 1964, AVIA 65/1860.
45 Andrew minute, 2 April 1964, DS 2/3–32/1, AVIA 65/1882.
46 *Flight International*, vol 85, No 2876, 23 April 1964, 640; available at www.flightglobal.com.
47 *Hansard*, HC, vol 694, cols 66–7, 29 April 1964; and cols 587–9, 30 April 1964; see also 'Britain can make Polaris warheads,' *The Times*, 30 April 1964.
48 Memorandum by C. B. Benjamin, 'Polaris: Supplementary Questions put to the Prime Minister on 30th April 1964,' DB/385/01, 6 May 1964, PREM 11/4737.
49 See 'Labour Accusation of Waste,' *The Times*, 5 May 1964.
50 *Hansard*, HC, vol 695, cols 222–3, 12 May 1964; and see 'Warheads,' *The Times*, 13 May 1964.
51 Zuckerman minute for Douglas-Home, 'Polaris Warheads,' SZ/371/64, 14 May 1964, PREM 11/4737.
52 Harrison minute, 'Polaris Penetration Aid Study,' XY/412/013, 4 May 1964, LSW/728/02 Part A, MoD records.
53 HR 169 Study Report, Part 1, November 1964, p8, AW2005/164, AWE archive.
54 HR 169 Study Report, Part 1, November 1964, p11, AW2005/164, AWE archive.
55 Ministry of Aviation memorandum, 'Re-Entry System for UK Polaris Missiles,' 6 February 1964, AVIA 65/1882.

56 HR 169 Study Report, Part 2, November 1964, pp. 28–9, AW2005/164, AWE archive.
57 East letter to G. L. Hutchinson, 'Polaris Penetration Aids,' 27 April 1964, LSW/728/02 Part A, MoD records.
58 See, for example, Polaris Management Board: Minutes of Third Meeting at Ministry of Aviation, Wednesday, 29th April 1964, ZH/16/08, 1 May 1964, LSW/738/04 Part A, MoD records.
59 East letter to Harrison, 'Polaris Penetration Aid Study,' 27 April 1964, LSW/728/02 Part A, MoD records.
60 The relevant papers were PC/P(64)4, 'Polaris Penetration Aids,' 15 June 1964, and for official approval of the parameters of the requirements, PC/M(64)2, 10 June 1964, both referred to in HR 169 Study Report, Part 1, November 1964, p8, AW2005/164, AWE archive.
61 See background information, untitled Ministry of Aviation covering note for HR 169 study in XY/412/013, Part B, 7 April 1965, AVIA 65/1860.
62 HR 169 Study Report, Part 2, November 1964, p26, AW2005/164, AWE archive.
63 HR 169 Study Report, Part 1, November 1964, p13, AW2005/164, AWE archive.
64 HR 169 Study Report, Part 1, November 1964, p16, AW2005/164, AWE archive.
65 HR 169 Study Report, Part 2, November 1964, p67, AW2005/164, AWE archive.
66 See Polaris Management Board: Note of a meeting on 17th September 1964, AVIA 65/1845; RAE Weapons Department memorandum, 'Penetration Aids for Polaris,' 7 October 1964; AVIA 65/1860; HR 169 Study Report, Part 1, November 1964, p22–30, AW2005/164, AWE archive.
67 HR 169 Study Report, Part 1, November 1964, Appendix E: Effects of Defensive Nuclear Explosions Against Mk. 2 Mod. 0 Re-entry Body, AW2005/164, AWE archive.
68 HR 169 Study Report, Part 1, November 1964, pp. 30–34, AW2005/164, AWE archive. Untitled Ministry of Aviation covering note for HR 169 study in XY/412/013, Part B, 7 April 1965, AVIA 65/1860.
69 HR 169 Study Report, Part 1, November 1964, p42–6, AW2005/164, AWE archive; and see Polaris Management Board: Note of a meeting on 17th September 1964, AVIA 65/1845.
70 HR 169 Study Report, Part 1, November 1964, pp. 47–50, AW2005/164, AWE archive.
71 COS 262/64, 'Nature of Military Operations, 1968–1980,' note by the Secretary, 9 October 1964, DEFE 5/154.
72 Henry Tanner, 'Soviet Parades Six New Rockets at Celebration,' *New York Times*, 8 November 1964.
73 See NIE 11–3–64, 'Soviet Air and Missile Defense Capabilities Through Mid-1970,' 16 December 1964, *FRUS, 1964–1968, Volume X: National Security Policy* (Washington, 2002), 194–7 (full version available at LBJL).
74 See 'Special Report: Current Aspects of the Soviet Antiballistic Missile System,' 26 March 1965, CK3100577570, DDRS.
75 NIE 11–3–64, 'Soviet Air and Missile Defense Capabilities Through Mid-1970,' 16 December 1964.
76 See, for example, David S. Yost, *Soviet Ballistic Missile Defense and the Western Alliance* (London, 1988), 27.
77 NIE 11–3–64, 'Soviet Air and Missile Defense Capabilities Through Mid-1970,' 16 December 1964.
78 See Podvig, *Russian Strategic Nuclear Forces*, 414.

79 Draft memorandum from McNamara for Kennedy, 14 November 1963, *FRUS, 1961–1963*, VIII, 526–33.
80 See Kaplan et al., *McNamara Ascendancy*, 320–2.
81 Hockaday letter to de Zulueta, 13 September 1963; Hockaday letter to Bligh, 'Underground Tests,' 17 September 1963, PREM 11/5173. Macmillan's laconic comment was merely, 'This seems sensible.'.
82 ND(63)7, 'British Nuclear Test Programme,' note by the UK Atomic Energy Authority, 25 September 1963; ND(63) 4th meeting, 30 October 1963, CAB 134/2240.
83 See Thorneycroft minute for Douglas-Home, 'British Underground Nuclear Tests,' 26 November 1963, PREM 11/5173.
84 See ND(63)10, 'A British Programme of Underground Nuclear Tests,' note by the UK Atomic Energy Authority, 16 December 1963, CAB 134/2240; ND(64) 1st meeting, 1 January 1964, CAB 134/2241.
85 See Thorneycroft minute for Douglas-Home, MO/12/2/1, 20 January 1964; John Boyd-Carpenter minute for Douglas-Home, 'British Underground Nuclear Tests,' 2-DM 40/771/01, 22 January 1964; Oliver Wright minute for Douglas-Home, 'British Underground Nuclear Tests,' 27 January 1964; Wright minute for Hockaday, 29 January 1964, PREM 11/5173.
86 Levin letter to A. E. Drake, 'Future Size of Aldermaston,' 125/64/D, 9 April 1964, AB 16/3977.
87 Zuckerman minute for Douglas-Home, 'Annual Nuclear Stocktake,' SZ/323/64, 5 May 1964, PREM 11/5170.
88 See Hockaday minute for Bligh, 'British Underground Nuclear Tests,' 7 May 1964, PREM 11/5173; and also Walker, *British Nuclear Weapons and the Test Ban*, 224.
89 See ND(64)8, 'Economy in Weapon Use of Fissile Material,' 22 June 1964, and ND(64) 5th meeting, 25 June 1964, CAB 134/2241; Penney letter to Glenn T. Seaborg, CH/WGP/64, 21 July 1964, DEFE 13/291; Thorneycroft minute for Douglas-Home, 'British Nuclear Test: Courser,' 14 September 1964; Hockaday minute for Malcolm Reid, 'British Nuclear Test: Courser,' 22 September 1964, PREM 11/5173.
90 See, for example, Scott George memorandum for Llewellyn Thompson, 'Test of UK Nuclear Device at Nevada Test Site,' 30 April 1965; Thompson letter to Seaborg, 30 April 1965, in Bureau of European Affairs, Office of North European Affairs, Records Relating to the United Kingdom, 1962–1974, box 2, RG 59, US National Archives.

13 The MLF, the size of the Polaris force and the approach of the general election, May 1963–October 1964

British policy and the dilemmas of the multilateral force

One of their key achievements as far as the British negotiators of the Polaris Sales Agreement were concerned was their success in decoupling US willingness to move ahead with support for the UK's Polaris programme from the other, more contentious aspects of the Nassau accord, including the establishment of a multilateral nuclear force, with its new mixed-manned element. In contrast with the relatively smooth trajectory of the UK Polaris programme, the fate of the MLF scheme was to be determined from the spring of 1963 onwards by the numerous military, political, technical and financial reservations that were raised over the proposal. To some MoD officials, the conclusion of the PSA in April 1963 meant that British opposition to the MLF could now be more openly voiced. Admiral Mountbatten, for one, as Chief of Defence Staff, had few qualms about dismissing with disdain, to anyone who would care to listen, the whole notion that Britain might associate itself with such a force. However, there were dangers to the UK's wider network of military and diplomatic relationships in the North Atlantic Alliance if it was the British who were seen to be the key state holding up positive movement. From Washington, for example, Ormsby Gore continued to warn that substantial political damage would occur if Britain was not to offer a contribution to the MLF, which if it went ahead without British involvement would serve to consolidate US–German ties to the detriment of UK interests.[1]

Not wanting to display outright opposition to the MLF, and with the Foreign Office concerned that rejection might have an adverse impact on Anglo-American relations and leave Britain on the sidelines if such a force was in any case established by its other potential members, the government therefore sought to continually delay its serious consideration. Nevertheless, the champions of the MLF scheme, largely to be found in the US State Department, were determined to press its features on the Alliance whenever possible and continued to lobby the White House in the search for more wholehearted presidential support. Amongst such US officials, Adenauer's obvious attraction to the MLF – and the dangers to Washington's relationship with Bonn if he was spurned, where there was growing talk of a potential Franco-German axis – was helping to create a momentum of its own. Their efforts began to bear some fruit when on 10 May 1963 President Kennedy wrote to Macmillan again, asking for an express British commitment to take part in the MLF, though no timescale was put on the request.[2] The Prime Minister and his senior advisers remained unimpressed. De Zulueta was dismissive, noting that the American arguments for an MLF were

> quite specious. Naturally the Germans are in favour of the multi-lateral nuclear force if only because it takes them one stage further along the road to nuclear power. It is not much prize for us and while the Americans no doubt attach primary importance to defeating the French 'force de frappe' and to stopping the Germans joining with the French in this I am by no means convinced that our interest lies in the same direction.

Nevertheless, as the MLF 'was in a sense the price for Polaris', de Zulueta did not think British opposition could be expressed in too forthright a fashion.[3]

Senior British ministers and officials, with Ormsby Gore recalled from Washington for the occasion, gathered in mid-May 1963 at Chequers to consider the government's response to the latest US pressure over moving ahead with the mixed-manned component of an MLF. Preparing Macmillan for the meeting, de Zulueta asked in rhetorical fashion: 'Do we wish to prevent the mixed manned force coming into being at all? The honest answer to this is that we do and this for three reasons:

i   We do not believe that it will have any military utility;
ii It will be expensive and whether we participate or not will inevitably divert resources from more useful military needs;
iii It will start the Germans on the road to nuclear power.

Yet up to that point British officials had by necessity adopted an 'equivocal' attitude to the MLF because of their desire to secure a Polaris deal and the promises made to the Americans to give the project 'a fair wind'. As blame for the MLF's ultimate failure might eventually be placed on Britain, de Zulueta was forced to the conclusion that a 'nominal' contribution (perhaps in terms of facilities) might have to be offered.[4]

During the Chequers discussions, ministers recognised that the military and financial arguments against participation in the MLF still seemed very strong, but there remained important political considerations which meant an accommodating attitude was advisable. 'If we failed to respond to this invitation,' it was noted, 'the project might fail completely; in which case the international odium would be laid at our door. Alternatively, if it were brought to fruition but we played no part in it, there was a risk that it would ultimately be dominated by the German Government.' Distrust of ultimate German intentions, once they became involved in the operation of such a multilateral force (and where they might contribute about 40 per cent of the costs), was once more an important factor lying behind official reservations about the creation of the MLF.[5]

In the event, Macmillan answered Kennedy's invitation by appealing for delay and arguing that no decisions should be made before the President's European tour in June. The Prime Minister was able to cite political uncertainty in Italy as an additional reason for why early decisions were not yet warranted.[6] It was also the case that British ministers and officials, as had been announced in January 1963, were determined to press ahead with the formal assignment of the entire V-bomber force to NATO, to form part of an 'Inter-Allied Nuclear Force', allowing SACEUR to integrate its weapons into his own nuclear strike planning. Thus on the final day of the gathering of NATO foreign and defence ministers held in Ottawa, on 23 May 1963, Mountbatten despatched a message to SACEUR, General Lyman L. Lemnitzer (who had taken Norstad's place the previous year), assigning to him the whole of the V-bomber force 'for targeting, planning, co-ordination and execution of strikes in accordance with your Nuclear Strike Plan.' This step, it was explained, was being taken, to begin the process outlined in paragraph 6 of the Nassau communiqué of bringing about closer arrangements for the control and organisation of NATO's nuclear forces. The caveat was added, however, that, 'Bearing in mind ... the dual role of the [V-bomber] force and the United Kingdom's commitments outside NATO for the defence of the free world,' the Government still retained the right to 'order the use of these British forces at discretion, if they decide that supreme national interests are at stake.' Moreover, 'in conditions of lesser emergency', it was stipulated the forces must also be available 'to meet national commitments outside NATO' (envisaged here was a contingency where elements of the V-force might have to be employed in a conventional bombing capacity).[7]

Assignment was therefore to be on terms which had very little substance in terms of operational control and consultative mechanisms for member states. The actual running and operation of the force – or what was called 'states of readiness, deployment and dispersal, logistics and support' – would remain a UK national responsibility.[8] The declaration made at Ottawa resulted in the arrangements for coordination of nuclear strike planning between Bomber Command and the US Strategic Air Command, which dated back to 1958, being superseded by new procedures. SACEUR would now have a new deputy responsible for nuclear affairs, and representation from other NATO members on SACEUR's own nuclear targeting staff, which operated a cell attached to SAC Headquarters at Omaha in Nebraska, was widened (so that by 1964 four NATO officers, from Italy, West Germany, France and the UK, alongside three US officers from SACEUR's staff, were assigned to the Joint Strategic Target Planning Staff at Omaha to ensure that SACEUR's nuclear plans were coordinated with those of the main US strategic nuclear forces).[9]

The Ottawa assignment of the V-bomber force, which would eventually be followed by the UK's Polaris submarines when they entered service, allowed British ministers to argue that they were moving forward with the understandings reached at Nassau.[10] It was nevertheless recognised that the Ottawa commitment was no more than a stop-gap measure that did not meet the requirements for shared control or mixed-manning of a commonly-owned nuclear force. Moreover, in some readings of the Nassau accord, the creation of an 'Inter-Allied Nuclear Force' (a description about which some NATO members had deep reservations, the French eventually vetoing its use as a label) did not invalidate the paragraph 8 undertaking to make the UK Polaris force available for inclusion in a wider 'NATO multilateral nuclear force' when one was eventually formed. Macmillan explained the latest position to the Cabinet on 23 May, saying that with the declaration made at Ottawa, Britain was under no further obligation to contribute to a NATO nuclear force. Nevertheless, although the military value of the mixed-manned MLF was 'open to serious question,' as the US Government attached such political importance to the project 'we could not refrain from endorsing it in principle.'[11]

The Kennedy administration, while recognising that the British Government had reservations concerning the MLF, was unclear about London's ultimate intentions. At the Ottawa meeting, Rusk had expressed his perplexity to Home over Macmillan's recent message to the President: did this represent some major problem in principle about taking part in an MLF? Backed into a corner, the Foreign Secretary had replied that the Government

> thought there was a lot in the political ideas behind the force and that we would continue to support it provided it was workable. But frankly there were difficulties, military, financial and Parliamentary.

On a personal basis, Home informed Macmillan that he did not think that Britain could avoid joining with other interested parties in discussions over the practical issues involved with setting up the seaborne mixed-manned component of an MLF, but the Cabinet would have to be fully behind whatever course was adopted.[12] Nevertheless, Macmillan still felt the best approach was to shun any further message to Kennedy about entering detailed talks, or offering even a conditional commitment to take part, and to 'play this along' until after the President's European tour.[13]

Reflecting dominant opinion in the Foreign Office, Home thought that this might not be the wisest course. Towards the end of May he submitted a paper for the Cabinet which attempted to lay out the political issues which were at stake. The Germans, Home had argued, were not prepared

> to remain indefinitely in the position of a second-class Power. United States diplomacy and the French *force de frappe* have stimulated the Germans into this mood, but I am convinced that they will not for very

much longer be content to have no share in the control of nuclear weapons. It is to meet this problem in a way that does not give the Germans an independent nuclear capacity that the United States have proposed the multilateral force.

American prestige was now firmly tied up with the success of the project, and it had become an important part of their overall European policy. The choice for the UK, as the Foreign Secretary now saw it, boiled down to either

> (a) joining the multilateral force and controlling the Germans from inside it or (b) standing aloof from it in the hope that it will be stillborn and that the Germans will not acquire nuclear weapons in other ways; or that it will come into being, but that it will not lead to a German national capacity or be detrimental to us in other ways.

Other NATO members, apart from France which wanted nothing to do with the MLF, hoped Britain would take part in the force's management and control, and Home believed it was certain the MLF would be formed (even if only by the United States and Germany alone), whatever stance the UK took. From the foreign policy point of view, Home saw a British contribution to the force 'of the first importance.' As an initial step, he therefore proposed 'a multilateral examination of the idea of mixed manning.'[14]

Thorneycroft countered the Foreign Office line with a paper which made the point there was no military case for a new mixed-manned force of surface ships, warned about the financial costs, and cast strong doubts over whether the scheme would have the positive political effects its supporters claimed. Indeed, its creation, he argued, would lead to the risk of putting nuclear weapons under effective German control (if the principle of unanimity of voting in the political arrangements accompanying the force were relaxed over time), intensify East-West tensions, and weaken the unity of the Atlantic Alliance. The Minister of Defence thought it should be British policy to bring about the abandonment of the whole plan: 'we must consider our attitude with the utmost care before we proceed with proposals for which the military case is non-existent and the political case both doubtful and controversial.'[15]

Another consideration, however, was the wider realm of Anglo-American relations as a whole. Now back at his post in Washington, Ormsby Gore was anxious that if the Government did not make a more positive contribution to the MLF idea and equivocation continued, it would create considerable ill-will within the Kennedy administration, telling Home that

> ...although the Americans could never claim that we had broken the letter of any agreement with them by not contributing to the force, I fear that they would feel we had broken the spirit of the agreement which

was reached at Nassau. While the President is fairly restrained on the topic when talking to me, I know that he feels this way.

For his own part, Ormsby Gore felt that the costs of any British contribution to the MLF had been exaggerated, and that participation would be worthwhile considering the 'political risks both to our relations with America, with the Germans and with the rest of Europe' if Britain were to eschew involvement.[16]

On the same day that the Ambassdor had composed his letter, Kennedy had despatched another message to the Prime Minister urging him to join with the United States in maintaining momentum behind the scheme. After defending the military case for the force, Kennedy then deployed what he saw as the key political issue:

> every day that passes makes it plainer that a clear move from the United Kingdom toward participation in the MLF will be a major forward step in our joint effort to bind the alliance safely and strongly together, in the face of General de Gaulle's opposite course. The Germans are the heart of the problem, and I simply cannot escape the conclusion that of the courses available to us in dealing with them, the MLF is the only safe one. If it fails the Germans are bound to move in much more dangerous directions. In the long run even toward some partly clandestine arrangement with the French or, if this should not work, toward an independent nuclear effort in Germany – not now but in time.

Although acknowledging that definite agreements leading to an MLF could not be made ready for his upcoming European trip, the President still expressed the hope that work on the necessary arrangements could be completed by the end of the year.[17]

Subsequent discussion of the issues by the full Cabinet revealed no consensus, with some ministers reluctant to be associated with a venture which carried such obvious drawbacks from the British point of view, but involvement in which seemed to be essential if harmony in Anglo-American relations was to be maintained. As the Cabinet Secretary's notes recorded Home saying: 'If we stand aside, will force be created? Yes. And if we stay outside we forfeit share of control. US may cheat on Polaris. But more likely if we stay outside.' Maudling, the Chancellor of Exchequer, also thought that if the MLF was going to be formed, Britain should be in, despite his concerns over the costs. Duncan Sandys, now Commonwealth Secretary, agreed with Thorneycroft's military objections, but viewed it as 'politically v[ery] dangerous to stay out. Fr[ance] has contracted out of Nato; if we do too, alliance may well disintegrate. In any case we shd. be bypassed on a good many Nato discussion and decisions.' The decision, Sandys said, should rest on the amount of money involved. As for Heath, he felt that European opinion was confused because after Nassau the UK had emphasised its nuclear independence almost as much as de Gaulle:

> If we stay out, we alienate US, Germany and our friends in Europe. We shall play into de Gaulle's hands: and we shall be isolated. France's object is to consolidate Six on basis of Fr-G. Treaty. If so, this means Fr-G arrangement about the deterrent. Our strategy needs rethinking before we can dismiss project as military nonsense.

The Prime Minister's final comment was that he was still unsure whether mixed-manning 'really was a military nonsense or not.' The Americans seemed less disposed to rush, and so Macmillan saw this as an opportunity to look at mixed-manning more closely, and to consider the issues again later. A temporising reply to Kennedy was once more delivered, explaining that the government was not yet in a position to give a final view on whether they would participate in the mixed-manned force.[18]

Despite the entreaties coming from the British Embassy in Washington, by the summer of 1963 there were in fact signs that the White House's immediate enthusiasm for the MLF was beginning to slacken. One significant development here was the visit of the French Foreign Minister, Couve de Murville, to Washington at the end of May. Asked directly by Kennedy if the French would provide nuclear help to Germany if the MLF scheme should not materialise, Couve gave a flat negative in reply – a response which received wide coverage in the press.[19] Another factor was the official attention that was consumed by the final stages of the negotiation of a partial nuclear test ban treaty, and US realisation that there was a growing conflict between the MLF and the future hopes of an accord with the Soviet Union over non-proliferation (Moscow rejecting any steps which might involve Germany any more closely in the control of nuclear forces, however indirect).[20]

While discussions over the MLF were conducted in the private communications between NATO governments, the Labour Opposition lost few chances to harass senior ministers over progress made in implementing all the features of the Nassau Agreement. In response to probing in the House of Commons on 20 June, for example, Macmillan replied that as UK nuclear forces had been assigned to SACEUR at the Ottawa meeting the previous month, the Government now considered it had fully carried out is obligations under the Agreement to use its 'best endeavours' to bring about the creation of a multilateral force amongst NATO members.[21]

Study of the possibilities of a mixed-manned force had meanwhile continued by officials and led to the conclusion by the COS that notwithstanding other military objections, the practical difficulties involved could, in fact, be overcome. As preparations were made for what was to prove Kennedy's final meeting with Macmillan, at the latter's home at Birch Grove in the Sussex countryside, the Foreign Secretary continued to press the case for British willingness to engage in technical talks with the United States and others over how the MLF could be formed, but without any political commitment to join any force which might eventually be created.[22]

Macmillan's own officials felt that joining such talks was premature, and would in any case be opposed by the Cabinet as a whole.[23] Indeed, subsequent Cabinet discussion saw several ministers referring to the basic issue that ultimately Parliament would not support a proposal for the UK to join a mixed-manned force as currently conceived. Yet at the same time the Prime Minister recognised, as he told his colleagues, that the Government could not ignore 'the growing feeling in Europe, which was not confined to Germany, that the European partners in NATO were entitled to some more effective share in the control of nuclear weapons on which their ultimate defence depended.' An offer to engage in a discussion of the management and control of NATO nuclear forces might be 'open to less political objection' than involvement in talks over a mixed-manned force. The idea was even mooted by Thorneycroft that an alternative to the MLF was a 'genuinely European nuclear deterrent' founded on Anglo-French nuclear cooperation – the Minister of Defence had said 'if we can persuade US to defer MLF, we cd. try to get talks with Fr. going, and some Eur. Alt[ernative] might emerge … if we go on with MLF without France, we shall move still further away from Fr. – without whom we can't have a Eur. defence policy'. But objections to this were raised by Home who argued that it would take many years and much expense to get anywhere close to US deterrent capabilities, while an Anglo-French monopoly over control would be unwelcome to the Germans.

Given the conflicting views on offer and his own doubts, Macmillan could do no more than say that in his forthcoming talks with Kennedy he would seek to delay further action over the mixed-manned force until the much wider current review of NATO strategy and force goals had demonstrated whether a military requirement for it existed. He would emphasise the domestic political opposition that would greet British involvement in technical talks concerning the mixed-manned force, and that the prime goal of Western policy should be negotiations with the Soviet Union aimed at the banning of nuclear testing, and stopping the further proliferation of nuclear weapons, objectives which could be undermined by promotion of the MLF in the face of Moscow's strenuous opposition.[24]

At their Birch Grove meeting at the end of June 1963, President Kennedy again indicated his support for the MLF scheme to Macmillan, saying that without it there would be 'strong pressure from the Germans for a bilateral arrangement with the US for medium range ballistic missiles on their territory,' and that he hoped Britain would agree to join with other Alliance members in studying proposals for creation of a mixed-manned force. Emphasising the parliamentary opposition he would face if he were to proceed in this way, Macmillan had reiterated the many problems attached to the arrangements that would accompany the MLF. Wanting to avoid disagreement, Kennedy did not seem disposed to press matters, predicting less pressure from Germany in the future and no urgent need to make decisions: 'He did not want to kill the idea of the multilateral force at this particular moment. He felt that to do so would be a bad mistake. In six months the idea might not have such an appeal.'[25]

The Prime Minister professed to want to address the political problem of the non-nuclear powers in NATO, rather than the technical matter of setting up a new force. Britain could not take part in any conference which had a mixed-manned force as its central subject but could participate in more general talks about nuclear arrangements in the Alliance, a proposition with which Kennedy was happy to agree.[26] Hence, the final communiqué issued after the Birch Grove meeting had reaffirmed in anodyne terms that the President and Prime Minister had 'agreed that a basic problem facing the NATO Alliance was the closer association of its members with the nuclear deterrent of the Alliance. They also agreed that various possible ways of meeting this problem should be further discussed with their Allies. Such discussions would include the proposal for a multilateral seaborne force, without prejudice to the question of British participation in such a force.'[27]

Kennedy himself was divided at this time between his appreciation of the crucial political factors that lay behind the project, and his belief that the MLF had major practical drawbacks and could never be made to work unless the British were willing and active participants. During June, for example, he was receiving very cautious assessments from McGeorge Bundy, his influential national security adviser, who thought that the US approach should switch 'from pressure to inquiry.' Many obstacles lay in the scheme's path (including overcoming the practical problems related to the force's composition and functioning, while major political capital would have to be used to surmount Congressional opposition), and even if it could be forced through, Bundy thought that it would be at the cost of damaging many key US relationships – not least with the UK – since the MLF would be regarded as the unwanted product of American pressure. Most importantly, Bundy's view was that there was 'no strong affirmative German sentiment for the MLF as something the Germans themselves want.... If we press the MLF through in the next 12 months, we shall have only grudging support among the very people on whose interest the force has been designed.' Instead, Bundy advised continuing study of the various features of the MLF, but a gradual retreat from the overt political commitment to its success that had been exhibited (mainly at the behest of enthusiasts in the State Department) over the previous few months.[28]

By July, in the wake of the Kennedy visit, and in view of the aspirations expressed in the resulting communique, the Foreign Secretary was keen to move forward with a British initiative to discuss the political control of nuclear forces within NATO. Anxious to show that the UK was not exhibiting a wholly negative attitude to the problem, the Foreign Office proposals included a 'NATO Nuclear Control Commission', representing all countries contributing either existing nuclear forces allocated to the Inter-Allied force inaugurated at Ottawa, or any new mixed-manned element that might be formed in the future. Home envisaged five permanent members on the Commission, the US, UK, France, West Germany and Italy, and one or two rotating members. Its functions were to include providing SACEUR with political guidance on nuclear matters, approving SACEUR's nuclear planning, drawing up guidelines for the use of nuclear weapons, and authorising SACEUR to execute his nuclear plans.[29]

However, the Minister of Defence thought any move to open this kind of discussion in NATO would be premature, while it was recognised wider ministerial approval would be required before the proposal could go any further. In the event, the Cabinet, at a meeting on 11 July, merely asked officials from the two concerned departments to study once again the problems of the management and control of nuclear weapons in NATO and to assemble an agreed set of views for further consideration by ministers. Advised by the British ambassadors in Bonn and Paris that the Commission scheme would be seen as 'setting up an alliance within the alliance' and that the French would not agree to join, the proposal was, in fact, to be dropped by the Foreign Secretary in September.[30] With the negotiation of the Partial Test Ban Treaty in Moscow in mid-July consuming the majority of official attention, moreover, there seemed no great urgency to launch a new initiative over the remainder of the summer.

In the meantime, however, US State Department officials had already begun to circulate the outline of a draft charter for the MLF, and to hold separate discussions with the Germans, Italians, Greeks and Turks on how to take matters forward. From these talks emerged an Italian proposal to form working groups, one to meet in Paris with a focus on the political and legal issues connected with establishment of an MLF, and the other to meet in Washington, where military and technical problems were to be of prime concern. American officials volunteered to compose terms of reference for the groups, and overtures were made in Washington about British attitudes to participation.[31]

The emergence of concrete proposals to form working groups intended to give practical shape to the MLF scheme again provoked much inter-bureaucratic conflict in Whitehall. Alternative moves to convince the Germans to take an interest in British ideas for the political management of nuclear weapons within NATO having obviously proved fruitless, an evidently alarmed Foreign Secretary told Thorneycroft towards the end of August that it was

> now becoming clear that the Multilateral Force is by no means dead ... We are thus faced once more with what our action should be if the caravan moves off without us ... In considering our attitude, I think we have to remember that we welcomed the concept of the MLF in principle. I did so in NATO and you did so in the House of Commons. We

cannot go back on that and I think we might reasonably be expected at least to give such a force facilities, even if we could not join it.

Home was inclined to favour attendance at the technical working group, saying,

> I do not like being left out of the force with no say in the management and therefore no influence on the amount of control of it, which may fall into German hands. I hope therefore that you will feel that our presence at the technical level, without any commitment, is possible. The only alternative would be a message from the Prime Minister to the President, asking him to bury the idea, but I am quite sure that it would not succeed.[32]

Thorneycroft, however, was plainly unhappy with the whole notion of involvement with the working groups, and he was joined by Treasury voices calling for greater reserve.[33]

When British officials received the US-composed terms of reference for the new working groups in early September concerns grew. As well as examining political, legal and administrative questions, the Paris group looked more like an overall steering committee whose task would include formulating agreed language between those NATO members represented that might be included in the draft text of an eventual treaty establishing the MLF. 'Whatever the exact status of the resulting documents,' the Washington Embassy reported, 'the Paris Group would aim to reach inter-governmental agreement covering such things as ownership of the new nuclear weapons and the political arrangements for their use.'[34] Both Home and Thorneycroft were asked to prepare papers for the Cabinet on the issue of whether Britain should be represented on the working groups.

By now the Foreign Office was convinced, given American determination to proceed, that some form of MLF was probably inevitable, even in the face of British objections, and that it would be far better if Britain joined at the outset in order to influence its development. Sir Harold Caccia, the PUS, sent strongly worded advice to Home that if the UK did not join the discussion groups,

> We shall have sacrificed something of the intimacy of our relationship with the United States in nuclear matters and ... we shall not only have put a strain upon the direct relations between the United Kingdom and the United States, we shall also have abstracted ourselves from what we must reckon is now a likely development in the Atlantic relationship between Europe and the United States. There is also the European aspect. General de Gaulle has kept us out of the European Community, but we have done what we can to maintain the closest links with the other members of the Community and the principal of these is Germany.

We must reckon that failure to participate in the committees on the MLF will put a strain on our relations with Germany. It is for these reasons that we risk to lose power and influence by standing aside.³⁵

Presenting the matter in his paper for Cabinet, the Foreign Secretary informed his colleagues that when he had seen Rusk in Moscow for the signing of the Partial Test Ban Treaty in August, the latter had said 'that the United States Government had committed their prestige and their good name to the Germans on the multilateral force and they could not go back; indeed he was inclined to reproach us for having changed our attitude since the Nassau meeting…' All the alternatives, including using existing nuclear systems under different forms of control, were not considered viable because of objections from other Alliance members. In an attempt to be positive and constructive, Home wanted his colleagues' agreement to his recommendation that the UK take part in meetings of the two working groups, on the understanding it would not be committed to membership, and that British objectives for the MLF (such as retention of the American veto, and that as far as possible existing rather than planned weapons systems should be used) were promulgated to the other participants.³⁶

MoD officials, as well as the Chiefs of Staff, held altogether different views, however, believing that a basic decision on whether the UK wanted to see an MLF created or not had to be taken before attendance at any meetings to discuss how it might be set up. Capital costs of a new mixed-manned MLF could amount to £400–500 million in total, with Britain expected to contribute £10–20 million over at least a decade. Moreover, a whole series of political and military objections could be raised against it, and Thorneycroft could see no prospect of gaining support in the House of Commons for British involvement. He discerned no genuine support from Germany for the MLF, except on the basis of conforming with American wishes, and did not believe that the Germans would do a bilateral deal with the US to establish the MLF if the British stayed out. Not surprisingly, Thorneycroft wanted the Cabinet to support his view that Britain should refrain from joining any further talks dealing with the MLF.³⁷

Cabinet meetings on 19 and 20 September saw Home and Thorneycroft rehearsing their familiar arguments, with Macmillan stating that the Government now faced a major dilemma over what course to adopt. Thorneycroft thought that 'we are being gradually manoeuvred into false posn. We are already regarded, abroad and at home, as largely committed to force. Attendance at confce [sic] will confirm this.' Heath, for one, disagreed with this approach. Considering the previous statements of ministers, particularly at the time of Merchant's visit to London in March 1963, he argued that Britain *was* at least morally committed to the MLF. If the MLF was considered militarily a 'nonsense', then so, he thought 'is our own independent deterrent – wh[ich] is equally unnecessary.' The only reasons for the UK's own nuclear capability, he argued, lay in the political domain and this was the same rationale for the MLF, Heath adding that, 'Dog shouldn't eat dog.' He also observed that MLF costs, even if underestimated, were small in relation to the total defence spending of the Alliance. The only alternative, in his view was a 'Franco-Br. independent deterrent', and if this was rejected then Britain could not afford to be left out of the US-German project. Macmillan, however, was very reluctant to take a full part in the working groups, instinctively feeling that technical discussions would be the start of a slippery slope. Ministers eventually decided to try to find an 'intermediate course' which would avoid accusations of a breach of faith by the US Government, 'exert some influence over the development of the project', and circumvent any commitment to contribute to the force. The Foreign Secretary would be instructed to make clear to Rusk, when he next saw him in New York for the meeting of the UN General Assembly at the end of the month, that Britain considered it had fulfilled its Nassau obligations, and that no undertaking to contribute to a mixed-manned MLF could be assumed. But he should also explain that in an attempt to give as much support to the US as possible, and as their closest ally, the UK was prepared to send observers to the working group meetings, without commitment to later steps.[38]

Over the next few days, a tortuous process of compiling a draft directive and supporting statements for Home's meeting with Rusk was undertaken. By now, Macmillan was becoming increasingly disturbed by press reports of splits between ministers – at a time when his Government was still reeling from the shocks of the Profumo scandal – and angry at the situation that US policy toward the MLF had created. On 21 September he minuted Sir Burke Trend, the Cabinet Secretary, to express his anxieties, complaining that all Kennedy's advisers 'wish to drive Britain out of being an independent nuclear power,' and that they had never reconciled themselves to his success at Nassau in convincing the President to supply Polaris. They would even, he alleged, prefer that a Labour Government emerge after the next election because it would be more amenable over such issues.[39] Another minute to Home expressed similar visceral feelings: 'The Administration as a whole, especially the State Department and the Pentagon, wish to stop us ever being an independent nuclear power. They think the President was over-persuaded by me and they have never forgiven me. So long as we have any power we must stand for Britain. If Mr Wilson and Co want to sell out Britain's interests and become a satellite of the United States let them do so.'[40]

When the Cabinet convened on 23 September to reconsider the terms of British participation in the working groups, the Foreign Secretary argued against the idea of just sending 'observers'. It would be better, Home felt, to have full representation with a specific reservation over any commitment. Sandys also agreed with this approach, maintaining that the aim should be to influence the talks, and drawing comparisons with Britain's failure to be involved at the outset when the European Economic Community was being formed. The Prime Minister again complained that the US Government, apart from Kennedy himself, 'want to destroy our independent deterrent and resent Nassau decision. They wd. welcome a Labour Govt. from this point of view!'[41]

Nevertheless, Home's position won the day, and the idea of sending observers was dropped in favour of full participation in the working group discussions. With the Cabinet Secretary's expert drafting skills fully employed, a statement was compiled which would explain the basis for British involvement for the benefit of the other working group participants, be suitable for public consumption, and provide formal guidance for Home when he saw Rusk. The statement stressed that the Government considered that it had already fulfilled its Nassau obligation to help with forming a multilateral force through the assignment earlier in the year of the V-bombers and, when they were produced, Polaris submarines, to NATO. With the value of forming a new mixed-manned element to an MLF having been publicly questioned, the Government could not join discussions about its practicalities under terms of reference which suggested that those involved would eventually be willing to participate. But, having reiterated this strong reservation, the statement concluded by offering to join in an 'objective examination' of the MLF scheme 'in all its aspects and possible variations.'[42]

When asked for his comment after being presented with this draft formula by Home in New York (a text that had been the source of such prolonged angst), a bemused Rusk could only affirm that final national decisions to take part in the MLF would in any case only come at the end of the process, and it was understood by other governments that involvement in the working group discussions was wholly without commitment. At the same time, he hoped that British involvement in the working groups would not lead to fundamental questioning of the whole MLF concept.[43] Cabinet agreement to the final text of a statement was secured on 1 October, and when ten days later the first meeting of the Paris MLF working group was convened (which included the US, West Germany, Italy, Belgium, the Netherlands, Greece and Turkey), Sir Evelyn Shuckburgh, the UK Permanent Representative to NATO, was present on Britain's behalf.

Thorneycroft was clearly unhappy with this whole drift of events. He wanted to supply Shuckburgh with a series of questions about wider aspects of the MLF, such as its aim and purpose, as well as its basic viability, to throw into the Paris group's deliberations, and was anxious that the Foreign Secretary still seemed to accept its formation as a *fait accompli*.[44] The Ministry of Defence was also keen to use the leeway afforded by the working group's acceptance that 'variants' to the MLF mixed-manned surface ship proposals could be considered to introduce new ideas about the different patterns of nuclear forces that could be allocated by national governments. Thus in the guidance issued to Shuckburgh it was specified that if discussion in the working group moved on from first principles to details of the desirable force, his position should be that the UK did not necessarily accept the original model of 25 surface ships, each equipped with eight Polaris missiles. 'In order to allow flexibility,' the guidance ran, 'we should wish to discuss the possibility of using other weapons or weapons systems, the number and type of carriers needed for the weapons to be used and the ancillary units or facilities which will be needed. In order to keep costs to a minimum, it would be preferable that the weapons used should as far as possible be found from existing or planned weapons systems. The aim and purpose might be better achieved by the establishment of a multilateral tactical force consisting of short-range land-based missiles or aircraft or even by constituting part of the force in this way.' Whether such units could also be mixed-manned by different nationalities would also have to be studied.[45]

For some, such ideas were little more than an elaborate spoiling operation, designed to slow down and distract members of the working groups, but in any event British defence officials were to expend major amounts of time and energy over the next year in devising different variants to the MLF, using the existing nuclear resources already deployed by NATO members in the European area. In December 1963, at the ministerial meeting of the North Atlantic Council held in Paris, Thorneycroft began to float the notion of using tactical weapons already in existence or planned as the basis for the MLF, suggesting that the mixed-manning principle could be extended to these units.[46]

By January 1964, while still finding it militarily unnecessary, the COS were informing Thorneycroft that if political factors required the UK to take part in an MLF, the idea of a mixed-manned force of land-based missiles and/or aircraft was to be preferred to a seaborne force, and appropriate weapons should be selected for such a force with SACEUR's interdiction mission in mind. An experiment involving the mixed-manning of a V-bomber was even discussed as a parallel to the surface ship exercise that the Americans had been proposing since the summer.[47]

Whitehall's reading of the US position on the MLF during the summer and autumn of 1963 was not helped by the different signals emerging from the US administration. The State Department seemed as determined as ever to push forward with the idea of creating an entirely new nuclear force (or a so-called 'hardware' solution), and there was no obvious enthusiasm for the Foreign Office's earlier notions of building on the start made at Ottawa in May by reforming the existing structures of the North Atlantic Alliance to give its non-nuclear members a greater say in political guidance over nuclear use and nuclear planning more generally (or a 'software' solution). At the same time, the strong reservations of the Pentagon and the US Joint Chiefs of Staff over the whole MLF project were well known, and, closer to the White House, Bundy's scepticism has already been noted. As for the President himself, Kennedy tended to steer a middle course.[48] He was ready to see a start made with experiments over the mixed-manning of surface ships, and to discussions in the working groups, but he was evidently satisfied that this all should proceed at a very measured and deliberate pace and his mind was open to variants, if the initial conception was to prove unworkable. At the start of October, for example, he told the Foreign Secretary that he hoped Britain would take part in the mixed-manning experiment as it would help to convey the impression of momentum, but it would also, in fact, be a useful time-consuming exercise.[49]

Meanwhile, and as Adenauer moved aside to be replaced as Chancellor by Ludwig Erhard, the German position over the MLF had begun to shift, in Alastair Buchan's words, from 'one of intelligent interest to something more closely resembling a demand.' As far as many officials in Washington saw it, the MLF had become a vital instrument to wean Bonn away from the temptations of a closer Franco-German partnership toward a strengthening of its Atlantic ties with the United States.[50] Nevertheless, it increasingly seemed that, with progress so slow, high-level political decisions over the future of the MLF would have to wait until after the two sets of elections that were anticipated in the United States and Britain in the autumn of 1964. The unexpected departure through illness of Macmillan as Prime Minister in mid-October 1963, moreover, and his replacement by Lord Home – now re-styled Sir Alec Douglas-Home to enable him to sit in the Commons – gave further cause for delay on the British side, and Kennedy's assassination the following month meant that American attentions were understandably diverted in the final part of the year. If British officials thought that American interest in the MLF would relax during 1964, however, they were to be sadly disabused. Kennedy's successor in the White House, Lyndon B. Johnson, was to prove similarly concerned over the potential for German nuclear ambitions to destabilise the North Atlantic Alliance, and by the spring diplomatic pressures would once more build for progress to be made with the scheme.[51]

Changes to the central organisation of defence and foreign policy

The protracted debates over the MLF during 1963, where the Ministry of Defence had often been pitted against the Foreign Office, with Downing Street acting as arbiter, were another illustration of the inextricable linkages between defence and foreign policy. It had long been recognised that some new Whitehall machinery which could accommodate this basic fact was required, especially as the challenges of controlling the defence budget amid reassessments of Britain's global and Cold War commitments grew during the early 1960s. Since its establishment in 1947, the Cabinet's Defence Committee had served a useful purpose, but its remit was considered too narrow, and it was supported by no formal and permanent committee structure on the official side. The other great organisational transformation mooted in the general area of defence policy, and given zealous backing by Mountbatten and Thorneycroft in 1962, was the centralisation of the Ministry of Defence so that the power of the separate service ministries was reduced, and control consolidated over the Navy, Army and Air Force. Decisions in principle on these matters were announced to the House of Commons by Thorneycroft in March 1963, and a more detailed White Paper specifying the changes proposed was published in July. This argued that the reforms introduced after the 1958 Defence Organisation White Paper had not, in practice, achieved the necessary degree of central control over defence policy, not least so that the defence budget could be rationalised. Moreover, new arrangements were 'needed for formulating requirements for weapons and for controlling the defence research and development programme.'[52]

Although the Navy, Army and Air Force would preserve their separate identities, a unified Ministry of Defence was to be created which would absorb the three service ministries, bringing them together in one building under the control of a single PUS. The evocative names of the old ministries – Admiralty, War Office, and Air Ministry – were to be supplanted with the neutral and more bureaucratic nomenclature of Navy, Army, and Air Force Departments, and their individual Secretaries of State (or in the case of the Navy, First Lord of the Admiralty) abolished. A new position of 'Secretary of State for Defence', with improved powers over administration, planning, and allocation of resources, was to replace the previous 'Minister of Defence', with support from three subordinate ministers of state, who might oversee a particular service or exercise responsibility in some functional area. A Defence Council, consisting of the new Secretary of State, the ministers of state, the COS, the PUS, and CSA, would replace the ineffective Defence Board that had been formed in 1958, and 'exercise the powers of command and administrative control' previously held by the Board of Admiralty, and the Army and Air Councils.

The post of Chief of the Defence Staff was also enhanced by giving its holder an increased staff, but otherwise remained little altered as it was the COS Committee that was still 'collectively responsible to the Government for professional advice on strategy and military operations and on the military implications of defence policy.' The CDS was to present the collective views of the Committee, and could offer his own advice to the Secretary of State when appropriate, but the effectiveness of the role tended to depend more on the personality of the individual that filled it than on its formal constitutional position. The fact that its occupant during this period continued to be Mountbatten ensured that the CDS would become a powerful voice in the new defence arrangements that were ushered in during the early 1960s. The nerve centre of the revamped MoD would be its Defence Secretariat, which brought together the civil administrative staffs of the old service ministries which had been concerned with questions of major defence policy. Now placed under the MoD's PUS, the secretariat would be responsible for dispensing advice on the defence programme and budget, as well as matters of major policy, and be the main conduit to the oversea policy departments, including the Foreign, Commonwealth, and Colonial Offices. Encapsulated by legislation in the autumn, the new arrangements at the MoD would come into effect from 1 April 1964.[53]

Complementing Mountbatten's imperious qualities at the top of the new defence machinery was Zuckerman, who continued in his important role as

CSA at the MoD. Indeed, the White Paper confirmed that under the changes the CSA was to join the CDS and PUS as one of the three principal advisers to the Secretary of State. Reflecting the ever-increasing prominence of science and technology to the MoD's concerns, and the rising costs of defence equipment, the CSA was accorded the right of direct access to the Secretary of State, giving him co-equal status to the CDS and PUS within the Ministry's hierarchy. As he had since first joining the MoD in 1960, Zuckerman continued to enjoy assistance with nuclear matters throughout this period from the influential but little recognised figure of Robert Press.[54] Born in 1915, Press had graduated from Queen's University in Belfast and worked as a research physicist at Trinity College, Dublin, in the early years of the Second World War. In 1941, he entered the scientific civil service and spent much of the war in the Far East, returning to research work at Trinity after 1945 which led to the award of his PhD. He joined the Atomic Energy Department at the Ministry of Supply in 1948, and during the 1950s became a leading technical expert on nuclear testing issues (and heading the atomic intelligence unit for period), by the end of the decade working in Washington on liaison with the Americans under the 1958 Agreement.[55] During the 1960s, Press served as Zuckerman's unstinting and loyal aide, providing technical advice, briefings, and the drafts of minutes on nuclear matters which would finally emerge under Zuckerman's name. 'His memory about who had said what at international meetings, both with our American allies and also at informal discussions in which the Russians were involved,' Zuckerman wrote after his death in a fulsome tribute, 'was formidable, and his attention to detail meticulous. He was always level-headed and his briefs were invariably succinct and complete.'[56]

Under the new White Paper dispensation, the CSA's Defence Scientific Staff was to be increased in size, and two deputies to Zuckerman were eventually appointed, one responsible for 'Projects' (covering the MoD's research and development programmes), and the other for 'Studies' (for broad matters of operational research and longer-term thinking). Alan Cottrell, a professor of metallurgy at Cambridge, was brought in to fill the amorphous 'Studies' brief in January 1965, while Sir William Cook, formerly Penney's deputy at AWRE, was made Chief Adviser (Projects), taking up his appointment on 1 August 1964.[57] As preparations for the reorganisation of the MoD advanced during the summer of 1963, Press's main concern was that the status and role of his own small Nuclear Group within Zuckerman's bolstered Defence Scientific Staff should not be reduced. Apart from maintaining bilateral nuclear cooperation with the Americans (where the CSA operated as the principal custodian of the 1958 MDA within the MoD), the work of the Nuclear Group served the CSA's needs when it came to considering the policy aspects of the nuclear requirements of the services, the defence research and development programme, the supply of special nuclear materials for defence purposes, safety of weapons storage, handling and transport, advice on nuclear security and classification, and control over the dissemination of nuclear information to other countries. There were also likely to be many new areas where technical assistance and advice was required, as the Partial Test Ban Treaty had to be monitored, and fresh negotiations over further measures of arms control and disarmament were instigated between the Superpowers. Appealing to a receptive Zuckerman, Press argued that this all amounted 'to a formidable commitment worthy of a clearly defined field of responsibility, in your new organisation, and one which should in no way be regarded as heading for early redundancy.' As well as looking for enhanced status for his Nuclear Group, Press wanted to ensure that he continued to enjoy a line of direct reporting to Zuckerman. Seeing that new scientific posts for Projects and Studies were to be created under the CSA, Press wondered if he could adopt the title Assistant Chief Scientific Adviser (Nuclear), or ACSA(N), to reflect the prominence that nuclear affairs should enjoy under the new organisational arrangements (nomenclature which Zuckerman was happy to approve).[58]

The July 1963 White Paper also dealt with reforms to the high-level policymaking machinery in the area of defence and foreign affairs. It had argued, in widely accepted fashion, that

> major questions of defence policy cannot be discussed in purely military terms; they also need to be examined in relation to foreign and economic policy, and in this wider context they often raise further issues which have a considerable political content. Conversely, our political relations with the other members of the Commonwealth and with foreign countries bear directly on our defence policy; and the requirements of the Government's financial and economic policies equally affect the size, disposition, and equipment of the Services.

So that the relevant ministers could collectively examine such issues, and though still subject to the 'supreme authority' of the Cabinet, a new Defence and Oversea Policy Committee (DOPC) was to be formed, chaired by the Prime Minister. This ministerial committee would be supported by an official counterpart, with the Cabinet Secretary usually taking the chair, and the permanent secretaries of the major departments represented on its parent body in attendance.[59] To general approval, the DOPC formerly came into existence on 1 October 1963, superseding both the Defence Committee and a short-lived Oversea Policy Committee which had met only briefly earlier in the year.

A five boat Polaris force?

One of the first nuclear subjects to be considered by the new DOPC machinery was the size of the Polaris force. By June 1963 it had become widely recognised by ministers that current levels of defence spending could not be sustained over the long term and were having a deleterious effect on the economy.⁶⁰ Among the suggestions for controlling spending circulated by Thorneycroft among the services at this time, and which helped to crystalise positions, was a proposal to finally settle for a four boat Polaris force. Certainly, Treasury thinking was predicated on the assumption that the programme was to involve only four boats.⁶¹

However, by the autumn of 1963 Admiralty views over the eventual size of the force had been influenced by the recognition, based on the latest studies and information available to the CPE, that a four boat force would not allow two boats to be kept on continuous station and ready to fire at all times. A five boat force, in contrast, would allow two to be kept on constant station throughout the year, which would also have the advantage of presenting two different and widely dispersed launching platforms, so complicating the task of anti-missile defence. Five boats also provided some insurance against the possibility that accident, malfunction or even sabotage could render a portion of the force non-operational, but these considerations had to be set against the cost for another boat (about an 18 per cent increase in capital and running costs), the additional manpower demands it would make on the already stretched resources of the Navy, and further delays to the nuclear hunter-killer submarine programme.

The Admiralty's Polaris Committee recognised that ministers had expected to have two boats permanently on patrol from a force of four when they initially approved the programme, but even with one boat available 'a very significant level of deterrence could be achieved without necessarily having two on station at all times, so long as reaction from one could be assured.' The difference lay between the 20-city damage capability offered by two boats, as against the seven to eight cities which would be threatened by one boat on continuous station.⁶² The latter figure derived from the calculation that, given Polaris reliability rates of about 70 per cent from one boatload of 16 missiles, 11 on average could be expected to find their assigned targets. Due to their size, Moscow and Leningrad were deemed to require four and two missile hits respectively, leaving five other cities receiving a single missile strike each; depending on target priorities, a salvo of 11 Polaris missiles would therefore constitute a seven city-deterrent.⁶³

At the end of October 1963, Thorneycroft was given notice by the Earl Jellicoe, who had just taken over from Carrington as First Lord of the Admiralty, about the importance of making a decision by end of the year about the eventual size of the force. For the first time Thorneycroft was given the information that four boats would only permit two to be kept on continuous station for 'something less than 50%' of the time, at least in the initial years of the force's operation. Jellicoe thought if the Cabinet decided that two boats on continuous station was an essential minimum for the level of deterrence required, then the Admiralty would have to advise that five boats were needed. Four boats 'theoretically' offered a 20-city deterrent for about 300 days of the year, when two boats could be available for firing, and a seven or eight-city deterrent for the remainder of the period, with only one boat available. Variations in the operational sequence of deployment, necessary to complicate the task of an adversary who might try to anticipate when only a reduced force was available, meant that in practice the period when two boats could be on station at the same time would be reduced from these estimates.[64]

By the end of the year, in fact, the Admiralty's calculations had been revised to take all the relevant factors into account, such as preserving reactor core life, refit schedules, and the need for trials and a 'working up' period before patrolling. Operating on the preferred US pattern of 56-day patrols, a Polaris force of four boats could, it was estimated, maintain two boats on continuous station for only about 250 days of the year. With five boats it was confirmed that two boats could be kept on station all year round.[65]

During November, at Thorneycroft's request, the Admiralty set about preparing a paper which laid out the pros and cons of a four or five boat fleet, so that a final decision could be made by the end of the year; an important factor bearing on the urgency of a decision was the knowledge that extra orders for long-lead items in the US would have to be placed before production lines for submarine fire control and launching equipment were closed in 1964.[66]

From his berth at the Admiralty, Jellicoe thought that the issue turned on whether the Polaris force was considered to be primarily in terms of its contribution to the Western deterrent as a whole, or as an independent national nuclear deterrent. If the former, the difference between having four and five boats was seen as negligible, but if the latter, then a five boat force was viewed as far preferable, since Jellicoe did not see anything less than two boats on station as a credible deterrent; the question involved such imponderable matters as 'whether we need a 15 or 20 city independent national deterrent or whether we can make do with less.'[67] In this context it will be recalled that by the spring of 1962, ministers had lowered the sights for the capability of any successor system to a 15 city-standard, while in June the Defence Committee had taken a decision to produce only 90 Skybolt warheads, effectively reducing the existing V-force standard even further to 50 per cent destruction of between seven and ten Soviet cities. The driving force in much of this process had been the need for greater economies, and there had been no serious and sustained discussion about how a particular level of damage related to a generally agreed criterion of deterrence.[68]

In theory, at the centre of the four or five boat issue in late 1963, therefore, was whether the deterrent criteria should be restored to the level suggested in early 1962 for a Skybolt-successor system. In practice, however, other considerations weighed equally heavily. The COS, for example, were torn between their desire to have some margin against the unexpected loss by accident or enemy action of a boat from the force, and their concerns over the financial consequences for the overall defence budget of a decision in favour of a fifth boat (which might cost up to £44 million, including £36 million for the boat itself, and £6 million for another part-outload of missiles). An additional consideration was that the anticipated arrival of TSR-2 in RAF service in the mid-1960s, with its high speed low-level capability and ability to carry the new high-yield laydown bomb being developed by AWRE, could give Bomber Command a better chance of penetrating Soviet air defences than it would otherwise have done than if forced to persevere with using V-bombers in the strategic nuclear role into the 1970s. Indeed, after a full discussion, the military advice of the COS was against acquisition of the fifth boat, though they hoped that Thorneycroft would remind the Prime Minister of the 'obvious political implications of any apparent weakening in the credibility of our deterrent.'[69]

After further discussion with his senior officials, on 20 December 1963 Thorneycroft reported the reluctance of the COS to recommend a fifth boat – despite the cogent arguments about the margin against contingencies this provided – because of concerns over pressures on the defence budget. This was advice that the Minister of Defence was prepared to endorse, though he added there were 'important implications to such a decision', and that he would be ready to discuss them with the Prime Minister. Moreover, Thorneycroft's minute had again underlined the dangers raised by the fact that 'the eggs will be in fewer baskets', and that an accident could easily remove a submarine from the patrol cycle, which with a four boat force would lead to gaps where no submarine was on patrol.[70] Earlier draft versions of the minute for Douglas-Home composed on the Minister of Defence's behalf had rehearsed the arguments over the lowering of the damage capability of the force, as compared to earlier assumptions, and included an expression of Thorneycroft's own view that 'a 7 or 8 city deterrent is adequate and on this score therefore I think that four boats would suffice.' This explicit reference to numbers of cities and the Minister of Defence's attitude was removed, however, after Thorneycroft had discussed the matter with Zuckerman.[71]

As might be expected, opposition to a fifth boat also came from the Treasury, the Chancellor of the Exchequer pointing out that since previous ministerial consideration of the size of the Polaris force in January 1963, the cost of the programme had risen by about a third from the original estimate, while the pressures on the defence budget had only increased, with weapons systems becoming ever-more sophisticated.[72] The Prime Minister's own thinking was revealed by the handwritten comment that he made on Thorneycroft's minute asking for information on the overall defence budget picture, and adding that, 'I lean towards the fifth submarine.'[73]

The advice that the Cabinet Secretary offered to the Prime Minister was also unequivocal: 'There is no point in having an independent deterrent unless it can be relied on to deter for every minute of 365 days a year. (Would we contemplate a four-day hiatus in the availability of the V-bombers?)' That said, the extra cost was seen by Trend as 'formidable', meaning that it could only be met if adjustments were made to the existing defence programme so that a fifth boat could be accommodated within current spending plans.[74] Meanwhile, press reports were beginning to appear that construction of a fifth boat was under consideration by the Government.[75]

The Cabinet's newly-created Defence and Oversea Policy Committee discussed the question of the size of the Polaris force during several of its meetings in February 1964. It was first agreed by ministers, on the basis of a paper furnished by the Minister of Defence, that in view of the costs involved in relation to the defence programme as a whole, and despite the argument that a force of four boats would not provide a fully credible independent deterrent, and gave only a small margin for refits and servicing, an order for a fifth boat could not be justified (a view reinforced by the COS's assurance that the introduction of TSR-2 would represent a major enhancement of the RAF's nuclear strike capability). Nevertheless, it was still considered prudent to purchase a complete spare set of submarine-installed Polaris weapons system for about £6.5 million, as a backup for support of the systems which would be installed on the four boats that had already been authorised.[76]

Negotiations over disarmament between the Superpowers soon, however, intruded and served to have a significant bearing on the Government's thinking at this time. On 21 January 1964, in a very public demonstration of his private convictions, President Lyndon Johnson despatched a message to the UN's Eighteen Nation Disarmament Committee, which was about to gather for another session in Geneva. Making his announcement also to a television audience, Johnson had reaffirmed the commitment of the United States to the cause of disarmament and, among other ideas, called for a 'verified freeze on the number and characteristics of strategic nuclear offensive and defensive launch vehicles.' New weapons developments would be allowed under the proposal, but only with close restrictions.[77] Moscow finally objected to Johnson's plan as it provided for intrusive on-sight inspections to verify compliance, and because it did not include short-range nuclear systems, including the many thousands of US nuclear weapons deployed in Europe. Most obviously, however, was the basic point that a freeze would have left the Soviet Union at a marked inferiority in terms of numbers of strategic launchers compared to a US inventory that had expanded enormously during the Kennedy years.

In an immediate sense, nevertheless, the Johnson Administration's proposals for a nuclear freeze had a direct bearing on the British Government's discussions over the eventual size of the Polaris force. On 7 February, Oliver Wright, the Prime Minister's Principal Private Secretary for Foreign Affairs, was informed that Thorneycroft was concerned by the implications of any freeze for the supply of Polaris to the UK, and that any 'defaulting ... would quickly give rise to another crisis comparable with that over Skybolt.' Although US officials had claimed that the Nassau arrangements would not be affected by the proposals, one had, however, floated the notion that there could be 'burden sharing' over any freeze, so that if only a proportion of the Polaris inventory had been delivered to the US Navy when a freeze was introduced, the UK, for example, might receive only three sets of 16 Polaris missiles for its submarines, rather than four.[78] Hence, a week later, during the Prime Minister's visit to Washington for his first meetings with Johnson as

President, Douglas-Home looked for and received assurances that the President's recent proposals for a freeze in nuclear delivery vehicles would not apply to plans to supply the UK with Polaris.[79]

Despite this, British officials returned from the trip not entirely convinced that the Americans had worked out how the provision of Polaris might fit in with their disarmament proposals. By the middle of February, the Prime Minister had come back to the DOPC with a recommendation that the order for an extra Polaris weapons system should go ahead, and that the whole position regarding a fifth boat should be reviewed once again, as one could still be built in the future if this was thought desirable. He cited the Johnson Administration's recent proposals as reason for a further review, and that if ceilings were placed on the numbers of US and Soviet nuclear delivery vehicles the inferiority of European nuclear strength would appear even more marked.[80]

Within the Foreign Office, although it was recognised that the Russians had shown no interest in the freeze proposals, they could be seen as dangerous in that the Soviet Union might eventually argue that the existence of the UK Polaris programme was an obstacle to agreement, or that as part of any freeze arrangements, the UK could be asked to reduce the size of the programme. A fifth submarine might then offer some bargaining room against the latter kind of pressures.[81]

Influenced by the strength of opinion of his colleagues, as well as the military arguments over the need to have a safeguard against accidents, and mindful of the Prime Minister's preferences, Thorneycroft performed a *volte face*, and produced a further paper for the DOPC which now advocated construction of a fifth Polaris submarine. Though he acknowledged that compensating savings (of perhaps £60 million in total) would have to be found in the defence costings over the next decade, Thorneycroft gave no clear indication of where they were going to be found.[82]

At the Defence and Oversea Policy Committee meeting on 25 February, Thorneycroft pointed out the dangers of relying on a force of only four submarines, while also noting that 'we should not wish to be inferior to the French,' who were then planning a force of five boats. He could also, he explained, begin to offset some of the extra cost by changes to the naval construction programme, and postponing the building of another hunter killer submarine. Opposition came from the Chancellor of the Exchequer who, concerned over the rising trend of the defence budget, could see no justification for a fifth boat and cited the views of the COS in his support. In the discussion that ensued, the point was made that there was no margin for error with a four boat force, in terms of either accidents or the overrun of the refit cycle, while 'the Government were committed to the maintenance of an independent nuclear deterrent and there were therefore strong political grounds for removing any doubt about the ability of the Polaris submarine fleet to constitute a credible deterrent.' Questions were also raised over the claim that TSR-2 (first envisaged as a replacement for the Canberra) could genuinely offer a strategic, as opposed to tactical, nuclear strike capability. With no consensus emerging in the Committee, the Prime Minister decided to refer a final decision to the full Cabinet which was due to meet later that same morning.[83]

The Cabinet were told by the Prime Minister that US proposals for a nuclear freeze between the Superpowers now made it 'even more essential that we should be seen to retain an independent capacity to inflict an unacceptable degree of nuclear damage upon an enemy.' A fifth submarine would offer a margin against the risk that one submarine from a four boat force could be put out of action by accident, leaving it impossible to maintain one boat from the remaining three on continuous station. The French, moreover, had decided to build a force of not less than five SSBNs. On the other hand, the construction of a fifth boat would put more strain on the defence budget and would have to be offset by savings elsewhere in the defence programme. The Prime Minister's presentation was embellished by Thorneycroft who argued that recent American experience had shown that the refit period for the submarines would be longer than had been supposed, and that this had caused the COS to reconsider their views on the need for a fifth boat. After the Chancellor had put forward his own position that there were strong financial objections to such an additional commitment, when there was already a heavy burden of new defence equipment programmes to sustain, the Cabinet decided to approve the order for a fifth submarine, provided compensating reductions could be found elsewhere in the forward defence costings.[84]

While US proposals for a freeze in nuclear delivery vehicles certainly played an important role in influencing the early 1964 decisions over the size of the Polaris force, they reinforced what was clearly the Prime Minister's own conviction that four boats would not represent a credible national deterrent. As regards the extra expenditure involved for a five boat force, as long as the Ministry of Defence could find the resources from within their own budgetary targets, he considered it was for them to decide how to allocate resources. Noticeable also in these ministerial deliberations was the absence of any overt discussion of the optimum criteria of deterrence as it related to whether one or two boats on station would provide enough destructive capability. Indeed the key issue for many ministers and officials was the need to provide a force that offered some safeguard against an accident or other mishap which might put the only submarine able to patrol in a four boat force out of action.

The Cabinet's final decision over a fifth boat came too late for the detail to be included in the annual Defence White Paper, which was published on 14 February 1964. This merely recounted the fact that even a small number of Polaris submarines 'would possess immense destructive capacity.' The White Paper extolled the Government's policy of maintaining an independent deterrent, and argued that those who called for its abandonment overlooked the fact that 'if there was no power in Europe capable of inflicting unacceptable damage on a potential enemy he might be tempted – if not now then perhaps at some time in the future – to attack in the mistaken belief that the United States would not act unless America herself were attacked.' But the White Paper, in its coverage of the trouble-spots in Africa, Asia and the Middle East where British forces had engaged in recent operations, also served as a powerful reminder of Britain's onerous world-wide defence commitments, for which well-equipped and flexible conventional forces were essential.[85]

Speculation over the number of Polaris boats to be built was resolved during the two day debate on the defence estimates that followed, when Thorneycroft told the Commons that Britain would go ahead with plans for a fifth boat irrespective of whether the United States and Soviet Union came to an agreement over freezing the deployment of nuclear delivery systems.[86] Labour claims that spending on the nuclear side of the defence budget was distorting Britain's overall defence effort were countered with figures which showed that only about 7 per cent of the total projected defence spending of just under £2,000 million for 1963/64 would be absorbed by the deterrent.[87]

The MLF and the approach of the October 1964 election

At the beginning of 1964, and despite the arrival of a new president in the White House, the Americans still seemed determined to press ahead with their original conception of the MLF. Indeed, responding to MoD speculation that the new administration might be prepared to play the issue 'long', the Foreign Office was telling Downing Street officials at the end of January 1964 that the impression of the Embassy was that, if anything the American position had 'strengthened' since Lyndon Johnson's arrival in the White House, and that it remained firm US government policy. By early March 1964 it was being reported by US officials in Washington that it was too late to present the MLF for Congressional approval that year, but that there was the expectation that enough preparatory work could be done so that a draft Charter could be ready for consideration just after the November presidential elections.[88]

In fact, at an important White House meeting held on 10 April 1964, fresh impetus was given to US policy over the MLF. Having reviewed the reasoning that informed the scheme, Ball reported to the President and other senior officials that preliminary soundings of Congressional opinion had been favourable and he now wanted to broaden consultations. Thomas Finletter, the chief US negotiator at the Paris working group, told Johnson that the 'educational phase' had reached an end, and the time had now come to move into 'the action phase' if the President would give the necessary instructions to proceed. There was particular concern that in the UK, the leader of the Labour Party, Harold Wilson, might have gained the impression that the administration was losing interest in the project and that this should be corrected. Finletter (unaccountably, given the recent declarations of Labour spokesmen) felt that 'even a Wilson Government would join the MLF. He was sure that in the long run Wilson would do what the US wanted and therefore it was important to tell him that the MLF was good for the Alliance.' The meeting concluded with Johnson directing that consultations with Congress should be deepened and the Europeans told it was his judgement that the MLF was 'the best way to proceed.' But at the same time, the President warned against 'trying to shove the project down the throats of the potential participants.'[89]

An outline of British ideas for variants to the MLF, including lower numbers of sea-based missiles, and the incorporation of existing land-based aircraft and missile systems (under new mixed-manning principles), was formerly presented by Shuckburgh to the Paris working group in mid-April 1964. This was also accompanied by the offer of several Valiant bombers which could form a mixed-manned trials unit to examine the practicality of forming an air component of a new force.[90]

Shuckburgh had asked that the UK's ideas for variants be discussed 'in parallel' with studies of a seaborne force, but he was immediately met with the wish that they should be considered as an 'add-on' extra to the original scheme. The principal point of contention within the working group thereafter became whether the introduction of the UK's new proposals regarding NATO's existing land-based nuclear systems should be considered as an alternative scheme to the mixed-manned seaborne MLF, or as complementary and for later addition. Related to this was whether discussions about such variants should be conducted by a separate group, in parallel with consideration of the MLF, or be included in the mix of alternatives and models that the main working group should tackle. Lying behind such arcane matters of procedure was the belief by some US officials that the alternative models suggested by the British were designed to drag out working group meetings, and delay early agreement over aspects of the mixed-manned MLF; or as Shuckburgh put it, 'our attempts to complicate the whole matter are easily interpreted as sabotage.'[91]

The somewhat surreal proceedings of the Paris MLF working group were conducted against the backdrop of the complicated triangular relationship between the calculations of political leaders in Washington, Bonn and London. US State Department officials were now anxious to reach some outline agreement on the MLF by the summer or autumn of 1964, so that formal signature by participating governments could take place in the first few months of 1965. They were driven above all by German domestic political considerations, as unless such a timetable was followed, the German elections due in the autumn of 1965 would prevent Bonn from passing the necessary legislation before the campaigning season began.

In late April 1964, Butler, who had moved to the Foreign Office when Douglas-Home became Prime Minister, travelled to the US capital where he was presented by Rusk with Washington's views on the MLF timetable. The US Secretary of State explained that inter-governmental decisions over the

MLF were needed by the end of the year, or the start of 1965 at the latest, to allow for the necessary legislation to be prepared for ratification in some of the key potential participants. As Rusk realised, this left very little time after the election which would have to take place in Britain during October 1964, and Butler was at pains to stress that no British decisions on the MLF could be expected before the poll. Rusk nevertheless wanted assurances that consideration of the UK's ideas on variants to the MLF would not hold-up agreements regarding the seaborne force. When Butler re-iterated that no formal British decisions could be expected and more time was needed to consider all the options, Rusk

> asked frankly whether the United Kingdom proposals were intended to be a contribution to mixed-manning, an alternative to ships or simply a procedure for procrastination. The United States Government could certainly consider United Kingdom ideas, but not as an alternative to the mixed-manned vessel nor as a procedure for delay.

The recent British proposals to the Paris working group, Butler, replied, had been presented in 'good faith' and were designed as an amendment and not as an alternative to the initial plans for a seaborne force.[92]

With little choice but to accept Butler's responses at face value, and not wanting to exercise undue pressure on the British Government, Rusk and US officials came around to accepting that the new British proposals would be examined alongside the original scheme, and that no commitment could be expected from London on any matter connected with the MLF until after the general election. At the same time, Rusk hoped that the working group could devise language which might eventually be included in a treaty with the aim of converting this rapidly into a formal agreement in November or December 1964.[93] Downing Street officials were not deceived by the polite language of these latest exchanges. As Oliver Wright observed, the Americans regarded the latest British proposals as 'at the worst, wrecking tactics, and at the best, delaying tactics.'[94]

It is possible to find evidence, however, suggesting that leading British policymakers, above all the Prime Minister himself, were by no means adamantly opposed to some kind of multilateral force, with new control arrangements, eventually emerging. While Butler was fending off American queries in Washington, Douglas-Home was receiving the Italian Prime Minister in London. In line with his attitude when at the Foreign Office, the Prime Minister told his visitor that, even though its military rationale was weak, he could see that the political case for the MLF was 'very strong indeed'. However, he was convinced that if he were to ask Parliament to approve British participation at the present time he would be defeated:

> At all costs, therefore he wanted to defer a decision until after the October Elections. If then the Conservative Party were returned to

power he was quite convinced that Britain would be able to join the MLF, although he felt that it would have to have certain modifications. At the moment it was very expensive and required too great a diversion of resources ... the fact was that the Labour Party was flatly against the proposal and so were a good number of Conservatives.[95]

In early May, Douglas-Home was informing an American visitor, Senator J. William Fulbright, that there were many reasons why the MLF was

> politically so important. From the British and American point of view the object of the MLF was to prevent Germany from wishing to acquire a nuclear capacity of its own. From the German point of view it would tie the US irrevocably into a nuclear defence of Europe. For everybody, the MLF would be a cohesive force in the Alliance.

In February 1964, the Prime Minister recalled, he had told President Johnson during his visit to Washington that an MLF would not receive approval from the current Parliament, 'If, however, the Conservative Party were returned to power that would be something quite different.'[96]

The Defence Secretary, for one, was alarmed by the positive tone of both these conversations. Thorneycroft informed the Prime Minister in unmistakable terms that he thought any advance commitments over post-election attitudes were unwise, not least as they could be used to electoral advantage by the Opposition if they should leak, and would certainly cause dissension on the Conservative backbenches.[97] Douglas-Home brushed aside such mild criticism, however, affirming that his overriding consideration was the need for delay. He wanted Shuckburgh in Paris told, for example, that he should not rush with the presentation of more detail on the UK's proposals for variants to the seaborne force. After hearing that the Americans and Germans had been conducting private bilateral talks over MLF arrangements, the Prime Minister also wanted President Johnson warned that the subject was 'political dynamite' in the UK, and that the Americans could not be lead to believe that they could 'steamroller us into a decision at a politically sensitive moment.'[98]

When the US Ambassador in London, David Bruce, was given this latest reminder of the British position in June 1964, Bruce responded that the US administration fully understood the domestic political issues. At the same time, Bruce emphasised, President Johnson was now committed to the project and would press ahead if re-elected in November. The most concerning part of this exchange was that the Ambassador reported that Johnson was now, even if the UK refused to join, prepared to work with the Germans alone and was beginning to lay the Congressional groundwork for presentation of legislation early in 1965.[99]

All this cut little ice with Thorneycroft who wanted British reservations over the whole scheme to be made far more explicit to the Americans.[100] The warning from the British Ambassador in Washington, nevertheless, was that President Johnson was committed to going ahead with a seaborne MLF by the end of the year. 'It has been an uphill fight here to convince people that our idea of a land-based MLF is anything more than a stalling tactic,' Lord Harlech (as Ormsby Gore had now become) continued. 'On the whole I think we have been pretty successful, but there are certainly still more doubters. If at the end of the year we are still talking about variants without commitment, it will almost certainly be concluded unanimously in Washington that we have indeed been stalling all along, and that there is no point in waiting for us any longer.'[101] Replying to such concerns, the Foreign Secretary had written to Harlech telling him that the gravity of the situation was recognised in some quarters: 'Here in the Foreign Office we all hold the same view as you that the political consequences of Britain standing aside from the multilateral force would be serious.'[102]

In a similar vein, Butler told the Prime Minister that same day that the Americans and Germans were clearly determined to press ahead without the British, and that after the election the new Government 'will be faced with the invidious choice of joining the Force, however imperfect it may be, or seeing it come into being without them.' The Foreign Secretary wanted to keep all options open up to the election, and was clearly drawn to a scheme which combined elements of the original seaborne force, though reduced in size, with British ideas for mixed-manning of existing land-based systems. In order to deflect US pressure for a rapid timetable toward agreement it was necessary, he felt, to push forward for discussion the British variants in Paris 'making clear that we genuinely believe in them and that our eventual decision about the MLF is bound to be influenced by the consideration which our Allies give to these ideas.'[103] Indeed, Butler saw a British decision to stand aside from an MLF as potentially a 'self-inflicted wound' which would further reduce Britain's influence in Europe in the wake of exclusion from the EEC.[104]

With the Foreign Office and MoD once more at odds over the most appropriate tactics to pursue in the MLF negotiations, at the start of July 1964 Shuckburgh introduced a more detailed set of British proposals for the land-based variants to the Paris working group. They were put forward, Shuckburgh told his fellow NATO ambassadors in a 'constructive spirit' and the fact that the British were asking them to be studied should be taken as 'proof that the British Government is genuinely and seriously interested in the broad political concept of a multilateral force, designed to bring the European and American nations together in a new form of cooperation in nuclear matters at a time when some of the NATO bonds appear to be loosening.'[105]

While Shuckburgh tried to make the case for proper consideration of the variants in Paris, Mountbatten continued to denigrate the whole project and was happy for the British Defence Staff in Washington to spread the ultra-sceptical MoD position to any US officials they encountered. All this placed Shuckburgh in a difficult position, and at the end of July he wrote to the CDS reminding him that he was conducting a serious negotiation on behalf of the Government and that 'while my object is of course to gain time and not to commit Britain to anything before we have a Government which is ready (and I mean ready) to take considered decisions, I am operating here in good faith and not as a pre-determined opponent of the MLF idea.' Shuckburgh's opinion – and one which made him suspect at the MoD for pursuing the Foreign Office line – tended to be that it would only be possible to block or modify the worst aspects of the scheme identified by the MoD, and most critically, ensure that there was no relaxation in the American veto over use of the MLF's nuclear weapons, if the UK was a full participant.[106]

As it found itself under inter-Alliance pressure to involve itself in a seaborne mixed-manned MLF, the Conservative Government spent its final few months in office during 1964 brandishing its commitment to maintaining an independent deterrent to its domestic political audience. For Douglas-Home, in particular, the issue seemed a personal one, and he was insistent that only its possession gave Britain a place at the top table in the councils of the world.[107] The Conservatives positioned the future of the independent deterrent as one of the key themes of their campaign for re-election, believing it would resonate with patriotic voters who associated the party with a strong defence policy (public opinion polls still registered high levels of support for Britain's continued possession of nuclear weapons). As well as seeking electoral advantage, Conservative Party strategists also saw encouragement of debate over the issue as a way to open up tensions and divisions within the Labour Party over whether they would immediately abandon Britain's nuclear capabilities. After the fifth Polaris boat decision was announced in February 1964, George Brown claimed in the Commons debate on the Defence White Paper that the 'so-called independent British strategic deterrent' was part of the 'electoral strategy' of the Conservatives rather than the 'defence strategy' of the country.[108] During the debate, Denis Healey, the shadow defence spokesman, was asked in pointblank fashion by Thorneycroft whether Labour would cancel Polaris. Healey had replied that he could not say in advance, but certainly would not continue the programme as a contribution to an independent British deterrent, but that 'whether or not it is any value as part of an alliance effort we cannot make up our minds until we negotiate the question with the United States.' If it was decided to abandon the idea of building a Polaris force, Healey ventured that a Labour Government would convert the boats that had just begun construction into sorely-needed hunter/killer submarines.[109]

Two months later, in April 1964, Patrick Gordon Walker, Labour's shadow Foreign Secretary, published an article in the influential US journal *Foreign Affairs* which proclaimed that the Party accepted the need for the Western nuclear deterrent but did

> not believe that Britain herself should seek to make or possess nuclear weapons of her own. Here we have changed our policy. The cancellation of Blue Streak [in 1960] was the turning point. It then became

obvious that Britain had not the means to remain in the nuclear race.... We do not accept Sir Alec Douglas-Home's argument that we must continue to buy an American weapon as a sort of status symbol that would purchase a place for us at the peace table. It seems to us pointless and wasteful to have a weapon that could not be used by itself and which adds nothing to the power of the American nuclear armory. Moreover, the British Prime Minister's argument is an open invitation to other countries to do likewise and must, therefore, tend to the dissemination of nuclear weapons.

At the same time, Gordon Walker made clear that Labour could not simply 'disassociate' Britain from nuclear weapons, and so would not 'throw away' the existing V-bombers, which constituted 'a formidable but wasting strike force.' Instead, the aim of a Labour Government would be to 'renegotiate' the Nassau Agreement so that a 'far-reaching new arrangement' was reached with the US where a 'real share' in 'shaping nuclear policy and strategy' was given to the UK, including over deployment and targeting. In exchange, Labour would 'recognize and support the ultimate nuclear monopoly of the United States in the West,' and play a constructive role in helping to prevent the spread of nuclear weapons.[110] The following month, despite the pressing need to make economies if the rising costs of defence spending were to be held in check, the Prime Minister ruled that the option of abandoning the Polaris programme should not be among those examined by official studies which were then being carried out under the direction of the Cabinet Secretary into the long-term future of defence policy.[111]

The long-anticipated general election campaign finally opened on 15 September 1964. The Conservative manifesto delivered the straightforward message that, 'Britain must in the ultimate resort have independently controlled nuclear power to deter an aggressor. We possess this power today. Only under a Conservative Government will we possess it in the future.' In pursuit of the concept of interdependence the UK's V-bombers had been assigned to NATO, but this was 'subject to our right to deploy them at discretion if supreme national interests are at stake. The Polaris submarines when operational will be assigned in the same way and subject to the same reservation.'[112] Conservative election broadcasts pressed the theme that Labour would abandon Britain's nuclear weapons, so weakening the nation's defences.

During the long election campaign, the Labour Party leadership endeavoured to adopt a low-key approach over questions of nuclear policy. The Party's own manifesto had invoked the criticism that the Nassau Agreement underlined Britain's 'utter dependence' on the US for supply of Polaris missiles, and would 'add nothing to the deterrent strength of the western alliance'. For good measure, it had asserted that all the spending on Polaris would not produce an 'independent British deterrent', instead proclaiming, in now-famous lines: 'It will not be independent and it will not be British and it will not deter. Its possession will impress neither friend nor potential foe.'

Britain's nuclear 'pretence,' it was alleged, only served to encourage more nuclear proliferation, not least within Germany. Dwelling on the implicit meaning of the supreme national interests clause of the Nassau Agreement, the manifesto noted that the Conservative Government based its policy 'on the assumption that Britain must be prepared to go it alone without her allies in an all-out thermo-nuclear war with the Soviet Union, involving the obliteration of our people.' By putting so much emphasis on this unilateral role for the Polaris force, it was claimed that the Western alliance, on which Britain's security depended, was undermined. The manifesto pledged there would be no wasting of the country's resources 'on endless duplication of strategic nuclear weapons', and advocated a 're-negotiation of the Nassau Agreement.' Expressing opposition to the development of national nuclear deterrents, and to the proposals for an MLF, it propounded that, 'We believe in the interdependence of the western alliance and will put forward constructive proposals for integrating all Nato's nuclear weapons under effective political control so that all the partners in the alliance have a proper share in their deployment and control.'[113]

The ambiguities of Labour's nuclear stance helped to engender deep anxieties within the Ministry of Defence over the attitudes that might be adopted by a future Labour Government. At the end of September, with the election campaign having been underway for a fortnight, Mountbatten informed the COS that he had prepared a study on the importance of retaining an independent nuclear deterrent which could be presented (as long as his fellow Chiefs approved) to any new Government which proposed its abandonment. He considered it was a 'moral obligation' of the COS to put forward the military arguments in favour of maintaining such a capability. After speaking to the Cabinet Secretary about the matter, Mountbatten's particular concern was that a Labour Government might try to carry through its 'election manifesto pledge to abolish the deterrent', by transferring naval crews being trained for the Polaris programme to meet the manpower requirement for the surface-ship seaborne component of the MLF. Wilson, the CDS claimed, 'was known to be in favour of abolition; the majority of the party were in agreement and abolition was included in their election manifesto.' However, there was 'a body of opinion in the party who were uncertain on this point and it was possible that, if a strong case could be made for retention, Labour policy on the subject could be reversed, provided that a face-saving formula could be found.' What Mountbatten had in mind was 'convincing an incoming Labour Government that the Polaris submarine project was so far advanced that very large nugatory expenditure and impracticable conversion problems' would arise if an effort were made to convert the submarines into hunter-killers. It was believed that about half the money for the Polaris submarine-building programme would in fact have been committed by the end of the year.

Mountbatten's idea was that all members of the COS Committee might sign a paper, yet to be assembled, which sought to dissuade an incoming Labour Government from abandoning Polaris. The essence of the paper would be that the COS could see no foreseeable way to discharge their responsibilities to defend the UK from all forms of attack except through possession of a nationally-controlled nuclear deterrent force capable of inflicting major damage against a potential aggressor. The paper would end with the request that if the Government wanted to abolish the deterrent they should 'absolve the Chiefs of Staff from responsibility for the defence of the United Kingdom against attack.' As well as agreeing to the idea that such a paper should be prepared for the eventuality of a Labour Government, the COS thought that any paper should also address Labour's claim that the deterrent was not truly independent by stressing that there were 'no strings' attached to the use of Polaris in the kind of contingency that had been acknowledged at the Nassau Conference. Mountbatten noted that complete reliance could not be placed on US assistance, and that the current UK V-bomber deterrent and its Polaris replacement 'would be a self-sufficient force in its own right which we were entitled to use in the last emergency.'[114]

A few days later, a suitable draft of a paper and a shorter covering note (prepared by the CDS's own staff) was circulated amongst the COS. The covering note began by underlining the responsibilities of the COS for defending the British Isles, and providing the best possible defence of British interests overseas, and that in these tasks, though allies had assisted in the past, 'we have often had to stand alone.' It was contended that the advent of nuclear weapons had made all previous strategic concepts 'outdated', and that with the Soviet Union capable of destroying the UK

> the only practical method of preventing direct attack at home or blackmail abroad available to us now and in the foreseeable future is the possession of a nuclear retaliatory capacity which can clearly inflict upon any potential enemy a degree of damage patently unacceptable as the price of aggression. It is this fear of inescapable consequences that provides the only certain way of influencing nations against pursuing policies hostile to the survival of another and which thus provides the best guarantee of preserving world peace. This is the true meaning of deterrence.

In the absence of a single political authority for the western world, the ability to defend the UK alone had to be retained at a national level:

> we cannot rely on triggering a nuclear response from an ally however close and satisfactory our ties with them might be. In the final analysis our ability to deter depends upon whether our potential enemies can see clearly that the decision whether or not to go to war over an issue of over-riding national importance, rests squarely upon HMG and none other.

The note continued by stating the 'unanimous opinion' of the COS that the only sure means to deter an attack upon the UK or its vital interests was to maintain national nuclear forces 'under our ultimate sovereign control.' Without such a capability, it was suggested that the COS could see 'no other rational method by which we can continue to discharge our classical and collective responsibility for preventing attack on these islands or of exercising an effective military influence over any nuclear power that might oppose us.'

The most arresting part of the outline paper that accompanied the covering note was its concluding section which attempted to reconcile avowed Labour Party policy with the existence of a deterrent under ultimate national control, as provided for by the Nassau framework. Retaining a national nuclear force, it found, was

> in no way incompatible with assignment of elements of such a force to International Alliances. All forces so assigned – whether nuclear or non-nuclear – can in practice be withdrawn for use nationally if so required and there is no reason for a special codicil to this effect (e.g. the 'Supreme National Interest' clause).

It was parenthetically noted that this final point could 'provide the basis for a Labour Prime Minister, if elected, to reconcile a decision to retain a national capability with pre-election policy.' In other words, by emphasising the practical point that 'assignment' to NATO was a very loose concept, and that such forces would still be subject to national control, it was possible to argue that renouncing the objectionable 'supreme national interests' clause of the Nassau Agreement would not necessarily involve repudiation of a strategic nuclear force under ultimate national control.[115]

When the COS next met on 6 October to consider the paper Mountbatten was away on a West African tour, and General Sir Richard Hull, the Chief of the General Staff, took the chair as Acting CDS. Hull – who held a hearty disdain for the flamboyant Mountbatten (a feeling which was reciprocated) – thought it might be premature for the COS to deploy their complete set of arguments against abolition since a new government's attitude could not be known for certain 'until it had gained access to the true facts of the matter', and it could also be 'tactless to present an in-coming Labour administration with a bald statement flatly opposing what had been a major plank in their Election platform.' More preferable would be to supply Labour ministers with a set of factual briefs on the size and capabilities of Britain's nuclear forces; only if they persisted in considering the abolition of the strategic nuclear force altogether were they to be given a paper presenting arguments for retention, and this was to take the form of a straightforward update of the less emotive December 1962 COS paper – COS(62)486 – on the need for a British strategic nuclear force. If abolition remained on the cards, a third stage was then envisaged – as Mountbatten had earlier proposed – of a direct appeal, with even fuller arguments, from the COS to the new Prime Minister. In a sign of party political sensitivities, it was, furthermore, felt advisable that future papers and discussion on the subject of British strategic nuclear forces

530   *The approach of the general election*

were to avoid the word 'independent' as a prefix and to instead use the phrase 'British strategic nuclear capability.'[116]

Despite the Conservative Government's rhetorical commitment to an independent nuclear deterrent, on the technical side there was still a degree of uncertainty over the future British nuclear weapons programme by the time the polls opened on 15 October 1964. After the Skybolt debacle and a series of difficult negotiations with the United States, commitments had been made to acquire the Polaris weapon system, and a decision taken in early 1964 to increase by one boat the initial order for four new submarines to carry the strategic nuclear deterrent. The design of a new British-manufactured Polaris warhead had also been chosen in the spring of 1964 and, with some reservations, the existing American Mk 2 Mod 0 re-entry system selected for procurement. AWRE were also working on the designs for two versions of the WE 177 air-delivered bomb, one a high-yield variant which was to equip the RAF's V-bombers during the interim period before the requisite number of Polaris submarines were ready to assume their primary strategic deterrent role. Moreover, approval had been given for AWRE to conduct a research programme involving the testing of the ideas for new weapon designs. Plans to reduce the numbers of staff at Aldermaston, encouraged in 1962 by a Treasury forever on the look-out for savings, would have to be put on hold.

However, despite this intense post-Nassau spell of activity, no decisions had yet been taken for work on a new class of thermonuclear warhead that could supersede the design used for Polaris, or a series of proposals from the services for a new generation of tactical nuclear weapons. Moreover, the vulnerability of Polaris to Soviet ABM defences had become a topic of major concern to several defence scientists at RAE and the Ministry of Aviation during 1963–64, with few prospects, given the financial constraints of a defence budget already stretched to cope with the capital costs of the Polaris submarine programme, and the tight timetable for the introduction of Polaris by 1968, that steps would be taken in the short term to improve its penetration capabilities. Without some efforts made to enhance Polaris performance some officials were already beginning to question whether the system could offer a credible deterrent where it was expected to operate alone against Soviet targets.

Set beside these technical uncertainties over the future path of British nuclear development, at a politico-diplomatic level was the continuing controversy within the North Atlantic Alliance over the MLF proposals. As the next volume will show, there was no sign by the time of the 1964 election that US pressure to make progress with the scheme was about to relent, if anything the reverse. The MLF proposals were also representative of a strain of opinion in Washington which was uneasy with the whole notion of a UK independent deterrent since its existence was felt to fuel the nuclear ambitions of other members of NATO, with Germany the prime concern. In this atmosphere the future disposition of a British strategic nuclear force, and how it would operate within whatever new Alliance nuclear arrangements might eventually be created, was still far from clear.

The outcome of the October 1964 election would, in fact, see a new group of Labour ministers returned to office, who would have to grapple with this complicated nuclear inheritance. But they would face this task, ostensibly at least, with a very different policy agenda from that of their Conservative predecessors. Not only was the validity of the whole notion of independence disparaged by Labour, when the UK relied on the United States for the means of delivery of its nuclear weapons and crucial technical assistance, but the plausibility of national, unilateral use – as implied by the 'supreme national interests' clause of the Nassau agreement secured by Macmillan – was attacked as a fantastical proposition which only served to undercut Britain's alliance commitments. A deep-seated scepticism over the strategic rationale of the Polaris programme, and its financial costs, was combined with explicit rejection of any further nuclear weapons development beyond those systems currently under development. How the Labour Governments led by Harold Wilson were to handle strategic nuclear policy over the subsequent six years, as ministers tried to influence the evolution of the NATO Alliance's nuclear arrangements in ways which best served British interests, and while Britain continued its withdrawal from a world power role, will form the subject of the next volume in this series.

Notes

1 See Ormsby Gore letter to Caccia, 25 April 1963, PREM 11/4161. Still one of the best guides to the debates within the North Atlantic Alliance over the MLF during 1963, despite being written so close to the events concerned, is Alastair Buchan, 'The Multilateral Force: A Study in Alliance Politics,' *International Affairs*, 40, 4, October 1964, 619–37; and see also Schwartz, *NATO's Nuclear Dilemmas*, 82–135.
2 See Home minute for Macmillan, 'NATO Mixed-Manned Force,' PM/63/68, 9 May 1963; Kennedy message to Macmillan, T.207/63, 10 May 1963, PREM 11/4161.
3 De Zulueta minute for Macmillan, 9 May 1963, PREM 11/4161.
4 De Zulueta minute for Macmillan, 'NATO Multi-Lateral Force: Meeting on 17 May,' 16 May 1963, PREM 11/4161.
5 GEN 798/2nd Meeting, 17 May 1963, CAB 130/191.
6 Foreign Office telegram No 4883 to Washington, 20 May 1963, containing Macmillan message for Kennedy, T.222/63, 20 May 1963, PREM 11/4162.
7 Mountbatten memorandum for Lemnitzer, 'Assignment of V-Bombers,' 23 May 1963, DEFE 25/250; for the final communique outlining the plans for assignment of forces to SACEUR, see Ottawa telegram No Codel NATO 42 to Foreign Office, 24 May 1963, PREM 11/4162.
8 See, for example, Wynn, *RAF Nuclear Deterrent Forces*, 550–51.
9 SACEUR's area of interest was in targets in the Eastern European Soviet satellite states, and western portion of the Soviet Union; see 'History of the Joint Strategic Target Planning Staff: Revisions 1–8 to SIOP 64,' History and Research Division, Headquarters Strategic Air Command, 31 January 1967, www.dod.mil/pubs/foi/joint_staff/jointStaff_jointOperations/336.pdf.

10 GEN 798/4th Meeting, 19 May 1963, CAB 130/191.
11 CC(63) 34th Conclusions, item 4, 23 May 1963, CAB 128/37.
12 Ottawa telegram No Codel NATO 4 to Foreign Office, 21 May 1963 (personal for Prime Minister from Foreign Secretary), PREM 11/4161.
13 Foreign Office telegram No Codel NATO 35 to Ottawa, 22 May 1963 (for Foreign Secretary from Prime Minister), PREM 11/4161.
14 See C(63)95, 'NATO Nuclear Force: Mixed-Manned Component,' memorandum by the Secretary of State for Foreign Affairs, 28 May 1963, CAB 129/113; Home minute for Macmillan, 'The NATO Meeting at Ottawa,' PM/63/77, 26 May 1963; Macmillan minute for Home, M.207/63, 28 May 1963, PREM 11/4162.
15 C(63)96, 'NATO Nuclear Force: Mixed-Manned Component,' memorandum by the Minister of Defence, 28 May 1963, CAB 129/113.
16 Ormsby Gore letter to Home, 'Multilateral Force,' 29 May 1963, PREM 11/4166.
17 Foreign Office telegram No 5181 to Washington, 29 May 1963, containing Kennedy message to Macmillan, 29 May 1963, PREM 11/4162.
18 CC(63)36th Conclusions, item 1, 30 May 1963, CAB 128/37; CC(63)36, 30 May 1963, CAB 195/22.
19 See memorandum of conversation, 25 May 1963, *FRUS, 1961–1963, XIII*, 773; 'France Gives Assurances on Nuclear Arms,' *The Times*, 27 May 1963.
20 See Kaplan et al., *McNamara Ascendancy*, 411.
21 *Hansard*, HC, vol 679, cols 642–3, 20 June 1963.
22 See CC(63)42nd Conclusion, item 2, 25 June 1963, CAB 128/37.
23 See de Zulueta minute for Macmillan, 26 June 1963, PREM 11/4163.
24 CC(63)43rd Conclusions, item 5, 27 June 1963, CAB 128/37; CC(63)43, 27 June 1963, 1030am, CAB 195/22.
25 'Record of a Meeting at Birch Grove House at 11.15pm on Saturday, June 29, 1963,' PREM 11/4163.
26 'Record of a Meeting at Birch Grove House at 10.30am on Sunday, June 30, 1963,' PREM 11/4163; and see memorandum of conversation, 30 June 1963, *FRUS, 1961–1963, XIII*, 599–601.
27 See Foreign telegram No 1185 to Rome, 30 June 1963, PREM 11/4163.
28 Bundy memorandum for Kennedy, 'The MLF and the European Tour,' 15 June 1963, *FRUS, 1961–1963, XIII*, 592–5.
29 Home minute for Macmillan, 'NATO Nuclear Force: The Next Step,' PM/63/89, 7 July 1963, PREM 11/4163; C(63)121, 'NATO Nuclear Force: The Next Step,' memorandum by the Secretary of State for Foreign Affairs, 9 July 1963, CAB 129/114.
30 CC(63)46th Conclusions, item 5, 11 July 1963, CAB 128/37; and for the demise of the Control Commission idea see C(63)151, 'The Multilateral Force,' memorandum by the Secretary of State for Foreign Affairs, 16 September 1963, CAB 129/114.
31 See Washington telegram No 2594 to Foreign Office, 20 August 1963, PREM 11/4163.
32 Home minute for Thorneycroft, 'Multilateral Force,' FS/63/84, 24 August 1963, PREM 11/4163.
33 Thorneycroft minute for Home, 'Multilateral Force,' 2 September 1963; Boyd-Carpenter minute for Thorneycroft, 2 September 1963, PREM 11/4163.
34 Washington telegram No 2764 to Foreign Office, 5 September 1963, PREM 11/4163.
35 Caccia minute for Home, 20 September 1963, PREM 11/4163.
36 C(63)151, 'The Multilateral Force,' memorandum by the Secretary of State for Foreign Affairs, 16 September 1963, CAB 129/114.

37 C(63)153, 'Multilateral Nuclear Force,' memorandum by the Minister of Defence, 16 September 1963, CAB 129/114.
38 CC(63)55th Conclusions, item 2, 20 September 1963, CAB 128/37; CC(63)55, 20 September 1963, 10am, CAB 195/23.
39 See Macmillan minute for Home, 'Multilateral Force,' M.334/63, 18 September 1963; Macmillan minute for Trend, 'Multilateral Force,' M.339/63, 21 September 1963, PREM 11/4163.
40 Macmillan minute for Home, 'Multilateral Force,' M.340/63, 21 September 1963, PREM 11/4163.
41 CC(63)56th Conclusions, item 2, 23 September 1963, CAB 128/37; CC(63)56, 23 September 1963 5pm, CAB 195/23.
42 Macmillan minute for Home, 'Multilateral NATO Force,' M.342/63, 24 September 1963, and attached 'Multilateral NATO Nuclear Force: Statement of Her Majesty's Government's Position,' PREM 11/4163.
43 New York telegram No 1549 to Foreign Office, from Prime Minister from Secretary of State, 27 September 1963, PREM 11/4163.
44 Thorneycroft minute for Macmillan, 4 October 1963, PREM 11/4739.
45 See Trend minute for Bligh, 'Multilateral Force,' 7 October 1963, and attached 'Draft Directive to the United Kingdom Permanent Representative on the Multilateral Force Steering Group,' PREM 11/4739.
46 See 'Britain Suggests Tactical Extension of Multilateral Force Idea,' *The Times*, 18 December 1963.
47 Acting Chief of Defence Staff minute for Thorneycroft, 'Variants to the Multilateral Force,' 24 January 1964, DEFE 11/314; COS 34/64, 'Variants to the Multilateral Force,' Note by the Secretary, 30 January 1964, DEFE 5/147.
48 See Kaplan, et al., *McNamara Ascendancy*, 412.
49 See Washington telegram No 3121 to Foreign Office, 10 October 1963, PREM 11/4739.
50 Buchan, 'Multilateral Force,' 630.
51 See Glenn T. Seaborg, *Stemming the Tide: Arms Control in the Johnson Years* (Lexington, MA, 1987), 95–8.
52 Cmnd 2097, *Central Organisation for Defence*, paragraph 6, July 1963.
53 See Howard, *Central Organisation of Defence*, 14–17.
54 See Zuckerman, *Monkeys, Men and Missiles*, 195.
55 'Dr Robert Press,' obituary, *The Times*, 3 September 1984.
56 'Dr Robert Press,' Zuckerman letter, *The Times*, 14 September 1984.
57 Zuckerman, *Monkeys, Men and Missiles*, 364; and see also 'Sir W. Cook's New Defence Post,' *The Times*, 12 June 1964.
58 Press minute for Zuckerman, 'Status of the Nuclear Group in the new CSA Organisation,' RP/315/63, 20 August 1963, DEFE 19/111.
59 Cmnd 2097, paragraphs 15–6, *Central Organisation for Defence*, July 1963.
60 See, for example, D(63)3rd meeting, 9 February 1963; D(63)8th meeting, 19 June 1963, CAB 131/28.
61 See W. R. Darracott letter to K. T. Nash, 26 September 1963, ADM 1/28842.
62 Hill-Norton minute, 'Polaris Submarines: Size of Force,' 13 September 1963, and attached paper, ADM 1/28842.
63 F. G. Thatcher minute, 'Polaris Submarines – Size of UK Force,' No 633/10, 29 November 1963, and attached note by Vice Chief of Naval Staff, 'Polaris Submarines – Size of UK Force,' ADM 1/28842; Confidential Annex to COS 68th Meeting/63, 3 December 1963, DEFE 4/160; 'Polaris Submarines: Size of UK Force,' Appendix to Annex to COS 3200/12/12/63, DEFE 13/296.
64 Jellicoe minute for Thorneycroft, 'Polaris submarines – size of force,' 28 October 1963, ADM 1/28842.
65 F. G. Thatcher minute, 'Polaris Submarines – Size of UK Force,' No 633/10, 29

534 *The approach of the general election*

  November 1963, and attached note by Vice Chief of Naval Staff, 'Polaris Submarines – Size of UK Force,' ADM 1/28842; Confidential Annex to COS 68th Meeting/63, 3 December 1963, DEFE 4/160; Secretary to First Sea Lord minute for Secretary to COS Committee, 'Size of the UK Polaris Force,' No 633/10, 9 December 1963, and attached 'Part II: Implications of having only one submarine on station', ADM 1/28442.
66 Jellicoe minute for Thorneycroft, 'Polaris Force: Number of Boats,' 13 November 1963, DEFE 13/296.
67 Jellicoe minute for Thorneycroft, 'Polaris Force: Number of Boats,' 2 December 1963, DEFE 13/296.
68 For a retrospective comment, see W. I. Tupman letter to H. Godfrey, 17 December 1963, ADM 1/28442.
69 See Confidential Annex to COS 69th Meeting/63, 10 December 1963, ADM 1/28842; Mountbatten minute for Thorneycroft, 'Size of the Polaris Force,' 12 December 1963, and attached paper 'Polaris Submarines: Size of UK Force,' Appendix to Annex to COS 3200/12/12/63; Hockaday minute, 'Size of the U.K. Polaris Force,' 13 December 1963, DEFE 13/296.
70 Thorneycroft minute for Douglas-Home, 'Size of the UK Polaris Force,' 20 December 1963, DEFE 13/296, and in PREM 11/5104; also reproduced in DO(64)3, 'Polaris Submarines,' memorandum by the Minister of Defence, 10 January 1964, CAB 148/1.
71 See A. D. Peck minute for Hockaday, 'Size of UK Polaris Force,' 19 December 1963, with attached draft minute, and handwritten note by Hockaday, 23 December 1963, DEFE 13/296.
72 Maudling minute for Douglas-Home, 1 January 1964, PREM 11/5104; also reproduced in DO(64)3, 'Polaris Submarines,' 10 January 1964, CAB 148/1.
73 Douglas-Home handwritten annotation on Thorneycroft minute for Douglas-Home, 'Size of the UK Polaris Force,' 20 December 1963, PREM 11/5104; and see Hockaday minute for Secretary, 'Size of UK Polaris Force,' 24 December 1963, DEFE 13/296.
74 Trend minute for Douglas-Home, 'Polaris Submarines,' 13 January 1964, PREM 11/5104.
75 See 'Another Polaris Submarine?' *The Times*, 20 January 1964.
76 See DO(64)10, 'The Defence Programme,' memorandum by the Minister of Defence, 5 February 1964; DO(64)7th Meeting, 7 February 1964, CAB 148/1.
77 Seaborg, *Stemming the Tide*, 9–14, 391–2.
78 Hockaday letter to Wright, 'Freeze of Nuclear Delivery Vehicles,' 7 February 1964, PREM 11/4737.
79 See PM(W)(64) 1st Meeting, Record of a Meeting held at the White House, 12 February 1964, CAB 133/247; and also memorandum of conversation, 13 February 1964, *FRUS, 1964–1968, Volume XI: Arms Control and Disarmament* (Washington, 1997), 19–20.
80 DO(64)8th Meeting, 19 February 1964, CAB 148/1.
81 Rose minute, 'Polaris Submarine Programme,' 24 February 1964, PUSD records, FCO.
82 DO(64)14, 'Polaris Submarine Programme,' memorandum by the Minister of Defence, 24 February 1964, CAB 148/1; Trend minute for Douglas-Home, 'Polaris Submarine Programme,' 24 February 1964, PREM 11/5104.
83 DO(64)9th Meeting, 25 February 1964, CAB 148/1.
84 Confidential Annex, CM(64)14th Conclusions, item 4, 25 February 1964, CAB 128/38; CM(64)14, 25 February 1964, CAB 195/23.
85 See Cmnd 2270, *Statement on Defence, 1964*, February 1964, paragraphs 7 and 20.
86 See 'Britain Will Stick to Polaris Plan,' *The Times*, 27 February 1964.

87 See 'Deterrent Takes 7% of £2,000M. Defence Bill,' *The Times*, 14 February 1964.
88 J. A. Thomson letter to W. N. Hugh-Jones, 2 March 1964, CAB 21/5172.
89 Memorandum of discussion of the MLF at the White House at 5.30pm on Friday, April 10, 1964, *FRUS, 1964–1968, Volume XIII: Western Europe Region* (Washington, 1995), 35–7.
90 See UK Delegation NATO Paris telegram No 168 to Foreign Office, 7 April 1964, PREM 11/4739; UK Delegation NATO Paris telegram No 181 to Foreign Office, 17 April 1964, PREM 11/4740.
91 UK Delegation NATO Paris telegram No 191 to Foreign Office, 21 April 1964, PREM 11/4740.
92 'Extract from Record of Meeting between Foreign Secretary and the US Secretary of State in Washington on April 26, 1964,' PREM 11/4740; see also memorandum of conversation, 26 April 1964, *FRUS, 1964–1968*, XIII, 41–3.
93 'Extract from Record of Meeting between Foreign Secretary and the US Secretary of State in Washington at 4pm on April 27, 1964,' PREM 11/4740.
94 Wright minute for Douglas-Home, 'Multilateral Force,' 28 April 1964, PREM 11/4740.
95 'Record of a Conversation between the Prime Minister of Great Britain and the Prime Minister of Italy at 10, Downing Street, on Monday, April 27, 1964,' PREM 11/4740.
96 'Record of a Conversation between the Prime Minister and Senator Fulbright at 11am at No 10 Downing Street on Tuesday, May 5, 1964,' PREM 11/4740.
97 Thorneycroft minute for Douglas-Home, 'MLF,' 9 May 1964, PREM 11/4740.
98 Douglas-Home minute for Butler, M.70/64, 16 June 1964, PREM 11/4740.
99 See Caccia minute for Butler, 17 June 1964, PREM 11/4740.
100 See Thorneycroft letter to Douglas-Home, 'Multilateral Force,' 30 June 1964, PREM 11/4740.
101 Harlech letter to Caccia, 19 June 1964, FCO 73/173.
102 Butler letter to Harlech, 30 June 1964, FCO 73/173.
103 Butler minute for Douglas-Home, 'Multilateral Force,' PM/64/77, 30 June1964, PREM 11/4740.
104 Butler letter to Douglas-Home, 30 June 1964, PREM 11/4740.
105 UK Delegation NATO Paris telegram No 280 to Foreign Office, 2 July 1964, PREM 11/4740.
106 Shuckburgh letter to Mountbatten, 31 July 1964, DEFE 25/102; and for the COS's unhappiness with Shuckburgh's role, see Confidential Annex to COS 42nd Meeting/64, Part I, item 4, 16 June 1964, CAB 21/5173.
107 See Pierre, *Nuclear Politics*, 253–4.
108 'Labour principles for defence policy,' *The Times*, 28 February 1964.
109 *Hansard*, HC, vol 690, col 481, 26 February 1964.
110 P. C. Gordon Walker, 'The Labor Party's Defense and Foreign Policy,' *Foreign Affairs*, 42, 3, April 1964, 392–3.
111 See Trend minute for Douglas-Home, 30 April 1964; Trend minute for Bligh, 5 May 1964, PREM 11/4731.
112 *Prosperity with a Purpose*, in F. W. S. Craig (ed.), *British General Election Manifestos, 1918–1966* (Chichester, 1970), 214–5.
113 *Let's Go With Labour for the New Britain*, in Craig, *British General Election Manifestos*, 245–6.
114 Confidential Annex to COS 58th Meeting/64, item 2, 'Future Policy,' 29 September 1964, DEFE 32/9.
115 'The Future of the United Kingdom's Independent Nuclear Forces: Cover Note by the Chiefs of Staff,' Annex A to COS 2971/2/10/64, and 'Outline of Paper on the Future of the United Kingdom Independent Nuclear Forces,' Annex B

to COS 2971/2/10/64, both attached to Air Vice-Marshal J. H. Lapley minute for COS, 'Future Policy,' COS 2971/2/10/64, 2 October 1964, DEFE 4/175.

116 Confidential Annex to COS 59th Meeting/64, 6 October 1964, DEFE 4/175, and in DEFE 24/78. On the relationship between Mountbatten and Hull, see Ziegler, *Mountbatten*, 615–6.

Index

Absolute Weapon, The: Atomic Power and World Order (Brodie) 6
Acheson, Dean 246, 248, 355, 366
Adenauer, Konrad 249, 336, 367, 376, 428, 495, 510
Advanced Research Projects Agency (ARPA) 78–9
Advisory Committee on Atomic Energy 8
'Agreement on the Uses of Atomic Energy for Mutual Defence Purposes' (MDA) of 1958 71, 116, 117–18, 119, 143–9, 191, 243, 342–3; amendments to (1959) 145
Air Ministry 9, 23, 34–7, 39–51, 48, 50–4, 66, 69, 127, 139, 149, 156–7, 161, 163, 173, 183, 201, 284, 287, 291–2, 295–6, 305–6, 318–20, 352; Strategic Scientific Policy Committee of 184
air power/aircraft 4–5, 9, 18, 23, 25, 310; TSR-2 352, 354, 515–16, 517, 518–19; V-force 34–5, 36–7, 38–9, 40–1, 42, 43, 51–2, 139, 140, 149, 161–2, 163–4, 178–9, 180–1, 213, 238, 239, 287, 296–7, 308, 310, 315, 318–20, 324, 331–2, 340, 341–2, 373–4, 427–8, 497–8, 526; VC10 aircraft 287–8, 290–1, 292; *see also* Valiant aircraft; Vulcan aircraft
Amery, Julian 320, 392–3, 412, 422–3, 436
Anderson, Sir John 8
Anglo-American nuclear collaboration x–xi, xii, 1–2, 9–10, 24, 42–3, 96–154, 348–9, 489–90; on ABM defence 70–1, 72, 77, 80, 260–5, 271–3; air forces 340, 341–2; atomic testing 147, 269–70, 271–5, 414; Blue Streak and the Thor option 130–3, 137, 141–2; Britain's independent deterrent 120, 121–2, 123, 127–9, 131, 134–5, 137, 148–9, 170–7, 204, 209, 216–17, 239–40, 244, 249–50, 308–9, 311–15, 317–18, 331–2, 345, 359, 360, 376, 378–80, 381–2, 384–6, 388, 393–4, 525, 527–9; common purpose, declaration of 96–102; development of collaboration 114–18; discussions on the size of Britain's deterrent 200–1; exchange of information 99–101, 115–17, 144, 285, 342–3, 369, 451; future nuclear programme, formation of 108–14; Future Policy Study view of 196–7; joint arrangements on targeting 50–3; joint study/working groups (JOWOGS) 146, 278, 467; and the NATO MRBM scheme 218–27, 228–9, 231–5; preventing the spread of nuclear weapons technology 168; priorities in an age of nuclear sufficiency 102–8; revision of Western strategic concept 103–4, 106; Skybolt and the Camp David meeting 202–10; Skybolt cancellation 346–60, 371–2, 373, 374; UK defence spending and the future of Blue Streak 118–27; US need for a Polaris base in Scotland 204–5, 206, 218–19, 221, 222, 223–4, 229, 230–1; *see also* multilateral force (MLF) proposal; Polaris Sales Agreement 1963; Polaris system
anti-ballistic missile (ABM) defence xii–xiii, 62–95, 110, 147, 450–1; OR/1135 (air staff target) 66; Anglo-American collaboration 70–1, 72, 77, 80, 260–5, 271–3; Anglo-American

anti-ballistic missile (ABM) *continued*
views on, at the start of the Kennedy era 260–5; array radars 263; British ABM research programme 1962–4 447–50; British perspectives 283–7; decoys 68, 69, 70, 72, 89, 263, 264–5, 284, 479, 481; funding and costs 66–7, 71–3, 80, 90; HR 169 study, May–November 1964 475–83, 483–4; intelligence 285–6, 483–7; missile defence, early development of 62–75; Nike II project 63; Nike-X 282; Nike-Zeus system 63–4, 78, 79–80, 83, 261, 262, 264, 268, 277, 280, 281–2, 448, 487; Project Wizard 63; re-entry (RV) design 68–9, 87, 262–3, 265–6; Soviet ABM programme xiv, 80–90, 261–2, 268–9, 274, 285–6, 469, 475–6, 477–9, 482–3, 483–7; Soviet ABM threat and Polaris re-entry options 458–66; System A-35 81–2, 87, 88, 263, 279; testing 265–75, 270–1, 279–80, 281–2, 447–50; US-Soviet competition over ABM systems 275–83; vulnerability issue 75–80; X-ray kill 262–3

anti-nuclear movement 28, 142, 217, 254

arms race intensification January 1961–January 1962 260–302; ABM defence, British perspectives 283–7; atmosphere testing and ballistic missile defence, resumption of 265–75; ballistic missile defence, Anglo-American views on 260–5; BNDSG and the criteria of deterrence 287–97; US-Soviet competition over ABM systems 275–83

Arnold, Lorna ix, x, xiv

Atomic Energy Act 1954 (US) 116

Atomic Energy Authority (AEA) ix, 25, 32, 99, 112, 191–2, 220, 319, 468, 487–8, 489

Atomic Energy Commission (US) 75, 115, 247, 487

Atomic Energy Intelligence Division 267

Atomic Weapons Production Committee 192

Atomic Weapons Research Establishment (AWRE) xi, xii, 15, 29, 32, 73, 191, 193, 194, 237, 269–70, 415–16, 466–7, 530; future of 487–90

Attlee, Clement 2–3, 7, 10, 13, 17

Ball, George 332, 371, 372, 377, 428, 520

ballistic missiles 214; Black Knight launcher system 68, 80, 284, 386–7, 447–50, 482; decoys 68, 69, 70, 72, 89, 263, 264–5, 284, 479, 481; Galosh Soviet missile 483–5, 486–7; Gammon Soviet missile 485; Griffon Soviet missile 459–60, 476; penetration aids (and decoys) 68–9, 69–70, 72, 209, 265, 276, 277–8, 280, 283–4, 435, 436–7, 438–41, 445, 462, 463–4, 469–71, 472–3, 475, 478, 481–3; Thor 49–50, 54, 70, 112, 114–15, 123, 125–6, 132–3, 141–2; US development of 38; *see also* anti-ballistic missiles (ABM); Blue Streak; intermediate range ballistic missiles (IRBM); medium range ballistic missiles (MRBMs); Polaris system; Skybolt programme (WS138A)

Bell Laboratories 63

Bethe, Hans 276

Bevin, Ernest 8, 11, 13, 17

Bishop, Frederick 111–12, 200, 222–3, 225, 232

Black Knight launcher 68, 80, 283–4, 386–7, 447–50, 482

Blackett, Patrick 26

Bligh, Tim 318

Blue Danube nuclear weapon 25, 29, 39, 54, 146

Blue Steel rocket 122, 130, 166, 178–81, 183, 194, 209, 312, 315, 318, 351–3, 373, 405, 407, 238287

Blue Streak ballistic missile 37–8, 49, 54, 66, 110, 112, 122–3, 124, 125–6, 130, 131–2, 133, 157–8, 179, 229, 346; aftermath of cancellation 213–18; cancellation of 136–43, 181, 182–3, 185–6, 198–9, 200, 207–9, 371, 525; decoys and 68–9, 70, 72, 265, 283–4, 435, 447, 483; as a 'fire first' weapon 184–6; vulnerability of 166, 167, 179–81, 182, 185–6, 387

Blue Water nuclear weapon 111

Bourges-Maunoury, Maurice 167

Bowie, Robert R. 227–8

Boyle, Air Chief Marshal Sir Dermot 42, 105, 107, 127–8, 134, 176–7, 186

Bravo nuclear test (1954) 28, 30, 31

Brezhnev, Leonid 486

Britain: ABM defence, British perspectives 283–7; Anglo-French

Index   539

nuclear collaboration possibilities 323–5, 326, 337–8, 349, 368–9, 393; contribution to thermonuclear development 33–43, 99; decision to develop nuclear weapons 1–2, 6–9, 10–12; dependence on US xii, 2, 18, 20, 22, 39, 41–2, 47, 48, 50, 80, 97–8, 119, 123, 144, 172, 182, 207–9, 216, 312, 315, 343, 351, 359, 388–90, 392, 395–6, 397, 420, 423–7; great power status 11–12, 22, 108–9; missile defence, early development of 64–75; role in NATO's nuclear effort 106–7, 108–9, 207, 243–4, 246, 382–5; Soviet threat over Egypt 96

British Nuclear Deterrent Study Group (BNDSG) 166, 213–14, 215, 230, 232, 263–4, 265, 303, 304–5, 308–9, 346, 415; analysis of maintaining a deterrence system into the 1970s 308–9; and the criteria of deterrence 287–97, 318–19; formation of 155–65; interim report on the deterrent up to the 1970s 178–86; and Polaris 347; review of options if Skybolt cancelled 352–3

Brodie, Bernard 6

Brook, Sir Norman 28, 30, 99, 111–12, 121, 124–5, 136, 140, 159–60, 177, 195, 195–6, 237–8, 244, 317, 324

Brown, George 216, 371, 424, 525

Brown, Harold 266, 277

Bruce, David 371–2, 391, 523–4

Brundrett, Sir Frederick 32, 47, 49, 66, 67, 69, 73, 77, 99, 109, 115, 125, 147, 159, 191, 193; on Thor 132–3

Bundy, McGeorge 250–1, 322, 325, 330–1, 370, 428, 503

Burke, Admiral Arleigh 38, 155

Butler, R. A. 372–3, 381, 521–2, 524

Buzzard, Anthony 27, 107

Cabinet 3, 13, 22, 23, 25, 28, 31, 35, 236, 250, 254, 273–5, 346, 372; and MLF 432, 472, 498, 500, 502, 504, 506–8; and Nassau Conference 381, 386–7, 388, 391, 393–5

Caccia, Sir Harold 229, 324, 368, 505–6

Campaign for Nuclear Disarmament 142, 254

Carrington, Lord 291, 293, 407, 435, 443, 445

Central Intelligence Agency (CIA) 84–5, 86, 486

Central Organisation for Defence White Paper of 1958 45, 46, 128

Central Organisation for Defense White Paper of 1946 12

Central Treaty Organization (CENTO) 39, 365

Challens, John 415, 460

Cherwell, Lord 23, 24–5, 30

Chevaline programme x–xii, xiii, 143

Chief of the Defence Staff (CDS) 45, 511

Chief Polaris Executive (CPE) x, 411, 412, 446, 451, 464, 465–6, 514

Chiefs of Staff (COS) 6, 7–8, 8, 11, 12, 13–14, 20, 39, 44, 67, 213–14, 373; and Blue Streak cancellation 185–6; concerns about a future Labour government and the independent deterrent 527–30; concerns over size of the Polaris force 515–16, 519; 'Defence Policy and Global Strategy' paper (1952) 21–2, 22–3, 46, 64, 159; and nuclear sufficiency 103–8, 119, 127–9, 133–5, 148, 176–7; report on future defence policy 1947 17; and the requirements of deterrence 52–4, 176–7, 364–6; 'Strategy for the Sixties' paper 303–11; and thermonuclear development 31

Chilver, Richard 182–3, 229

Christmas Island 101, 270, 273, 275

Churchill, Winston 8, 10, 12, 14, 21, 23, 24, 28, 29–30, 31–2, 33–4, 35–6

Cockburn, Robert 67, 69–70, 72, 276, 288, 410

Cold War 3; Berlin, status of 142, 252, 254; Paris Summit 1960, collapse of 220; strategic context of 9, 11–12, 16–25, 26–8, 33–4, 39, 147–8, 266

Commissariat a l'energie atomique (CEA) 167

Congressional Joint Committee on Atomic Energy (JCAE) 10, 99–100, 101, 115, 116–17, 203

Conservative Party: electoral strategy 1964 525; manifesto (1964) 526; and Nassau Conference 366, 371, 427

Controller of Guided Weapons and Electronics (CGWL) 65, 74, 464–5

conventional forces, policy on 104–5, 107, 129, 329–30

Cook, Sir William 32, 117, 125, 160, 183, 305, 468, 512

Cottrell, Alan 468, 512

540 Index

Couchman, Admiral Sir Walter 213, 214–15
Couve de Murville, Maurice 343–4, 501

Daniel Webster USS 281
de Gaulle, Charles 168, 169, 203, 210, 242, 250–1, 253–4, 313, 317–18, 321, 324, 343, 393, 428–9; attitude to Britain joining the EEC 337, 367–8, 370, 400–1, 420; meetings with Macmillan 245–6, 337–8, 367–70; and the Nassau agreement 396–401
De L'Isle, Lord 35
Dean, Sir Maurice 288
Dean, Sir Patrick 118–19, 148, 160, 161, 165, 169, 172, 174, 200, 226
Defence Committee 12, 20, 46, 102, 109, 111, 123–5, 126, 129, 135–41, 155, 156, 199–200, 204, 208, 221, 239, 303–4, 311, 317, 320, 408–9, 410, 510, 513, 515
Defence Council 511
Defence and Overseas Policy Committee (DOPC) 513, 517, 518–19
Defence Planning Staff (was Joint Planning Staff) 483
Defence Research Committee 468
Defence Research Policy Committee (DRPC) 13, 64, 65, 67, 69, 71, 72–3, 76–7, 80, 448–9, 468; reputation of 74–5
Defence Scientific Staff 512
Defence Secretariat 511
defence spending and costs 40–2, 44, 46, 66–7, 111, 118–27, 136–7, 144–5, 209–10, 303–4, 347–8; ABM defence 66–7, 71–3, 80, 90, 261, 282–3; Blue Streak 49, 112, 136–7, 140–1, 198; Future Policy Study view of 197, 198–9; independent deterrent 173, 175, 176–7; information, lack of 110; Polaris system 180, 387–8, 407, 409–10, 416–22, 464, 470, 473, 482, 519; proposed cuts to the nuclear programme 236–8; Skybolt 315–20, 348, 349; United States (US) 79–80, 261; VC10 aircraft 292
Defence White Paper 1955 33, 37
Defence White Paper 1957 45, 46, 48, 107, 120
Defence White Paper 1958 106–7, 109–13
Defence White Paper 1959 135, 157
Defence White Paper 1960 198
Defence White Paper 1962 312–14
Defence White Paper 1963 510–13
Defence White Paper 1964 519–20
Defense Atomic Support Agency 261–2
Defense Reorganization Act 1958 (US) 79
deterrence 6–8, 10–11, 33; criteria of 50–4, 161–5, 169–72, 174–7, 287–97, 405–6, 408–9; damage capability reduction 315–17, 318, 319–20; definition of independent deterrent 174–5; graduated 27; revision of criteria 303–35; Sandys White Paper and creation of a national strategic target policy 43–54; Skybolt and the defence budget 315–20; 'Strategy for the Sixties' and the future of the deterrent 303–11
deterrent policy February 1959–March 1960: BNDSG interim report and the fate of Blue Streak 178–86; formation of British Nuclear Deterrent Study Group (BNDSG) 155–65; future policy aims 169–70; Future Policy Study and the independent deterrent 165–78; nuclear weapons, effects of 163–5; size and purpose of a future system 161–4, 287–97, 364–6
Dickson, Marshall of the Royal Air Force Sir William 40–1, 42, 43, 44, 105, 107, 128–9, 133, 135, 160
Director of Defense Research and Engineering (DDRE) 79
Dixon, Sir Pierson 337, 368, 398–9, 400
Dog House ABM radar 88, 485
Doggett, F. J. 410, 416, 417
Dossor, Rear Admiral Frederick 412, 446, 447, 465–6
Douglas-Home, Sir Alec 474, 510, 517–18; and the NATO MLF proposal 522–3; *see also* Home, Lord
Downey, W. G. 436
Dulles, John Foster 26, 100, 102, 116, 168

East, F. H. 460–1, 475, 476
Eden, Anthony 22, 44
Eisenhower, Dwight D. 20, 70, 85, 97, 98–9, 100, 202, 205–6, 220, 223–4
Elliott Automation Space and Advanced Military Systems (EASAMS) 476–7
English Electric 65–6
European Economic Community (EEC) 90, 241–2; British application to join

254, 315, 323, 325, 326, 337, 340–1, 344, 366, 367–8, 370, 400–1, 420

Festing, General Sir Francis 134–5
Finletter, Thomas K. 337, 520–1
Flight International 474
Foreign Affairs 525–6
Foreign Office 19, 118–19, 432; and deterrence criteria 161, 169–72, 310–11; doubts about nuclear collaboration with France 168–9, 243, 246; and independent deterrent 170–2, 177, 317–18, 322–3; and the MLF 495, 498–9, 503–4, 505–6, 507–8; Nassau agreement, appraisal of 395–6; NATO's control of Britain's nuclear capability 243–4
France 202, 203, 221, 241, 245, 317–18; Anglo-French nuclear collaboration possibilities 168–9, 323–5, 326, 337–8, 349, 368–9, 393; Franco-German treaty 1963 428–9; and the Nassau agreement 372, 396–401; nuclear collaboration with Germany 348, 500, 501; possible information exchange with US 326,.331; possible supply of Polaris to 377–8, 396–7; sharing of nuclear responsibilities and Britain's desire to join the EEC 168, 242–3, 244, 369–70; US attitudes to French nuclear ambitions 168, 202, 246, 247–8, 249–51, 321–2, 339–40, 343–4
Future Policy Steering Committee 176–7
Future Policy Study 165–78, 194, 237, 239; reception of 195–202

Gaither Report 77–8, 97
Gaitskell, Hugh 216, 217, 345–6, 424
Galantin, Rear Admiral I. J. 411, 418, 440, 443
Gates, Thomas S. 166–7, 204, 207, 221–2, 240
GEN 163 13
George Washington, USS 38
Germany 227, 245, 250, 311, 313, 336, 338, 344, 367, 376, 377–8, 431, 432–3, 496–7, 498–9, 510; Berlin, status of 142, 252, 254; Franco-German treaty 1963 428–9; nuclear collaboration with France 348, 500, 501
Gordon Walker, Patrick 424–5, 525–6
Gowing, Margaret ix, 8, 11, 16

'Grand Design' memorandum 1961 241–54, 323
Grapple nuclear test series (1957–8) 32, 48–9, 75, 99, 101, 115, 117, 209, 270
Grundy, Air Vice Marshal Sir Edouard 464–5, 466

Harding, Field Marshal Sir John 27–8
Hardtack nuclear test series (1958) 75–7, 261–2
Harrison, James 475
Healey, Denis 474, 525
Heath, Edward 323, 353, 394–5, 397, 432–3, 500–1, 506–7
Heathcoat Amory, Derick 121, 124, 140, 215–16
Hen House ABM radar 88
Herter, Christian 205–6, 233, 235
Home, Lord 233–4, 246, 247–8, 253, 316–17, 337, 344–5, 350, 353, 368, 377, 390, 394; and the NATO MLF proposal 432, 498–9, 500, 502, 504–6, 507–8; *see also* Douglas-Home, Sir Alec
Hoyer Millar, Sir Frederick 177
HR 169 study, May–November 1964 475–83, 483–4
Hudleston, Air Vice Marshal Sir Edmund 181, 306–7, 309–10
Hull, General Sir Richard 529
Hunt, John 293, 296
Hunwicks, Sidney A. 435, 446, 461
hydrogen bomb 13, 26, 28, 29–30, 31–2, 33–5

intelligence: ABM defence 285–6; Soviet ABM programme 84–7, 89, 267–8, 460, 483–7
intercontinental ballistic missiles (ICBM) 5, 96; Minuteman 158, 260, 266, 277, 280, 351, 352, 353, 356, 415, 480
intermediate range ballistic missiles (IRBM): Thor 49–50, 54, 114–15, 123, 125–6, 132–3, 141–2; *see also* Blue Streak; Polaris system

Jellicoe, Earl 514, 515
Johnson, Lyndon B. 510, 517–18; and the NATO MLF proposal 520–1, 523–4
Joint Chiefs of Staff (JCS) 200, 202, 261–3, 265, 282, 350, 373, 434, 509
Joint Congressional Committee on Atomic Energy (JCAE) 10, 100, 101, 116–17, 203

Joint Global War Committee 162–3
Joint Intelligence Bureau (JIB) 53, 267, 294–5, 460
Joint Intelligence Committee (JIC) 12, 18, 85, 293–4, 458; JIC(62)10 295–7, 306, 307; Missile Threat Coordination Subcommittee 285–6; paper on nuclear sufficiency 103
Joint Inter-Services Group for the Study of All Out War (JIGSAW) 163, 164
Joint Planning Staff (JPS) 12, 18, 40, 45, 50, 67; maintenance of a UK strategic nuclear capability after 1970, paper on 364–6; nuclear sufficiency, paper on 103–4, 105
Joint Re-entry System Working Group (JRSWG) 446–7, 460–2, 463, 464, 481
Joint Steering Task Group (JSTG) 444, 446
Joint Technical Warfare Committee 9

Kennedy, John F. 223, 234, 246, 247, 260, 322–3; on ABM defence 283; assassination 510; attitude to MLF scheme 433–4, 509–10; and Britain's independent deterrent 311–15, 322–3, 331–2; correspondence with Macmillan 250–1, 253, 313–14, 496, 500; and de Gaulle 248–51, 321–6, 348, 376, 383, 396–400; meeting with Khrushchev 252, 254; meetings with Macmillan 247, 248–9, 271–4, 322–3, 325–6, 359–60, 502–3; Nassau meeting with Macmillan, opening stages 372–81; Nassau meeting with Macmillan, reaching an agreement 381–93; personal qualities 391; and a replacement for Skybolt 371–2; speech to Canadian parliament on NATO policy 251–2
Khrushchev, Nikita 82–4, 142, 147–8, 220, 252, 254, 272, 275, 279, 389, 459, 486
Kisunko, Gregory Vasylovych 81, 82, 87, 88
Kohler, Foy 331–2

Labour Party 340, 345–6, 371, 374–5, 474; anti-nuclear mood in 28, 142; Commons debate on Nassau agreement 424–7; criticism of Conservative nuclear policy 107, 216–18, 392; manifesto 526–7; and MLF 520, 523; nuclear policy 525–7, 531
Lambe, Admiral Sir Charles 177
Le Fanu, Vice Admiral Michael 373, 386, 389, 405–6, 411, 449–50
Lemnitzer, General Lyman L. 497
Lighthill, James 373, 386–7, 390, 391, 437
Limited Test Ban Treaty *see* Partial Test Ban Treaty
Lippmann, Walter 341
Lloyd, Selwyn 41, 123, 168, 226
Lockheed Missiles and Space Company (LMSC) 277, 438–9, 444, 461, 463–4, 474, 482
Long Term Study Group (formerly JIGSAW) 274–5
Lyons, D. J. 440–2

McElroy, Neil H. 78, 131–2
Mackenzie, Rear Admiral Hugh S. 410, 411–12, 464–5
McMahon Act 1946 2, 10, 47, 70–1, 99
Macmillan, Harold 28–9, 35, 43, 44, 46–7, 70–1, 71–2, 115–16, 136–7, 510; advice to Kennedy on de Gaulle 250–1, 253; on Anglo-French nuclear collaboration possibilities 324–5, 326, 337–8; Blue Streak cancellation 208–9; on Britain's independent deterrent 121–2, 123, 249–50, 345, 376, 378–9, 380, 381–2, 384–5, 393–4, 507–8; on Britain's nuclear policy 108–9, 199–200; Commons debate on Nassau agreement 423–8; criticised by Wilson 217; and France 168–9; on future wars 114; 'Grand Design' memorandum 1961 241–54, 323; and the MDA 143–4; meetings with de Gaulle 245–6, 337–8, 367–70; meetings with Eisenhower 50, 54, 70, 98–9, 100, 205–7; meetings with Kennedy 247, 248–9, 271–4, 322–3, 325–6, 359–60, 502–3; Nassau meeting with Kennedy, opening stages 372–81; Nassau meeting with Kennedy, reaching an agreement 381–93; and the NATO MRBM scheme 223–4, 226–7; on numbers of required warheads 113–14; on Skybolt 304; and US need for a Polaris base in Scotland 205, 223–4, 231
McNamara, Robert 240–1, 252, 260–1,

266, 277, 280, 282, 321, 367, 371, 390, 406, 434, 487; on Anglo-American nuclear collaboration 342–3, 348–9; Ann Arbor speech, June 1962 339–42, 345–6, 360, 369; on Polaris costs 417–18, 422; Skybolt cancellation 350–1, 353–4, 355, 357–9; speech to NATO, May 1962 326–9, 330, 339
Main Special Machine-Building Directorate, Design Bureau 1 81
Makins, Sir Roger 192, 319, 488
Malinovsky, Marshal Rodion Y. 81, 267, 281, 486
Marconi Wireless Telegraph Company 65–6
massive retaliation 26–7, 82, 107, 118–19, 147–8
MAUD Committee 1
Maudling, Reginald 41, 387, 410, 500
MC 14/2 106
MC-48 26–7
medium range ballistic missiles (MRBMs) 202–4, 205, 206–7, 354; NATO scheme 218–27, 228–9, 231–2, 321–2, 329, 367
Merchant, Livingston 431–2, 434
Mills, Air Chief Marshal Sir George 35–6
Ministry of Aviation (MoA) (formerly Supply) 74, 80, 410–11, 412, 416, 447–8; MoA/Admiralty report on warheads and RES for Polaris 469–72; and Polaris project management 464–6; report on ballistic missile countermeasures 264–5
Ministry of Defence (MoD): central organisation of 12–13, 43–6, 135, 166, 510–13; creation of Central Scientific Staff 467–8; and future nuclear programme 109–14, 120–4, 191–5, 235–9; Nassau meeting brief 373–4; NATO MBRM scheme, attitude to 225, 226; NATO MLF proposals, views on 506
Ministry of Supply 13, 14, 15, 24, 32, 37, 49, 65, 66, 67, 192, 194, 276, 472; reform and renaming of 74; role of 72–3
Moore, Richard 156, 181
Morgan, Lieutenant General Sir Frederick 24
Mountbatten, Earl, of Burma 38, 45, 52, 104, 105, 107, 118, 119, 176, 213, 495, 497, 524–5; and Blue Streak 133, 134; on Britain's contribution to the Western deterrent 128–9; interest in submarine launched missiles 155–6; study on the independent deterrent and 1964 election 527–9
multilateral force (MLF) proposal 228–9, 232–3, 235, 252, 336–7, 344–5, 367, 377–8, 379–81, 383–4, 397, 495–536; Anglo-American relations, effects on 499–500; and the approach of the October 1964 election 520–31; assignment of V-force to NATO 497–8; British ideas for variants 508–10, 521–2, 524; British policy and the dilemmas of the MLF 495–510; British response to US pressure 496–8, 500–1; confused US thinking about the MLF 509–10; mixed manning idea 499, 501–3, 508–10, 521; 'NATO Nuclear Control Commission' proposals 503–4; Polaris force, size of 513–20; reactions to the proposal 328–34; working groups 504–9, 521
Mutual Defence Agreement (MDA) see 'Agreement on the Uses of Atomic Energy for Mutual Defence Purposes'

Nailor, Peter x
Nassau negotiations, December 1962–January 1963 364–404; aftermath of 393–401; agenda arrangements for the Nassau meeting 370; Cabinet concerns about the agreement 387–8; Cabinet meeting to discuss the agreement 393–5; Commons debate on the agreement 423–7; criticism of the agreement 392–3; Foreign Office appraisal of the agreement 395–6; forging of an agreement 381–93; Kennedy's views on a UK replacement for Skybolt 371–2; maintenance of a UK strategic nuclear capability, JPS paper on 364–6; Ministry of Defence (MoD) brief 373–4; MoD delegation's concerns about the agreement 386–7; multilateral force proposals, reactions to 428–34; opening rounds of the negotiations 372–81; personal memorandum from Macmillan to Kennedy 384–5, 386; Rambouillet meeting between Macmillan and de Gaulle 367–70; 'Statement on Nuclear Defence Systems' 388–90; wording of joint communiqué 383–4, 386

544   Index

Nassau, prelude to, June–December 1962 336–63; Anglo-French nuclear collaboration possibilities 337–8; Ann Arbor speech (McNamara), build up to 336–46; maintenance of a UK strategic nuclear capability after 1970 364–6; NATO multilateral force (MLF) proposal 336–7, 344–5; Skybolt cancellation and the deterrent gap 346–60

National Intelligence Estimates (NIEs) 84–5, 86–7, 89, 459; Soviet ABM programme 484–6

New York Herald Tribune 341

Nike-X ABM system 282, 469, 476, 487

Nike-Zeus ABM system 63–4, 71, 78, 79–80, 83, 88–9, 261, 262, 264, 268, 277, 279–80, 281–2, 448, 487

Nitze, Paul H. 418, 419

Norstad, General Lauris 202–3, 205, 207, 218, 222, 226–7, 228, 231, 344, 497

North Atlantic Treaty Organization (NATO) 17, 19, 20, 23, 26–7, 42, 135, 231–2, 313; atomic stockpile proposal 102; collective nuclear capability proposals 202–4, 205, 206–8; control of Britain's nuclear capability 243–4, 245, 253; MC 14/2 106; MC-48 26–7; MRBM scheme 218–27, 228–9, 231–2, 321–2, 329, 367; NATO policy, Acheson's proposals 248–9; 'Statement on Nuclear Defence Systems' (Nassau agreement) 388–90; UK position 47, 48; US concern about NATO's problems 246–7; *see also* multilateral force (MLF) proposal

nuclear forces, control of, March 1960–May 1961 213–59; Blue Streak cancellation, aftermath of 213–18; future nuclear programme and Skybolt prospects 235–41; Macmillan, Kennedy and the 'grand design' 241–54; multilateral force (MLF) proposal and the Holy Loch agreement 227–35; Polaris and the NATO MRBM scheme 218–27; *see also* multilateral force (MLF) proposal

nuclear programme, future plans for 23–5, 108–14, 120–7, 129–31, 143–7, 193–5, 198–200, 235–9, 315–20; UK underground nuclear test programme and the future of AWRE 487–90

Nuclear Requirements for Defence Committee (NRDC) 191–5, 238, 270–1, 416, 488–9, 490

nuclear testing 113; atmosphere testing and ballistic missile defence 265–75; Bravo 28, 30, 31; Christmas Island, 101, 270–1, 273–5; Dominic 278; doubts about resumption of 275–7; France and 168, 203; Grapple test series 32, 48–9, 75, 99, 101, 115, 117, 209, 270; Hardtack 75–6; high altitude 75–7, 87; Operation Hurricane 25; Orange 76, 262; Pampas 269; Partial Test Ban Treaty 278, 459, 504, 506, 513; Soviet Union and 17–18, 20, 27, 81, 84, 87, 266–7, 268–9, 274, 281, 459, 484–5; Starfish Prime 278; suspension of 115, 147, 265–75; Teak 76, 262; Tendrac 414; underground 269–70, 487–90; United States (US) 26, 28, 75–6, 261–2, 266, 269, 278, 281–2; Yucca 76

Operation Hurricane 25

Operational Requirements Committee (ORC) 468

Ormsby Gore, Sir David 311, 340–1, 350, 350–1, 355–6, 370, 390, 391, 398, 399–400, 422, 433, 444, 495; on the MLF proposal 499–500, 524; relations with Kennedy 374

Partial Test Ban Treaty 278, 459, 504, 506, 513

Penley, W. H. 267–9, 283, 284, 285, 447, 451

Penney, William 15–16, 24, 29, 30, 32, 76, 99, 115, 143–4, 270, 271–2, 274, 275–6, 451, 459

Playfair, Sir Edward 193, 213, 215, 289

Plessey UK 476, 477

Plowden, Sir Edwin 99, 100, 101, 109, 115, 116, 117, 143–4, 145, 192

Polaris Interdepartmental Policy Steering Committee (PIPSC) 412, 461–2

Polaris Sales Agreement 1963 xiv, 405–57, 465, 495; British contributions to research and development costs 416–22; Nassau agreement, Commons debate on 423–7; penetration aids, the Williams mission, and conclusion of the agreement 434–47; Polaris force configuration and organisational

arrangements 405–13; study on British production of own missiles 422–3; terms of the agreement 445–6; Zuckerman mission and the Polaris surcharge debate 413–28
Polaris system x, xi, xii, 124, 125, 137, 140, 142, 155–6, 186, 201, 214–15, 260, 289, 347, 530; ABM threat and re-entry system options 458–66; advantages of 138–9, 391; British contribution to research and development costs 416–22; costs 180, 387–8, 407, 409–10, 419–22, 464, 470, 473, 482, 519; first British approach on 166–7; Galosh and intelligence appreciations of the Moscow ABM system 483–7; HR 169 study, May–November 1964 475–83, 483–4; Joint Re-entry System Working Group (JRSWG) 446–7, 460–1, 462, 463, 464, 481; Joint Steering Task Group (JSTG) 444, 446; and the Labour Party 525–7; multilateral force (MLF) proposal 228–9, 232–3, 235, 252, 336–7, 344–5, 367, 377–8, 379–81, 383–4; Nassau agreement, aftermath of 393–401; and the NATO MBRM scheme 218–27, 231–5; penetration aids 435, 436–7, 438–41, 445, 462, 463–4, 469–71, 472–3, 475, 478, 481–3; Polaris A1 missile 38; Polaris A2 missile 201, 277, 280, 413–15, 418, 442; Polaris A3 missile 280–1, 291, 413, 414–15, 416–17, 418, 435–6, 442–3, 445–6, 469; Polaris force, size of 513–20; project management issues 464–6; PX-1 package 277; re-entry body 277; re-entry (RV) design 414–15, 416, 434–5, 437, 439–40, 441–2, 444, 447, 458, 460–4, 466–75; as a replacement for Skybolt 351–3, 354–5, 356–7, 358–9, 373–4; 'Statement on Nuclear Defence Systems' (Nassau agreement) 388–90; submarine options 406–10; supply to France 377–8, 396–7, 398; supply to the UK 206–7, 208–9, 228–9, 231, 372, 376–7, 381; technical training and support 416, 418–19; US need for a Polaris base in Scotland 204–5, 206, 218–19, 221, 222, 223–4, 229, 230–1; warhead design 413–14, 415–16, 466–75

Potts, Archibald 267, 460, 469
Powell, Sir Richard 100, 101, 156–7, 158–9, 160, 162, 177, 192
Press, Robert 436, 462, 512–13
Project Defender 78–9
Project Wizard 63, 64

Quebec Agreement 1943 1, 8

radar 65–6, 75; blackout techniques 479; confusion of 479–81; discriminating radar 72, 264–5, 464, 479–81; Dunay-2 (Hen Roost) 88; Dunay-3 (Dog House) 88, 263, 485; penetration aids 68–9, 69–70, 89; phased array radars 263, 485
Ramsbotham, Peter 170, 317
re-entry (RV) design 68–9, 87, 262–3, 265–6, 283–5; Dazzle 284; Gaslight 284; HR 169 study, May–November 1964 475–83, 483–4; Mark 2 re-entry system 280–1, 434–5, 437, 439–40, 441, 442, 461, 463–4, 471, 473, 478, 479, 480, 483, 530; Polaris system 414–15, 416, 437, 439–40, 441–2, 444, 447, 458, 460–4, 466–75; vulnerability 278
Re-entry System Study Group 460–1, 463–4
Red Beard nuclear weapon 146, 414
Red Snow nuclear weapon 194, 238
Rose, Clive 395–6
Rostow, Walt 332
Royal Air Force (RAF) x, 4, 19, 21, 25, 38–43, 51–4, 106, 181, 186, 199–200, 213, 287–8, 352, 393, 415
Royal Aircraft Establishment (RAE) 68, 73, 80, 209, 267, 284, 411, 434, 435, 437, 439, 440–2, 460, 461, 464, 470, 471, 482; HR 169 study, May–November 1964 475–7
Royal Navy 19, 21, 38, 115, 143, 155, 201, 411–12, 416, 440, 469; Polaris Committee 477, 514
Royal Radar Establishment (RRE) 68, 80, 267, 476
Rusk, Dean 247–8, 321, 325, 329, 340, 343–5, 348–9, 354, 428, 444, 498, 506, 508, 521–2
Russia see Soviet Union

Sandys, Duncan 37, 43, 44, 53, 107, 109, 111, 112, 165–6, 372, 386, 390, 500, 507; and Blue Streak 49, 125–6,

546 *Index*

Sandys, Duncan *continued*
  130, 131–2, 133, 137, 138, 140–1, 157–8; and BNDSG 158–60; and defence spending 121; and Defence White Papers 45, 46, 48, 67, 102, 107; and departure from MoD 165–6; and Polaris 156; on Thor 133; on US support for Europe 134–5
Sary Shagen (Soviet ABM testing site) 81–2, 84, 86–8, 266–7, 271, 274, 281, 286, 484, 485
Schlesinger, Arthur 375
Scott, Sir Robert 289–90, 293, 305, 306, 307–8, 310, 315, 346–7, 353, 354, 359, 387, 407
Seaborg, Glenn 247, 271
Selkirk, Lord 120
Shuckburgh, Sir Evelyn 24, 508–9, 521, 524–5
Skybolt programme (WS138A) xii, 179, 181, 183, 185–6, 198, 199, 202, 204, 205–6, 207–8, 209–10, 213, 214, 215, 218–19, 290–1, 292, 296–7, 304, 312, 392; cancellation 240, 346–60, 366–7, 369, 370–1, 372, 373, 374, 391; cost-sharing proposal 374, 376, 379; costs 348, 349; decoys 284; and the defence budget 315–20; formal agreement 229; technical problems and doubts about 230–1, 332, 349–50, 376
Slessor, Air Chief Marshal Sir John 21, 24
Slim, General Sir William 16–17
South East Asia Treaty Organization (SEATO) 39, 114, 365
Soviet Union xii, 6, 11; ABM programme xiv, 80–90, 261–2, 268–9, 274, 285–6, 437–8, 440–1, 458–66, 469, 475–6, 477–9, 482–3; air defence 82, 85; atomic testing 17–18, 20, 81, 84, 87, 266–7, 268–9, 274, 281, 459, 484–5; cities as potential targets 9, 18, 51–2, 53, 112, 161–2, 163–4, 178, 287–8, 291–2, 294–5, 306, 307, 308, 315–17, 318, 408–9, 478, 481, 514, 515; and Cold War context 9, 11–12, 16–25, 26–8, 33–4, 39, 147–8, 266; espionage 10, 14; Galosh missile 484–5, 486; Gammon missile 485–6; Griffon Soviet missile 459–60, 476; nuclear sufficiency, effects of 103; Sputnik satellite 70, 77, 78, 82–3, 96, 100; surface-to-air missile and radar installations 80–1, 88, 438; technological advances 147–8;

  US-Soviet competition over ABM systems 275–83
Special Projects Office (SPO) 38, 411–12, 413, 416, 418
Sputnik satellite 70, 77, 78, 82–3, 96, 100
Stephenson, Sir Hugh 293, 294, 296, 306
Stevenson, A. W. 474
Strath, Sir William 112
submarines 38, 138–9, 180, 223, 289, 291, 292, 305, 347, 356, 373; nuclear submarine reactor technology 115, 117; for the Polaris force 406–10, 451, 513–20
Suez crisis 1956 43, 44, 47, 96, 98
Sulzberger, C. L. 83
Supreme Allied Commander Europe (SACEUR) 23, 102, 132, 202–3, 206, 207, 221, 225, 226–7, 228, 231–2, 233–4, 248, 427–8, 497, 504
surface-to-air missile (SAM) systems 80–1, 438

targeting 42; and assured destruction 487; counterforce targeting 35–6, 39–40, 326–30; countervalue targeting 36–7, 54; national and alliance plans 204, 232, 246, 341–2, 415, 427, 478, 497; national strategic target policy, creation of 50–4; against Soviet Union 9, 51–2, 112–13, 140, 161–4, 178, 201, 287–8, 291–7, 308–10, 316, 319–20, 408–9, 438, 477, 515
Taylor, General Maxwell 279
Templer, Field Marshal Sir Gerald 104–5, 107, 119, 127, 128–9, 134
testing *see* nuclear testing
thermonuclear revolution 25–32, 99
Thor ballistic missile 49–50, 54, 70, 112, 114–15, 123, 125–6, 132–3, 141–3
Thorneycroft, Peter 346, 380–1, 394, 417, 419, 423, 429, 430, 444, 473, 502, 506, 523; meetings with McNamara 348, 357–9, 366–7; options for Polaris submarines 407–10, 514, 516, 518; paper on mixed manning 499; paper on reducing the nuclear weapons programme 236–7; Skybolt cancellation 350, 351–2, 353–4, 356–7, 358–9, 371, 373
Times, The 157, 339, 341–2, 370, 371
Tizard, Sir Henry 6–7, 13, 64
Trachtenberg, Marc 329–30
Trident programme xi; C4 missile system x; D5 x

Tripartite Technical Cooperation
  Programme 71, 77, 101
Truman, Harry S. 7, 9–10, 24

U-2 aircraft 84–6, 220
unilateral nuclear disarmament 28, 106,
  171, 172–3, 174, 217–18, 517–18, 519
United Kingdom (UK) *see* Britain
United States (US): atomic testing 26, 28,
  75–6, 261–2, 266, 269, 278, 281–2;
  attitudes to French nuclear ambitions
  168, 202, 203, 246, 247–8, 249–51,
  339–40, 343–4, 396–400; attitudes to
  independent nuclear deterrent 246–7,
  331–2, 354–5, 371–2, 507; British
  reliance on 22–3, 39, 41–2, 47, 48;
  defence spending 79–80, 261; missile
  defence, early development of 62–4,
  77–80, 89–90; 'New Look' defence
  policy 26–7; nuclear guarantee to
  Western Europe 39, 48, 96–7, 98, 101,
  246; possible information exchange
  with France 326, 331; State
  Department 202, 203, 205, 206, 218,
  227, 229, 247, 251–2, 321, 331, 336,
  344, 349, 354, 371, 374, 377, 390,
  429–30, 431, 434, 495, 503, 504, 507,
  509, 521; United States Air Force
  63–4, 79; United States Army 63, 79;
  United States Navy 38, 115, 201, 204,
  214, 277, 413, 414, 416, 435, 438,
  440, 461, 517; US-Soviet competition
  over ABM systems 275–83
uranium 235 111, 145–6, 319, 321
US Supreme Allied Commander Europe
  (SACEUR) 23, 102, 132, 202–3, 206,
  207, 221, 225, 226–7, 228, 231–2,
  233–4, 248, 427–8, 497, 504

V-2 rocket 5, 62–3, 64, 65
Valiant aircraft 25, 48
Valiant, HMS 451
Vulcan aircraft 9, 51, 52, 161, 186, 238,
  287, 306, 320, 410
vulnerability, of warheads 75–80, 261–3,
  268, 278, 460, 467, 480, 484–5

Ward, George 120, 156, 186
Warhead Safety Coordinating
  Committee 466–7
warheads 63, 72, 191–2, 193, 194; ABM
  warheads 147; kiloton range warheads
  111, 123, 126–7, 238–9; megaton
  range warheads 109–10, 111, 113, 123,
  124, 126, 238; Polaris system 413–14,
  415–16, 443, 466–75; and radar
  blackout techniques 479; radiation
  output 278; Red Snow 194, 238;
  Short Granite 48–9, 99; Tony 239; US
  designs 146–7; US Mark 47 194, 413,
  415; US Mark 58 413, 415–16, 435,
  445, 466–7, 469, 471–2, 473–4, 488;
  warhead hardening 480; and X-rays
  262–3, 267–8, 278, 480
Watkinson, Harold 166–7, 181–2, 185,
  193, 198–9, 201, 204, 205, 208, 329;
  Anglo-French nuclear collaboration
  possibilities 323–4; damage capability
  reduction 315–16, 318, 320; on de
  Gaulle 253–4; deterrent options
  290–1; dismissal of 346; on
  McNamara's Ann Arbor speech
  339–40, 341–2; meeting with Gates
  1960 221–2; and the NATO MRBM
  scheme 219–20, 221–2, 226, 235, 329;
  and Polaris 214, 231, 289; report on
  future defence requirements 238–9;
  and Skybolt 218–19, 220–1, 230, 231,
  240–1; on Thorneycroft's proposed
  defence cuts 236–7
WE-177 nuclear weapon 407, 469, 489,
  530
Weapons Development Committee
  (WDC) 468, 469; Nuclear Sub-
  Committee 472–3
Williams, Leslie T. D. 435, 436–7,
  438–40, 442–3, 444
Wilson, Charles 37, 53
Wilson, Harold 216–17, 314–15, 345,
  520–1, 527; at the Commons debate
  on Nassau agreement 425–7
Wright, Oliver 517, 522
Wynn, Humphrey x

X-rays 76–7, 262–3, 267–8, 278, 460, 480

York, Herbert F. 79, 261

Ziegler, Philip 170
Zuckerman, Sir Solly 74–5, 183–5, 230,
  264, 266, 267, 270, 271, 275–6, 277,
  357, 387, 410–11, 450, 462, 468,
  472–3, 475, 511–12; on Anglo-
  American nuclear collaboration
  489–90; Polaris mission to US 410–11,
  413–18; on warheads for Polaris 474–5
Zulueta, Philip de 223, 224, 226, 315,
  324, 368, 431, 496

Taylor & Francis eBooks

Helping you to choose the right eBooks for your Library

Add Routledge titles to your library's digital collection today. Taylor and Francis ebooks contains over 50,000 titles in the Humanities, Social Sciences, Behavioural Sciences, Built Environment and Law.

Choose from a range of subject packages or create your own!

Benefits for you
- Free MARC records
- COUNTER-compliant usage statistics
- Flexible purchase and pricing options
- All titles DRM-free.

Benefits for your user
- Off-site, anytime access via Athens or referring URL
- Print or copy pages or chapters
- Full content search
- Bookmark, highlight and annotate text
- Access to thousands of pages of quality research at the click of a button.

REQUEST YOUR FREE INSTITUTIONAL TRIAL TODAY

Free Trials Available
We offer free trials to qualifying academic, corporate and government customers.

eCollections – Choose from over 30 subject eCollections, including:

Archaeology	Language Learning
Architecture	Law
Asian Studies	Literature
Business & Management	Media & Communication
Classical Studies	Middle East Studies
Construction	Music
Creative & Media Arts	Philosophy
Criminology & Criminal Justice	Planning
Economics	Politics
Education	Psychology & Mental Health
Energy	Religion
Engineering	Security
English Language & Linguistics	Social Work
Environment & Sustainability	Sociology
Geography	Sport
Health Studies	Theatre & Performance
History	Tourism, Hospitality & Events

For more information, pricing enquiries or to order a free trial, please contact your local sales team:
www.tandfebooks.com/page/sales

The home of Routledge books

www.tandfebooks.com

Printed in Great Britain
by Amazon